The CASSELL

DICTIONARY of
ENGLISH USAGE

The CASSELL

DICTIONARY of ENGLISH USAGE

LORETO TODD

CASSELL

This edition first published in the UK 1997 by
Cassell
Wellington House
125 Strand
London WC2R 0BB

Copyright © Loreto Todd 1997

British Library Cataloguing-in-Publication Data
A catalogue record for this book is available from the British Library

ISBN 0–304–34446–X

Typeset by Ben Cracknell Studios
Printed and bound in Great Britain by Mackays of Chatham

Contents

Introduction

The English language is currently the most widely-used language in the world. It is spoken as a mother tongue on every continent; employed as the medium of instruction in over half of the world's universities; and utilized as the link language of business, the media and international relations. We cannot be certain of the exact number of its users, but we do know that one in every six people on this planet uses English on a daily basis. Over 350 million of us speak it as a mother tongue, and an estimated 650 million use it for purposes of business, communication, education, entertainment and literature. With over one billion speakers, the need for accuracy, clarity and precision in its use has never been greater.

English, like all living languages, changes. New words are coined in the wake of illnesses such as AIDS or in the research and manufacture of new drugs; meanings are modified; spellings are simplified; pronunciation reflects media influence; and styles and structures that would have been inappropriate in the past have been accepted and sanctioned. A brief examination of any publication dealing with computers illustrates many of the changes referred to. We have coinages such as 'BASIC' (Beginners All-Purpose Symbolic Instruction Code), 'byte', 'macro' and 'RAM'; the semantic modification of 'cache', 'drive', 'mouse' and 'window'; and the widespread use of 'disk' and 'program' by people who would otherwise prefer 'disc' and 'programme'.

Many of the changes create uncertainty in the minds of users. Is it now acceptable to spell the past tense of 'travel' with one 'l'? What exactly is the meaning of 'enormity'? When is it permissible to use abbreviations? How can we know whether a word ends in '-able' or '-ible'? Why do some people leave spaces before their punctuation marks? Where do borrowed words come from and how should they be pronounced? When should I use 'I' and when should I use 'me'? Does any of this matter? Are there any rules left?

In addition, virtually all speakers have their pet hates and preferences. We may know that for most verbs the endings '-ise' and '-ize' are interchangeable, but we may have a strong preference for one of them; we have all known teachers who have advised their pupils not to use 'get' or 'nice'; some people are content to acknowledge that 'silly' no longer means 'holy' but are irritated when speakers use 'aggravate' to mean 'annoy'; and many of us may criticize the 'loss' of 'l' in some pronunciations of 'vulnerable' but do not notice its earlier loss from words such as 'calm' or 'walk'.

The Cassell Dictionary of Usage has been compiled to provide helpful, unambiguous guidance. We have aimed to offer readers the information necessary to clarify a single point of usage or to explore, in depth, the grammar of the world's *lingua franca*. As the size of this book shows, we have aimed to be comprehensive, but we have excluded all items that are obsolete and all structures that are rarely, if ever, used by ordinary speakers or which owe their continued existence to their immortalization in other usage books. We have attempted to write objectively about current usage and to distinguish clearly between mistakes and local or idiosyncratic usage; we have based our information on modern description rather than on outmoded prescriptivism; and we have acknowledged that changes are under way, especially in verb forms, so that Britain's 'fitted' and 'shrank' are likely to bc influenced and perhaps replaced by America's 'fit' and 'shrunk'.

We have, of course, had to make decisions. To avoid doubling the size of the *Dictionary*, we have put most of the words ending in either '-able' or '-ible' under one entry; we have dealt with the main differences between British and American usage in a set of entries such as 'UK and US English'; and we have often treated pairs of related words under the one that occurs first in the alphabet.

Our dual aims have been to clarify without over-simplifying and to avoid any terminology that might be familiar only to the linguist. We have avoided phonetic symbols, for example, preferring to give rhymes to indicate variant pronunciations and have used only two conventions that may require a brief explanation:

the use of SMALL CAPITALS indicates that there is a dictionary entry on this topic

the use of *See* directs the reader to the actual location of the entry for the topic and *See also* at the end of an entry refers the reader to entries with additional or related information.

Many people have contributed time, energy and information to the development and insights found here. In particular, I should like to thank Dr Mary Penrith for advice, criticism and help with proofreading, and Professor Ian Hancock for in-depth collaboration and co-operation. A special word of thanks is also due to my students from many parts of the English-speaking world. They have shared with me their knowledge of the usage habits of the younger generation and I have, I hope, shared with them my enthusiasm for this – infinitely flexible and often frustrating – language.

Loreto Todd
Reader in International English
University of Leeds

Acknowledgements

It would be difficult to list all the people who have talked or written to me about usage, yet each of them has contributed to this dictionary and so deserves my thanks. There are some, however, whose contributions have been extensive and I should like to record my gratitude for their help. Among those to whom I owe most are:

Mireille Canu (France)

George Cave (Guyana)

Sarah Chatwin (England)

Carol Clarke (South America)

Barbara Engels (Germany)

Carol Galvez (Central America)

Beatrice Honikman (South Africa)

Professor Devindra Kohli (India)

Professor Derry Jeffares (Scotland)

Professor Munzali Jibril (Nigeria)

Christopher Jowett (England)

Professor Ian Hancock (USA)

Professor Tometro Hopkins (USA)

Dr Tony Hung (Singapore)

Ruth Jones (Wales)

Professor Paul Mbangwana
  (West Africa)

Moira McCartney (Scotland)

Dr Mona McCausland (Ireland)

Dr Azmi Megally (North Africa)

Tony Richards (England)

Professor Gildas Roberts (Canada)

Celia Roig-Jimenes (Spain)

Joanne Todd (Ireland)

Dr Richard Watkins (Australia)

and Nigel Wilcockson (England).

The Dictionary

A

a

A is the first letter of the alphabet and a vowel whose pronunciation varies in words such as *arm, at* and *ate*.

A can be used to mean '(for) each/every' in such phrases as:

three times a week (i.e., every week)
$1 a dozen (i.e., for each dozen)
10 pence apiece (i.e., for each one).

The last example, *apiece*, which is normally written as one word, is no longer common in spoken English but is frequently found in literature.

See also A- WORD

a, an

A and its variant *an* are indefinite articles:

This is a book.
This is an apple.

An is used before words that begin with *a, e, i, o* or *u*:

an apple
an elephant
an inkwell
an orange
an umbrella
an easy target
an unusual event.

If the vowel sound is pronounced as *y* or *w*, however, *a* is used:

a ewe (sounds like a *yew*)
a euphemism
a one-man band
a one-way ticket.

Occasionally nouns beginning with a vowel or the letter 'n' were incorrectly segmented, and so:

'a napron' became 'an apron'
'an ewt' became 'a newt'

and

'a norange' became 'an orange'.

There is sometimes confusion about which article to use before *h*. The rules are, however, simple. *A* is used when the *h* is pronounced:

a heavy burden
a high hill
a hospital.

An is used before words when the *h* is silent:

an heir

an honest child
an hour.

In the past, it was usual to use *an* before certain words beginning with *h* when the first syllable was not stressed. Thus:

an historical event
an hotel.

This usage is now regarded as old-fashioned.

When pronouncing letters or groups of letters, the same rules apply:

an aitch
a BA degree
an FA meeting
an NBC announcement
a U-turn.

See also ARTICLE, 'H' SILENT AND DROPPED

à la

The phrase *à la* is usually italicized and is sometimes used to mean 'in the manner and style of':

This is salmon *à la* Dunowen.

It is a shortened form of the French phrase *à la mode de*. The commonest uses of the construction are:

à la carte (having dishes listed and priced separately)
à la king (cooked in a cream sauce)
à la mode (in fashion; of meat: braised with vegetables in wine; of pies: with ice cream).

a side, aside

Aside is an adverb meaning 'to one side':

I took him aside to explain the problem.

This adverb should not be written as two words. Nor should it be confused with *a side* meaning 'on each side':

There were only twelve of us so we played six a side.

a- word

A- occurs as a prefix with a range of meanings. It can precede body parts and a number of common nouns to indicate direction or location:

abreast, ahead, aside, abed, abroad, aloft.

Some 'a + body parts' are now used only figuratively in the standard language:

He was taken *aback* (i.e., surprised)
There was something *afoot* (i.e., going on).

It is found in a number of nautical items indicating position:

abaft, aboard, astern

condition:

adrift, afloat, aground

or a desire to establish contact:

ahoy.

The prefix *a-* is also found in a number of words indicating a state or process:

ajar, alive, atingle.

The *a-* form in these words derives from Old English. It is no longer productive as a prefix, and although many such words, such as:

aloud, aloof, asleep

are commonly used, others, such as:

ablush, aflame, alight

are found mainly in literature. *A-* forms are occasionally derived from other Germanic languages. *Akimbo*, for example, which is used adverbially to mean 'with hands on hips and elbows sticking out', probably comes from the Old Norse expression *i keng boginn*, meaning 'bent in a curve'.

There is also an 'a-/an-' prefix that derives from Greek *a-/an-* meaning 'not' or 'without' and that is still in use. It occurs in such words as:

amoral, asocial, asymmetrical.

The an- form is used before vowels:

anaemic, anarchy, anastigmatic.

See also AFFIX

Å

Å is the symbol used to indicate an Ångström unit of measurement. The Ångström measures the wavelengths of electro-magnetic radiation and is equivalent to one hundred millionth of a centimetre or 10^{-10} of a metre.

See also ABBREVIATION

a priori

The phrase *a priori* comes from Latin and means 'from the previous'. It is used in English to mean deductive reasoning from cause to effect:

It is my job to make out an *a priori* case for changing from a three-term to a two-semester system.

The phrase is generally pronounced to rhyme with 'day high awe rye', but the more Latinate pronunciation rhyming with 'Ah! tree glory' is also acceptable. Latin phrases, like this, should be avoided if there is any danger of their being misused or misunderstood.

See also LATIN

ab initio

Like many Latin phrases used in English, this phrase is usually written in italics. The phrase means 'from the beginning':

It is important to have a contingency plan *ab initio*.

Latin phrases should normally be avoided because they can cause uncertainty or mis-understanding.

See also LATIN

abbreviation

Abbreviations occur widely in technical writing

and in casual or journalistic styles. Abbreviations can be extremely useful, but they should be avoided where they might cause uncertainty or misunderstanding.

It is useful to distinguish between contractions, which end with the last letter of the word:

Dr (Doctor)
Ltd (Limited)
Rd (Road)

and abbreviations, which do not:

Prof (Professor)
ms (manuscript)
Sept (September).

In the past, abbreviations were followed by full stops. Contemporary usage prefers to avoid full stops except in special cases or unless ambiguity would occur. Americans are, however, more likely to preserve the full stops in all abbreviations, especially after a lower case letter:

Fr.
Lat.

Here too, however, the tendency is to drop punctuation marks where this will not cause confusion.

There are several types of abbreviation, including the use of initial capital letters of the significant words in a phrase:

AA (Automobile Association)
BBC (British Broadcasting Corporation)
FBI (Federal Bureau of Investigation)
QC (Queen's Counsel)
RIP or R.I.P. (*Requiescat/requiescant in pace* = Rest in peace).

In speech, the main stress normally falls on the last letter of the abbreviation. Sometimes the letters used can combine to form a new word or an acronym:

AIDS (Acquired Immune Deficiency Syndrome)
NATO (North Atlantic Treaty Organization)
UNESCO (United Nations Educational Scientific and Cultural Organization)
WASP (White Anglo-Saxon Protestant).

Only one full stop is necessary after an abbreviation that occurs at the end of a sentence:

His name was David Anders Jr.

rather than:

*His name was David Anders Jr..

The article used before an abbreviation is determined by the pronunciation of the first letter:

a UFO (an unidentified flying object)
an MA (a Master of Arts).

The plural forms of abbreviations are occasionally specialized:

MSS (= manuscripts)
pp. (= pages)

but they generally take a lower case *s*:

JPs (= Justices of the Peace)
MPs (= Members of Parliament).

Titles
Abbreviations are commonly used for titles:

Dr (Doctor)
Mr (Mister)
Rev. or Revd (Reverend).

The titles Doctor, Mister and Mistress are always abbreviated when used with names:

Dr Mary Adams
Mr Michael Jones Jr
Mrs Mary Jones.

The convention of referring to a married woman as

Mrs Michael Jones

is no longer widely practised, although a woman who marries into the British Royal Family may take her husband's first name:

Princess Michael of Kent.

Messrs (Messieurs) is still occasionally used in business letters, and Ms is not strictly an abbreviation but a blend of Mrs and Miss.

Measurement
Abbreviations are used for measurements, especially in tables and lists:

cc (cubic centimetre/s)
ft (foot or feet)
g or gm (gram/s)
km (kilometre/s)
mpg (miles per gallon)
yd (yard/s).

Time and dates
Phrases denoting time frequently appear in abbreviated form:

AD (*Anno Domini* = in the year of the Lord; appears before the date)
am or a.m. (*ante meridiem* = before noon)
BC (Before Christ; appears after the date)
hr (hour/s)
pm or p.m. (*post meridiem* = after noon)
sec (second/s).

Abbreviations for days of the week and months of the year should normally be avoided, but the following are the accepted forms when space is limited:

Mon Tues Wed Thurs Fri Sat Sun
Jan Feb Mar Apr May Jun Jul Aug Sept Oct Nov Dec.

Many people prefer to spell March, April, June and July in full.

Education
In educational and academic circles, abbreviations are used for examination boards, examinations and degrees:

JMB (Joint Matriculation Board)
GCSE (General Certificate of Secondary Education)
MA (Master of Arts).

Academic degrees may combine capital and lower-case letters:

BSc (Bachelor of Science)
DPhil (Doctor of Philosophy)
MEd (Master of Education).

Abbreviations may vary in different countries or in different institutions. A Bachelor of Arts degree, for example, is referred to as a BA in Britain and in many universities in the United States, but as an A.B. in Harvard.

Cardinal points
The abbreviations for compass directions are:

N (north)
S (south)
E (east)
W (west)

and combinations of these initials are used for more precise directions:

NNW (north by northwest)
SSE (south by southeast).

Latin words and phrases
English has adopted many expressions from Latin, some of which are used in abbreviated form:

c. (*circa* = about)
e.g. (*exempli gratia* = for example; not italicized)
i.e. (*id est* = that is; not italicized)
infra dig. (*infra dignitatem* = undignified).

These abbreviations continue to take full stops, and the abbreviations of most Latin phrases tend to be written in italics.

Place-names
In general, abbreviations of place-names should be avoided, although they are widely used as a space-saving device in addresses for English counties:

Bucks (Buckinghamshire)
Glos (Gloucestershire)
Oxon (Oxfordshire)
Salop (Shropshire).

In the United States, zip codes use capital letters and no full stop for the names of states:

AL (Alabama)
FL (Florida)
MS (Mississippi)
WA (Washington).

Incidentally, many Americans prefer the use of 'United States of America' to US or USA, although the abbreviations occur frequently.

Languages
It is always preferable to give the name of a language in full, although abbreviations are sometimes used in scholarly and technical writings:

AN (Anglo-Norman)
AS (Anglo-Saxon)

Fr (French)
Ger (German).

Religious writing
The names of sacred writings should be written in full. In scholarly works, however, abbreviated forms are sometimes used:
Gen (Genesis)
Lev (Leviticus).

See also ACRONYM, APOSTROPHE, BIBLE, CLIPPING, CONTRACTION, COUNTY, US STATES

aberration
This word is often incorrectly spelled. It means 'deviation from the norm':
His behaviour was totally out of character. It was an aberration.

See also SPELLING

abet
The word *abet* means 'help', 'assist', especially with a crime. It is often used as part of the phrase to 'aid and abet'. The noun form is 'abettor'.

abide
The verb *abide* has three different meanings. It can mean 'live', 'remain', 'stay with', as in the hymn 'Abide with me'. This meaning of the verb is almost obsolete and is preserved mainly in liturgical and literary language. This verb was irregular and had the forms:
abide, abides, abode, abiding, abided
The word *abode* occurs as a noun, meaning 'home, dwelling', especially in the phrase 'of no fixed abode'.

The second meaning of *abide* is 'to accept', 'put up with':
They have agreed to abide by the decision of the court.
When the verb is used with this meaning, it is regular:
He abided by the rules.
Colloquially, *abide* is used with the negative form of the verb 'can' to mean 'dislike over strongly':
I can't abide this sort of behaviour.
I couldn't abide John when we first met.

-ability, -ibility
These endings indicate that the words are nouns. They correspond to adjectives that end in -able or -ible:
durability, durable
eligibility, eligible.

See also -ABLE/-IBLE

abjure, adjure
These words are occasionally confused. *Abjure*

comes from Latin *abjurare*, 'to deny on oath'. Its English meaning is similar and implies the formal renouncing or retracting of an earlier belief or statement:
Joan of Arc refused to abjure her earlier statements.

Adjure comes from Latin *adjurare*, 'to swear to', and is used to mean 'appeal earnestly to':
I adjure you by the living God that you tell us if you are the Christ.

ablative
Latin nouns could differ in form to reflect both number and case, as we can illustrate by selecting the word *dominus*, 'lord':

	Singular	Plural
Nominative	*dominus* (lord)	*domini* (lords)
Vocative	*domine* (O lord!)	*domini* (O lords!)
Accusative	*dominum* (lord)	*dominos* (lords)
Genitive	*domini* (lord's)	*dominorum* (lords')
Dative	*domino* (to a lord)	*dominis* (to lords)
Ablative	*domino* (by a lord)	*dominis* (by lords)

The ablative case ending could imply 'by, with, from'. In the English noun, case is much less significant than in Latin. We tend to use prepositions to fulfil many of the roles of case in Latin. It is unnecessary and, indeed, unhelpful to describe English grammar according to a Latin model, although some grammar books still apply the Latin case terms to English.

See also LATINATE MODELS OF GRAMMAR

able, capable
Able is followed by an infinitive verb in English:
I won't be able to come.

Capable is, however, followed by 'of + -ing':
She was capable of inspiring her students.

-able, -ible
In spoken English there is little or no difference in pronunciation between the suffixes -*able* and -*ible*, and this fact adds to the uncertainty many people have about spelling. Etymology is of little help. It is true that many '-able' endings derive from the Latin suffix -*abilis* whereas '-ible' endings are from -*ibilis*. Such information, however, only puts the problem back one language. There is, unfortunately, no easy set of rules, although the more recent the compound word the more likely is the suffix to be '-able':
permute: permutable
televise: televisable.
This is because '-ible' is no longer used to create words and because '-able' is meaningful not only as a morpheme but also as a word that allows compounds to be rephrased:
permutable = able to be permuted

televisable = able to be televised.

The following information will help to prevent spelling errors, but the wisest course of action is to check the spelling in a dictionary.

Adjectives can be formed by adding -able to many verbs:

laugh: laughable
interpret: interpretable
think: thinkable

and negative adjectives may be formed by prefixing un-:

unflappable, unsinkable, unworkable.

Where the verb ends with a silent 'e', as in 'like' or 'shake', the 'e' is dropped before '-able' and before all suffixes beginning with a vowel. A number of words, such as likable/likeable, have two acceptable forms, the former more widely used in the United States, the latter in Britain. It is probable that the form without 'e' will become accepted worldwide. Where variants are possible, however, they are listed below. The only exceptions to this rule are words whose base forms end in '-ce', '-ee' or '-ge':

pronounceable, agreeable, gaugeable.

When the base form ends in a vowel + y, the 'y' is retained:

employable, enjoyable, playable

and where the base form ends in a consonant + y, the 'y' is changed to 'i':

deny: deniable
justify: justifiable
vary: variable.

The exceptions to this rule are:

flyable, fryable

neither of which is widely used. The adjective 'friable', meaning 'easily broken up', should be distinguished from 'fryable', 'capable of being fried'.

The soil in this area is friable; it crumbles easily.
These vegetables are fryable.

When the base form of a polysyllabic word ends in '-ate', the '-ate' was originally dropped before '-able' was added:

alienate: alienable
calculate: calculable, incalculable
demonstrate: demonstrable.

This rule does not apply, however, to monosyllabic words:

date: datable

or to disyllabic words:

debate: debatable.

In recent coinages, however, and frequently in speech '-atable' forms occur, even with polysyllabic words:

infiltrate: infiltratable
inundate: inundatable.

Base forms ending in a single consonant usually double the consonant before adding '-able':

forgettable, battable (of a ground capable of being batted on).

This rule applies only to one verb ending in '-er', thus:

conferrable.

All the others have '-erable':

preferable, referable, transferable.

-ible endings occur in a fixed number of words deriving from Latin, such as:

audible, compatible, destructible, incorrigible, risible.

It is no longer a living suffix and often we find pairs occurring with '-ible' in the Latin-derived (and usually formal) word and '-able' attached to the more frequently used verb:

credible, believable
edible, eatable
risible, laughable.

A useful though not infallible rule is that when we delete '-able' we are usually left with a recognizable English word. This is not true when we delete '-ible':

buyable: buy
edible: *ed
laughable: laugh
legible: *leg.

The following lists give the recommended spellings of words that people are often confused about.

Ending in -able

abominable, accountable, adaptable, adorable, advisable, agreeable, alienable, amiable, appreciable, approachable, arguable, assessable, available, believable, bribable, bridgeable, calculable, capable, changeable, chargeable, collectable (adjective or, less frequently, noun), conceivable, conferrable, consolable, curable, datable, debatable, definable, demonstrable, desirable, despicable, dissolvable, drivable, durable, educable, equable, excitable, excusable, expendable, finable, foreseeable, forgettable, forgivable, gettable, givable, hirable, immovable, immutable, impalpable, impassable (meaning 'that cannot be passed'), impeccable, implacable, impressionable, indefatigable, indescribable, indispensable, inflatable, inimitable, insufferable, irreplaceable, justifiable, knowledgeable, losable, malleable, manageable, measurable, noticeable, operable, peaceable, penetrable, perishable, permeable, pleasurable, preferable, pronounceable, readable, reconcilable, regrettable, reliable, removable, reputable, serviceable, suitable, tolerable, transferable, undeniable, unexceptionable, unknowable, unmistakable

Ending in -able, -eable

likable/likeable, lovable/loveable, salable/saleable, sizable/sizeable, usable/useable

Ending in -ible
accessible, admissible, audible, avertible, collapsible, collectible (noun or, less frequently, adjective), combustible, compatible, comprehensible, contemptible, contractible, controvertible, convertible, corruptible, credible, deducible, defensible, destructible, digestible, discernible, divisible, edible, eligible, extensible, fallible, feasible, flexible, forcible, fusible, gullible, illegible, impassible (meaning 'that cannot feel'), incorrigible, incredible, indelible, indigestible, intangible, intelligible, irascible, irresistible, legible, negligible, ostensible, perceptible, perfectible, permissible, plausible, possible, reprehensible, reproducible, resistible, responsible, reversible, risible, seducible, sensible, susceptible, tangible, transmissible, unintelligible, vendible, visible

The derived nouns ending in *-ability* and *-ibility* also cause difficulties and many people do not know when to use *-ability* and when to use *-ibility*. As with the adjectives, there is no simple rule that will help in all circumstances. The best generalizations are summarized below.

Recent coinages, such as those associated with computers, use *-able* and, less frequently, *-ability*:
bootable, computable, scannable/scannability.
All drawings are scannable if you have enough memory.

Words that are formed from recognizable English words use *-able* and, rarely, *-ability*:
drinkable, eatable, thinkable.
Many thoughts previously unthinkable have become not only thinkable but doable.
The loss of the *Titanic* in 1913 destroyed the myth of unsinkability.

Words using Latin roots often use *-ible/ -ibility*
credible (from *credo* = I believe)
risible (from *risibilis* = laughable).

See also -ABILITY/-IBILITY

abnormal, subnormal

These words are often used both loosely and insensitively. *Abnormal* means 'not normal', 'deviating from the norm':
This section of the B156 road will be closed between 2 and 6 a.m. to allow three lorries with abnormal loads to travel to Bryant's.
She always says she dislikes the abnormal, it is so obvious. She says the normal is so much more simply complicated and interesting.
> Gertrude Stein,
> *The Autobiography of Alice B. Toklas*, 1933

Subnormal means 'below the norm':
She had a subnormal temperature for the first forty-eight hours.
He had a subnormal curiosity.

Because of their negative connotations, it is often better to avoid these words.

aboriginal, Aboriginal

The word differs in meaning depending on whether or not it begins with a capital letter. The adjective beginning with a lower-case 'a' means 'indigenous, having existed in a place from the earliest times':
Who were the aboriginal inhabitants of South Africa?

Aboriginal with a capital letter is used as both an adjective and a noun to refer to the original inhabitants of Australia.
Most Aboriginals prefer to be called 'Native Australians'.

Aborigine

This word is probably derived from Latin *ab origine*, 'from the beginning', although it is possible that the word actually comes from *Aborigines*, the name given to a pre-Latin tribe in Italy. It is generally used with a capital letter to refer to the indigenous inhabitants of Australia. The abbreviation *Abo* is condescending and is similar to the use of 'Mick' for an Irishman or 'doll' for a woman.

about, around

Both *about* and *around* can function as adverbs and prepositions and, when they mean 'here and there', they are usually interchangeable:
We wandered around/about for hours.
We wandered around/about the house for hours.

When the meaning is 'approximately', British speakers prefer 'about' and American speakers 'around':
She left at around/about five o'clock.
Some British purists argue that 'around' in the sense of 'approximately' is unacceptable:
*I have around 60 CDs.
However, many young users of English use such sentences as:
I have about 60 CDs.
I have around 60 CDs.
interchangeably.

above, over

These words are almost synonymous, but they have slightly different meanings and can be used in different contexts. *Above* means 'higher than':
The plane was above the clouds.
Over means 'vertically on top of':
The helicopter hovered over the house.
Occasionally, the words are interchangeable:
Put it above/over the door.
Some writers dislike the use of *above* as in:
See above

although this usage is perfectly acceptable when there is no possibility of confusion.

See also BELOW/BENEATH/UNDER/UNDERNEATH, OVER

abstract

An *abstract* is a brief summary of a thesis, dissertation or learned article. It provides details of the content, development and conclusion of the data in language that can be understood by the non-specialist.

abstract noun

An abstract noun is a noun that refers to non-material concepts (*justice*), emotions (*despair*), ideas (*existentialism*) and relationships (*marriage*). These are in contrast to concrete nouns such as *ball*, *hammer*, *newspaper* and *aunt*.

See also NOUN

abuse, misuse

These words, both of which can be used as a verb and as a noun, are not synonyms. As a verb, *abuse* means 'use wrongly', and it occurs with abstract nouns:

She will not abuse her position as director.

Misuse means 'use incorrectly', and it tends to occur with concrete nouns:

Don't misuse the printer. Doing so inconveniences everyone.

Because *abuse* has been used so frequently in phrases such as 'child abuse', many speakers and writers use *misuse* with both abstract and concrete nouns:

There were suggestions that he misused his knowledge for insider trading.
        Sunday Times

abyss

This noun refers to a gulf, chasm, bottomless pit, either in the literal or metaphorical sense:

In the dark, the climbers failed to see the abyss.
He fell into the abyss of grief.

Many purists dislike the second use. The adjective from *abyss* is *abysmal* with only one 's':

The project was an abysmal failure.

AC, DC

The letters AC stand for 'alternating current', and are distinguished from DC, meaning 'direct current'.

academic

This term can be a noun or an adjective. As a noun, it is sometimes confused with 'intellectual', although it refers to someone who teaches at tertiary level:

An academic is a teacher at a university or college.

As an adjective, it usually relates to teaching and learning in any institution:

The academic year lasts for approximately nine months.

Some writers distinguish between 'academic' subjects, which tend to be theoretical, and 'technical' subjects, which tend to be practical:

All pupils are required to take courses in both academic and technical subjects.

Academic subjects might include biology, literature and mathematics; technical subjects might include carpentry, cookery and typing.

The adjective also means 'of theoretical interest only':

I have already signed the contract so your views on it are academic.

Academy

The word *academy* goes back to ancient Greece, where it referred to the Platonic school of philosophy. It is now often used to name an institute of learning or to refer specifically to the French Academy, l'Académie Française. This is an association of scholars and writers that is concerned with maintaining the standards, purity and eloquence of the French language. There is no equivalent academy for the regulation of English, although several authoritative bodies have tried to introduce formal controls. The Royal Society, for example, was established in 1660 and it encouraged its members, scientists and writers alike, to develop 'a close naked, natural way of speaking; positive expressions, clear senses, a native easiness'.

America, too, has had its informal 'academicians'. Noah Webster (1758–1843), for example, helped to modify spelling conventions, preferring '-or' to '-our' in words such as 'colour' as well as the simplification of endings in words such as 'catalogue' and 'programme'.

Today, the media, especially in the quality press and the news programmes of radio and television, function like an academy in that they arbitrate on what is acceptable and they influence the entire population, encouraging a modification towards NETWORK NORMS.

accent

The word *accent* refers to a person's pronunciation. Everyone who speaks a language has an accent, but people often think that prestigious accents are clearer, better or even accentless:

She speaks English perfectly, with no trace of an accent.

The term *accent* is often popularly confused with DIALECT, so that someone speaking Standard

English with a regional accent may be described, inaccurately, as speaking a dialect. In England RECEIVED PRONUNCIATION is still a prestigious accent and is the accent used by many television and radio presenters. Every English-speaking community has an accent sometimes referred to as the NETWORK NORM. Such accents are associated with education, power and privilege and are often thought of as being the standard accent for the particular community.

accent mark

Accent marks, such as é, ö and ï, are not used to represent English sounds, but they are occasionally found in words borrowed from other languages or to indicate that a syllable is long or short. The most widely-used accent marks are:

the acute ('), as in *risqué*. This mark indicates that the é is pronounced like 'ay'.

the bar (¯)as in *machīne*. This mark indicates that the vowel is long.

the breve (˘)as in *hĭd*. This mark indicates that the vowel is short.

the cedilla (̧)as in *façade*. This mark indicates that the ç is pronounced like 's'.

the circumflex (^) as in *maître d'hotel*

the dieresis (¨)as in *naïve*. This mark indicates that the word has two syllables.

the grave (`)as in *à la mode*

the wedge (ˇ) as in many Polish names. This mark indicates that the c is pronounced as 'ch' and the 'z' as /ʒ/ as in French 'rouge'.

the umlaut (¨) as in *Köhler*; sometimes 'e' is used instead as in *Koehler*.

accessary, accessory

In American English, these forms are alternative spellings for words that are occasionally distinguished in careful British English. The word *accessary* was traditionally used as a noun to refer to a willing helper in a criminal act:

He was convicted of being an accessary after the fact.

Increasingly, the word with 'o' is gaining ground. It can be used as a noun or adjective to mean 'an additional feature, additional':

He provided material that was accessory.

Accessory is the only acceptable form for the meaning of 'items of clothing':

She wore a grey suit with blue accessories.

and it is becoming the preferred form for 'criminal helper'. It has been extended to refer to additional features on such goods as cars and electronic equipment:

Such accessories come as standard with the Daewoo. Other accessories include a double-speed disc drive.

accidence

This term was used in traditional grammar to refer to what many contemporary linguists call *inflectional morphology*. Both terms refer to the variation that can occur in nouns:

boy, boys, boy's, boys'
girl, girls, girl's, girls'

in pronouns:

I, me, mine
she, her, hers

and in verbs:

go, goes, went, going, gone
see, sees, saw, seeing, seen.

accommodate

This word and its related noun 'accommodation' are frequently misspelled. They both have double 'c' and double 'm'.

accompany

This verb tends to be followed by a different preposition depending on whether the company is animate or inanimate:

I was accompanied by Michael.

Malaria is often accompanied with fever and loss of appetite.

The musician who accompanies a singer is an *accompanist*.

accusative

This term is taken from traditional grammar. In Latin, nouns and pronouns often differed in form depending on whether they were the subject (in the nominative case) or the object (in the accusative case):

Nominative	Accusative
dominus	*dominum*
domini	*dominos*

In English, nouns have the same form in the nominative and accusative:

The lord saw me.
I saw the lord.

but all personal pronouns except 'you' and 'it' change form depending on their role in the sentence:

Nominative	Accusative
I	me
he	him
she	her
we	us
they	them

See also NOUN, PRONOUN

acetic, ascetic

These words are sometimes confused. *Acetic* is associated with vinegar:

The acetic acid can turn wine into vinegar.

An *ascetic* is a person who exercises rigorous self-control:

It would be hard for us to imagine the privations endured by early Christian ascetics.

acknowledgement, acknowledgment

These are variant spellings. The form *acknowledgement* is probably more common in Britain and *acknowledgment* in America, but both spellings are found in both countries. Whichever spelling is selected, consistency is recommended.

SEE ALSO JUDGEMENT/JUDGMENT, SPELLING

acme, acne

The word *acme* is singular and refers to the summit of achievement, the highest point, the culmination of one's efforts:

That particular novel marks the acme of his achievement as a writer.

Acne is a skin disorder commonly found in teenagers:

His acne was a temporary condition. In a few months his skin was totally free of spots.

acoustics

The word is singular when it refers to the science of sound:

Acoustics is sometimes studied in departments of phonetics.

It can be used as a plural noun to refer to the sound qualities of a room:

The acoustics in the new lecture theatre are atrocious.

acronym

An *acronym* is a special type of ABBREVIATION in which the initial letters of a phrase are joined and pronounced as a word:

NATO (North Atlantic Treaty Organization).

There is often no logical reason why one abbreviated phrase becomes an acronym, as in:

SOAS: School of Oriental and African Studies

and another remains an abbreviation where the letters are pronounced individually, as in:

TUC: Trades Union Congress.

Often, groups select a name that will produce a memorable acronym:

Action on Smoking and Health: ASH
Surface to Air Missile: SAM
Mutually Assured Destruction: MAD.

As the above examples show, acronyms often omit prepositions. Other grammatical words such as articles are also omitted if their inclusion would make the pronunciation more difficult:

TEFL: Teaching (of) English (as) (a) Foreign Language.

Alternatively, some acronyms use two letters from one word as in:

LASSO: Laser Search (and) Secure Observer.

When acronyms are first introduced into the language, they are written with capital letters:

UNESCO

but, if they become widely used, they are eventually written with lower-case letters:

laser: Light Amplification by Stimulated Emission of Radiation

quango: Quasi-autonomous Non-Governmental Organization

radar: Radio Detecting and Ranging

and people often cease to be aware of their origin as acronyms.

acrophobia, agoraphobia

The two words, both derived from Greek, are sometimes mistaken. *Acrophobia*, derived from *acro* + *phobos*, is the fear of high places.

Agoraphobia is the fear of open spaces. The word derives from *agora*, 'market place' + *phobos*, 'fear'. The first part of the word is misspelled by people who mistakenly believe that it derives from Latin *ager*, 'a field'.

active voice, passive voice

These terms occur frequently in traditional grammatical descriptions. They were applied to sentences of a particular structure. If we look at such related sentences as:

John broke the window.
The window was broken (by John).

we can see that in the first sentence the agent, John, is the subject of the sentence:

S (subject)	P (predicate)	O (object)
John	broke	the window

whereas the recipient of the action, the window, is the object. This is called an *active* sentence. In the second sentence the recipient of the action occurs in the subject position and we can omit the agent. This type is called a *passive* sentence. Thus the category of VOICE is applied to the relationship between the agent or performer of an action and the recipient of an action. Generally, active voice has the structure:

Noun Phrase (Agent) + Verb Phrase + Noun Phrase (Recipient)

whereas passive voice has the structure:

Noun Phrase (Recipient) + 'be' + past participle of Verb

or

Noun Phrase (Recipient) + 'be' + past participle of Verb + by a Noun Phrase (Agent).

See also ERGATIVE, GRAMMAR, INTRANSITIVE

actor, actress

Many English nouns have male and female forms:

actor/actress, author/authoress, masseur/masseuse, poet/poetess.

See also GENDER, POLITICAL CORRECTNESS

actor, agent

These terms are both used to describe the person or animal who performs the action in a sentence:

John ate a biscuit.

She sang a song.

The dog barked.

In the above examples the actors/agents are 'John', 'She' and 'The dog'.

In English, the actor/agent is usually animate but, occasionally, the term is applied to the non-animate subjects in sentences such as:

The sun was shining.

It was raining.

The wind howled all night.

The sea lashed the shore.

In the above examples, the actors/agents are 'The sun', 'It', 'The wind' and 'The sea'.

Often, the actor/agent is the subject of a sentence but the agent may also occur as an adjunct:

The biscuit was eaten (by John).

or it may be omitted:

The song was sung.

In active sentences, the actor/agent is usually the subject:

Mary (actor/agent) loved the lamb.

In the passive equivalent, the agent may be included:

The lamb was loved by Mary.

or it may be omitted:

The lamb was loved.

See also CASE, GRAMMAR, VOICE

actually

This word has been criticized because it is so frequently used as a filler:

Well, actually, no.

I didn't actually go.

To condemn this usage because 'actually' is semantically redundant is to forget that speakers often use fillers to help with the rhythm of speech. The early users of Français Fondamental, for example, had to introduce fillers such as *Alors* or *Eh bien* to help learners speak naturally and confidently.

There are, however, differences between speech and writing. Whereas words such as *actually* and 'well' are acceptable in everyday speech, it is probably best to avoid them in formal writing.

See also DEFINITELY, FILLER, IN FACT

AD, BC

The convention is to use AD and BC without full stops. AD stands for *Anno Domini*, 'in the year of the Lord', and refers to a specified number of years after the birth of Jesus Christ. It is placed before the year as in:

AD90 or AD 90

When a date is not certain, a question mark is used as in:

She died in ?AD90.

BC, standing for Before Christ, however, comes after the year as in:

27BC or 27 BC

He died in ?27BC.

Although BC can be applied to centuries:

She lived in the third century BC.

it is customary to omit AD from references to the periods of this era:

She died in the third century.

AD can, however, be inserted if its omission could cause ambiguity:

He lived in the second century BC and she in the third century AD.

Some writers prefer to avoid the religious connotations of AD and BC and use instead CE (common era, Christian era) and BCE (before common era, before Christian era).

ad hoc

This Latin phrase, meaning 'to this', is used mainly as an adjective to suggest 'for a specific purpose':

They set up an *ad hoc* committee to deal with the student's complaint.

There is a tendency also to use the phrase to mean *improvise*:

It's just an *ad hoc* get-together.

Many purists disapprove of this usage.

ad infinitum

This Latin phrase, meaning 'to infinity', is used adverbially to suggest 'endlessly', 'without limit':

I thought his lecture went on *ad infinitum*.

ad lib

Ad lib is an abbreviation of Latin *ad libitum*, 'according to pleasure'. It is sometimes used as a verb meaning 'extemporise', 'improvise':

She ad libbed wonderfully.

When it is used as an attributive adjective, it is hyphenated:

The ad-lib performance was well received.

Ad lib is not hyphenated when it is used as a predicative adjective or as an adverb:

The performance was ad lib.

She played ad lib.

ad nauseam

This Latin phrase, meaning 'to the point of nausea', is normally written in italics:

They went on and on *ad nauseam*.

It has been so overused as an adverb that it should be avoided in formal contexts.

adapt, adept, adopt

The two verbs *adapt* and *adopt* are occasionally confused. *Adapt* means 'change', 'modify', 'make more suitable':

I've adapted the script to suit our needs.
We can adapt our policies to your current needs.

Adopt means 'take as one's own':

We're so lucky. We've been able to adopt a baby.
We've adopted Michael's plan and it will become departmental policy.

The noun from *adapt* is 'adaptation', not *adaption:

Have you seen her adaptation of *Sense and Sensibility*?

The noun from *adopt* is 'adoption':

The adoption will take at least twelve months.

The adjective *adept* means 'skilled', 'expert' and is followed by 'at':

They're adept at finding methods of recycling rubbish.

adherence, adherent, adhesion, adhesive

The verb *adhere*, 'to stick to', can be used both literally and metaphorically:

The label failed to adhere to the envelope.
The students adhered to their campaign plan.

The nouns *adhesion* and *adhesive* are used literally:

The envelopes won't stick. The adhesion is minimal.
You'll have to use a strong adhesive to hold this heavy paper.

The nouns *adherence* and *adherent* are used metaphorically. The first noun implies loyalty:

His adherence to the cause – even when it seemed doomed – was praiseworthy.

Adherent refers to a person:

He's a willing adherent to the cause.

adjacent, adjoining

These adjectives are near synonyms but they are not interchangeable. *Adjacent* means 'near each other', 'close'. Items that are adjacent need not necessarily touch:

Jean lived in an adjacent street.

Adjoining, on the other hand, means 'joined on to':

They lived in adjoining rooms.

Rooms that are adjoining share a wall or passage; rooms that are adjacent are merely close. This is a useful distinction in the language and so the terms should not be equated.

adjective

An *adjective* is a descriptive word. In English, adjectives belong to a large open class of words, and they can function in two main ways: before a noun or after a COPULA verb (such as 'to be' and 'to seem'):

a tall building, the green door
The building is tall. The door was green.

Adjectives that precede nouns are called *attributive*. Adjectives that follow copula verbs are called *predicative*.

Most adjectives can occur in both positions:

the clever child
The child seems clever.

but some adjectives occur in one position only. Among the adjectives that can only be used attributively are *elder*, *mere* and *utter*:

her elder brother	*Her brother is elder.
a mere token	*The token is mere.
an utter fool	*The fool is utter.

Among those adjectives that occur only predicatively are *afloat*, *asleep* and, usually, *well*:

*an afloat raft	The raft was still afloat.
*an asleep baby	The baby is asleep.
*a not well man	The man is not well.

Most adjectives can have comparative and superlative forms:

Positive	Comparative	Superlative
big	bigger	biggest
delightful	more delightful	most delightful
good	better	best

but some adjectives, such as *alive*, *dead* and *unique*, cannot logically have comparative or superlative forms. In practical terms, one is either dead or alive, and if an object is unique, then there are no others with which to compare it. In colloquial English, however, a number of uses of such 'impossible' forms occur:

He was more dead than alive when they found him.
I've known walking sticks that were more alive than Peter.

Some speakers tend to regard *unique* as a synonym for 'excellent' or 'wonderful':

It was the most unique experience of my life.

Care should be taken, however, not to use language loosely.

Most monosyllabic adjectives form their comparative by adding -er and their superlative by adding -est:

long, longer, longest
low, lower, lowest

however monosyllabic adjectives that end in a single consonant (excluding 'w' and 'y') double the consonant before the suffixes:

big, bigger, biggest
fat, fatter, fattest
thin, thinner, thinnest.

Commonly occurring disyllabic adjectives and all disyllabic adjectives ending in 'y' form their comparatives and superlatives by adding -er and -est:

gentle, gentler, gentlest
lovely, lovelier, loveliest
mellow, mellower, mellowest.

Other adjectives prefix 'more' and 'most':

suitable, more suitable, most suitable
useful, more useful, most useful.

In a certain number of fixed collocations derived from other languages, the adjective follows the noun:

attorney general (French)
Princess Royal (French)
Father Almighty (Latin)
whisky galore (Gaelic).

Many dialect speakers use adjectives where the standard language requires adverbs:

Dialectal	Standard
He sings real good	He sings really well.
She walks quick.	She walks quickly.

See also ADVERB, MODIFIER, SPELLING

adjudge, judge

These verbs both derive ultimately from Old French *ajuger*, meaning 'judge', 'adjudicate'. *Adjudge* means 'declare officially', 'decide by law':

The court adjudged him to be liable and fined him.

Judge is now used much more widely than in connection with the legal system. It can mean 'form an opinion about', 'estimate':

As far as I can judge, the full extent of the damage will never be known.

adjure

See ABJURE/ADJURE

administer, administrate

The verb *administer* was borrowed in the fourteenth century from Old French *amynistre*, 'to administer', and means 'direct or control affairs'. Often the affairs relate to business, government or the law:

The Senior District Officer was responsible for administering justice.

The derived forms are:

administration, administrative(ly), administrator.

The verb *administrate* seems to have been coined in the seventeenth century from Latin *administratus*, the past participle of *administrare*, 'to administer'. The verbs are used in similar contexts, but *administer* is used more widely and is often thought to be more correct. The derived adjective *administrable*, not *administratable, is used to mean 'capable of being managed':

The inland districts proved to be just as administrable as the coastal areas.

admission, admittance

The noun *admission* is used when the meaning relates to 'confession', 'permission to enter' or the price paid to enter:

Such a statement is not an admission of guilt.
Admission restricted to members.
I can't afford the price of admission.

Admittance is a more technical and restricted term referring to the 'physical right to enter' a place or an area. It is often used negatively:

No admittance to unauthorized personnel.

admit

This verb comes from Latin *ad* + *mittere* meaning 'to let come or go'. It is used in English with three main meanings: first, 'permit entrance to':

We have a policy of refusing to admit men who are not wearing ties.

second, 'allow to be part of':

After much discussion, his testimony was admitted.

and third, 'confess':

She admitted her association with the accused but refused to accept that she had in any way participated in the crime.

Many usage experts dislike the use of *admit* to mean 'confess' but such changes in meaning are commonplace in English.

See also SEMANTIC CHANGE

admittance

See ADMISSION/ADMITTANCE

admonish, admonition, admonishment

The verb *admonish* means 'reprove firmly', 'warn', 'caution':

I was admonished for behaving in such a way while I was wearing the club's colours.

The usual derived noun is *admonition*:

He paid no attention to the Head's admonition.

A second noun *admonishment* is also used:

He resented the admonishment but had been advised 'to take his medicine like a man'.

Many stylists dislike *admonishment*, but the form has come about by analogy with other derived nouns:

astonish, astonishment
banish, banishment
fulfil, fulfilment.

See also ANALOGY

adolescence, adolescent

The noun *adolescence* and the relative adjective and noun *adolescent* are often misspelled. There is a 'c' after the 's':

Adolescence is the developmental period between puberty and maturity.

I thought you were too mature for such adolescent behaviour.

Adolescents often have problems coping with their new responsibilities.

adopt

See ADAPT/ADEPT/ADOPT

adopted, adoptive

These two adjectives are occasionally misused, partly because there is an overlap of meaning. If John and Mary adopt a child called Kim, then Kim is their *adopted* son, while they are Kim's *adoptive* parents.

adult

The noun *adult* may be stressed on either syllable. The British tend to stress the second syllable, the Americans the first.

The word is often used as an adjective (with the stress on the first syllable) as a synonym for pornographic when it is applied to films, magazines, videos or computer data:

At the moment, there is no way to stop children downloading adult material from the Internet.

It is also used in expressions like 'that wasn't adult behaviour'.

adulteration, adultery

These nouns have little in common now, although they both derive from Latin *adultare*, 'to corrupt'. *Adulteration* means 'debasing by adding something less valuable':

There was widespread adulteration of the milk. Water had been added.

The police fear the adulteration of this drug may lead to the death of other young people.

Adultery means 'sexual relations between a married person and someone who is not his or her spouse':

Adultery was cited as the reason for the divorce.

advance, advanced

These words can both be used as adjectives. As an adjective, *advance* means 'before it is normally due':

Advance payments will be made from the Monday before the Bank Holiday.

The company received advance warning but failed to act upon it.

The phrase 'advance guard' is used in military circles to refer to a unit sent ahead of an advancing group:

The advance guard tries to facilitate the progress of the following force.

Advanced means 'highly developed', 'being ahead in one's development':

The rocket was already at an advanced stage of development.

She is advanced for her age. She is only 24 months old but she is already producing four- and five-word sentences.

advantageous

The adjective *advantageous* is frequently misspelled. There is an 'e' between the 'g' and the '-ous'.

advent

This noun means 'coming' but it carries with it associations of formality and seriousness:

We anticipated the advent of the Millennium.

When *Advent* refers to the period before Christmas, it is given a capital letter:

The Sunday closest to St Andrew's Day is the first day of Advent.

adverb

An *adverb* is a word or group of words that modifies a verb, a sentence, an adjective or another adverb:

He spoke *quietly*.

We shall need to see your certificates, *however*.

It was *very* small.

He spoke *very* quietly.

Adverbs are often morphological variants of adjectives:

Adjective	Adverb
clever	cleverly
happy	happily
graceful	gracefully
quick	quickly

Adjectives most frequently modify nouns:

the *happy* child
The child is *happy*.

whereas adverbs frequently modify adjectives:

She is an *extraordinarily* happy child.
The child is *extraordinarily* happy.

other adverbs:

He responded *extremely* quickly.
She danced *exceptionally* gracefully.

preposition phrases:

They were *unbelievably* out of sorts.

sentences:

Interestingly, he forgot to mention his part in the affair.

and verbs:

He responded *quickly*.
She danced *gracefully*.

Like adjectives, adverbs have comparative and superlative forms:

Positive	Comparative	Superlative
cleverly	more cleverly	most cleverly
fast	faster	fastest

as in:

He drove fast.
He drove faster when I complained
He drove fastest when he thought I might overtake him.

Although the form of an adverb often differs from its related adjective:

quick, quickly
sweet, sweetly

several words can function, without change of form, as both adjectives and adverbs. The most frequently occurring items in this category are:

cheap, clean, dead (= completely), easy, fast, fine, free, hard, high, late, loud, low, pretty, quick, sharp, slow, straight, sure, well, wide, wrong.

Several other words, such as *fair*, *just* and *tight*, can be used adverbially in certain collocations:

Fight fair.
He has just arrived.
Hold tight.

Adverbs are among the most mobile elements in a sentence and can occur in three main positions. First, at the beginning of the sentence:

Yesterday, upon the stair,
I met a man who wasn't there.

Second, in the middle of the sentence:

He arrived yesterday just as I was about to go out.

Finally, at the end of the sentence:

I arranged to meet him yesterday.

As we might expect, however, not all adverbs can occur in all positions. The adverbs that are most likely to occur in the initial position are discourse markers such as:

actually, alternatively, apparently, briefly, finally, frankly, however, perhaps, surely, unfortunately

adverbs of time:

next week, today, tomorrow, yesterday

adverbs that indicate frequency:

occasionally, rarely, sometimes.

In literary style and for emphasis we often foreground adverbs:

Surely some revelation is at hand;
Surely the Second Coming is at hand.
      W.B. Yeats, 'The Second Coming'

Gently does it.
There he goes!

When adverbs occur in the middle of a sentence, they usually precede all verbs except 'be', 'have' and the auxiliaries:

The old man rarely went out of his house.
The old man was rarely out of his house.
The newspaper boy invariably tears my Sunday paper.
My Sunday paper is invariably torn.
My younger brother usually wins something.
My younger brother has usually won something.

Adverbs can, however, precede auxiliaries, especially in speech, if extra emphasis is required:

They will really try. (unemphatic)
They really will try. (emphatic)

The tendency to use adjectives as adverbs as in:

She talks very nice.

has been so frequently stigmatized that many speakers hypercorrect by using inappropriate '-ly' forms such as:

*fastly, *thusly.

See also ADJECTIVE, HYPERCORRECTION, SENTENCE

adverse, averse

These two adjectives are occasionally misused. *Adverse* means 'unfavourable', 'hostile' and it tends to premodify abstract nouns:

adverse circumstances
adverse weather conditions.

Averse means 'against', 'opposed to', 'unwilling'. It tends to be applied to people and is used predicatively:

She was averse to repeating her lectures.
I'm not averse to your suggestion.

advertise

Advertise is one of the few *-ise* verbs that cannot be spelled with the alternative suffix *-ize*. The derived noun is *advertisement*, and the abbreviated forms 'ad' and 'advert' should be avoided in formal speech and writing.

See also -IZE/-ISE

advice, advise

The noun *advice* is spelled with a 'c' and rhymes with 'mice':

She gave me some wonderful advice. I wish I had taken it!

Advice is an uncountable noun. This means that it cannot be preceded by an indefinite article:

*I wanted an advice.

Instead, we must use either 'some' or 'a piece of':

I wanted some advice.

I wanted a piece of advice.

The verb *advise* is spelled with an 's' and rhymes with 'eyes':

I would not presume to advise you.

Advise is a regular verb:

advise(s), advised, advising.

adviser, advisor

A person who is consulted for advice tends to be called an *adviser* in Britain and an *advisor* in America. Both spellings are acceptable but a writer should aim to be consistent.

-ae-, -e-

The digraph *-ae-* is frequently used in words from Greek and Latin:

Aesop, caesarean.

It is now written as two separate letters and not as æ. The æ is used, however, for Old English:

Cædmon, sing me hwæþwuga.

In many words where British English has *-ae-*, American English prefers *-e-*:

aesthetic/esthetic
aetiology/etiology
anaesthetic/anesthetic.

The *-e-* spelling is currently preferred throughout the English-using world in such words as:

eon (formerly aeon)
ether (formerly aether)
hyena (formerly hyaena)
medieval (formerly mediaeval)

and it seems likely that the *-e-* will gradually replace *-ae-*, just as '-e' has replaced '-oe'.

See also SPELLING

aeon, eon

These are alternative spellings and are both correct. *Aeon* used to be the preferred form in Britain but the simpler spelling *eon* is replacing it:

It happened eons ago, long before our ancestors stood upright.

aerial, antenna

The noun *aerial* is the usual word in Britain for the mechanism used for sending or receiving radio waves. The adjective *aerial* is used as a derived adjective from 'aeroplane' and also 'air':

We were shown the film of the aerial bombardment.
The Japanese have invested heavily in aerial railways.

Antenna is the preferred form in America and its plural is *antennas*:

There was a rapid growth in the number of television antennas in the 1960s.

When *antenna* is used to mean an insect's feeler, the plural is *antennae*.

How many antennae has an ant?

See also UK AND US ENGLISH

aerie, eyrie

There are several acceptable spellings for this word, which refers to an eagle's nest, possibly because the word had several forms in medieval Latin:

aerea, aeria, airea, airia, eyria

The preferred form today seems to be 'eyrie', although 'aery', 'eyry' and 'aerie' are also acceptable. It has two acceptable pronunciations: it can rhyme with 'dearie' or 'fiery'.

aerobics

The noun *aerobics* refers to an energetic form of physical exercise, often accompanied by music. The noun was formed by analogy with 'aerobatics', which was itself modelled on 'acrobatics'.

aeroplane, airplane

The spelling *aeroplane* was the original term for a fixed-wing aircraft. Britain retains this spelling in formal writing, whereas most Americans use *airplane* or *plane*. The abbreviated form, without an apostrophe, is also acceptable in Britain.

The noun *aircraft* is used for both planes and helicopters.

See also UK AND US ENGLISH

aerosol

This noun is a blend of aero (air) + sol(ution) and means 'a suspension of particles in a gas', 'a substance packed under pressure in a container with a spraying device' and 'the can containing the gas'. It is spelled *aerosol* throughout the English-using world:

These aerosols do not contain CFCs.

See also WORD FORMATION

aesthetic(s), esthetic(s)

The form without '-s' is an adjective:

We should not overlook aesthetic considerations.

and the form with '-s' is a singular noun:

Aesthetics is the branch of philosophy that is concerned with the study of such abstract concepts as beauty and refinement.

Both spellings are acceptable, although *aesthetics* is more likely to be used in Britain and *esthetics* in America.

See also -AE-/-E-, UK AND US ENGLISH

aetiology, etiology

These nouns refer to 'the study of causation, especially the cause of diseases':

The aetiology of Bêchet's Disease is unknown.

Both spellings are acceptable, but *aetiology* is more likely to appear in Britain and *etiology* in America.

See also UK AND US ENGLISH

affect, effect

Affect can function as a verb meaning 'have an influence on':

She doesn't seem to be affected by the high humidity.
The humidity affected the camera.

'move or disturb emotionally':

She was deeply affected by her father's death.

and 'attack (of pain, disease)':

My entire lymphatic system was affected.

Effect can function as a noun or a verb. As a noun, it means 'result', 'power or ability to influence a result', 'efficacy':

What effect did the Viking settlement have on the English language?

As a verb, *effect* means 'cause to occur', 'bring about', 'accomplish', 'perform', 'produce':

He will try to effect changes in the running of the department.
The thieves effected a rapid getaway in a stolen car.

The plural, *effects*, is used in such collocations as:

special effects (costume, lighting or sound to enhance a film or play)
personal effects (personal property).

affectation, affection

These nouns are occasionally misused. *Affectation* refers to an assumed manner of behaviour, dress or speech that is intended to impress people:

His huge bow tie is an affectation. His tutor used to wear a small one and he feels that he has to outdo his tutor.

Affection refers to feelings of warmth and tenderness:

I have always had a great deal of affection for John.

affinity

This word is widely – and loosely – used. *Affinity* can mean a relationship of liking or attraction between two people:

There has always been a close affinity between John and Michael, partly because of their similar backgrounds.

a close similarity in appearance or quality:

There's an obvious affinity between Flemish and Dutch.

or a relationship other than by blood:

Consanguinity implies a blood relationship; affinity implies that the link is by marriage or adoption.

The use of *affinity* where 'aptitude' would be more appropriate is often condemned, but many people write such sentences as:

She has an affinity for languages.

This usage might well be considered an extension of the first use above.

Affinity collocates with the prepositions 'between' and 'with':

There is an obvious affinity between adjectives and adverbs.
Jane Austen has a rapport, an affinity, with her readers.

The use of *affinity* with 'for' is limited to scientific English when a substance is said to have an affinity for another if it unites easily with it:

Carbon has an affinity for oxygen.

The use of 'for' in non-scientific English is stigmatized.

affirm, confirm

Affirm means 'state strongly and positively', 'assert':

I wish to affirm my support for both cabinet ministers.

Confirm means 'ratify', 'corroborate':

I am afraid I have not been able to confirm your hypothesis.

affirmative, negative

In English grammar, sentences are often classified as being declarative, imperative and interrogative, with all three being capable of occurring in the affirmative or the negative:

Affirmative	Negative
I saw him	I didn't see him.
Go home.	Don't go home.
Have you seen it?	Haven't you seen it?

Occasionally, to avoid misunderstanding on the phone or over the radio, the words 'affirmative' and 'negative' replace 'yes' and 'no':

Are you still in contact with the suspect?'
Affirmative. We are following at a discreet distance.
Negative. He has disappeared into the station.

See also GRAMMAR, SENTENCE

affix

The word *affix* derives from Latin *affixare*, meaning 'attach to', and describes a class of words that includes PREFIXES, SUFFIXES and INFIXES.

See also DERIVATION, MORPHEME, WORD FORMATION

afflict, inflict

These verbs are occasionally confused. *Afflict* means 'cause pain and distress':

The Black Death afflicted millions of people throughout Europe.

Although *afflict* can occur in active sentences, such as the one above, it is normally used in passive constructions where it means 'suffer from':

She was afflicted with arthritis from the age of eight.

The direct object of *afflict* as an active verb is the person who suffers:

Arthritis afflicts people of all ages.
People of all ages are afflicted.

Inflict means 'cause pain to be suffered by someone else':

Napoleon inflicted a crushing defeat on the Russians but he was ultimately beaten by the rigours of a Russian winter.

It collocates with 'on' in both active and passive sentences:

A heavy penalty was inflicted on those who could not pay their taxes.

The direct object of *inflict* is the suffering:

He inflicted pain on all those he knew.

In passive constructions, the suffering is the subject:

Pain was inflicted on all those he knew.

Afghanistan

An inhabitant of the country in eastern Asia is an 'Afghani'; the derived adjective is 'Afghan' or 'Afghani'. The capital is Kabul.

aficionado

This word, of Spanish origin, means 'fan, devotee'. It has been used recently, especially in the tabloid press, as a synonym for 'sports enthusiast':

Harry C., the well-known aficionado of boxing ...

In most uses the word is no longer italicized. The plural is *aficionados*:

Hemingway and his friends were aficionados of bullfighting.

See also BORROWING, FOREIGN LOAN-WORDS

Afro-

People of African origin have been referred to in many ways, including 'African', 'Black' and 'Negro'. The term 'Afro-American' was first used of Americans of African origin as early as 1853, but it did not become popular until the late 1950s, when the *Afro-* prefix gave rise to such coinages as:

Afro (African hairstyle)
Afro-American (Black American)
Afro-Asiatic (family of languages including Berber, Chad and Semitic)
Afro-Caribbean (Black West Indian)
Afro-comb (hand-shaped comb designed for African hair)
Afro-Cuban (music).

See also POLITICAL CORRECTNESS

afterward, afterwards

These adverbs are both acceptable in all styles, although *afterwards* is the preferred form in Britain:

Afterwards, we relaxed and enjoyed the lovely weather.

Afterward is preferred in America:

... and afterward you may like to take advantage of the sauna.

See also -WARD/-WARDS

age

Age can function as a noun with a range of meanings:

What age are you, Tom?
They took an age shopping.
Did they die out in the Mesozoic Age?

Age is a regular verb:

age(s), aged, ag(e)ing

The spelling 'ageing' is preferred in British English, while 'aging' is the preferred US usage.

Generally, a person's age is expressed according to the conventions that apply to numbers. There are some differences, however. When the age follows the verb, it is spelled out in full:

John is seventeen.
She was twenty-two years old at the time.

British people often omit the word 'old', while Americans tend to use it.

When the age is given as an attributive adjective, the elements are hyphenated and, to avoid excessive hyphenation, numbers are often preferred, although, of course, the use of figures should be consistent throughout any document:

The seventeen-year-old girl won the prize.
The 22-year-old was the author.

See also NUMBERS, SPELLING

aged

Aged can function as a verb and as an adjective. As a verb, it is monosyllabic and rhymes with 'paged':

He was aged about twenty at the time.

When the word is used as an adjective or noun meaning 'very old [people]', it is disyllabic:

Your aged aunt would enjoy a visit.
She works for Help the Aged.

agenda

Agenda is a noun meaning 'list of items, usually for a meeting':

We didn't receive the agenda for today's meeting until yesterday.

The word derives from Latin *agendum*, but although the English form derives from a Latin plural, it is treated as a singular noun with *agendas* as a plural:

This agenda is totally inadequate. Who used to prepare the agendas?

In recent usage, the expression 'hidden agenda' has taken on the extra meaning of 'secret plan':

I should be glad to know if there is a hidden agenda that could adversely affect my career prospects.

Agenda is also taking on the meaning of 'a personal plan of action':

Tell us about your current agenda and your plans for the future.

agent
See ACTOR/AGENT

aggravate
Aggravate derives from Latin *aggravare* 'to make heavier' and means 'make worse or more serious':

His lifestyle aggravated his medical condition.

Aggravate is also frequently used to mean 'annoy, irritate' but purists continue to argue that speakers and writers should avoid such sentences as:

His smarmy manner really aggravates me.

It is hard to explain why the people who criticize the semantic shift of *aggravate* from 'make worse' to 'annoy' do not condemn the change of meaning of *prevent* from 'come before' to 'inhibit' or the change of *silly* from 'holy' to 'foolish'. Purists tend to overlook two facts about language: that changes of meaning are inevitable and that no amount of dogmatic assertion will prevent users extending or modifying a word's meaning. To admit that change is inevitable is not, however, the same as claiming that any usage is acceptable. Care must always be exercised so that the language may be used with precision and appropriateness. Natural semantic change is very different from inaccurate or imprecise use of language.

See also ACADEMY, ETYMOLOGY, MALAPROPISM, PURIST, SEMANTIC CHANGE, SHIBBOLETH

agnostic, atheist
An *agnostic* is someone who believes that God's existence is and must remain an open question:

My father was an agnostic. He would like to have believed in God but he never found an argument that convinced him.

An *atheist* is someone who denies the existence of God:

Atheists claim that God does not exist.

ago, since
The adverb *ago* is sometimes incorrectly combined with the conjunction *since*:

*It was five years ago since I saw them.

Ago is used when people want to view a time in the past from the vantage point of the present:

I first saw her five years ago.

That happened a long time ago.

It is thus most frequently used with the simple past:

It happened two years ago.

Since is a conjunction introducing a clause that looks at the present from a point in the past:

It is two years since we met.

Ago can be followed by a clause beginning with 'that':

It was two years ago that we met.

but it should not be followed by a clause beginning with 'since':

*It was two years ago since we met.

Notice that the sentences using 'ago' and 'since' tend to occur with different tenses:

It was two years ago that we met.

It is two years since we met.

because 'since' involves looking at the present from a vantage point in the past and 'ago' reverses the viewpoint.

Since can also be used as a preposition:

We have been here since January.

If a specific period of time is mentioned, then the preposition 'for' should be used:

We have been here for two weeks/six months/five years.

See also SINCE

agoraphobia
See ACROPHOBIA/AGORAPHOBIA

agreement
The term *agreement* is used to describe a type of concord between different parts of an utterance. Thus, in the present tense in English, a singular, third person subject causes an 's' to be added to the verb:

The child sings.

whereas all the other persons require an unmarked verb:

I/you/we/they/the children sing.

In languages like French, determiners and adjectives agree with the nouns they modify:

le petit livre vert
la petite boîte verte
les petits livres verts
les petites boîtes vertes

whereas English has much less agreement, as we can see from the equivalents of the French phrases:

the little green book

the little green box
the little green books
the little green boxes.

There is little agreement left in contemporary English. We can deal with what remains under two categories: determiners, and person and number.

Determiners

Most determiners do not change to agree with the nouns they modify:

the table, the tables.

The exceptions are 'this' and 'that', which modify singular nouns only, and 'these' and 'those', which modify plural nouns:

this table, these tables, *this tables

that table, those tables, *those table

and 'a/an', which can only modify singular nouns:

a table, an awl.

When we need a plural equivalent of 'a/an' we use, depending on context, either 'some' or no determiner at all:

some tables, tables

some awls, awls.

Person and number

The rules for agreement that are most widely broken occur in the area of number. The rules are relatively easy but mistakes are made even by native speakers.

■ Subject + verb agreement

With the exception of the verbs 'to be', 'to have', the modal verbs (such as 'may') and, to a lesser extent, 'to do' and 'to say', agreement occurs only in the non-past tense when a third person singular subject triggers off the use of a marked form of the verb:

I/you/we/they/the children *walk*
he/she/it/the child *walks*.

There is no agreement between subject and verb in the past tense where all subjects take the same verb form:

I/you/he/she/it/we/they/the child/the children *walked*.

'To be' is the most irregular verb in the language and shows more agreement. In the present, we have the following pattern:

Person	Singular	Plural
1	(I) am	(we) are
2	(you) are	(you) are
3	(he/she/it) is	(they) are

The past is simpler:

Person	Singular	Plural
1	(I) was	(we) were
2	(you) were	(you) were
3	(he/she/it) was	(they) were

'To have' is more regular than 'to be'. In the pre-sent, there are two forms, 'have' and 'has'. If the verb were regular, we would expect 'have' and 'haves':

I/you/we/they *have*
he/she/it *has*.

In the past tense, all subjects take the same form of the verb:

I/you/he/she/it/we/they *had*.

'To do' is more regular still. In the present, we have the forms 'do' and 'does' (pronounced to rhyme with 'fuzz'):

I/you/we/they *do*
he/she/it *does*.

The invariable past tense form is 'did':

I/you/he/she/it/we/they *did*.

'To say' is regular in the written medium:

I/you/we/they *say*
he/she/it *says*
I/you/he/she/it/we/they *said*

but, in speech, 'says' is pronounced to rhyme with 'Jez' and not, as one might predict, with 'jays'.

The modal verbs, 'can', 'could', 'may', 'might', 'must', 'shall', 'should', 'will' and 'would', show no agreement whatsoever between subject and predicate:

I/you/he/she/it/we/you/they *can*
I/you/he/she/it/we/you/they *could*.

■ Subject + verb + complement agreement

Subject complements are usually in concordial agreement with both subject and predicate:

Michael is a farmer.
Michael and John are brothers.
Mary and Rosie are sisters.
It wasn't my book.
They weren't my books.

It is, however, possible to find sentences such as:

Her recordings are now a national asset.
His children are a worry.

The subject and the predicate, however, must be in agreement:

*His children is a worry.

■ Agreement with 'each', 'everyone', 'no one'

Many people are uncertain about agreement with these items. Briefly, they are all singular and should trigger off the agreement of a singular form:

Each book *is* numbered.
Each of the books *is* numbered.

If 'everyone' occurs as a subject, it triggers off a singular form of the verb:

Everyone *is* coming.
Everyone *was* worried.

Problems occur in such sentences as:

Everyone must do *her* best.

Everyone must do *his* best.

Everyone must raise her or his hand.

Many people now sacrifice grammatical agreement and use a sentence that is neither clumsy nor sexist and say:

Everyone must raise their hand.

■ Agreement with 'either', 'neither'

There are two agreement problems with 'either' and 'neither'. The first is very easy to deal with. In balanced sentences, 'either' requires 'or' and 'neither' requires 'nor':

I want either green or blue.

I want neither green nor blue.

The tendency to use 'or' with 'neither' as in the following BBC news report is incorrect:

*They will neither release the hostages or even confirm that they are still alive.

The second problem with 'either' and 'neither' relates to agreement between a compound subject and a verb. Few people find difficulty with sentences such as:

Either John or Michael is the culprit.

Neither William nor Mary was happy with the arrangement.

but there is often confusion when the compound subject contains a single and a plural element as in:

Either John or the twins is/are the culprit(s).

The rule is that the verb agrees with the noun that is closer to it, thus:

Either John or the twins are the culprits.

Either the twins or John is the culprit.

■ Agreement with 'there is/are'

'There is' should be used only when the following noun is singular:

There is a bird on the roof.

There are birds on the roof.

In recent grammatical analyses the term 'concord' is often preferred to *agreement*.

See also COMPLEMENT, EVERYBODY/EVERYONE, MODALITY, NO ONE/NOBODY/NONE, THERE ARE/THERE IS

aid, aide

Aid can function as a noun meaning 'help', 'assistance':

These countries need aid immediately.

and as a regular verb:

aid(s), aided, aiding.

Aid and its plural *aids* occur in many compounds including:

audiovisual aid(s)

first aid

hearing aid(s)

legal aid.

Aide is most often used of a person. It means 'assistant':

One of the prince's aides was responsible for the leak.

It also functions in a number of French-derived compounds such as:

aide-de-camp (officer who assists a general)

aide-mémoire (reminder).

See also FOREIGN LOAN-WORDS

ain't

Ain't is one of the most widespread nonstandard forms in English. It occurs as a regional and class variant throughout the English-speaking world. It is used in three main ways. First, as an undifferentiated present tense negative form of the verb 'be':

I ain't leaving here without her.

She ain't saying nothing.

He ain't heavy; he's my brother.

second, as an undifferentiated auxiliary where the standard language requires 'have':

I ain't seen him today.

She ain't got it yet.

and third, without an overt subject in some forms of American speech:

Ain't seen nothing yet!

Ain't misbehaving, saving all my love for you.

Ain't got no loving to call my own.

'Ain't' occurs most frequently in speech, but it has been employed by fiction writers as a stereotyping word to signal a speaker's social status or regional origins. In *Great Expectations*, for example, Dickens uses a literary variant, *an't*, as a device to emphasize Joe Gargery's humble origins:

And I a'nt a master-mind ...

and Mark Twain employs *ain't* as one of the characterizing elements in the speech of Tom in *Tom Sawyer Abroad*:

Why the Holy Land – there ain't but one.

Occasionally 'ain't' is adopted by educated speakers, especially young ones, as a marker of group solidarity .

See also NONSTANDARD ENGLISH, SPEECH AND WRITING, STILE/STYLE

airplane

See AEROPLANE/AIRPLANE

aisle, isle

These nouns are homophones and they are occasionally confused. An *aisle* is a passage in a church or a large vehicle:

The bride walked slowly down the aisle towards the altar.

The aisles must be kept clear at all times.

An *isle* is an island. This word is rarely used now except in place-names:

Isle of Man

Isle of Wight

and in poetry:

Can you recite 'The Lake Isle of Innisfree'?

Albania

An inhabitant of the east European country is an 'Albanian'; the derived adjective is the same. The capital is Tiranë (but Tirana is also used).

albeit

This word derives from fourteenth-century 'al be it', meaning 'although it be'. Today, it is occasionally used as a conjunction to mean 'even though':

Mine is an original, albeit a small, contribution to knowledge.

See also COMPOUND

albumen, albumin

Careful users of language distinguish between these words. They use *albumen* to refer specifically to the white of an egg, and *albumin* for any water-soluble proteins that are coagulated by heat and found in a variety of substances, including blood plasma and egg white. For most language users, these are variant spellings and they are both acceptable.

alfresco

Alfresco derives from Italian and means, literally, 'in the cool'. In English, it is used both adjectivally and adverbially to mean 'in the open air':

Let's have an alfresco meal.

It was so hot that we had all our meals alfresco.

See also FOREIGN LOAN-WORDS

algae

The plural form of alga is *algae*. The word, which refers to simple stemless plants that grow in water or moist ground, almost invariably occurs in the plural:

Some algae, like seaweed, can be highly nutritious.

Algae is normally pronounced as in 'Algie' from 'Algernon' but the spelling pronunciation, where the 'g' is pronounced as in 'algorithm', is also heard.

See also SPELLING PRONUNCIATION

Algeria

An inhabitant of the north African country is an 'Algerian'; the derived adjective is the same. The capital is Algiers.

algorithm

The word *algorithm* derives ultimately from Arabic. It is now used, especially in mathematics and computing, to describe a method or procedure to carry out a complex operation by breaking it down into a series of simpler steps:

I've been experimenting with an algorithm for explaining how negatives are formed in Indo-European languages.

alias

The word derives from Latin *alias*, 'otherwise'. It is used as an adverb to mean 'known as at another time or place':

John Gregory, alias Gregory Johns, alias Greg Jones, is wanted for grand larceny in five states.

It is also used as a noun (plural 'aliases'), meaning 'assumed name':

His aliases were always modifications of his original name.

The abbreviation 'aka' (also known as) is sometimes used instead of alias:

John Gregory, aka Gregory Johns ...

See also LATIN

alibi

The word derives from Latin *alibi*, 'elsewhere'. The normal meaning of *alibi* (three syllables, the last one rhyming with 'fly') is 'evidence in support of one's claim', 'defence by an accused person that he or she was elsewhere when a crime was committed':

My client could not have committed the crime with which he is charged. He has a watertight alibi proving that he was in London when the Leeds robbery occurred.

The word has been popularized by detective films and it is occasionally used to mean 'excuse':

I have no alibi. I simply forgot to do my homework.

Many disapprove of this usage as it weakens the meaning of an otherwise useful addition to English.

See also LATIN

align

This verb is frequently misspelled. It is pronounced like 'a line' and means 'bring into line', but it has a 'g' in it, like 'sign':

I can't quite align the items in this table.

See also SPELLING

alive, live

A *live* and *live* (pronounced to rhyme with 'hive') are closely related in form and meaning but they differ in the ways they function. A *live* means 'living', 'active'. It functions as a predicative adjective, that is, it tends to occur only after a verb:

The rescuers could hardly believe that she was alive and well in spite of spending four nights alone on the mountain.

If we wish to use an attributive adjective, we could choose:

a living person.

The phrase:

*an alive person

is only marginally acceptable in such sentences as:

She was the most alive person I've ever met.

Live meaning 'living' functions as an attributive adjective:

Few people have seen a live emu.

It can be used both attributively and predicatively when it means 'unrecorded and, usually, unedited' and thus modifies an inanimate noun:

They call it a live programme but even the applause is rehearsed.

The programme was live.

In the context of broadcasting *live* is frequently used adverbially:

The President's visit was transmitted live.

In contemporary usage, there is a tendency for *live* to be used almost exclusively as a modifier of inanimate nouns.

See also A- WORD, ADJECTIVE

all, all of

All can function as a pre-determiner:

All the children were in bed by 8 o'clock.

as a determiner:

All people who on earth do dwell …

and as a noun:

He gave his all.

People sometimes worry about when to use *all* and when to use *all of* before noun phrases. The answer is simple. Both are correct:

All (of) the children were in bed by 8 o'clock.

You can't fool all (of) the people all (of) the time.

In Britain, *all* is preferred; in America *all of* is more widely used; but both structures are used in both countries. However, *all of* is obligatory before pronouns:

He will see all of us on Monday.

All occurs in a wide range of compound adjectives, such as:

all-American boy
all-night shopping
all-risks insurance policy
all-round sportswoman
all-seater stadium.

All can also function adverbially, especially in colloquial usage:

I'm all in a dither.
I'm all washed up.

See also ADJECTIVE, ALL/BOTH/EACH, DETERMINER, NOUN, PRONOUN

all, both, each

All, *both* and *each* can function in parallel constructions, when *all* means more than two, *both* means two only, and *each* refers to more than two. The words can function as adjectives:

All girls like rugby. (NB the plural noun)
Both girls like rugby. (NB the plural noun)
Each girl likes rugby. (NB the singular noun)

They can all be followed by 'of + plural noun' in what used to be called 'partitive constructions':

All of the girls sing well.
Both of the girls sing well.
Each of the girls sings well.

They can be used as determiners:

I saw all applicants.
I saw both applicants.
I saw each of the applicants.

They can be used as pronouns:

I ordered all.
I ordered both.
I ordered each.

Although *all* and *each* refer to more than two, they are not interchangeable:

Give each person the right to earn a living.
They all received extra shares when the company was privatized.

All, *both* and *each* can occur as the subject or object of a sentence:

All/both/each (of them) seemed quiet.
It attracted all/both/each (of them).

but

It attracted us all/both.

When a personal pronoun occurs before *all* or *both*, 'of' is not required:

We invited all/both (of them).
They invited us all/both.

When *all* and *both* occur in the subject position there are some differences and restrictions on the methods of forming negative equivalents. A sentence such as:

All (of) the children arrived late.

can be negated as:

Not all (of) the children arrived late.

A sentence such as:

Both (of) the children arrived late.

can be negated as:

Neither of the children arrived late.

or (but not idiomatically):

Both (of) the children didn't arrive late.

Thus, where *all* means 'more than two', *all* and *both* function in very similar ways. Some of their roles are distinct, however. As well as meaning 'everyone', *all* can mean 'complete, entire':

I eat my peas with honey. I've done it all my life.
It makes the peas taste funny but it keeps them on the knife!

In this role, *all* resembles 'whole' and not *both*:

She worked hard all her life/her whole life.

and it takes a singular noun.

See also ADJECTIVE, ADVERB, ALL/ALL OF, AMBIGUITY, BOTH, DETERMINER, EACH, EITHER/NEITHER, PRONOUN

all in, all-in

All in can be used in colloquial speech to mean 'exhausted':

After a day spent in the sea, I was all in by 8 o'clock.

All-in is a colloquialism for 'inclusive':

I was led to believe that the all-in price was £560, but when I arrived at my holiday destination I discovered that breakfast was not included.

all most, almost

These items should not be confused. *All* and *most* can co-occur, but only in such sentences as:

It was all most enjoyable.

meaning:

All of it was very enjoyable.

The 'all' can be omitted with little change of meaning:

It was most enjoyable.

Almost (one word and one 'l') can appear in a similar structure:

It was almost enjoyable.

but the meaning is different, being equivalent to:

It was very nearly enjoyable.

all-purpose

This hyphenated adjective meaning 'useful for many tasks' is quite widely used in advertising language:

The gadget you've been waiting for! This all-purpose grater makes mincemeat ...

all ready, already

All ready is used as an adjective meaning 'totally prepared':

I was all ready to go by 6 o'clock.

Already is an adverb meaning 'by or before a stated time':

They're here already. It is only 7.45.

See also ALREADY/STILL/YET

all right

This phrase occurs as a predicative adjective meaning 'adequate', 'satisfactory', 'well':

The first chapter was all right but the rest was unreadable.

It is also used to express assent or agreement:

All right, I'll do it.
She's the backbone of the firm all right.

Occasionally, in American-influenced, casual speech, *all right* can occur in front of a noun:

He's an all-right guy.

but this usage is not widely accepted. In Britain the form 'alright' is not acceptable but it is so widely used that it is likely to become an alternative spelling in the future.

all together, altogether

These items are frequently confused and yet their meanings are markedly different. *All together* means 'all at the same time and/or place':

They were all together when it happened.

Altogether means 'completely':

It was an altogether new experience.

allay, alleviate

These verbs are similar in meaning. *Allay* means 'calm', 'offer relief, usually permanent relief':

We must quash the rumours and allay their fears.

Alleviate means 'offer temporary help or relief':

These tablets should alleviate the pain but surgery offers the best hope of a permanent cure.

alliteration

Alliteration involves the systematic repetition of consonants, as with the patterning of 'w', 's' and 'p' in Wilfred Owen's poem, 'Disabled':

He sat in a wheeled chair, waiting for dark,
And shivered in his ghastly suit of grey,
Legless, sewn short at elbow. Through the park
Voices of boys rang saddening like a hymn,
Voices of play and pleasure after day,
Till gathering sleep had mothered them from him.

Alliteration was used in oral literature as an aid to memory, but it has been systematically used and exploited as a rhetorical device in written English literature for about 1500 years. It is currently popular in advertising and in tabloid headlines:

Choose Snickers for snacks.
Bolton Bonanza.

See also PARALLELISM, RHETORIC, STILE/STYLE

allot

Allot is a regular verb meaning 'give a share to someone'. It doubles the 't' before '-ed' and '-ing':

allot(s), allotted, allotting.

allow, allow of

The sentences:

The question allowed only one answer.

The question allowed of only one answer.

are both acceptable. The second one is slightly more formal than the first.

allude, elude

These verbs are sometimes confused. *Allude* means 'refer to something, often in an oblique way' and it is followed by 'to':

Do you think she was alluding to my pink socks?

Elude, which derives from Latin *eludere*, 'to play away', means 'escape or avoid' or 'fail to grasp' and it takes a direct object:

The prisoners eluded their guards.

The name eludes me for the moment.

See also ALLUSION/DELUSION/ILLUSION

allusion, delusion, illusion

These nouns sometimes cause problems for users, although they should be clearly distinguished. An *allusion* is a passing reference:

Was that 'pastures new' bit an allusion to Milton?

A *delusion* is a strong belief that something is true, although it is false.

His delusions of grandeur hurt nobody and they help him to cope with an unhappy life.

It often collocates with 'suffer':

She suffers from delusions of grandeur.

He suffers from the delusion that he is God's gift to women!

An *illusion* shares some of the meaning of *delusion* in that it is a deceptive impression of reality:

I wonder how they perform the illusion that they are sawing the girl in half.

I wanted to believe that he was a politician who shared our ideals and values, but his commitment to honesty and kindness was an illusion.

We frequently talk about an 'optical illusion' when we see something that may not have been there:

It was a mirage, an optical illusion. Or, at least, that's what they say the UFO was.

See also ALLUDE/ELUDE

alms

Alms is an uncountable noun, meaning 'charitable donations':

They encouraged us to give alms to the poor.

alone, lone

Alone means unaccompanied:

Alone, alone, all, all, alone,
Alone on a wide, wide sea!

S.T. Coleridge, 'The Rime of the Ancient Mariner'

It is used mainly as a predicative adjective and tends to modify people:

She was alone.

They were alone on a hillside.

It can also occur as an emphatic emphasizer after a noun or pronoun:

She was a woman alone and must now learn to fend for herself.

She alone agreed with me.

Alone can also be used as an adverb:

I found him alone on the hillside.

The phrase *let alone* is sometimes used to mean 'even less':

I could hardly afford the rent, let alone a holiday!

Lone has poetic overtones. It means 'solitary' and is used as an attributive adjective, whereas *alone* is used predicatively:

All I could see was a lone sail in the distance.

I saw a lone shepherd, high up on the hills.

He was totally alone, except for the sheep.

See also A- WORD, ADJECTIVE, LONELY/ LONESOME

alphabet

The word *alphabet* derives from the first two letters of the Greek alphabet, *alpha* and *beta*. It designates a set of letters (or signs) that correspond, often very roughly, to the sounds of a particular language. An alphabet that provided a one-to-one correspondence between letters and sounds would be a 'phonemic' alphabet. No European language has a phonemic alphabet, although the Spanish alphabet is much closer to being phonemic than the English one is.

The alphabet used for English was based on the Latin alphabet, modified by influences from Irish and French scripts. It is non-phonemic in that the same sound can be represented by different letters. The vowel sound /i/, for example, is represented by:

ea in meat

ee in feet

ei in receive

i in machine

ie in chief

and the consonant sound /s/ can be represented by:

c in ceiling

s in sill

sc in scion.

In addition, the same letter can represent different sounds. The letter 's', for example, can represent:

s in sat

sh in sugar

z in cabs.

Linguists have constructed the International Phonetic Alphabet (IPA), which offers a set of letters and diacritics that can, in combination, represent all the sounds of every language.

See also ORTHOGRAPHY, PHONEME, PRONUNCIATION, SPELLING, SPELLING PRONUNCIATION

alphabetization
Alphabetization is a method of organizing words or phrases into lists that are alphabetically ordered. There are some conventions associated with alphabetization, including the following: Mac, Mᶜ and Mc are listed as if they were all spelled 'Mac':

MᶜBride
MacTavish
McWilliams

and abbreviations are alphabetized according to their full form:

St John
Sinclair
Smithers.

already, still, yet
Some speakers experience difficulty in distinguishing these three adverbs. *Already* implies that something has happened earlier than might have been expected and often implies surprise:

You haven't finished it already, have you? That was quick.

Still is used to imply that the action is continuing:

We are still negotiating.

Yet is used when we talk about something we expect to happen:

He hasn't come in yet (but we are expecting him).

See also ADVERB, YET

also
Also is an adverb that is more commonly used in the written than in the spoken medium, where 'too' or 'as well' are preferred:

I have also written to Michael.
I have written to Michael too/as well.

In such sentences as the first, the context will usually make it clear whether the meaning is 'I have written to Michael (as well as talking to him)' or 'I have written to Michael (as well as to several other people)'.

Also can occur in different parts of the sentence; the rules are as follows:

■ It usually occurs after the copula verb when the verb is simple, that is, a single word:

I was also a waitress.

■ It usually occurs after the first auxiliary when the copula is complex:

I have also been a waitress.

■ It usually occurs before the verb when the verb phrase is simple, that is, a single word:

I also wrote to Michael.

■ It usually occurs after the first auxiliary in a complex verb phrase:

I have also written to Michael,
I have also been writing to Michael.

Occasionally in speech *also* is used as a conjunction suggesting that what follows it is an afterthought:

I want some cheese, also bread and milk.

This usage is less acceptable in writing than:

I want some cheese, bread and milk.

Also can occur at the beginning of a sentence to offer special prominence to a phrase:

Also invited were the Chancellor and the Heritage Minister.

The use of *also* followed by a comma in the initial position in a sentence is regarded as stylistically inappropriate:

Also, I should like to know the fees for a PhD.

Also, like 'too' and 'as well', tends to occur only in affirmative sentences:

She also invited the twins.

In the negative equivalent, 'either' is the preferred choice:

She didn't invite the twins either.

altar, alter
An *altar* is a noun referring to a special table in a church or temple:

I will go in unto the altar of God, unto God who giveth joy to my youth.

Alter is a verb meaning 'change':

I wish you wouldn't alter the agenda at the last minute.

altercation
An *altercation* is a verbal row, not a physical one:

I did not know how to avoid altercations with John. We could not discuss anything without arguing.

alternate, alternative
Alternate can function as both an adjective and a verb. The adjective rhymes with 'alter it' and means 'in turns':

He showed alternate feelings of love and hate.

The verb rhymes with 'alter fate' and is usually followed by 'with':

There are no seasons to speak of, but a rainy season alternates with a dry period.

Alternative can function as a noun or an adjective. They both involve choice, usually between two things:

What alternative did I have? If I hadn't taken the job I would have been unemployed.

The first option was unpleasant but the alternative option was even less appealing.

Recently, there has been a tendency – and one that has not been welcomed by purists – to widen the meaning of *alternative* in its roles as noun and adjective, especially in speech:

How can he choose when he has so many alternatives?

He has at least three alternative options.

The expression *have no alternative but* is a frequently used extension of 'alternative'. It implies that one has no choice:

I had no alternative but to go.

This usage is illogical, in view of the meaning of *alternative* but it is quite firmly established, especially in speech.

alternately, alternatively

These adverbs are frequently confused. *Alternately* means 'first one and then the other in sequence' and refers to an ordering of two:

She studied language and literature alternately, claiming that she stored the information on different sides of her brain.

Alternatively means a choice between two mutually exclusive possibilities:

We may go to Greece or, alternatively, we might save our money and buy a piano.

Although *alternatively* refers to a choice between two, its meaning has been widened to include a choice of several possibilities:

He says he might be very late or alternatively he may only be a little late or not late at all.

Some people dislike this widening.

although, though

Although and *though* are closely related in form and meaning and are freely interchangeable in most contexts. The following differences should, however, be noted. *Although* is used as a conjunction – that is, it always introduces a subordinate clause – with the meaning 'despite the fact that':

Although you are angry now, you will understand one day why I have to do this.

Although can be used in any style from extremely formal through casual to informal:

I continued to employ them although I was no longer making a profit.

I kept them on although I was nearly broke.

Though can be used in the same way:

I went home though I knew there would be trouble.

As a conjunction, *though* can always be replaced by *although* unless *though* is preceded by 'even':

He did what he thought was right although it was not always the popular thing to do.

*He did what he thought was right even though it was not always the popular thing to do.

'Even' can co-occur with *though*:

I went home, even though I knew there would be trouble.

He did what he thought was right, even although it was not always the popular thing to do.

Many careful users insist that 'even' cannot co-occur with *although*, but sentences using 'even although' are frequently heard and will almost certainly become acceptable. They are regarded as unacceptable because *although* is seen as an emphatic form of *though*, with the 'al-' performing a similar role to 'even'.

As though can function as a compound conjunction equivalent to 'as if':

She looked as though she hadn't eaten for weeks.

Although cannot be substituted for *though* in this context.

Though can also be used at the end of a sentence as a marker of emphatic concession:

He was a brilliant player, though.

Although can never be used in this context. *Though*, but not *although* can function as an adverb meaning approximately the same as 'however' or 'nevertheless':

She cannot paint; she sketches beautifully, though.

Though, but not *although*, can be used as a sentence adverbial:

The best solution of all, though, may not be to your taste.

The clipped forms *altho* and *tho* occur, but are acceptable only in very informal letters and notes.

See also ADVERB, CONJUNCTION

aluminium, aluminum

Aluminium is the British spelling of the metal. *Aluminum* is the American spelling. The British stress the word on the third syllable, the Americans on the second.

See also UK AND US ENGLISH

a.m., p.m.

The abbreviation *a.m.* or *am* stands for the Latin *ante meridiem*, 'before noon'. The abbreviation *p.m.* or *pm* stands for Latin *post meridiem*, 'after midday'.

See also ABBREVIATION, TIME

amateur

Amateur can function as a noun and an adjective. The noun refers to a person who performs an action for pleasure rather than for payment:

Many athletes who compete in the Olympic Games are amateurs in name only.

If she accepts money directly, she will lose her amateur status.

The adjective *amateur* is sometimes used loosely as a synonym for 'amateurish' meaning 'of a poor standard':

The last thing we need is another amateur approach to the problem!

Amateur has two main pronunciations. The 't' may be pronounced like the 't' in 'water' or like the 'tch' in 'watcher'.

See also LATIN

ambi-

This prefix derives from Latin *ambo*, 'both'. It occurs in a number of words, including:

ambidextrous (equally competent with both hands)
ambilingual (equally competent in two languages)
ambivalent (equally strong but opposing attitudes).

'Ambilingual' is less widely used than 'bilingual', but a 'bilingual' speaker may prefer to use the different languages in different situations.

ambidextrous

The adjective *ambidextrous* means 'equally competent with both hands':

My colleague is so ambidextrous that he can write on the left of the blackboard with his left hand and on the right with his right hand.

It is often misspelled *ambidexterous.

ambiguity

Ambiguity means 'capable of more than one interpretation'. There are two main types of ambiguity in English: lexical ambiguity and syntactic ambiguity.

Lexical ambiguity is a common feature of many languages and derives from the fact that many words have more than one meaning. *Neuf*, for example, can mean 'new' or 'nine' in French just as 'foot' can mean 'part of a leg' and '12 inches' in English. Lexical ambiguity is rarely a problem in speech, because the context suggests one meaning rather than another. In the context of map reading, for example, we would interpret 'key' in:

I can't find the key.

as 'explanations', but in the context of opening a door it would refer to a metal object that fits in a lock.

With syntactic ambiguity, we find structures capable of more than one interpretation. In English, there are several ambiguous structures, including:

■ Adjective + noun + noun

old men and women
= old men and old women
= old men and women of any age

Irish eggs and cheese
= Irish eggs and Irish cheese
= Irish eggs and cheese of any origin

■ Adjective + adjective + noun

American film stars
= American stars of films
= stars of American films

■ -ing form + noun

visiting relatives
= relatives who visit
= relatives who are visited

■ Phrasal verbs

tear up the dotted line
= tear along the perforations
= run quickly up the middle of the road.

Ambiguity is often cultivated by advertisers:

Go to work on an egg.

by newspaper headlines:

Giant waves down tunnel

and by poets. John Donne (1573–1631) punned on the pronunciation of his own name in 'A Hymn to God the Father':

When Thou has done, Thou hast not done,
For I have more.

See also PUN, ZEUGMA

ambiguous, ambivalent

These adjectives are occasionally confused. *Ambiguous* means 'having more than one possible meaning'. In spite of the prefix 'ambi-', ambiguous sentences may be capable of several interpretations, not just two. The sentence:

I upset his plans.

has at least four interpretations, in that 'upset' may refer to the past or the present and 'plans' may mean 'drawings' or 'intentions'.

Ambivalent means that one experiences two opposite and conflicting feelings or emotions at the same time.

Perhaps it's because I'm a Libran that I have ambivalent responses to Hamlet. I'm attracted by his poetry and repelled by his behaviour.

This adjective now tends to be overused and is being weakened to mean 'having mixed feelings, being undecided':

I've been asked out for the weekend but I'm ambivalent about whether or not to go.

amenable

Amenable means 'open to suggestion', 'likely to listen', 'cooperative'. It is followed by the preposition 'to':

I'm amenable to persuasion on this point.

amend, emend, mend

These verbs are occasionally misused. *Amend* means 'improve something':

I amended the engine design so as to make the car more fuel efficient.

The law was amended to take account of the verdict from the Court of Human Rights.

The expression 'make amends' means 'compensate for an injury':

How can anyone make amends for such a terrible crime?

Emend means 'make corrections in a text by critical editing':

We estimate that a good editor will emend this sort of text in three to four weeks.

Why has he still not emended his text? The errors are still here.

Mend means 'repair', 'reform':

Do you think I could get these shoes mended?

He'll have to mend his ways if he wants to be a politician.

America, American

America and its related adjective *American* can be ambiguous. *America* can refer to the continent of America, north and south (an area also referred to as 'the Americas') or it can be used as an abbreviated form of the United States of America.

American can function as an adjective and a noun. The noun can refer to an inhabitant of the United States of America, an inhabitant of the Americas or the English used in the United States of America. The term *American* can thus, in certain circumstances, be applied to Canadians, Mexicans and the people of Central and South America.

The adjective relates to any or all of the above:

I love American football.

How many American languages are spoken by more than one million people?

I'd like a copy of *The American Language*, please.

See also US/USA

American English

American English is as ambiguous as the word 'American', but it regularly refers to the English used in the United States of America. English became established as a mother tongue on the North American mainland in the early seventeenth century, and many varieties of African, Irish, Scottish and Welsh English have contributed to the language originally transported from England.

See also US ENGLISH

Americanism

The term *Americanism* is applied, often by British writers, to sounds, words or structures that are, or are thought to be, characteristic of the speech of people from the United States of America. We can examine these under four main categories: sounds, words, spelling and structures:

Sounds

The sounds that are thought to be quintessentially American are, in fact, found also in parts of Britain. These include the use of post-vocalic 'r' in words such as 'fourth' and 'four'; the use of an 'oo' rather than a 'yoo' pronunciation in words such as 'new', 'stew' and 'Tuesday'; and the use of different stress patterns in such words as 'cigarette' or 'laboratory'.

Words

Words are most frequently invoked in the discussion of *Americanisms*. These include words borrowed into US English from Amerindian languages:

cashew, coyote, kayak, moccasin, squaw, wampum

words borrowed into US English from African languages:

banjo, cola, jazz, okra, voodoo, zombie

words borrowed from European languages:

cookie, pizza, prairie, pretzel, rodeo, sombrero

words coined in the United States of America:

blur, bunkum, gimmick, hobo, palimony, realtor

words that have UK synonyms:

candy (sweets), condo (flat), elevator (lift), gas (petrol), store (shop), truck (lorry)

words that have different meanings:

	UK	US
blank	space	form
grip	firm clasp of hand	bag
purse	small bag for holding money	handbag
vest	underwear	waistcoat

Spelling

The majority of words are spelled the same in both communities but there are some systematic differences:

color/colour; program/programme; traveled/travelled.

Structures

Most grammatical patterns are identical, but there are a number of differences, including the use of 'gotten':

I've gotten a new computer.

the use of different past tense forms such as 'dove' and 'fit' for British 'dived' and 'fitted':

He dove into the water.

He fit a new fender to the car.

and the use of 'Do you have' instead of 'Have you (got)':

Do you have any sisters?

The overlap between British and American English is large and growing. Even people who disapprove of the Americanization of world English find themselves using words and structures that would once have characterized only the speech of Americans.

See also UK AND US ENGLISH

amiable, amicable
These two adjectives are confused because they both derive ultimately from Latin *amare*, 'to love', and they both involve pleasantness. *Amiable* means 'pleasant', 'friendly', 'agreeable' and is applied to people:

She is one of the most amiable people I have ever met.

Amicable means 'characterized by goodwill'. It is applied to events, relationships or agreements:

They've managed to reach an amicable settlement.

amoeba
An *amoeba* is a single-cell organism capable of changing shape. The word derives from Latin *amoeba* and has *amoebae* as its plural. This plural is mostly restricted to scientific writings and *amoebas* is now the preferred plural:

Amoebas are able to change shape because of the movement of cell processes.

The usual American spelling is *ameba(s)*.

See also SPELLING, UK AND US ENGLISH

amok, amuck
These spellings are both acceptable, although the former is more widely used. *Amok* derives from Malay *amoq*, 'furious assault', and is used to mean 'run about in a frenzy':

They drank heavily and then began to run amok.

Amok and *amuck* are both pronounced to rhyme with 'a duck' but one also hears a spelling pronunciation, where the word is rhymed with 'a dock'.

See also BORROWING

among, amongst, between
These three words are prepositions. The first two are variants and are interchangeable:

Blessed art thou among(st) women.
You are among(st) friends.

It seems probable that *amongst* may be preferred by older speakers, but it is perfectly standard and acceptable in all contexts. *Among* is preferred in US English.

The word *between* is a preposition and is historically related to 'two' and 'twain', as the spelling still suggests. It should thus be used only to relate two items that are often joined by 'and':

John divided the money between Mary and Ella.
Leeds is between Hull and Liverpool.
I can't choose between the car and the boat.
The robbery occurred between six o'clock and midnight.

It is correct to say:

They divided the cake between the two of us.

but the frequently heard:

*between you and I

is not correct. It breaks the grammatical rule whereby prepositions are followed by object pronouns:

from me, for her, near him, to us, with them.

Although it is etymologically incorrect to use *between* for more than two, many people do it. This usage should, however, be avoided in formal contexts.

Among(st) is the equivalent preposition for any number over two:

John divided the money among Mary, Sam and Ella.
They divided the cake among the four of us.

The archaic form *betwixt*, meaning 'between' is sometimes found in literature and in the tautologous cliché, *betwixt and between*.

See also PREPOSITION, WHILE/WHILST

amoral, immoral
These two adjectives are based on 'moral'. *Amoral* means 'without morals', 'lacking in morals':

Chaucer's fabliaux may be amoral but they have an animal vitality.

Immoral means 'wicked':

Immoral conduct may be understood but not condoned.

An *amoral* person may not be wicked; an *immoral* person invariably is.

ampersand
The symbol & is known as *ampersand*. It should be avoided in formal writing unless it forms part of a name:

I've had a letter from Brown, Jones & Co.

-an, -ean, -ian
The SUFFIX *-ian* is a variant of *-an* and *-ean* and can denote a person belonging to a place:

Canadian, Mexican, Singaporean

a person typical of a period:

Edwardian, Elizabethan, Shakespearean

and characteristics similar to those of a well-known individual:

Cromwellian, Machiavellian.

The *-ian* suffix is also widely used to indicate an adherent of a religion:

Christian, Presbyterian

and an expert in a subject:

magician, physician.

See also -IST/-ITE

anacoluthon

Anacoluthon comes from the Greek word *anakolouthon*, 'inconsistency in logic'. It involves a deliberate or an accidental change from one syntactic structure to another within a single sentence:

She was extremely affable and – for heaven's sake what's going on?

Most speakers produce *anacolutha* in spontaneous speech and in unedited writing. Stylists usually consider such sentences to be both inelegant and confusing.

See also DANGLING PHRASE OR CLAUSE, FUSED SENTENCE

anaesthetic, anesthetic

An *anaesthetic* is a drug that causes general or local loss of bodily sensations:

I'm a believer in the powers of acupuncture but, if I needed a major operation, I think I'd prefer the doctor to use an anaesthetic.

The normal American spelling is *anesthetic*.

See also SPELLING, UK AND US ENGLISH

analogue, analog, analogy

An *analogue* is something that is similar to something else in certain ways. Researchers often look for *analogues* as a means of expressing complex ideas in ways that non-specialists can understand.

A dripping tap is an analogue for the constant passing of time.

The usual American spelling is *analog* and this spelling is increasingly used in British computer manuals.

The term *analogue/analog* is also used for a cognate word, that is, a word that is parallel to a word or form in another language. For example, the English, French, Irish and Latin words below are cognates and therefore analogous:

English	French	Irish	Latin
heart	coeur	croidhe	cor
hound	chien	cú	canis
three	trois	trí	tres

and they almost certainly derive from common Indo-European roots.

An *analogy* is a similarity between items that are otherwise different. Children often create past tense forms by analogy with the ones they know. Thus, if they know 'mend' and 'mended', they may produce 'bend' and 'bended'.

Analogizing is evident at all levels of the language. In vocabulary it may be seen in the development of BACK FORMATIONS such as 'globetrot' from 'globetrotter'; in pronunciation it is found in the anglicizing of non-English sounds, making 'trait' rhyme with 'gate'; in morphology it helps to account for the formation of new compounds such as 'refusenik' or blends such as 'happenstance'; and in syntax it is apparent in every speaker's ability to form unique sentences and utterances in accordance with the rules of the language. Analogy is a motivating force for both comprehensibility and change.

The noun *analog(ue)* rhymes with 'fog' but the 'g' in *analogy* or the related verb 'analogize' is pronounced like the 'g' in 'pigeon'.

analyse

We can *analyse* items into their constituent parts:

The students are trying to analyse a particular salt.

We also use *analyse* for breaking sentences down into smaller units:

I can't analyse these sentences; they are complex.

The American spelling is *analyze*, but this is not used in UK English.

analysis

The result of analysing a sentence or a product is an *analysis* and the plural is *analyses*:

Our analyses are different. Could we both be right?

Linguists often use the terms 'analytic' and 'synthetic' when they describe languages. Contemporary English is often described as an analytical language because most words and phrases can be separated into meaningful units or morphemes. If we compare Latin *amavero* with English 'I shall have loved', we can see that the Latin is more synthetic than its English equivalent.

anaphora

In connected speech and writing, many items refer back to others in the discourse. A sentence like:

She was very pleased with it.

can be interpreted fully only if both 'she' and 'it' refer back to, for example:

Jane finished her homework. She was very pleased with it.

See also ANTECEDENT, DISCOURSE

ancillary

The word *ancillary* meaning 'subsidiary, supplementary' is often misspelled. It does not have an 'i' before '-ary':

The ancillary services have all been privatized.

and

And is a coordinating conjunction, that is, it joins units of equal value:

adjective + adjective: fine and dandy

noun + noun: Peter and Paul

phrase + phrase: the good, the bad and the ugly

pronoun + pronoun: she and I

sentence + sentence: She was smart and he was brave.

Stylists used to condemn the use of 'and', 'but' or 'so' at the beginning of sentences, insisting that a joining word could not, logically, occur as the first element in a sentence. Creative writers have, however, broken such rules. William Blake's poem gains considerably by the use of 'and' as the first word in:

And did those feet in ancient time
Walk upon England's mountains green?
And was the holy Lamb of God
On England's pleasant pastures seen?

The practice of using sentence-initial *and* is more acceptable today, especially in the representation of colloquial styles, but it should be used sparingly.

Many people dislike the use of *and/or* as in:

Please supply your phone and/or e-mail number.

They prefer the more explicit:

Please supply either your phone or your e-mail number or both.

See also COMMA, CONJUNCTION, OR, PUNCTUATION

Andorra

An inhabitant of the European co-principality is an 'Andorran'; the derived adjective is the same. The capital is Andorra la Vella.

anecdote, antidote

These words are occasionally confused because of their similarity in sound and appearance. An *anecdote* is a short story:

I think I must have heard all his anecdotes by now – twice!

An *antidote* is a medicine to counteract a poison:

There is no known antidote for the venom from a black mamba.

anesthetic

See ANAESTHETIC/ANESTHETIC

aneurysm, aneurism

An *aneurysm* is a sac formed by the abnormal dilation of the weakened wall of a blood vessel. The spelling *aneurysm* is preferred in Britain but the American form, *aneurism*, is now widely used in both countries.

Anglicism

An *Anglicism* is a word, structure or idiom that is, or is thought to be, characteristic of the English language. All languages have unique characteristics. English, for example, has two methods of indicating possession:

my child's mother

and:

the mother of my child.

The former is an *Anglicism*, the latter is found also in French:

La mère de mon enfant.

Idioms, too, are often language specific. In English, for example, we have a number of idiomatic expressions meaning 'he died':

he passed away

he passed on

he popped his clogs

he went to his eternal reward.

All languages have a verb 'to die' and all languages can deal with death in a straightforward or metaphoric way. No other language uses the same set of idioms.

The word *Anglicism*, or more often 'Briticism', is applied also to a usage that is non-American, for example:

boot/trunk; lift/elevator; railway/railroad.

See also AMERICANISM

Anglo-

The prefix *Anglo-* is used to denote 'English' or 'England'. It is found in such compounds as:

Anglo-American (relationship between England and the US)

Anglo-Catholic (high Anglican)

Anglo-French (relationship between England and France).

We also find the unhyphenated forms:

Anglophile (lover of England and English things)

Anglophobe (hater of England and English things)

Anglophone (speaker of English).

A number of compounds are used by linguists with special reference to language. Among them are:

Anglo-English (varieties of English spoken in England)

Anglo-Irish (a variety of English spoken in Ireland)

Anglo-Romani (an English-influenced variety of Romani)

Anglo-Welsh (a variety of English spoken in Wales).

Some English people dislike the compound 'Anglo-English', but the term 'English' can sometimes be ambiguous: 'It's an English expression' can mean 'It's an expression that occurs in the English language' or 'It's an expression used in England.'

Angola

An inhabitant of the southwest African republic is an 'Angolan'; the derived adjective is the same. The capital is Luanda.

angry, mad

These adjectives are occasionally misused. In Britain, *angry* means 'annoyed', 'vexed':

I was very angry that my opinion was ignored.

The adjective *angry* functions with both 'at' and 'with'. We get *angry* at things and *angry* with people:

I was angry at the interruption.

I was angry with you for interrupting me.

Mad derives from Old English *gemædan*, 'to make insane', and it has a range of meanings, including 'insane' and 'silly':

It was believed that a genius was often mad.

John has such mad ideas.

Don't be mad! It would be crazy to spend so much money on a balloon ride!

Society was not kind to mad people. They were locked away like criminals.

In American English *mad* is often used where British speakers would prefer *angry*:

Don't be mad with me.

I was really mad when I missed the bus.

See also BLEACHING, SEMANTIC CHANGE

Anguilla

An inhabitant of the island in the Leeward group is an 'Anguillan'; the derived adjective is the same. The capital is The Valley.

annex, annexe

Annex usually functions as a verb:

Germany annexed Cameroon in 1884.

In America *annex* can also function as a noun meaning 'extension to a main building'. In Britain, the noun usually takes an 'e':

She has a room in the nurses' annexe.

but the use of *annex* as a noun is spreading.

The stress falls on the second syllable of the verb and on the first syllable of the noun.

annual, perennial

These words can function as adjectives and nouns. The adjective *annual* means 'once a year', 'every year':

It's my annual break.

The noun *annual* is used also to refer to a book that comes out once a year:

The new bumper *Beano* annual.

Perennial can function as an adjective meaning 'lasting through several years', 'perpetual':

The constantly changing sea is a perennial source of pleasure to me.

It's the perennial trouble.

Both nouns are used of plants. An *annual* is a plant that lives for only one year and dies in winter. A *perennial* is a woody or herbaceous plant that lasts for several years:

We planted some perennials last year.

annunciation, enunciation

An *annunciation* is a 'proclamation' or 'important announcement'. The word is most frequently used with a capital letter to refer to the announcement made to the Blessed Virgin Mary by the angel Gabriel:

The Annunciation is celebrated on 25 March.

The noun *enunciation* means 'clear, distinct articulation and pronunciation':

Her enunciation was crystal clear. Every syllable could be heard at the back of the hall.

He'll have to work on his enunciation if he wants to be a newsreader.

anonymous

This word means 'of unknown origin or identity':

Many of the early ballads are anonymous.

The donor wishes to remain anonymous.

Anonymous is frequently misspelled.

another

The compound word *another* may be used as a determiner meaning 'one more':

He was caught red-handed but we decided to give him another chance.

It can also be used as a pronoun:

He was offered one and then helped himself to another.

As an adjective, *another* can mean 'a different example of':

I think we are dealing with another Dickens.

Another is sometimes misused. It should not replace 'other' in the structure 'some way or other':

They are looking for some way or other round the problem.

There is also a marked difference in meaning between 'one other' and 'one another'. 'One other' can be replaced by 'an additional':

I saw one other flaw that I might mention.

'One another' is similar to 'each other' but, whereas 'each other' applies to two only:

John and Bill loved each other.

'one another' applies to more than two:

John, Bill and Harold loved one another.

See also EACH OTHER/ONE ANOTHER

-ant, -ent

The SUFFIX -*ant* derives from Latin -*ant*, a present participle ending of a first conjugation verb. It can be used to form nouns:

claimant, Protestant

or adjectives:

discordant, pleasant.

The -*ent* suffix also derives from a Latin present participle ending, -*ent*. It, too, can help form both nouns:

antecedent, gradient

and adjectives:

competent, decadent.

The two suffixes are pronounced the same in rapid speech and the difference between them depends more on Latin than on any intrinsic difference of meaning or usage.

The words that seem to cause the greatest spelling problems are:

ascendant, attendant, intendant, relevant, repellent, superintendent, transcendent.

Sometimes the -*ant* spelling is the noun and the -*ent* spelling the adjective. This applies to the following:

Noun	Adjective
dependant	dependent
descendant	descendent
pendant	pendent
propellant	propellent

See also SPELLING

ante-, anti-

These PREFIXes have markedly different meanings and uses. *Ante-*, from Latin, means 'before in time or position', 'in front of'. It occurs in large numbers of compounds, including:

antecede (go before), antedate (precede in time), antenatal (before birth), antepenultimate (two before the last), antechamber (room before a larger room), anteroom (room before a larger room).

Anti- derives from a Greek prefix meaning 'against', 'opposing'. It, too, occurs in a wide range of compounds, including:

antibiotic, anticipate, antidote, antifreeze.

See also SPELLING

antecedent

The term *antecedent* describes a word or phrase to which a later word refers. Most sentences make use of antecedents. If we look at:

Mary decided to stop dancing because it was wearing her down.

we can see that 'Mary' is the antecedent of 'her' and 'dancing' is the antecedent of 'it'.

The personal pronouns 'he', 'she', 'it' and 'they' and the relative pronouns 'who', 'whom' and 'which' always have antecedents. Auxiliary verbs frequently have antecedents:

I said I will go and I will [go].

See also ANAPHORA, DISCOURSE, PRONOUN

antenna

See AERIAL/ANTENNA

anti-

See ANTE-/ANTI-

anticipate, expect

Anticipate means 'foresee and act in advance of':

She was a wonderful woman, always able to anticipate my wishes.

Many people incorrectly use *anticipate* as a synonym for 'foresee':

I don't anticipate any delays.

or *expect*:

I'll anticipate a letter by Friday.

Such changes in meaning are not 'wrong', but we should not use *anticipate* as a synonym for *expect*.

Expect is a regular verb meaning 'look forward to', 'regard as probable':

I expect that John will arrive later this evening.

See also BLEACHING

anticlimax

An *anticlimax* is a figure of speech in which we have a sudden change from serious to humorous or from important to frivolous:

Not louder shrieks to pitying heav'n are cast,
When husbands, or when lap-dogs breathe their last.

        Alexander Pope, *The Rape of the Lock*

See also FIGURE OF SPEECH

antidote

See ANECDOTE/ANTIDOTE

Antigua

An inhabitant of the Caribbean island, properly known as Antigua and Barbuda, in the Leeward group is an 'Antiguan'; the derived adjective is the same. The capital is St John's.

antisocial, unsociable, unsocial

These adjectives are often confused. *Antisocial* means 'contrary to the interests of society in general':

This noise pollution is antisocial and unacceptable.

Unsociable means 'not liking to mix with other people':

He rarely goes out. He appears unsociable but, in fact, he is extremely shy.

Unsocial most frequently occurs in the fixed phrase 'unsocial hours', meaning times that fall outside the normal working day:

I wanted to be a doctor but I was worried that I might not be able to cope with the unsocial hours.

antithesis

Antithesis forms its plural with '-es' – that is, 'antitheses'. It is a noun whose basic meaning is 'contrast' or 'one thing set against another'. The word is applied to a figure of speech where contrasting words, phrases or ideas are juxtaposed to produce an emphatic balance:

More haste, less speed.

Yes; I am proud, I must be proud to see
Men not afraid of God, afraid of me.
                Alexander Pope, Epilogue to the Satires

When poverty comes in through the window, love goes out through the door.

See also FIGURE OF SPEECH

antonym

An *antonym* is a word that is opposite in meaning to another word:

hot/cold
love/hate
quickly/slowly.

The word *antonymy* comes from Greek *anti-*, 'against' + *onyma*, 'name'. Contemporary scholars tend to distinguish three types of 'oppositeness': implicitly graded antonyms such as 'big' and 'small'; complementarity such as 'female' and 'male'; and converseness such as 'buy' and 'sell'.

Implicitly graded antonyms are so called because they involve pairs of words where a norm is implied. For example, if we say that someone is 'big' or 'kind' or 'old' we are implicitly establishing a continuum:

big, less big, small
kind, less kind, cruel
old, less old, young

and the meaning is established, in large measure, by the noun they modify. Thus 'a big book' is only 'big' in the context of 'books' and is almost certainly smaller than 'a small bull'.

Complementarity is applied to such pairs as 'male' and 'female', 'single' and 'married'. The characteristic of such pairs is that the denial of one implies the assertion of the other:

'X is not female' implies that X is male.
'Y is not male' implies that Y is female.

This is different from implicitly graded antonyms, where:

'X is not bad' does not necessarily imply that X is good.
'X is not young' does not necessarily imply that X is old.

In certain contexts, the following can be complementary pairs:

black and white (piano keys)
red and white (wines)
transitive and intransitive (verbs).

Converseness tends to be applied to the relationship that holds between such related pairs of sentences as:

I borrowed £10 from John.
John lent me £10.

where 'borrow' and 'lend' are in a converse relationship. English has a number of conversely related verbs and therefore sentence converseness is quite common. Verbs in this category include:

borrow/lend, loan
buy/sell
command/serve
give/take
teach/learn.

Sometimes we find converse nouns corresponding to converse verbs:

borrow, lend/borrower, lender
teach, learn/teacher, learner, student
treat, consult/doctor, patient.

See also GRADABLE, HOMOGRAPH/HOMONYM/ HOMOPHONE, SEMANTICS, SYNONYM

any

Any can function as a determiner that can modify both singular and plural nouns:

Have you any wool? (singular)
Have you any potatoes? (plural)

and as a pronoun with both singular and plural reference:

I don't want any. (e.g., money)
I don't want any. (e.g., French francs)

Because of its ability to be used with either singular or plural reference, some people are not sure which form of the verb to use. The rule is simple. Check to see whether *any* refers to a singular or a plural noun and use the correct form of agreement for such a noun. For example, the questions:

Is there any left?
Are there any left?

are both correct if the first *any* refers to a single noun such as 'tea' or 'coffee' and if the second refers to a plural noun such as 'bananas' or 'bicycles'.

Any is found in a range of compound words, including:

anybody, anyhow, anyone, anything, anywhere.

Because of its tendency to form compound words, many users also produce:

*anymore, *anyplace

but these are not acceptable in British English, where the required forms are:

any more, any place.

In American English, the compound 'anymore' is widely used when it means 'any longer':

Mary doesn't live here anymore.

The forms:

anyways (variant of 'anyway'), anywise (in any way at all), anywheres (variant of 'anywhere')

occur also, mainly in the United States of America, but these are not acceptable in formal speech or writing.

any one, anybody, anyone

The compound forms *anybody* and *anyone* are synonyms and are interchangeable in all contexts, although some speakers feel that *anyone* is slightly more formal and *anybody* slightly more emphatic:

I haven't seen anybody all week.
I haven't seen anyone all week.
Is anybody in?
Is anyone in?
She's not just anybody. She's the star.
She's not just anyone. She's the star.

Some people worry about which pronoun to use when *anybody* or *anyone* is replaced:

If anybody wants it, he can have it.
If anyone wants it, she can have it.
If anybody wants it, they can have it.

Since *anybody* and *anyone* refer to a single person, the pronoun should be singular, but many people who wish to avoid gender bias use 'they'.

It is important, however, to distinguish between *anyone* and *any one*. *Anyone* can only be applied to people:

Can anyone go to the party?

Any one can refer to animate and inanimate nouns:

Any one of the students could have seen it.
You can sit at any one of the tables.

Any one is followed by a phrase such as 'of us' or 'of the nouns':

It could have happened to any one of us.
It could have happened to any one of the small children.

See also GENDER, NO ONE/NOBODY/NONE, POLITICAL CORRECTNESS, SOMEBODY/SOMEONE

any way, anyway

Any way and *anyway* have distinct meanings. The two-word compound *any way* means 'in any manner', 'by any method':

Decorate the house any way you like.

Anyway means 'in any case' and is more mobile in a sentence. It can usually be deleted from

a sentence without altering its grammatical acceptability:

I went home early. I had work to do and (anyway) I wasn't enjoying myself (anyway).

Anyway tends to be colloquial and it usually implies a dismissal of what has preceded it:

I didn't go to see her. She wouldn't have wanted to see me anyway.

Anyways is regarded as nonstandard.

aphasia

Aphasia, like 'dyslexia', has been popularized by the media in the recent past. The word means 'without speech', but it is now applied to the sudden or gradual loss of language due to age, an accident or a stroke. All users of language, even children, have some experience of *nominal aphasia*, the temporary loss of nouns. This reveals itself in two main ways: the inability to remember the name for something:

What's the word for that thingummy I need?

and the use of the wrong word in essentially the right context, such as when we use 'cooker' when we mean 'cupboard'.

See also A- WORD, COMPETENCE AND PERFORMANCE, DYSLEXIA

aphesis

Aphesis comes from Greek *aphienai* meaning 'to let go', and it involves the dropping of a short, unaccented vowel from the beginning of a word:

because: cos
esquire: squire.

Aphesis is relatively common in speech. It differs from CLIPPING in that clipping can involve the loss of a stressed syllable or the loss of several syllables.

See also APOCOPE, CONTRACTION, ELISION, PIDGIN AND CREOLE, SYNCOPE

aphorism

The word *aphorism* comes from Greek *aphorismos* meaning 'definition'. It tends to be used today to refer to a general truth that is expressed concisely and memorably. Shakespeare uses an aphorism when, in *Twelfth Night* (Act II, Scene 5), Malvolio says:

Some are born great; some achieve greatness; and some have greatness thrust upon 'em.

See also MAXIM, PROVERB

apocope

Apocope comes from Greek *apokoptein* meaning 'to cut off'. It refers to the loss of one or more sounds or letters from the end of a word. It has occurred historically in English when, for example, verbs such as 'bindan' became 'bind'. It is also a marked feature of colloquial speech. It is acceptable in writing when 'Robert' becomes 'Rob', but not when 'and' becomes 'an' or 'n'.

See also APHESIS, CLIPPING, ELISION, SYNCOPE

apostrophe

There is considerable confusion about the correct use of the *apostrophe*. The rules governing its usage, however, are consistent and straight-forward. Apostrophes must be used in the following circumstances:

■ To indicate ownership or possession by adding 's to a singular noun or noun phrase:

Jan's book(s)
the boy's boot(s)
the princess's poetry
George I's accession

and by adding s' to a plural noun or noun phrase:

kings' ransoms
the boys' boot(s)
the Men of Harlech's choir.

■ To indicate that letters have been omitted:

she is not = she isn't
I cannot = I can't
I have lost it = I've lost it
influenza = 'flu' = flu.

■ To indicate time or quantity:

in a month's time
this week's opportunities
a pound's worth of petrol.

■ To indicate the plurals of abbreviations, letters, numbers and words that are being discussed as words:

There are two a's in 'separate'.
How many s's are there in Massachusetts?
There are three the's in the first two lines of 'The Second Coming'.
The his's must all be replaced by 'his and/or her'.

The apostrophe is not, however, used to indicate the plural of abbreviations or numbers, and it is not used in decades:

There are two 7s in 14.
three 12s = six 6s
Two of the local MPs are not standing for re-election.
three MDs
the 1990s.

■ To indicate the past tense of abbreviations that are being treated as verbs:

I OK'd the draft.
He has OD'd. (He has overdosed.)

Many people have problems with the use of the apostrophe in specific instances, which can be dealt with as follows:

■ 'It's' always means 'it is'.

■ An apostrophe is never required when 'its' functions as a possessive adjective:

The lion licked its paws, stretched its legs and returned to its lair.

■ Apostrophes are not needed with possessive pronouns:

It is hers.
It is theirs.

■ 'Who's' always means 'who is':

Who's coming to dinner?

but the possessive adjective and pronoun 'whose' never needs an apostrophe:

This is the author whose book was shortlisted.
Whose is this? = To whom does this belong?

■ Singular names ending in 's' add 's to indicate possession:

Yeats's publications.

■ The use of 's to form the plural of words ending in vowels is incorrect:

*Pizza's delivered to your door.
*Half Price Radio's.

Many writers avoid the use of apostrophe + s to indicate the possessive of nouns that have more than one 's' or 'z' in the last syllable, preferring:

Jesus' followers to Jesus's followers
the Jones' families to the Jones's families
Moses' law to Moses's law.

It is also customary to avoid the use of the apostrophe + s in forming the possessive of classical names that end in 's'. Thus:

Achilles' heel is preferred to *Achilles's heel
Archimedes' finding is preferred to *Archimedes's finding
Euripides' plays is preferred to *Euripides's plays
Pythagoras' theorem is preferred to *Pythagoras's theorem.

However, the official name of the Royal court in London is:

the Court of St James's

not, as one might expect:

*the Court of St James'.

See also CONTRACTION, PUNCTUATION

appal, appall

This widely-used verb is frequently misspelled. *Appal*, with one 'l', is British:

That sort of behaviour appals me.

Appall with 'll' is American:

That sort of behavior appalls me.

In Britain, the 'l' is doubled before '-ed' and '-ing':

appalled, appalling

so that the past tense of the above sentence is correct in both countries:

That sort of behaviour appalled me.

See also UK AND US ENGLISH

apparatus

Apparatus can now be both singular and plural:

Set up this apparatus for me, please.

The apparatus were set up in the Chemistry Department.

Many people prefer to use *apparatuses* as the plural form.

The pronunciation of this word is also variable. Most people rhyme the third syllable with 'date', but some speakers prefer to rhyme it with 'dart'. A similar variability is heard in the pronunciation of 'data'.

appendices, appendixes

The noun *appendix* comes from Latin *appendere*, 'to hang something from'. The word is widely used with two meanings in English, 'a small organ in the abdomen':

I had my appendix removed in the General Infirmary.

and 'additional material at the end of a book':

This supplementary information should be presented in an appendix.

Appendix has two plurals, *appendices* and *appendixes*. The first tends to be preserved for 'supplementary material':

How many appendices are there in her book?

The second is mainly used in anatomical contexts:

Six appendixes in the one day! It's like an epidemic.

applicable

This word is pronounced with different stress patterns. Some people stress the first syllable, as they do with 'apple'; others stress the second, as they do with 'apply'. Both pronunciations are acceptable.

apposite, opposite

These adjectives both derive from Latin *ponere*, 'to put or place'. *Apposite* means 'well suited for the purpose', 'apt':

Your comments were apposite and extremely well timed.

Opposite means 'contrary to', 'face to face':

We sometimes evoke a reaction that is almost the opposite of what we expected.

She sat opposite me in the train.

appraise, apprise

These verbs are occasionally confused. *Appraise* means 'assess the worth or value of':

Few universities enjoy being appraised but most realize that such appraisal can benefit both staff and students.

Apprise is occasionally spelled as *apprize* and means 'make someone aware of something':

I was not apprised of the problem until earlier today.

The Chairman should be apprised of any development.

appreciate

The verb *appreciate* usually means 'value highly', 'feel grateful for':

Children do not always appreciate classical music.

Children do not always fully appreciate their parents.

Recently, *appreciate* has also been used to mean 'understand':

I appreciate that the bus service is not always reliable but you must take that into account in planning your journey.

Although such changes in meaning are common in the language, many users dislike this usage.

See also BLEACHING, SEMANTIC CHANGE

approve, endorse

These verbs are occasionally misused because there is some overlap of meaning. *Approve* means 'think well of' or 'authorize or sanction':

I approve of her cheerful attitude to work.

All cash payments must be approved by the Administrative Officer.

Endorse means 'sign one's name', 'support in writing':

Please endorse your cheque. (i.e., sign your name on the back)

I have pleasure in endorsing his candidature.

Endorse is also used in Britain to mean 'record details of motoring offences on the back of a driving licence':

He should have lost his licence rather than simply having it endorsed.

The spelling *indorse* should be avoided.

apt, liable

These words are frequently confused. *Apt* means 'suitable, appropriate':

I can always find an apt couplet in Pope.

It is also applied to one's disposition:

She's apt to go off at a tangent.

and it is in this sense that it can be replaced by *liable*.

Liable means 'responsible for':

I am liable for any expenses incurred.

A man is liable for his wife's debts.

See also LIABLE TO/LIKELY TO, SEMANTIC CHANGE

Arab, Arabian, Arabic

These three words can be used as nouns and adjectives. *Arab* refers to the Semitic people originally from Arabia who spread throughout the Middle East and North Africa from the seventh century:

Ahmed was born here but he thinks of himself as an Arab and often chooses to wear Arab dress.

Arabian means 'of or relating to Arabia':

Have you read *The Arabian Nights' Entertainment*?

Arabic is a language spoken by perhaps 80 million people:

He writes Classical Arabic but uses a more demotic variety when he speaks.

See also HAMITIC/SEMITIC

Arabic influence

The English language contains many words of Arabic origin. Some of these have entered the language directly, and others have come in through French, Persian, Spanish, Turkish or Urdu. The oldest borrowings date back to the Crusades and are found in almost all west European languages. Among these are:

albatross, admiral, alchemy, alcohol, alkali, algebra, cipher, elixir, jar, sugar, zenith, zero

Such words emphasize the eminence of Arabic scholars of the period in astronomy, mathematics, medicine, science and navigation. The numbers, too, were borrowed, and thus all literate Europeans would recognize 1, 2, 3, although English speakers would call them 'one, two, three', French speakers 'un, deux, trois' and Gaelic speakers 'aon, do, trí'.

See also BORROWING

arbiter, arbitrator

These nouns are both related to the verb 'arbitrate'. *Arbiter*, the older form, refers to a person who has the authority to resolve a dispute or who is thought to be an expert on matters of judgement or taste:

She has been selected as an arbiter because of her diplomatic skills.

He thinks he's an arbiter on all matters concerning etiquette and good taste.

An *arbitrator* is a person who is chosen to settle a dispute. It is now used more frequently in this context than *arbiter*:

It was not easy to find an arbitrator who was acceptable to all sides in the dispute.

arbitrarily

The adverb *arbitrarily* normally has its main stress on the first syllable in Britain and on the third syllable in America. Both pronunciations are acceptable.

See also STRESS

arbitrate, mediate

These verbs have much in common. *Arbitrate* means 'have authority to settle a dispute':

He has again been chosen to arbitrate between the factions.

To *mediate* is to 'intervene between conflicting parties in the hope of settling a dispute':

I do not feel able to mediate because my sympathies are almost entirely with the people who have been overrun.

arc, ark

An *arc* is part of a circle:

The arc of the circle cuts the hypotenuse of the triangle.

An *ark* is an old-fashioned word for a wooden chest:

They used to keep blankets in a wooden box called an ark.

When *Ark* is given a capital letter, it refers to Noah's Ark or the Ark of the Covenant.

'Ark.' is the abbreviation for the state of Arkansas.

archaeology, archeology

These nouns both refer to the study of the past through the analysis of material remains. The first spelling is still quite widely used in Britain but the second is usual in America and is gaining in popularity in Britain.

archaism

An archaism is a word, expression or style that was formerly in use but no longer occurs naturally in contemporary speech or writing. When A.H. Clough (1819–61) wrote 'The Latest Decalogue', for example, he deliberately employed archaic vocabulary and structure:

Thou shalt have one God only; who
Would be at the expense of two?
No *graven* images may be
Worshipped, except the currency:
Swear not at; for *thy* curse
Thine enemy is none the worse:

Some *archaisms* have a certain amount of prestige, largely because of their antiquity value, although it is not easy to draw a simple distinction between forms that are 'old-fashioned' and forms that are *archaic*. The following are examples of well-known archaisms:

anon (soon, immediately)
boot (gain, profit)
delve (dig with a spade)
durst not (does not dare)
puissance (power)
spake (spoke)
thou/thee (you (singular))
wax and wane (grow bigger and smaller)
willy nilly (whether he wishes it or not).

See also BIBLE

archetype

The first syllable of *archetype* rhymes with 'park'. The word has two main uses in English. It can refer to a prototype or to one of the inherited mental images, such as a cave, that is thought to be part of our collective unconscious. The associated adjective *archetypal* is popularly used to mean 'typical':

Here we have an archetypal piece of Beleek china.

This usage is often criticized because it weakens the meaning of a term that is useful in literary and psychoanalytical commentary.

See also BLEACHING

Arctic, arctic

The word *Arctic* has a capital letter when it refers to the region near the North Pole (Antarctic refers to the region round the South Pole):

Many Inuits live in the Arctic Circle.

The word *arctic* is used as an adjective to mean 'extremely cold':

The arctic conditions continue. Last night a temperature of -15°C was recorded at Glasgow airport.

aren't

The form *aren't* is a CONTRACTION that should be avoided in formal writing. It is used in negative interrogative tags with 'I', 'you', 'we' and 'they':

I am, aren't I?
You are, aren't you?
We are, aren't we?
They are, aren't they?

Argentina

Many usage experts insist that *Argentine* is the only acceptable form for both noun and adjective:

She married an Argentine.
He was in the Argentine navy.

However, the two forms *Argentinean* and *Argentinian* are increasingly used for both:

I have an Argentinean as a penfriend.
Buenos Aires is the Argentinean capital.

The form *Argentinian* is probably by analogy with such words as 'Amerindian', 'Canadian', 'Indonesian' and is now acceptable at all levels of language.

argot

The term *argot* has derogatory connotations and, like 'PATOIS', it tends to be used by educated speakers to describe the language of a socially inferior group. An *argot* is often equated with cant and may be described as the special, sometimes secret, vocabulary and idioms used by a particular group. The group is often involved in illegal activities. The term is sometimes mistakenly confused with JARGON.

argue

The verb *argue* is frequently misspelled. The 'e' should be dropped before '-ed', '-ing', '-able' and '-ment':

We argued about the meaning of the poem but the argument remained friendly.

argument

The word *argument* can refer to verbal repartee as in the previous example. It can also, however, be used technically to refer to the process by which a writer or speaker attempts to convince a reader or listener of the validity of some conclusion, principle or point of view. The term normally applies to the sequence of points through which a case is presented and illustrated:

The argument presented in this thesis is that Walcott's Caribbean heritage is the single most important contribution to his status as a poet.

arise, arouse, rise

These three verbs are occasionally confused. *Arise* is an irregular verb:

arise(s), arose, arising, arisen.

It means 'come into being', 'originate', 'happen':

I'm sorry for disturbing you but a matter has arisen that requires urgent attention.

Arouse is a regular verb meaning 'stimulate', 'give rise to':

My suspicions were aroused when he claimed to have studied at Cambridge but could not remember the name of his college.

Arouse and 'rouse' can also mean 'wake someone up':

I was aroused from a deep slumber.

This usage is obsolescent.

Rise is an irregular, intransitive verb meaning 'get up' or 'increase':

rise(s), rose, rising, risen

I have been rising at 6:30 every morning for the last six years.
The water level is beginning to rise again in Yorkshire.

As well as people, animals, dough, hair and prices can *rise*:

The hair rose on the back of my neck!

See also RAISE/REAR/RISE

ark

See ARC/ARK

Armenia

An inhabitant of this east European country,

formerly part of the USSR, is an 'Armenian'. The capital is Yerevan.

armour, armor

The spelling of the word for the protective metal covering worn by knights in the Middle Ages is *armour* in Britain and *armor* in America.

around

See ABOUT/AROUND

around, round

There is considerable overlap in the meaning and use of these words, although *round* is more versatile in that it can function as an adjective:

I designed a round house.

as an adverb:

No, I didn't drive. I walked round.

as a noun:

We played a relaxing round of golf.

as a verb:

He rounded the corner at 90mph!

and as a preposition:

I showed them round the house.

Around can occur as an adverb:

I used to live around here.

and as a preposition:

We've been walking around the town for hours.

Round and *around* are usually interchangeable when used as adverbs and prepositions, although *round* is still probably the preferred form in Britain and *around* in the United States:

UK: The tree is six feet round.
US: The tree is six feet around.
UK: I strolled round the gardens.
US: I strolled around the gardens.

Some British speakers claim that, for them, the sentences:

I strolled round the gardens.
I strolled around the gardens.

have different meanings, the first one implying that one walked inside the gardens and the second suggesting that one walked on the outside. If this distinction is still valid, it seems to be disappearing, and *around* and *round* are virtually interchangeable, with *around* becoming the preferred form in Britain as well as in the United States of America.

See also UK AND US ENGLISH

arouse

See ARISE/AROUSE/RISE

artefact, artifact

These spellings are both acceptable for 'some-thing that has been made', usually something from an earlier period:

They've dug up a variety of artefacts, including flints and shards.

The usual British spelling is with an 'e'. Americans use *artifact* and British students who use American books on archaeology also use the 'i' variant. Both spellings are correct.

article

There are two articles in English: the definite article *the* and the indefinite article *a* or *an*. Both *the* and *a* have two pronunciations. When stressed, *the* rhymes with 'she', and stressed *a* rhymes with 'may'.

See also A/AN, DETERMINER, THE

artist, artiste

An *artist* is a person who paints, draws or sculpts:

Why did fourteenth-century artists always draw feet that were vertical rather than horizontal?

Occasionally, the word is used to describe someone who is talented in an artistic way:

She's an artist in the kitchen.
He's an artist with words.

An *artiste*, pronounced to rhyme with 'priest', is a professional entertainer, especially one who performs on the stage or in a circus. The word *artiste* is less widely used now than in the past, partly because the music-halls with which *artistes* were associated have almost all disappeared.

as

As can function as a conjunction:

I met him as I was leaving the house.

as a preposition:

I worked as a teacher.

and in comparisons:

She is as tall as her brother now.

The items compared are often fixed:

as good as gold
as white as snow

and sometimes alliterate or chime:

as cool as a cucumber
as happy as Larry.

In comparisons such as:

She is taller than X.

if X is a pronoun, many traditionalists claim it should be:

She is taller than I.
She is taller than he.
She is taller than we.

Most speakers, however, say:

She is taller than me.
She is taller than him.
She is taller than us.

but write:

She is taller than I am.
She is taller than he is.
She is taller than we are.

Comparative constructions can often be ambiguous:

He likes John more than Peter.

This sentence may mean:

He likes John more than he likes Peter.

or:

He likes John more than Peter does.

'So ... as' can be substituted for *as ... as* in negative sentences, especially in speech:

She is not as/so tall as her mother.
She is not as/so tall as her mother was at that age.

Most speakers prefer 'so ... as' when the '... as' is followed by the infinitive, e.g., 'to try':

He won't be so foolish as to challenge you.
She isn't so obstinate as to go out alone.

The first *as* is usually omitted when *as* is used to mean 'although/though':

(As) hungry as I was, I waited until eight before eating.

Occasionally, the second *as* is omitted in constructions with comparative forms of the adjective or adverb:

My cooking is as good (as) or better than yours.
I drive as fast (as) or faster than you.

As is also sometimes used to suggest a reason. In this context, many users prefer 'because' or 'since':

She would not go as she had a headache.
I stayed in as I had a lot of work to do.

In very formal styles *as* can be followed by inversion:

She was a brilliant doctor, as was her husband.

See also COMPARISON AND CONTRAST, CONDITIONAL, THAN

as, because, for, since

These words have similar meanings and they can all be used to introduce clauses that provide a cause or explanation:

I took an umbrella because rain was forecast.
As she had another appointment she couldn't stay.
We tried to be on time since we knew he valued punctuality.
You must have told him for nobody else knew.

For is sometimes used as a conjunction meaning 'because':

I wanted to leave for I knew I'd stand a better chance in a city.

Many people dislike this usage.

Because can be used in all the above sentences and it tends to be the most acceptable con-

junction. Sometimes the use of *as* can be ambiguous in that *as* can also mean 'while':

*She could not do the cleaning as she was minding the baby.

See also AS, BECAUSE, CONJUNCTION, FOR, SINCE

as if, as though

The phrases *as if* and *as though* are used in comparisons and are interchangeable, but *as if* is slightly less formal:

They danced as if/though they were one person.
It looks as if/though we may get snow.

Often, in formal contexts, 'were' is used instead of 'was' in subordinate clauses, especially if the comparison is extravagant or unreal:

He looked as if/though he were about to float away!
I must have looked as if/though I were mad!
He looked as if/though he were about to burst.

In less formal circumstances, 'was' is used and is perhaps gradually ousting 'were'.

In colloquial speech 'like' is sometimes used instead of *as if* or *as though*:

I must have looked as if/though I had seen a ghost!
I must have looked like I'd seen a ghost.

While many stylists accept 'like' before a noun or noun phrase, they dislike its use in introducing clauses:

You came out best as you always do.
*You came out best like you always do.

The colloquialism *As if!* implying 'As if I would do such a thing!' is popular with young speakers:

Don't do anything foolish.
As if!

See also COMPARISON AND CONTRAST, CONDITIONAL, SUBJUNCTIVE

as regards

As regards is used especially in business or legal correspondence as a method of highlighting information:

As regards your request, addressed to us on ....

Other words serve a similar function but indicate varying degrees of formality. The most widely used of these are:

about, concerning, regarding, with reference to, with regard to.

as such

As such is an overused phrase with relatively little meaning. It may be used to mean 'in the strict sense of the word':

He is not a doctor as such but he makes us feel better just by visiting us.

Often, the phrase has little semantic or syntactic value:

Poetry as such is not easy to define.

as though
See AS IF/AS THOUGH

as to
The phrase *as to* is occasionally used in formal writing:

Could you give me any additional information as to the likely outcome of the meeting?

In most cases, 'about' is more natural:

Could you give me any additional information about the likely outcome of the meeting?

as well as
As well as, meaning 'in addition to', can be followed by a noun or a pronoun:

As well as the children, there were twenty people at the class.

As well as that, she added the juice of two lemons.

When it is followed by a verb, the -ing form of the verb is used:

The thief stole my bag as well as breaking the lock on my car.

as yet
The phrase *as yet* is frequently used where 'yet' would be sufficient:

I haven't heard from him as yet.

It is better to omit the 'as'.

ascender, descender
An *ascender* is a typesetting term for the top portion of letters such as 'b', 'd', 'f', 'h', 'k' and 'l'. A *descender* is the part of a letter such as 'p' or 'q' that is written or printed below the level of a letter such as 'a' or 'm'.

ascent, assent
The noun *ascent* is occasionally confused with its homophone *assent* but the meanings are markedly different:

The first recorded ascent of Everest was in 1953.

I gave my assent because I agreed with their proposal.

ascetic
See ACETIC/ASCETIC

Asian, Asiatic
These two words are occasionally misused. The derived noun and adjective from 'Asia' is *Asian*:

I have an Asian penfriend.

She speaks three Asian languages: Hindi, Korean and Japanese.

Asiatic is not normally used of people. It is, occasionally, used of languages:

He has skills in one or two Asiatic languages.

See also POLITICAL CORRECTNESS

aside
See A SIDE/ASIDE

aspect
The noun *aspect* is used in English to mean visual effect:

The bleakness was the most immediately striking aspect of the landscape.

a distinct element in a problem:

This is the aspect of your solution that I find most disturbing.

and a position facing a particular direction:

The distant river enhances the southern aspect of our home.

It can also refer to a grammatical distinction. English can make two types of distinction in the verb phrase: aspectual distinctions and temporal distinctions. The latter relates to time:

I walked to work yesterday. (time = past)

and the former to progression and completion:

I was walking to work …

I had walked to work …

See also VERB

assay, essay
These words can both function as nouns and verbs. *Assay* is associated with testing minerals:

How long will it take to assay these rock samples?

The assay will be finished in approximately 48 hours.

Essay is most frequently used as a noun to mean 'prose essay':

The essays must be no longer than 2,500 words.

As a verb, it means 'attempt':

They essayed a climb on the north face.

assent, consent
These words can both be used as nouns and verbs meaning 'agree'. *Assent* is a formal word and it suggests less reluctance than *consent*:

We readily assented to her request.

After much thought we consented to her request.

See also ASCENT/ASSENT

assignation, assignment
These nouns can, occasionally, be used as synonyms:

We witnessed the assignation of troops in Bosnia.

We witnessed the assignment of troops in Bosnia.

More usually, however, they are differentiated. *Assignation* is most frequently applied to a secret meeting, usually of lovers:

We knew all about their assignations in the woods.

Assignment is most frequently applied to a piece of work, often set by a teacher:

For your next assignment, I'd like you to do some fieldwork.

assimilate
This verb is often misspelled. It means 'integrate' and has a double 's':

The first immigrants were assimilated and gave up their languages.

assimilation
The noun *assimilation* has been widely used in the media to mean 'harmonious settlement into a community':

Both local and immigrant communities deserve credit for the latter's easy assimilation into Yorkshire society.

Evening Post

The noun has a different meaning when applied to speech. In normal speech, adjacent sounds often affect each other so that they become more alike and thus less of an effort to produce. In slow, careful speech, for example, the second 'n' in 'London Bridge' is pronounced 'n', but in casual speech it is pronounced 'm', because of the influence of the /b/ in 'Bridge'.

See also ACCENT, PRONUNCIATION

assonance
Assonance is a mnemonic device that involves the repetition of vowel sounds in words or stressed syllables that have different consonants. The words 'nine' and 'ninety' and 'losing' and 'blues' are examples of assonance in:

There must be ninety-nine ways of losing the blues. (song)

See also ALLITERATION, SOUND SYMBOLISM

assume, presume
Some purists have claimed that Stanley's greeting to Livingstone:

Dr Livingstone, I presume.

should have been:

Dr Livingstone, I assume.

because *assume* suggests a hypothesis whereas *presume* suggests a conclusion based on evidence. In fact, where the meaning is 'suppose' or 'take for granted', either verb is acceptable.

I presume you'd like to eat now.

I assume you'd like to eat now.

The verbs do, however, also have different meanings. *Assume* can mean 'adopt' and 'undertake':

He assumed a new identity.

She assumed full responsibility for the children.

Presume can mean 'dare' and 'take advantage of':

I would not presume to argue with someone of your eminence.

They presumed on our generosity.

assurance, insurance
Both these nouns can refer to financial arrangements with a company to guarantee a certain amount of protection. *Assurance* is used to refer to an arrangement where money is paid out after one's death:

Without assurance, your wife and children could be robbed of the lifestyle you would wish them to have.

Insurance refers to protection against accidents, fire and theft:

Motor insurance is likely to rise by 10 per cent this year because of a rise in claims during January.

Insurance is the more widely used of the two nouns and is often employed with both meanings.

assure, ensure, insure
These verbs are sometimes confused. *Assure* means 'promise and guarantee, convince':

I assure you that I shall look into the matter immediately.

We often use it when we wish to convince a reader or a listener of our sincerity.

Ensure means 'make sure' or 'guarantee':

Please ensure that your seat belt is fastened, that your seat is in the upright position and that your tray is stowed.

Coming third in the London Marathon ensured his place in the team travelling to the Olympics.

Many Americans use insure for this meaning and for the one listed below.

Insure means make arrangements to cover life and possessions in case of death, injury or damage:

You are strongly advised to insure any item valued at £1000 or above separately. We shall be happy to quote for any additional item.

asthma
Asthma is often misspelled, partly because it is unusual to have four consonants in a cluster:

It is estimated that one in three children suffers from asthma or an asthmatic complaint.

The 'th' in *asthma* is not pronounced.

at
At is one of the most frequently used prepositions in the language. Confusion sometimes occurs in the use of *at* or 'in' before place-names. The rule is not absolute, but the tendency is to use *at* before the name of a small village:

They have a cottage at Littlemincham.

and 'in' before towns, cities, counties and countries:

I was born in Coalisland.

I lived in County Tyrone.

I worked in Scotland.

When in doubt, it is best to use 'in'.

The cliché 'at this moment in time' meaning 'now' is best avoided.

See also IN, PREPOSITION

ate

Ate is the past tense form of the irregular verb 'to eat':

eat(s), ate, eating, eaten.

In parts of Britain, the pronunciation rhymes with 'let'. This pronunciation is considered nonstandard in America, where *ate* and 'eight' are homophones and rhyme with 'late'.

atheist

See AGNOSTIC/ATHEIST

attach

Attach is often misspelled. People often write '-atch', by analogy with 'catch' or 'match'.

attribute

This word can function as both a noun and a verb. The noun is pronounced with the stress on the first syllable; the verb is stressed on the second syllable.

See also STRESS

au fait

This French phrase is used in English to mean 'acquainted with something':

I am not yet *au fait* with the running of the department.

auger, augur

An *auger* is a tool for boring holes:

I'd never heard of an auger before I bought one but it's the most useful little tool I've ever had.

Augur with a 'u' was an official in Rome who observed and interpreted omens:

Interpreting omens was of significance in Rome and an augur was both respected and feared.

Today, we use *augur* as a verb meaning 'foreshadow':

There is a lot of evidence against Tom so it doesn't augur well for him.

aural, oral

These adjectives are sometimes confused. *Aural* comes from Latin *auris* meaning 'ear' and relates to the ear and to hearing:

The aural examination suggests that you could benefit from a hearing aid.

An *aural* examination is where one has to show that one understands the spoken language:

The aural examination will consist of dictation followed by six spoken questions to which you will supply a written answer.

Oral comes from Latin *os, oris* meaning 'mouth', and means 'of the mouth', 'spoken' and relates to the mouth and to speaking:

Children are encouraged to take an interest in oral hygiene.

An *oral* examination is one in which one must show that one has a command of the spoken language:

All students should have an oral as well as a written examination.

Oral can be used as a noun, usually standing for 'oral examination':

Our French oral is on Wednesday and the German and Spanish orals are next week.

The two words are sometimes pronounced the same, to rhyme with 'coral', and sometimes differentiated so that the first syllable of *aural* is identical with that in 'aura'. *Oral* is sometimes pronounced to rhyme with 'choral'.

See also VERBAL

Australia

An inhabitant of the island continent in the southern hemisphere is an Australian; the derived adjective is the same. The capital is Canberra.

Australianisms

Australia has given world English a large number of words, many from Aborigine languages. Among the best known of these are:

boomerang, budgerigar, dingo, kangaroo, koala, kookaburra, wallaby, wombat.

In addition, Australians are associated with such expressions as:

G'day (rhyming with 'high')
I'm crook. (I'm not well.)

and:

I'm taking a sickie this arvo. (I'm taking the afternoon off because I'm ill.)

Austria

An inhabitant of this central European republic is an 'Austrian'; the derived adjective is the same. The capital is Vienna.

author, authoress

Many female writers prefer to be called 'authors' and not 'authoresses' because the -ess ending is thought to be a diminutive that reflects badly on their status.

Many Americans use *author* as a verb:

List the titles of books authored entirely or in part by you.

Many British people dislike this usage.

See also GENDER, POLITICAL CORRECTNESS

authoritarian, authoritative

These adjectives are sometimes confused. *Authoritarian* means 'favouring or characterized by strict obedience to authority', 'dictatorial and domineering':

He was brought up by an authoritarian father who insisted that he should be obeyed unquestioningly, even in matters of religious belief.

Authoritative means 'recognized and accepted as true and reliable':

Their authoritative paper on the link between smoking and cancers is still a recommended text.

Some people use *'authorative' when they mean *authoritative* – that is, they omit an '-it-'. They incorrectly derive the adjective from 'author' rather than from 'authority'.

automaton

The noun *automaton* has two plurals, *automata* and *automatons*. The former plural, although correct, is now rarely used:

I've been reading about androids, automatons and cyborgs.

automobile

The noun *automobile* is now not the usual word for 'car', even in the United States of America. It is retained, however, in such collocations as:

automobile centre, automobile industry

and in the blend:

automart (automobile mart).

auxiliary

This word is frequently misspelled: it has only one 'l'. It means 'supporting', 'supplementary':

She's working as an auxiliary nurse.

In the study of English, the word *auxiliary* or the phrase *auxiliary verb* is applied to a verb that is used with another to help make distinctions. In a verb phrase such as:

might be going

'might' and 'be' are auxiliaries and 'going' is the head verb or main verb.

See also BE, DO, HAVE, MODALITY, QUASI-MODAL, STRONG AND WEAK FORM, VERB

avenge, revenge

These verbs, both associated with repaying an injustice, are occasionally confused. *Avenge* tends to be used in reference to a third party's attempts to exact justice:

Hamlet sought to avenge his father's murder.

The person who *avenges* a crime usually retaliates on behalf of someone else. When Milton wrote the sonnet:

Avenge, o Lord, thy slaughtered saints

he was asking God to punish the killers.

Revenge is most frequently used as a noun but, whether noun or verb, it is the person who has been injured who seeks retribution:

He will revenge himself on all those who have deprived him of his rights.

Hamlet's failure was that he could not find the will to revenge himself on the man who had killed his father, seduced his mother and stolen his crown.

Revenge is more frequently used as a noun than as a verb:

I don't want justice. I want revenge.

The noun 'vengeance' is used in similar contexts to *avenge*:

Hamlet sought vengeance for his father's murder.

Careful users distinguish these words, but there is a growing tendency for *avenge* to take over the roles of both verbs and for *revenge* to be used as a noun.

averse

See ADVERSE/AVERSE

avoid, evade

These verbs can all occur in similar collocations but they can and should be distinguished. *Avoid* means 'stay away from':

I try to avoid the people I don't like. Life's too short to be wasted on rows.

Evade means 'avoid by cunning':

He evaded capture by hiding in a grandfather clock.

await, wait

These verbs are similar in meaning. *Await* is formal and becoming obsolete. It takes a direct object:

We shall await your reply.
We are eagerly awaiting your arrival.

Wait does not take a direct object. It can be followed by an adverb:

Please wait outside.

or by a preposition, such as 'for' or 'on' and, less frequently, 'at', followed by a pronoun or noun phrase:

I'll wait at the corner.
I'll wait for you in the foyer.
Wait for me. I'll be with you in five minutes.
He's waiting at tables in a large hotel.

See also WAIT FOR/WAIT ON

awake, awaken, wake, waken

Many speakers are uncertain about which of these verbs to use and also how they are inflected. The four verbs, *wake, awake, waken, awaken*, have overlapping uses and meanings. In Britain, they are inflected as follows:

Present	Past	Present participle	Past participle
wake(s)	woke	waking	woken
waken(s)	wakened	wakening	wakened
awake(s)	awoke	awaking	awaked, awoken
awaken(s)	awakened	awaking	awakened

In UK and UK-influenced English, *wake* is an irregular verb with the past time form *woke* and the past participle *woken*:

I woke up in the middle of the night.

I was woken by the noise of a helicopter circling overhead.

Although in US English this verb is usually irregular, as in the UK, there is a growing tendency for it to be regularized:

The desk clerk waked us at 9:30am.

The forms *woke* and *woken* are still, however, the preferred forms throughout the world.

Wake can be used both transitively and intransitively:

She woke me (up) to tell me her news.

She woke (up), as usual, at 7:00am.

Awake is also an irregular verb, although some US speakers regularize it to *awaked*. It can also be used transitively and intransitively:

It awoke feelings that I thought were dead.

I awoke to find that I had never left the hotel!

Awake is most frequently used in the past tense and as a predicative adjective:

Why did you tell me that tonight? I'm wide awake now!

Try ringing now. He's certain to be awake at this time.

Waken is a regular verb and shares with *wake* the meanings of 'rouse someone from sleep' and 'be in an alert state':

You might as well try to waken the dead as my son!

It is often thought to be more literary than wake:

For Peel's view-hollo would waken the dead,
Or a fox from his lair in the morning.
          J.W. Graves, 'D'ye Ken John Peel'

Awaken is also a regular verb and is much less frequently used than the other verbs:

I was awakened by the sound of church bells.

It, too, is often thought to be literary.

In some parts of the world, the word *wake* can mean 'keep a vigil over the dead', and in this circumstance it is both regular and transitive:

They were both waked in the front room.

although the noun is probably more widely used than the verb, as in the following adage:

The sleep that knows no waking is followed by the wake that knows no sleeping.

See also A- WORD

awful, awfully

These words derive from the noun 'awe', but they have been so widely used that they are now loosely synonymous with 'bad' and 'very':

She has an awful cold.

He sang awfully well.

It would now be impossible to recapture the meaning of 'awe' that was inherent in Shelley's use of *awful*:

The awful shadow of some unseen Power
          'Hymn to Intellectual Beauty'

and so the best advice is to avoid these words in all but the most informal of contexts.

See also BLEACHING

ax, axe

The usual British spelling is *axe*:

We need an axe for the play but we don't know anyone who has one.

Ax is the usual American spelling for both the noun and the verb and both countries use the same forms before verb endings:

axes, axed, axing.

The verb *axe* is very popular in headlines:

Council to axe 400 teachers.

The noun plural *axes* is identical in form with the plural of *axis*, 'a real or imaginary line'.

axil, axle

These words are pronounced alike. An *axil* is the upper angle between the leaf and the stem or between the branch and the trunk. It occurs mainly in references to botany and derives from the Latin word *axilla*, meaning 'armpit'.

An *axle* is a bar on the ends of which wheels revolve:

I'm afraid it's serious. The axle has been damaged in the crash.

Azerbaijan

An inhabitant of the east European country, formerly part of the USSR, is an 'Azerbaijani' (plural 'Azerbaijanis'), and the derived adjective is 'Azerbaijanian'. The capital is Baku.

B

b

B is a consonant and the second letter of the alphabet.

bachelor

This word may derive ultimately from a Celtic source. Irish, for example, has *bachlach*, meaning 'a peasant'. It usually implies an unmarried male:

Mr X, a lifelong bachelor, refused to be drawn on the issue.

Occasionally, the phrase *bachelor girl* occurs for a young, unmarried, self-supporting woman, but many women would regard this usage as, at best, coy, and at worst, demeaning.

The word *bachelor* is frequently misspelled in Britain. It is possible that the form *batchelor has been influenced by the trade name 'Batchelors'.

See also FEMININE FORM/MASCULINE FORM

back formation

Back formation is a linguistic process involving the creation of a new word from the assumed root of an existing word. A change of word class always occurs. The verbs:

burgle, edit, televise

are back formations from the nouns:

burglar, editor, television.

The newly created words are formed by analogy with other existing words:

burgle is analogous to gurgle

edit is analogous to audit

televise is analogous to revise.

Because back formations resemble existing words, the new formations are readily acceptable and indistinguishable from words with conventional roots. Thus *burgle* seems as regular as *gurgle* or *bungle* and only students of etymology know that *burglar* existed first. Other well-known back formations include:

automate from automation

craze from crazy

donate from donation

fax from facsimile

flab from flabby

enthuse from enthusiasm

liaise from liaison

perv from perverse/perverted

psych from psychology.

See also ANALOGUE/ANALOG/ANALOGY, CLIPPING, WORD FORMATION

back of, behind

American speakers often use the phrase *in back of* where a British speaker would prefer *behind*:

UK: I saw him behind the house.

US: I saw him in back of the house.

Some writers dislike one or other usage but the dislike is not linguistically motivated. Both American and British speakers use similar constructions without adverse comment:

UK/US: I saw him in front of the house.

UK/US: I saw him before 2 o'clock.

See also AMERICAN ENGLISH, BRITISH

back slang

Back slang is a form of slang in which words are pronounced backwards:

net, ten

owt, two

spoc, cops

yob, boy.

See also SLANG

backward, backwards

Many adverbs of motion have two forms, one ending in '-ward', the other in '-wards'. In British English, the form in '-wards' is often preferred:

She moved backwards and forwards.

The words with '-ward' tend to be preferred in America:

She moved backward and forward.

It is not, however, uncommon to find British speakers using '-ward' forms as adverbs or even vacillating in their usage. The form *backward* is the only acceptable form for the adjective:

She left without a backward glance.

See also ADJECTIVE, ADVERB, AFTERWARD/AFTERWARDS, -WARD/-WARDS

bacteria

This word is the plural of *bacterium*, and should be used with a plural verb form:

Bacteria are typically unicellular organisms.

There is a tendency to use *bacteria* as a singular noun, partly because some other Latin singular nouns, such as *formula*, are singular. In May 1995, for example, a BBC news reporter claimed:

This bacteria is transmitted by body fluids.

Such usage should be avoided.

See also BORROWING, LATINISM

bade

Bade is the past tense form of *bid* and tends to be restricted to such structures as:

She bade him a fond farewell.

This word normally rhymes with 'glad' but there is a growing tendency to rhyme it with 'glade'. The former pronunciation is to be preferred.

baggage

Baggage, like 'luggage' is an uncountable noun:

I have two pieces of baggage only.

In form, it is a singular noun:

this baggage

but it is plural in meaning and can refer to several suitcases:

Put all my baggage here.

There is no absolute distinction between *baggage* and 'luggage' although the former tends to be used when people travel by air.

See also COUNTABLE AND UNCOUNTABLE

Bahamas

An inhabitant of the island group in the West Indies is a 'Bahamian'; the derived adjective is the same. The capital is Nassau.

Bahrain

The preferred spellings for the country and the derived noun and adjective are 'Bahrain' and 'Bahraini'. 'Bahrein' and 'Bahreini' are also sometimes seen. The capital is Manama.

bail, bale

There is some confusion about these words but the following distinctions should help. Both words can be used as nouns and verbs. *Bail* is associated with courts of law. Sometimes a judge permits the temporary release of an accused person on *bail*, that is, on the deposit of a fixed sum of money or other security. The verb *bail* can be used to cover the related meanings of providing *bail* and releasing on *bail*:

The family pooled their money to bail their son.

He was bailed on condition that he reported daily to his nearest police station.

The verb *bail* can also mean 'remove water from a boat':

They tried to bail out the water but the boat eventually capsized.

The noun *bale* is an archaic word for 'evil', 'harm', 'disaster'. A *bale* is also a large bundle:

There were six bales of cotton waiting to be collected.

The verb *bale* can mean 'make into a large bundle':

They baled the cotton ready for shipment.

Both spellings are used with 'out' to mean 'jump out of a plane':

The pilot had no alternative but to bail/bale out.

baited, bated

These past participles are sometimes confused. *Baited* derives from the verb *bait* and can mean 'angered, provoked or teased':

He was baited unmercifully by the other children.

Bated is a reduced form of 'abated' and is used as an adjective in the collocation 'with bated breath'. This phrase is a cliché and should be avoided in formal styles.

balance

In some parts of the English-speaking world, the noun *balance* is used to mean 'change':

The goods cost 1500 francs and so your balance is 500.

Although this usage is comprehensible, it is not regarded as standard.

bale

See BAIL/BALE

baleful, baneful

These adjectives are rarely used in the spoken medium and this may partly explain why they are sometimes confused. *Baleful*, deriving from the noun *bale*, which is now archaic, means 'harmful', 'menacing', 'vindictive'. *Baneful*, deriving from the noun *bane*, means 'poisonous, destructive'. Both adjectives are becoming archaic.

balk, baulk

These words are acceptable variants. They mean 'stop suddenly or unexpectedly':

The horse balked at the first jump.

In Britain, the form *baulk* is used in billiards to refer to the line that is 29 inches from the bottom cushion. The space between the line and the cushion is sometimes described as the *baulk*. The spelling without 'u' is becoming more widely used in all contexts.

balmy, barmy

In British English, these two words tend to be homophones and so there is a tendency to confuse them. The adjective *balmy* derives from *balm* and means 'pleasant', 'mild', 'fragrant':

The air was balmy rather than bracing.

Barmy derives from the noun *barm* and means 'foolish', 'mad', 'unacceptable':

How did he come up with such a barmy idea?

In the United States and, increasingly in Britain, *balmy* is often used for both meanings.

baluster, balustrade, banister

A *baluster* is the upright that supports an upper rail, usually of stone and generally outside. A *balustrade* is a series of *balusters* supporting a rail or coping.

A *banister* is a handrail, supported by *balusters*, fixed along a flight of stairs. The spelling 'bannister' is acceptable but unusual:

She needed to hold on to the banister for support as she climbed the stairs.

baneful
See BALEFUL/BANEFUL

Bangladesh
This is the name of the Asian republic, formerly known as East Pakistan. The inhabitants are 'Bengalis' or 'Bangladeshis' and the derived adjective is 'Bangladeshi'. The capital is Dhaka (not Dacca).

banister
See BALUSTER/BALUSTRADE/BANISTER

banjo
This word has two acceptable plurals, *banjos* and *banjoes*. The form without 'e' is the more widely used.

banzai, bonsai
Both these words come from Japanese and they are sometimes spelled incorrectly and confused. *Banzai* means 'May you live'. It is a greeting that has been used as a battle cry. The phrase 'banzai attack' refers to an attack in which the troops show little or no concern for their own safety.

Bonsai is the art of growing dwarf varieties of trees and shrubs:

The bonsai oak was 12 inches tall and perfect in every detail.

baptismal name
This is the name given to a child when it is baptized. It is the equivalent of CHRISTIAN NAME. Because these terms are specifically Christian, they are now normally avoided on forms and non-religious equivalents are used. The best-known equivalents are FIRST NAME, 'forename' or 'given name'. These terms are in contrast to the family name or surname.

Barbados
An inhabitant of the island in the West Indies is a 'Barbadian'; the derived adjective is the same. The capital is Bridgetown.

barbaric, barbarous
These words are sometimes confused. They both derive from Latin *barbaricus*, meaning 'foreign, outlandish'. *Barbaric* means 'relating to or characteristic of barbarians' and, from this,

'primitive, unsophisticated'. Greeks and Romans shaved their faces and they regarded those people who did not as uncivilized. The word *barbarian* literally meant 'a man with a beard'. The Romans regarded the British as *barbaric*.

Barbarous tends to mean 'brutal, coarse, ignorant':

Imprisonment without trial is essentially barbarous. The custom cannot ever be condoned.

barbarism
Barbarism is a term used to condemn words that are popular rather than learned. For example, 'disassociate' is regarded as a *barbarism* because an etymologically more correct form 'dissociate' exists. It is not, however, difficult to see how 'dis + associate' came into being or to find analogous words (dis + agree, dis + allow, dis + appoint). Other so-called barbarisms are:

Barbarism	Prestige form	Analogous word
adaption	adaptation	adoption
educationalist	educationist	nationalist
grievious	grievous	devious
orientate	orient	meditate
preventative	preventive	tentative
pronounciation	pronunciation	pronounce
reoccur	recur	reaffirm
untactful	tactless	unhelpful

It is likely that some *barbarisms* will oust their more respectable counterparts. Ultimately, it is general usage, rather than etymological pedigree, that determines the survival of a word.

The term *barbarism* is sometimes used to refer disparagingly to foreign, vulgar, uneducated or impolite expressions.

See also ANALOGUE/ANALOG/ANALOGY, COGNATE, ETYMOLOGY

barbecue
This word was borrowed into English from American Spanish. It is sometimes misspelled. The past tense is 'barbecued' and the present participle is 'barbecuing'.

barely, hardly, scarcely
These adverbs, which are close synonyms that are used to mean 'almost not' or 'only just', are unusual in a number of ways. They cause inversion when they occur at the beginning of a temporal clause:

Hardly had I mentioned his name when John appeared.

If they are used after the auxiliary, however, there is no inversion:

I had hardly mentioned his name when John appeared.

This usage is similar in meaning to sentences using 'no sooner ... than':

I had no sooner mentioned his name than John appeared.

and such constructions have brought about the colloquial use of *barely/hardly/scarcely ... than*:

I had barely turned the corner when I saw him.

*I had barely turned the corner than I saw him.

*I had hardly mentioned his name than John appeared.

Barely, hardly and *scarcely* include a negative in their meaning, although some users incorrectly use a negative with these adverbs:

I hardly know you.

*I can't barely/hardly/scarcely see the outline.

*I don't hardly hear you.

When they are used as adverbs of degree, they tend to occur after the subject but before the auxiliary:

I can hardly see you.

*I can see you hardly.

I can barely see the outline of the building.

She was barely sixteen when she left school.

See also ADVERB, HARD/HARDLY, NEGATION, NO SOONER

bark, barque

These are variant spellings of a poetic word for 'boat'. The form *barque* is preferred in Britain. The two forms are found in American English.

barmy

See BALMY/BARMY

base, basis

These words have the same written plural, *bases*, although some speakers pronounce the plural of *base* to rhyme with 'cases' whereas they pronounce the plural of *basis* to rhyme with 'bay seas'. *Base* is used to refer to a literal foundation or support:

There is evidence of damp on the base of the column.

Basis refers to metaphorical foundations or support:

The basis for the argument was not carefully explained.

base form

The *base form*, which is also known as the 'root' or the 'stem', is the unmodified word, that is, the singular form of a noun:

'bird' and not 'birds'

the imperative form of a verb:

'go' and not 'goes', 'going' or 'gone'

and the positive form of an adjective:

'tall' and not 'taller' or 'tallest'.

Affixes are added to the base form:

taste: dis + taste + ful

man: un + man + ly.

See also AFFIX, DERIVATION, INFLECTION/INFLEXION

Basic English

C.K. Ogden (1889–1957) created *Basic English*, a reduced and simplified form of English, which he believed would be easy to teach and learn. *Basic English* consisted of 850 words:

600 'things', ranging from 'account' to 'year'

150 'qualities', including 'able', 'bad', 'good' and 'young'

100 'operators', containing 16 full verbs such as 'be' and 'put', two modals, 'may' and 'will', a number of pronouns, adverbs, determiners, conjunctions, prepositions and the words 'yes', 'no' and 'please'.

Basic English failed to find wider acceptance because the English produced was judged 'unnatural':

I have love for you.

and not:

I love you.

It did not lead on to the mastery of natural English; the 850 words are the minimum one can use, but 150 extra words were necessary for the translation of the Bible. (A normal Bible uses approximately 6,400 words.) In addition, many words were allowed to be used both literally and metaphorically.

See also PIDGIN AND CREOLE

basically

Basically is sometimes described as a buzz word in that it is often used simply because it is fashionable and not because it is necessary. In sentences such as:

Well, basically, I haven't anything to add.

it adds nothing to the meaning. The meaning of the word *basically* is roughly the equivalent of 'fundamentally' as in:

She was basically correct in her assessment.

This is how the adverb should be used.

basinet, bassinet

Both these words can be traced back to Old French *bacinet*, 'a little basin', and neither is widely used in contemporary English. The form with one 's' has the alternative spelling *bascinet*; it means a 'light steel headpiece'. The word with 'ss' refers to a wooden or wickerwork pram or cradle with a hood. It was borrowed from modern French *bassinet* and has been influenced in meaning by *barcelonnette*, 'a little cradle'.

basis

See BASE/BASIS

bated

See BAITED/BATED

bath, bathe

Bath can be both a noun and a verb:

I haven't had my bath yet.
Can I bath (i.e., give a bath to) the baby?

The verbs *bath* and *bathe* cover different but overlapping semantic areas in the UK and the USA. Because their spelling differs only in the present tense, the distinctions between them are becoming blurred.

Bath as a verb is used in the UK. It means 'wash oneself or someone else' usually in a bathtub:

I'll bath after you.
Shall I bath the baby?

Many American speakers would prefer *bathe* in the above examples or would use such periphrastic constructions as:

I'll take a bath after you.
Shall I give the baby a bath?

UK speakers also use the expressions 'have a bath' and 'take a bath'.

Bathe is used more extensively in the USA than in Britain. Its meanings include 'give a bath to' and 'apply a liquid to something':

I'll bathe the baby.
Bathe your eyes in a saline solution.

In conservative UK usage bathe tends to be confined to moistening with liquid or alleviating pain, as in the second example. Increasingly, however, US usage is spreading among the young.

The verb *bathe* is found throughout the world with the meaning of 'swim in the sea':

I try to bathe every morning because sea water is so stimulating.

but it is much less widely used than 'swim'.

bathos

Bathos is a FIGURE OF SPEECH involving the sudden switch from an exalted to a more mundane style:

Here thou great Anna! whom three realms obey,
Doth sometimes counsel take – and sometimes Tea.
    Alexander Pope, *The Rape of the Lock*

bathroom

This word is used differently in the UK and the USA. In the UK it refers to a room containing a bath and, usually, a lavatory and wash basin. In the USA it is used as a synonym for 'lavatory'.

See also LAVATORY/TOILET/WASHROOM

baton, batten

These two words refer to pieces of wood and so are sometimes confused. A *baton* is used to refer to:

the stick used by a conductor of a choir or orchestra
the short stick carried by athletes in relay races

the long stick with a knob that is carried and thrown into the air by a leader of a parade, a drum major or majorette
a staff carried by an officer as a sign of rank.

A *batten* is a sawn piece of wood used in the building trade often to cover joints or for flooring. It is frequently used as a verb in the fixed phrase 'batten down the hatches':

We'd better batten down the hatches. There's going to be a storm.

baud, bawd, bawdy

These words occur infrequently in English, and this fact may help explain their confusion. A *baud* is the name of a unit to measure the speed of telegraphic code messages:

A baud is the equivalent of one unit interval per second.

Its use has been extended into computer technology.

The word *bawd* is now archaic but is found in the writings of Shakespeare. It refers to a person, usually a woman, who runs a brothel or who is a prostitute. The derived adjective *bawdy*, meaning 'humorously obscene', continues to be used:

Modern readers miss many of the bawdy puns in Shakespeare because of changes in pronunciation.

and has been extended to act as a noun meaning 'eroticism, especially in drama':

She's the professor who wrote a book on Shakespeare's bawdy.

baulk

See BALK/BAULK

bay window, bow window

Both these windows protrude from the wall. The *bow window* is curved, whereas the *bay window* is not.

bayonet

When the word *bayonet* is used as a verb, it does not double the 't' before suffixes:

bayonet(s), bayoneted, bayoneting
He bayoneted the dummy.

bazaar, bizarre

The word *bazaar*, occasionally *bazar*, is a noun borrowed from Persian *bazar* and means a market area, usually with small stalls. Originally, the word was applied to Middle Eastern and Oriental markets but it is now also applied to sales of second-hand items, usually for charity:

The Church Bazaar brought in an extra £524.

The word *bizarre* is an adjective, adopted from French in the seventeenth century and meaning 'odd', 'unusual', 'strange':

There's something bizarre about his recent behaviour.

BC
See AD/BC

---

be

The verb 'to be' is the most irregular and also the most frequently used verb in the language. It has eight morphologically distinct forms:

Present	Past	Non-finite
am	was	to be
are	were	been
is	being	

The verb 'to be' has three main roles in English. It can function as a linking verb (sometimes called a COPULA). In this role, it introduces a complement:

I am a painter.
She is a doctor.
You are very intelligent.

When the copula introduces a noun, noun phrase or pronoun, it is sometimes referred to as 'equative be' because the subject and the complement refer to the same person or thing:

Michael is a dentist. (Michael = dentist)
That's you as a baby. (That = you)

It can be used with the -ING FORM of the verb to create what linguists call 'progressive aspect'. Traditionally, this *be* was referred to as 'continuative be' because it was used to indicate the continuing nature of the action described:

I am dancing.
She was driving a Jaguar.
You weren't working all the time.

It can be used with the past participle of a verb to create the passive voice:

I was followed home.
It was written in 1546.
The cat is called Felix.

Some languages use the verb 'to be' existentially, that is, with the meaning of 'exist'. This is rare in English except in translations from Hebrew:

I am who am.

or from Latin, as when Réné Descartes (1596–1650) wrote:

Cogito, ergo sum ('I think, therefore I am').

See also ASPECT, AUXILIARY, IRREGULAR VERB

---

beat, win

Beat and *win* are verbs which are occasionally misused. *Beat* has several meanings:

The Welsh team beat the visiting Irish team.
Schoolchildren used to be beaten with a cane to punish them.

The bird rose into the air, beating its wings rhythmically.
The gamekeeper organized a team to beat the hillside to drive the gamebirds into the air.
The conductor beat time with his baton.

Win is an irregular verb:

win(s), won, winning, won
He has won two prizes already and his team is winning the cricket match.

This verb is occasionally misused:

*He won me at running.

Win cannot take a human object. We can win a prize or a match or even an animal:

She won a kitten in the competition.

If we wish to imply 'overcome an opponent', then we must use *beat*:

He regularly beats me at scrabble.

---

beau

This word comes from French and forms its plural with 'x', as in *beaux*. Both the singular and the plural forms are pronounced to rhyme with 'show' although the plural is also rhymed with 'shows'. The words are now regarded as old-fashioned or dated:

Don't you think *beau* was an attractive word for an escort?

Similar borrowings are:

chateau(x), gateau(x), plateau(x).

See also BORROWING, FOREIGN LOAN-WORDS

---

beautiful

The words *beautiful* and *beauty* are sometimes misspelled. They are both derived from French *beau* meaning 'beautiful', 'fine'.

---

because

Because is a conjunction that means 'for the reason that':

I applied there because it has a good reputation.

Some people use 'because' when 'that' would be more appropriate:

*Her reason for leaving was because she was bored.
*The full significance of the data is because it vindicates her position.

rather than:

Her reason for leaving was that she was bored.
The full significance of the data is that it vindicates her position.

Many stylists also dislike starting a sentence with *because*. They point out that, logically, it should follow the clause it depends on:

I played well because I had practised.

The reversed order:

Because I had practised, I played well.

is, however, perfectly acceptable and can serve the

useful function of emphasizing the cause of the main action.

See also AS/BECAUSE/FOR/SINCE

beefs, beeves

The word *beef* is normally a mass noun and so it is not pluralized:

a kilo of beef
two kilos of beef
*two kilos of beefs.

Recently, in the British press, it has been treated as a count noun and given a plural:

The customers will only buy the imported beefs.

Such usage is not to be recommended.

The plural *beeves*, meaning 'cattle', is now archaic and found only in liturgical language:

Only the beeves in the field did Him homage.

been

Been is the past participle of the verb 'to be':

Where have you been?

In Britain, the word rhymes with *seen* when it is stressed and with *sin* when it is unstressed, as in:

I've been working all the day ...

In many parts of America, *been* always rhymes with *sin*.

befriend

This word is often loosely used to mean 'become friendly with'. It is more correctly used to mean 'help' or 'comfort':

Gladstone befriended many women who had been degraded by circumstances beyond their control.

beg the question

This phrase is often misused. It means 'assume the thesis under discussion is proved':

To claim that Pythagoras' theorem was known when the pyramids were built because the building involved the use of right-angled triangles is to beg the question.

Recently, the phrase has been widely used to mean 'evade the issue'. Some purists dislike this usage, but it appears to be growing in popularity.

beggar

The spelling of this word is unusual. It ends in '-ar' not '-er'. The other widely-used nouns ending in '-ar' are 'liar' and 'pedlar'.

begin, start

The past tense of this verb is 'began' and the past participle 'begun':

I began work on the garden yesterday.
Work on the garden has only just begun.

Some users are uncertain about the correct forms

of the verbs *begin*, 'sing' and 'swim'. They are as follows:

Present	Past	Past participle
begin/begins	began	(have) begun
sing/sings	sang	(have) sung
swim/swims	swam	(have) swum

The use of 'begun', 'sung', 'swum' as the simple past tense is incorrect.

For most people, *start* and *begin* are close synonyms, but there are also differences.

■ *Start* can mean both 'begin' and 'cause to begin':

They started to walk.
They began walking.
They started the ball rolling.
*They began the ball rolling.

■ *Start* can be transitive or intransitive:

I started the book.
I began the book.
I started up the engine.
*I began (up) the engine.

There is a tendency to use *start* with animate or animate subjects:

I started school when I was four.
The car started immediately.
The article begins on page 96.

■ *Start* can mean 'move involuntarily':

I started when I heard the bang.

(on) behalf (of)

The phrase *on behalf of* means 'as the representative of':

I am speaking on behalf of all taxpayers.

In American English, careful speakers distinguish between *on behalf of*, 'as a representative of' and *in behalf of*, 'in the interests of':

I am speaking on behalf of my fellow workers.
I am speaking in behalf of children as yet unborn.

The meaning of this phrase is similar to *on the part of* but the two should not be confused:

That was a bad move on the part of the Prime Minister. (i.e., The PM acted unwisely.)
*That was a bad move on behalf of the Prime Minister.

behind

See BACK OF/BEHIND

behove

This word is now archaic although it sometimes occurs in the fixed collocation:

It behoves me ...

meaning 'It is fitting for me ...'. The word is

usually spelled *behoove* in the United States and pronounced to rhyme with 'move'.

beige
This word refers to a colour in the light brown or fawn range. It is sometimes misspelled, because it breaks the spelling rule 'i before e, except after c'. It is also occasionally mispronounced to rhyme with 'wage'. The 'ge' in *beige* is pronounced like the 's' in 'pleasure'.

Belau
An inhabitant of the island country in the west Pacific is a 'Belauan' or 'Pelauan'. The capital is Koror.

Belgium
An inhabitant of the European country is a 'Belgian'; the derived adjective is the same. The capital is Brussels.

Belize
An inhabitant of the Central American country (formerly British Honduras) is a 'Belizean'; the derived adjective is the same. The capital is Belmopan.

bellicose, belligerent
These words both derive from the Latin word *bellum*, meaning 'war'. *Bellicose* is the stronger of the two words and it means 'warlike', 'likely to wage war':
We would be foolish to disarm and to disregard the bellicose statements of the new President.

Belligerent used to mean 'waging war' as in:
The talks broke down and they continued their belligerent campaign of 'ethnic cleansing'.
More recently, it has been used to mean 'aggressive, ready to argue or fight':
He has become so belligerent that it is impossible to discuss anything with him.

Belarus
An inhabitant of the east European country, formerly part of the USSR and sometimes called 'Belarrussia', is a 'Belarussian'; the derived adjective is the same. The spellings 'Byelarussia' and 'Byelarussian' are also accepted. The capital is Minsk.

beloved
The adjective *beloved* tends to be confined to literary or religious language. It is pronounced with three syllables:
This is my belovèd Son in Whom I am well pleased.

See also -ED FORM

below, beneath, under, underneath
These words can all be used as prepositions meaning 'lower down than':
She lives in the flat below mine.
Such actions are beneath contempt.
I studied under Noam Chomsky.
I lived underneath a shop.

It is usually possible to substitute *under* for *below*, especially when the meaning is literal:
She lives in the flat under mine.

Often, however, we cannot substitute *below* for *under* without making the sentence literal:
*I studied below Noam Chomsky.

We often use *below* in the expression:
See below.
to refer to written material that follows.

Under means 'directly below, lower in rank than':
I work under Jay Brown.

Beneath means 'lower than':
The small plain was beneath us.
but except in fixed phrases, *beneath* is not widely used in contemporary English. Both prepositions are used in idioms where they are not interchangeable:
under cover; *beneath cover
under sail; *beneath sail
one degree under; *one degree beneath
beneath contempt; *under contempt
beneath his dignity; *under his dignity.

Underneath is used almost exclusively for physical descriptions:
I found it underneath the passenger seat.
It tends to suggest that 'it' was less accessible than if:
I found it under the passenger seat.

See also ABOVE/OVER

beneficent, beneficial, benevolent
These adjectives all use the Latin prefix *bene-*, meaning 'good' or 'well' and they are all associated with good actions or intentions. *Beneficent* means 'doing good', 'charitable', 'generous' and it applies to the actions of people:
David's beneficent behaviour was well known, so it was not surprising that he left all his money to the orphans of the parish.

Beneficial applies to things and means 'advantageous', 'causing a good effect':
I've persevered with the lotion for weeks but it doesn't seem to have any beneficial effect.

Benevolent applies to people and means 'well-intentioned', 'generous':
She was a benevolent person and her kindness was expressed in the many practical ways she found to help people.

Benin
An inhabitant of the West African republic (formerly Dahomey) is a 'Beninan'. The derived adjective is 'Beninan' or 'Benin'. The capital is Porto Novo.

benzene, benzine
These words are pronounced alike and sometimes confused. *Benzene* is a colourless, flammable, poisonous liquid that is sometimes used as a solvent for fats and resins. *Benzine* is a mixture of petroleum hydrocarbons, also sometimes used as a solvent. *Benzine* is occasionally used as a synonym for petrol.

Bermuda
An inhabitant of the north Atlantic island is 'Bermudan'; the derived adjective is the same. The capital is Hamilton.

beside, besides
Beside is always a preposition. It means 'at the side of', 'close to':

Oh, I do like to like to be beside the seaside …

Besides can be a preposition meaning 'in addition to':

There were ten men besides my father.

Besides can also be used as an adverb, meaning 'anyway', 'moreover':

He deserved to win and, besides, it's not going to affect his position in the table.

better
Better can be a noun meaning 'one who bets'. The word can also be the comparative form of both the adjective *good* and the adverb *well*:

You are a much better (good) player now than you were last year.
I played better (well) than I have ever played before.

Better can be ambiguous. The question 'How are you?' can elicit an answer such as 'I'm better now', which may mean 'better than before but still not well' or 'completely recovered'. This type of ambiguity can be resolved either by the context or by the addition of a word or phrase to clarify the meaning:

I'm a lot better now but I'm still very tired.
I'm completely better.

Better can also function as a quasi-modal, similar in meaning to 'must'. In this function it collocates with 'had' and the base form of the verb:

You'd better check the time.

This usage does not imply a comparison but is a means of offering advice or indicating an intention. It occurs more frequently in speech than in writing.

See also ADJECTIVE, ADVERB, QUASI-MODAL

between
See AMONG/AMONGST/BETWEEN

Bhutan
An inhabitant of the Asian kingdom is a 'Bhutani'; the derived adjective is 'Bhutanese'. The capital is Thimphu.

bi-
English adopted two prefixes meaning 'two', *bi-* from Latin, as in 'bicycle', and *di-* from Greek, as in 'carbon dioxide'. The prefix *bi-* occasionally becomes *bin-* before vowels, as in 'binoculars' (Latin *oculus* = eye). The Latin prefix *bi-* meaning 'two' should not be confused with the Greek prefix *bio-* or *bi-* before words beginning with 'o'. This prefix means 'life', as in 'biography', meaning an 'account of someone's life', and 'biology', which is 'the study of living organisms'.

See also BIO-, PREFIX

biannual, biennial
Biannual means 'twice a year' or 'half yearly', and it is sometimes used to describe regular payments:

This publisher has changed from annual to biannual payment of royalties.

Biennial means 'every two years':

The last biennial conference was in 1996 so the next one will be in 1998.

biased
Many people worry unnecessarily about whether the 's' in *bias* should be doubled before a suffix beginning with a vowel. The answer is that it is not necessary but it is acceptable:

Usual spelling	Acceptable spelling
biased	biassed
biases	biasses
biasing	biassing

Note, however, that 'focuses', 'focused' and 'focusing' should never be spelled with 'ss'.

Bible
When the word Bible applies to the Old and New Testaments it is conventionally written with a capital letter but without quotation marks, and the same rule applies to the individual books of the Bible. When its meaning is extended to an authoritative work, an initial capital letter is not required:

This book has become the cricketer's bible.

The adjective biblical also takes lower case:

Milton frequently wrote on biblical themes.

The same orthographic conventions apply to the sacred writings of other major religions, such as the Koran, the Talmud and the Vedas.

The usual forms of reference to parts of the Bible are:

the Old Testament
the New Testament
the Ten Commandments
the Gospels
the Epistles

and references are given in the form of book + chapter + verse, as in:

Genesis 2:8–10 (i.e., verses 8 to 10 of the second chapter of the book of Genesis)
II Kings 4:34
St Luke 21:3–7.

For the psalms, it is enough to quote the number:

Psalm 22

although care should be taken because the numbers given to the psalms by different denominations are not identical.

The accepted abbreviations of the names of the books of the Bible are:

Old Testament (OT): Gen, Exod, Lev, Num, Deut, Josh, Judg, Ruth, I Sam, II Sam, I Kgs, II Kgs, I Chron, II Chron, Ezra, Neh, Esther, Job, Ps, Prov, Eccles, S of S, Isa, Jer, Lam, Ezek, Dan, Hos, Joel, Amos, Obad, Jonah, Micah, Nahum, Hab, Zeph, Hag, Zech, Mal;

Apocrypha: Tobit, Judith, Wisdom, Ecclesiasticus, Baruch, I Maccabees, II Maccabees;

New Testament (NT): Matt, Mark, Luke, John, Acts, Rom, I Cor, II Cor, Gal, Eph, Phil, Col, I Thess, II Thess, I Tim, II Tim, Tit, Philem, Heb, Jas, I Pet, II Pet, I John, II John, III John, Jude, Rev/Apocalypse.

The language and imagery of the Bible, in Hebrew, Greek, Latin and English translations, have had a profound effect on literature and on popular usage. Although tradition suggests that biblical translations in Britain go back to the eighth century, complete translations date only from the sixteenth century. The translations by William Tyndale (1525) and Miles Coverdale (1536) provided the basis for all subsequent translations up to and including the Authorized King James Version of 1611, with the result that the language of the King James Version was archaic even in its own day.

References and allusions to the Bible permeate literature in English, much of which (such as Metaphysical Poetry, *Paradise Lost* or *The Scarlet Letter*) cannot be fully understood without a knowledge of the Bible. A number of expressions involving biblical names are in common usage, among them:

Babel
the mark of Cain
David and Goliath
Job's comforter
a Judas
as wise as Solomon.

Many felicitous words and expressions are also derived from translations of the Bible. Among these are:

beautiful
die the death
eat, drink and be merry
the fatted calf
a land flowing with milk and honey
the powers that be
to see eye to eye.

Some fixed biblical phrases calqued from Hebrew are also now part of the English language. These include possessives such as:

a man of sorrows
rock of ages

and superlatives of the form:

king of kings
holy of holies.

See also ARCHAISM, CALQUE

bibliography

A *bibliography* is a list of books or articles on a particular subject. The way in which it is organized and the items that are included depend on the purpose and scope of the compiler. The style of a bibliography should follow existing conventions, should harmonize with that of any notes or footnotes and should be consistent.

There are two main styles of bibliographical form: the author–date or Harvard system and the author–title system. When it is taken in conjunction with notes or footnotes, the first system (author–date):

Holm, John (1988) *Pidgin and Creole Languages*, Cambridge, Cambridge University Press.

is simpler and more economical, and a reference may be contained within the main body of the text in the form 'Holm (1988:15)' or '(Holm 1988:15)'. With the second system:

Holm, John *Pidgin and Creole Languages*. Cambridge: Cambridge University Press, 1988.

full footnotes are necessary within a text.

Each entry in a bibliography should be considered a sentence, opening with a capital letter and ending with a full stop; titles of books and journals should be italicized (or underlined) and those of articles and short poems should be given within quotation marks.

Some publishers omit the place of publication, but this habit can cause problems if a reader wishes to trace the item but does not know the country of origin. It is useful and informative to be clear, comprehensive, precise and consistent.

biceps

In spite of the ending, *biceps* can be a singular noun:

His biceps was strained during the exercise.

The word has two acceptable plurals, *biceps* and *bicepses* but the former is the more widely used:

Biceps derive their name from Latin and mean 'two-headed' muscles.

The form *triceps* can also be both singular and plural.

bid

The past tense of *bid*, meaning 'make an offer', is also *bid*:

They bid seven million dollars for the painting.

Many verbs ending in 't' or 'd' have the same form for the present, the past and the past participle:

Infinitive	Present	Past	Past participle
to bid	bid	bid	bid
to put	put	put	put
to set	set	set	set
to spread	spread	spread	spread

The verb *bet* is, for most people, also in this category:

I bet £20 on the lottery every week.
I bet £20 yesterday.
I have bet all my money and lost.

Some speakers still use *betted* as a past tense and past participle form when there is no overt object:

I betted on the winner.
I have never betted on a winner.

Most users of the language, however, treat *bet* as they do *put*.

See also INFINITIVE, PARTICIPLE, TENSE

biennial

See BIANNUAL/BIENNIAL

bight, bite, byte

These words are pronounced the same and, occasionally, confused. A *bight* is a large bay:

The Bight of Benin is south of Nigeria.

A *bite* is made with the teeth:

The dog's bite was much worse than his bark.

A *byte* is a term used in talking about computers. It refers either to a sequence of bits (i.e., binary digits) processed as a single unit of information, or to the storage space in the memory that is allocated to one character.

In contemporary journalism, the phrase *sound-bite* refers to a short, memorable utterance often made by politicians to be quoted on the news and in the press. During his visit to Northern Ireland in 1995, President Clinton was repeatedly quoted as saying:

'Engaging in honest dialogue is not an act of surrender'

and

'Don't let the ship of peace sink on the rock of old habits.'

billion, million, thousand

In the United States *billion* means 'one thousand million', that is, a one followed by nine zeros:

1,000,000,000.

In Britain *billion* traditionally referred to a million million, that is, a one followed by twelve zeros:

1,000,000,000,000.

The American meaning has virtually replaced the earlier British usage, even in government documents and school textbooks. Wherever there is even a slight risk of misunderstanding, an explanation of *billion* should be provided.

A *million* is represented by a one followed by six zeros:

1,000,000.

In financial dealings the letter 'K' is often used to signify *thousand*, so that £2,000 is referred to as £2K.

See also NUMBERS

bio-

Bio- comes from Greek *bios* meaning 'life'. It is widely used as a prefix:

bio + chemistry = biochemistry
bio + sphere = biosphere.

When *bio-* is prefixed to words beginning with 'o', only one 'o' occurs:

bio + opsis = biopsis
bio + osis = biosis.

See also BI-

birth date, birthday

Our *birth date* is the day on which we were born:

My birth date is 10 December 1947.

Our *birthday* is the anniversary of the day we were born:

My birthday is on 10 December.

In Britain the phrase 'date of birth' is normally preferred to *birth date*, although the latter is becoming more common.

bisect, dissect

The verb *bisect* comes from *bi* (two) + *sect* (cut) and means to cut in two:

The river almost bisects the town.

The verb *dissect* (notice the -ss-) comes from Latin *dissecare* 'to cut open'. It does not mean the same thing as *bisect*:

We were asked to dissect frogs but I could not cut up an animal.

Dissect can also be used metaphorically to mean 'examine minutely':

The students dissected the play.

Dissect has two acceptable pronunciations. The first rhymes the first syllable with 'kiss'; the second rhymes it with 'die'.

bit
This noun is widely used in computer language. It is a blend of *bi*nary + dig*it*. In the binary notation system, two numbers, 0 and 1, are used to express all numbers. The binary system is used in computing because the numbers can be represented electrically as *off* (0) and *on* (1). The word *bit* can be used to refer to either of the two digits, 0 or 1. Information is sometimes expressed in *bits* or in *bytes*, that is, a number of *bits*.

See also BIGHT/BITE/BYTE

bite
See BIGHT/BITE/BYTE

bizarre
See BAZAAR/BIZARRE

black
The word *black* can be used as an adjective:
my black suit
and as a noun to refer to a person of African, African-American or Afro-Caribbean descent:
Blacks make up just under 50 per cent of the population of Guyana.

The adjective *black* has many negative uses in English. It can suggest pessimism in:
black comedy, a black day
or disapproval in:
a black list, a black mark (against someone).
In trade union circles, a 'blackleg' is synonymous with a 'scab', and if any goods are 'blacked', trade unionists will not touch them.

Black can also imply cruelty:
Black Shirts
illegal actions:
blackmail, black market
unnatural spiritual activities:
black magic, black Mass
trouble or pain:
black eye, black ice
and people who do not behave as they should:
blackguard, black sheep.

In traditional European descriptions of heaven and hell, God is white, the devil is black and sin is thought to 'blacken' the soul.

Some of the words and phrases cited above are derived from the colour of the clothes worn, black shirts by Nazis, black vestments by exponents of the black Mass. Nevertheless, the equation of *black* with negative associations in so many phrases and idioms probably contributes to unconscious racism.

See also POLITICAL CORRECTNESS, RACIST LANGUAGE

Black English
Black English is the term used by many linguists to describe the spectrum of Englishes used mainly by Americans of African descent. The origins of Black English are claimed by some to be dialects of English, and by others the continuum of New World Englishes and creoles. Black English includes the following features:

■ The 'r' is not pronounced in such words as 'far' or 'farm'.

■ There are fewer vowel contrasts in Black English than in the pronunciation of most American broadcasters.

■ Consonant clusters, such as 'nd' or 'pt' tend to be reduced, especially when they occur at the end of a word.

■ It is probable that Black English has given world English words like 'banjo', 'boogie-woogie', 'bug' (annoy), 'jamboree', 'jazz', 'jive' and 'okay'.

■ Nouns may not be marked for plurality or possession:
I got too many rabbit.
He on my daddy chair.

■ There are fewer contrasts between pronouns:
I ain know he lose he wife. (I didn't know he lost his wife.)

■ There is a tendency not to use the verb 'to be' in such sentences as:
I tired.
She sick.

The study of Black English is sometimes referred to as 'Ebonics', a blend of 'Ebony' and 'phonics'.

See also AMERICAN ENGLISH, CREOLE, PIDGIN AND CREOLE, US ENGLISH

blanch, bleach, blench
The verbs *blanch* and *blench* are sometimes confused. *Blanch* derives from Old French, 'to make white', 'to remove the colour from'. It can be used as a transitive verb, that is, a verb with an object:
For this dish, we recommend that you blanch the vegetables.
It can also be used intransitively:
She blanched at the thought of her future ordeal.
This last sentence helps explain why the two verbs are sometimes confused. *Blench* comes from Old English *blencan*, 'to deceive', and it now means

'to quail', 'to flinch, as in fear'. Clearly, fear could cause one to *blanch* and *blench*.

The word *bleach* comes from Old English *blæcan*, 'to make white or colourless'. The main difference between *blanch* and *bleach* is that people can blanch but only things can be bleached.

blatant, flagrant

The meanings of these adjectives are similar, and this similarity, in part, explains why they are sometimes confused. *Blatant* means 'glaringly conspicuous', 'showy', 'contrived':

They showed no shame when I realized that their statement had been a blatant lie.

Flagrant means 'outrageous'. It is often used of a disregard for rules and regulations:

It was a flagrant breach of the traffic rules.

bleaching

Bleaching is a term used by some linguists to refer to the weakening of meaning in words such as:

	Original meaning	Current meaning
awful	awe-inspiring	unpleasant
dead	not alive	very (e.g., dead right)
fabulous	legendary	extremely good
interface	electrical circuit linking one device with another	overlap, meeting

blench

See BLANCH/BLEACH/BLENCH

blend

Blending is a type of word formation. It combines CLIPPING and compounding, often creating new words by the overlap of all or part of the existing words:

education + entertainment = edutainment
work + welfare = workfare.

The fragments are not necessarily morphemes at the time of the blend, although they may become so later if several blends are made with the same fragments:

motor + pedal = moped
motor + town = Motown

even leading to the jocular:

motor + bike = mobike
motor + park = mopark.

Many blends are created for specific purposes, such as advertising or punning, and are therefore unlikely to become fully integrated into the language. Among these are such words as:

decol(l)eenization derived from decolonization + col(l)een = the removal of the colleen symbol from Irish literature
stakisfaction derived from stack + satisfaction = chairs that stack easily.

Others have become or may become part of the language:

Afroamerican from African + American
breathalyser from breath + analyser
chortle from chuckle + snort
citrange from citrus + orange
smog from smoke + fog.

See also COMPOUND, DERIVATION, PORTMANTEAU, WORD FORMATION

blessed

This word is usually pronounced differently as an adjective and as a verb. The adjective is normally disyllabic, especially in religious titles:

Blessèd Michael
the Blessèd Virgin Mary.

This is also the pronunciation of the word in the Beatitudes:

Blessèd are the poor in spirit: for theirs is the kingdom of heaven.
Blessèd are they that mourn: for they shall be comforted.
    Matthew 5:3–4

When *blessed* is the normal past tense or past participle, it is pronounced as one syllable:

He blessed the crowds.
She had blessed the food before we arrived.

Blest is an alternative to the past participle 'blessed', but many usage experts dislike its use as a past tense form.

See also -ED/-T

bloc, block

The noun *bloc* (without a 'k') can only be used to refer to a group of people or nations united by a common purpose or ideology:

Phrases like 'the Eastern bloc countries' have almost disappeared from the language.

All other *blocks*, whether they are:

a block of flats
a block of ice
a block of marble
a block of wood

take a 'k' in the spelling.

blond, blonde

These words were borrowed from French and they are still used, in part, in the French way. Both can be used as adjectives and nouns. *Blond* is used for men:

He has blond hair.
He is a blond.
Tom and Jerry are blonds.

for inanimate objects, except lace:

blond wood

and for groups of people:

Many Scandinavians are blond.

Blonde is used for females:

She has blonde hair.
She is a blonde.
Tina and Teri are blondes.

and for a type of silk lace:

Blonde lace or pillow lace was made of unbleached, cream-coloured, Chinese silk.

blue-chip

In some nineteenth-century games of chance the blue chips had the highest value. The term *blue-chip* is now usually applied to Stock Market trading. A *blue-chip* stock is both safe and profitable. It is therefore highly regarded and much sought after. The adjective has recently been extended to refer to a company with an excellent reputation:

IBM is trying to rebuild its blue-chip image.

blueprint

A *blueprint* was a type of print used mainly by draughtsmen for drawings and designs. The meaning has now been extended to refer to any plan, physical or intellectual, which may be regarded as significant:

The government has today published its blueprint for the NHS.

blurb

This word was once considered slang. It is now, however, the standard term for a short promotional description of a book, usually on the back cover or the fly-leaf. A *blurb* is a type of advertising, and so it is usually an attractive and sympathetic résumé of the book's contents.

boat, ship

In theory, the difference between a *boat* and a *ship* is size. A vessel that holds only two rowers is a *boat*; a vessel that carries two hundred passengers is a *ship*. In practice, though, the word *boat* is often applied to larger vessels, especially submarines, frigates and cross-Channel ferries:

John is joining his boat in Portsmouth and will be at sea for three months.
The best thing about crossing the Channel by boat is the space. I don't like being cramped.

bodge, botch

Botch can function as a verb or noun to mean '(make) a bad job of something':

He means well but he botches everything he touches.
She made a terrible botch of the tiling.

Bodge is a variant form of *botch* and, although many purists do not like it, it is popular in Australia and, through the influence of soap operas, it is becoming the more widely-used form in Britain.

bogey, bogie, bogy

These words are not often used by the general public and so writers sometimes use one form when they mean another. A *bogey* (with 'ey') is a term used in golf to refer to the standard score for a hole or a course. A *bogie* is used in Britain for a vehicle with a short wheelbase, used for carrying coal, bricks and other heavy loads. A *bogy* or *bogyman* is an evil spirit. He still appears in children's rhymes:

O the wind and the rain brings my Daddy home again.
Keep away from the window, bogyman.

There is a growing tendency to use *bogey* and *bogeyman* for the evil spirit.

Bolivia

An inhabitant of the South American country is a 'Bolivian'; the derived adjective is the same. The seat of government is La Paz, and the legal capital is Sucre.

bombast

Originally, *bombast* was a soft material used for padding clothes. By metaphorical extension it was applied to extravagant, insincere language.

bon mot

This phrase comes from French and has the literal meaning of 'good word'. It is used now for witty or clever sayings such as those associated with Oscar Wilde:

In married life three is company and two is none.
There is no sin except stupidity.
To love oneself is the beginning of a lifelong romance.

bona fide

This phrase comes from Latin and means 'in good faith, genuine'. It is often used adjectivally in such constructions as:

He did not believe that it was a bona fide offer.
She owns a bona fide Salvador Dali.

The phrase with an 's', *bona fides*, is used as a singular noun:

She believes in checking things out. Asking for proof of his claims does not mean that she doubted his bona fides.

In Britain the first syllable in *fide* is generally pronounced to rhyme with 'fee'; it tends to rhyme with 'high' in America. In both countries the first syllable of *fides* generally rhymes with 'high'.

bonsai
See BANZAI/BONSAI

born, borne, bourn(e)
Born is an adjective and can be used both predicatively:

I was born in Yeovil.

and attributely:

She was a born leader.

Borne is not frequently used in contemporary English. It is the past participle of the verb 'to bear', meaning 'carry', 'give birth to':

They have borne their troubles with great courage.
She had borne eleven children in as many years.

Bourn(e) is a noun, meaning 'destination, boundary or limit'. The place where we are most likely to encounter its use today is in Hamlet's 'To be or not to be' speech:

… from whose bourn
No traveller returns.

This element also occurs in place-names such as 'Eastbourne'.

borrow, lend, loan
These words are related in meaning. *Borrow* is a verb meaning 'take something for a period of time with the owner's permission':

I borrowed Sam's car for the afternoon.

We borrow something *from* someone:

I borrowed the car from Sam.

The use of *off* with borrow is not acceptable in Standard English:

*I borrowed the car off Sam.

Lend is a verb that means 'give something to someone for a period of time':

lend(s), lent, lending
I lent John that novel last week.
Sam lent me his car for the afternoon.

Lend and *borrow* are reciprocal verbs:

I lent John that novel last week.
John borrowed that novel from me last week.

Occasionally, *borrow* is used where *lend* is the appropriate choice:

*John borrowed me his book.
John lent me his book.

Loan is a noun for the thing that is lent:

I asked the bank for a loan of £500 but the manager would not lend me the money because I was already in the red.

We can have something *on loan*:

The car is on loan from Sam.

Although many usage experts disapprove, *loan* is being used increasingly as a verb substitute for *lend*, especially if the *loan* is significant:

loan(s), loaned, loaning

He loaned me his car.
I wonder if you could loan me some money.
The museum has loaned its Rembrandts to Holland.

Logically, there is no need to use *loan* as a verb since we already have *lend*, but the process by which nouns become verbs is extremely common in the language:

foot: He left me to foot the bill.
head: She will head our mission to Peru.
man: Will you help me to man the telephones?
wall: They decided to wall the garden.

See also SEMANTIC CHANGE

borrowing
The words *borrowing* or *loan* are used in language studies to refer to words or phrases taken from another language:

There is evidence that *penguin* ('head + white') is a borrowing from Welsh.

The metaphor of 'borrowing' is misleading in that the item borrowed does not deprive the donor language. Nor is it usually given back. English speakers have borrowed words from every group of people with whom they have been in contact. One only has to think of food to realize how extensive the borrowing has been:

avocado, banana, cannelloni , deli, egusi, frankfurter, guava, halva, taco.

See also FOREIGN LOAN-WORDS, FRENCH, LATIN

Bosnia Herzegovina
An inhabitant of this European country, formerly part of Yugoslavia, is a 'Bosnian'; the derived adjective is the same. The capital is Sarajevo.

botch
See BODGE/BOTCH

both
In addition to the uses discussed under ALL/BOTH/EACH, *both* can also function as an adverb:

He was both frightened and thrilled by the prospect.

It is occasionally used loosely in colloquial speech to mean more than two:

He can both cook, clean and sew.

This usage is unacceptable in Standard English.

Both can create ambiguities when it precedes two noun phrases, such as:

Both parents and the MP attended the concert.

This could mean:

The two parents and the MP

or:

The parents (number unspecified) and the MP.

In speech we may know exactly what is intended,

but the structure is ambiguous in the written medium.

See also ADJECTIVE, ADVERB, AMBIGUITY, EACH, PRONOUN

Botswana

An inhabitant of this southern African republic (formerly Bechuanaland) is a 'Botswanan'; the derived adjective is the same. The language of the Botswanan people is Tswana. The capital is Gaborone (not Gabarone).

bottleneck

This word was originally extended metaphorically to narrow stretches of road where traffic hold-ups were likely to occur. It has recently been expanded to mean any hold-up, however caused:

The bottleneck caused by the work-to-rule in the hospital has resulted in the cancellation of all non-essential operations.

and any situation from which there is no escape:

The human race has already entered the bottleneck. Even if the world population falls, humanity is doomed.

Like many clichés, *bottleneck* has been overused and should, if possible, be avoided.

See also CLICHÉ

bottom line

This phrase was metaphorically extended from the bottom line of a financial report to mean 'the most salient point to consider':

We've heard a lot about the past greatness of the firm, but the bottom line is that no firm can live on memories.

The phrase has been so overused that it is now a cliché and should be avoided.

bouquet

This word, borrowed from French, rhymes with 'hay'. It is sometimes pronounced with the stress on the first syllable and sometimes with the stress on the second. Both pronunciations are acceptable.

Bouquet can be used to mean a 'bunch of flowers' or the 'fragrance of wine or liqueur':

She was presented with a magnificent bouquet of roses.

This wine has a rather astringent bouquet.

bourgeois

The word *bourgeois* comes from an Old French word meaning 'merchant'. It is etymologically related to *burgher*. In contemporary English, it means 'middle class' but with negative overtones:

Universities are now governed by the bourgeois mentality that profit is more important than standards.

The middle class are sometimes referred to as the Bourgeoisie.

bourn(e)

See BORN/BORNE/BOURN(E)

bow window

See BAY WINDOW/BOW WINDOW

bowdlerize

This verb has the meaning of 'delete or modify texts that are thought to be rude or offensive'. It developed from the surname of a publisher called Thomas Bowdler (1745–1825), who removed anything from Shakespeare that he felt might cause offence. The *damned* in:

Out, damned spot

for example, was replaced by *crimson*.

boy

The noun *boy* normally refers to a male child under sixteen:

The boys' eleven gave the adults a thrashing.

Informally, however, especially in the plural, it can be used to refer to men:

He's gone for a night out with the boys.

As an address term, *boy* should be avoided because it has frequently been used with classist and racist overtones.

See also POLITICAL CORRECTNESS, RACIST LANGUAGE

boycott

The word *boycott* can be used as a noun and a verb:

They organized a boycott of all oil products.

They intend to boycott the next match as a protest against the huge increase in the season tickets.

The word ends in 'tt' because it was adopted into the language from the surname of Charles Boycott (1832–97). He was a land agent in Ireland whose tenants managed to bring down their rents by refusing to cooperate with him.

See also EPONYM

bra

This abbreviation of *brassiere* is now more widely used than the full form of the word. In this it resembles 'bus' (omnibus = for everyone) and 'pram' (perambulator).

See also ABBREVIATION, CLIPPING

brackets

The word *bracket* is one of the few punctuation words in English not derived from Greek or Latin. It is a Germanic word, coming from the same root as 'brace' and 'breeches'. The term is applied to a pair of marks used in writing or printing to enclose a piece of material. There are four main types of bracket:

angle brackets <...>
brace brackets {...}
round brackets (...)
square brackets [...].

Angle brackets are regularly used to supply text that is either illegible or missing:

The handwriting is unclear at this point. The phrase may be <myne owne> or <my sone>.

Brace brackets are used to enclose alternatives:

Many prefixes can be used in front of '-duce':

de
in
pro   } + -duce
re

Round brackets are the most frequently used brackets. They are properly called 'parentheses' because they enclose information that is explanatory, optional or supplementary:

He is (to the best of my knowledge) the most successful golfer of all time.

Square brackets are used mainly to enclose remarks or interpolations in a text that were not in the original text or as brackets within parentheses:

He was an almost exact contemporary of Shakespeare (?1564 [or 1565]–1618).

brain, brains

The human *brain* is singular:

The brain has two hemispheres. The speech centre is in the left hemisphere.

The word is also singular in many fixed phrases:

brain-child, brain drain, brainpower, brainwash, brainwave.

The plural form of the word tends to be used when we equate the brain with intelligence:

They have no brains or they couldn't possibly do such things.
She has both the brains and the beauty of the family.

braise, braze

Braise is a term used in cooking:

First, braise the steak. (i.e., Brown the steak lightly in oil or fat and then cook slowly in a covered pan using a small quantity of liquid.)

Braze is used in welding. It means 'join two metals together by fusing them with a solder, usually brass':

I wasn't able to braze the metals together because the melting point of the solder was too low.

Braze can also mean 'decorate with brass' or 'make something like brass':

We should try to braze the candlesticks.

brake, break

Both these words can be verbs and nouns. *Brake* is a regular verb meaning 'stop, slow down':

brake(s), braked, braking
She braked gently.

A *brake* is a device used to slow or stop something:

Put your foot on the brake, not the accelerator!

Break is an irregular verb with several meanings, including 'fracture', 'cause to disintegrate', 'transgress against the rules':

break(s), broke, breaking, broken
You've broken my favourite mug.
I have broken my leg.
That's what happens when you break the law.

A *break* can mean a 'rupture' or 'an intermission':

There has been a break in communications.
Let's have a coffee break.

bravado, bravura

Bravado is a noun meaning 'ostentatious or boastful behaviour, swagger':

Getting the cat off the roof may have started off as an act of bravado but she showed real courage in walking along the gutter with a struggling cat under her arm.

Bravura is a noun meaning 'showy display of boldness or daring':

I accept that sword swallowing is an act of bravura but I don't like it.

Bravura is also applied to a musical passage that requires considerable spirit and technical skill:

It was a bravura piano performance.

braze

See BRAISE/BRAZE

Brazil

An inhabitant of the South American country is a 'Brazilian'; the derived adjective is the same. The capital is Brasilia.

breach, breech

A *breach* is a gap, a hole or a breaking of a rule:

They were able to survive within the walled city because the attacking army could not find a breach in the fortifications.
Such breaches in the rules will not be tolerated.

Breech has two main uses in current English. We talk about 'a breech birth' when a child is not delivered head first. In this usage, *breech* refers to the buttocks. We can also talk about 'the breech of a gun', meaning 'the rear end of a gun barrel'.

break

See BRAKE/BREAK

breakthrough

This word has become a CLICHÉ in popular journalism for 'significant and unexpected advance in our knowledge':

Breakthrough in computer technology!

All clichés should be avoided in formal speech and writing.

See also JOURNALESE

breath, breathe

There should not be a problem with this pair but they are sometimes confused. *Breath* is the noun and it rhymes with 'death':

I had to get out for a breath of fresh air.

Breathe is the verb and it rhymes with 'seethe':

It's lovely to breathe clean air.

The confusion arises partly because the verb loses the 'e' before affixes:

to breathe, breathed, breathing.

breech

See BREACH/BREECH

bring, take

These verbs are irregular:

bring(s), brought, bringing, brought

take(s), took, taking, taken

and they are occasionally misused. *Bring* implies movement towards the speaker, so:

Bring your mother to the supermarket.

implies that the speaker is at the supermarket.

Take implies movement away from the speaker, so:

Take your mother to the supermarket.

implies that the speaker is not at the supermarket.

Take occurs frequently in phrasal verbs:

take after (resemble)

take away/out (sell for consumption outside)

take off (remove, become airborne, go, imitate).

Britain

The name *Britain* is often used loosely for British Isles, Great Britain and the United Kingdom. These terms refer to different combinations of countries and care should be used not to cause ambiguity.

British Isles: Eire, England, Isle of Man, Northern Ireland, Scotland and Wales

Great Britain: England, Scotland and Wales

United Kingdom: England, Isle of Man, Scotland, Wales and Northern Ireland

British

British is even more ambiguous than *Britain* in that it can designate citizenship as well as nationality. Many people from former British colonies have British passports, with or without the right of residence in the United Kingdom. Some English people use 'English' when they mean 'British'. There is, for example, no such thing as an 'English passport'. English people, like Scots, are entitled to use a 'British passport'.

The term 'British English' is often used by people from the United States to refer to written English which does not follow American spelling rules.

The term 'Briticism' is often used for a linguistic usage that is thought to be quintessentially British. The word *vest* for an undergarment, for example, is a Briticism.

See also AMERICANISM, POLITICAL CORRECTNESS, UK AND US ENGLISH

broad

The noun associated with this adjective is *breadth*. Many of the common adjectives of size have nouns that end in '-th':

broad, breadth

deep, depth

long, length

wide, width.

High has a related noun, *height*, to which some people incorrectly add an 'h'.

broadcast

This word can be a noun or a verb:

I missed the broadcast last night.

The Prime Minister will broadcast to the nation.

Some people are uncertain about the past tense and past participle forms of the verb. The answer is simple: we can use either *broadcast* or *broadcasted*, but the former is used more frequently. *Broadcast*, like many verbs ending in '-t' or '-d', now does not form its past tense or past participle by adding -ed':

She broadcast yesterday.

She has already broadcast to the nation.

See also -ED/-T, FIT

brochure

This noun has two acceptable pronunciations, one that rhymes with 'kosher' and one where the second syllable is stressed and pronounced like 'sure'.

broken

See BRAKE/BREAK

Brunei

An inhabitant of the sultanate in northwestern Borneo is 'Bruneian'; the derived adjective may be either 'Brunei' or 'Bruneian'. The capital is Bandar Seri Begawan.

budget

Budget can be both a noun and a verb. As a verb, it is sometimes incorrectly spelled. It does not double the 't' before suffixes:

I budgeted for a family of four.

I wasn't budgeting on so many people staying.

See also SPELLING

buffet

The English noun and the verb *buffet* are borrowed from unconnected French words. The noun usually rhymes with 'ay' and can mean a 'meal where people help themselves' or a 'counter from which food is served'. The noun is frequently compounded as in:

buffet car, buffet meal.

The verb *buffet*, meaning 'batter', 'knock against', rhymes with 'pit' and does not double the 't' before suffixes:

buffet(s), buffeted, buffeting

He was buffeted by the storm.

See also SPELLING

Bulgaria

An inhabitant of the east European country is a 'Bulgarian'; the derived adjective is the same. The capital is Sofia.

bulk

Some purists object to the word *bulk* being used to mean 'majority':

The bulk of the orders come from Germany.

It is, however, widely used in this context, and the metaphorical extension from 'bulk' meaning 'large size' to 'quantity' is not unusual or logically untenable.

bullet

This term is used for a punctuation mark like a large dot, which is sometimes used before items in a list:

- comprehensive
- computer-based
- informative

bulletin

This word is often misspelled. It has 'll' and a single 't':

The hospital issued regular bulletins.

buoy

This word and all its derived forms, such as 'buoyancy', 'buoyant' and 'life buoy', are often misspelled because the spelling of 'u' followed by 'o' is not a pattern in English.

bureaucracy

This word comes from French *bureau* and is often misspelled. The suffix is '-cracy' as in 'democracy' and not '-crasy' as in 'idiosyncrasy'.

burgle, burglarize, rob, steal

These verbs all involve taking other people's property without their consent.

Burgle means 'break into a house and steal property':

Insurance premiums are high in this area because so many of the houses have been burgled.

Burglarize is the American equivalent of *burgle*. Both verbs derive from the noun *burglar*, the preferred British form by back formation and the American form by the addition of '-ize':

burglar, burgle, burglarize.

Rob is a regular verb meaning 'take something illegally from someone', and it can have the connotation of 'taking something by force or by threatening violence':

rob(s), robbed, robbing

He robbed me of my good name.

They robbed the bank after threatening the staff with a sawn-off shotgun.

Rob often takes a person as a direct object:

He robbed me.

Steal is an irregular verb meaning 'take unlawfully, without permission', 'take something, usually in a secret manner':

steal(s), stole, stealing, stolen.

It can be used with both concrete and abstract nouns:

He stole £7 million in gold bullion.

How can you prove that he stole your idea?

He stole my good name from me.

Steal takes an inanimate object as a direct object:

He stole my car.

There are many near synonyms of *steal* in English, some of them dialectal:

He nimmed my pen.

some colloquial:

He pinched my pen.

some slang:

He nicked my pen.

He half-inched my pen.

Steal has the metaphorical meanings of 'move quietly so as to avoid being noticed':

It was after midnight when we stole up the stairs, hoping that no one would hear us.

'gain an advantage':

We stole a march on our competitors.

and 'win unexpected acclaim':

She had only a minor role in the play but she stole the show.

The use of *rob* to mean 'steal', 'shoplift' is common in some parts of Britain:

*The children went to rob in the arcade.

*He robbed my pen.

but such usage is not standard.

Burkina Faso

An inhabitant of the West African republic (formerly Upper Volta) is a 'Burkina Fasoan'; the derived adjective is the same. The capital is Ouagadougou.

Burma, Myanmar

The new name for *Burma* is *Myanmar*, but the older name is still widely used. A native of Burma is a 'Burmese' or a 'Myanmari'; the derived adjective is 'Burmese' or 'Burman' or 'Myanmari'. The capital is Rangoon or Yangon.

burned, burnt

Some purists worry about the use of '-t' instead of '-ed' as a past tense form, but British writers use *burnt* as both a past tense form and as a past participle:

She burnt all his letters.

She has burnt all his letters.

The acceptable rules are that when the verb takes an object, *burnt* is preferred in the UK, *burned* in America:

UK: She burnt his letters.

UK: She has burnt his letters.

US: She burned his letters.

US: She has burned his letters.

and when the verb does not take an object, *burned* is preferred in both:

UK/US: The house burned down.

UK/US: The house has burned down.

The adjective *burnt* always ends with a 't' in both countries:

burnt fingers, burnt offerings.

See also -ED/-T

burst, bust

The verb *burst* has the same form for its past tense and past participle:

I burst the balloon yesterday.

The balloons have burst.

In the USA, the verb *bust* is derived from *burst* but is now acceptable in its own right:

We'll have to bust open the door.

Its past tense form may be either *bust* or *busted*:

They bust/busted into the house.

In Britain, *bust* is not regarded as standard but it is acceptable in the colloquial phrases 'bust-up' and 'bust a gut' :

They've had a bust-up.

I bust a gut working for him but got very little thanks.

See also -ED/-T, UK AND US ENGLISH

Burundi

An inhabitant of the east-central African republic is a 'Burundi'; the derived adjective is 'Burundian'. The capital is Bujumbura.

buses, busses

There is considerable disagreement about whether or not the 's' in *bus* should be doubled before a suffix, such as '-ed', '-es' or '-ing'. Generally, when a monosyllabic word ends in a single consonant, the consonant is doubled before suffixes as in:

bag, bagged

big, bigger

hum, humming.

The usual plural in Britain is *buses*. This spelling is found in American English, although *busses* is also used. In both countries, it is acceptable to use 's' or 'ss' before verbal affixes:

bus, buses/busses, bused/bussed, busing/bussing.

The forms with 's' seem to be growing in popularity and are preferred in Britain.

business

This noun, meaning 'commercial undertaking', is often spelled incorrectly. It derives from *busy*:

busy + ness = business

fussy + ness = fussiness.

Because *business* has diverged in meaning from *busy*, a new noun, *busyness*, meaning 'the state of being busy', has been introduced into the language.

bust

See BURST/BUST

but

But is used as a coordinating conjunction linking two grammatically equal but opposed units:

He can sing but he can't dance.

I saw not one but three swallows.

Some stylists object to the use of *but* in sentences with 'however' because they serve similar purposes:

His comments on cancer treatment were well received, but his views on the use of vitamin C were treated with suspicion.

His comments on cancer treatment were well received; his views on the use of vitamin C, however, were treated with suspicion.

*His comments on cancer treatment were well received but his views on the use of vitamin C, however, were treated with suspicion.

This is, however, a matter of stylistic preference, rather than a matter of standard or nonstandard usage. Others insist that, since the role of *but* is contrastive, it should not be used to open a sentence. Many writers, however, regularly 'break' this rule:

But, my good master Bates …

    Jonathan Swift, *Gulliver's Travels*, Book 1, Chapter 1

But can also be used as a preposition, meaning 'except', in which case it is followed by a noun or pronoun:

There was nobody there but Jonathan.

There was nobody there but me.

They found everyone but him.

Like all prepositions, *but* is followed by the object form of the pronoun. However, when we transform such sentences into:

Nobody but me was there.

Everyone but him was found.

some stylists prefer to use the subject pronoun instead:

Nobody but I was there.

Everyone but he was found.

It is worth pointing out that if we substitute 'except' for 'but', we do not change the form of the pronoun:

Nobody except me was there.

Everyone except him was found.

See also CONJUNCTIONS, PREPOSITIONS

buzz word

When certain words and phrases become popular and are then overused, they are often referred to as *buzz words* or 'vogue words'. There is nothing intrinsically wrong with any word but, if words and phrases are overused, then there is a tendency for them to lose much of their force and meaning. Words such as 'basically', 'interface' and 'situation', for example, have been so overused that some argue that they have been virtually bleached of meaning.

See also BLEACHING

by, bye

By is an adverb and a preposition:

I wasn't in when John came by.

We walked by the river.

Bye is a noun used to refer to an extra run in cricket:

Byes are not actually scored by the batsman so they are awarded to the team rather than to the player.

Bye is also sometimes used informally as a reduced form of 'Goodbye':

Bye for now.

Both *by-* and *bye-* are acceptable as prefixes in:

by-election, bye-election, by-law, bye-law

but *by* is still the acceptable form in:

bygone (Let bygones be bygones), byline, bypass, byproduct, byroad, bystander, byway, byword.

The expressions 'by the bye' and 'by the same token' are clichés and so best avoided.

by, with

These prepositions can occur in almost identical constructions:

She was hit by a child.

She was hit with a stone.

With should be used to introduce the instrument; *by* should introduce the agent. The instrument is almost invariably an inanimate noun whereas the agent is almost invariably human. It is not always necessary to indicate the agent or the instrument of an action. If, for example, John breaks a window with a stone, we can express the information in a variety of ways including:

John broke the window with a stone.

John broke the window.

A stone broke the window.

The window broke.

The window was broken.

The window was broken by John.

The window was broken with a stone.

See also CASE, PREPOSITION

byte

See BIGHT/BITE/BYTE

C

c

The letter *c* is a consonant that has two main pronunciations: it is normally pronounced like an 's' when it is followed by an 'e' or an 'i':

ceiling, citrus

and as a 'k' when followed by an 'a', 'o' or 'u':

cat, cot, cut.

c.

When the letter 'c' is italicized and followed by a full point, it is an abbreviation for Latin *circa*, 'about', and is most often used with dates:

Tiglath-peleser I (reigned c.1150–c.1077BC)

The use of *c.* to mean 'about' in such constructions as:

The article had c.20 pages.

should be avoided.

See also CC

°C

A capital *C* is used for both Celsius and centigrade:

The maximum temperature today will be 16°C.

See also CELSIUS/CENTIGRADE/FAHRENHEIT

cabriole, cabriolet

These two words are occasionally confused. The first is most frequently used as an adjective meaning 'curved'. It derives from French *cabrioler*, 'to caper':

The chair is probably not genuine. This type of cabriole leg only became popular in the early eighteenth century.

Cabriole can be used as a noun to refer to a leap in ballet:

A cabriole is a leap with one leg outstretched.

A *cabriolet* is a small carriage with a folding hood:

A cabriolet was originally a horse-drawn vehicle but the word is also applied to some motor cars.

cacao, coco, cocoa

The noun *cacao* (stressed on the second of the word's three syllables) is a small tropical American tree:

The *Theobroma cacao* has reddish-brown seed pods from which cocoa and chocolate can be prepared.

The word derives from Nahuatl, an Amerindian language, and came into English from Spanish.

The English word *cocoa* is a modification of the Spanish word *cacao*, 'chocolate', which is an approximation to the Aztec word *kakaua*, and it is applied to the powder made from *cacao* or *cocoa* beans and also to the drink made from the powder:

I find that a cup of cocoa helps me to sleep.

The homophones *coco* and *cocoa* are both nouns but they can also be used attributively:

coconut, cocoa butter.

The spelling *cocoanut* for the palm tree resulted from a confusion of *cocoa* from Spanish *cacao* and *coco* from the Portuguese word *coco*, 'grimace', which was applied to the fruit of certain palm trees.

I've got a lovely bunch of cocoanuts.

Today, the form without 'a' is preferred so that *cocoa* can be used unambiguously to refer to the powder and the beverage.

cache

The word *cache* is a homophone of 'cash'. It was borrowed from the French verb *cacher*, 'to hide', and is applied to a hidden store of food or weapons, and to the hiding place:

The soldiers came across a cache of weapons.

Cache can also be used as a verb:

This is where they used to cache the paintings.

cachet

This word also derives ultimately from French *cacher*, 'to hide'. It was borrowed into Scottish English in the seventeenth century to refer to an 'official seal on a document'. Later, it developed the meaning of a 'distinguishing mark' and came to be associated with 'prestige':

Many teenagers feel that these logos add a cachet to their clothes.

cactus

A *cactus* is a spiny plant. The word comes from Latin and the plural was originally *cacti*. The more usual English plural *cactuses* is now widespread and acceptable.

caddie, caddy

The noun *caddie*, meaning 'a person who carries a golfer's clubs', was a seventeenth-century Scots borrowing from French *cadet* 'younger son, junior':

Many young golfers support themselves by acting as caddies for professionals.

This word is occasionally spelled *caddy*.

A *caddy* meaning a small box in which tea is kept derives from Malay *kati*, 'weight of about two-thirds of a kilo'.

Caesarean, Caesarian

These two spellings are acceptable in both Britain and the United States of America, although the forms *Cesarean* and *Cesarian* are also found in America. The word means 'relating to Caesar', but it occurs most frequently in the phrase 'Caesarean section', 'a surgical procedure for delivering a baby', because Julius Caesar was supposed to have been delivered in this way. The word *caesarean* is sometimes used as an abbreviation of 'Caesarean section':

She had to have caesareans for both her children.

café

The noun *café* refers usually to a small, inexpensive restaurant where light meals are served. The word derives from French *café*, 'coffee', and it is customary for it to be written with the 'é' in English and for the second syllable to be pronounced to rhyme with 'day' either in its stressed or unstressed form. The colloquial and humorous pronunciation 'caff' should be avoided.

cagey

The adjective meaning 'cautious', 'wary', 'not frank' is sometimes spelled without the 'e', *cagy*:

It's nothing personal. He's cagey with everyone.

calculate

Calculate is a regular verb that derives ultimately from Latin *calculus*, a pebble used in counting. The derived adjectives are 'calculable' and 'incalculable' and not *(in)calculatable:

The damage done by such advertisements is incalculable.

caldron, cauldron

A *cauldron* is a large pot, usually with handles. It was originally used for boiling water. The American spelling is *caldron*, and that form is increasingly being used in Britain.

calendar, calender, colander

A *calendar*, ending in '-dar', is a system used to indicate divisions of time. We use the word most frequently to refer to a table showing days, months and years:

I'll always keep the 1961 calendar because it's the last time for thousands of years that the date looks the same upside down.

A *calender*, ending in '-der', is a machine with rollers to smooth paper or cloth:

People who control these machines are called 'calenderers'.

Calender can also be used as a verb, meaning 'make smooth'.

A *colander* or, less frequently, *cullender* is a vessel with holes that is used for straining food:

If you'd used a colander, the vegetables wouldn't be so soggy.

calf

The plural of *calf* is *calves*:

There were four calves in the picture.

Old English nouns that ended in '-f' formed their plurals by changing '-f-' to '-v-' and we have a relic of this in contemporary English in such sets as:

half, halves
wife, wives.

More recent English words ending in '-f' simply add 's' to form the plural:

goof, goofs.

See also NOUN, ROOF, SPELLING

calibre, caliber

The normal British spelling is *calibre*, although the American spelling *caliber* is sometimes found, especially when the meaning refers to the diameter of a bullet:

It was a 32-caliber pistol.

See also SPELLING

calliper, caliper

The usual British spelling has '-ll-':

I've tried measuring this figure with callipers but I am still uncertain of its dimensions.

The form with one 'l' is preferred in the United States of America.

See also SPELLING

callous, callus

The adjective meaning 'unfeeling, insensitive' is spelled with an 'o':

I didn't expect such a callous reaction.

The related noun, meaning an area of the skin that is hard or thickened, is *callus*:

I've worked so hard that I've got calluses on both hands.

Both words derive ultimately from Latin *callum*, 'hardened skin'.

calorie

A *calorie* can be defined as the amount of heat required to raise one gram of water by 1°C under standard conditions. The word is normally used in connection with food:

One-Cal drinks are popular because they contain only one calorie.
This cake must have 1000 calories!

The word is normally spelled *calorie* throughout the English-speaking world, but the spelling *calory* is also acceptable.

calque

A *calque* is a loan translation, that is, a direct translation of a word or phrase from one language into another:

cordon bleu: blue ribbon
Übermensch: superman.

calyx

A *calyx* is 'a cup-shaped cavity, the outer floral envelope that protects the bud':

The sepals of a flower are collectively known as a 'calyx'.

The word has two acceptable plurals, *calyxes* and *calyces*, with the 'x' variant being more widely used

Cambodia

The official name of the southeast Asian republic is 'Kampuchea'; it was also formerly known as the Khmer Republic. An inhabitant of the country is a 'Cambodian'; the derived adjective is the same. The capital is Phnom Penh.

camel

The term *camel* is applied to both the one-humped Arabian camel from north Africa and the two-humped Bactrian camel from Asia. A 'dromedary' is a one-humped camel that has been bred for racing.

camellia

This word is frequently misspelled. It has -ll- and is pronounced to rhyme with 'Celia'.

cameo

A *cameo* is a small engraving, usually on a brooch or ring:

My mother used to collect cameos.

The word is also used to refer to a short literary work or a small acting part in a film or play:

He wrote one major work of criticism in his life but a number of cameo sketches, several of which were performed in his college.

Film directors sometimes have cameos in their own films.

camera-ready

The adjective *camera-ready* has been widely used in printing for many years, but it has become popular since the introduction of desk-top publishing:

Camera-ready copy is printed material ready to be photographed for plate-making and reproduction.

The expression 'mechanical copy' or, more often, 'mechanicals' is also used in the United States of America.

Cameroon

An inhabitant of the west-central African republic is a 'Cameroonian'; the derived adjectives are either 'Cameroon' or 'Cameroonian'. The capital is Yaoundé.

can, may

These two modal verbs are often used interchangeably:

Can I have the salt, please?
May I have the salt, please?

although usage experts emphasize their difference and the value of preserving the distinction between them.

Can implies ability:

I can sing. (= I am able to sing.)
Can you swim? (= Are you able to swim?)

whereas *may* involves either permission:

May I swim in your pool this afternoon? (= Have I permission to swim?)

or suggests doubt:

I may go on Saturday. I still haven't made up my mind.

In practice, many people use *can* with the meaning of permission, especially in informal conversations or writing:

Can I borrow that book?

People are particularly likely to select *can* when a negative tag is required:

I can go, can't I?

rather than the more formal:

I may go, mayn't I/may I not?

See also AUXILIARY, MAY/MIGHT, MODALITY, VERB

Canada

An inhabitant of the North American country is a 'Canadian'; the derived adjective is the same. The capital is Ottawa. Canadian English has much in common with the English of the United States, and the similarities have grown largely due to media influence and the free access between the two countries.

canapé, canopy

A *canapé* is usually a pastry case containing a savoury filling or a small piece of toast covered with a savoury spread:

We'll bring some canapés and vol-au-vents for the party.

A *canapé* differs from a *vol-au-vent* in the lightness of the pastry. A *vol-au-vent* is normally made of such light puff pastry that it might 'fly in the wind'.

A *canopy* is usually a roof-like structure:

There was a highly ornate canopy over the altar.

cancel

This regular verb doubles the 'l' before '-ed' and '-ing':

cancel(s), cancelled, cancelling.

The noun 'cancellation' also has '-ll-':

Have there been any more cancellations?

In American English, one 'l' is acceptable:

The blizzards caused hundreds of flight cancelations.

candelabra

This form of the word was originally a plural:

candelabrum, candelabra

but *candelabra* is often used as a singular:

A candelabra is a large, branched candle holder.

Various plurals occur, including 'candelabrums', 'candelabra' and 'candelabras'.

Few people criticize the use of *candelabra* as a singular although they criticize a similar use of DATA.

cannibal

This word and its associated forms are often misspelled. They have '-nn-' and one 'l':

cannibalize, cannibalization.

Some critics suggest that the name Caliban from Shakespeare's *The Tempest* is an anagram of an earlier spelling that used only one 'n'.

cannot, can't

Can't is the abbreviation of *cannot*. In British English, *cannot* is written as one word:

I cannot believe you said that.

whereas it is often written as two words in the United States of America:

I can not believe you said that.

The only times when *cannot* is written as two words in British English are when the 'not' is being stressed:

I'm afraid I can not be present at the inauguration.

or when the 'not' is part of such a structure as 'not only but':

I can not only cook but I can also drive a car.
It can not only wash but spin dry as well.

Many people believe that reduced forms such as *can't* should not be used in formal writing.

canoe

Canoe can be used as a noun and a verb:

The canoe was not strong enough for the turbulent waters.
Can I canoe you down the river? (song title)

The 'e' is maintained before '-ing' and '-ist':

I enjoy canoeing although I'm not an experienced canoeist.

canon, cannon, canyon

These words are occasionally confused. A *canon* has three main meanings. It can refer to a churchman:

A canon is higher than a parish priest but lower than a dean.

to a law, especially a church law:

He completed his doctorate on canon law.

and to a body of work:

Some critics subscribe to the idea of a literary canon while others insist that one piece of writing is as worthy of study as another.

A *cannon* is a large gun:

Cannon to right of them,
Cannon to left of them,
Cannon in front of them,
Volleyed and thundered
Into the valley of Death
Rode the six hundred.
> Alfred, Lord Tennyson, 'The Charge of the Light Brigade'

When *cannon* is used as a verb, it means 'crash into someone, collide with someone':

He rushed round the corner and cannoned into the policeman.

A *canyon* is a 'ravine':

We flew over the Grand Canyon.

canopy

See CANAPÉ/CANOPY

cant

The term *cant* is applied to JARGON, especially the jargon spoken by society's outcasts:

I've just bought a book called *Tinkers' Cant*.

by criminals:

Certain ordinary terms such as 'porridge', 'screw' and 'snout' have entered prison cant with the meanings of 'time', 'guard' and 'tobacco'.

and by people who say one thing but mean another:

Love, love, love – all the wretched cant of it …
> Germaine Greer, *The Female Eunuch*

See also ARGOT, PATOIS

canto

The word *canto* is from Italian *canto*, 'a song'. Today, it is used mainly for divisions in a long poem:

Is the 'Rime of the Ancient Mariner' divided into parts or cantos?

or for the highest part in a piece of choral music.

canvas, canvass

At the moment, these words are clearly differentiated. *Canvas* is a noun meaning a particular type of heavy material:

Canvas can be made of cotton, hemp or jute and has been used for centuries for sails and tents.

Canvass is a verb meaning 'solicit votes':

I got a part-time job canvassing voters on behalf of our local MP.

Both words derive ultimately from the Latin *cannabis*, 'hemp'.

canyon
See CANON/CANNON/CANYON

capable
See ABLE/CAPABLE

Cape Verde
An inhabitant of the West African republic is a 'Cape Verdean'; the derived adjective is the same. The capital is Praia.

capers
The word *capers*, meaning 'a type of plant with an edible part', was originally a singular form deriving from Latin *caparis*. Like many nouns that look plural, we now have a new singular, *caper*. A similar change can be seen in:

Original singular	New singular
chives	chive
pease	pea

capitalization
The term *capital* is derived from Latin *capitalis*, meaning 'head', 'foremost'. It was applied in the fourteenth century to letters that appeared at the beginning or head of a text. Capital letters can be used for emphasis and are frequently used in headlines, especially in tabloid newspapers:

PRINTS CHARMING
TALK TO BE CHEAPER.

There is some flexibility in the use of capital letters but the rules below are widely accepted. Capital letters should be used in the following circumstances.

Punctuation
■ The first word of a sentence or sentence fragment:

I like cheese.
One person, one vote.

■ The first personal singular pronoun, *I*:

My husband and I have travelled widely this year.

■ The first word in a direct quotation:

She walked over and said, 'You don't know me but ... '

■ The first word in the greeting of a letter:

Dear Nick,
My dear Nick,

■ Abbreviations and acronyms:

the AUT
the BBC
NATO

although some acronyms, such as 'laser' and 'radar', have become assimilated into the language are not written with capitals.

■ The first letter of exclamations and interjections:

Goodness me!
Heck!

'O' is always capitalized:

O my foot and O my leg!

'Oh' is capitalized only at the beginning of a sentence:

Oh my word!

Nouns
Proper nouns are usually given a capital letter:

■ Days of the week:

We work Mondays through Thursdays.

■ Months of the year:

I was born in October.

but not usually the seasons:

I was born in winter.

■ People's names, surnames and given names, whether in full, or as initials:

Jan Pater
Jan F.J. Pater

■ Titles that precede a name:

Bishop Blunt (but John Blunt, the bishop)
Doctor Wicklow (but my present doctor)
President Lind (but the president of the country)

■ The names of countries and states:

Armenia, Cameroon, Delaware

■ The names of languages:

Armenian, Bikom, English

■ The names of the inhabitants of a country:

Armenians, Cameroonians, Americans

■ Place-names, whether cities, towns or villages:

Brisbane, Dungannon, Greystone

In British English, it is usual to write political abbreviations, such as UK and USA, without full stops. Many Americans prefer to write U.K. and U.S.A.

■ The names of houses, avenues, roads and streets:

'Dunroamin', Moor Road, Church Street

■ Individual rivers, mountains and major geographical features:

the Seine (but the rivers of France)
Mount Fako (but the mountains of Cameroon)
Lake Ontario (but the Canadian lakes)

- The titles of books:

Jane Eyre
Translations

- Historical periods and events:

the Ice Age, the Great War, the Reformation

- The names of significant astronomical bodies:

Mars
the Orion Nebula
the Van Allen Belt

- The names of air, sea and space vehicles:

the *Saint Patrick*
the SS *Ulysses*
the *Starship Enterprise.*

Religion

A capital letter is often used to indicate respect for God and religions.

- Religious titles such as:

Our Lord, the Prophet Mohammed

- Religious writings such as:

the Bhagavad Gita, the Bible, the Koran

- Books of the Bible:

Genesis, Exodus

although adjectives deriving from *Bible*, *Gospel* and *Scripture* are not capitalized:

a biblical story
the gospel truth
scriptural study.

Poetry and verse

The first word in a line of poetry is generally capitalized:

He ruined me, and I am re-begot
Of absence, darkness, death; things which are not.
John Donne, 'A Nocturnal upon St Lucie's Day'

Occasionally, especially in contemporary poetry, writers make use of verse paragraphs, using capital letters as we do in prose:

O was the conch-shell's invocation, mer was
both mother and sea in our Antillean patois,
os, a grey bone, and the white surf as it crashes
and spreads its sibilant collar on the lace shore.
Derek Walcott, 'Omeros'

and some poets, following the example of e.e. cummings, use punctuation marks idiosyncratically:

my sweet old etcetera
aunt lucy during the recent
war could and what is more did tell you just
what everybody was fighting for

Capital letters were sometimes used in poetry when a noun, usually an abstract noun, was being personified:

So long, sure-found beneath the sylvan shed,
Shall Fancy, Friendship, Science, rose-lipped Health ...
William Collins (1721–59), 'Ode to Evening'

carat, caret, carrot

These words are homophones but they have distinct meanings. The word *carat* refers to a measure of purity of gold or the weight of precious stones. When we say that something is '24 carat gold', we mean that it is pure gold. If we talk about a '14-carat gold nib', we mean that the nib is 59.5 per cent gold and 40.5 per cent non-gold, perhaps copper. The spelling *karat* is often found in American English:

US: 24-karat gold jewelry.
UK: 24-carat gold jewellery.

A gem is measured in *carats*. A 50-carat diamond, for example, weighs 10 grams and a ten-carat ruby weighs 2 grams.

A *caret* is a mark used to indicate that an omission has occurred in a text. It looks like $\wedge$, and its position indicates the point of the omission:

early   a
Jane Austen's ∧novels are m∧ked by a vitality that is missing in later works.

A *carrot* is a root vegetable:

I've just bought some lovely baby carrots.

carburettor, carburetor

In British English *carburettor* has '-tt-' but it has only one in American English.

See also SPELLING, UK AND US ENGLISH

carcase, carcass

In British English the noun *carcase* is used to refer to the body of a dead animal, often an animal used as meat:

The cow's carcase was removed yesterday.

The preferred spelling in America is *carcass* and this spelling is increasingly widely used in Britain, possibly because people feel it is a better reflection of the pronunciation. It rhymes with 'canvass'.

cardinal

Cardinal numbers are 'one', 'two', 'three' and so on.

See also NUMBERS

care about, care for, care to

The verb *care* can collocate with 'about', 'for' and 'to' and the meaning changes according to each usage.

Care about means 'like', 'be fond of', 'be concerned for':

He cares deeply about Mary.
He really cares about his parents.

Care for means 'look after':

It is not easy or, indeed, possible to care for all old people in their own homes although that is our ideal.

Care to means 'want to'. The 'to' is part of an infinitive verb:

Would you care to take your seats now?

careen, career

In British English, *career* can be used to mean 'move quickly without proper control':

The car careered down the hill and over the cliff.

Americans can also use *careen* in similar constructions:

The truck careened down the hill.

This use of *careen* is growing in popularity in Britain.

carefree, careless

These adjectives are occasionally confused. *Carefree* means 'free from worry':

Do you remember how carefree we were when we were students?

Careless means 'sloppy, unwilling to take sufficient care':

This work is unbelievably careless. You have not paid attention to spelling, punctuation or structure. You would be well advised to re-do the essay.

caretaker

A *caretaker* is a person who looks after premises such as a school or an office block:

I can't find the caretaker anywhere. Can you bleep him for me, please?

When the word is used adjectivally, it is applied often to temporary governments or politicians:

Do you think this caretaker government has a chance of being returned to power?

cargo

Cargo forms its plural by adding '-es':

The ships come to Victoria to collect cargoes of bananas, palm kernels and rubber.

See also SPELLING

Carib

The *Caribs* were Amerindian people who lived in the north of South America and in parts of the area now known as the Caribbean. Their languages have contributed a number of words to world English, including 'canoe', 'curare' and 'hammock'.

Caribbean

This word is used to refer to the sea south of Mexico and north of South America; the islands in the sea; and the islands in the sea + the 'Guianas' (now French Guiana, Guyana and Surinam). In Britain the word is stressed on the third syllable, which is pronounced 'bee'. In America the word is stressed on the second syllable, which is pronounced 'rib'.

caries

Caries is the dental term for 'tooth decay':

The incidence of dental caries in Britain has steadily decreased since fluoride has been added to tap water.

The same form of the word is both singular and plural, and a sentence such as:

Caries is a common ailment even among children.

is perfectly acceptable. However, because the word appears plural to most speakers of English, it often appears in such constructions as 'cases of dental caries' even in dental pamphlets:

Cases of dental caries have been documented in children as young as eighteen months.

caring

Caring has become a vogue adjective in such phrases as:

a caring community

a caring profession

a caring society.

Like all such overworked words, it is becoming increasingly meaningless.

carpal, carpel

These words are often confused by children who study biology and botany. A *carpal* is a wrist bone:

The carpal bones had been crushed in the accident.

A *carpel* is the female reproductive organ of flowering plants:

A carpel usually consists of an ovary, style and stigma. Carpels may be fused to form a single pistil.

carrot

See CARAT/CARET/CARROT

carte blanche

The French expression *carte blanche*, literally 'white card', 'blank paper', is used to mean 'total freedom', 'complete discretion':

She has *carte blanche* to sign all contractual documents.

carton, cartoon

A *carton* is a cardboard box or packet:

Will you bring home a carton of cigarettes?

A *cartoon* is used to mean a satirical drawing:

Have you seen my book of cartoons?

a full-size preparatory sketch for a mural or fresco:

Have you seen the exhibition of da Vinci's cartoons?

and a short film containing comic characters:

I've got a collection of 'Tom and Jerry' cartoons.

case

The word *case* is used in descriptions of grammar to refer to relationships in a sentence that are marked by patterns of agreement. There is relatively little *case* marking in English. We can distinguish two cases for nouns:

Unmarked		Genitive/possessive	
singular	plural	singular	plural
boy	boys	boy's	boys'

and three for many pronouns:

Nominative	Accusative	Genitive
I	me	mine

The phrase *in case* is often used to introduce a clause:

I'll wear a raincoat in case it rains.

Occasionally, especially in informal speech, it is used on its own, without a following clause:

Take this with you just in case.

See also GENITIVE, POSSESSION, PRONOUN

cassock, hassock

These words are occasionally confused, probably because they are both associated with churches. A *cassock* is an ankle-length garment worn by clerics and choristers. It comes from French *casaque*, meaning 'a long coat'.

A *hassock* is a small, upholstered cushion used for kneeling. It comes from an Old English word *hassuc*, 'matted grass'.

caster, castor

A *caster*, ending in '-er', is a container with a perforated top, used for sprinkling sugar or flour:

The trouble with my sugar caster is that the perforations clog easily in damp weather.

A *castor* is a small swivelling wheel attached to a piece of furniture to make it easier to move:

The settee is much easier to move since I attached castors to it.

This word is also often spelled *caster*.

The lubricant 'castor oil' can only be spelled *castor*.

casual, causal

These adjectives and their associated nouns, 'casualty' and 'causality', are occasionally confused. *Casual* means 'informal, not premeditated':

The style of dress is usually casual although some people enjoy dressing for dinner.
It was only a casual remark but it caused me a lot of pain.

Causal means 'being a cause of, implying a cause':

'Because' is a causal conjunction.

cataclysm

This word has become popular in the recent past and its meaning modified. A *cataclysm* is a violent upheaval:

The Krakatoa cataclysm affected the earth's climate for at least five years.

The word derives from Greek *kataklusmos*, 'deluge', and it can still be applied to a disastrous flood:

This flooding has cost the lives of over ten thousand people and the government is appealing for help in dealing with this cataclysm.

Recently, the term has been applied, often in its adjectival form, to political upheavals:

The government was heading for a cataclysmic defeat in the local elections.

catalyst

A *catalyst* is a substance that accelerates a chemical reaction without being chemically changed in the process. The term is metaphorically applied to a person or event that seems to have brought about significant changes:

The death of the four children acted as a catalyst for a change in the law.

catarrh

This noun, which describes inflammation of the mucous membrane, is commonly associated with the common cold. It is widely misspelled.

catch

This is an irregular verb:

catch(es), caught, catching.

See also VERB

catch phrase

A *catch phrase* is a well-known phrase particularly associated with a person or a group. Comedians often use catch phrases, such as:

It's the way I tell 'em!

The phrase is undergoing the process of hyphenation, *catch-phrase*, and will soon be written as one word, *catchphrase*.

catch-22

A *catch-22* situation is one that is characterized by obstacles. The phrase 'no-win situation' is often used as a synonym. The phrase derives from the name of a novel, *Catch 22*, written by Joseph Heller and published in 1961.

Catholic, catholic

The adjective *catholic*, with a small 'c', means 'universal, comprehensive':

I have, I suppose, catholic tastes in poetry. I like everything from Chaucer to Walcott via Milton and Pope.

The word *Catholic* with a capital letter usually refers to the Roman Catholic Church and can be both a noun and an adjective:

Have you always been a Catholic?
I had a typical Catholic education.

cattle

The noun *cattle* meaning 'cows' is used with a plural verb:

The cattle are left out in the fields in the summer months.

cauldron

See CALDRON/CAULDRON

causative

The term *causative* is used in grammar to refer to forms, usually verbs, that indicate cause:

She made me do it. (= She caused me to do it.)

See also GRAMMAR, MAKE, VERB

cauterize

This word, referring to the treatment of a wound by burning or searing with a hot iron or caustic agent, may also be spelled *cauterise*:

The wound will have to be cauterized if we are to prevent the spread of infection.

caviare, caviar

Both these spellings are used to refer to the roe of the sturgeon:

It's believed that the best caviare comes from the Beluga sturgeon.

cavil

The verb *cavil* means 'carp', 'raise petty objections'. In British English, the 'l' is doubled before '-ing' and '-ed' but a single 'l' is preferred in America:

UK: cavil(s), cavilled, cavilling
US: cavil(s), caviled, caviling.

cc

The abbreviation *cc*, generally without full points, is used for cubic centimetre/s:

First, 20cc of the blue copper sulphate solution was placed in a conical flask.

-ce, -cy

The endings *-ce* and *-cy* usually indicate abstract nouns. There is often a tendency for *-ce* to turn adjectives ending in '-ant' and '-ent' into nouns, as in the following list:

Adjective	Noun
different	difference
diligent	diligence
ignorant	ignorance
intelligent	intelligence
magnificent	magnificence

but some words (not necessarily adjectives) ending in '-ant' or '-ent' replace the 't' by *-cy* in the formation of nouns:

agent (noun): agency
clement (adj): clemency
decent (adj): decency
infant (noun): infancy
vacant (adj): vacancy.

There is no easy, fixed rule about these nouns. Their form depends largely on the date of their introduction into English. Occasionally, two nouns exist with approximately the same meaning, as in:

coherence, coherency
consistence, consistency
lenience, leniency
valence, valency.

Other pairs have different meanings:

dependence, dependency
emergence, emergency
excellence, excellency.

cease

The regular verb *cease*, meaning 'end', 'stop', tends to be used in formal contexts:

Our little systems have their day;
They have their day and cease to be.
> Tennyson, 'In Memoriam'

I must insist that the noise ceases immediately.

Occasionally, it is used humorously in such sentences as:

Stop! Cease! Desist!

cede

The regular verb *cede* comes from Latin *cedere*, 'to give way, yield':

This area of Cameroon was ceded to Nigeria in 1961.

cedilla

A *cedilla* is an ACCENT MARK placed under a 'c' to show that the 'c' is pronounced as an 's' and not a 'k':

garçon (boy).

The same punctuation mark is sometimes used under 's' to indicate that the 's' is pronounced 'sh'.

ceiling

This word, which rhymes with 'feeling', is frequently misspelled. It follows the rule 'i before e except after c'.

celibate

The word *celibate* derives from Latin *caelebs*, 'unmarried', and tends to be applied to one who has taken a religious vow of chastity:

The Catholic church insists on a celibate clergy.

It can be used as an adjective or a noun:

a celibate priest

These men are celibates.

Celibate is sometimes used as a synonym for 'virgin(al)' but a *celibate* need not be a virgin:

Some people responded to the AIDS crisis by deciding to become celibate.

Celsius, centigrade, Fahrenheit

These nouns all refer to temperature scales. The first two are different names for the same system, which was developed by the Swedish scientist Anders Celsius (1701–44). In this temperature system, water freezes at 0° and boils at 100°.

English-speaking countries used the Fahrenheit system in the past. This system was invented by a German scientist, Gabriel Daniel Fahrenheit (1686–1736). According to this scale, water freezes at 32°F and boils at 212°F. It is still common in America to hear:

The temperature will hit a high of 75° today.

whereas, in Britain, weather forecasters have moved from Fahrenheit, to centigrade to Celsius:

The temperature today is expected to rise to 25° Celsius.

In the written medium, the degree mark is occasionally omitted:

Maximum temperature 5C (41F).

Celtic

The adjective *Celtic* derives from the noun *Celt* and is used to refer to a language such as Breton, Cornish, Irish Gaelic, Scots Gaelic and Welsh and to items that are characteristic of the Celts or their languages. Most Celts pronounce the initial 'C' as 'k', but some people, including the Celtic Football Club in Glasgow, pronounce it 's'.

It has often been claimed that the Celtic languages of Britain have added very little to the vocabulary of English. This is a debatable issue. They have certainly provided many of the names of rivers and towns, including:

Avon, Leeds, Ouse, Thames

as well as the following from Gaelic (Irish and Scots) and Welsh:

Gaelic: banshee (fairy woman), bog (marshy ground), brogue (shoe), cairn (pile of stones), coracle (boat)

Welsh: bard (poet), corgi (dog), cromlech (stone circle), eisteddfod (festival), penguin (white head).

See also BORROWING

censer, censor, censure

The first two of these are homophones and so sometimes confused; the meanings of *censor* and *censure* overlap and so they are often used incorrectly.

A *censer* is a vessel in which incense is burned. It is also called a 'thurible':

Have you noticed how high that altar boy swings his censer?

Censor can be both a noun and a verb. As a noun, it refers to an official who examines material such as books, plays and films and may suggest cuts:

I didn't recognize the film after the censors had got hold of it.

The verb means 'examine material with a view to deleting sections':

All written material entering or leaving prisons is liable to be censored.

The activity of censoring is known as 'censorship'.

Censure is a verb meaning 'criticize strongly', 'condemn':

If I had committed such an act, I might deserve to be censured, but I am innocent.

The adjective from *censure* is 'censorious':

Don't criticize her so much. Your tone is always too censorious.

centenary, centennial

Both these words relate to periods of one hundred years. *Centenary* usually refers to anniversaries:

The centenary of Yeats's birth was celebrated in 1965.

The victory is celebrated every year but the centenary celebrations are on a much grander scale than the annual events.

In the United States of America, *centennial* is the preferred equivalent of *centenary*:

The biggest centennial celebrations were held in Boston in 1976.

center, centre, middle

The forms *centre* and *center* are identical in meaning. The spelling *centre* is the only acceptable form in Britain and *center* is the preferred form in the United States of America. Both forms mean 'equidistant from other points' and they have a precise meaning in geometry:

The radius is the distance between the centre of the circle and the circumference.

The term *centre* is used to refer to a place where a certain activity is concentrated:

the business centre

the main shopping centre

and also to indicate approximate positions in politics:

I'm not on the left or the right. I'm somewhere near the centre.

I suppose I'm slightly right of centre.

The verb *centre* is regular:

UK: centre(s), centred, centring
US: center(s), centered, centering

and takes the preposition 'on':

The discussion centred on the increased costs of the project.

Many people say and write *centre (a)round*:

*The criticism of structuralists centres around their unwillingness to accept at least two levels of language.

Stylists insist that since the *centre* is a point, it cannot logically go 'around' or 'round' something.

The term *middle* is used more loosely and can mean 'somewhere near the centre':

Put it in the middle of the pile.
We were dropped off in the middle of a field.

Middle can be used for times, places and for periods in the development of languages:

the Middle Ages, the Middle East, Middle English.

Middle and *centre* can be synonymous in sentences such as:

There's a flower in the centre of this tablecloth.
There's a flower in the middle of this tablecloth.

but *middle* tends to be less precise.

centigrade
See CELSIUS/CENTIGRADE/FAHRENHEIT

Central African Republic
Both the noun and derived adjective are 'Central African'. The capital is Bangui.

centrifugal, centripetal
Centrifugal means 'moving away from the centre' and comes from Latin *centrum*, 'centre', + *fugere*, 'to flee from':

The clearest example of a centrifugal force is shown in an explosion where material is hurled away from the centre of the blast.

The usual pronunciation stresses the third syllable and rhymes the word with 'bugle'.

Centrifugal is sometimes used (and confused) with *centripetal*, which means 'moving towards the centre':

When an electric light bulb implodes, it is an illustration of centripetal force.

century
This word comes from Latin *centum*, 'hundred', and refers to a period of one hundred years:

Why were there so many good novelists in the nineteenth century?

People are sometimes confused about the meaning of such phrases as 'the nineteenth century'. It means dates such as 1810, 1815 or 1880. Thus, the phrase 'the nineteenth century' is virtually synonymous with 'the 1800s'.

The most widely-used system of dating counts from the birth of Christ. Thus, '225 or AD225' means 'two hundred and twenty-five years since the birth of Christ' and '225BC' means 'two hundred and twenty-five years before the birth of Christ'. In strict usage, the first century of our current era began in AD1 and lasted until 101. According to this system, the twenty-first century begins on 1 January 2001 and ends on the 31 December 2100. Care should, however, be exercised in reading such references, because most people regard the expressions 'the twentieth century' and 'the 1900s' as being synonymous. Celebrations of a new century traditionally begin on the 31 December 1899 or 1999.

The term *century* is also traditionally applied to one hundred runs in cricket:

Gooch has scored more first-class centuries than any other English cricketer.

See also CENTENARY/CENTENNIAL

ceramics
The noun *ceramics* can be used to refer to the art and techniques of producing clay and porcelain artefacts and to the artefacts so produced.

When the first meaning is intended, the word is used as a singular noun:

Ceramics is studied at Leeds.

The second sense requires that the word is used as a plural:

Ceramics of this quality are rarely seen on the *Antiques Roadshow*. They should be insured for £5,000.

cereal, serial
These words are homophones but are otherwise unrelated. *Cereal* derives ultimately from Ceres, the Roman goddess of agriculture. The word is applied to edible grain such as maize, oats, rye and wheat:

We used to set aside 20 acres for cereal crops.

More recently, *cereal* has been applied to breakfast foods that are made from cereal crops:

Corn Flakes and Rice Crispies are the most popular breakfast cereals in Britain.

The word *serial* derives from Latin *series*, 'a series, a group of connected items, usually arranged in order'. It is used for a story that is presented in separate instalments:

Have you been watching the Jane Austen serial?

The adjective *serial* is often used in the phrase 'serial killer' and refers to a person who kills a number of people one after the other over a period of time.

ceremonial, ceremonious
These adjectives both derive from Latin

caerimonia, 'religious rite'. *Ceremonial* means 'relating to ceremony or ritual':

I enjoy the pomp and splendour of such ceremonial occasions.

Ceremonious suggests 'excessive observation of formalities':

Ten years ago, everyone wore formal academic dress on such occasions. Now, such dress is regarded as ceremonious and out of place.

certainty, certitude

There is a considerable overlap of meaning between these nouns. They both derive ultimately from Latin *certus*, 'fixed, sure'. *Certainty* is the more widely used of the two. It means 'the condition of being sure, without doubt':

I know for a certainty that we'll have rain on 15 July.

Certitude suggests 'fixed convictions':

It must be consoling to hold views with such certitude.

cervical

This adjective derives from Latin *cervix*, 'neck', and is most frequently applied to the lower part of the uterus that extends into the vagina:

Women patients were encouraged to have regular cervical smear tests.

Cervical has two equally acceptable pronunciations. It may have its main stress on the second syllable and rhyme with 'Michael' or on the first syllable and rhyme with 'conical'.

Chad

An inhabitant of the African republic is 'Chadian'; the derived adjective is the same. The capital is N'Djamena. The French spelling, *Tchad*, should be avoided.

chafing, chaffing

These words are occasionally misused. *Chafing* comes from Old French *chaufer* 'to warm' and can be used both literally and figuratively to mean 'irritating':

The seatbelt is chafing my shoulder.

I can't stand this critical chafing.

The etymology of *chaffing* is uncertain, but it can be used to mean 'light-hearted teasing', 'bantering':

She enjoys the chaffing more than we do. That type of humour wears thin after a while.

chain reaction

The expression *chain reaction* refers literally to the process in which a neutron collides with an atomic nucleus, causing fission and the splitting of other nuclei. The metaphorical meaning of a series of rapidly occurring events, each of which triggers off the next, is probably more widely used than the literal:

The failure of the municipal authorities to react speedily to the Kobe earthquake caused a chain reaction that brought about several resignations.

chair, chairman, chairperson

The noun *chairman* used to refer to the person who presided over a company or committee, irrespective of gender:

She was the obvious choice for chairman.

Many people objected to the usage because of its sexist overtones and other terms were tried. *Chairperson* was suggested and used with varying degrees of acceptability:

The chairperson will serve for three years.

To avoid any reference to 'man', 'woman' or 'person', the word *chair* was suggested. It is perfectly acceptable as a verb:

Who will be chairing the meeting this afternoon?

but can produce unintentional humour and ambiguity as a noun:

We have a three-year rotating chair in our department.

See also GENDER, PERSON, POLITICAL CORRECTNESS, SEXIST LANGUAGE

chamois, shammy

A *chamois* is an antelope. The noun was also applied to the soft leather made from its hide and to a soft leather cloth used for polishing:

The shine on the car is always better if a chamois is used.

The word for the leather has two main pronunciations. It may be pronounced 'sham + wah' or 'shammy'. Because the leather is no longer made from the chamois, it is also being written 'shammy'.

Why don't you pick up that shammy and help me shine the car?

change

Change retains its 'e' before the suffixes '-able' and 'ling':

This country is renowned for its changeable weather patterns.

Yeats wrote a poem about a changeling. It was called 'The Stolen Child'.

See also -ABLE/-IBLE, SPELLING

channel

This regular verb doubles the 'l' before suffixes in British English:

channel(s), channelled, channelling

but uses one 'l' only before suffixes in American English:

channel(s), channeled, channeling.

See also SPELLING

chaperon, chaperone

These spellings are equally acceptable for a person, usually a mature woman, who accompanies and supervises a younger woman or a group of young people. The word derives ultimately from Old French *chape* meaning 'protective covering' and it is pronounced like 'shapper + own'.

character

The noun *character* comes ultimately from Greek *kharakter*, 'engraver's tool', and it has been used in English to refer to a letter of the alphabet as well as to the combined traits and qualities of a person, to moral integrity and to individuals in fiction:

My new phonetic fonts give me thirty-two additional characters.

He's a complex person. I'm only beginning to understand his character.

She was renowned for the gentleness of her character.

Elizabeth is the name of the main character in *Pride and Prejudice*.

The word is increasingly used to mean 'quality', 'nature' or 'type' as in:

I was impressed by the constructive character of her comments.

I was embarrassed by the acrimonious character of their row.

Programmes of a serious character are usually relegated to the less popular channels.

(in) charge (of)

In British English the phrases *in charge of* and *in the charge of* can have very different meanings. When we say:

I am in charge of Michael.

we mean:

Michael is under my care.

On the other hand, when we say:

I am in the charge of Michael.

we mean:

I am under Michael's care.

In American English, however, the sentence:

I am in charge of Michael.

means:

I am under Michael's care.

Because of the potential for confusion between British and American speakers, this phrase should be used with care.

The legal use of *charge*, meaning 'accuse officially', always collocates with the preposition 'with':

He was charged with manslaughter.

charisma

Charisma and the related adjective *charismatic* derive from liturgical Latin *charisma* meaning 'a divinely bestowed power':

Each of us has at least one charisma, one special talent bestowed on us by a loving God.

We belong to a charismatic church that needs each of us to exercise the special gifts we have received.

Recently, the liturgical meaning has been replaced by a meaning of 'special quality or power of an individual' similar to 'magnetism':

The Kennedy charisma is still very much in evidence in Senate debates.

She is such a charismatic person. Everybody admires her energy.

This word has been so overused that it is now clichéd.

chassis

This noun meaning 'the steel frame of a motor vehicle' is a borrowing from French *chassis* 'frame'. The word is identical in form in the singular and the plural:

The chassis includes the wheels, engine and mechanical parts.

The chassis were rusting because they had been left in the open for months.

The pronunciation differs, however, in that the singular rhymes with 'lassie' and the plural with 'lassies'.

chauvinism

The noun *chauvinism* derives from Nicolas Chauvin, a nineteenth-century French soldier noted for his devotion to Napoleon. It originally meant 'unthinking patriotism', then 'jingoism', then 'any prejudiced belief in the superiority of a race, country, party or gender':

Gender chauvinism is no more acceptable than racism.

See also POLITICAL CORRECTNESS, SEXIST LANGUAGE

cheap, cheaply

There is a simple theoretical distinction between these words. *Cheap* is an adjective meaning 'inexpensive':

I bought a cheap dress.

and *cheaply* is an adverb meaning 'inexpensively':

They sold it cheaply.

In colloquial speech, however, many people use *cheap* as an adverb:

Stack 'em high and sell 'em cheap.

check

Check can be a regular verb meaning 'examine' and also 'hold back':

We checked the windows for any sign of a forced entry.

The illness checked his progress.

As a noun, *check* can mean 'cursory examination':

We had a quick check through the books.

Check can also combine with 'in', 'out' and 'up':

The check-in desk is now open.
Where is the check-out?
It's time for my annual check-up.

cheque, check

In Britain a *cheque* is a bill of exchange drawn on a bank by the holder of a current account. The equivalent word in the United States of America is *check*:

UK: She gave me a cheque for my birthday.
US: She gave me a check for my birthday.

See also UK AND US ENGLISH

cherub

The noun *cherub* comes from Hebrew and means a type of angel, often painted as a winged child. The 'ch' is pronounced as in 'cherry' and the word has two acceptable plurals, *cherubs* and *cherubim*. The '-im' suffix is a Hebrew plural that is found also in:

kibbutz, kibbutzim
seraph, seraphim.

chickenpox

Chickenpox is a viral disease characterized by a rash and a fever. The word is not hyphenated. The word 'pox' is a fifteenth-century spelling of 'pocks', the plural of 'pock'.

chide

Chide is almost obsolete and means 'scold':

Chide me not for my lack of birth.

Originally, the verb was irregular:

chide(s), chid, chiding, chidden

but it has become regular:

chide(s), chided, chiding, chided.

chilblain

This word is often misspelled. The first syllable is *chil-* and not 'chill'.

childish, childlike

These adjectives are rarely applied to children and they are occasionally misused. *Childish* suggests 'immature', 'unbecoming in an adult':

He didn't object to their high spirits but he thought that their practical jokes were childish.

Childlike, on the other hand, is usually a positive adjective implying innocence and all that is attractive in a child:

She has a childlike simplicity and directness, qualities not often found in someone of her age.

Chile

An inhabitant of the South American country is a 'Chilean'; the derived adjective is the same. The capital is Santiago.

chilli, chili

Both these spellings are acceptable. The first is the usual British spelling and the second is the preferred form in the United States of America, although the form 'chile' is also found. The word was borrowed into English from Spanish, which had adapted it from an Amerindian word for a dried capsicum pod. The plural is formed by adding '-es', *chil(l)ies*.

China

Britain has had trading links with China for almost 400 years, and so it is not surprising that some Chinese words have entered English. The best known of these are words associated with culture:

kow-tow, kung fu, mandarin, tai chi, yin and yang

with food and cooking:

chop suey, chow mein, longan, lychee, wok

and with items of trade, including:

char (tea), kaolin, silk, tea.

An inhabitant of China is a 'Chinese', and the derived adjective is the same. The word 'Chinaman' is now regarded as patronizing and not politically correct. The need to transliterate the several thousand characters of the Chinese system of writing has led to the development of two main phonetic systems, Pinyin and Wade-Giles. Pinyin was accepted by the People's Republic of China in 1956 and is now widely used in the West. Beijing (the Pinyin form) is now accepted as the spelling of the capital city, instead of Peking.

chiropodist

This word can cause problems because many people do not know how to pronounce it. The 'ch' is pronounced as a 'k'. The usual American equivalent is 'podiatrist', and the main stress is on '-di-', which is pronounced 'die'.

choir, quire

These words are homophones but there is no overlap of meaning. A *choir* refers to a group of singers:

He joined the Cathedral choir when he was eight.

A *quire* is a quantity of paper, usually twenty-five sheets.

cholesterol

Cholesterol is a fatty substance found in animal fluids and tissue. The word is frequently misspelled.

A high level of cholesterol in the blood is thought to contribute to heart disease and hardening of the arteries.

choose

Choose is an irregular verb:

choose(s), chose, choosing, chosen.

The associated adjective is 'choosy' without an 'e'.

chord, cord

These homophones are occasionally confused. A *chord* has two main uses. In music, it refers to a combination of notes, usually sounded together in harmony:

I can play only a few chords on the guitar.

In mathematics, a *chord* is a straight line that joins two points on the circumference of a circle:

The chord was dissected at right angles by the radius.

A *cord* is a strong, flexible piece of material, usually thicker than string but thinner than rope. It is frequently called a 'flex' in the United States of America:

I've pulled the cord (flex) out of the kettle.

The word *cord* is also applied to parts of the body that are thin and flexible:

the spinal cord, the umbilical cord, the vocal cords.

Cord is frequently misspelled in the phrase 'vocal cords'. In this context, it does not have an 'h'.

chordate, cordate, cordite

These words are sometimes misused. *Chordate* is a technical term for any animal that has at some stage of its development a dorsal tubular nerve cord. It derives from Latin *chorda*, 'a string':

All the vertebrates, including human beings, are chordates.

Cordate derives from Latin *cor*, 'heart', and means 'heart-shaped':

I was sent a lovely cordate Valentine's card.

Cordite derives from 'cord' and is a smokeless explosive:

Nitro-cellulose is the technical name for cordite.

chorus

When *chorus* is used as a verb, it does not double the 's' before suffixes:

chorus(es), chorused, chorusing.

Christian name

A *Christian name* is, etymologically, the name given at baptism to a Christian. The term is also used for a first name and, where the speaker is Christian, this is perfectly appropriate. It is not, however, appropriate to use the term when referring to Hindus, Jews, Muslims, followers of other faiths or atheists.

Many people now use such terms as FIRST NAME or 'given name', but 'surname' remains perfectly acceptable for 'family name'.

See also BAPTISMAL NAME

chronic

The terms *chronic* and *acute* are occasionally confused when they are applied to medical conditions. A *chronic* condition is one that has been giving trouble for some time. It may well be serious but it is not sudden:

He has been suffering chronic back trouble for eighteen months.

An 'acute' condition is one that flares up suddenly and is often of short duration:

He woke up with such acute pain that we rushed him to hospital.

The term *chronic* is often applied to long-standing social ills such as:

chronic overcrowding, chronic unemployment.

chute, shoot

A *chute* is a sloping channel or passageway down which food, liquid, packets or other products may be dropped:

He was cleaning out the coal chute when he slipped.

The builders' rubbish is dropped in a covered chute from the roof to the bins.

This word is frequently spelled *shoot* in America and this spelling is increasingly common in Britain, too.

A *shoot* is a new bud or twig on a plant:

After the rain, the new shoots can be seen on all the hedgerows.

chutzpah

The word *chutzpah* is usually pronounced 'hoots + pa' and means something like 'arrogant effrontery'. It was borrowed into American English from YIDDISH because there is no English word to describe the mixture of 'nerve' or 'gall' and 'intelligence' that are combined in *chutzpah*.

cipher, cypher

Cipher with an 'i' is the usual spelling, but *cypher* is also acceptable. The normal meanings of *cipher* are a code or secret language:

I can't understand this: it's written in cipher.

a zero or nought:

The word *cipher* comes from Arabic *çifr*, meaning 'zero'.

and a person of little value:

He's a mere cipher in the firm and does as little as he can.

circumcise

This is a regular verb, spelled '-ise' in all varieties of English:

circumcise(s), circumcised, circumcising.

The noun is *circumcision*.

circumflex

A *circumflex* is an accent mark represented by ˆ. It occurs in words borrowed from French and is often optional:

fête (fete), rôle (role)

The accents are retained, however, in tête-à-tête.

See also ACCENT MARK

circumlocution

Circumlocution is the use of an excessive number of words to say something that could be said more succinctly. The phenomenon is seen in the use of redundant words:

He is 6 feet in height. = He is 6 feet.
It was green in colour. = It was green.
There were six in number. = There were six.

and in the use of roundabout expressions:

at this moment in time = now
in the event that = if
in this day and age = today/now.

See also PERIPHRASIS, PLEONASM, REDUNDANCY, TAUTOLOGY

cirrhosis

This word is frequently misspelled. It comes from Greek *kirrhos*, 'orange-tawny', and refers to a degenerative disease in an organ of the body, especially the liver:

Hepatitis is a disease of the liver but it is usually not as serious as cirrhosis.

cist, cyst

These words are homophones. A *cist* is related to the English word 'chest' and means 'early tomb, burial chamber'.

Cyst derives from Greek *kystis*, 'sac, bladder', and refers to any sac or pocket in the body, especially if filled with fluid or diseased matter:

The cyst that they removed was benign.

cite, sight, site

These words are homophones. *Cite* derives from French *citer*, 'to summon', and usually means 'quote a text, refer to an authority', or 'mention for bravery in an official military report':

I hadn't read half the texts she cited.

He was cited twice for outstanding bravery i n the field.

Sight is associated with the verb 'to see':

Sight is probably our most valuable sense.

Site can function as a noun meaning 'piece of land where something was or is located':

We're looking for the site of the Roman amphitheatre.

and as a regular verb 'to locate':

The council still hasn't decided where to site the new supermarket.

city, town

It is not always easy to say when a conurbation is a town or a city. The modern criteria include size and its own system of local government. Usually a town is smaller than a city, but some small conurbations with cathedrals have been given city status. When the phrase 'the City' is used, it refers to the financial centre of London:

He used to work in the City but he cracked under the pressure.

The expression 'town house' can be ambiguous. British estate agents use the term for a terraced house. It is also used to refer to the London residence of the rich who have their main estate in the country.

civil

Civil is an adjective deriving from Latin *civis*, 'citizen'. It means 'urbane, courteous':

I was given an extremely civil reception.

The related verb is 'civilize', which may also be spelled with '-ise'.

clamour, clamor

Clamour can function as a noun and a verb:

The noise and clamour were deafening.
They clamoured for more food.

The preferred spelling in the United States of America is *clamor*:

UK: clamour(s), clamoured, clamouring
US: clamor(s), clamored, clamoring.

The adjective is *clamorous* in both countries.

clandestine

This adjective derives from Latin *clandestinus*, 'hidden', and means 'secretive, furtive':

I don't want to be involved in any clandestine negotiations.

The word is normally stressed on the second syllable but some people stress it on the first.

class

There are problems associated with the word *class* when it refers to social divisions based on rank, economic status or a set of such criteria because it is difficult to define with precision. The most frequently used divisions are:

upper, middle, lower

upper, middle, working

and:

A, B, C¹, C², D, E.

classic, classical

Classic can function as an adjective and a noun. As an adjective, it can mean 'of lasting value' and 'typical':

Hers was a classic piece of research.

She is showing all the classic symptoms of glandular fever.

As a singular noun, it means 'a work of enduring excellence':

Black Beauty is a classic. Every child who has read it loves it.

When the plural form is used, the noun refers to the language, literature and culture of ancient Greece and Rome:

He studied Classics at Oxford before going into the City.

The adjective *classical* can refer to the language, literature and culture of Greece and Rome:

She had a classical education and always felt that it served her well in her study of world languages.

It is also widely applied to serious music and the arts:

They had never listened to classical music before last summer.

clause

The term *clause* refers to a grammatical unit that includes a verb phrase:

Come in.

I saw John.

when I saw John.

Clauses are usually subdivided into 'main clauses', which are independent grammatical units, and 'subordinate clauses', which are not independent. Our first two examples above are main clauses; our third is a subordinate clause.

There are various types of subordinate clause in English. The following sentences illustrate the range (the clauses are enclosed in brackets):

■ Adverbial clauses:

[When she arrived] the concert began.

I went [because I had to].

■ Noun clauses:

[What you did] was foolish.

He said [that he was tired].

■ Relative clauses:

The man, [whom we met yesterday], has gone.

The ship, [which has all the safety features], is being bought by several countries.

See also DEFINING RELATIVE CLAUSE, GRAMMAR, RESTRICTIVE CLAUSE/NON-RESTRICTIVE CLAUSE

claustrophobia

Claustrophobia means 'the fear of being in restricted spaces':

I hate flying or using lifts. I suppose I suffer from claustrophobia.

clean, cleanse

Clean can function as an adjective, noun or verb:

We wanted to live in a clean environment.

The house needs a really good clean(ing).

I'll give you a hand to clean up the mess.

It can also, occasionally, function as an adverb, meaning 'completely':

I clean forgot.

Cleanse functions only as a verb. Its meaning is similar to *clean* but it has overtones of purification:

Cleanse my lips and my heart, O Lord.

cleanliness

Cleanliness is the habit of keeping things clean:

Cleanliness is next to godliness.

The noun *cleanness* exists but is rarely used. It refers to something being clean at a particular moment:

The cooking was good but I worried about the cleanness of the hired crockery.

cleave

Cleave is one of a small group of verbs that can have two opposite meanings. *Cleave* can mean 'stick to':

They have always cleaved to each other.

It can also mean 'divide, split in two':

Our swift frigate cleaved through the water.

These verbs, which are obsolescent, derive from different Old English verbs. The first comes from *cleofian* and is related to 'clay'. The second comes from *cleofan*, meaning 'to peel'. Two parts of this verb continue to be used adjectivally. These are 'cleft' and 'cloven' as in:

a cleft palate

a cloven hoof.

The nouns 'cleavage' and 'cleaver' as in 'meat cleaver' are related to the second verb.

clench, clinch

These words are occasionally confused. *Clench* means 'close tightly':

I clenched my teeth to prevent myself shouting out in pain.

Clinch can mean 'settle a deal' or 'hold someone tight':

We clinched the entire deal in twenty minutes.
You'll hurt her if you hold her in such a tight clinch.

clerk

This word is pronounced to rhyme with 'dark' in Britain but with 'perk' in the United States of America. In Britain, a *clerk* tends to be an office worker but the phrase 'sales clerk' for a 'shop assistant' is widely used in America.

clever

The adjective *clever* is sometimes misused. It means 'ingenious', 'quick-witted' rather than 'well-educated':

Let's ask Michael. He's bound to come up with a clever excuse!

cliché

A *cliché* is a stereotyped expression. The word is borrowed from French *cliché*, meaning 'a stereotype printing plate composed of moveable type'. *Cliché* is used to comprehend trite, hackneyed words or phrases. Such terms may once have been innovative but they are now stale from overuse. There are several types of clichés, including:

■ Single words or even morphemes:

grassroots, as in 'support from the grassroots'
situation, as in 'a no-win situation'
-wise, as in 'timewise'

■ Phrases:

a pitched battle
at this moment in time
a foregone conclusion

■ Metaphors:

to leave no stone unturned
to be at death's door
to beat about the bush

■ Formulaic expressions:

as far as I can see
that's how the cookie crumbles
to be perfectly frank

■ Catch phrases:

a catch-22 situation
by and large
keep a low profile

■ Quotations or misquotations:

fresh fields and pastures new
lend me your ears
a poor thing but mine own.

There are no objective criteria by which we can say 'This is a cliché' any more than there are objective criteria for defining a work of art. If a word or phrase is frequently used, however, so that it has lost most of its original power, then it has one of the properties of a cliché.

See also CATCH PHRASE, FAD WORD, PHATIC COMMUNION

click, clique

These words are homophones in some regions, although many people pronounce the second word to rhyme with 'leek'. A *clique* is a group of people who tend to exclude others:

I wanted to join a committee, not a clique.

A *click* is a short, sharp sound:

I heard something click. Did you hear it?

client, customer

A *client* is someone who purchases professional time:

Our firm has many doctors among its clients.

A *customer* is someone who buys goods from a shop or services from a manual worker:

I have my statutory rights as a customer and can return any goods that are substandard.

In Britain the word *client* is being used increasingly for 'patient', 'student' or 'unemployed person', reflecting the citizen's charters and the culture of the market economy, while the word *customer* is being used for 'passenger' and 'consumer'.

climactic, climatic

These adjectives are often misused. *Climactic* derives from 'climax':

We were all waiting for a climactic ending but the play just fizzled out.

Climatic relates to 'climate':

Every time we have a good summer, we hear stories about climatic changes and the 'greenhouse effect'.

The word 'climate' has been extended metaphorically to include 'trend, feeling':

a climate of hope
the moral climate
the political climate.

clinch

See CLENCH/CLINCH

cling

Cling is an irregular verb:

cling(s), clung, clinging, clung.

clipping

Clipping is a type of word formation in which a shorter word or phrase is made from a longer one. Clipped words are normally colloquial and are more often spoken than written. Thus we hear:

Dip Ed (Diploma in Education)
pram (perambulator)

but not, usually:

caps (capital letter)
para (paragraph)
univ (university)

because these latter examples tend to be written abbreviations.

Clipped forms may often be based on pronunciation:

nuke (nuclear weapons/power)
telly (television)

and because they are used as full words, they take the same morphological endings as other English words:

Their nukes are being dismantled.
Most homes have at least two tellies.

Clipped forms are often part of an in-group vocabulary:

students: exam, lab, prof, vac
football: footie, goalie, ref, sub.

Because of their usefulness, some clippings have become very much a part of our everyday vocabulary:

bus (omnibus)
piano (pianoforte)
sport (disport)
flu (influenza)

while others coexist alongside their more formal sources:

phone/telephone
photo/photograph
specs/spectacles.

Clipping of compound words and phrases also occurs, although this tendency is limited by the need to have within the expression a word that is unlikely to occur in many other contexts:

car (motor car)
inter-city (inter-city train)
laptop (laptop computer)
typo (typographical error).

As with other subdivisions of language, clippings are not a totally discrete category. Some involve the clipping of more than one English word:

perm (permanent wave)

or of a Latin tag:

ad lib (*ad libitum*, 'to speak extempore')
infra dig (*infra dignitatem*, 'beneath one's dignity')
mob (*mobile vulgus*, 'unstable crowd')

or the conjoining of two clippings:

hifi (high fidelity)

and others may change as the items they describe become more familiar:

stereophonic record player: stereo record player, stereo
television set: TV, telly.

Clipped forms may vary between the UK and the US:

advertisement: advert, ad (UK), ad (US)
chipped/French fried potatoes: chips (UK), French fries (US)
mathematics: maths (UK), math (US).

See also ABBREVIATION, ACRONYM, CONTRACTION, UK AND US ENGLISH, WORD FORMATION

clique
See CLICK/CLIQUE

clone

The word *clone* derives ultimately from Greek *klon*, 'twig'. It is used as a noun and a verb to refer to asexual reproduction, as by cuttings or graftings on plants. Today, it is also used to mean the creation of genetically identical organisms:

Some science fiction writers suggest that scientists will achieve immortality when they can clone themselves.

The word is occasionally extended to mean something that is indistinguishable from something else:

There was a time when we had a dozen really different daily newspapers. Now we have three sets of clones.

close, shut

Virtually every dictionary gives *shut* as the meaning of *close* and *close* as the meaning of *shut* and, in virtually all instances, this is the case:

We couldn't close/shut the door.
I'm sure the door was closed/shut when I left.

Close is a regular verb:

close(s), closed, closing.

Shut is an irregular verb. Like many verbs ending in '-t' or '-d', its past tense form is the same as the infinitive without 'to':

shut(s), shut, shutting
Shut the window, please.
He shut all the windows a few minutes ago.

Shut cannot be substituted for *close* when it is used to mean 'terminate successfully':

We've just closed a deal for nearly a million dollars.

or when *close* is used adjectivally:

close to Leeds not *shut to Leeds
a close shave not *a shut shave
a close friend not *a shut friend.

cloth, clothe, clothes

A *cloth* rhymes with 'moth' and is a piece of material or fabric:

Don't use the drying cloths as dusters, please.

Clothe is a verb and rhymes with 'loathe'. It means 'dress' or 'cover with material':

And they realized that they were naked and clothed themselves with fig leaves.

Clothes rhymes with 'loathes' and means 'garments':

You've spilt milk on my best clothes!

clothes

The terms for some items of clothing can differ in Britain and the United States, even though many of the garments are essentially the same. The reason for this is probably that dress has changed radically since the political separation between UK and US speakers and both groups have introduced their own terms for the new garments.

See also AMERICANISM, ANGLICISM, DRESS, UK AND US ENGLISH, UK ENGLISH, US ENGLISH

co-

Co- is a prefix meaning 'together'. It is a variant of the Latin prefix *com-*, which comes from *cum*, 'with', as in *cum patre et filio*, 'with the father and the son'. The *co-* prefix occurs frequently in English and has been reinforced by the 'Co.' in names such as 'Wilkins and Co.'

Originally, *co-* occurred before Latin-derived words beginning with vowels, 'h' or 'gn':

coagulate, coalesce, coexist, cohere, cognition.

More recently, *co-* has been used as a prefix meaning 'with', 'joint':

co-heir (coheir)

'partner':

co-author (coauthor)

or 'lesser partner':

co-pilot (copilot).

So extensively has *co-* been used that it can even occur with a word that already has a 'com-' prefix:

co-composer, co-conspirator, co-contributor.

The hyphen is optional.

See also COM-, HYPHEN, PREFIX

Co.

Co. is the abbreviation for 'Company' and, in Ireland, for 'County':

Brighton, Stern and Co.
They live in Co. Down.

See also COUNTY

coarse, course

These words are homophones and rhyme with 'source'. *Coarse* is an adjective meaning 'rough, unrefined':

I couldn't wear the jacket because the coarse material was unpleasant to the touch.
We were put off by a string of coarse jokes.

Course is a noun with a range of meanings including 'action':

Which course of action have you agreed?
'dish':
I think I'll skip the fish course.
'place where a certain activity occurs':
golf course, racecourse
and 'series of lectures':
The undergraduate course lasts three years.

coastal, costal

Coastal is an adjective derived from 'coast':

In spite of the coastal defences, Spurn Point became an island in the storms of 1996.

Costal rhymes with 'hostel'. It derives from Latin *costa*, 'a rib' and refers to the ribs:

I'm studying the intercostal muscles.

coco, cocoa

See CACAO/COCO/COCOA

coconut, cocoanut

These are alternative spellings of the nut of some varieties of palm tree. The form without the 'a' is more widely used today.

cocoon

This word is a diminutive of Latin *coca*, 'a shell', and refers to the silky case spun by an insect larva to protect itself. *Cocoon* has been extended metaphorically to a soft, protective covering:

We were far away from all the harshness of life, cocooned in our well-appointed mobile home.

code

A *code* is a system of letters, words or signs used for secret messages or for presenting information succinctly and unambiguously. Groups of letters can sometimes be misheard and misunderstood. The group ACC, for example, can sound like SEC. The following set is used by police forces and other agencies to prevent misunderstandings:

A Alfa, B Bravo, C Charlie, D Delta, E Echo, F Foxtrot, G Golf, H Hotel, I India, J Juliet, K Kilo, L Lima, M Mike, N November, O Oscar, P Papa, Q Quebec, R Romeo, S Sierra, T Tango, U Uniform, V Victor, W Whiskey, X Xray, Y Yankee, Z Zulu.

codex

A *codex* is now used almost exclusively to mean a 'manuscript volume':

She's working on an Anglo-Saxon codex.

Occasionally, it refers to a systematic collection of laws:

This liturgical codex was also called 'the commandments of the church'.

The plural of *codex* is 'codices'.

codicil, corollary, rider

The words *codicil* and *corollary* are occasionally confused. A *codicil* is a diminutive form of 'codex' and refers to an 'addition to a will':

The will has been complicated by the recent codicil that seems to change the main beneficiary of the will.

A *corollary* is a conclusion drawn from something that has been proved:

The second corollary to this theorem is that triangles on the same base and between the same parallels are equal in area.

The noun *rider* usually refers to a person on a bicycle or horse, but it also has the meaning of 'addition' as in:

The jury added a rider urging the judge to take the defendant's previous good character into account.

The word *rider* is also used in mathematics as a near synonym of *corollary*, that is, 'a logical extension of something that has already been proved':

The rider to this is that parallelograms on equal bases and between the same parallels are equal in area.

cognate

The term *cognate* is used to refer to languages or units of languages that derive from the same source. Irish Gaelic, Welsh and Breton are cognate languages, all deriving in part at least from a Proto-Celtic language. Words such as Latin *cor* (heart), French *coeur* and Gaelic *croidhe* are cognate words deriving from a common Indo-European root.

See also ANALOGUE/ANALOG/ANALOGY

cohere

The verb *cohere* derives from late Latin *cohaerere*, 'to cling together'. It is a relatively formal word and can mean 'stick together in a logical or systematic way':

These ideas don't cohere properly.

coherence, cohesion

Both these nouns derive from 'cohere' but they now have different meanings. *Coherence* means 'logical connection, consistency':

She was so frightened that there was absolutely no coherence in anything she said.

Cohesion tends to suggest 'sticking together':

There was no cohesion in the group. It was bound to break up.

See also ANAPHORA, DISCOURSE, LINKAGE

coinage

Coinage refers literally to coins:

The coinage is sometimes used as a synonym for 'currency'.

The word is used metaphorically to refer to newly created words. Such new words are formed according to the phonological possibilities of the language. Because of the many methods of word formation available to English users, coining is relatively rare, except in advertising and in the creation of trade names. Monosyllabic coinages tend to exploit hitherto unused slots in the language. For example, there are a number of monosyllabic words consisting of a consonant + '-ot':

cot, got, hot, jot, lot

but not all possibilities are used. We do not find, for example, such words as:

*bot, *fot, *kot, *mot, *vot

although there is no logical reason for their non-existence. A coinage could be created by using one of these vacant slots. Such a word would be analogous in form with other '-ot' words but it would also be novel. Thus, Lewis Carroll's *snark* and *toves* in *Through the Looking Glass* resemble 'spark', 'stark', 'shark' and 'coves', 'doves', 'loves' respectively.

Polysyllabic coinages tend to combine novel elements with conventional morphemes, so that the roots of *decombubelize* and *spifflicate* are novel but the affixes are regular. An extended example of polysyllabic coinages is Lewis Carroll's 'Jabberwocky', where many of the roots are coined but word classes are signalled by conventional affixes.

A number of well-known words were originally coinages:

fun, pun, posh, quiz, slang, snob

but we no longer notice their novelty because they do not break any rules and are thus indistinguishable from other words.

See also AFFIX, DERIVATION, WORD FORMATION

colander

See CALENDAR/CALENDER/COLANDER

collaborate, corroborate

These words are occasionally confused. *Collaborate* means 'work willingly with someone' and it comes from Late Latin *collaborare*, 'to work with'. In English, 'collaborate with' and the associated noun 'collaborator' are usually pejorative and suggest working with the enemy:

They are ashamed to admit it, but they collaborated willingly with the invaders.

Corroborate means 'confirm what someone else has said'. It too derives from Late Latin, from *corroborare*, 'to strengthen':

We can't find anyone who can corroborate your version of events.

colleague

Colleague means 'a work partner'. It tends to refer to professional workers:

My colleagues and I should like to invite you to lecture to us on 19 April.

collective noun

A *collective noun* is a noun that is singular in form but plural in meaning:

The audience was attentive.

The group is receiving therapy.

The troop has not yet engaged in any military activity.

The category *collective noun* is not, however, as discrete as our definition suggests. 'Team' is clearly a collective noun and 'flour' is clearly a mass noun, but it is not so easy to decide the status of such nouns as:

cattle, hair, linen, royalty.

A *collective noun* takes a singular verb and is replaced by a singular pronoun in formal and written English:

The jury is having difficulty reaching its verdict. It has been out for seven days.

In informal styles, there is a tendency to use a plural verb form:

The jury are having difficulty.

but, although this is acceptable in the spoken medium, there should be consistency of reference. To mix singular and plural usage as in:

My family is moving house but they are not leaving until Friday.

would be regarded as an error of style and syntax. There is a strong risk of a shift in number when a plural modifier comes between the collective noun and the verb:

The family was represented by the local solicitor.

The family of seals were under threat from the oil spillage.

In colloquial styles, words such as 'family', 'government' and 'team' are often used with plural verbs, but this usage should be avoided in writing.

Some apparently plural subjects may take singular verbs if the subject is regarded as a single unit:

Two years is a long time.

The United Nations has ruled on the matter.

Nouns of assembly may be regarded as a sub-category of collective nouns. Many of these, such as:

a flock of sheep

a herd of cattle

are well known, but others are much rarer and are known only to collectors. Among these are:

a cete (pronounced 'seat') of badgers

an exaltation of larks

a herd/bevy of swans

a kindle of kittens

a plump of waterfowl

a gaggle of geese on the ground

a skein of geese in the air.

For practical purposes, the ordinary speaker needs relatively few nouns of assembly, several of which seem the result of light-hearted creativity rather than observation:

a charm of goldfinches

a malice of lecturers

an unkindness of ravens.

See also COUNTABLE AND UNCOUNTABLE, EVERY, MASS NOUN

collision, collusion

These nouns are occasionally confused. *Collision* comes from Latin *collidere*, 'to clash together' and means 'violent impact':

I was involved in a collision with another car and we were lucky to escape with our lives.

Collusion comes from Latin *colludere*, 'to play together, connive' and means 'connivance, secret agreement for a fraudulent purpose':

Collusion between the witnesses was suspected but could not be proved.

collocation

The word *collocation* comes from Latin *collocare*, 'to place together' and means 'a grouping together of words in a certain order'. In English, we have fixed collocations such as:

bread and butter not *butter and bread

fish and chips not *chips and fish

hale and hearty not *hearty and hale

kick the bucket not *kick the pail

and we also have collocations that are not usual but are acceptable:

a small elephant

Jane, Jane, tall as a crane

kick the tennis ball.

Because of the rules for English word order, certain collocations are less acceptable than others:

a tall tree

*a tall banana

*a tall idea

I saw three ships come sailing by.

*Three ships I saw come sailing by.

*I three sailing ships come by saw.

There is, however, a certain 'poetic licence' that allows poets and users to modify the language in such a way that Dylan Thomas, for example, could write:

Once below a time

and many speakers who would reject 'a tall idea' might accept 'a tall story'.

colloquial English

Colloquial comes from the Latin verb *colloquor* meaning 'to converse, to speak with'. Its primary meaning, therefore, relates to the spoken medium, so that a colloquialism is characteristic of conversation. The word 'English' is a form of shorthand for the many different varieties and styles within the language. Martin Joos divided English styles into five main sub-styles – frozen, formal, consultative, casual and intimate – and *colloquial English* is most likely to be found in the two last categories. It implies 'informal' and carries the additional feature of 'conversational'. It is not, however, inferior to 'formal'. Cricket is not inferior to football but its rules would be inappropriate in a soccer match.

Colloquial is a more general term than 'slang'. Whereas slang usually relates to nonstandard forms, a colloquialism may be standard or nonstandard. For example, the term 'loo' is a colloquial variant of the more formal 'toilet', but both are standard. In contrast, the terms 'comfort station' and 'john' are less widely known in Britain and the second, in particular, might be described as nonstandard.

Colloquial English is marked by spontaneity, simple vocabulary, reduced forms ('aren't' rather than 'are not', 'don't' rather than 'do not'), fillers ('actually', 'you see'); and the use of words and structures that are acceptable in speech but less so in writing ('Who to?').

See also FORMAL ENGLISH, FORMALITY, SLANG, SPEECH AND WRITING

colloquialism

A *colloquialism* is a word, phrase or idiom that is appropriate to conversation or to informal writing but may be out of place in formal contexts. Greetings such as:

Hi!

How's the form?

would not, for example, be acceptable in a formal interview. Such idioms as:

Get your choppers going on this (eat up)

Not on your nelly (definitely not)

are colloquialisms and not acceptable in all contexts.

collusion

See COLLISION/COLLUSION

Colombia

A native of the South American country is a 'Colombian'; the derived adjective is the same. The capital is Bogotá. The country is often wrongly spelled *'Columbia'.

colon

A *colon* is a punctuation mark represented by two full stops, one on top of the other (:). It is used for the following purposes:

to separate a list from a main clause:

You will be provided with all necessary hard furniture: beds, chairs, cupboards, wardrobes.

to separate main clauses when the second is an illustration of the first:

The students were eager for the new term: they had missed their friends over the long vacation.

to introduce examples, illustrations or quotations:

Remember the old adage: A bird in the hand is worth two in the bush.

to write the time:

Meet me at 3:30.

to separate the title and subtitle of a book:

The English Language: from 450 to 2000.

See also PUNCTUATION

coloration

Coloration refers to the colouring and/or marking of insects, birds and animals:

I've never seen such exotic coloration as on a Papua New Guinea bird of paradise.

The word is spelled without 'u' in both Britain and America, although the associated word 'colourant' retains the 'u' in Britain.

colour, color

Colour is the standard spelling in Britain and *color* is standard in the United States of America. Britain uses the 'u' also in such forms as:

colourable, colourant, coloured, colourful, colouring, colourist, colourless

but not COLORATION.

com-

Com- is a prefix deriving from Latin *com-* meaning 'together with, jointly':

combine, commit, complain.

In compound words of Latin origin, the *com-* becomes 'co-' before words beginning with vowels, 'gn' or 'h':

co-administration, cognate, cohort.

Com- becomes 'col-' before words beginning with 'l':

collocate, colleague

'con-' before words beginning with consonants other than 'b', 'l', 'm', 'p' and 'r':

conduct, conspire

and 'cor-' before words beginning with 'r':

correct, correspond.

See also CO-, HYPHEN, PREFIX

comatose

This word derives ultimately from Greek *koma*, 'heavy sleep'. When used medically, it means 'in a state of unconsciousness':

The patient is still comatose but we are hopeful that he will regain consciousness after treatment.

The adjective is now also used to mean 'torpid and lethargic', although many purists dislike this dilution of meaning.

See also PURIST, SEMANTIC CHANGE

combat

Combat can function as a noun and a verb:

They were involved in unarmed combat.
It is hard to combat such ideas.

The word normally means 'fight against an enemy', and it is not a synonym for 'contest' or 'competition', which are more neutral in their implications.

In Britain, the 't' is not doubled before suffixes:

combated, combating, combative.

In American English, the 't' is sometimes doubled:

We're still combatting racism and sexism.

but the '-tt-' forms are less widely used than the forms with a single 't'.

See also SPELLING

combustible

Combustible means 'capable of igniting and burning':

Campers have been banned from the moors because, after months of dry weather, the moss and heather are combustible.

come

Come is an irregular verb:

come(s), came, coming, come.

The past participle is 'come':

We have come to a decision.

comic, comical

Comic can be an adjective or a noun:

Shakespeare's comic characters are given many of the most memorable lines in the plays.
He earns his living as a comic.
I used to love the *Beano* and the *Dandy* comics.

Comical can function only as an adjective. The chief difference between the two adjectives is that *comic* implies 'intentionally funny' whereas 'comical' suggests that the humour is unplanned or unintentional:

He looked so comical in that strange old suit.

comma

The *comma* is the most frequently used punctuation mark in the language. The word *comma* was adopted into the English language in 1554 and derives ultimately from Greek *komma* meaning 'clause', 'segment of sentence'. In English the comma is represented by a full stop with a tail, viz. [,], and it is used for eleven main purposes.

Separating items

Words in lists, phrases or clauses are separated by a comma:

a happy, cheerful child
I bought milk, sugar, tea and coffee.
He sang in pubs, in clubs, in village halls and in churches.
She took the book, put it in her briefcase, locked it and went out.

In Britain, a comma is not normally used between the last two items in a list if they are joined by a conjunction. Thus, the next two sentences are correct in both Britain and America:

He bought shoes, socks, shirts, shorts.
He bought shoes, socks, shirts and shorts.

but the third one is more widely acceptable in America:

He bought shoes, socks, shirts, and shorts.

This kind of construction, known as the Oxford comma or serial comma, is also used in Britain, especially in some academic writing. It is not, however, an impediment to the understanding of the sentence. A comma is, however, used to avoid ambiguity when the last item in a list contains 'and':

I tried Debenhams, Schofields, and Marks and Spencers.

Separating clauses

A comma is used to separate introductory clauses from the rest of the sentence:

When the fields are left fallow, wild flowers soon return.
If you do your best, you'll be fine.

Reduced clauses are separated from the rest of the sentence by a comma. These clauses generally contain either the infinitive (e.g. *to go*), the present participle (e.g. *going*) or the past participle (e.g. *gone*):

To put an end to the quarrel, I agreed to disagree.
Writing in my best style, I tried my hand at a short story.
Bought for a few pounds, the painting sold for thousands.

Foregrounding

A comma can be used to highlight or emphasize a part of the sentence that does not normally come first. This is sometimes referred to as foregrounding or fronting:

Tomorrow, the results will arrive.
An absolute idiot, you made me feel.

Separating insertions

Insertions into a sentence or utterance are

separated by commas. The insertion may be a word:

I suggested, however, that we should both go.

or a phrase:

She is, in fact, my father's cousin.

or a clause:

I think, but I can't be certain, that the quotation is from Milton.

The commas, like brackets, are used both before and after these insertions.

Separating parts of noun phrases

The two parts of a noun phrase that is composed of a proper noun and a designation are separated by commas:

Michael Manning, the voter's choice.

This type of structure is often called *noun phrases in apposition*. If such a structure occurs in a sentence, then commas are used before and after the explanatory phrase:

Lois Lane, the renowned journalist, failed to recognize Superman in quiet Clark Kent.

Separating non-defining clauses

Non-defining (non-restrictive) clauses are separated from the rest of the sentence by commas:

The children, who went to nursery school, were able to read.

A non-defining clause expands the noun it modifies, whereas a defining clause limits or reduces its application. Thus, in:

The children, who went to nursery school, were able to read.

we can delete the non-defining clause and make the correct deduction that:

The children (i.e., all of them) were able to read.

The sentence with a defining clause, where commas are not used, limits the reference of the noun *children*. Thus, in the sentence:

The children who went to nursery school were able to read.

the relative clause is essential to our understanding that only *some* of the children were able to read. In speech, non-defining clauses are signalled by pauses and a change of tone.

Separating main clauses

Long main clauses linked by *and*, *but* and *so* are separated by commas:

I rang the television company in New Zealand, and they confirmed the news release.

Commas are not used when the linked units are short:

I rang and heard their news.

In dates

A comma is used to separate the year from the month:

1 October, 2002

It was in October, 1989, that we met.

Increasingly, the commas before and after the year are omitted:

It was in October 1989 that we met.

In long numbers

Digits in long numbers are separated by commas:

11,000,000 yen

£1,654

Traditionally, the comma has been used, as above, to mark off thousands and millions. This convention continues to be applied, except with one thousand, which tends to be written *1000*, and not *1,000*.

In letters

The salutation in a letter may be separated from the body of a letter:

Dear Gladys,

It was good to ....

See also BRACKETS, DASH, NUMBERS, PUNCTUATION

commando

The plural of *commando* is 'commandos'. It is often misspelled. This word takes an 's' to form its plural, not an '-es' like 'tomatoes'.

commence

Commence is a formal equivalent of 'begin' or 'start':

All-party talks commenced this morning.

It should be reserved for the opening of formal ceremonies.

commensurate

This adjective comes from Late Latin *commensuratus*, 'measured with', and is used to mean 'equal in extent', 'proportionate':

The new Professor will receive a salary commensurate with the recognized value of the key role Language Studies will play in the next decade.

comment, commentate

When *comment* is used as a verb, it means 'express an opinion' and the opinion may be expressed in speech or writing:

Please stop commenting on my behaviour.

My comments on this book are to be read in the spirit in which they were written.

Commentate is a back formation from 'commentator' and is widely used to mean 'provide a commentary on':

He has been invited to commentate on the match.

Many people dislike this use but its frequent occurrence in sports journalism suggests that it has become part of the language.

See also WORD FORMATION

commercialese

Commercialese is a pejorative term for the jargon associated particularly with business and commerce. The items most frequently selected for criticism are abbreviations:

inst (this month)
Thank you for your letter of the 12th inst.

re (about, concerning)

and fixed phrases:

advise (inform, tell)
as per your instructions
beg to inform you
effect such (do this)
enclosed please find (I enclose)
further to your letter
in respect of
please find enclosed.

Most of these items are now regarded as old-fashioned and few modern businesses employ them.

See also JARGON

commissionaire

A *commissionaire* is an attendant in uniform, often found at the entrance of a theatre or hotel:

I've asked the commissionaire to get us a taxi.

The word is frequently misspelled.

commit

The verb *commit* is frequently used in the collocation:

commit an offence/sin.

It is a regular verb and doubles the 't' before '-ed' and '-ing' in all varieties of English:

I committed the offence.

The verb has a different meaning when followed by a reflexive pronoun:

I committed myself to the group.

means 'I gave the group my allegiance and strong support'.

To *commit* something to a person or a cause means 'entrust it' for a specific purpose:

I didn't feel that I could commit all my funds to the one venture.

commitment, committal

Both these nouns derive from the verb 'commit'. *Commitment* has one 't' before the 'm' and is most frequently used to mean 'pledge, obligation, firm support':

His commitment to the welfare of the children was never questioned.

Committal has '-tt-' and means 'official consignment of a person to be tried or to be sent to prison or to a mental institution'.

committee

This word is frequently spelled incorrectly. It has three sets of doubled letters, '-mm-', '-tt-' and '-ee'.

See also SPELLING

common, mutual

The adjective *common* derives from Latin *communis*, 'general, universal', and means 'ordinary, widely known':

Lowering interest rates with little advance warning is common practice in building societies.

It can also mean 'belonging to or shared by two or more people':

Why do so few people look after common property?

Mutual derives from Latin *mutuus*, 'reciprocal', and refers to something that is experienced by or shared by two or more people:

Their mutual hatred was palpable.

Tom is a mutual friend. (i.e., He is a friend of both or all the people involved.)

The correct use of *mutual* has worried careful users for over a hundred years. The rule is that *mutual* denotes a response, attitude or action that is equal, contemporaneous and shared by two people:

mutual affection/assistance/attraction
mutual dislike/distrust/distaste

If the response, attitude or action is shared by more than two, then *mutual* must not be used:

Everyone noticed the mutual trust between John and Joan.

*Everyone noticed the mutual trust shown by John, Joan and Joshua.

The advice often given is that *common* should be used when dealing with more than two:

their common interests

but in addition to meaning 'shared', *common* means 'coarse', 'vulgar', and its use may be ambiguous. *Mutual* is now widely used to mean 'shared', losing its original meaning of 'shared by two', but SEMANTIC CHANGE is a feature of a living language.

Careful users also take care to distinguish between *mutual* and 'reciprocal'.

Mutual love is shared; reciprocal love is given in return.

See also INDIVIDUAL, SHIBBOLETH

common noun

Nouns are often divided into *common* and 'proper'. A *common noun* is the name of a member of a whole class:

banana, brick, tree.

A proper noun refers to a particular person, place or thing:

Ben, Cairo, Thatcherism.

Common nouns always begin with a lower-case letter.

See also NOUN

common sense

Common sense is a noun meaning 'ordinary good judgement':

Common sense is, in spite of its name, a rare gift.

The hyphenated form *common-sense* is adjectival:

Let's adopt a common-sense approach to the problem.

commoner

This noun is most frequently used to mean 'one who is not a member of the nobility':

Several members of the Royal Family have married commoners.

communiqué

A *communiqué* is a an official announcement or communication:

The following communiqué was issued by the Palace a few moments ago.

The word is spelled with an acute accent on the 'e' but is not normally written in italics. It is a borrowing from French, once regarded as the language of diplomacy, and it was in the context of diplomacy that the word originally occurred.

comparable

Traditionally, this word is stressed on the first syllable. The tendency to stress *comparable* on the second syllable is disliked by many speakers.

comparative, superlative

Adjectives and adverbs can occur in three forms, traditionally called 'positive', 'comparative' and 'superlative':

Adjective: black, blacker, blackest
Adverb: fast, faster, fastest.

Short adjectives and adverbs form their comparatives and superlatives by adding '-er' and '-est'. Longer adjectives and most adverbs use 'more' and 'most':

Adjective: extravagant, more extravagant, most extravagant
Adverb: recklessly, more recklessly, most recklessly.

Short adjectives ending in a single consonant double the consonant before suffixes. Those ending in 'y' change the 'y' to 'i':

big, bigger, biggest
fat, fatter, fattest
funny, funnier, funniest
happy, happier, happiest.

Some of the most widely used words in the language have irregular comparatives and superlatives. The following are the most widely used:

bad, worse, worst
badly, worse, worst
good, better, best
little, less, least
well, better, best.

Although one often assumes that there is an increase from positive to superlative, each word takes its meaning from the word it modifies. Thus, the positive can imply more than the comparative, and the comparative is often greater than the superlative:

His speech is better but it's still not good.
Norway has made the design of the roll-on-roll-off ferries safer, but it has not made them safe.
It was longer than the longest story I'd ever heard.
He's the tallest boy on the team but the new captain is taller still.
Only the best is good enough for our customers.

The adjective *superlative* is used generally to mean 'truly excellent':

It was a superlative performance. Washington came back from being two sets down to win the match.

See also ADJECTIVE, ADVERB, SPELLING

comparatively

This adverb is often used loosely as a synonym of 'rather' or 'quite':

She was a comparatively good swimmer.
We've had a comparatively mild winter.

compare

The verb *compare* comes from Latin *comparare*, 'to couple together, match'. Its meaning changes depending on which preposition it occurs with. *Compare to* is used when we wish to point out the similarity between two things:

Shall I compare thee to a summer's day?

Compare with is used when we wish to point out both resemblances and differences:

I'd like to compare our results with those of our competitors.

In such sentences, the direct object comes between *compare* and 'with'. When there is no direct object, we use *compare with*:

Nothing can compare with home-made bread.

comparison and contrast

Comparison and *contrast* are procedures for determining the similarities and differences between two or more people, ideas, objects or things. *Comparison* focuses on likeness:

You can't compare a silk purse and a sow's ear.

Many popular sayings are comparisons:

as bold as brass
as strong as an ox.

Contrast explores differences and is frequently employed in logical and/or persuasive writing in order to establish distinctions:

No man can serve two masters for either he will love the one and hate the other, or he will serve the one and despise the other. You cannot serve God and Mammon.

Luke 17:13

There is, however, some overlap between the words 'compare' and 'contrast' in that 'compare to' stresses similarity and 'compare with', like 'contrast', stresses difference.

See also AS

compass, compasses
A *compass* is an instrument for indicating location:

My compass doesn't seem to be working. The needle seems to be swinging randomly between north and south.

A pair of *compasses* is an instrument used for drawing circles:

Don't draw circles free-hand. Use a pair of compasses.

compass directions
The main compass points are North, South, East and West, often referred to by an initial capital letter:

N (north), S (south), E (east), W (west)

Subdivisions can be indicated:

NE = halfway between north and east
NNE = halfway between north and north east.

A northerly wind blows from the north; a southerly wind blows from the south and rhymes with 'motherly'.

See also -WARD/-WARDS

compatible
This adjective is frequently misspelled. It can occur on its own:

John and Joanna have decided that they are no longer compatible.

or it can be followed by 'with':

His words were not compatible with his actions.

compel
Compel is a regular verb meaning 'force':

I was compelled to put a stop to the libel.

It doubles the 'l' before suffixes throughout the English-speaking world:

compel(s), compelled, compelling.

competence, competency
These nouns are variants borrowed into the language from French at different times. *Competence* is the more widely used and can be used

in all contexts. *Competency* tends to be used in legal language and implies 'capacity to testify in a court of law' or 'eligible to be sworn in'. *Competence* can also be used with these meanings.

competence and performance
This distinction was introduced into linguistics by Noam Chomsky. *Competence* is defined as 'the ideal speaker-hearer's knowledge of his language' and *performance* as the 'actual use of language in concrete situations'. *Competence* is, as it were, the complete and perfect storehouse of linguistic knowledge, a knowledge that allows a speaker to perform the following tasks:

■ To produce and understand an infinite number of well-formed sentences.

■ To recognize errors and classify the degree of error involved, whether a slip, an understandable extension or a usage that breaks grammatical rules.

■ To recognize similarity of meaning under dissimilarity of form:

Lois loved Superman.
Superman was loved by Lois.

and differences of meaning under similarity of form:

Lois asked Clark what to wear.
Lois advised Clark what to wear.

■ To recognize the possibility of one structure having several meanings:

I upset his plans. (This can have at least four meanings: the verb, for example, can be either past or present and the noun can mean 'drawings' and 'intentions'.)

See also LANGUE AND PAROLE, SPEECH AND WRITING

competition, contest
These words are approximately synonymous. The suggestion in both words is of an open struggle, which may be between friends or enemies or strangers. In both, there will be winners and losers.

complement
This noun has a specific meaning in linguistics. In its most general application, the term *complement* refers to anything that completes the predicate. It therefore comprehends everything that follows the verb and that is necessary to complete the state or action specified by the verb. According to this view, all the underlined items in the following sentences are 'complements':

I rang the chemist.
I am the chemist.
I went into town.

Most contemporary linguists give *complement* a more restricted meaning. They apply the term 'subject complement' to words or phrases that follow a COPULA as in the following examples:

Ben is <u>a student</u>. (noun phrase complement)

Ben is <u>angry</u>. (adjective complement)

Ben was <u>away</u>. (adverb complement)

Ben was <u>in a good mood</u>. (preposition phrase complement)

All of these complements provide information on the subject.

In such sentences as:

They elected Ben <u>President</u>.

She called her son <u>Benjamin</u>.

She made them <u>happy</u>.

the underlined items provide extra information on the object and are called 'object complements'.

See also BE, PREDICATE

complement, compliment, supplement

These three words can function as both nouns and verbs. They are often misspelled. *Complement* is related to the verb 'complete' and is used to refer to something that goes well with something else or that completes it:

The beautiful setting complemented the meal.

We now have a full complement of students.

Compliment relates to praise, respect, approval:

The judge complimented me on my lovely roses.

I want to pay him a compliment but I don't want to sound fulsome.

Supplement can function as a noun and a regular verb meaning 'add to something that is already complete':

They are bringing out a supplement to the Oxford English Dictionary, providing details of all the items collected over the past two years.

supplement(s), supplemented, supplementing

She supplements her grant by working on Saturdays.

complete and utter

This phrase is widely used and widely criticized as being tautological:

I felt a complete and utter idiot!

Logically, it is tautological. *Complete* came into the language from French and *utter* is from Old English. There are many fixed phrases like this in the language such as:

bits and pieces

goods and chattels

hale and hearty

might and main

part and parcel

wear and tear.

Originally, many of these dyads had one word from English and one word from French and would have been extremely useful in post-

Norman Conquest England, when both English and French were in daily use. Later, the dyads became a stylistic feature in the language.

See also DYAD

complex, complicated

These adjectives are often used as synonyms but careful speakers distinguish between them. If something is *complex*, it is intricate and made up of many parts:

He spent hours working on complex mathematical problems.

If something is *complicated*, it is also made up of several parts but often has overtones of 'confused' or 'confusing':

I asked how to get to their house and got the most complicated set of instructions. We've arranged to meet at the theatre.

Complex is frequently used as a noun meaning 'a group of buildings':

Have you seen the plans for the new shopping complex?

complexion

Several words in English may be spelled either '-xion' or '-ction':

connection, connexion

inflection, inflexion.

Complexion is spelled only with '-xion'.

See also -CT-/-X-, SPELLING

compliment

See COMPLEMENT/COMPLIMENT/SUPPLEMENT

compose, comprise, consist, constitute

These words have overlapping meanings in that they all suggest parts coming together to form a whole.

Compose can have a range of meanings. One can *compose* music or poetry or one can *compose* oneself – that is, calm oneself in preparation for some activity. When the meaning of 'parts coming together' is required and a passive construction is needed, it is advisable to use *compose*:

The new School is composed of the departments of Linguistics and Modern Languages.

Comprise implies 'to contain, include, be composed of':

The new School comprises the departments of Linguistics and Modern Languages.

Comprise does not combine with 'of' so it is incorrect to say:

*The new School is comprised of the departments of Linguistics and Modern Languages.

Consist, which means 'be made up of', may be followed by both 'in' and 'of' although the meaning of the verb changes depending on the preposition. *Consist in* means 'have its existence in' and is followed by an abstract noun:

The success of the technique consists in its blend of well-known ideas and unconventional innuendo.

Consist of means 'be made up of':

The list consists of six hundred words ending in '-ant'.
The course consists of four modules.

Constitute means 'come together to make a whole'. It tends to be used in active sentences:

Such a combination does not constitute a balanced meal.

compound

A *compound* is a lexical item formed by the process of combining words:

black + bird = blackbird
book + case = bookcase
not + with + standing = notwithstanding.

The process of combining words and affixes is known as 'derivation':

ante + room = anteroom
in + sight = insight
re + view = review.

Compounding is a highly productive type of word formation and so it is not possible to make too many generalizations about compounds. We can, however, offer a few guidelines.

The strongest stress normally falls on the first element of a two-word compound:

'blackbird (contrast: black 'bird)
'Whitehouse (contrast: white 'house)

but it may occur on a different syllable in polysyllabic words:

notwith'standing
photo'phobia.

Compounds may be single words:

bookcase, cupboard

hyphenated words:

bone-meal, book-plate

separate words:

book club, egg cup

or hyphenated phrases:

a down-and-out, a back-to-back.

These forms represent a continuum between the word and the phrase, many being in the process of change. Thus we find both:

book-maker and bookmaker
lion-tamer and liontamer

with UK users favouring more hyphenation than US speakers.

One group of compounds uses morphemes borrowed from Greek. Though usually full words in Greek, they may be bound morphemes in English. This type of compounding is a frequent source of new names for scientific and techno-logical inventions and discoveries:

astronaut, biorhythms.

Several modern compounds are formed from a letter + a word:

A-frame, T-square, U-bend.

Compound words may function as adjectives:

an off-the-shoulder dress

as nouns:

a doorway

and verbs:

typeset

and they can be composed of:

adjective + noun: blackboard
noun + noun: treetop
verb + noun: walkman
verb + adverb: takeaway.

See also DERIVATION, HYPHEN, WORD FORMATION

comprehensible, comprehensive

These words are sometimes confused. *Comprehensible* is applied to something that can be understood and it can often be replaced by 'capable of being understood':

I have a mental block about it. No matter how clear the explanation is, I still do not find it comprehensible.

Comprehensive means 'inclusive' and it is applied to something that is complete:

His description was comprehensive: no detail was omitted.

compute

The verb *compute* is used with two basic meanings, 'to calculate a result, often with the help of a computer':

We shall need at least two days to compute the results of the questionnaires.

and, more recently, 'to use a computer':

I've got a problem. I've been asked to compute my essays but I'm not computer literate.

It is, however, more usual to use a phrase involving 'computer', such as:

I need two additional hours of computer time to finish my work.

The verb 'computerize' is used to mean 'convert something to a computer system':

Our records have been computerized.

computerese

Computerese is a word used to mean 'computer terminology'. Like some other words ending in '-ese', such as 'headlinese' and 'journalese', it is often used with pejorative overtones:

I suppose you understand all this new-fangled computerese?

Samples of *computerese* include the use of abbreviations:

PC (personal computer), CD (compact disc)

the use of acronyms:

RAM (random access memory), ROM (read only memory)

the use of computer terms:

disc drive, monitor

the use of words with specialized meanings:

mouse (device for moving the cursor), windows (method of organizing the screen).

con-

Con- is a prefix, a variant of 'com-'.

See also COM-, HYPHEN, PREFIX

concave, convex

These words are frequently confused. *Concave* means 'curved inwards like the inside surface of a ball'. *Convex* means 'curved outwards like the outside surface of a ball'.

The inside of a spoon is concave. It is hollow like a cave.

concept

The word *concept* is used widely today to mean 'accepted idea':

the concept of holistic medicine
the concept of interior design
the concept of money management.

concerned

The meaning of *concerned* changes depending on the preposition that follows it. *Concerned in* means 'involved with':

We believe him to be concerned in criminal activity.

Concerned for/about means 'worried about':

We are concerned for his safety.

Concerned with means 'associated with':

Linguistics is concerned with the scientific study of language.

concerning

Concerning can be used to mean 'on the subject of'. In such contexts, it is a formal equivalent of 'about':

For all advice concerning investments, ring the following number.

concession, concessive

A *concession* is 'an act of yielding, something granted', 'an exclusive right to market a product':

We have been unable to wring any concessions from our dealers.

They have a concession to sell our cars.

A *concessive* clause suggests that something is conceded and is often introduced by words such as 'although', 'as', 'but', 'though' to imply a contrast:

Although we lost, we were pleased with our performance.

conch

A *conch* is a shell. The word derives from Latin *concha*, 'mussel, oyster, shell'. The word has two pronunciations. It may rhyme with 'clonk' or with the first syllable of 'poncho'. *Conch* has two plurals, 'conchs', pronounced like 'conks', and 'conches'. The latter plural is the more widely used.

concord

Concord refers to a system in language where the choice of one element triggers off the use of a particular form of a subsequent element. For example, in the following French sentences, the noun determines, by concord, the forms of the adjectives and the verbs:

Le livre est petit. (The book is small.)
La porte est petite. (The door is small.)
Les livres sont petits.
Les portes sont petites.

There is little concord in English but we find it in the following circumstances:

Verbs

In the present tense of the verb, the subject sometimes conditions the form of the verb:

I/you/we/they remember
he/she/it remembers.

The base form of the verb is used for all persons except the third person singular. There is no concord between subject and verb in the past:

I/you/he/she/it/we/you/they remembered.

Slightly different forms of concord affect the verbs 'be', 'do' and 'have':

Person	Present	Past
I	am	was
you/we/they	are	were
he/she/it	is	was
I/you/we/they	do	did
he/she/it	does	did
I/you/we/they	have	had
he/she/it	has	had

Subject complements

Subject complements sometimes agree with the subject:

She is a student.
They are students.

Pronouns

Certain pronouns trigger off the use of a particular form of the verb:

Neither (of them) has gone.
None of them has gone.

'None' is the equivalent of 'not one' and so it takes a singular verb. Increasingly, however, speakers use 'none' as the negative equivalent of 'all' and so they use a plural verb:

None of them have gone.

'Everyone' causes problems of concord. Most speakers say:

Everyone (everybody) has their problems.

but purists argue that since 'one/body' is singular, the correct form is:

Everyone has his problems.

Feminists have pointed out the inequity of such usage and the problems inherently involved in such sentences as:

Anyone can do it if he/she tries/if they try.
Everyone has equal rights, hasn't he/she/haven't they?

See also AGREEMENT, ASPECT, AUXILIARY, EVERY, NO ONE/NOBODY/NONE

concur

Concur means 'agree'. It normally co-occurs with 'with' and 'in':

We concur with you in your assessment of his work.

The 'r' is doubled before suffixes:

concurred, concurring, concurrence.

conditional

This term is applied to clauses that hypothesize:

If I won the Lottery, I'd be a different person.

or imply conditions:

Unless your work improves, you will be asked to leave.

The use of 'if I were/was' is partly determined by the likelihood of the hypothesis:

If I were a millionaire ... (unlikely)
If I was there now ... (likely)

Many traditional grammarians insist on the use of 'were' after 'if', claiming that in such constructions we must use the subjunctive form of the verb. However, the subjunctive only occurs in a few fossilized retentions in English:

Be that as it may ...
... as it were
If such be the case ...
Long live the king!

all of which involve either the base form of the verb (e.g., 'live') or 'be', which is, in any case, the most irregular verb in the language.

The modal verbs are frequently used in expressing conditions:

You can do it if you try.
I can't do it unless I have help.

In the past, the term 'conditional tense' was applied to constructions involving the modals 'would/should':

I should do it at once, if I were you.

Most scholars now accept that there is no conditional tense in English and that conditionality can be expressed in a variety of ways including:

the use of modals:

I might let you go if you're good.

the use of such subordinate conjunctions as:

as if, if, on condition that, unless.

See also MODALITY

condominium, condo

The term condominium used to mean 'joint sovereignty' as in:

Cameroon became a condominium after World War I, with Britain and France being the joint rulers.

Nowadays, it is used, mainly in America, to refer to an apartment:

We are renting a lovely condominium/condo in a block close to Ben's house.

conducive

The adjective conducive is followed by 'to' and not 'of':

Such actions are not conducive to good government.

conductor

This noun is always spelled with '-or':

He wants to be the conductor of a light orchestra.

See also SPELLING

conduit

Many native speakers are uncertain how to pronounce this word, which means 'pipe' or 'channel':

The occupier will also be responsible for all conduits leading to or from the said dwelling.

The most popular pronunciation rhymes the word with 'bond it' but it is also pronounced to rhyme with 'pursue it'.

confer

Confer is a formal equivalent of 'give officially':

Her degree was conferred in absentia.

The 'r' is doubled before '-ed' and '-ing', but 'conference' is spelled with one 'r' only.

confetti

Although confetti is the plural form of Italian confetto, 'a bonbon', it is treated as a singular noun in English:

The confetti was forgotten.

confidant(e), confident

A *confidant* is a person in whom one confides:

I seem to have been selected as Jane's current confidant.

Confidant is now generally applied to both males and females although *confidante* is also used for women:

Marje Proops was a confidante to generations of British women.

The two forms are pronounced alike and rhyme with 'aunt'.

Confident is an adjective meaning 'assured, sure of oneself':

He is so confident of success that I envy him.

confide in, confide to

Confide means 'disclose a secret', 'entrust'. It can combine with both 'in' and 'to'. When we *confide in* someone, we confess something to them:

I did not feel that I could confide in anyone. There are some things that are better kept to oneself.

When we *confide* something *to* someone, we entrust that person with something:

I have confided all our secrets to Ben.

confirm

See AFFIRM/CONFIRM

conform

This verb usually combines with 'to':

Your plans do not conform to my specifications.

but there is growing evidence that it is also being used with 'with':

?*I don't conform with the stereotype of the stiff upper lip.

Many careful users find this usage unacceptable.

confrontation

Confrontation means 'face-to-face meeting involving opposition or hostility':

There was a confrontation between the representatives of the council and the tanker owners.

The meaning of this word has been weakened, mainly by use in the popular press, so that it has become a synonym for 'row':

Yesterday there was a serious confrontation between previously friendly neighbours. The cause? Music ...

conga, conger

In many British accents, these words are homophones. A *conga* is a dance usually performed by a group of people in single file. The name *conga* comes from American Spanish and is derived from 'Congo':

I enjoy the conga. You don't have to be able to dance. You just have to follow the rhythm.

A *conger* is a large marine eel. The word comes ultimately from Greek *gongros*, 'sea eel':

Are conger eels edible?

congenial, congenital, genial

The adjective *congenial* means 'friendly', 'pleasant', 'agreeable':

The building is beautifully appointed and offers congenial working conditions.

I enjoy working with such congenial people. We share the same views on most subjects.

Congenital means 'a non-hereditary but inherent condition, existing since birth':

In spite of congenital deafness, she has become a world-class musician.

The adjectives *congenial* and *genial* overlap in meaning and one is sometimes used where the other would be more appropriate. *Genial* means 'cheerful, easy-going':

Everyone likes Roger. He's such a genial, courteous man.

Congo

An inhabitant of the Central African People's Republic of Congo is a 'Congolese'; the derived adjective is the same. The capital is Brazzaville.

conjunction

A *conjunction* is a joining word. In English, there are two types: coordinating conjunctions (also called 'coordinators') and subordinating conjunctions (also called 'subordinators').

The chief coordinating conjunctions are:

and, but, either ... or, neither ... nor, or, so, then, yet

and they join units of equal status. The units may be:

adjective + adjective: big and brave

adverb + adverb: smoothly and carefully

noun + noun: men and women

verb + verb: sang and danced

phrase + phrase: on the floor or behind the chair

sentence + sentence: Either you toe the line or you leave the club.

Subordinating conjunctions introduce subordinate clauses (also referred to as 'dependent clauses'), often providing information on when, where, why or how an action or event occurred. The commonest subordinating conjunctions are:

after: They arrived after we did.

(al)though: (Al)though they were poor, they were happy.

as: The meeting ended as I entered the room.

as ... as: Do it as quietly as you can.

as if: She looked as if she hadn't a care in the world.

because: I did it because I needed the experience.

before: I had to leave before the guest speaker arrived.

if: If I buy a car, I'll be able to get to work in 20 minutes.

in case: I bought it in case we needed it.

since: I haven't seen him since we left school.

so that: I took the job so that we'd be able to afford a holiday.

till/until: Don't touch them until they're cool.

when: When you're smiling, the whole world smiles with you.

where: I don't know where I've put it.

while: Stay in the car while I get the paper.

Many subordinating conjunctions can also function as prepositions:

Subordinator	Preposition
They came after we did.	They arrived after us.
She left before you did.	She left before you.

See also CLASS, CLAUSE, SENTENCE

conjurer, conjuror

Both spellings are acceptable for a person who performs tricks, although the '-or' form is more frequently used in Britain.

connection

Connection means 'union, something that joins, links, unites':

What's the connection between John and Jo? Does he work for her?

I have missed my connection to Paddington.

The normal spelling in America and Britain is '-ection' but the alternative '-exion' is acceptable.

See also -CT-/-X-

connoisseur

This noun derives ultimately from Latin *cognoscere*, 'to know', and refers to an expert or person with a special knowledge of a particular field:

He's a connoisseur of fine wines.

The first two syllables are pronounced as for 'Coniston'.

connotation

The noun *connotation* is often misused. *Connotation* refers to the extra association(s), usually emotional or social, that a word or phrase may have in addition to its denotative or referential meaning. For example, the words 'induce', 'persuade', 'urge' and 'wheedle' may all be used of the act of encouraging someone to behave in a particular way, but their connotations vary from open (persuade) to hostile (wheedle). The emotional load of a word such as 'home' in contrast to 'apartment' or 'house' lies in its connotation. Social attitudes may affect the connotations of a word. Victorian prudery, for example, gave the words for trousers and underwear such strong taboo connotations that they

could not be used in polite company. Today, attitudes to race are often implied in the terms selected by a speaker or writer.

The connotative force of words is often exploited in persuasive language such as advertising and PROPAGANDA.

See also CLICHÉ, DENOTATION, EUPHEMISM, SYNONYM

conscientious

This adjective derives from the noun 'conscience' and is frequently misspelled because writers carry over the '-ienc' from the noun.

See also SPELLING

conscious

Conscious is widely used in the popular press as an adjective meaning 'aware':

My son has suddenly become clothes-conscious.

I wasn't conscious of the weather.

Careful users of language disapprove of such usage, pointing out that *conscious* should relate to a part of the human mind and mental activity:

He was comatose for three weeks but is now fully conscious.

consensus

Consensus is frequently misspelled as *concensus*. The problem can be avoided by remembering that the word derives from Latin *consentire*, 'to consent', and has nothing to do with the noun 'census', meaning 'population count'.

See also SPELLING

consent

See ASSENT/CONSENT

consequent, subsequent

These words both derive ultimately from the Latin verb *sequor*, meaning 'follow', and because of their overlapping meanings they are sometimes confused. *Consequent* means 'following on as a direct result of':

They were badly injured and their consequent inability to look after themselves was not taken into full account by the tribunal that decided their level of compensation.

Consequent is followed by the preposition 'on':

There has been a four-fold increase in population consequent on better healthcare facilities.

Subsequent means 'following':

Their meeting and subsequent friendship had a marked effect on the lives of both young poets.

Subsequent is followed by 'to':

His promotion was subsequent to, but did not depend on, his new book.

conservative, Conservative

When we spell *conservative* with a lower-case 'c', the word means 'cautious, moderate, favouring the preservation of established customs and values':

Rural people are often conservative by nature, preferring evolution rather than revolution.

When the word is spelled with a capital letter, it relates to a supporter of a Conservative party:

He's been a Conservative since he joined the party at university.

See also CAPITALIZATION

considerable

The adjective *considerable* is often used as a variant of 'great' or 'large':

There was a considerable crowd at the football stadium.

This loose use of *considerable* is disliked by many who claim that it should be used before abstract nouns to mean 'worthy of respect':

She has made a considerable contribution to the world of science.

or before concrete nouns to mean 'significant':

Collins is not, perhaps, a considerable poet: he is, however, an enjoyable one.

consist

See COMPOSE/COMPRISE/CONSIST/CONSTITUTE

consistent, persistent

These words are occasionally confused. *Consistent* means 'in agreement or harmony with':

Such an action is totally consistent with my knowledge of his character.

Persistent means 'continuous, enduring':

We moved house because of the persistent noise.

consonant

A *consonant* is a letter or speech sound that is not a vowel. There are 21 consonants in the English alphabet.

See also ALPHABET, PRONUNCIATION

consonant cluster

A *consonant cluster* involves the co-occurrence of two or more consonants as in the beginning sequences of:

slap, splat, state.

English permits up to three consonants at the beginning of a syllable:

screw, spring, strike.

In word-final position, English permits up to four consonants in a cluster:

pre-empts, thousandths.

Consonant clusters can cause pronunciation problems to both native and non-native speakers. The standard orthography illustrates how many clusters have been simplified in the past:

knack, sought, thumb

and the simplification continues: clusters are often reduced in speech:

anae(s)thetist, fi(f)ths, s(c)lerosis

and intrusive vowels are introduced:

ath(e)lete, chim(i)ney, sprink(e)ler system.

See also EPENTHESIS

consonant doubling

The rules about when we should double consonants are clear but there are two problems for writers of English in that there are exceptions to the rules and American and British rules often differ. The general rules are these:

■ Words of one syllable that end in a consonant preceded by a single vowel double the consonant when the word is followed by a suffix beginning with a vowel:

big, bigger, biggest
flat, flatter, flattest
grit, gritted, gritter, gritting.

■ Words of one syllable that contain two vowels do not double the consonant when a suffix is added:

fleet, fleeter, fleetest
great, greater, greatest
hoot, hooter.

■ Words of one syllable that end in two consonants do not double a consonant when followed by a suffix:

bend, bender, bending
cold, colder, coldest
milk, milked, milking.

■ Words of two or more syllables follow the above rules when the main stress falls on the final syllable:

forget, forgetting
redeem, redeeming
implant, implanted, implanting.

In Britain, words of more than one syllable double the consonant when the stress falls on the first syllable:

kidnap, kidnapped, kidnapping
travel, travelled, traveller, travelling.

See also SPELLING

constable

Constable is sometimes preferred to 'policeman' or 'policewoman' because it is unmarked for gender. The traditional British pronunciation rhymes the first syllable with 'done', but a spelling pronunciation that rhymes it with 'don' is spreading.

constitute
See COMPOSE/COMPRISE/CONSIST/CONSTITUTE

constrain, restrain
These words are occasionally confused. *Constrain* means 'force someone to do something':

The law constrains me to charge you with Grievous Bodily Harm for attacking the burglar, even though I can sympathize with your behaviour.

Restrain means 'hold back':

Don't restrain her. She has every right to express her opinion.

constructional, constructive
These adjectives are both derived from 'construction' but have markedly different implications. *Constructional* means 'pertaining to the construction':

We met the architect and the builder yesterday to talk about a number of constructional problems that have arisen with the angle of the roof.

Constructive means 'helpful, useful':

I am grateful for the many constructive comments you have offered on the text.

consult (with)
Sometimes British and American English can be distinguished by the use or non-use of a preposition. British speakers *consult* a dentist, a doctor or a supervisor when they need help or advice, whereas Americans *consult with* such people:

UK: I had to consult my doctor yesterday.
US: I had to consult with my doctor yesterday.

When British people use *consult with* it means 'inform and discuss options with':

Naturally, we shall consult with all the elected parties before drawing up details of the election process.

contact
The meanings of the noun and verb *contact* are beginning to diverge. The noun often means 'the act of touching physically':

The trains are always crowded in the morning and I don't like being in such close contact with strangers.

The verb is most frequently used now to mean 'get in touch with, communicate with':

I've contacted the candidates and they can all attend the interview on Friday, 22 March.

contagious, infectious
Many people use these words as synonyms but careful speakers distinguish between them. *Contagious* is related to 'contact' and means

'capable of being passed on by direct physical contact with a diseased individual or by handling something that has been contaminated':

This form of hepatitis is highly contagious.

Infectious means 'capable of being passed on by micro-organisms that are carried in the air or by water':

This strain of influenza is highly infectious and we recommend all vulnerable patients to make an appointment for an injection.

contemporary, contemporaneous
Contemporary refers to 'the same period of time, simultaneous' and may be used as a noun and an adjective:

Auden and MacNeice were contemporaries.
Keats is often described as the most mellifluous of contemporary poets.

The adjective *contemporary* is increasingly used to mean 'modern', 'current' so that 'contemporary poets' in the example above could be ambiguous, meaning both 'poets of Keats's time' and 'poets of today'. Since both interpretations are possible, we should use 'contemporary' with care.

Contemporaneous is an adjective meaning 'occurring at the same time'. It normally refers to events:

The Great Strike and the Wall Street Crash were almost contemporaneous.

contemptible, contemptuous
These adjectives are sometimes misused. They both derive from *contempt* but they have different meanings and uses. *Contemptible* means 'despicable':

I find it hard to believe that anyone could behave in such a contemptible manner. Nothing can excuse this cruel attack on a helpless old woman.

Contemptuous means 'scornful', 'haughty', 'feeling or showing contempt':

We could not make him see that such behaviour was unacceptable. He listened to us in silence but with a contemptuous smirk on his face.

content(s)
The singular noun *content* can mean 'meaning and significance':

It is hard to refer to the content of a poem without commenting on its form.

The plural noun *contents* means 'everything that is inside':

I have examined the contents of the trunk carefully and have found nothing of any interest to our investigation.

contest
See COMPETITION/CONTEST

context

The term *context* is used most specifically in linguistic and stylistic studies, where it refers to the words, structures and punctuation surrounding a particular word or usage. Out of context, words seldom have precise meanings, a fact that can be illustrated by the word 'bear'. On its own it may evoke very different responses in the minds of different people, but in the following contexts we have no difficulty in giving it very specific meanings:

The baby can't sleep without her bear.
The bear hibernates throughout the winter.
I can't bear it! I'm going to own up.
Thou shalt not bear false witness against thy neighbour.

In the first example, the use of 'bear' as a noun and its collocation with 'child' and 'sleep' suggests 'teddy bear' and eliminates other possible interpretations. Similarly, in the third sentence, where 'bear' is a verb and collocates with 'can't', the meaning 'tolerate/endure' is clearly indicated. The functions and relationships between words thus constitute a very specific meaning of 'context'.

See also COLLOCATION

contingency

A *contingency* is 'an unforeseen possibility', 'something that may happen but is not very likely':

We must try to cater for every contingency, however unlikely.

The word has occurred so frequently in the phrase '*contingency* plans' that it is often applied to future events that can be predicted:

The hospital has contingency plans for dealing with all major accidents.

continual, continuous

These words have related meanings. *Continual* and its derived adverb 'continually' refer to actions that occur often, but with interruptions:

The continual noise upsets me to such an extent that I can't even enjoy the periods of quiet when they occur.
She is continually asking for new clothes.

Continuous refers to an uninterrupted action or activity:

We were late and the film was half over when we went in. The continuous programme meant that we could watch the film in its entirety, however, rather than having to leave when the first show ended.
It has rained continuously for 18 hours.

contra-

The prefix *contra* derives from Latin *contra* 'against'. It occurs in many words including:

contraband (prohibited goods)

contraception (prevention of conception)
contradict (to affirm the opposite of).

See also WORD FORMATION

contraction

The noun *contraction* is used in language descriptions to refer to a process whereby a word is reduced and attached to an adjacent form. It can be illustrated by:

I + am = I'm
I + have = I've
you + are = you're
cannot = can't
will + not = won't.

Contractions are a feature of colloquial speech and informal writing.

See also APHESIS, APOSTROPHE, ELISION, STRONG AND WEAK FORM

contrary

Contrary derives from Latin *contrarius*, 'opposite'. When it means 'opposed in nature or position', it is stressed on the first syllable:

How can we ever reconcile such <u>con</u>trary views?

When *contrary* means 'perverse' or 'obstinate', it is stressed on the second syllable:

I come from a family of con<u>tra</u>ry individuals. We can't even see eye to eye with each other.

contrast

See COMPARISON AND CONTRAST

contretemps

This French word is now quite widely used in English to refer to 'an awkward, difficult or embarrassing situation'. The same form is used for both singular and plural and, like 'restaurant', it tends to keep its French pronunciation:

We try to encourage a spirit of harmony and cooperation and so we tend to avoid contretemps.

Many purists dislike the use of *contretemps* to mean 'disagreement':

We had a little bit of a contretemps about what she should wear but we've found a compromise.

See also BORROWING

contribute

The usual pronunciation of *contribute* puts the main stress on the second syllable as we do with 'condition' or 'contrition'. Many people dislike the tendency of some speakers to put the main stress on the first syllable as we do with such disyllabic words as 'contour' or 'convent'. The noun 'contribution' has the main stress on the third syllable.

control

Control is a regular verb that doubles the 'l' before suffixes beginning with a vowel:

control(s), controlled, controlling, controller.

controversy

A *controversy* is a dispute, argument or debate, especially one in which strong opinions are held:

There is controversy about whether or not the press has the right to reveal details about an individual's private life.

The usual pronunciation in both Britain and America puts the main stress on the first syllable, but many speakers in Britain prefer to stress the second syllable.

controvertible

This adjective, which means 'capable of being denied or refuted', is frequently misspelled. It ends in '-ible' not '-able':

No matter how well established this view is, if you have found controvertible evidence, you have a duty to reveal it.

See also -ABLE/-IBLE

convalescence

This noun, which means 'period of recovery after an illness', is often misspelled. It comes from Latin *convalescere*, 'to grow strong':

I strongly advise a period of convalescence.

conversion

The word *conversion* comes from the verb 'convert' and means 'a change in form, character or function'. It is often used in language descriptions to refer to one part of speech being used in a different role. For example, 'Herod' is a proper noun, but Shakespeare uses it as a verb in: ... outHerod Herod.

See also WORD FORMATION

convertible

This adjective, meaning 'capable of being changed', is often misspelled. It ends in '-ible', not '-able'.

I've always wanted a convertible car.

See also -ABLE/-IBLE

convex

See CONCAVE/CONVEX

convince, persuade

These verbs are occasionally misused. If we *convince* someone, we make them understand the validity of something:

You can't convince people of the validity of your views if they are unwilling to listen to reason.

Persuade means 'encourage someone to accept something':

I am persuaded by the beauty of the presentation, rather than by the power of the argument.

co-operate, cooperate

Both the above spellings are acceptable. The hyphenated form is more likely to occur in British English, but is being increasingly superseded by the unhyphenated form, which is the norm in America. If we co(-)operate, we work together in a friendly way:

If we don't learn to co(-)operate, we will never achieve anything.

co-ordinate, coordinate

Both these spellings are acceptable but, as with *co-operate* and *cooperate*, the unhyphenated word is the norm in America and among younger British writers. *Coordinate* is used as a verb to mean 'organize and integrate diverse elements':

Who will undertake the job of coordinating the conference papers, ensuring that they are arranged in order of topic and ensuring that copies of all papers are available for each participant?

See also ANAPHORA, CONJUNCTION

copula

This word, which derives from Latin *copula*, 'bond', refers to verbs such as 'to be' that link a subject and a complement:

Sam is a moody person.

Sam is moody.

Sam is in a bad mood.

The following verbs can also be used as copulas:

Appear: He appeared tired.

Become: He became a nurse.

Get: He is getting very tall.

Grow: He is growing taller all the time.

Look: He looks a nice person.

Seem: He seems content.

See also BE, COMPLEMENT, VERB

copyright

Copyright can function as a noun or a verb meaning 'having the exclusive right to produce copies':

The normal copyright in Europe lasts for seventy years after the death of the artist, composer or writer.

We use the symbol © to copyright a particular work.

cor-

Cor- is a prefix, a variant of 'com-'.

See also COM-, HYPHEN, PREFIX

cord

See CHORD/CORD

cordate, cordite
See CHORDATE/CORDATE/CORDITE

co-respondent, correspondent
Whereas the spelling of 'co(-)operate' with or without a hyphen is optional, the use of a hyphen is essential in *co-respondent*. A *co-respondent*, where 'co-' rhymes with 'no', means 'a person cited in a divorce case as the spouse's partner in adultery':

Wasn't Parnell cited as the co-respondent in a famous divorce case?

A *correspondent*, with no hyphen but with '-rr-', means 'a person who writes letters or regular news reports':

I'm not a good correspondent. I prefer to talk to people on the phone.
Our foreign correspondent has filed this report.

corn, maize
In America and Australia, *corn* refers to *maize* and British people use it with this reference when they talk about 'sweet corn' or 'corn on the cob'. Britain's *maize* is America's 'corn':

UK: Maize is grown in many parts of Oklahoma.
US: Corn is grown in many parts of Oklahoma.

In Britain, *corn* is the general term for any cereal crop, including barley and maize.

corollary
See CODICIL/COROLLARY

coronary
Coronary derives from Latin *cor*, 'heart'. It can be used as an adjective to refer to the arteries leading to the heart:

His coronary arteries were blocked.

As a noun, it can be used to mean 'heart attack'. In this context, it is an abbreviated form of 'coronary thrombosis':

He had a severe pain in his left arm and side, and so the doctor thinks it was probably a coronary.

corps, corpse
A *corps* is a group or 'body' of people, often military or diplomatic:

The 6th Army Corps is made up of two divisions.
She has got a job working for the diplomatic corps.

The word comes from French *corps*, 'body'.

A *corpse* is a dead body:

I'd never seen a corpse before my visit to the morgue.

Both words derive ultimately from Latin *corpus*, 'body'.

correction, corrigendum, erratum
Correction is the general word for 'corrected error':

I've marked my corrections in red.

The two Latin words *corrigendum* and *erratum* are usually used in the plural. *Corrigenda* is a formal word for a list of corrections included in a book when there has not been the time or the opportunity to correct them in the text. *Errata* means 'errors'. They are both plural and therefore need a plural form of the verb:

The errata are given at the end of the book.
The corrigenda were integrated into the text in the second edition.

correspond
This verb has two main meanings. It can refer to 'writing letters':

We correspond once or twice a year.

It can also mean 'conform to, be consistent or compatible with':

These essays correspond so closely that they suggest collusion.

corroborate
See COLLABORATE/CORROBORATE

cortège
This French word is sometimes spelled without the grave accent. A *cortège* is a formal procession:

There were hundreds of mourners in the funeral cortège.

cortex
The plural of *cortex* is 'cortices'. The *cortex* is the outer layer of an organ and the word most frequently occurs in the collocations:

cerebral cortex (the grey matter in the brain)
renal cortex (the outer part of the kidney).

cosmetic
Cosmetic can be used as an adjective to mean both 'something designed to improve one's looks':

Cosmetic surgery is no longer limited to the rich.

and 'something that makes only a superficial improvement':

These improvements are merely cosmetic. They do not deal with the fundamental problems of our society.

Costa Rica
An inhabitant of the Central American republic is a 'Costa Rican'; the derived adjective is the same. The capital is San José.

costal
See COASTAL/COSTAL

cosy, cozy
This word, meaning 'warm and snug' is spelled with an 's' in Britain and with a 'z' in America:

UK: It was the cosiest house I'd ever been in.
US: It was the coziest house I'd ever been in.

couch, divan, settee, sofa

These words are often used as synonyms but careful speakers distinguish them. A *couch* is a long, upholstered seat with a low back and an arm at one end. A *divan* is a long, upholstered seat with no back or arms and most frequently used as a bed. A *settee* is a long, upholstered seat with a back and arms and usually with two matching armchairs. A *sofa* is virtually the same as a *settee* but usually without the matching armchairs. The word *couch* was borrowed from French, *divan* from Turkish, *settee* from older English *settle*, and *sofa* from Arabic.

See also BORROWING

could, might

These modals can often occur in the same context:

The examinations could be postponed.
The examinations might be postponed.

but there slight differences in meaning. The first tends to imply that it would be possible to postpone the examinations; the second has overtones of 'permission'.

See also MODALITY

council, counsel

These words both derive from Latin *consilium*, 'assembly'. They were in free variation in the Middle Ages but developed distinct meanings from about the sixteenth century. *Council* is a noun referring to a deliberative body of people who control a particular area of government and whose members are known as 'councillors':

She's a member of Leeds City Council.
I've just been elected to the University Council.

Council may also be used before a noun to denote a facility or service administered by a local council:

council houses
council spending.

Counsel can function as a noun and a verb meaning 'advice, advise':

We have always benefited from your wise counsel.
I must counsel you against such precipitate action.

The person performing such a function professionally is known as a 'counsellor':

You will need special training if you want to become a qualified counsellor.

In legal English the phrase *counsel for the prosecution* refers to a barrister or group of barristers engaged to conduct a court case and/or to give advice on legal matters:

I've been asked by the counsel for the prosecution to evaluate the evidence submitted by the forensic linguist.

In British English, the 'l' is doubled before '-ed' and '-ing' but it remains single in American English:

UK: counsel(s), counselled, counselling
US: counsel(s), counseled, counseling.

See also UK AND UK ENGLISH

countable and uncountable

These terms are applied to certain types of nouns. *Countable* nouns are individual items that we can easily differentiate, number and pluralize. The singular can also be prefixed by 'a':

a/one banana, two bananas, ten bananas
a/one chair, two chairs, ten chairs
a/one donkey, two donkeys, ten donkeys.

Uncountable or 'mass' nouns denote amounts that can be divided but not separated into entities that can be numbered. We do not, for example, usually count sand by the grain or milk by the drop. Examples of uncountable nouns are:

bread, furniture, sugar

Uncountable nouns may be used with 'some':

some bread, *a bread
some furniture, *a furniture
some sugar, *a sugar.

with 'the':

the bread

with a phrase equivalent to 'an amount of':

a loaf of bread
a jar of coffee
a suite of furniture
a kilo of sugar

or without an article:

I was filled with remorse.

Such nouns are treated as singular and do not normally have a plural:

The bread is delicious.
*The furnitures are not ready.

The distinction between countable and uncountable nouns is neither wholly logical (some languages treat 'hair', 'knowledge' and 'luggage' as countable nouns, whereas others treat them as uncountable) nor wholly linguistic ('news' is uncountable but 'news item' is countable). Moreover, a noun normally treated as uncountable may become countable when we refer to a variety:

a bread with no additives

or to a specified amount:

One sugar or two?
Let's have a coffee.
Two coffees and three teas, please.

See also DETERMINER, FEWER/LESS/LESSER, MASS NOUN, NOUN

counter-
Counter- is a prefix deriving from Latin *contra*, 'against'. It means 'against, contrary, opposite' and it occurs in a variety of compounds, some hyphenated:

counter-attack, counter-intelligence, counter-productive, counter-revolutionary.

countless
Many purists object to the use of *countless* where 'many' would be more appropriate:

We received countless invitations to join in.
> Sunday Times

Clearly, the meaning of countless is 'incapable of being counted' but many words in English change their meanings. 'Bye and bye' used to mean 'immediately' and 'silly' meant 'holy'.

See also SEMANTIC CHANGE

county
The term *county* is used in Britain to refer to administrative subdivisions, such as Durham or Fermanagh. In England, Scotland and Wales, the term county rarely prefaces the subdivision:

Cornwall not *County Cornwall

Clwyd not *County Clwyd

Fife not *County Fife

although 'County Durham' is used to distinguish the county from the city.

County, usually abbreviated to 'Co.', traditionally precedes the names of the Irish administrative divisions:

Co. Antrim, Co. Tyrone.

In the USA a *county* is the largest territorial division for local government within a state, and the term tends to follow the name of the division, as in:

Orange County.

coup, putsch
English has no indigenous word for 'a sudden, violent or illegal seizure of government' and uses either *coup* from French *coup d'état*, 'stroke of state', or *putsch* from Swiss German *Putsch*, 'a push'.

coup de grâce
The French word *coup* occurs in many English borrowings. *Coup* rhymes with 'who' and *grâce* with 'grass'. The phrase came into the language almost three hundred years ago and meant 'blow of mercy' or 'blow that put an opponent out of his misery'. Today, it tends to mean 'decisive stroke':

But the coup de grâce was delivered by Cantona when he drilled the second goal into the back of the net.

couple
When *couple* functions as a noun, it refers to two people who live together or associate regularly with each other:

Walter Matthau and Jack Lemmon were in *The Odd Couple*.

Couple is singular in form but, although one finds examples such as:

This couple is planning to buy our house.

it also frequently occurs with a singular determiner and a plural verb:

That couple are coming back tomorrow

Careful users of the language dislike this usage just as they dislike:

The government are voting on the referendum issue.

See also NOUN

course
See COARSE/COURSE

courtesy, curts(e)y
These nouns are occasionally confused, possibly because they are variants of the same French word. In contemporary English, *courtesy* refers to polite, respectful behaviour, as in Hilaire Belloc's verse:

Of courtesy, it is much less

Than courage of heart or holiness;

But in my walks it seems to me

That the grace of God is in courtesy.

Curts(e)y can be spelled with or without an 'e'. It refers to a female bow, usually involving bending the knees:

Women are asked to curtsey to the Queen when they are introduced.

cousin
There are relatively few English kinship terms and many of the ones we use come originally from French:

aunt, uncle, cousin, nephew, niece, grandparent.

The word *cousin* can be used on its own to refer to the children of an uncle or an aunt. It can also occur in such combinations as:

first cousin = cousin, child of one's aunt or uncle

second cousin = child of one's parent's first cousin

first cousin once removed = child of one's first cousin.

See also FAMILY RELATIONSHIP

crèche
This word rhymes with 'mesh'. It derives from

French *crèche*, 'crib', but is used in English to mean 'a day nursery for very young children':

The university offers crèche facilities for both students and staff. The crèche is staffed from 8:00 until 5:00, Mondays to Fridays. Children must be three months or more.

credence, credibility

These nouns both derive from Latin *credere*, 'to believe'. *Credence* means 'acceptance, belief' and it frequently occurs with 'give … to':

It's hard to give credence to anything they say.

Credibility refers to 'trustworthiness, the quality of being believable'. It appears often in the phrase *credibility gap*, meaning 'the disparity between claims and facts':

People use 'credibility gap' as a polite equivalent of 'lies'.

credible, credulous

These adjectives derive from Latin *credere*, 'to believe'. *Credible* means 'believable':

I know it's a strange story but it's credible.

Credulous is applied to a person who tends to believe things very easily. It is similar in meaning to 'gullible':

It's hard to believe that anyone could be so credulous! He probably believes that the moon is made of green cheese.

credo

Credo is the Latin equivalent of 'I believe'. It is used as a noun to mean 'system of belief, set of principles':

That's my credo. It may not suit anyone else but it helps me to cope.

If one uses *Credo* with a capital 'c', the reference is to the Apostle's or the Nicene Creed, the opening words of which are:

Credo in unum deum … (I believe in one God …).

creep

Creep is an irregular verb:

creep(s), crept, creeping, crept.

The noun *creep* is a slang expression for someone who is obnoxious or servile:

I can't stand him! He's a creep!

creole, Creole

A *creole* is a pidginized language adopted as a mother tongue of a speech community. In the process of becoming a mother tongue, the language is modified so as to fulfil all the linguistic needs of a specific community. We have historical evidence of the creolization of many European-related pidgins over the last five hundred years: creole Englishes are found in the Caribbean, creole Dutch in South Africa, creole French in Mauritius and creole Portuguese in the Moluccas.

The processes by which people learn the rudiments of a language not their own and are forced (by large-scale social disruption such as that caused by the Slave Trade) to pass this newly-acquired language on to their children as a mother tongue have been better documented since the fifteenth century than at any other period in the past. Nevertheless, the linguistic features associated with pidginization and creolization (such as the loss of redundancies, the dropping of inflection and concordial agreement, the exploitation of linguistic common denominators) have occurred many times in history, especially during times of conquest. The changes that became apparent in the English language in England after the Norman Conquest differ more in degree than in essence from the changes that occurred in the English of Jamaica during the period of the Slave Trade.

The noun *Creole*, with a capital 'C', is used for two main purposes: to designate a particular language:

She speaks Jamaican Creole but not the creole of Guyana.

and to designate a person, often of mixed race, especially a person from an area where a French creole is spoken:

Napoleon's wife, Josephine, was a Creole.

See also PIDGIN AND CREOLE

crescendo

Crescendo is a noun that is used in music to refer to a gradual increase in volume. It is also applied to the musical symbol that indicates this increase in sound. It has been extended to refer to an increase in noise or even to a climax:

The noise from the classroom was increasing but just as it reached its crescendo, the headmaster appeared.

Like many musical terms, *crescendo* is borrowed from Italian.

crisis

Crisis derives from Greek *krisis*, 'decision, judgement', and is used in English to mean 'a vital stage in events' or 'a turning point in a disease':

The crisis has passed. The child is now responding to treatment and the prognosis is good.

The plural is *crises*:

Life seems to be a long series of crises.

criterion

The noun *criterion* is singular and means 'standard of judgement'. The plural is *criteria* but this form is sometimes incorrectly used as a singular, as in the BBC news report:

*This criteria has been applied here and found wanting.

critic, critique

These nouns both came into English via French *critique*, 'critical art'. The earlier borrowing, *critic*, now means 'a person who writes reviews of a work':

He's a critic for *The Times*.

The meaning of *critic* has been influenced by 'criticize' and extended to anyone who comments adversely on a person or a thing:

Everybody's a critic these days! Why can't we concentrate on the positive aspects of life?

Critique has been reborrowed from French to mean 'a critical review':

I'd like you to write a 1500-word critique of the play.

critical

This adjective has three widely-used meanings. It can mean 'fault-finding':

I wish you wouldn't make so many critical comments. They are often very hurtful.

It can also be used as the derived form of 'critic' and so refer to the art of making artistic judgements:

I have to read a selection of Eliot's critical essays.

The third meaning is 'decisive, crucial':

The opportunity came at a critical point in my life.

The expression *go critical* is used of nuclear reactors:

A reactor goes critical when it reaches a state where a nuclear action can sustain itself.

Croatia

An inhabitant of the European country (formerly in Yugoslavia) is a 'Croatian'; the derived adjective is the same. The capital is Zagreb.

crochet

This word derives from French *crochié*, 'hooked', and refers to a type of handiwork involving a hooked needle:

My mother taught me to crochet.

Like 'ricochet', it rhymes with 'shay' and the past tense rhymes with 'shade' or 'hid', as in:

I've crocheted a little matinée coat.

crocus

The name of this flower derives from Latin *crocus*, 'crocus plant', 'saffron', and its plural was *croci*. This form is still found in English, but the more usual plural is 'crocuses':

I've planted more crocuses this year.

crosier, crozier

A *crosier* is a shepherd's staff with a cross on top. It derives ultimately from Latin *crux*, 'cross', and is meant to symbolize a bishop's role as the 'pastor' or 'shepherd' of his flock. Both spellings are acceptable.

crow

The verb *crow* used to be irregular:

crow(s), crew, crowing

but it is now treated as a regular verb:

The cock crowed loudly.

The only time that one is likely to meet the form 'crew' as the past tense of *crow* is in an old version of the story of Peter's betrayal of Christ:

Then began he to curse and to swear, saying, I know not the man. And immediately the cock crew.
    Matthew, 26:74

crucial

Crucial is an adjective that derives from Latin *crux*, 'cross'. It means 'decisive, critical, at the turning point':

The crucial clause in the will specifically excluded his children.

Like many adjectives, the meaning of *crucial* has been weakened so that, for many speakers, it means little more than 'important':

And now we come to the crucial point of my story ...

In British Black English, *crucial* is sometimes used as an indicator of approval:

Crucial, brother!

crumpet

The terms for bread, cakes and biscuits can differ from one part of the country to another, or from one country to another. Most people know that an English 'biscuit' is an American 'cookie' and that an American 'biscuit' is like an English 'scone'. A *crumpet* is normally described as 'a soft light yeast cake with small holes on the top', but this description could be applied to a 'pikelet'.

crux

This noun is pronounced to rhyme with 'flux'. Although it derives from the Latin word for 'cross', it now means 'a vital or decisive stage':

The crux of the matter is this.

The word is rarely used in the plural, but two plurals exist, 'cruces' and 'cruxes', the latter being the more usual.

-ct-, -x-

There is some vacillation in English spelling with regard to the use of -*x*- or -*ct*- as in:

connection, connexion
deflection, deflexion

genuflection, genuflexion
inflection, inflexion.

We cannot replace the suffix -*ct*- with its alternative -*x*- in such words as 'confection', 'election', 'reflection', 'resurrection' and 'section'. In British English the -*ct*- variant is generally the preferred form, but the -*x*- form is the only acceptable form for 'complexion' and 'crucifixion'.

See also SPELLING

Cuba

An inhabitant of the island in the West Indies is a 'Cuban'; the derived adjective is the same. The capital is Havana.

cubical, cubicle

Cubical is an adjective meaning 'shaped like a cube':

She described him as 'cubical' and I'm trying to decide whether she was referring to his figure or to his strait-laced character.

This adjective is rare outside mathematics.

Cubicle is a noun meaning 'enclosed section of a room', 'tiny room':

There were twenty-two of us in the dormitory but we each had a curtained cubicle.

cue, queue

These words are homophones.

Cue can mean 'signal to an actor':

She has missed her cue again.

This usage probably comes from the letter 'q', which was an abbreviation of Latin *quando* meaning 'when' and was written in early scripts to indicate when an actor was to perform a particular action. The word *cue* that is used in connection with billiards and snooker derives from French *queue* meaning 'tail'.

In Britain, *queue* can function as a noun meaning 'line of people':

The queues in the bank are longest on Monday.

and as a regular verb:

queue(s), queued, queuing
We queued in the rain for hours.

This word is often spelled *cue* in America.

See also UK AND US ENGLISH

cuisine

The word *cuisine* comes from French, where it means 'kitchen'. In English, it is used to refer to a style of cooking:

She's devoted to French cuisine.

and also to the food prepared by a particular restaurant or chef:

The Ritz is renowned for its cuisine.

cul-de-sac

This word derives from French, where its literal meaning is 'bottom of the bag'. It is used in English to mean 'a dead end', 'a road closed off at one end':

We're lucky to live in a cul-de-sac. We don't suffer from through traffic.

The word has two plurals, the French 'culs-de-sac' and the English 'cul-de-sacs'. The 'cul' rhymes with 'pull' or 'gull', both pronunciations being acceptable, and *sac* is a homophone of 'sack'.

See also HYPHEN

culminate

The verb *culminate* is often misused. It derives from Latin *culminare*, 'to reach the highest point', and it was used both literally and metaphorically:

The steeple culminated in a spire.

His meteoric rise culminated in a directorship at the age of thirty.

The word has been weakened by overuse so that many people think of it as a synonym for 'conclude, end, result':

The performance culminated with the playing of the National Anthem.

cultivated, cultured

These adjectives both derive from Latin *cultus*, 'cultivated, tilled' and they both suggest 'educated, refined'. *Cultivated* is often applied to behaviour ar.d accents:

Alvar Liddell had the most cultivated accent of all BBC announcers.

Cultured tends to be applied to people:

She was a highly educated, cultured woman.

and to pearls:

Cultured pearls are artificially grown.

curb, kerb

The verb *curb* means 'restrain' and comes from Latin *curvus*, 'curved', because the 'curb' or 'bit' that was put in a horse's mouth was curved:

I don't want to curb your enthusiasm but could you try to make a little less noise?

In Britain the stone edge of a pavement is called a *kerb*. This word also derives from Latin *curvus*:

The car swerved and hit the kerb.

In America *curb* is used for the pavement edge as well as the horse's bit:

The car swerved and hit the curb.

This spelling is spreading in Britain.

currant, current

A *currant*, ending in '-ant', is a small dried grape or a small fruit:

I bought currants for the cake and some lovely fresh blackcurrants for jam.

A *current*, ending in '-ent', is a mass of air, water or electricity that has a steady rate of flow in a particular direction:

The water looks inviting but there is a strong current to the left.

curriculum

A *curriculum* is a course of study:

The National Curriculum is very specific about what children are required to know at a particular age.

The plural is 'curricula', although one also finds 'curriculums':

How are teachers expected to prepare properly when they are forced to teach new curriculums each year?

Careful users dislike the plural in 's'.

curse, swear

Many speakers regard these words as synonymous, but careful speakers distinguish between them. *Curse* comes from Old English *cursian* meaning 'to curse', 'to wish evil on someone':

May he rot in hell!
May the devil take you.

And such curses have the same syntactic form as blessings:

May he rest in peace!
May the Lord keep you safe.

Swear also comes from an Old English word, *swerian*, originally meaning 'take an oath', 'calling on God to witness that what is said is true', a meaning it still has in:

I swear by Almighty God that the evidence I give will be the truth, the whole truth and nothing but the truth.

Casual swearing, when the names of heavenly beings were invoked in exclamations:

God Almighty!
Lord God!

was condemned by law in England in 1606. (Breaking the law could result in a fine of £10, which was a great deal of money in the seventeenth century.) This law had three effects on the language. First, it brought about the use of classical deities, a device used by Shakespeare and still found today in expressions like:

By Jove!
Jumping Jupiter!

Second, we find hidden swearing:

Bloody (= By Our Lady)
Drat (= God rot you).

Third, people use substitutes (often alliterating substitutes):

Crikey! (= Christ)
Gee whiz! (= Jesus).

More recently, *swearing* has taken on the

meaning of exclamations involving 'four-letter words'.

See also EUPHEMISM, EXCLAMATION, TABOO VOCABULARY

curtsey, curtsy

See COURTESY/CURTS(E)Y

customer

See CLIENT/CUSTOMER

c.v.

The abbreviation of curriculum vitae, which means 'the course of one's life', is *c.v.*, and it refers to an outline of a person's educational and professional history and is prepared as part of an application for a job:

Please include an up-to-date c.v. and the names and addresses of two referees.

The full points are usually included to distinguish between c.v. (curriculum vitae) and cv (cultivar).

See also ABBREVIATION

-cy

See -CE/-CY

cyclical

The word *cyclical*, meaning 'occurring at regular intervals', has two acceptable pronunciations of the first syllable, the first rhyming with 'bike' and the second a homophone of 'sick'.

cymbal, symbol

These homophones are occasionally confused, although there is no overlap in their meanings. A *cymbal* comes from Latin *cymbalum* 'hollow instrument' and is a percussion instrument consisting of thin circular pieces of brass, which vibrate when they are clashed together:

O the drums they bang and the cymbals clang
And the music is simply grand ...

A *symbol* means a mark or sign that represents something else, ranging from characters to mathematical symbols.

Until recently the symbol of the dagger, †, was used to indicate a footnote.

cynical, sceptical

These adjectives are often misused. *Cynical* comes from 'cynic'. The original Cynics were Greeks, who belonged to a sect founded by Antisthenes (?445–365BC) and who believed that goodness depended on self-control and on indifference to material things. In English *cynical* means 'distrustful or contemptuous of virtue' and it is usually applied to people who expect the worst of others:

He has become extremely cynical and seems to believe that all our acts are based on selfishness.

The adjective *sceptical* also derives ultimately from a Greek school of philosophy. The Sceptics believed that all our knowledge is partial and can never be anything more than this. *Sceptical* means 'doubting' and it is applied to people who doubt the authenticity of accepted beliefs:

She acknowledges that religion must be a comfort to believers, but she is sceptical of the intellectual value of any religion.

In America, 'sceptic' and its derived forms are spelled with a 'k':

skeptic, skeptical, skepticalness, skepticism.

See also SCEPTIC/SKEPTIC/SEPTIC, SPELLING

cypher
See CIPHER/CYPHER

Cyprus
An inhabitant of the Mediterranean island is a 'Cypriot'; the derived adjective is the same. The capital is Nicosia.

cyst
See CIST/CYST

czar, tsar, tzar
The title of the Russian emperors derives ultimately from Latin *Caesar*. It is spelled in several ways including *czar*, *tsar* and, less frequently, *tzar* and is pronounced to rhyme with 'bar'. *Czar* is the preferred form in America and *tsar* is generally preferred in Britain. However, both are acceptable. The form *tsar* is often preferred by scholars because it corresponds more closely to the Russian spelling in the Cyrillic alphabet.

Similar spelling problems arise with the related words 'tsarevitch' (son), 'tsarina' (wife) and 'tsarism' (system). Either 'ts-' or 'cz-' is acceptable but one should always be consistent in one's use.

Czech Republic
The noun and derived adjective are 'Czech'. The capital is Prague.

D

d
D is a consonant, pronounced 'dee'. In casual speech, it is occasionally pronounced like 'j' in words such as 'dew' and 'dune'. Careful British speakers tend to pronounce such 'd's as 'dy'.

d.
The letter 'd', sometimes italicized, is used as an abbreviation for 'died':

Charles II (d.1685) had no legitimate children.

dado
The word *dado* is used to describe the lower part of an interior wall that is decorated differently from the upper part. It is pronounced to rhyme with 'fade + oh'. Nobody is absolutely certain of the etymology of *dado* but it probably comes from an Arabic word *dad*. English borrowed it from Italian in the seventeenth century. The usual plural is 'dados' but 'dadoes' is also acceptable.

See also ARABIC INFLUENCE, BORROWING

dagger
Dagger is the name given to the symbol †, which used to occur in books as a means of indicating a cross-reference, especially to a footnote. A double dagger, ‡, was used to indicate a second such reference on a page. Numbering is now the acceptable method of indicating both endnotes and footnotes.

dahlia
A *dahlia* is a perennial tuberous plant called after the Swedish botanist Anders Dahl (1751–89). It is pronounced to rhyme with 'regalia'.

daily, diurnal
These adjectives both relate to the noun 'day'. *Daily* means occurring every day:

The milk is delivered daily.

Diurnal tends to refer to the entire day and to be used in contrast to 'nocturnal':

A badger is not a diurnal animal, is it?

The noun *daily* is often used of a newspaper that is published on weekdays or, colloquially in Britain, of someone who helps with housework:

I don't get a daily but I often buy a Sunday paper.

She was their daily for five years, and when she left, they realized how much housework she had been doing for them.

dairy, diary
There is no logical link between these words except that they are often confused when misspelled. A *dairy* is a place where milk products are produced and sold:

I get my milk and cheese directly from the dairy.

A *diary* is a personal record of events:

He's kept a diary since the beginning of his political career.

dais
A *dais* is a raised platform used by public speakers:

I thought it was only a simple talk. I didn't realize that you'd want me to stand on a dais and speak to 300 students!

The word is usually pronounced as disyllabic, to rhyme with 'day + iss', but it is occasionally pronounced as monosyllabic, rhyming with 'lace'.

damage, injury
Generally, if there is a car crash, a car is *damaged* but a person is *injured*:

The dead and injured were carried to the hard shoulder but the damaged vehicles could not be removed until daylight.

We can, however, use *damaged* for part of the body:

Most rugby players damage their collar bones.

I've damaged my knee ligaments.

Colloquially, *damage* can be used to mean 'cost':

What's the damage for the meal?

dangling phrase or clause
A phrase or clause is described as *dangling* or 'hanging' when it is inappropriately attached to a word, or when it is not related structurally to any part of the sentence. The clause 'because they are deadly poisonous' in:

Pesticides should be locked away when there are children about because they are deadly poisonous.

refers logically to 'pesticides' but its position suggests that it applies to 'children'.

The effects of such phrases and clauses may be ambiguous, comic or, in some instances, colloquially acceptable.

Ambiguous
In a sentence such as:

Walking through the woods I saw a strange man.

the group of words 'walking through the woods' modifies 'I', but if the order is changed to:

I saw a strange man walking through the woods.

the group is called a 'dangling modifier' because

it is unclear whether it modifies 'I' or 'strange man'. There is similar ambiguity in the following sentence, which occurred in a news bulletin:

He said that industry was bleeding to death in a debate calling for tougher measures.

Comic

Sometimes, the implications of a dangling modifier are absurd:

I saw the little cottage walking through the woods.
He walked on his head in the air.

Colloquially acceptable

Some dangling modifiers such as the following, are colloquially acceptable:

Assuming that there are no interruptions, the job shouldn't take long.
Knowing her generosity, the gift was not surprising.
Roughly speaking, the house is about five miles away.

These modifiers all 'dangle'. 'Assuming' does not modify 'the job', nor does 'knowing' modify 'the gift'. However, these constructions, and others like them, are distinguished from the ambiguous and comic examples by the facts that their verbs involve estimation, perception or mental processes and the dangling sections all imply a first-person subject.

The essential rule is to use modification carefully, ensuring that there is no chance of misinterpretation.

See also FILLER, INFINITIVE, -ING FORM, MODIFIER, PARTICIPLE

dare

The verb *dare* has three different meanings. It can mean 'challenge someone to do something':

I dare you to dive in backwards.

In this usage, *dare* is a regular verb:

dare(s), dared, daring, dared.

It can also mean 'be courageous enough to do something':

I wouldn't dare climb that tree.

and it can mean 'be cheeky enough to do something':

He dared to say it in front of the entire class!

When *dare* is used with these meanings, it can be followed by the infinitive with or without the 'to':

I didn't dare to do it.
I didn't dare do it.

It also acts like a modal verb in being able to form questions and negatives without the use of an auxiliary verb:

Dare I go? Do I want to go?
I daren't do it! I didn't want to do it.

Increasingly, however, *dare* is being regularized:

Do I dare?
I don't dare!

The expression 'I dare say' is often used to suggest that the speaker thinks that a particular outcome is probable:

I dare say he'll win.

This structure is limited to the subject 'I' and the two verbs are often written as one word:

Has he come back yet? I daresay he has.

See also MODALITY, QUASI-MODAL, VERB

dash

A *dash* is a punctuation mark that is longer than a hyphen. Single dashes are used to indicate an explanation or expansion:

We ordered fruit – apples, bananas and cherries.

to emphasize a point:

This was a tragedy – a modern tragedy.

to indicate disjointed speech or thought:

Will you – will he …

to show that letters have been omitted:

Bl—y cheek!

and to indicate a link between dates, pages, teams and similarly linked items:

the 1914–1918 war
The details are on pp. 16–24.
I missed the Manchester–Newcastle match.

A pair of dashes can be used as an alternative to brackets or a pair of commas:

The question – if it was a question – is unhelpful.
The question (if it was a question) is unhelpful.
The question, if it was a question, is unhelpful.

See also PUNCTUATION

data

The Latin singular *datum*, 'something given', means 'one piece of given information'. It occurs rarely in this form. Instead, the plural form *data* is used with plural agreement in the USA:

These data were not easy to obtain.

Increasingly in Britain, especially in speech, *data* is used as a collective noun with singular determiners and a singular form of the verb:

This data suggests that further research is required.
This computer data is confidential.

See also COLLECTIVE NOUN, DETERMINER, NOUN

date

British and American conventions differ slightly in the preferred method of writing dates, although we find some overlap:

UK	US
1st April, 1999	April 1, 1999
1 April, 1999	1 April 1999
1 April 1999	

The following rules apply:

- A form with commas can be used when the full date is written within a sentence:

She planned to leave on 1 April, 1999.

although many people prefer:

She planned to leave on 1 April 1999.

- When the day of the week is added, another comma is used:

She planned to leave on Monday, 1 April, 1999.

- When only the month and year are used, the month is usually followed by a comma but this is not obligatory:

She planned to leave in April(,) 1999.

- Except in formal and legal documents, the day and year are usually expressed in Arabic numerals.

- In business letters, months with more than four letters are sometimes abbreviated:

1 Apr, 1999.

- When the complete date is given in numbers, the conventions are:

UK	US
1.4.1999	4.1.1999
1.iv.99	4.i.99
1/4/99	4/1/99

- When dates are spoken or read aloud, they should be:

the first of April nineteen ninety-nine

or:

April first nineteen ninety-nine.

- Years and centuries should be written as follows:

59BC
AD432
the 1990s
the nineties
between 1066 and 1312
from 1997 to 2003
twentieth-century verse
the sixteenth century.

datum

Datum is part of the Latin verb meaning 'give':

do, dare, dedi, datum.

In English, *datum* is used as a noun meaning 'one given piece of information'.

See also DATA

day

The English noun *day* is cognate with German *Tag* and Latin *dies*. It combines freely, sometimes with and sometimes without hyphens:

daybreak, day-dream, day return.

See also COMPOUND, HYPHEN, NIGHT

DC
See AC/DC

de

The usual convention for writing *de* as part of a person's name is not to use a capital letter unless the *de* occurs as the first word in a sentence:

Guy de Maupassant
De Maupassant was highly regarded.

However, some English people of French descent prefer to use a capital letter for De, and we should follow the style preferred by the individual.

de-

The prefix *de-* comes from Latin. It is most frequently used in the formation of verbs and verbal derivatives and has a wide range of meanings in English, including removal:

de + forest = deforest
de + throne = dethrone

reversal:

de + brief = debrief
de + construct = deconstruct

and departure from:

de + camp = decamp
de + train = detrain.

The prefix also occurs in words of Latin origin, including:

deceive, defect, deter.

de la

In names such as 'de La Fontaine', practices vary for capital letters:

Delacroix
De la Mare
De La Ware.

As with the use of DE, the wishes of the person whose name it is should be followed.

de rigueur

The French phrase literally means 'of strict- ness' and it is usually italicized in English, where it means 'required by etiquette':

A straw boater used to be *de rigueur* at Henley.

de trop

The French phrase *de trop* is often written in italics. It literally means 'of too much' and is used in English as an emphatic way of describing something that is unwanted or superfluous:

I can't stand any more humour. We've had comedy *de trop*.

Some speakers do not like French phrases in English and they should never be used to impress or confuse. Some are, however, often difficult to avoid.

deacon

The noun *deacon* has different meanings in different churches. In the Roman Catholic Church, a *deacon* is an ordained minister who can perform some, but not all, of the duties of a priest. In certain Protestant churches, a *deacon* is a lay person who assists the minister, often in secular matters. It is no longer usual to refer to a female *deacon* as a 'deaconess'.

The office of a deacon is referred to as a 'diaconate'.

deadly, deathly

These words both derive ultimately from Old English *diegan*, 'to die'. *Deadly* implies 'likely to cause death, either of the body or the soul':

Many household products contain deadly poisons.

The Seven Deadly Sins are Pride, Avarice, Lust, Envy, Gluttony, Anger and Sloth. They make up the acronym 'pale gas'.

In colloquial speech, *deadly* suggests 'boring':

The lecture was deadly. Most of us dozed off after a few moments.

Deathly implies 'resembling death':

She turned a deathly white.

deal

Deal is a slightly irregular verb:

deal(s), dealt, dealing, dealt.

We tend to *deal* in commodities:

I believe he deals in silver.

and we *deal* with people:

I enjoy dealing with clients from other parts of Europe.

dear, dearly

Dear can function as an adjective meaning 'loved' or 'expensive':

He's a dear and trusted friend.

Fruit is dear at this time of the year.

Dear is used adverbially in the expression 'cost dear':

That single act of stupidity has cost me dear.

For some speakers 'pay dear' is also acceptable as in:

You'll pay dear for that act of vanity!

but careful users of English dislike this usage.

Dearly is an adverb meaning 'much loved', 'very much' and 'costly':

Dearly beloved brethren

I would dearly love to own a sports car!

I paid dearly for my indiscretion.

Many careful users prefer to use *dearly* and not *dear* in all adverbial positions.

death

Death and serious illness have often been regarded as taboo subjects and so there are many euphemisms for 'death':

passing away, passing over, departed.

See also EUPHEMISM, TABOO VOCABULARY

deathly

See DEADLY/DEATHLY

debacle

Debacle is usually written without accents in English although it is often pronounced in the French way, *débâcle*, with the first two syllables rhyming with 'day + baa'. It means a sudden, disastrous failure:

It was a complete and utter debacle in spite of all our efforts. We failed miserably.

debar, disbar

These verbs are occasionally confused. *Debar* is usually followed by 'from' and means 'exclude from, prevent':

His earlier activities were used as an excuse for debarring him from the club.

Disbar means 'expel a lawyer from the Bar, deprive someone of the status of barrister':

It is still relatively unusual for a barrister to be formally disbarred.

debatable

This word has two acceptable spellings, *debatable* and *debateable*.

See also -ABLE/-IBLE, SPELLING

debauch, debouch

Debauch comes from an Old French verb *desbaucher*, which literally meant 'shape timber roughly'. Today it means 'lead someone into a life of depravity':

Television has been accused of everything including debauching the youth of the country!

It is most frequently used adjectivally in such structures as:

He led a debauched life.

Debouch is ultimately from French *bouche*, 'mouth'. It rhymes with 'vouch' and means 'flow from a valley into a larger area' or 'move from a confined space into a larger one':

The troops debouched from the narrow canyon where they had been lying in wait for the enemy.

debit

Debit comes from Latin *debitum*, 'a debt'. It can function as a noun or verb:

I don't understand this debit in my account.

You have incorrectly debited my account.

The 't' is not doubled before endings:

debit(s), debited, debiting.

See also SPELLING

debris

The noun *debris* comes from an obsolete French verb *débrisier*, 'to break into small pieces'. In English, it means 'rubble, fragments of something broken':

The debris from the bomb blast covered an area of seven square miles.

People are often unsure how *debris* should be pronounced. British people tend to put the stress on the first syllable and to pronounce the '-e-' as either the sound of 'e' in 'get' or as the vowel sound in 'hay'. Americans often stress the second syllable and this pronunciation is also heard in Britain.

debug

This verb was first used in America to mean 'remove insects from':

People do not always appreciate the value of bugs and would willingly debug the region if they possibly could.

It has been extended to mean 'locate and remove hidden microphones':

He would not use his phone even after his room had been debugged.

and 'to remove defects from computer software':

I don't buy new software until it has been on the market for a year or two and I can be sure that it has been thoroughly debugged.

debut

A *debut* means 'a first appearance':

She made her debut in the 1985 production of Friel's *Translations*.

Like DEBRIS, the first syllable has two acceptable pronunciations. It may be pronounced with the vowel sound that we have in 'get' or 'day'.

dec(a)-

The prefix *dec(a)-* comes from Greek *deka* and denotes 'ten':

decade = period of ten consecutive years
decagon = ten-sided figure
decalogue = ten commandments
decapod = crustacean with ten limbs.

When *deca-* is used in the metric system, it means 'ten times':

UK: decametre = ten metres
US: decameter = ten meters

whereas *deci-* means 'one tenth of':

UK: decimetre = one-tenth of a metre
US: decimeter = one-tenth of a meter.

See also DECI-

decade

A *decade* means a period of ten consecutive years. The usual pronunciation stresses the first syllable, which is a homophone of 'deck'. Many people now stress the second syllable and make no distinction between *decade* and 'decayed'.

deceitful, deceptive

These adjectives both derive from 'deceive' and they are occasionally confused. *Deceitful* implies intentional misleading or misrepresentation:

The trouble with this type of deceitful behaviour is that it is often hard to spot.

Deceptive, on the other hand, may apply to unintentional misleading:

Appearances can be deceptive.

deceive

Deceive is a regular verb that is frequently misspelled:

deceive(s), deceived, deceiving.

It follows a traditional spelling rule: 'i' before 'e' except after 'c'.

See also SPELLING

decent, descent, dissent

These words are occasionally confused. *Decent* is an adjective meaning 'respectable', 'proper', 'suitable', 'fitting':

She is a thoroughly decent human being.
We must leave a decent interval before advertising his post.

Descent is a noun meaning 'the act of going down'. It has an 's' before the 'c':

Climbers often say that the descent can be as hazardous as the climb.

Dissent is a homophone of *descent* and means 'disagree', 'disagreement':

We rarely had this amount of dissent before Jay joined the firm.

See also SPELLING

deceptively

This adverb is very widely used and misused in the popular press and in house advertisements. It means 'misleadingly' and so:

a deceptively fit person = a person who is not fit
a deceptively large room = a room that is not large.

Many people use *deceptively* to suggest 'contrary to appearances', 'surprisingly':

The French windows give access to a deceptively large rose garden. [Actual dimensions 2 x 2.4 metres]

deci-

Deci- is a prefix meaning 'one tenth'. It comes

from Latin *decimus* 'tenth' and occurs in a variety of words including:

decimal = relating to powers of ten

decimate = kill one in every ten

decimetre = one tenth of a metre.

See also DEC(A)-

decided, decisive

These adjectives both derive from the verb 'decide' meaning 'to determine', 'settle' but they have developed distinct usages. *Decided* means 'unmistakable' or 'definite':

She is a decided asset to the team.

She's a lady with very decided views on politics.

Decisive means 'capable of making decisions quickly, influential':

He is intelligent, industrious and capable of decisive action.

decidedly, decisively

These adverbs are, like their adjective counterparts, distinct in meaning. *Decidedly* means 'definitely, without doubt':

She has decidedly clear views on the subject.

Decisively means 'conclusively, without hesitation':

We must act decisively to end these rumours.

decimate

Decimate comes from Latin *decimare* and means 'reduce by one tenth'. Originally it applied to the practice of punishing troops for cowardice or mutiny by killing every tenth man. The word was generalized to mean the reduction by a tenth of anything countable, from parrots to profits:

The parrot population could be decimated if the disease spreads.

Decimate is now often used loosely as an emphatic and emotive word for the destruction of a large proportion of something:

The population of Sarajevo has been decimated. Every family has been touched by death.

Many people dislike this usage but, in a world where Latin is rarely learnt, the etymology is no longer apparent.

declarative

The word *declarative* comes from Latin *declarare*, 'to make clear'. In traditional grammar, sentences were often categorized as *declarative*, IMPERATIVE and INTERROGATIVE:

Declarative

She went home yesterday.

She didn't go home yesterday.

Imperative

Go home.

Don't go home.

Interrogative

Did she go home?

Did she not go home?

decline

The word *decline* can function as a noun or a verb:

The recent decline in our market position must be reversed.

I declined their invitation.

Decline is used in grammar to mean 'list the inflections of a noun, pronoun or adjective':

The first Latin noun I ever learned to decline was *mensa*, 'a table'.

We *decline* nouns and we conjugate verbs. A list of noun inflections is called a 'declension'.

décor

The noun *décor* comes from French *décorer*, 'to decorate'. It is used to mean 'a style or scheme of interior decoration':

Have you seen their new décor? Tony called it 'Buy-a-style' but I thought it was warm and tasteful.

The word is normally written with an acute accent and is stressed on the first syllable, which is pronounced like 'day'.

decorative, decorous

These adjectives are occasionally confused. *Decorative* derives from 'decorate' and means 'ornamental, serving to decorate':

I suggest that we use a decorative border on this wall, to mirror the staircase.

Decorous comes from Latin *decorus*, 'elegant', and means 'characterized by propriety':

The word 'decorous' is becoming obsolete in English because the virtues associated with 'decorum' are no longer prized in our society.

decry

This verb is not used often in contemporary English, a fact that accounts for its misuse when it does occur. *Decry* means 'disparage, express open disapproval of':

Jonathan Swift decried the debasement of the coinage in 'A Drapier's Letters'.

The opposition spent most of their time decrying the feeble achievements of the government.

deduce, deduct

These verbs both derive from Latin *deducere*, 'to lead away, derive'. *Deduce* means 'reach a conclusion by reasoning, infer':

Would it be reasonable to deduce from your c.v. that you are becoming increasingly interested in English Language teaching?

Deduct means 'take away':

There won't be much left when we deduct all our costs.

defecate

This verb comes from Latin *defaecere*, 'to cleanse from dregs'. (Latin *faex* meant 'dregs, sediment'.) It is normally used in English to mean 'discharge waste from the bowels' although it is occasionally used also to mean 'clarify or remove impurities from a solution'. The verb is spelled *defecate*, but the related noun continues to be spelled 'faeces' in British English.

defect

Defect comes from Latin *deficere*, 'to fail', 'to forsake'. As a noun, it means 'lack', 'deficiency', 'imperfection':

There's a defect in my braking system. I have to pump the brake twice before it responds.

As a verb *defect* means 'leave one's country or cause in order to join another with very different ideals':

Several Russian ballet dancers defected to the West.

defective, deficient

These adjectives both derive ultimately from Latin *deficere*, 'to fail', 'to forsake', but they now have distinct meanings. *Defective* means 'faulty', 'having a flaw':

My car failed its MOT because the brakes were defective.

Deficient means 'lacking, incomplete':

Parents are advised to ensure that their children's diet is not deficient in iron. Beef, sausages, red meat, spinach and wholemeal bread are rich in iron.

defence, defense

These alternative spellings of the noun meaning 'protection', 'shelter' or 'justification' derive from Latin *defendere*, 'to defend':

UK: I was advised that I had no defence against such a claim.

US: I was advised that I had no defense against such a claim.

In both countries, the adjectives 'defensible' and 'defensive' are spelled with 's'.

See also SPELLING

defer

There are two verbs *defer*, which are identical in form but different in meaning:

defer(s), deferred, deferring.

One verb comes from Old French *differer*, 'to be different', 'to postpone', and means 'delay, postpone':

We may have to defer the interviews until a new chairman has been chosen.

The other *defer* comes from Latin *deferre*, 'to bear down'. It means 'yield', 'comply with the wishes

of someone else'. This *defer* is always followed by 'to':

I must defer to your superior knowledge in this field.

The derived forms are:

deferential (-r-): His behaviour was deferential.
deferment (-r-): The deferment was unavoidable.
deferral (-rr-): The deferral is temporary.
deferred (-rr-): She bought a deferred annuity.

See also SPELLING

deficient

See DEFECTIVE/DEFICIENT

defining relative clause

Relative clauses are subdivided into *defining relative clauses* and non-defining relative clauses. In general, a *defining clause* limits and reduces the applicability of the noun it modifies. In the following sentence, for example:

The children who do not eat red meat may have to supplement their iron intake.

we are referring only to the children who do not eat red meat. A non-defining clause extends our knowledge of the antecedent so that the sentence:

The children, who do not eat red meat, may have to supplement their iron intake.

refers to all of the children, implying that none of them eats red meat.

Defining clauses are not separated from their antecedents by commas and, in the spoken medium, the main and the defining clause constitute one tone group. Non-defining relative clauses are marked off in the written medium by punctuation – commas, dashes or parentheses. In speech, such sentences would have two tone groups and pauses equivalent to the punctuation marks. A non-defining clause may be deleted without fundamentally altering the meaning and implication of the antecedent.

The distinction between defining and non-defining clauses is a significant one. The distinctions made by such clauses are carried by punctuation in the written medium and by intonation in speech.

See also ANTECEDENT, CLAUSE, THAT/WHICH

definite, definitive

These adjectives both derive from 'define', but they now have distinct meanings. *Definite* means 'certain', 'exact', 'precise':

He has very definite views on the value of teaching foreign languages in primary schools.

Definitive means 'authoritative', 'final':

There can never be a definitive book on English as long as it remains a living, changing language, but this one comes close.

definite article

English has two articles: a *definite* article 'the' and an indefinite article 'a/an':

Once upon a time there was a wicked witch. The witch lived in the middle of a large forest.

See also A/AN, DETERMINER, THE

definitely

Many adverbs, such as ACTUALLY, *definitely* and REALLY are overused:

I'm definitely going to buy that CD if I can.

is little more emphatic that:

I'm going to buy that CD if I can.

Emphatic adverbs should be reserved for occasions when emphasis is required.

definition

All definitions involving language are circular, a fact that is quickly ascertained if we look up any word in a dictionary. If we want to know the meaning of 'gibberish', for example, and use *The Concise Oxford Dictionary*, we are told that 'gibberish' is:

Unintelligible speech, meaningless sounds, jargon, blundering or ungrammatical talk.

If we seek further clarification we find that 'jargon' is defined as:

Unintelligible words, gibberish ...

See also DICTIONARY

deflection, deflexion

The noun *deflection* has an alternative form 'deflexion', although the '-x-' variant is not widely used in either Britain or the United States.

See also -CT-/-X-

defuse, diffuse

Defuse is a verb that means 'remove the triggering device from a bomb', and it has been extended metaphorically to mean 'remove the cause of tension or friction':

One cannot overestimate the courage of the soldiers who regularly defuse the mines that litter Bosnia.

I thought that the meeting would break up in chaos but the chairman quietly defused the situation.

Occasionally, this verb is spelled *defuze* in America. The first syllable is usually pronounced to rhyme with 'bee' in both countries.

Diffuse can be a verb and an adjective. The ending of the verb is pronounced /z/ whereas the adjective ending is /s/. *Diffuse* means 'scatter', 'disseminate', 'disperse':

The light was diffused over a wide area.

The adjective is used more frequently than the verb and means 'lacking conciseness or focus':

That was the most diffuse talk I'd ever had the misfortune to attend!

degree

The term *degree* is applied to adjectives and adverbs because they can occur in three different forms or 'degrees': positive, comparative and superlative:

Positive	Comparative	Superlative
awful	more awful	most awful
fast	faster	fastest
good	better	best
stupidly	more stupidly	most stupidly

Occasionally, the constructions:

as awful as
as fast as
less good than
less stupidly than

are included in discussions of degree, the first described as 'equative', the second as 'negative comparison'.

See also ADJECTIVE, ADVERB

degrees

Academic *degrees* are normally given after a person's name only in formal circumstances directly connected with an individual's academic or professional activities.

The conventions for indicating degrees are:

John Brown, BA (A.B. if the degree is from Harvard)
Mary Jones, Ph.D.
J. Smith, BA (London), MA (Leeds), PhD (Texas)
Dr Mary Brown

The title 'doctor' and the degree are mutually exclusive and so the following should not be used:

*Dr Mary Jones, PhD

In the past, full stops were regularly used in the marking of degrees:

B.A.

but these full stops are regularly dropped, especially in Britain.

See also ABBREVIATION

deity

Many people use *deity* as a means of referring to God or divine beings, whether male or female. The word comes from Latin *deus*, 'God':

We cannot with our human intellect comprehend the infinite wisdom of the deity.

There are two widely-used and acceptable pronunciations of this word. The first pronounces 'de-' as if it were 'day'; the second pronounces 'de-' to rhyme with 'bee'.

deixis

The term *deixis* is used as a shorthand expression for words and phrases relating to place and time. It can thus refer to:

- Adverbs such as 'here', 'now'

- Anaphoric reference such as 'the former', 'the latter'

- Demonstratives such as 'this', 'that', 'these', 'those'

- Pronouns such as 'we', 'you'

- Verbs such as 'bring/take', 'come/go'.

The word derives ultimately from Greek *deiknunai*, 'to show', 'point out', and is related in form and meaning to 'index' as in 'index finger'. The unit that carries *deixis* is called a 'deictic'.

See also ANAPHORA

déjà vu

This widely-used French expression literally means 'already seen' but refers to the sensation of perceiving something new as if it had occurred before. It is normally italicized and written with both accent marks:

I can't explain it. Perhaps it's *déjà vu* but I could swear I've been in this house before.

The usual pronunciation rhymes the phrase with 'say ya too'.

deletion

Certain items can be deleted from sentences without interfering with the grammatical acceptability of the structure:

The (beautiful) girl ran towards me (quickly) and (she) asked me the way.

The items that can be deleted are adjectives, adverbs and coordinating conjunctions. In addition, shared constituents of compound phrases, clauses and sentences can be deleted:

my mother and my father: my mother and father

That's the book that we bought and that we paid £5 for: That's the book we bought and paid £5 for

She was tall; she was clever; and she was happy: She was tall, clever and happy.

delicatessen

This word, which is borrowed from German *Delikatessen*, is frequently applied to a shop that sells various foods already prepared and cooked:

I haven't the time to cook so I'll get a quiche and some salads from the delicatessen.

The word is often misspelled, a fact that may account for its being abbreviated to deli:

I haven't the time to cook so I'll get a quiche and some salads from the deli.

delimit

Delimit means 'demarcate', 'mark off the boundaries':

Our potential is clear; our commitment is absolute; our achievements will be delimited only by financial constraints.

The derived noun is 'delimitation' and this has given rise, by back formation, to an alternative verb form 'delimitate'. Many people dislike this form but its use continues to grow.

delineate

The verb *delineate* means 'sketch, outline, represent'. The derived adjective is 'delineable', not *delineatable:

Shakespeare found Cleopatra's beauty hard to delineate.

Her beauty was not delineable.

deliverance

This word is rarely used outside liturgical circles:

The deliverance of his soul from the snares of Satan is due entirely to the prayers of the faithful.

The word ends in '-ance', not '-ence'.

delusion

See ALLUSION/DELUSION/ILLUSION

delve, dig

Delve derives from the Old English verb *delfan*, 'dig', but has been replaced by a later verb *diggen*. *Delve* survives in the dyad 'dig and delve' and in the verse attributed to John Ball, who took part in the Peasant's Revolt and was executed in 1381:

When Adam delve and Eve span
Who was then the gentleman?

Dig is an irregular verb:

dig(s), dug, digging, dug.

It is one of the few verbs in the language that used to be regular, having 'digged' as its past tense.

The noun 'digs' meaning 'rented lodgings' is almost exclusively British.

demarcation

This noun, which means 'establishing the boundaries', is occasionally spelled 'demarkation' because of the influence of 'mark'. Many people dislike the '-k-' spelling.

demean

The verb *demean* means 'humble or debase oneself':

I would not demean myself by asking for their help.

demeanour, demeanor

The noun *demeanour* has a 'u' in British spelling but not in American. It means 'conduct, the way a person behaves':

One could see from his demeanour that he was totally at peace with himself and the world.

Demeanour does not derive from 'demean', as in

the previous entry, but from an Old French verb *demener*, 'to lead', 'to drive'.

demi-

Demi- is a prefix meaning 'half'. It derives from Latin *dimidius*, 'half', and is semantically linked with HEMI- as in 'hemisphere' and SEMI- as in 'semi-quaver'. *Demi-* is no longer a productive prefix but occurs in such words as:

demigod (part god, part mortal)

demimonde (social group that is not totally respectable; i.e., half in and half out of polite society)

demitasse (small cup).

demise

The noun *demise* is used only in formal circumstances. It derives ultimately from Latin *demittere*, 'to send away'. It is used formally and euphemistically for 'death':

We have all been affected – deeply affected – by the demise of our friend and colleague.

It is most widely used now to mean 'termination, failure':

We must accept that this response marks the demise of our hopes and aspirations.

demon

The noun *demon* comes ultimately from Greek *daimon*, 'spirit, deity'. This spelling has become associated with 'evil spirit' or 'devil' whereas the variant spellings *daemon* and, less often, *daimon* are used for 'mythological spirit'.

demonstrable, demonstrative

The adjective *demonstrable* derives from the verb 'demonstrate' and means 'capable of proof or demonstration':

Their demonstrable courage is being honoured today.

The word is now almost universally stressed on the second syllable, but many argue that it ought to be stressed on the first syllable. Both pronunciations are acceptable.

The other adjective derived from 'demonstrate' is *demonstrative*, which means 'tending to express one's feelings easily and overtly':

She's a demonstrative child. I wish I could show my feelings as easily.

demonstrative

The word *demonstrative* is used as a noun to refer to the words 'this', 'that', 'these' and 'those', which can be used as determiners:

this book

that child

these books

those children

and as pronouns:

This is the answer.

That is a problem.

These are my children.

Those were very expensive.

'This' and 'these' imply proximity to the speaker while 'that' and 'those' imply distance from the speaker. None of the demonstratives is marked with regard to closeness or distance from the listener. English used to have a tripartite system with 'yon' implying distance from both speaker and listener (and paralleling 'yonder' in spatial orientation), but for most contemporary users of the language 'yon' and 'yonder' are archaic or regional.

See also DEIXIS

demur, demure

These words are occasionally misspelled. *Demur* is a regular verb, meaning 'hesitate', 'show reluctance':

demur(s), demurred, demurring

They went along with most of the schemes but demurred at the thought of doing anything illegal.

Demure is an adjective meaning 'sedate', 'modest', 'reserved':

Come pensive nun, devout and pure,

Sober, steadfast and demure.

John Milton, 'Il Penseroso'

denizen

This noun means 'inhabitant' but is now rarely used except in the clichés:

denizens of the deep

denizens of the woods.

Denmark

An inhabitant of the European country is a 'Dane'; the derived adjective is 'Danish'. The capital is Copenhagen.

denotation

A word's *denotation* is its referential meaning, as distinct from its emotional, social or regional associations. For example, the word 'immigrant' may be defined referentially as a person who comes into a country of which he/she is not a native with the intention of permanent residence. This is the kind of denotative information given in most dictionaries. However, the word 'immigrant' may also carry a range of emotional implications (such as colour, poverty) that vary according to personal experience, location and political or social attitudes. The additional associations are not the *denotation* but the connotations of the word.

Few words are exclusively denotative. Even scientific or technical words may arouse strong feelings, as is clear from such words as:

chromosome
ecology
inter-continental ballistics.

See also CONNOTATION, STILE/STYLE, SYNONYM

dénouement

The noun *dénouement* is used in English with or without the acute accent to refer to the clarification or resolution of a plot in a work of literature. It derives from French *dénouer*, 'untie a knot':

I've always enjoyed the dénouement in a Jane Austen novel. It always seems so natural, so uncontrived.

deny, refute

There is an overlap of meaning between these verbs. *Deny* means 'declare that something is untrue', 'reject as false':

My client totally denies any complicity in the crime.

I denied the charge that I had stolen the cheque but I could not refute it because I had no proof.

Refute is a regular verb meaning 'prove that something is untrue':

refute(s), refuted, refuting

We have refuted all accusations against my client. He leaves court today with an unblemished character.

I was able to refute all the allegations laid against me.

dependant, dependent

Dependant is a noun referring to a person who depends on someone else for food and shelter:

I have two dependants: my daughter and son.

Dependent is an adjective with a related meaning:

Babies are totally dependent on the care of their parents.

There is a growing tendency, partly inspired by American English, for the spelling *dependent* to be used for the noun as well as the adjective, and it seems likely that the distinction between noun and adjective will gradually be lost.

See also -ANT/-ENT

dependent

The term *dependent* is used in sentence analysis to refer to clauses other than the main clause. It is synonymous and in free variation with 'subordinate'. In a sentence such as:

I heard what you said.

the clause 'what you said' may be described as either 'dependent' or 'subordinate'.

Dependent clauses, as their name implies, cannot

occur independently but rely structurally on another unit in a sentence. The term 'embedded sentence' is also used as a synonym for 'dependent clause', especially in modern grammars.

See also CLAUSE, EMBEDDING, GRAMMAR, SUBORDINATION

deplete, reduce

These verbs are similar in meaning but are not synonymous. *Deplete* means 'empty, use up almost completely':

We'll have to go shopping tomorrow. We've depleted the food stock.

Reduce is a regular verb meaning 'lessen' but not necessarily exhaust:

reduce(s), reduced, reducing

We have reduced the risk of road accidents but we can never entirely eliminate risk.

The adjective is 'reducible', ending in '-ible'. The phrase 'reduced circumstances' is sometimes used as a euphemistic or genteel equivalent of 'impoverished':

We found them living in very reduced circumstances.

See also -ABLE/-IBLE

deploy

The verb *deploy* was originally an exclusively military term meaning 'adopt a battle formation, distribute forces to or within a particular area':

After the formal agreement, British forces were deployed in the Sarajevo area.

The verb became popular in the 1980s in relation to acts of civil disobedience:

More women have recently been deployed to Greenham Common.

Greenpeace volunteers are being deployed to every whaling port.

depot

In Britain a *depot* refers to a warehouse or a building for servicing buses. It is pronounced to rhyme with 'pep + oh':

Turn left at the bus depot.

In America, it usually rhymes with 'peep oh' and is also used for a railway station:

She is now the manager at the Buffalo train depot.

deprecate, depreciate

These verbs are occasionally confused, although their meanings should be distinguished. *Deprecate* comes from Late Latin *deprecari*, 'to avert, ward off by prayer', and means 'express disapproval of':

We wrote to the Vice-Chancellor to deprecate the university's intention to sell off greenfield sites for commercial development.

Depreciate comes from Latin *depretiare*, 'to

lower the price of', and can mean both 'fall in value' and 'lessen the value of by criticism':

Sterling has depreciated 15 per cent over the last five years.

I do not mean to depreciate your efforts. You did your best, I'm sure, but your best was not good enough.

deprived

The adjective *deprived* has undergone a change of meaning in the late twentieth century. It originally meant that something had been taken away from someone or something:

This area of Dublin was once the wealthiest part of the city. Then it became a deprived section. It is now highly sought after by the upwardly mobile.

Now, *deprived* tends to be used as a synonym for 'very poor':

This is one of the most deprived areas on earth. The average annual income is less than £12.

derisive, derisory

These adjectives both derive from Latin *deridere*, 'to laugh', 'to scorn'. *Derisive* means 'mocking, scornful' and it frequently co-occurs with 'laughter':

My effort wasn't good but it didn't deserve to be treated in such a derisive way.

Derisory has come to mean 'so small that it is laughable':

We were offered the derisory increase of 2 per cent but there were strings attached. The 2 per cent would not be phased in until October and had to be paid for by productivity.

derivation

Derivation is a type of word formation involving the use of affixes:

man

man + ly = manly

un + man + ly = unmanly.

Thus 'manly' and 'unmanly' are derivations of 'man'.

The word *derivation* is also used in the study of the relationships between languages or between one stage of a language and another. Many words in English, for example, derive from French; and modern English 'duck' derives from Old English *duce*.

See also AFFIX, BASE FORM

descendant, descendent

Only *descendant*, ending in '-ant', is widely used. It means 'a person, animal or plant that is in a direct line of development from an older form':

The Duke of Edinburgh is a descendant of Queen Victoria.

Our modern horse is thought to be a descendant of an animal that was the size of a modern terrier.

Descendent is virtually obsolete but means 'coming or going downwards':

The experienced climbers chose a descendent path that far exceeded my powers.

See also -ANT/-ENT

descender

See ASCENDER/DESCENDER

descent

See DECENT/DESCENT/DISSENT

desert, deserts, dessert

These words are occasionally misused or misspelled. *Desert* can function as a noun and as a verb. Both forms come ultimately from Latin *deserere*, 'abandon', 'forsake'. The noun is stressed on the first syllable and is most frequently used to mean an arid, infertile region:

Many early Christians sought solitude in the desert.

The Kalahari Desert is one of the most inhospitable regions in Africa.

but it can also be used metaphorically to describe a place that is not what one is used to:

This town used to be a cultural desert.

He lived for nineteen years on a desert island.

The verb *desert* is stressed on the second syllable and means 'leave', 'abandon people or places that one has an obligation or duty to support':

He deserted his wife and children three years ago.

Many young soldiers deserted because they could not bear the thought of returning to the battlefield.

It can also be used, usually with an inanimate subject, to mean 'leave', 'fail':

My common sense deserted me!

Deserts meaning 'reward' comes from Old French *deserte*, which was from a verb meaning 'deserve'. The main stress is on the second syllable:

I believe that we all, eventually, get our just deserts.

Dessert derives from French *desservir*, 'to clear a table', and is used by some English speakers for the last course of a meal. It is stressed on the second syllable and is a homophone of the verb *desert*:

I couldn't afford a full meal so I just had the soup and the dessert.

desiccate

This word is frequently misspelled. It comes from Latin *desiccare*, 'to dry up', and has one '-s-' but '-cc-':

Then add 4 tablespoons of desiccated coconut.

designer

This word was popularized in the 1980s and

applied to goods that were produced by prestigious or fashionable companies:

The advertisers have done a wonderful job on my daughter. She's only eleven but she insists on designer labels: she's got designer jeans, designer trainers, designer sweaters and now she wants a designer watch.

desolate, dissolute

These adjectives are occasionally misused and misspelled. *Desolate* comes from Latin *desolare*, 'to leave alone', and means 'lonely, wretched':

It's the most desolate place I've ever seen, barren, isolated and depressing.

Dissolute comes from Latin *dissolutus*, 'loose', and can only be applied to people. It means 'lacking restraint', 'self-indulgent', 'promiscuous', 'dissipated':

He now leads a totally dissolute, debauched life.
The tradition is that the poet Francis Thompson led a dissolute life until he was rescued and cared for by a prostitute.

despatch, dispatch

These are alternative spellings for both noun and verb:

The soldier was sent to deliver an official dispatch.
The parcel was dispatched on Friday.

The spelling with 'i' is more common throughout the English-speaking world.

desperate, disparate

These adjectives are occasionally confused and often misspelled. *Desperate* means 'despairing, reckless':

I'm desperate. Please help me.
No one in a caring society should be allowed to become so desperate that death is preferable to life.

Disparate is related to 'separate' and it may help to remember that it refers to things that are not on a 'par' but *disparate*, meaning 'different or distinct in kind':

I can't understand why the two children have been given such disparate treatment.

despicable

Despicable, not *despisable*, is the derived adjective from 'despise':

It was despicable behaviour. We have a right to expect people to behave with courtesy and decorum.

despite, in spite of

Despite and *in spite of* are virtually synonymous, although *despite* is a little more formal and a little less likely to occur in speech. They can be substituted for each other in almost all cases:

Despite his cold, he played brilliantly.
In spite of his cold, he played brilliantly.

Despite does not need to be followed by a preposition and neither structure needs to be prefaced by 'but'.

destined

Destined derives from Latin *destinare*, 'to appoint'. In English, the word suggests 'being determined in advance':

From childhood he was destined for a life of service.

Some people object to 'destined' being used as a synonym of 'intended':

I was destined to be a teacher.

but the usage is widespread.

desultory

Desultory means 'unmethodical, haphazard':

I couldn't work with someone whose activities are so desultory, but I must admit that he achieves results.

The word should be stressed on the first syllable and many users dislike the growing tendency to stress the second syllable.

détente

This noun derives from Old French, where its literal meaning was 'loosening'. It is often used to refer to the easing of tension, especially between countries:

The current détente between Russia and Germany was largely due to the efforts of Gorbachev.

deter

Deter means 'to discourage someone from doing something':

No matter what problems there are, I won't be deterred from going to college.

Deter is a regular verb and doubles the 'r' before '-ed' and '-ing':

deter(s), deterred, deterring.

deteriorate

Deteriorate means 'become worse':

Her health has deteriorated recently.

There is a tendency to pronounce the word as if it were *deteriate. This pronunciation is popular but unacceptable.

determiner

Structuralist grammarians coined the word *determiner* to refer to a group of words such as 'a', 'my', 'the' and 'this' that regularly precede nouns and help to specify their meanings. *Determiners* can be divided into several categories:

articles: a/an, the
demonstratives: this, these, that, those
numbers: two, second

possessives: my, your, their

interrogatives: which? what?

indefinites: any, some.

See also ARTICLE, DEMONSTRATIVE, NUMBERS, POSSESSIVE

detour

Detour rhymes with 'see your' and can be used as a noun or a verb:

We'll have to make a detour to avoid the fair.
We detoured to avoid the M62 bottleneck.

detract, distract

These verbs are occasionally confused. *Detract* means 'take away from', 'diminish':

The building site detracts from the natural beauty of the moors.

Distract means 'divert attention from':

I'm sorry. What did you say? I was totally distracted by the fireworks.

See also DISTRACTED/DISTRAUGHT

develop

Develop is a regular verb:

develop(s), developed, developing.

It means 'grow gradually, elaborate, improve':

She is developing into a first-class researcher.

The 'p' is not doubled before verb endings or in derived forms such as:

developer, development.

developing countries

Common courtesy, as well as political correctness, suggests that we find words and expressions that do not hurt or insult the people we wish to describe. Some countries that are economically weaker than others have been referred to as 'undeveloped' or 'underdeveloped' and, most recently, *developing countries*. The last phrase is meant to be positive and to stress the potential of the countries.

device, devise

A *device* is a machine or piece of equipment:

I need a device for undoing the washers on a tap.

The noun can also be used metaphorically to mean 'clever plan':

What device can we use to explain that this character's father didn't really die in a car crash?

Devise is a regular verb:

devise(s), devised, devising

and means 'work out, contrive, think something up':

We have devised a plan to get over these difficulties.

Devil

The *Devil* with a capital letter is equated with Satan and Lucifer:

Do you renounce the Devil and all his works and pomps?

When the word is used without a capital letter, it can mean 'imp' or 'mischievous person':

He's a little devil, always getting into mischief, but we wouldn't have him any other way!

dextrous, dexterous

Both these spellings are acceptable for the adjective meaning 'skilful, good with one's hands':

She is without doubt the most dextrous member of the family. The rest of us are very clumsy.

The spelling without the 'e' before the 'r' is the more widespread in this word and in related words such as:

ambidextrous, dextrously, dextrousness.

diagnosis, prognosis

These medical nouns are occasionally confused, partly because they both derive from Greek *gignoskein*, 'to know', 'to perceive'. *Diagnosis* involves the identification of a disease or problem from an examination of the symptoms:

I should like to send you for a series of X-rays as a means of verifying my diagnosis. Please don't worry. As far as I can tell, you are suffering from nothing more malign than stress.

The noun *prognosis* means 'prediction of the course or outcome of an illness'.

I'm afraid the prognosis is not good. It is likely that the disease will spread quite rapidly in the next few months.

It is occasionally extended to mean any prediction:

Our prognosis is that base rates will have to rise within three months.

The plurals of both words are formed by changing '-is' into '-es':

I've been to three different specialists and got three different diagnoses.

diagram

The word *diagram* comes from Latin *diagramma* and means 'sketch, outline, plan'. It can be used as a noun or verb:

My diagram is very flat. I find it difficult to indicate depth.

The verb is regular and doubles the 'm' in British English:

UK: diagram(s), diagrammed, diagramming
US: diagram(s), diagramed, diagraming.

dial

The word *dial* comes from Latin *dialis*, 'daily'. It

is most frequently used as a noun to refer to the face of a clock or watch and as a verb for 'ring a number'. Since we no longer normally have dials on telephones, the expression may disappear. *Dial* is a regular verb that doubles the 'l' in British English:

UK: dial(s), dialled, dialling
US: dial(s), dialed, dialing.

---

dialect

No brief definition of this term will be totally satisfactory because the word *dialect* has been used in so many different ways. It derives ultimately from a Greek word *dialektos* meaning 'speech, discourse, conversation, a way of speaking, a language of a country or district' and all these meanings, and several more, are implied by the term today. Indeed, *dialect* is so ambiguous that several linguists have tried to replace it with other terms such as:

cryptolect = a secret variety

ethnolect = an ethnic variety

idiolect = a variety used by an individual

lect = any variety of language without social or regional implications

register = a variety of language defined according to use

sociolect = a variety used by a social class or occupation.

Dialect has both scholarly and popular connotations. Scholars have used the word to imply all of the following:

a language at different periods in its evolution

regionally marked varieties of a language

socially marked varieties of a language

the language of literature

the speech of the uneducated

the idiosyncratic language use of an individual

non-standard varieties of a standardized language

languages of the third world

languages of minority groups.

The popular view of dialects overlaps the scholarly in that the term is usually applied to:

regionally marked speech

the speech of lower socio-economic groups

regional pronunciations.

Popularly, dialects are also often associated with warmth, humour, vitality, incorrectness, slovenliness and lack of intelligence. With so many and such varied implications, the term *dialect* needs to be used with care and it is worth our while to clear up some misconceptions.

A *dialect* is not just a form of pronunciation. It relates to a variety of language and comprehends pronunciation, vocabulary choice and syntax. A Yorkshire woman, seeing some children may say:

When I was standing at the shop, I saw the boy playing in the park.

or:

When I were stood at t'shop, I seen t'lad leikin in t'park.

The first is Standard English with a regional accent; the second is an example of Yorkshire dialect.

Dialects are in no way linguistically inferior to any other mother-tongue speech. They are perfectly adequate for the needs of their speakers and can be easily modified to accommodate changes in society. Usually, dialects do not have their own orthography and, since most remain unwritten, they lack the prestige that accrues to a standard language with a recognized system of writing. All dialects can be given orthographies and any dialect could be moulded to suit the needs of any society. Standard English was once a regional dialect, considered by many to be incapable of expressing cultural or literary aspirations.

As well as regional dialects, there are class dialects. Working-class people tend to have less formal education than their more affluent peers and often use a variety described as 'non-standard'. As far as English is concerned, working-class dialects show considerable similarities. First, they are all being influenced by the media and so are coming closer to network standards. Second, there is a 'standardness' about the nonstandard features that are found in working-class English from London to Adelaide or the Appalachians:

■ A tendency to use 'them' as a demonstrative:

Pass me them books.

■ A tendency to simplify verb forms:

I do, I done, I have done

I go, I went, I have went

I see, I seen, I have seen

■ A tendency to use multiple negation:

I never said nothing to nobody.

■ A tendency to use the local rather than the network pronunciation.

See also NETWORK NORM, PRONUNCIATION, SPEECH AND WRITING

---

dialectal, dialectic, dialectical

These words are occasionally confused. *Dialectal* is an adjective relating to 'dialect':

We've been asked to pick out the dialectal features on the tape.

I hadn't realized there was so much dialectal variation in the north of England.

Dialectic is a noun and means 'logical argument', 'the art of assessing a theory by discussion':

The phrase Hegelian Dialectic implies a method of debate in which the contradiction between the thesis and its antithesis is resolved in the synthesis.

Dialectical is the adjective derived from *dialectic*:

Ben always tried to use dialectical procedures in his debates with students.

dialogue

This word derives ultimately from Greek *dialegesthai*, 'to converse'. It is used to mean 'conversation, discussion' and is spelled *dialogue* in Britain and *dialog* in America:

I'm trying to write some dialogue for my little play. It's not easy to make it sound realistic.

The verb is less widely used than the noun and is regular:

UK: dialogue(s), dialogued, dialoguing
US: dialog(s), dialoged, dialoging.

dialysis

This word is frequently misspelled. It ends in '-alysis' like 'analysis':

He goes into hospital twice a week for kidney dialysis.

diaphragm

This word is frequently misspelled because it rhymes with 'diagram'. It comes from Greek *dia*, 'through', 'between', + *phragma*, 'fence', and has two main meanings in English. It can refer to any separating membrane in the body:

The dome-shaped muscular partition that separates the abdominal and thoracic cavities is called a 'diaphragm'.

and is widely used as the name of a contraceptive membrane placed over the opening of the cervix.

diarrhoea, diarrhea

This word derives from Greek *diarrhein*, 'to flow through', and is frequently misspelled. The most widely-used spelling in Britain is *diarrhoea* and Americans prefer the spelling without the '-o-', *diarrhea*. However, both forms occur in both communities. *Diarrhoea* is pronounced to rhyme with 'buy a Tia (Maria)'.

diary
See DAIRY/DIARY

Diaspora

This word is related to 'disperse' and was originally applied to the dispersal of the Jews after the Babylonian captivity (*c*.597– *c*.538BC). Later, the term was applied to the early Christians who lived outside Palestine. Most recently, it has been applied, with or without a capital letter, to people who originally came from one place or shared one culture:

the Black Diaspora
the Irish diaspora.

diatribe

Although the original Greek word *diatribe* meant 'discourse', 'pastime', this word has taken on the meaning of a bitter or violent criticism:

I don't agree with these views either but I can't condone the cruelty of the diatribe and invective levelled at the speaker.

Diatribe is increasingly being used to mean 'verbosity bordering on stupidity':

I have never heard such a diatribe in my life!

Many people dislike this extension of meaning but it is frequently heard, even on news broadcasts.

dice, die

The word *dice* is now used as both the singular and the plural form of the cube that has numbers of dots from one to six on its faces:

Where are the dice? We want to play ludo.

The original singular was 'die' from Old French *dee*, 'a piece in a game' and this usage still occurs in the simile 'as straight as a die' or in the translation of the quotation attributed to Julius Caesar:

The die is cast.

Dice is also used as a regular verb:

dice(s), diced, dicing

Dice the carrots and parsnips before adding them to the stew.

dichotomy

Dichotomy means 'division into two parts, especially when the parts are opposed':

The dichotomy between eastern and western art can, in part, be accounted for by the shift in power from Rome to Constantinople.

The first vowel is usually pronounced as a homophone of the vowel in 'Dick', but some speakers prefer to pronounce the first syllable as 'die'.

diction

Diction comes from Latin *dictio*, 'a saying, mode of expression', and has two widely-used meanings in English. It can refer to the enunciation of words by a speaker or singer:

Her top notes have begun to wobble but her diction is crystal clear.

It can also be applied to the selection of words, especially in the teaching of writing skills:

The purpose of this course is to improve your diction and writing skills, helping you to write clearly and effectively.

The term POETIC DICTION refers, usually disparagingly, to hackneyed words and phrases often found in poor poetry:

feathered friend (bird)
vernal (spring).

dictionary

There are two main types of *dictionary*, both capable of providing a variety of information.

A bilingual *dictionary* aims primarily at the sort of translations that will help a person who is using two languages. This aim is usually fulfilled by dividing the book into two halves, each organized alphabetically. Thus an English–Spanish dictionary will devote the first to English words for which Spanish equivalents are provided and the second half to Spanish words for which English equivalents are given.

A monolingual *dictionary* provides alphabetically arranged information on meaning and contextualization. Definitions usually include synonyms and the most widely-used collocations in which a word occurs. The monolingual dictionary may also include information on etymology and pronunciation.

dictum

A *dictum* is a formal or authoritative statement:

What's the dictum from the management this week?

The plural is, as in Latin, 'dicta', but 'dictums' is also acceptable.

die

See DICE/DIE

die of, die from

The slightly irregular verb *die*:

die(s), died, dying, died

can be followed by a variety of adverbs:

die away = fade
die back = suffer from a disease of plants
die out = disappear.

When people contract a disease that will result in their death, *die* normally takes the preposition 'of':

She's dying of pneumonia.
They died of old age.

Increasingly, many speakers use 'from' rather than 'of' and many careful speakers dislike this usage.

dietician, dietitian

Both spellings are acceptable, although many people prefer *dietitian* since the scientific study of food intake is 'dietetics'. *Dietitian* is the older spelling but the *-ician* form was influenced by such nouns as:

clinician, mortician, physician.

differ from, differ with

Differ from is normally used in the sense of 'be dissimilar in quality or nature, show a difference':

Cultivated primulas differ from wild primroses in colour, size and shape.

Differ with normally means 'disagree with':

I differed with her on the manner of approach, not on the principle.

The colloquialism 'agree to differ' means 'ending an argument amicably but in such a way that both sides maintain their views':

We'll have to agree to differ on her place in history.

different from, than, to

There is some uncertainty about which of three prepositions should follow 'different'. The simplest rule, if in doubt, is to use *different from* in preference to *different to* in Britain:

The food was different from anything I'd ever eaten.
Her house is different from mine.

American usage has both *different from* and *different than*, depending on the construction:

The book was very different from what I expected.
The book was very different than I expected.
These are in a different order than I expected.

The structures involving *different* can arouse strong feeling and many speakers in England object to *different to* and *different than*. There is little justification for such an attitude since all of these structures have been used since the seventeenth century, often in the writings of prestigious authors. Prejudice is, however, a strong force and the *different from* structure is least likely to be criticized.

differential

The noun *differential*, especially in the plural form, was popularized by the British press in the 1970s to refer to different pay rates for different types of work:

Many trade unionists dislike Jones's idea of a £6 rise for everyone. It erodes the differentials.

diffraction, refraction

These two nouns are often confused, especially by students of physics. *Diffraction* involves passing light through a narrow aperture:

Cameras use the principles of diffraction.

Refraction involves bending light by passing it from one transparent medium to another:

Refraction involves the bending of light although it may also separate it into its constituent colours.

The regular verb *refract* is sometimes confused with 'reflect':

Light can be reflected, that is, sent back; or it can be refracted, that is, broken up into its constituents.

diffuse

See DEFUSE/DIFFUSE

dig

See DELVE/DIG

digest

Digest is a regular verb meaning 'absorb, assimilate':

I have difficulty digesting cheese.

I have difficulty digesting some of his ideas.

The noun *digest* refers to a magazine or periodical that summarizes information, often in a simple and pleasant way.

digit

A *digit* is a finger or toe:

Some of the Stuarts had an extra digit on their right hand.

or a character or number:

The new clock has digits instead of hands on a dial.

The main derived forms are 'digital' and 'digitize'. In computer technology, 'digital' means 'using discrete signals to represent data in the form of numbers or characters'. The term 'digitize' means 'to transcribe data into a digital form so that it can be processed by a computer'.

diglossia

Diglossia comes from Greek *di* + *glotta*, 'two + tongue' and is used to describe a speech community where two varieties of the same language coexist, each with its own range of functions. Usually one of the varieties has more prestige than the other. Sometimes, Standard English and a pidgin or creole English are in a diglossic relationship.

See also PIDGIN AND CREOLE

digraph

When two letters or characters are combined to represent a single speech sound, the combination is called a *digraph*. In the following words, 'ch', 'gh' and 'ph' are *digraphs*:

Christmas, roughly, pharmacy.

dike, dyke

These are alternative spellings for an 'embankment'. *Dike* is the usual spelling in America and *dyke* is the preferred form in Britain:

UK: What was the name of the boy who put his finger in the dyke?

US: What was the name of the boy who put his finger in the dike?

The noun *dyke*, almost invariably spelled with a 'y', is a twentieth-century synonym for 'lesbian'. Its etymology is uncertain. In the past, it has frequently been used as a negative term, but some lesbians have begun to use it with pride.

dilapidated

Dilapidated is an adjective meaning 'in a poor state of repair, run down':

They bought a dilapidated cottage for a few thousand pounds and spent years turning it into a dream home.

Because the word includes the Latin word *lapis* 'stone', some etymologists do not like the adjective *dilapidated* applied to things that are not made of stone as in:

Everything in the house was dilapidated, even the curtains.

Few speakers of English reserve this adjective exclusively for items constructed of stone but many misspell it, assuming that it begins with 'de-'.

dilate

This verb means 'expand', 'cause to expand'. The first syllable is most frequently pronounced to rhyme with 'pile' but it is occasionally pronounced as if it were 'dill':

Do my pupils dilate in the dark?

We'll have to dilate the neck of the womb.

The noun from *dilate* is either 'dilator' or 'dilater', with the former spelling being preferred in Britain. The adjective 'dilatory', meaning 'inclined to delay or time-wasting', is not related.

dilemma

The noun *dilemma* comes from Greek *di*-, 'two', + *lemma*, 'situation', and it is used in English to refer to a choice between two equally unpleasant alternatives:

Our dilemma was not knowing whether to choose the operation or the chemotherapy.

Some people dislike the extension of this word to include more than two options:

My dilemma is a pleasant one. I have offers from four good universities and I'd be happy going to any one of them.

The first syllable of *dilemma* is normally pronounced to rhyme with 'pill' but, partly because of American influence, it is occasionally rhymed with 'pile'.

dimension

The noun *dimension* has both literal and metaphorical uses. Literally, it refers to measurement:

Please supply me with the precise dimensions of each room in the house.

Metaphorically, it means 'size, scope':

This is a problem of Europe-wide dimensions.

The press has popularized *dimension* and

extended its meaning to 'aspect', especially in the phrase 'a new dimension':

The fact that millions of pounds worth of trade hang on the decision has added a new dimension to the expulsion order.

diminish, minimize

These words have overlapping meanings because they both derive from the Latin verb *minuere*, 'to reduce'. *Diminish* means 'lessen':

The number of applications we receive has diminished steadily over the last five years.

Minimize means 'reduce to the least possible amount', 'talk down':

Don't minimize the risks involved in backpacking.

diminution

This noun meaning 'reduction, decrease' is much more widely used in the written medium because many speakers are uncertain of its pronunciation. It rhymes with 'dim in you shin':

King Lear was unwilling to accept the diminution in his power.

dinghy, dingy

A *dinghy* is a small boat and it has three acceptable spellings, *dinghy*, *dingy* and *dingey*, although the first is the most widely used. English adopted the word from Hindi *dingi*. The most widespread pronunciation rhymes with 'ring + gee', but the pronunciation that rhymes with 'ring + ee' is also heard.

The adjective *dingy* rhymes with 'binge + ee' and is related to the English word 'dung':

We used to live in a dingy little house but now we have a lovely home with a garden.

dingo

A *dingo* is a wild Australian dog. The word rhymes with 'bingo' and forms its plural in '-es':

It's lonesome away from your kindred and all
By the campfire at night where the wild dingoes call.
                    Song

dinner

There is little agreement among English speakers about when *dinner* is eaten, but for most speakers it is the main meal of the day:

Dinner was formerly eaten in the evening but many people now eat their main meal around one o'clock and refer to it as 'dinner'.

See also LUNCH/LUNCHEON, MEALS, TEA

diphtheria

Diphtheria is an acute contagious disease. It is often misspelled and even more often mispronounced. The first syllable should rhyme with 'if' and not with 'dip', although both pronunciations are heard.

diphthong

This word comes from Greek *di*, 'two' + *phthongos*, 'sound', and is applied to a sound that is made up of two vowels. In the word 'how', for example, the 'ow' sound begins as an 'a' and ends as an 'u'. This sound is a diphthong. The word has the letter sequence '-phth-' and the first syllable rhymes with 'if', rather than 'dip', although both pronunciations are heard.

diplomat, diplomate

A *diplomat* is an official or someone who is skilled in dealing tactfully with people:

He's a diplomat in China.

He has many excellent qualities but he's no diplomat when it comes to personal relationships.

A *diplomate* is someone who has been awarded a diploma:

Diplomates will be awarded their certificates at a ceremony in the Great Hall on Tuesday, 29 July.

The word *diplomat* rhymes with 'fat', and the word *diplomate* with 'fate'.

direct, directly

Direct can function as a regular verb meaning 'regulate', 'control', 'conduct':

He directed his business from home.

as an adjective meaning 'straightforward, non-circuitous':

He's extremely direct and always says what he means.

This is the most direct route between Leeds and Huddersfield.

and as an adverb meaning 'directly':

She went direct to the theatre.

The adverb *directly* can mean 'in a direct manner':

I drove home directly without any stops or detours.

but it is most frequently used to mean 'immediately':

I want you to type this directly.
She left directly she got your message.

direct speech

The term *direct speech* is used to describe a set of conventions by which we express what someone is supposed to have said:

'Walk on, Rover,' said Mary. 'We're late and so you'll have to hurry.'

The same conventions are employed to indicate thought:

'I'm going to be late,' thought Mary.

The creation of the category *direct speech* is a convenient way of referring to the commonest means of representing speech in novels and stories, but it is more a description of the impression created by such speech representation than an isolatable category of its own. *Direct speech* is seldom an actual record of what is said: we introduce conventions such as inverted commas and exclamation marks; we do not normally record such phenomena as hesitations, false starts, tempo, loudness or intonation; and what is given as 'thought' is an oversimplified stylization of mental processes.

The contrastive relation between *direct* and indirect (or reported) speech is more of an imposed idealization than a description of language use. The only direct speech samples that can be easily transformed into indirect speech (or vice versa) are those that are composed for the purpose. Live speech is hard to transform into indirect speech, as the following recorded utterance illustrates:

'You can never … ugh … never get these bloody lids off … you see! you see! all over the place … I'm sure the idiot got a whaddyacallit for a lid like it!

If we turn this into indirect speech we produce a version such as:

John fumbled with the lid on the bottle and swore that he could never get such lids off. He got it off, spilling the contents, and exclaimed that he had been right and that the designer of such lids had probably won a design award.

The reported version loses much of the quality of the original and the solution of replacing 'bloody' by 'swore' is only partly successful.

The dichotomy *direct/indirect speech* is a simplification of the many representations of speech and thought that occur in literature. It is not always possible to say whether some samples such as:

'Will she never come?' he wondered.

are meant to represent speech or thought because many attributive verbs such as 'hypothesized', 'mused', 'pondered' and 'theorized' can represent both.

In traditional terms, *direct speech* is characterized by quotation marks, which are usually double in older books and single in modern texts. A punctuation mark at the end of the speech precedes the closing quotation mark. The first line of direct speech is indented from the left-hand margin. If a speech consists of more than one paragraph, each paragraph starts with an opening quotation mark, but a closing quotation mark is used only at the end of the speech or before a verb of attribution. In the conversion of *direct* into indirect speech, time words such as 'now', place terms such as 'here', pronouns and verbs are changed. Thus, such sentences as:

'Bring the book here,' said the teacher.
'I arrived yesterday.'

become:

The teacher told him to take the book there.
She said that she had arrived the day before.

The conventions involved in transposing from one mode to another suggest that speech can exist in more than one form without alteration of meaning. Reported speech is, however, less precise. Such a report as:

She said she would not go.

does not distinguish between:

'I will not go,' she said.

and:

'I would not go,' she said.

Perhaps this is one reason why writers of detective stories often prefer reported speech. Moreover, some conversions from direct to reported speech require changes such as the deletion of titles:

'May I help you, sir?' he asked,
He asked (politely) if he could help him/be of help.

the substitution of more formal lexical items:

'Can I go too?' he asked.
She asked if she could also go.

the deletion of exclamations:

'Oh! You nearly gave me a heart attack!' he exclaimed.
He exclaimed that she had frightened him badly.

and the expansion of contractions:

'We'll go if it's a nice day,' I promised.
I promised that we would go if the day was pleasant.

Such changes inevitably affect meaning.

In reality, speech and its written representation are much more flexible, subtle and varied than the terms *direct* and 'indirect/reported speech' suggest.

See also INDIRECT SPEECH, MEDIA/MEDIUM, NARRATION/NARRATIVE

dis-

Dis- is a prefix that comes from Latin *dis-*, 'apart'. It is used to indicate reversal and negation:

appear, disappear
connect, disconnect
trust, distrust.

See also AFFIX, PREFIX

disadvantaged

In an attempt to avoid hurting anyone's feelings, certain adjectives such as *disadvantaged*, 'deprived' and 'underprivileged' are preferred to 'poor'.

See also POLITICAL CORRECTNESS

disappoint

Disappoint is a regular verb:

disappoint(s), disappointed, disappointing.

It is often misspelled with one 'p'.

disarmed, unarmed

Disarmed means 'having had one's weapons taken away':

Both sides have now been disarmed by NATO so there is a hope that peaceful negotiations can begin.

This word also has a figurative meaning 'allay criticism or hostility':

His pleasant manner disarmed his critics.

Unarmed means 'not bearing weapons':

Don't shoot. We're unarmed.

disarming

Disarming derives ultimately from Latin *arma*, 'arms, equipment' and it can still be used with a related meaning:

The troops are currently disarming the warring factions.

More frequently, *disarming* is used as an adjective meaning 'charming':

He has such a disarming smile that I find it hard to be angry with him.

disassemble, dissemble

These two verbs are occasionally confused although there is no overlap of meaning. *Disassemble* means 'take apart':

We had to disassemble the entire kitchen because we had used the wrong struts for some of the wall cabinets.

Dissemble is not an alternative form of 'disassemble'; it means 'conceal one's motives, pretend':

No one should be criticized for failing to see her shortcomings. She concealed her true motives by dissembling.

It is hard to explain why Iago dissembled with almost every character in the play. He was successful because few of us can distinguish between truth and a successful lie.

disassociate

Often, the prefix 'dis-' is placed in front of a verb to create a new verb:

like, dislike

regard, disregard.

With some verbs, however, we have two forms:

associate, dissociate, disassociate.

The older form in English is *dissociate* and this is still the preferred form for many careful speakers and writers:

I wish to dissociate myself from these remarks.

disastrous

The adjective *disastrous* is often misspelled because people add '-ous' to the noun 'disaster'. The creation of '-ous' adjectives from nouns is not, however, always straightforward in English:

Noun	Adjective
fable	fabulous
ridicule	ridiculous
sense	sensuous

disbar

See DEBAR/DISBAR

disbelief, unbelief

Careful speakers distinguish between these nouns. The commoner noun, *disbelief*, means 'inability to believe':

I stared at her in disbelief. Surely this could not be my oldest friend!

Unbelief is stronger and implies 'rejection of belief':

I believe. Help thou my unbelief.

disc, disk

A thin, flat, circular object is usually a *disc* in Britain but a *disk* in America:

UK: Why is the disc around a saint's head called a 'halo'?
US: Why is the disk around a saint's head called a 'halo'?

In both countries, it is usual to refer to a storage device for computers as a *disk*:

UK/US: I needed 15 disks.

disciple

Disciple comes ultimately from Latin *discere* 'to learn'. This word and its derived forms are often misspelled. Like their Latin source, they all have '-sc-':

disciplinarian, disciplinary, discipline.

disclose, expose

These verbs are both associated with the meaning of 'reveal'. *Disclose* means 'to make information available':

They disclosed their relationship to the press.

Expose, by contrast suggests 'bring to public notice, unmask':

The press is wonderful when it exposes fraud but there is often a thin line between a revelation that is in the public interest and a revelation that is mere titillation.

discoloration

Whereas most compounds of 'colour' in British English have '-our':

discolour, discolourment

the noun *discoloration* does not have a '-u-':

It's almost impossible to prevent discoloration in photographs.

See also COLOUR/COLOR

discomfit, discomfort

These words are occasionally confused. *Discomfit* is becoming obsolete but continues to have a limited role with the meaning of 'make uneasy, frustrate, thwart':

His role in life seems to be to discomfit the self-satisfied.

The derived noun 'discomfiture' continues to have currency:

It was hard not to feel sorry for their discomfiture.

Discomfort occurs as both a noun and a verb meaning 'distress, inconvenience, pain, upset':

It won't hurt although it may cause a little discomfort.

It's not just a slight inconvenience; it is discomforting the entire staff.

discourse

Grammatical analysis tends to be limited to the sentence. As F.R. Palmer expressed it: 'In a sense, then, what is meant by sentence is defined in practical terms. It is the largest unit to which we can assign a grammatical structure.'

Yet, it is clear to any sensitive user of language that there are many links between sentences in a continuous stretch of coherent speech or prose. *Discourse analysis* is the study of such links and of the patterns likely to occur in different types of discourse (narrative, conversation, religious ritual, political persuasion) and on certain occasions (such as marriages, funerals, christenings, bar mitzvahs).

Links between sentences add to the cohesion of a passage and these links are most apparent in:

■ Consistency of tone (voice quality may contribute to cohesion in speech; stylistic appropriateness may achieve the same end in writing)

■ Consistency of vocabulary (no item appears out of place in the context and lexical sets may occur, e.g., 'game, set, match, fifteen, thirty, forty, love, deuce, advantage' would form a lexical set in a description of tennis)

■ Consistency of syntax (we do not expect rapid and inexplicable changes in tense, aspect, location, narration)

■ Anaphora (backward and forward references involving pronouns, auxiliary verbs, adverbials such as 'finally', 'furthermore', 'later' and conjunctions, both coordinate 'and, but, either … or' and subordinate 'because, if, when'.

See also ANAPHORA, COHERENCE/COHESION, PARALLELISM

discover, invent

The regular verbs *invent* and *discover* are both associated with finding. *Discover* means 'be the first to find out about something', 'encounter for the first time':

Newton discovered the laws of gravity.

The quality of life of our ancestors must have been improved when they discovered fire.

Discover is sometimes used incorrectly as a synonym for 'invent':

*Fleming invented penicillin.

Fleming discovered penicillin.

Invent means 'bring something into existence':

We don't know who invented the first wheel.

discreet, discrete

These adjectives are frequently misspelled and misused. *Discreet* is related to 'discretion'. It means 'prudent, tactful, good at keeping confidences' and is applied to humans:

You can trust her absolutely. She is sensitive and utterly discreet.

Discrete means 'separate, distinct' and is applied usually to non-humans:

There are three discrete sections in this lecture.

discretion

Discretion is the usual noun derived from *discreet*, although 'discreetness' is occasionally used. It means 'prudence', 'tact':

We need someone with discretion, someone who will be able to listen and make constructive suggestions.

'authority':

I don't have the discretion to sign company cheques.

and 'maturity' especially in the collocations 'age of discretion' and 'years of discretion':

It's nice to think that the children have both reached the age of discretion.

discriminating, discriminatory

These adjectives derive from Latin *discriminare*, 'to divide'. *Discriminating* is a compliment. It suggests discernment and the ability to make fine distinctions:

They are both discriminating in artistic matters.

Discriminatory is now, usually, a synonym for 'prejudiced' although it is used positively in earlier texts:

They were not prepared to put up with such discriminatory treatment. They did not object to doing their fair share but they refused to be exploited simply because of their gender.

discus, discuss

These words are occasionally misspelled. A *discus* is a circular object used in throwing competitions. It has two acceptable plurals, *discuses* and *disci*, but the former is the more widely used:

A discus can weigh two kilos.

Discuss is a regular verb meaning 'have a conversation about':

We never discussed anything personal but we often had a chat about the weather.

dishevel

Dishevel is a verb formed from the adjective 'dishevelled' meaning 'untidy, unkempt'. The verb doubles its 'l' in British English but not in American English:

UK: dishevel(s), dishevelled, dishevelling

US: dishevel(s), disheveled, disheveling.

The first syllable is pronounced 'dish' because the word derives from *dis* + *chevel*, 'hair', and was originally used in Old French and English to describe untidy hair.

disinterested, uninterested

These adjectives are occasionally misused although they are different in meaning and application. *Disinterested* means 'free from bias', 'impartial', 'unprejudiced':

It is unlikely that she will give you a disinterested comment on double glazing. She had an appalling experience when her own house was being renovated.

Many people incorrectly use 'disinterested' as the negative equivalent of 'interested', but it is the adjective *uninterested*, meaning 'indifferent', 'unconcerned', which is the negative form of 'interested':

He seems totally uninterested in any musical instrument. We've encouraged him to have lessons but he would rather play football.

I've never met such uninterested participants. Why did they come to the conference if they are so bored with the subject?

See also NEGATION

disk

See DISC/DISK

disorient, disorientate

These verbs are both used to mean 'to lose or cause to lose one's bearings':

I was completely disoriented. I could not remember where I was or how I could get home. It was the most frightening experience of my life.

Disorient is the acceptable form in America and it is also acceptable in Britain. *Disorientate* is rarely used in America but is becoming acceptable in Britain.

disparate

See DESPERATE/DISPARATE

dispassionate, impassioned

These adjectives should not be confused. *Dispassionate* means 'calm, impartial, objective':

How is it possible to find five dispassionate judges for the book prize?

Impassioned means 'enthusiastic, showing a passionate commitment':

His plea was so direct, so clearly expressed, so impassioned that we had twice as many volunteers as we required.

See also IMPASSABLE/IMPASSIBLE/IMPASSIVE

dispatch

See also DESPATCH/DISPATCH

dispel, disperse

Dispel means 'drive away, scatter':

There have been so many problems with these machines that it will not be easy to dispel our customers' worries.

It is a regular verb that doubles the 'l' before '-ed', '-er' and '-ing' endings:

dispels(s), dispelled, dispelling.

Disperse means 'break up, separate, scatter over a wide area':

The Irish have been dispersed to all parts of the world.

Whereas *dispel* takes an abstract object, disperse can take both a human or a non-human object.

See also DIASPORA, DISPERSAL

dispense

Dispense is a regular verb, which is often misspelled with '-ence':

dispense(s), dispensed, dispensing.

It can mean 'give out or distribute', 'do away with' and 'exempt':

The Queen dispensed her Maundy gift to sixty-nine people on 4 April.

We are very sorry but we must dispense with your services.

We have been dispensed from attending these services.

dispersal

This noun derives from 'disperse' and tends to be applied to the spread of seeds, plants or animals to another area:

Wind is one of the methods of seed dispersal.

disperse

See DISPEL/DISPERSE

dispute

Dispute can function as a noun or a verb. It comes from Latin *disputare*, 'to contend verbally', and means 'argue', 'debate', 'quarrel':

They are involved in a long-running dispute about land boundaries.

The noun is normally stressed on the second syllable although there is a growing tendency to stress the first syllable so as to distinguish between the noun and the verb. The verb is regular and is always stressed on the second syllable:

dispute(s), disputed, disputing.

disrepair

This noun means 'the condition of being run down or worn out'. It is applied only to inanimate objects:

Your car is in a terrible state of disrepair. How could it have passed its test?

dissect

See BISECT/DISSECT

dissemble

See DISASSEMBLE/DISSEMBLE

dissent

See DECENT/DESCENT/DISSENT

dissociate

See DISASSOCIATE

dissolute

See DESOLATE/DISSOLUTE

distend

The noun from *distend* has two acceptable spellings, 'distension' and 'distention'. The former is the more widely used:

There are several illnesses associated with the distension of the stomach.

distil, distill

Both spellings of this word, meaning 'purify, separate, concentrate', are acceptable. The single 'l' is British and the double 'll' American:

UK: distil(s), distilled, distilling
UK: distill(s), distilled, distilling

The derived nouns 'distillation' and 'distillery' have the same spellings in both countries.

distinct, distinctive

These adjectives both incorporate the meaning of 'individual' but they have different, if overlapping, meanings and distributions. *Distinct* means 'clear', 'precise', 'separate':

There used to be a distinct smell of disinfectant that I always associated with hospitals.

Distinctive means 'characteristic', 'distinguishing':

She has a most distinctive way of pronouncing 'solve'. I think she picked it up at Cambridge.

distract

See DETRACT/DISTRACT

distracted, distraught

These adjectives are occasionally confused. *Distracted* means 'bewildered, confused':

She seemed so utterly distracted that I couldn't bear to tell her the bad news.

and it is frequently used to suggest a loss of attention:

I was distracted by the music.
Don't distract Mary from her studies.

Distraught is an older adjective from 'distract'. It tends to be restricted in meaning to 'agitated and worried' or 'extremely worried':

She was distraught at the news of her son's accident.
You should have rung us earlier! Your mother has been distraught!

See also DETRACT/DISTRACT

distribute

The pronunciation of this regular verb:

distribute(s), distributed, distributing

causes some friction. It is usually stressed on the second syllable and many users dislike the pronunciation that puts the main stress on the first syllable.

distrust, mistrust

These words can function as nouns and as regular verbs. They have overlapping meanings. *Distrust* suggests 'suspicion, strong doubt':

I have no evidence for my suspicions but I distrust this young man.

Mistrust is less widely used and suggests weaker doubts and suspicions:

They have only known each other for a few days so it is not surprising that they harbour slight feelings of mistrust.

disturb, perturb

These regular verbs both derive from Latin *turbare*, 'to confuse'. *Disturb* can mean 'intrude on', 'interrupt':

I'm not disturbing you, am I?

but also, especially when used passively, 'agitate', 'upset':

She was so deeply disturbed by his visit that we had to send for the doctor.

Perturb is less frequently used than *disturb*. It also suggests 'trouble' but it is stronger and includes the notion of destroying one's mental composure:

He was deeply troubled and perturbed by the thought of what he had to undergo.
I'm perturbed and perplexed by what you tell me.

disused, misused, unused

These adjectives all derive from 'use' but they have distinct meanings. *Disused* always rhymes with 'bruised' and means 'discarded, no longer used':

They've bought a disused mill and spend all their spare time in it.

Misused means 'not properly used' or 'ill-treated':

It's good to know that this poor, misused animal has found a good home.

Unused has two pronunciations and two main meanings. When it rhymes with 'bruised', it means 'new, not used yet':

That computer cost me a fortune and it has been sitting unused on the desk since I bought it.

For legal reasons, you cannot have the word 'new' in the advertisement but you can say 'unused present'.

When it rhymes with the first syllable of 'Euston', it means 'unaccustomed':

I was unused to such behaviour.

See also ABUSE/MISUSE

ditto

Ditto comes ultimately from Latin *dicere*, 'to say', and means 'the aforementioned'. It is symbolized by two small marks ["] called *ditto* marks and these are used to avoid repetition, especially in lists and accounts:

25 cartridges for HP printers
7 " " Epson printers.

divan

See COUCH/DIVAN/SETTEE/SOFA

dived, dove

In British English *dive* is a regular verb:

dive(s), dived, diving

but in American English it is often an irregular verb:

dive(s), dove, diving, dived.

diverge

This regular verb means 'separate, cause to separate':

Looking back, it is clear that our lives started to diverge at that time.

The stress falls on the second syllable and the 'di-' rhymes with 'by'.

divide

The usual adjective from *divide* is 'divisible':

Ten is not divisible by three.

An alternative adjective 'dividable' exists and can be found in some children's arithmetic books:

Three into ten doesn't go, so ten is not dividable by three.

divorcee

There is a tendency to use the unaccented form *divorcee* to refer to a divorced person of either sex:

David is also a divorcee.

The older French form 'divorcé' is exclusively male and the form 'divorcée' is exclusively female.

do

Do is an irregular verb:

do (does), did, doing, done.

It can occur as a full verb, meaning 'perform, complete':

Do your best.
Poets do their best work in their youth.

and it can also occur as a dummy auxiliary. It has been called the 'dummy auxiliary' because it is used where the structure requires an auxiliary. It has formal significance but little semantic value. It functions as follows to allow:

■ The formation of interrogative sentences:

He loves me. Does he love me?

■ The formation of negatives:

He loves me. He doesn't love me.

■ The formation of tag questions:

He loves me, doesn't he?
He doesn't love me, does he?

It is also used to mark emphatic affirmation or denial:

He doesn't love me. He does.
He loves me. He doesn't.

and to avoid repetition:

He loves me more than you do (i.e., you love me).

The use of *do* as a dummy auxiliary is a relatively recent development in English. In Shakespeare's time, the head verb could be negated and interrogated directly:

I love thee not. *(Henry IV, Part 1*, II.iii.91)
Goes the king? *(Macbeth*, II.iii.52)

At that time, apart from being a head verb, *do* was a marker of time and perhaps emphasis:

When I do count the clock that tells the time.
(Sonnet 12)

Writers traditionally commented on the fact that British and American speakers tended to use different auxiliaries in such structures as:

UK: Have you any wool?
US: Do you have any wool?

but many British speakers can use all of the following:

Have you any wool?
Have you got any wool?
Do you have any wool?

and advertisements, possibly imported from

America, are reinforcing the use of periphrastic *do* as in:

I didn't know you had dandruff.

I don't.

See also AUXILIARY, DUMMY, MODALITY, PERIPHRASIS

do's and don'ts

The words 'do' and 'don't' can be pluralized and used as nouns:

Here are the do's and don'ts of the job.

Usually, *do's* is spelled with an apostrophe before the 's' but don'ts has only one apostrophe and that is before the 't'.

docket

Docket can function as a noun and as a regular verb that does not double the 't' before endings:

docket(s), docketed, docketing.

In Britain, the noun can refer to a piece of paper accompanying a packet:

The docket lists the contents and the delivery instructions.

or to a receipt:

I am still waiting for the docket to show that all customs duties have been paid.

In America, the noun can refer to a list of things to be done:

I'm always making up dockets but I still fall behind with my chores.

and to a list of cases awaiting trial:

I've just seen the docket and it is unlikely that your case will be heard before January.

The verb can mean 'fix a docket to a package':

I docketed the package myself.

and, in legal language, 'make a summary':

The judgement will be presented in full to the legal teams but docketed for the press.

doctor

The verb *doctor* is regular:

doctor(s), doctored, doctoring

and in colloquial styles it covers a wide range of meaning from 'castrate':

We've had our tom cat doctored.

through 'add something to':

We doctored the food.

to 'falsify':

Somebody has doctored the accounts.

doctrine, dogma

These words both appear in religious contexts. *Doctrine* comes from Latin *doctrina*, 'teaching', and still refers to a body of teaching or belief:

The bishop is not repeating established church doctrine. He is offering a personal interpretation.

Dogma comes from Greek *dokein*, 'to seem good' and means 'a piece of religious teaching laid down as true':

The dogma of Our Lady's Assumption was not announced until the middle of the nineteenth century.

In colloquial language, *dogma* is applied to any authoritarian belief or set of beliefs:

That's Marxist dogma.

document

Document is often used as a regular verb with the meaning of 'provide evidence or factual support':

You have failed to document your thesis by providing any of your own data or authoritative referential support.

dodo

The *dodo* is an extinct, flightless bird. It has two acceptable plurals, 'dodos' and 'dodoes'. The former is the more frequently used form.

dogged

This word has two different pronunciations depending on whether it is used as a verb:

He dogged (i.e., followed) my steps.

or as an adjective:

She has shown dogged (i.e., tenacious) determination.

The verb *dogged*, whether past tense or past participle, is pronounced as one syllable and rhymes with 'logged'. The adjective *dogged* is two syllables and rhymes with 'log + id'.

See also -ED FORM

dogma

See DOCTRINE/DOGMA

dolman, dolmen

These nouns are not widely used and are occasionally misspelled. A *dolman* is a Turkish outer garment. The plural is 'dolmans'.

A *dolmen* is a prehistoric stone formation:

Dolmen probably comes from the Celtic words *tol* meaning 'table' and *men* meaning 'stone'.

domestic, domesticated

These adjectives are occasionally confused. They both come from Latin *domesticus*, 'belonging to the house'. *Domestic* means 'relating to the home':

I don't have much time for purely domestic chores.

Domesticated means 'adapted or modified to home life':

We weren't really domesticated when we lived in a flat but that changed when we got a home in the country.

Americans often use the verb 'domesticize' where British people use 'domesticate':

UK: It won't be easy to domesticate Tom.

US: It won't be easy to domesticize Tom.

dominating, domineering

These adjectives both involve the meaning of 'control' but only the second implies 'bullying':

He is a dominating character on most social occasions; people listen to him even if they don't like him.

Domineering suggests arrogance:

He can be a domineering bully to people who do not stand up to him; but, like many bullies, he's also a coward.

Dominica

An inhabitant of the island in the Windward group is a 'Dominican'; the derived adjective is the same. The capital is Roseau (with one 's').

Dominican Republic

An inhabitant of the country that occupies the eastern part of the island of Hispaniola is a 'Dominican'; the derived adjective is the same. The capital is Santo Domingo.

domino

A *domino* is a small rectangular block used in the game of 'dominoes'. (The game is occasionally spelled 'dominos'.) Although the game is plural in form, it is often used with a singular verb:

Dominoes is frequently played in confined spaces.

When we refer to several rectangular blocks, we must use a plural form of the verb:

The dominoes are all on the table.

don't

Don't is a CONTRACTION of 'do not'. It is perfectly acceptable in informal writing but the full form should be used in all formal styles.

double comparative

In English, we can have comparative and superlative forms of many adjectives and adverbs:

Positive	Comparative	Superlative
attractive	more attractive	most attractive
big	bigger	biggest
fast	faster	fastest
slowly	more slowly	most slowly

In contemporary English, it is regarded as incorrect to use double comparatives or superlatives as in:

*This one is more better than that.

*She is the most beautifulest girl in the world.

These forms do, however, occur in some dialects

and are found in older forms of English. Shakespeare, for example has 'more better' (I.ii) and 'most busiest' (III.i) in *The Tempest*.

double entendre

The phrase *double entendre* is usually written in italics. It derives from French and is used of puns or ambiguities where one of the meanings intended is indelicate or indecent. An example of *double entendre* is the variation on the nursery rhyme:

Mary had a little lamb
She also had a bear.
I've often seen her little lamb
But I've never seen her bear (bare).

double negative

Double negatives are often treated under the heading of 'multiple negation' or 'negative concord'. In earlier forms of English, double or multiple negation was used for emphasis. Chaucer used it:

He nevere yet no villeiny ne sayde
In al his lif onto no maner wight.
　　　Prologue to the Canterbury Tales

and so did Shakespeare:

This is no mortal business nor no sound
That the earth owes.
　　　The Tempest, Act I, Scene ii

Since the seventeenth century, however, it has been regarded as incorrect, and millions of schoolchildren have been taught that:

Two negatives make an affirmative.

In contemporary English, such structures as:

*I didn't see nothing.

are not acceptable in Standard English, but it is possible in certain types of understatement or LITOTES to use 'not' with some 'dis-' and 'un-' forms to suggest limited affirmatives:

She wasn't disliked.

He's not unintelligent.

The one structure that may seem to break this rule is the use of 'neither ... nor'. When we use 'neither', we must use 'nor':

I have heard from neither John nor Michael.

*I have heard from neither John or Michael.

See also NEGATION, UNDERSTATEMENT

doublespeak

The word *doublespeak* was coined on analogy with George Orwell's 'Newspeak'. It is the term used to describe language that is intended to conceal rather than to reveal information. It is applied, for example, to the warnings on cigarette packets that say:

Smoking can seriously damage your health.

where the 'can' implies that it might not, instead of the more accurate:

Smoking has been shown to contribute to cancer and heart and lung disease.

Doublespeak (occasionally also 'doubletalk') is a means of promoting a cause, whether political, commercial or ideological, by manipulating language. A well-known form of doublespeak relates to the use of unwarlike vocabulary in descriptions of war and weapons:

a cruise missile
fat man (a weapon)
the theatre (of war).

See also EUPHEMISM, GOBBLEDEGOOK, JARGON, NEWSPEAK, SEASPEAK

doublet

In a bilingual community, one of the easiest methods of ensuring comprehension is to provide the word in both languages. This is frequently done today in Cameroon when people ask for:

Essence, le plein; petrol, fill it up.
I followed up my *dossier*, my file.
I want a *mandat*, a postal order, please.

A number of fossilized doublets exist in English where two words from different languages (often meaning approximately the same) have been fused into a unit:

fit and able (Middle English 'fitten' + Norman 'able')
flagstone (Old Norse 'flaga' + Old English 'stan')
good and proper (Old English 'god' + Norman 'propre')
time and tide (Old Norse 'timi' + Old English 'tid').

Many doublets seem to have come into the language after the Norman Conquest and this technique led to other types of doublets. Some are linked by rhyme or alliteration:

by hook or by crook
highways and byways
through thick and thin
trials and tribulations.

See also DYAD

doubt

The verb *doubt* means 'be unsure of':

I doubt his motives.
I have always doubted her suitability.

Doubt can be followed by 'if', 'that' and 'whether' in positive statements. When *doubt* is negated it can be followed only by 'that':

I don't doubt that she is intelligent.
There can be no doubt at all that he committed the crime.

The related noun means 'uncertainty':

We all have doubts at some time in our lives.

doubtful, dubious

These adjectives both have the meaning of 'uncertain' but *dubious* carries overtones of 'questionable':

I am doubtful about whether or not to trust him.
He has been involved in some dubious business deals.

dour

The adjective *dour* rhymes with 'poor' and means 'stern', 'unsmiling':

There was an impish sense of humour under that dour exterior.

douse, dowse

These verbs are both connected with water. *Douse* means 'drench with water':

We quickly doused the flames.

Dowse means 'search for underground water':

He used a forked stick to dowse for water.

There is a tendency for both verbs to be spelled dowse, but the distinction is a useful one.

dove
See DIVED

downward, downwards

In British English, *downward* is an adjective and *downwards* an adverb:

a downward movement
We moved downwards.

In American English *downward* can be used both adjectivally and adverbially.

See also -WARD/-WARDS

dowse
See DOUSE/DOWSE

draft, draught

These words are homophones and they were once variant spellings. In contemporary British English, *draft* is used for 'a money order':

a bank draft

and 'an early or imperfect version':

This is just a rough draft.

Draught is used for 'a current of air':

I'm sitting in a draught.

and 'a pull, something that pulls or is pulled':

a draught horse
draught beer.
The game is called draughts.

In America *draft* is used for all these words, except the game, which is usually called 'checkers'.

A 'draughtsman' is someone who prepares drawings and plans. A 'draftsman' is one who prepares documents.

dramatist, playwright

These words are synonymous:

Shakespeare is our most famous dramatist/ playwright.

but *dramatist* is perhaps slightly more prestigious.

The noun *playwright* ends in '-wright', a word meaning 'maker' that now occurs only as a suffix in such words as:

cartwright, playwright, shipwright, wheelwright.

The '-wright' comes from an Old English word for 'worker' and has nothing to do with 'write'. As the trades like cart-making and wheel-making die out, the words involving '-wright' become less widely used.

draw

Draw is an irregular verb:

draw(s), drew, drawing, drawn.

drawing

This word is often rhymed with 'flaw + ring' by speakers from the south of England, especially those who speak what has been called ESTUARY ENGLISH. The intrusive 'r' is not generally acceptable.

See also INTRUSIVE 'R'

drawing room

Many words for rooms in the house, like the names of meals, are marked for class and region. The term *drawing room* is an abbreviated form of 'withdrawing room', a room where the ladies retired after a meal while the men smoked and drank brandy. Today, many people use *drawing room* for the room where they relax. Other names given to such a room are 'lounge', 'parlour', 'living room' and 'sitting room'.

dreadful

Dreadful used to mean 'capable of filling one with dread'. The adjective now means little more than 'unpleasant':

It's a dreadful day.

Many people dislike the way words such as 'awful' (which derived from 'awe' + 'ful'), *dreadful* and 'terrible' ('terror' + '-ible') have been bleached of meaning. Such BLEACHING, however, has occurred throughout recorded history.

dream

In British English *dream* has two acceptable past

tense and past participle forms, 'dreamed' and 'dreamt':

dream(s), dreamed/dreamt, dreaming, dreamed/dreamt.

'Dreamed' may be rhymed with 'seemed' or 'exempt'; 'dreamt' always rhymes with 'exempt'.

In American English, the '-ed' forms are the norm:

dream(s), dreamed, dreaming, dreamed.

See also -ED/-T

dress

As English has spread around the world, speakers have come into contact with people of many other cultures and have borrowed many of their words for local dress. Among these borrowings are:

anorak from Inuit
beret from French
bolero from Spanish
cashmere from Kashmiri
cheongsam from Chinese
kimono from Japanese
sari from Hindi
sarong from Malay.

See also CLOTHES

drier, dryer

The form *drier* is the only acceptable spelling for the comparative form of the adjective 'dry':

I can't get the clothes any drier.

Drier is also used in Britain as a noun meaning 'person or thing that dries'.

The variant *dryer* is acceptable and is widely used especially for the electrical apparatus:

I've bought a new washer-dryer.

drily, dryly

The adverb *drily* means 'in a dry manner', 'sarcastically':

'So, we can speak French!' he whispered drily.

The form *drily* is widely used in Britain but the form *dryly* is preferred in America.

drink

Drink is an irregular verb:

drink(s), drank, drinking, drunk
I drank my coffee.
I have drunk my coffee.

Many speakers use the past participle form as a past tense:

*I drunk my coffee.

This is unacceptable.

drive

Drive is an irregular verb:

drive(s), drove, driving, driven.

drivel

The regular verb *drivel*, 'flow from the mouth, speak foolishly', doubles the 'l' before the '-ed', '-er' and '-ing' endings in British English but not in American English:

UK: drivel(s), drivelled, drivelling, driveller
US: drivel(s), driveled, driveling, driveler.

drunk, drunken

Drunk can be used as a past participle and as an adjective:

He has drunk all the medicine.
He's drunk, I think.
We saw a drunk man.

Drunken is not widely used but it can occur before an abstract noun as in:

a drunken brawl
a drunken spree.

It occurs before the animate noun 'sailor' in the song:

What shall we do with the drunken sailor?

but *drunk* has replaced *drunken* before other animate nouns:

a drunk man.

dry

Dry forms its comparative and superlative by changing 'y' to 'i':

dry, drier, driest.

See also SPELLING

dryer

See DRIER/DRYER

dryly

See DRILY/DRYLY

dual, duel

Dual means 'relating to two':

All the cars in the Driving School have dual control.
Don't try to pass that car until we reach the dual carriageway.

Duel can function as a noun and a verb meaning 'arranged combat between two':

They fought a duel.
They duelled for over an hour.

In British English the 'l' is doubled:

UK: duel(s), duelled, duelling

but left single in American English:

US: duel(s), dueled, dueling.

dubious

See DOUBTFUL/DUBIOUS

due to, owing to

There are some strong prejudices associated with the use of *due to* and *owing to*. According to purists, *due to* should be used only adjectivally, as a nominal complement that follows the noun it relates to:

The accident was due to the combination of ice, fog and poor driving.
Her delay must be due to the heavy traffic.

Owing to should be restricted in function to phrases acting as adverbials:

Owing to the derailment, trains are running two hours late.
There may be a slight delay, owing to the unexpected increase in traffic.

Because of the stigma attached to the use of *due to* and *owing to*, some speakers and writers avoid both structures and use 'because of' instead.

See also PURIST

duly, dully

These two adverbs are not related in meaning but they are frequently misspelled. *Duly* derives from 'due' but it does not have an 'e':

The train duly arrived at 2:15.

Dully is an adverb that derives from 'dull':

He droned on dully for an hour.

dummy

The term *dummy* has been applied to the verb 'do' when it functions as an auxiliary. It has also been applied to a subject that is structurally significant but has little meaning. There are two *dummy* subjects, 'it' and 'there', in such sentences as:

It's raining.
There was once a beautiful maiden ...

Not all uses of subject 'it' are dummy, as is clear if we contrast:

The castle was in a large wood and it (i.e., the castle) was guarded by a fierce dog.

with:

It's going to rain. (It = ?)

See also ANAPHORA, AUXILIARY, DO, SUBJECT

duplication, duplicity

These words both derive from Latin *duplex*, 'double', but they are now used with distinct meanings. *Duplication* means 'copy':

Try to avoid too much duplication. It's wasteful.

Duplicity means 'deception, double dealing':

We have never before encountered such cunning and duplicity.

Dutch

See NETHERLANDS, THE

dwarf

Dwarf is an undersized person. The normal plural is 'dwarfs' as in:

Snow White and the Seven Dwarfs

but the form 'dwarves' also occurs and is acceptable.

dwell

Dwell has almost disappeared from the language although it still occurs as a synonym for 'live' in literature and storytelling and, occasionally, in songs:

I dreamt I dwelt in marble halls ...

Dwell is an irregular verb:

dwell(s), dwelt, dwelling

Americans also use 'dwelled' as both the past tense and the past participle form:

She dwelled among the untrodden ways.
She has dwelled here for years.

dyad

The word *dyad* comes from Greek *dyo* meaning 'two'. It is used in stylistic analysis to refer to pairs of words that habitually collocate:

chop and change
by hook or by crook
hue and cry
might and main
odds and ends
through thick and thin
tooth and nail
well and truly.

Dyads are also referred to as 'doubles' and 'doublets' and they are so frequently used that many of them have become clichés.

See also DOUBLET

dye

Dye means 'stain, colour':

I bought two new dyes to try on my shoes.

Dye is a regular verb:

dye(s), dyed, dyeing.

The present participle has an 'e':

He was dyeing his hair.

and this helps to distinguish it from the present participle of 'die' meaning 'cease to live':

He was dying from a bullet wound.

dyke

See DIKE/DYKE

dynamic

Some verbs in English can, and usually do, occur in the progressive, as in:

I am sitting and thinking about France.

I was walking home.

and are frequently used in imperative structures:

Sit down beside me.

These verbs are often called *dynamic*.

A second type of verb, often referred to as 'stative', 'essive' or 'static', rarely occurs in the progressive or the imperative:

I am a student.

rather than:

*I am being a student.

I have a horse.

rather than:

*I am having a horse.

I like you.

rather than

*I am liking you.

I remember.

rather than

*I am remembering.

Among the commonest stative verbs are 'be', 'have', 'resemble' and verbs of liking, verbs of mental processes, such as 'remember', 'think', and verbs of perception, such as 'hear' and 'see'.

Dynamic can also be described as a vogue (or 'buzz') word in such sentences as:

She has a dynamic personality.

As a metaphor, this is perfectly acceptable but, like 'nice' and 'charisma', it has been overused.

See also ASPECT, FAD WORD, STATIVE AND DYNAMIC, VERB

dys-

Dys- is a prefix meaning 'diseased, faulty':

dysentery: intestinal infection (literally 'bad bowels')
dysfunction: abnormality in the function of an organ.

dysfunction, malfunction

Both these nouns relate of faulty functioning. *Dysfunction* is limited to medical and psychological contexts whereas *malfunction* tends to apply to machinery:

They have been described as a dysfunctional family.
There has been a major malfunction of the primary rocket.

dyslexia

Dyslexia derives from Latin *dys*, 'bad', + *lexia*, 'speech', and is the technical term for a disability known also as 'word blindness'. It manifests itself early in a child's life: in the inability to differentiate between 'p' and '9', or 'b' and 'd' or any of the other letters that are similar in shape; or in an inability to remember the ordering of letters in a word. Thus a dyslexic child may write 'mna' or 'amn' or 'nam' for 'man'.

No one is certain how many people are affected by this problem, although the frequently-cited figure of 10 per cent is probably an underestimate. The danger is that children who confuse sets of letters and habitually misspell words will be considered unintelligent, whereas they seem to have visual problems associated with shapes, comparable, but not necessarily related, to colour blindness.

See also APHASIA

E

e

E is a vowel. In isolation, it is pronounced to rhyme with 'see', but it has this pronunciation in only a few words such as 'he', 'she' and, on occasions, 'the'.

-e-, -oe-

Many words have *-oe-* in British English and *-e-* in America:

foetus, fetus
oedema, edema.

each

Each can function as a determiner:

Each book is to be examined carefully.

and as a pronoun:

Each must be examined carefully.

When *each* is used as the subject of a sentence, it takes a singular verb and singular referents:

Each girl is asked to make her own bed.
Each has its own kennel.

In speech, the pronoun *each* is almost invariably followed by 'of':

Each of the girls is asked to make her own bed.
Each of them has its own kennel.

In such circumstances, people often use a plural form of the verb, especially when the verb is a long way from the *each*:

*Each of the remaining soldiers were asked to return to barracks.

Sometimes, to avoid sexist language, people use 'their' or 'his/her' rather than a gender-marked singular possessive adjective:

Each student is responsible for submitting their dissertation.
Each student is responsible for submitting his/her dissertation.

When *each* follows a plural noun, the verb and the referents are plural:

The students each have a dossier of their own.

See also AGREEMENT, ALL/BOTH/EACH, DETERMINER, EVERY, PRONOUN

each and every

Each and every is frequently used as an emphatic form of 'each', 'every', 'every one' or 'all':

I have examined each and every case.
I have examined each case.

I have examined every case.
I should like to thank each and every one of you.
I should like to thank each of you.
I should like to thank every one of you.
I should like to thank all of you.

The phrase is usually a cliché and should be avoided.

See also DYAD

each other, one another

Some speakers distinguish between *each other* and *one another*, claiming that the first relates to only two:

Do Peter and Paul know each other?

and the second to more than two:

Do the four children know one another?

In contemporary British usage:

They love each other.

and:

They love one another.

are used almost interchangeably. Even in Britain, however, the use of *each other* tends to emphasize the individuals involved in the act, whereas *one another* is less particular:

John and Mary love each other.
At this age, children find it easy to love one another.

If these phrases are used as possessives, *'s* is added:

They borrowed each other's books.
They borrowed one another's books.

See also ANOTHER

-ean

See -AN/-EAN/-IAN

earn

Earn is a regular verb:

earn(s), earned, earning.

Some speakers analogize with 'learn' and form the past tense and the past participle with 't'. This is not acceptable:

I earned a living as a guide.
I had earned a living as a guide.
*I earnt a living as a guide.
*I had earnt a living as a guide.

earth, Earth

When *earth* is written with a lower-case 'e', it refers to the land or to the world in general terms:

It was good to feel the earth beneath my feet!
I've been on this earth for forty years.

Earth, with a capital letter, is the preferred spelling when the reference is to the planet:

Apart from Earth, there are three planets that are 'terran' or earthlike: Mercury, Venus and Mars.

earthly, earthy

Earthly is an adjective meaning 'characteristic of the earth', 'worldly':

Our heavenly life will long outlast this earthly one.

Colloquially, *earthly* is used, often in negative expressions, to mean 'conceivable', 'possible':

This is of no earthly use to anybody!

Earthy is an adjective that means 'characteristic of the earth or soil' and has developed the meaning of 'lusty, unrefined':

He has an earthy sense of humour.

The older adjective 'earthen' is virtually obsolete and is usually only found in the fixed phrases:

an earthen floor
earthenware (pottery).

east, East, eastern, Eastern

When *east* is used as an adjective, adverb or noun indicating direction, it has a lower-case 'e':

Temperatures are below normal for April, especially on the east coast, where they are unlikely to rise above 4°C.
We decided to drive east.
When the wind's from the east
It's not good for man or beast.

East with a capital 'E' is used when it is part of a name:

East Africa

or when *East* refers to a geographical area:

The Dutch were once the dominant power in the East Indies.

Eastern is an adjective that means 'towards the east':

We followed the eastern shore until the road became little more than a track.

It is usually written with a lower-case 'e' when the reference is general, but with 'E' in such fixed phrases as:

the Eastern Front.

easy, easily

In general, *easy* is an adjective:

an easy journey
the easiest topic I ever set

but it is used adverbially in a few fixed utterances such as:

Easy come, easy go!
Easier said than done!
Take it easy!

Easily is always an adverb:

She passed easily.

See also ADJECTIVE, ADVERB

eat

Eat is an irregular verb:

eat(s), ate, eating, eaten.

In most parts of England, the past tense form usually rhymes with 'get', although some speakers, especially those in Scotland and Ireland, rhyme it with 'gate'. In America, the standard pronunciation rhymes with 'gate'.

eatable, edible

The meanings of these adjectives overlap. They can both imply 'fit to eat':

The fish wasn't eatable: it was covered in sauce.
The fish wasn't edible: it had clearly gone off.

but *eatable* suggests that it would not hurt one to eat the fish, whereas *edible* implies that it would not be dangerous to eat it:

These button mushrooms are edible but the ones with black spots are poisonous and therefore inedible.

echelon

The word *echelon* is borrowed from French *échelon*, meaning 'rung of a ladder'. It means 'level of command', 'responsibility' and is often used now with the adjectives 'higher' and 'upper' to mean 'grade', 'rank':

She has a position in the higher echelons of the diplomatic service.
I believe he works in the upper echelons of the Registry.

eclectic

This adjective derives from Greek *eklegein*, 'to select', and means 'composed of elements taken from a variety of sources':

We have not chosen to follow one particular model in this course. Rather, we aim to be eclectic, using insights from a variety of models in order to show how the English language works.

eco-

This prefix derives ultimately from Greek *oikos*, 'house, environment', and is now widely used to denote 'ecology' or 'ecological':

ecocide: 'destruction of an area of our environment'
eco-friendly: 'friendly to the environment'
ecosystem: 'interaction between community and environment'.

economic, economical

These adjectives both derive from the noun 'economics'. *Economic* has two main uses. It can suggest 'relating to the economy':

Britain's 'seven wise men' are discussing our economic future and the likelihood of further interest rate cuts.

It can also be used in contexts where it means 'likely to make a profit, profitable':

We are in a classic catch-22 situation. If we do not charge economic fees, we cannot pay suitable salaries; but if we do not reduce the fees, we cannot attract the right number of students.

Economical traditionally meant 'relating to economics', but recently it has been used almost exclusively to mean 'careful with money' and 'cheap, inexpensive':

I really will have to be more economical if I want to stay in the black.

We hadn't much money but we found an economical holiday in Spain.

Some speakers dislike the use of *economical* to mean 'cheap', but this usage is widespread.

ecstasy

This word is frequently misspelled. It refers to a state of intense emotion, a state of joy or rapture:

Medieval saints often described their trance-like states of ecstasy.

The related adjective is 'ecstatic':

She's ecstatic about her A-level results.

Ecuador

An inhabitant of the South American republic is called an 'Ecuadoran', 'Ecuadorean' or 'Ecuadorian'; the derived adjectives are the same. The capital is Quito.

eczema

This noun, which describes a skin disease, comes from Greek *ek* + *zein*, 'to boil out'. It is frequently misspelled and mispronounced. It is stressed on the first syllable and rhymes with 'ex-simmer'.

-ed form

Often the term *-ed form* is used as a brief description of past tense forms in the English verb. This is because many regular verbs form their past tense by adding '-ed':

ask, asked

cool, cooled

last, lasted

and most nouns that are converted into verbs are treated as regular:

arm, armed

bank, banked

land, landed.

The expression *-ed form* derives from the written medium and does not take pronunciation into account. When we pronounce the above sets, we realize that there are three endings, pronounced 'd', 't' and 'id' respectively.

Many adjectives are formed from verbs:

a deserted village

tired eyes

and when these end in *-ed*, they are normally pronounced 'd' after a vowel or a voiced consonant:

agreed (an agreed sale)

banned (banned substances)

't' after a voiceless consonant:

dressed (dressed lamb)

and 'id' after a '-d-' or a '-t-':

guided (a guided tour)

rated (an X-rated film).

The 'id' pronunciation can sometimes seem repetitive, a fact that may explain why verbs such as 'broadcast', 'fit' and 'wet' have lost their *-ed* endings in certain regions and why many verbs ending in '-t' or '-d' either do not take *-ed* endings or are in the process of losing them. The main verbs in this category are:

bet, burst, cast, cost, cut, hit, hurt, let, put, quit, set, shut, slit, split, thrust, upset, rid, shed, spread.

A number of adjectives also have 'id' forms, the most widely used being:

aged (an aged woman)

blessed (this blessed morn)

crooked (... and he walked a crooked mile ...)

dogged (dogged determination)

jagged (a jagged rock)

learned (our learned friend)

naked (naked ambition)

ragged (Round and round the rugged rock the ragged rascal ran.)

wicked (a wicked sense of humour)

wretched (a wretched existence).

When these *-ed* forms function as verbs, the *-ed* is not pronounced as a separate syllable:

They blessed the day they met!

She learned Greek in a matter of months.

The *-ed* ending is sometimes given a stress in poetry to complete a metrical pattern:

Love is not love

Which alters when it alteration finds,

Or bends with the remover to remove.

O, no! it is an ever-fixéd mark

That looks on tempests and is never shaken.

Shakespeare, Sonnet 116

It is possible that the pronunciation of the *-ed* endings of certain adjectives may have been reinforced by the set of adjectives that derive from Latin and end in *-id*. Among such adjectives are:

acrid, avid, fervid, horrid, lucid, lurid, morbid, pallid, rancid, torrid, torpid, turbid.

A number of adverbs also pronounce the *-ed* syllable as 'id'. The best known of these are:

allegedly, assuredly, supposedly.

See also -EN FORM, VERB

-ed, -t

A number of verbs in British English may form their past tense and past participle by adding either *-ed* or *-t*. These are:

burn, burned, burnt

dream, dreamed, dreamt
dwell, dwelled, dwelt
kneel, kneeled, knelt
lean, leaned, leant
leap, leaped, leapt
learn, learned, learnt
smell, smelled, smelt
spell, spelled, spelt
spill, spilled, spilt
spoil, spoiled, spoilt.

Most Americans use the -ed forms:

She spilled the beans.
She's spilled the beans.

and some British writers use the -ed for the past tense and the -t for the past participle:

She spilled the beans.
She's spilt the beans.

edema, oedema

This noun is normally spelled with 'oe-' in Britain and 'e-' in America:

UK: An oedema is an excessive accumulation of fluid in tissue. The plural is 'oedemata' although 'oedemas' is occasionally found.

US: An edema is an excessive accumulation of fluid in tissue. The plural is 'edemata' although 'edemas' is now more widespread.

edible

See EATABLE/EDIBLE

education

The descriptive terms used in education in Britain and in the United States overlap, but the differences can cause confusion to outsiders. Differences are found at all levels, so that a 'pupil' at a 'playschool' in Britain may be a 'student' at a 'nursery school' in the United States. The influence on British usage from America is, however, strong. In the 1980s it was still the norm to refer to 'postgraduate' students, but the American phrase 'graduate student' is now widely used throughout British universities: .

Leeds has a large and growing population of graduate students ...

See also AMERICA/AMERICAN, GRADUATE, UK AND US ENGLISH, UK ENGLISH, US ENGLISH

-ee, -er, -or

The SUFFIX -ee is used to form nouns that indicate:

■ The person who receives the action:

assignee (person to whom a right is transferred)

■ A person in a particular state or condition:

absentee, employee

■ A diminutive:

bootee (baby's boot)
goatee (small pointed beard on chin).

The suffix -er can function in a variety of ways. It can be used to form nouns that indicate:

■ The person or thing that performs an action:
reader, speaker

■ The person engaged in an occupation:
baker, writer

■ An inhabitant:
Londoner, New Yorker, villager

■ A trade or profession
join + er = joiner
write + er = writer.

And it can form the comparative of some adjectives and adverbs:
grand: grander
well: better.

Sometimes, the -ee and -er words form a reciprocal set:
assignee, assigner
employee, employer
tutee, tutor.

The suffix -or can be used to form nouns that indicate a person or thing that performs the action described in the verb. These words are less frequent than -er words and are often misspelled. The most frequently used of these are:

actor, censor, conductor, contributor, conveyor, creator, doctor, mentor, inventor, protector, professor, sailor, sensor, solicitor, surveyor, tailor.

There are a number of words where the suffix can be either -er or -or. The commonest words in this category are:

adviser/advisor, converter/convertor, conveyer/conveyor, superviser/supervisor.

The -er ending is increasingly commonly used except where a distinction is being made between an animate and an inanimate noun as with:

distributer (person), distributor (part of car).

The form -or is also the American equivalent of '-our' as in:
colour, color
favour, favor.

See also SPELLING, UK AND US ENGLISH

e'er, ere, err

E'er is the poetic abbreviation of 'ever':

Where'er you walk, cool gales shall fan the glade,
Trees where you sit, shall crowd into a shade:
        Alexander Pope, *Pastorals*, 'Summer' .

Ere is an archaic preposition meaning 'before':

This was done ere you were born.

Err is a verb meaning 'make a mistake':

To err is human; to forgive divine.

effect
See AFFECT/EFFECT

effective, effectual, efficacious, efficient

As with many words with related form and overlapping meaning, there is sometimes confusion regarding the use of these four adjectives. All relate to 'effect' in its meaning of 'result'.

The adjective *effective* is applied to someone or something that can produce a satisfactory result or solve a problem:

If we judge by examination results, she is the most effective teacher in the school.

We have tried for years to find an effective solution to the problems associated with condensation.

The adjective *effectual* is applied to an action that fulfils its purpose or to a person capable of producing a desired effect:

I was told that a little oil added to the petrol could be highly effectual in preventing engine knock.

He was a highly effectual administrator: everything ran so smoothly when he was in charge that many people thought the office ran itself.

The adjective *efficacious* is applied to something (usually a medicine) sure to produce a desired effect:

... For she invented a medicinal compound,
Most efficacious in every case.

Freshly ground pepper in warm milk is a most efficacious remedy for hay fever.

The adjective *efficient* is applied to people and instruments that function well:

She was extremely efficient. Everyone and everything in her office worked like clockwork.

My car's getting old. The engine is no longer as efficient as it once was.

effeminate

The adjective *effeminate* is sometimes misused. It is applied to a man who does not look manly. The equivalent adjective used of a woman is 'mannish'.

See also POLITICAL CORRECTNESS, SEXIST LANGUAGE

effete

The adjective *effete* is frequently misused. It comes from Latin *effetus*, 'having produced offspring' and thus 'tired'. It has two main uses. It can mean 'worn out', especially when applied to plants or animals:

This is an effete strain, most unlikely to reproduce.

It can also mean 'weak', 'ineffective', 'decadent':

Many of the portraits of Keats make him look effete, but when we consider how much poetry he wrote before he was twenty-six we must marvel at his vitality.

efficacious, efficient
See EFFECTIVE/EFFECTUAL/EFFICACIOUS/EFFICIENT

e.g., i.e.

These abbreviations are occasionally confused. They both derive from Latin, *exempla gratia*, 'for the sake of example' and *id est*, 'that is':

Many words in English derive ultimately from Latin, e.g., 'abbreviations', 'occasionally' and 'confused'.

Don't indulge in meiosis, i.e., understatement.

See also ABBREVIATION, LATIN

egoist, egotist

These nouns are often confused, partly because their meanings overlap. They both derive from Latin *ego*, 'I'. An *egoist* is someone who is preoccupied with his or her own interests:

He is an egoist: introverted and self-obsessed.

An *egotist* is a boastful, conceited person:

She is an egotist: totally convinced that she is the most articulate and intelligent person in the school.

The normal pronunciation for these words rhymes the first syllable with 'league' but the alternative pronunciation, which rhymes 'eg-' with 'leg', is also acceptable.

Egypt

An inhabitant of the northeastern African republic is an 'Egyptian'; the derived adjective is the same. The capital is Cairo.

-ei-

One of the best known spelling rules is:

'i' before 'e' except after 'c'.

This rule holds for the majority of the words in the language but not for the following:

beige, caffeine, casein, codeine, counterfeit, deign, eiderdown, eight, either, feign, feint, foreign, forfeit, freight, heifer, height, heinous, heir, kaleidoscope, leisure, Madeira, neigh, neighbour, neither, obeisance, plebeian, protein, reign, reindeer, seismic, seize, skein, sleigh, sleight, surfeit, their, veil, vein, weigh, weigh, weird.

eighth

This word is frequently misspelled. It has one 't':

eight, eighth.

Eire

Eire is the Irish Gaelic name for 'Ireland' ('Eire' + 'land'). It is now often applied to the Republic of Ireland:

There are thirty-two counties in Ireland: twenty-six in Eire and six in Northern Ireland.

either, neither

These words can function as adverbs, conjunctions, determiners and pronouns and they tend to be pronounced differently in Britain and America. In Britain, the first syllables usually rhyme with 'I' and 'nigh' but in America they rhyme with 'me' and 'knee'.

When *either* is an adverb, it tends to occur in negative structures, and often at the end of the sentence:

I liked her too. I didn't like her either.
We also went. We didn't go either.

Adverbial *neither*, by contrast, often occurs in the initial position:

I didn't like her. Neither did I.
We didn't go. Neither did we.

Either and *neither* can be paired with 'or' and 'nor' respectively and can function as coordinating conjunctions, implying two-part contrasts:

He was either French or Belgian.
He was neither French nor Belgian.

In practice, these 'two-part structures' often relate to more than two:

He was either French or Belgian or Swiss.

Normally, the elements in such structures are equivalent (e.g., two adjectives, two nouns, two phrases or two sentences):

I want either green or blue.
It was neither fish nor flesh.
He is either on top of the world or down in the dumps.
Either they sink or they swim.
They will neither work nor sleep.
Neither John nor Mary received an invitation.

Occasionally, for emphasis, the structures with *either ... or* are not balanced, but in these circumstances, 'else' is often introduced:

She is either very talented or else she has been incredibly lucky.

There has been much debate as to the correct position of adverbial *either* and *neither* in balanced structures. The following sentences are regarded as correct:

She'll either accept the position or form her own company.
He claimed to be neither lazy nor inactive.

while the following variants, although common in the spoken medium, are not altogether acceptable in formal contexts:

*Either she'll accept the position or form her own company.
*He neither claimed to be lazy nor inactive.

If *either* occurs in initial position in a clause, it can sometimes imply a threat:

Either leave at once or accept the consequences.

As determiners, *either* and *neither* cannot co-occur with other determiners and, since they are singular, they are correctly followed by a singular noun, verb and pronoun:

It was either Peter or Paul.
It was neither Mary nor Sam.
It was either Pat or John.
Neither Pat nor John was there.
Either book is fine and will make a lovely present.
Neither boy is eligible.
If either boy rings, tell him I'll be home at five.

In practice, however, to avoid using 'him' or 'her', 'them' is sometimes selected:

If either Mary or Mike rings, tell them I'll be home at five.

Either and *neither* also occur in the structure '(n)either' + 'of' + determiner + plural noun phrase:

Either of those books will do.
I want neither of the reports.

or '(n)either' + 'of' + plural pronoun:

Either of them will do.
I want neither of them.

A problem of agreement can arise when the coordinates would normally require a different form of the verb:

He is not going and I am not going.

The solution is either to rephrase:

John is not going and neither am I.
Neither of us is going.

or to use plural agreement:

Neither he nor I are going.

When a plural noun or pronoun is coordinated with a singular, as in:

neither the children nor my wife

the verb usually agrees with the subject closest to it:

Neither the children nor my wife is going.
Neither my wife nor the children are going.

The only exception to this is when the second part of the coordinated phrase is 'I' as in:

Neither he nor I are going.

Many people are, however, unhappy about this solution and prefer to rephrase it.

See also ADVERB, AGREEMENT, ALL/BOTH/EACH, CONCORD, DETERMINER, PRONOUN

eke

This word is virtually archaic but it is still found in the phrasal verb *eke out* meaning 'make something last by being frugal':

We'll have to be very careful so that we can eke out our food until the end of the month.

or 'add to something that is insufficient':

I was able to eke out my grant by working at weekends.

El Salvador

An inhabitant of the Central American republic is a 'Salvadorian', a 'Salvadoran' or a 'Salvadorean'. The derived adjectives are the same. The capital is San Salvador.

élan

This French word is used because there is no single English word that combines its meaning of 'style and vigour':

He was magnificent. He played with passion and élan.

elapse, lapse

These two words, which can function as nouns and verbs, are occasionally confused. They both derive from Latin *labi* 'to slip, glide'. *Elapse* means 'pass', 'expire' and it frequently occurs with 'time':

Your allocated time has elapsed. You must leave the car park or pay for a further period.

Your television licence has elapsed.

Lapse suggests 'drop standards' or 'fail to maintain a norm, often temporary':

I'd like to apologize for the lapse in my behaviour.

I've allowed my membership to lapse.

There was a two-week lapse between meetings.

elder, older

Most dictionaries give *elder* and *eldest* as synonyms of *older* and *oldest* and all four of them relate to age. *Elder* and *eldest* modify people and are often applied to family members:

my elder son: *my elder car

the elder of my two sons: *the elder of my two cars

the eldest child: *my eldest suit.

Elder and *eldest* cannot be used as predicative adjectives:

*She is elder.

*He is eldest.

although they can occur in such structures when they are preceded by 'the':

She is the elder.

He is the eldest.

Elder cannot be used in comparative structures such as:

*He is elder than my daughter.

In such a structure, *older* is required:

He is older than my daughter.

Older and *oldest* are the normal comparative and superlative forms of the adjective 'old':

He's three years older than Tim.

She's the oldest woman in the world.

Older and *oldest* can modify people and things and they can also be used both attributively and predicatively:

the older daughter; the older suit

my oldest child; my oldest car

She is older.

He is oldest.

Elder is often applied to or of people as a term of respect to indicate their age and experience:

an elder statesman

village elders

She has been a church elder for ten years.

electric, electrical, electronic

These adjectives all derive from Latin *electrum*, 'amber'. (Friction causes amber to become charged.) *Electric* means 'produced or powered by electricity':

an electric storm

an electric kettle

an electric light bulb.

Electrical is most frequently used to mean 'concerned with electricity':

It's probably an electrical fault.

He lectures in electrical engineering.

An electrocardiograph is an instrument for recording the electrical activity of the heart.

Electronic relates to equipment such as computers and CD players in which the current is controlled by microchips or transistors:

The children are surrounded by electronic equipment at school.

I've bought an electronic diary that I can even use for sending or receiving faxes.

elegant variation

Elegant variation describes a style that uses learned or polysyllabic vocabulary, choosing, for example:

He circumnavigated the planet.

I witnessed the acrimonious aftermath of the collision.

rather than:

He sailed around the world.

I saw the row that followed the crash.

Elegant variation is part of most people's repertoire of styles. It should, however, be used carefully so that it does not interfere with comprehension, give misleading information or evoke an unintentionally humorous response when the writer is aiming at sophisticated description.

See also CIRCUMLOCUTION, POETIC DICTION

elegy, eulogy

An *elegy* is a reflective poem, often dealing with a lament for the dead:

When did Thomas Gray publish his 'Elegy Written in a Country Churchyard?' Was it 1751?

A *eulogy* is a formal speech or piece of writing praising someone lavishly:

It was the most complimentary reference I have ever read. Indeed, it was more like a eulogy than a testimonial.

elemental, elementary

These adjectives are occasionally confused, partly because they derive from the same source, Latin *elementum*, 'a first principle'. *Elemental* means 'relating to the chemical elements or to air, earth, fire and water; basic, fundamental, primal':

Heathcliff represents the elemental forces in nature. He is strong, emotional, powerful and, ultimately, destructive.

Elementary means 'simple, introductory':

Where does one start? They have never studied grammar or acquired even the most elementary knowledge of how the language works.

elevator, lift

These words are often synonymous, the former being used in America, the latter in Britain:

UK: Take the lift to the third floor.

US: Take the elevator to the third floor.

Some British people claim to use *elevator* for 'goods' and *lift* for 'people' but a study of student usage does not support such a claim.

See also UK AND US ENGLISH

elf

It is not always clear what distinction there is between an *elf* and such other legendary beings as 'gnomes' and 'fairies'. The plural form is 'elves':

Are elves always drawn sitting on toadstools?

elicit, illicit

These homophones are occasionally confused. *Elicit* is a regular verb:

elicit(s), elicited, eliciting.

It derives from Latin *elicere*, 'to lure forth', and means 'draw out, give rise to, evoke':

My act of kindness didn't even elicit a 'thank you'.

I wrote several letters but could not elicit a response.

Illicit is an adjective meaning 'improper', 'unlawful':

My father makes counterfeit money
My mother brews illicit gin...

The authorities are trying to put an end to the trade in illicit drugs.

eligible, illegible, unreadable

The adjectives *eligible* and *illegible* are sometimes confused although they do not, in fact, share an overlap of meaning. *Eligible* comes from Latin *eligere*, 'to elect', and means 'fit, worthy, qualified to be chosen':

Is he eligible to apply for the post? He has been in the firm for only three weeks.

He spent years looking for an eligible princess.

Illegible comes from Latin *legere*, 'to read'. It means 'unreadable', 'indecipherable', 'written or printed in such a way that it cannot be read':

Are doctors trained to have illegible handwriting?

Is this letter an 'r' or an 's' or an 'e'? John should learn to type. His handwriting is almost completely illegible.

It is impossible to mark a script if the handwriting is illegible.

The adjectives *illegible* and *unreadable* are often used loosely and are therefore likely to cause confusion. *Unreadable* can include *illegible*. It can mean not only 'indecipherable' but also 'dull, tedious':

Is she a doctor? Her handwriting is unreadable.

I've never been able to read *Pilgrim's Progress* from start to finish. As far as I am concerned, parts of it are so boring that they are unreadable.

See also LEGIBLE/READABLE

elision

Elision involves the loss of sounds in speech or the loss of letters in writing:

is + not = isn't

will + not = won't

Worcester (pronounced 'Wooster').

Vowels, consonants and entire syllables can be elided.

The term *elision* comprehends APHESIS (the loss of an initial vowel or syllable):

about = 'bout

because = 'cos

SYNCOPE (the loss of a sound or syllable from the middle of a word):

apostle (the 't' is not pronounced)

Wednesday (two syllables)

and APOCOPE (the loss of a sound or syllable from the end of a word):

cup of tea = cuppa tea

fitted = fit.

elk, moose

The European and Asian *elk* is a large deer of the species *Alces alces*. This species includes the North American *moose*. The animal that the Americans call *elk* or 'wapiti' is also a deer, but from the species *Cervus canadensis*.

ellipsis

Ellipsis (plural 'ellipses') derives from Greek *elleipsis*, 'omission'. It has two main uses.

It refers to the omission from a quotation of words needed to complete it and to the three full stops that signal the *ellipsis*:

The speaker ... invariably used 'dump' where a British speaker would use 'drop' ... as in 'I've just dumped my cookies on the floor'.

When *ellipsis* occurs after a complete sentence, the full stop should be followed by three stops:

Whatever sentence will bear to be read twice, we may be sure was thought twice. ...

Henry Thoreau, *Journal*, 1842

It is used by some linguists for the omission of a part of a sentence that is recoverable:

Where did you put them?
In the drawer. (I put them in the drawer.)

See also ANAPHORA, PUNCTUATION, QUOTATION

else

Else is used after pronouns and interrogatives to mean 'in addition':

Nobody else can do it.
Who else should we invite?

The phrase *or else* is used to mean 'if not, then':

Start working or else you'll regret it.

When possession is indicated, the apostrophe + 's' is attached to the *else*:

I don't want to hear anybody else's problems!
Who else's work should I read?

When it is used elliptically, a threat is implied:

Get that piece of work in by tomorrow, or else!

See also APOSTROPHE

elude
See ALLUDE/ELUDE

elusive, illusive, illusory

These adjectives are sometimes confused or misspelled. *Elusive* means 'difficult to capture', 'difficult to understand or remember':

He was called 'the Elusive Pimpernel' because the French could not capture him.
The meaning of this word is elusive; it seems to change depending on the noun it is describing.

Illusive and *illusory* mean 'deceptive', 'based on illusion'. They are both used, but some writers prefer *illusory*:

Dreams of power are, ultimately, illusory. No position and no condition will last forever.

See also ALLUSION/DELUSION/ILLUSION

e-mail

E-mail is also written *email* and is an abbreviation of 'electronic mail'. It can be used as a noun:

Are you using e-mail or snail mail?

and as a regular verb:

e-mail(s), e-mailed, e-mailing
I'll e-mail the times as soon as they are confirmed.

embarrass

This regular verb and its derived adjective and noun are frequently misspelled. The words have '-rr-' and '-ss-':

embarrass(es), embarrassed, embarrassing
I was extremely embarrassed by my outburst.
Teenagers often suffer from pangs of embarrassment.

embedding

The term *embedding* is used in some modern grammars to refer to the process by which one sentence is included within another. For example, the sentence:

The boy who sings solo is twelve.

is a combination of two sentences:

The boy is twelve. + The boy sings solo.

The second sentence 'The boy sings solo' is embedded in the first:

The boy [the boy sings solo] is twelve.

and the repeated phrase 'the boy' is replaced by a relative pronoun, in this example 'who'.

Other types of embedding occur. Very often, sentences involving non-finite verbs (e.g., 'to write', 'writing' and 'written') can be shown to involve embeddings. Such sentences as:

His writing of short stories continues to be respected.
She advised me to write short stories.

are combinations of:

He wrote short stories. + The short stories continue to be respected.
She advised me. + I wrote short stories.

Embedding differs from coordination, which uses coordinating conjunctions such as 'and', 'but', 'either ... or' to join units of equal rank:

I saw the play and I enjoyed it very much.
I like coffee but I hate tea.
Either he's a saint or he's deaf to all criticism.

See also CLAUSE, DEPENDENT, SUBORDINATION, TRANSFORMATIONAL GRAMMAR

emend
See AMEND/EMEND/MEND

emigrant, immigrant, migrant

The nouns *emigrant* and *immigrant* are occasionally confused. *Emigrants* are those people who are leaving their country of birth whereas *immigrants* are coming into a foreign country:

Emigration from Ireland increased after the terrible famines of the mid-1840s. Some of the emigrants sought sanctuary in America; many did not get any further than Liverpool.

There are large numbers of immigrants in Port Moresby. Some have come from Australia, some from the Solomon Islands, some from Irian Jaya and some from other Pacific islands such as Fiji.

An easy way to remember the difference is to remember that the 'im-' in *immigrant* means 'in' and so an *immigrant* comes into a country:

Many of America's earliest immigrants were the downtrodden of Europe.

Most of the emigrants from Britain to America knew that they would never see their homeland again.

A *migrant* is a person who moves from one country to another, often in search of work:

Some of these migrants have worked in four or more different countries.

The related verbs are 'emigrate', 'immigrate' and 'migrate'.

eminent, immanent, imminent

These homophonic adjectives are frequently confused. *Eminent* means 'outstanding', 'distinguished', 'famous':

Many eminent scholars are nominated for Nobel Prizes.

Even eminent scientists have misinterpreted the calculations.

Immanent comes from Latin *immanere*, 'to remain', and means 'inherent', 'existing':

God's presence is immanent; it pervades the entire universe.

Imminent comes from Latin *imminere*, 'to project over', and means 'close in time', 'about to happen', 'impending':

Now that the examinations are imminent, I'm working as hard as I should have worked all semester.

The excitement grew as the plane appeared and they prepared for the imminent arrival of their hero.

emotional, emotive

These adjectives both derive from the noun 'emotion', but they have different meanings. *Emotional* means 'having emotions that are easily roused':

It's hard not to feel emotional about the destruction of the forests.

Emotive means 'tending to or likely to stir the emotions':

Freedom of speech is a wonderful ideal but should we tolerate the dissemination of emotive ideas that encourage racism and intolerance?

empathy, sympathy

These nouns are occasionally confused because their meanings overlap. *Empathy* describes an ability to understand and share the feelings of someone else:

Her most attractive quality was her empathy for others. She could sense their problems and their difficulties and was therefore in a position to offer help and guidance.

Sympathy describes the ability to feel pity or sorrow for someone else:

I'd like to offer my sympathy for her difficulties but it is not always easy to find the right words.

emphasis

The plural form of *emphasis* is 'emphases':

Few courses give as much emphasis to the written skills as this one does.

The equivalent verb is usually *emphasize*, which can be spelled with '-ise' in Britain.

In language study, the word *emphasis* comprehends the many methods of putting extra stress on a sound, word, phrase or idea so as to give prominence to it. *Emphasis* may involve choices from all areas of the language and its effect may depend on a statistical change, such as regular increased volume or an increase in the number of negatives per paragraph. *Emphasis* may be given by omission, so that speakers who avoid fillers such as 'um' or 'er' may use silent pauses to add significance to their utterances. The most widely-used forms of emphasis are summarized below.

Parallelism

This device uses repetition of sound, word or rhythm as in Tennyson's *In Memoriam*:

But what am I?
An infant crying in the night,
An infant crying for the light;
And with no language but a cry.

Word order

The normal word order of:

Subject	Predicate	Object	Complement
They	called	him	David

may be modified to:

(It was) David they called him.

thus emphasizing 'David'.

Figures of speech

Most of these are used for emphasis. For example, in the following rhyming couplet from Alexander Pope, apostrophizing, antithesis and bathos combine to highlight the trivial:

Here Thou, great Anna, whom three realms obey
Dost sometimes counsel take and sometimes tea.

Deviation

Deviations from the norm catch the reader's or listener's attention. The deviations may be in the imagery or in unexpected adjectives such as Dylan Thomas's:

Her fist of a face died clenched on a round pain.

Proportion

The amount of space devoted to each stage of an argument may indicate a writer's priorities. Similarly, the deliberate exclusion of something that is expected may represent a form of emphasis.

Emphasis is thus not simply, or even primarily, a matter of talking loudly or punctuating heavily. It permeates language at every level, reflecting and promoting certain attitudes and details. It may vary regionally and also socially, but most types of language involve *emphasis* of some kind.

See also DEVIATION, FIGURE OF SPEECH, FOREGROUNDING, PARALLELISM, WORD ORDER

empiric, empirical, empiricism

These words, which all derive from a Greek word *empeirikos*, 'experience', are frequently misused. *Empiric* is a derogatory term most frequently used by the medical profession with reference to a quack. The word has been adopted by literary critics so that 'empiric criticism' is untrained or unskilled criticism that does not take account of theoretical approaches to study:

Why didn't he just call him a quack instead of a charlatan and an empiric?

Empirical and *empiricism* are philosophical terms applied to the practice of evolving rules to fit experience. *Empirical* has, however, been generalized to denote any procedure that relies on experience or observation alone, and it is sometimes used of an experimental method:

His research is empirical rather than theoretical but such empiricism is not highly valued today.

The adjective *empirical* is often used inaccurately by speakers and writers as an equivalent for 'proven'.

emporium

This noun has become popular as a synonym for a large shop or trading centre. The word has two acceptable plurals, 'emporia' and 'emporiums':

I bought this electronic diary at the computer emporium.

empty, vacant

These adjectives both relate to 'absence' but they should be used differently. *Empty* means 'containing nothing':

My purse is empty. Every single thing has been taken from it.

Vacant suggests 'unoccupied' of a building:

The house that I grew up in is vacant now.
The house stood vacant for three years.

The word is also used metaphorically to mean 'expressionless':

He used to sit there with a completely vacant look in his eyes.
That child always has a rather vacant expression on his face.

The expression *vacant possession* is frequently used in the housing market to mean that the owner/occupiers will have left the house by the time the sale has been completed:

Vacant possession; no chain involved.

emulate, imitate

These regular verbs have similar meanings but *emulate* comprehends *imitate*. *Emulate* means 'try to do at least as well if not better than someone else':

I'm trying to emulate my father's sporting successes.

Imitate means 'copy someone's behaviour':

He's a wonderful mimic. He can imitate my speech and my mannerisms extremely well.

en-, in-

A number of nouns and verbs may begin with either *en-* or *in-*, the commonest of which are:

en-	in-
enclose	inclose
encrust	incrust
endorse	indorse
enquire	inquire

The verbs 'ensure' and 'insure' have different meanings and there is a growing tendency for 'enquire' and 'inquire' to be used with different meanings.

See also ASSURE/ENSURE/INSURE, ENQUIRE/INQUIRE

-en form

The term *-en form* is sometimes used as a synonym for 'past participle' because many irregular verbs have a past participle that ends in *-en*:

Verb	Past participle
be	been: I've been …
get	got/gotten: (UK) I've got/ (US) I've gotten
go	gone: I've gone …
put	put: I've put …
take	taken: I've taken …

As we can see from the list above, not all past participles end in *-en* but the term is used as a means of distinguishing between the past tense and the past participle of verbs. There is no difference in form between the past tense and the past participle of regular verbs (both of which end in '-ed'):

I looked it up.
I've looked it up.

but there is a difference in function.

The *-en* ending had two other uses in earlier forms of English. It could be used to create causative verbs from adjectives or nouns:

black + en = cause to become black
fright + en = cause to feel fright
haste + en = cause to make haste
thick + en = cause to become thick

Many of these verbs still exist but the technique is no longer available to modern speakers:

pink: *pinken (cause to become pink)

slim: *slim(m)en (cause to become slim).

Its other use was to create adjectives from nouns:

brass: brazen (made of brass)
gold: golden (made of gold)
wood: wooden (made of wood).

Occasionally, the spelling has diverged from the original noun and the adjective is often used metaphorically as with 'brazen', which has come to mean shameless or impudent:

a brazen act.

See also ASPECT, -ED FORM, VERB

en suite
This French phrase literally means 'in sequence' but is used as a shorthand phrase meaning 'with its own bathroom':

This delightful house comprises ... three large bedrooms, two en suite ...

It was originally italicized but is now so widely used in house descriptions that this is no longer required.

enable
The verb *enable* means 'make able, help':

My knowledge of French enabled me to get a good job in Paris.

Since the 1980s, *enable* has occasionally been used like 'empower' to mean 'raise someone's consciousness':

Political correctness may have flaws but it has enabled many people who were previously disadvantaged.

enclose, inclose
These are variant spellings of the same verb, as are their derived nouns 'enclosure' and 'inclosure'.

See also -EN/-IN

encyclopaedia, encyclopedia
These are variant spellings of the same verb. Due to the influence from America, the second has now become more widely used in Britain:

He bought his daughter *The Cambridge Encyclopedia of Language.*

endearments
Endearments, like insults, are often very personal and not easily described. It is probably true to say that we proliferate terms of address and reference for the people we love and hate most. It is therefore difficult to do more than indicate some of the endearments that occur widely in the language.

The most widely-used endearments are 'love', 'darling' (which originally meant 'little dear') and 'dear', which is identical in form and etymology

to the adjective 'dear' meaning 'expensive'. Other endearments, especially those for women, derive from the imagery of eating, especially items that are sweet:

honey, sugar, sweetie

from animals:

duck, hen, pet

from babies and dolls:

baby, babydoll, doll

and from flowers:

blossom, flower, petal.

See also POLITICAL CORRECTNESS

endeavour, endeavor
These variant spellings are regionally marked. *Endeavour* is the accepted form in Britain and *endeavor* is standard in America:

UK: Students must endeavour to register ...
US: Students must endeavor to register ...

See also SPELLING

endive
This plant, which is often eaten with salad, has several names and pronunciations. In Britain, it rhymes with 'heave'; in America with 'hive'. Its alternative names are 'chicory' and 'escarole'.

endorse
See APPROVE/ENDORSE

enervate
This verb is frequently misused. It means 'sap someone's strength or energy':

I find tropical heat less enervating than summer heat in England.

enforceable
Enforceable always has 'e' before the 'able':

Such rules are not easily enforceable.

England
England is one of the three countries making up Great Britain:

Since 1707, the term 'Great Britain' has regularly been applied to the large island that is made up of England, Scotland and Wales.

See also BRITAIN

English
English can function as both an adjective and a noun:

an English oak
English is now spoken by almost one in every six human beings on earth.

Inhabitants of England are English; the words

'Englishman' and 'Englishwoman' can be used instead.

The language is a mother tongue for many people in Australia, Britain, Canada, the Caribbean, India, Ireland, New Zealand, South Africa and the United States. It is also the most widely-used second language in the world.

enhance

This regular verb is sometimes misused. It means 'increase the good qualities of something', 'improve the look of':

Such behaviour will not enhance his reputation.
The new colour scheme has enhanced the appearance of the room.

enormity, enormousness

In strict usage, *enormity* refers to the great wickedness of a crime or action:

Words cannot describe the enormity of their crime against the child.
We were all shocked by the enormity of the killing.

Frequently, however, especially in speech and in loose writing, *enormity* is used as a synonym for 'very large':

Everyone who visits Disneyland is amazed at the enormity of this children's playground.

If we wish to use a word relating to size, we could select *enormousness*, but it seems likely that the second usage may oust the first except in legal and liturgical contexts:

The Prodigal Son's enormity was forgiven by his father.

enough

Enough can function as an adverb meaning 'sufficiently':

You've worked hard enough.

a determiner meaning 'adequate, sufficient':

We haven't enough bread.

as a pronoun:

Enough is always too much.

and as an intensifier:

Strangely enough, we met in Papua New Guinea.

enquire, inquire

For many speakers, these forms and their related nouns 'enquiry' and 'inquiry' are interchangeable:

I'd like to enquire/inquire about your advertised flat.

Some speakers, however, are beginning to distinguish these words and use *enquire* for simple requests for information:

I'll enquire about that for you.

and to use *inquire* for serious investigations:

The police plan to inquire into the seemingly natural deaths of a number of other pensioners in the Leeds area.

So far, this is only a tendency, but the meanings of these variants may diverge in the future in the same way that 'insure' has diverged from 'ensure'.

British speakers tend to stress the second syllable of both verb and noun and rhyme the first syllable with 'in'. Many Americans stress the first syllable and pronounce it like 'ink'.

See also INQUIRY

enrol, enroll

This regular verb, which is spelled with one 'l' in Britain and two in America, means 'note in a roll, become a member of an organization':

UK: enrol(s), enrolled, enrolling
US: enroll(s), enrolled, enrolling
I enrolled as a life member of the club.

The derived noun is 'enrolment' in Britain but 'enrollment' in America.

See also SPELLING

ensure

See ASSURE/ENSURE/INSURE

-ent

See -ANT/-ENT

enthral, enthrall

This regular verb meaning 'hold spellbound' has one 'l' in the present tense in Britain and two in America:

UK: enthral(s), enthralled, enthralling
US: enthrall(s), enthralled, enthralling.

The increasingly seldom-used derived noun 'enthral(l)ment' has one 'l' in Britain but two in America.

enthuse

Enthuse is a regular verb created as a BACK FORMATION from the noun 'enthusiasm':

enthuse(s), enthused, enthusing.

It means 'feel or show or inspire enthusiasm':

She's the only person I know who can enthuse about grammar.

entitled, titled

Entitled is used to mean 'named':

It was entitled The Charioteers in Britain.

Recently, first in America but now in many parts of the English-speaking world, *titled* has begun to be used in the same way:

My chapter is titled 'The Medium for the Message'.

Some scholars dislike this usage but it is becoming the norm.

The word *title* is most frequently used as a noun:

The title of the novel is Long Drums.

entomology

Entomology means the study of insects:

I could never have taken up entomology. I'm afraid of wasps.

entrance, entry

These nouns both derive from the French verb *entrer*, 'to enter', and they can both relate to a place for entering:

It had a wonderfully baroque entrance.

I made my way through the entry into the garden.

Entrance can also refer to the act of entering or to coming on to the stage:

He loves to make a grand entrance.

Applause always greets the entrance of the Dame.

Entry can refer to the result of going in:

He was accused of unlawful entry into the office.

The verb *entrance*, meaning 'fill with wonder', is stressed on the second syllable and derives from Latin *transire*, 'to go over':

The children were entranced! And the adults!

entrapment

Entrapment is the derived noun from 'entrap' and is the term given to the crime of deliberately ensnaring a criminal to perform an illegal act:

The case was thrown out on the grounds of entrapment. The policeman had asked the accused to supply him with cocaine.

entreat, intreat

These are alternative spellings for the regular verb meaning 'plead, implore'. The *en-* form is more widely used in Britain.

entrust, intrust

These are alternative spellings for the regular verb meaning 'put into the care of'. *Intrust* is an acceptable but less common variant. *Entrust* is to be preferred.

enumerable, innumerable

These adjectives are occasionally confused. *Enumerable* means 'countable':

The relative pronouns were easily enumerable.

Innumerable means 'uncountable':

The stars seem as innumerable as the grains of sand on the shore.

enunciation

See ANNUNCIATION/ENUNCIATION

envelop, envelope

These words are occasionally confused and misspelled. *Envelop* is a verb:

The mist began to envelop the climbers.

Envelope is a noun:

I need a large brown envelope.

The verb is stressed on the second syllable whereas the noun is stressed on the first. The first syllable of the verb is pronounced 'in-' and the first syllable of the noun is pronounced 'en-' or 'on-'. Both pronunciations are acceptable.

enviable, envious, jealous

These adjectives derive from 'envy', which comes ultimately from Latin *invidere*, 'to eye maliciously'. They have developed different uses and meanings. *Enviable* means 'capable of arousing envy' or 'likely to arouse envy':

She's in the enviable position of having two well-paid jobs.

Envious means 'feeling or showing envy':

He was envious of her good reputation.

Neither of these adjectives is synonymous with 'jealous', which means 'frightened of being displaced by a rival':

At the moment he's feeling a little jealous of his new brother.

See also ENVY/JALOUSIE/JEALOUSY

environment

Traditionally, the noun *environment* meant external conditions or surroundings:

It is easy to relax in the countryside. The environment is so attractive.

Recently, it has been widely used in ecological debates:

We are daily polluting our environment and spoiling the planet for plants and animals as well as other human beings.

environs

This noun is plural in form and means 'outskirts of a town, vicinity':

Looking for a home in the environs of Leeds? Look no further. We have homes of distinction to the north and west of the city.

envisage, envision

These verbs can both mean 'have a positive image of'. The former is more likely to be used in Britain and the latter in America:

I can envisage myself living here in peace and tranquillity.

He envisioned a time when racial harmony would be the norm.

Neither verb should be used as a synonym for 'expect, estimate':

*He envisages/envisions a rise in interest rates.

envy, jalousie, jealousy

The nouns *jealousy* and *envy* are sometimes used

as synonyms but they can be, and ought to be, differentiated. *Envy* suggests that one is aware of someone else's advantages and would like them for oneself. *Envy* need not necessarily be unpleasant:

I really envy you this beautiful home!
I envy his total self-confidence.

Jealousy is always unpleasant. It often involves rivalry and suspicion:

It is hard to accept jealousy as a tragic flaw. Whereas Macbeth's ambition is not in itself ignoble, Othello's jealousy is neither acceptable nor excusable.

A *jalousie* is a slatted blind or shutter:

Jean Rhys refers to 'jalousies' in *Wide Sargasso Sea*.

This noun comes from Old French *gelosie*, literally 'jealousy', but refers to a latticework screen.

eon
See AEON/EON

epenthesis
This noun refers to a process that is almost the reverse of 'syncope'. *Epenthesis* involves the inclusion of a vowel or consonant in the middle of a word, often making the word easier to pronounce:

film: *filim
scuttling: *scutteling.

It most frequently involves the insertion of a short neutral vowel into a group of consonants.

See also CONSONANT CLUSTER, SYNCOPE

epic
The noun *epic* derives from Greek *epos*, 'speech, song', and was originally applied to a long narrative poem recounting the deeds of a legendary hero:

The students rarely read epic poetry although most of them have dipped into the *Iliad* and *Paradise Lost*.

The novelist Henry Fielding described *Tom Jones* as 'a comic epic in prose' and the term has also been applied to lavish films often on biblical themes:

Few studios could now afford to make the epics that Hollywood created in the 1950s.

epigram, epigraph, epitaph, epithet
The prefix *epi-* derives from a Greek form meaning 'upon'. These four words are sometimes confused because of their similar appearance and because of a certain overlap in meaning.

An *epigram* originally meant an inscription (often on a tomb). The word is now used to describe a short, pithy saying, often in the balanced, antithetical structures favoured by Alexander Pope:

Yes; I am proud, I must be proud to see

Men not afraid of God, afraid of me.
'Tis with our Judgements as our watches, none
Go just alike, yet each believes his own.

An *epigraph* is an inscription in stone, on a coin or on a statue:

Look on my work, ye Mighty, and despair.
                    P.B. Shelley, 'Ozimandias'
E pluribus unum (From many one).

An *epitaph* is an inscription on a tomb:

Here lieth the mortal remains of X
The Lord hath given
The Lord hath taken away.

Epitaph is used in a broader sense to refer to a commemorative verse written in honour of someone who has died.

The term *epithet* refers to an adjective or adjective phrase describing a quality:

gilded tombs
honest toil.

See also HYPALLAGE

epitome
Epitome is a noun that derives from Greek *epitemnein*, 'to cut short'. It is used in English to mean a person or thing that is a perfect example of a quality or characteristic:

Mary is the epitome of generosity.

and a thing that shows in a small scale the characteristics of something greater:

This playground is the epitome of the world at large.

This second meaning is, however, more frequently expressed by means of a verb:

This playground epitomizes the world at large.

eponym
An *eponym* is any noun derived from the name of a person:

boycott from Charles Boycott
Constantinople from Constantine
Georgia from King George III
guillotine from Joseph Ignace Guillotin.

See also NOUN, WORD FORMATION

equable, equatable, equitable
These adjectives are occasionally misused and *equitable* is frequently misspelled. *Equable* comes from Latin *aequare*, 'to make equal'. It means 'even-tempered', 'placid':

My father had the most equable of temperaments. Nothing ever seemed to annoy or frustrate him.

Equatable is not widely used. It also comes from *aequare* and means 'can be equated', 'can be regarded as equal':

The ingredients are not equatable with the end product.

Equitable is the adjectival form of 'equity' and means 'fair', 'just':

I'm sure we can come to an equitable arrangement.

equal

Equal is a regular verb that doubles the 'l' before '-ed' and '-ing' in British English:

UK: equal(s), equalled, equalling
US: equal(s), equaled, equaling.

The derived forms 'equality', 'equalize/equalise' and 'equalizer/equaliser' have one 'l'.

equally

Equally is the adverbial form in both Britain and America:

John and Paul are equally intelligent.

Occasionally, *equally* is misused. We can say either:

John and Paul are equally intelligent.

or:

John is as intelligent as Paul.

but we should not say or write:

*John is equally as intelligent as Paul.

equator

The *equator* is not usually written with a capital 'e':

The trade winds blow between the tropics and the equator.

Equatorial Guinea

An inhabitant of the central African republic is a 'Guinean'. The derived adjective is '(Equatorial) Guinea'. The capital is Malabo.

equinox

The word *equinox* literally means 'equal night' and refers to the days in the year when there are approximately twelve hours of daylight and twelve hours of night:

There are two equinoxes in Britain: the vernal equinox on 21 March and the autumnal equinox on 21 September.

equip

Equip is a regular verb meaning 'supply with all that is necessary':

They equipped their kitchen with every gadget you could think of.

It doubles the 'p' before '-ed' and '-ing' in both Britain and America:

equip(s), equipped, equipping.

equitable

See EQUABLE/EQUATABLE/EQUITABLE

equivalent

Equivalent can function as an adjective meaning

'equal in value' and as a noun meaning 'something that is equal in value'. The adjective is followed by the preposition 'to' but the noun takes 'of':

The pound is equivalent to approximately 150 yen.

Slapping someone on the face with a glove was the equivalent of challenging him to a duel.

-er

See -EE/-ER/-OR

eradicate

Eradicate comes from the Latin word *radix*, 'root', and means 'obliterate', 'wipe out':

It's not possible to eradicate all traces of the pesticide from the land.

ere

See E'ER/ERE/ERR

ergative

The term *ergative* is used in language studies to describe the relationship that exists between such sentences as:

The plane landed in Paris.

and:

The pilot landed the plane in Paris.

where the subject of a verb becomes the object of the same verb and a new subject is introduced as the cause or agent of the action.

See also ACTIVE VOICE/PASSIVE VOICE, GRAMMAR, VERB

Eritrea

An inhabitant of the former province of Ethiopia is an 'Eritrean'; the derived adjective is the same. The capital is Asmara.

err

See E'ER/ERE/ERR

erratum

See CORRECTION/CORRIGENDA/ERRATUM

ersatz

This word was taken into the language from German *ersetzen* 'to substitute'. It is an adjective applied to an artificial (often inferior) substitute or imitation:

It's ersatz coffee. It looks good but it does not have the right smell.

erstwhile

Erstwhile is still occasionally used as an adjective meaning 'former':

my erstwhile associate

but it is becoming obsolete.

eruption, irruption

These nouns sound alike and are occasionally misused. An *eruption* is most frequently used in connection with volcanoes:

The science of predicting volcanic eruptions is still in its infancy.

It is also used for skin blemishes:

Brand X: safe for all skin eruptions.

Irruption is used in two contexts. It can refer to a sudden increase in population:

There has been a massive irruption in the mosquito population.

or to a forcible breaking through of defences:

Last night came the sea's inevitable irruption of the sea wall at Spurn Head.

escalate

Escalate is a BACK FORMATION from 'escalator', a moving staircase. It has been so widely used in journalism in the sense of 'increase', 'increase in intensity' that many careful users avoid it. In journalism, prices and wars frequently *escalate*:

Inflation caused house prices to escalate.

The conflict escalated from a local skirmish into a full-scale war.

Eskimo, Inuit

Eskimo can be either singular or plural but a plural with '-s' also occurs:

The Eskimo was building an igloo.
The Eskimo have lived for centuries in harsh conditions.
There were two Eskimos in a kayak.

Many of the people who inhabit Alaska, Northern Canada, Greenland and Siberia dislike being referred to as *Eskimo*, a word that probably comes from the Abnaki language and means 'eater of raw meat'. A more acceptable designation is *Inuit*:

The Inuit have their own language and their own culture.
The Inuit language is said to have dozens of words for different types of snow.

See also POLITICAL CORRECTNESS, RACISM

esoteric

The adjective *esoteric* means 'restricted to an initiated minority':

Fewer than five scholars are actively involved in deciphering this esoteric script.

The word has been popularized and is now sometimes used as a synonym for 'difficult' or 'private':

We have received no instructions since the second esoteric statement.
Both groups had their own esoteric ideas but they did not choose to divulge them.

especial, special

These adjectives and their associated adverbs 'especially' and 'specially' often cause problems for users. *Especial* is less widely used than *special*, which can be substituted for *especial* when the meaning is 'out of the ordinary' :

I paid (e)special attention to the punctuation.

Especial is, however, less common and so slightly more emphatic than *special*, and it continues to be the preferred form when the implied meaning is 'not general, peculiar':

a special talent
an especial talent
She had an especial affinity with spiders.

Especial cannot be substituted for *special* when the meaning implied is 'particular':

We have put on a special course for Thai graduate students.

To substitute *especial* here would change the meaning from 'particular' to 'extremely good'.

The adverbs too are often used interchangeably but 'especially' is more formal and must be used when the implication is 'more than usual', 'above all':

He was especially fluent on Monday.

'Specially' must be used when the implication is 'purposely', 'in this specific way':

The course has been specially created for mother-tongue speakers.

-ess

The suffix -*ess* indicates that the referent is feminine:

actor, actress
author, authoress
manager, manageress
poet, poetess.

Many people feel that this suffix is at best unnecessary and at worst patronizing. Most women prefer to be referred to by the unmarked noun:

She is one of the finest poets of the twentieth century.

There are still a few words ending in -*ess* that need the ending. These words are related to hereditary titles:

count, countess
duke, duchess
marquis, marchioness
prince, princess.

See also GENDER, POLITICAL CORRECTNESS, SEXISM

essay
See ASSAY/ESSAY

-est

The superlative suffix *-est* can be found on adjectives and adverbs:

Positive	Comparative	Superlative
small	smaller	smallest
fast	faster	fastest

It was the smallest horse I'd ever seen.
Who drove fastest?

See also ADJECTIVE, ADVERB

esthetic(s)

See AESTHETIC(S)/ESTHETIC(S)

estimable, estimatable, inestimable

These adjectives are occasionally confused, partly because they derive from the same Latin verb *aestimare*, 'assess the worth of'. *Estimable* is related to 'esteem' and means 'worthy', 'deserving of admiration':

An estimable friend is one who stands by you in times of difficulty.

Estimatable is derived from the verb 'estimate' and means 'capable of being counted or calculated':

The distance seemed huge, only just estimatable.

It is not widely used.

The negative adjective *inestimable* means 'too large to be counted':

Distances in space are virtually inestimable. Even when we use expressions like 'light years', we forget that this represents 186 million x 60 x 60 x 365 miles.

Estonia

An inhabitant of the Baltic republic, formerly part of the USSR, is an 'Estonian'; the derived adjective is the same. The capital is Tallinn.

Estuary English

Estuary English is a convenient term for a variety of spoken English, originally centred on London speech but now spread from the Greater London area to the Home Counties and beyond. It is found as far north as Norfolk and as far west as parts of Somerset and, because it is favoured by the young, it is likely to spread even further. It is marked by a number of features found in Cockney, including the use of glottals instead of /t/ in 'bottle' or 'water', the tendency to drop /h/ in 'harm' and 'hat', and the tendency for the vowel sound in 'may' to approximate to the vowel sound in 'my'.

See also DIALECT, PRONUNCIATION, STANDARD ENGLISH

et al.

The Latin phrase *et alii*, 'and others', is used most frequently in scholarly writing to indicate the omission of one or more names:

I've just read the Jones *et al.* book.
The book was written by Quirk *et al.*

etc.

The Latin phrase *et cetera*, 'and other similar things', is normally abbreviated to *etc.* in English. It tends to occur at the end of a list to indicate that the list is suggestive and not comprehensive:

They sold root vegetables: potatoes, carrots, turnips, etc.

A comma should be used before *etc.*

See also ABBREVIATION, PUNCTUATION

ethics

Ethics can be treated as a singular noun when it refers to the study of moral values:

Ethics is often used as a synonym for 'moral philosophy'.

It must be treated as a plural noun when it refers to the morality of a decision:

The ethics underlying such decisions are questionable.

See also -IC/-ICAL

Ethiopia

An inhabitant of the northeastern African republic is an 'Ethiopian'; the derived adjective is the same. The capital is Addis Ababa.

ethnic

The adjective *ethnic* means 'relating to or the characteristics of a human group':

There are several ethnic groups in China.

Recently, it has become a vogue adjective meaning 'non-white':

Ethnic costumes are frequently worn, especially for festivals.

We also find such phrases as:

ethnic food, ethnic speech.

ethnolect

The term *ethnolect* is used by linguists to refer to the linguistic behaviour characteristic of an ethnic group. The term has been applied to 'Black English', 'Gypsy English' and 'Hiberno-English'.

etiology

See AETIOLOGY/ETIOLOGY

etymology

The word *etymology* derives from the Greek *etumos*, 'true', 'actual'. The word now refers to the study of the origins and history of the forms and the meanings of words. We know a great deal about the etymology of certain words. For example, we know something of the etymology of 'Saturday', which derives from Old English *Saetern(es)daeg* from Latin *Saturni dies* (Saturn's day). 'Saturday' is etymologically related to 'saturnic' (affected by lead poisoning) and 'saturnine' (of a gloomy disposition) but few speakers of English would relate 'Saturday' semantically to either of these words.

However, not all etymologies are as clear as for 'Saturday'. Some words, such as the verb *bug*, have been adapted from African languages, which are less well documented than Latin, and others, like *hype*, 'the elaborate promotion of a record, book or film', have more than one etymology. 'Hype' may derive from Greek *hypo* meaning 'under', from 'hypodermic' (under the skin), and from the Greek prefix *hyper* meaning 'over', as in 'hypermarket'. Multiple etymologies are commonly invoked in the explanation of creole vocabularies. For example, the word *wuman*, which is found in most Atlantic pidgins and creoles related to English, almost certainly derives from Efik *uman* meaning 'woman, female' as well as from English 'woman'.

A further point should be made here relating to what might be called the 'etymological fallacy'. A number of people claim that the true meaning of 'grammar' should be 'the history of writing' because this is what it used to mean. Others insist that 'aggravate' should not mean 'annoy'. Earlier meanings are in no way better or more valid than their modern equivalents; they are just older. It is more important to describe meanings that are relevant today than to attempt to hold back or deny the tide of change.

A 'false etymology' is an incorrect account of the history of a word or phrase. To claim, for example, that 'ptarmigan' must derive from Greek because a number of words such as 'pterodactyl' are Greek in origin is a false etymology. The word actually comes from Gaelic *tarmachan*, 'a type of grouse'.

See also BORROWING

eulogy
See ELEGY/EULOGY

euphemism

A *euphemism* is an inoffensive word or phrase that is substituted for one that is regarded as too explicit, offensive or unpleasant:

fat = 'fuller figure', 'Junoesque', 'well-made'
poor ='low income group', 'underprivileged'.

Euphemisms may be ephemeral in that a new word may take on the connotations of the word that it replaced and thus no longer serve a euphemistic purpose. This has happened in English to what was originally called a 'water closet'. Among the euphemistic equivalents are:

bathroom, comfort station, restroom, toilet, washroom, WC.

Euphemisms can be useful. There are, for example, a great many related to death and dying, suggesting our reluctance to face the fact of non-existence. Some of these are serious and others pious or humorously dismissive, but all serve the purpose of distancing us from the reality:

Serious	Pious	Humorous
die	sleep in the Lord	kick the bucket
die	go to one's eternal reward	push up daisies

Some of the humorous equivalents for 'die' are callous and unfeeling and therefore, often, inappropriate. It is, however, acceptable to use euphemisms in expressing sympathy, when gentler expressions are preferred to the starkness of 'die' and 'death'.

Euphemisms may be described as a means of directing our thoughts away from unpleasant realities such as bodily excretions, death, obesity, old age, and poverty. Indeed, in English, the only excretions that can be talked about freely are tears and perhaps perspiration.

Euphemistic substitutions result from feelings of 'taboo' that are associated with certain bodily acts and functions. Euphemisms exploit the language's capacity for metaphorical expansion. This capacity is in itself neither good nor bad, but we should always be aware of the power euphemisms can have to reveal our thoughts and our attitudes to other people.

See also CLICHÉ, CONNOTATION, CURSE, PROPAGANDA, TABOO VOCABULARY

euphuism

The noun *euphuism* is sometimes incorrectly associated with 'euphemism'. The noun *euphuism* derives from a character called 'Euphues', who was created by John Lyly in 1579. It refers to a contrived, intricate prose style popularized in England in the late sixteenth century but having roots that go back to the fourteenth. *Euphuism* is characterized by ALLITERATION, elaborately balanced constructions and carefully selected words.

See also ASSONANCE, PARALLELISM, STILE/STYLE

Euro, Euro-

The word *Euro* and the prefix *Euro-* are back formations from 'Europe'. The noun *Euro* has been given to the currency that is acceptable in all countries of the European Community:

Britain fights to retain the Queen's head on the Euro.

As the term becomes more widely used, the capital letter is replaced:

We still do not know how many euros there will be in the pound or even whether we can retain the pound alongside the euro.

Euro-, with and without the hyphen, is used as a shorthand method of referring to anything related to the European Community:

We've got Eurobanks and Eurobonds, Euro-MPs and Euro-bureaucracy.

evade
See AVOID/EVADE

even
Even can function as adjective and an adverb. As an adjective, it can mean 'level':

When the snow lay roundabout
Deep and crisp and even.

or, when applied to numbers, it can be contrasted with 'odd':

Two, four and six are even numbers; one, three and five are odd.

Even can be used as an intensifying adverb:

Even a fool could answer that question.
She's even cleverer than I remembered.
He is highly unusual, even rather eccentric at times.

The positioning of adverbial *even* is significant. It should be placed as close to the word it modifies as possible. If we look at a sentence such as:

I enjoyed his version of that play.

we can emphasize various elements as follows:

Even I enjoyed his version of that play.
I even enjoyed his version of that play.
I enjoyed even his version of that play.
I enjoyed his version of even that play.

Each of these sentences has a different meaning and the differences are due to the positioning of *even*.

Even occurs in a number of fixed phrases, including:

break even (neither gain nor lose on a transaction)
get even (get revenge)
even as (at the very same moment)
even so (nevertheless)
even though (in spite of).

See also ALTHOUGH/THOUGH, DESPITE/IN SPITE OF

eventuate
The verb *eventuate* (in) means 'result in', and it has been popularized by journalists:

Such activities eventuate in military action.

Many careful writers dislike the usage, regarding it as an inelegant variation of 'result in'.

ever, -ever
Ever is an adverb meaning 'at any time':

If you are ever in Leeds, please give me a ring.

It is also frequently used as an INTENSIFIER of 'so' and 'such', especially in colloquial British English:

He is ever so tall!
She was ever such a clever girl!

The emphatic construction where *ever* comes at the end of an exclamation is largely American:

Did he ever! (He certainly did!)
Was she ever! (She certainly was!)

When *ever* modifies question words such as 'how', 'what', 'where', 'which', 'who', the *ever* is a separate word:

How ever did you get into this mess?
What ever did you say to hurt her so much?

When *-ever* is attached to such words as 'how', 'what', 'when', 'where', 'which', 'who', they occur in statements:

I can't do it however hard I try.
Whatever she said seems to have done the trick.

See also HOW EVER/HOWEVER, WHAT EVER/WHATEVER, WHEN EVER/WHENEVER, WHERE EVER/WHEREVER, WHICHEVER, WHO/WHOEVER

every
Every functions as a determiner:

Every person going through Customs was searched.

Every and the compounds involving *every-*, such as 'everybody', 'everyone' and 'everything', take singular nouns and verbs:

Every leaf was beautifully drawn.
Everybody is delighted.

The only exception to this rule is when *every* precedes a cardinal number:

They come home every five or six days.

This is in contrast to the usage before ordinals:

They come home every fifth or sixth day.

Every can cause problems of agreement in such structures as:

Every child should do —— best.

In the spoken medium, the usual construction is:

Every child should do their best.

but, since *every* + noun is singular, grammarians insist the construction should be:

Every child should do his or her best.

Many speakers feel uncomfortable with both solutions and are uncertain what to use here and in tag questions following sentences involving 'any-', 'every-', 'some-':

Anyone can enter, can't …? (he?, she?, they?)
Everybody has the same rights, hasn't he/she/haven't we?

There are no easy answers to this problem. The only general rule that can be given is that language should not be used to offend people or to reinforce stereotypes.

The expression 'every which way', meaning 'in all directions' is a colloquial Americanism that has found its way into some British speech styles:

I looked every which way for her but couldn't find her anywhere.

See also AGREEMENT, CONCORD, DETERMINER, EACH, EACH AND EVERY, SEXIST LANGUAGE

every one, everyone

The forms *every one* and *everyone* are distinguished by careful writers. *Every one* can usually be replaced by 'every single one'. It can refer to people, to animals and to inanimate nouns:

Every one of the children has asthma.

Every one of the books I bought was slightly damaged.

Everyone can be replaced by 'everybody'. It is singular and refers to people:

Everyone I know is under pressure at work.

Everybody I know is under pressure at work.

The main distinction between:

Everyone has asthma.

and:

Every one of the children has asthma.

is that the second focuses on each child individually, a fact that becomes clearer when modifiers such as 'blessed', 'last' or 'single' are introduced:

Every blessed/last/single one of the children has a cold!

everybody, everyone

The pronouns *everybody* and *everyone* are interchangeable:

Everybody likes to be happy.

Everyone likes to be happy.

In theory, they should both involve singular agreement:

Everybody is doing his/her best.

Everyone is doing his/her best.

See also AGREEMENT, EVERY

evocative, provocative, vocative

These adjectives all come from the Latin verb *vocare*, 'to call'. The adjective *evocative* relates to 'reviving or stimulating memories':

It's such an evocative painting. It makes me think of summer and childhood, when it was always summer.

Provocative suggests 'liable to arouse' and it is often unpleasant:

Did you have to make such a provocative speech?

Vocative is most frequently used in grammar to refer to the person or thing being addressed:

Come here, Mary.

Latin expressed grammatical relationships by means of inflections. The vocative case was used in addressing a person or a thing:

Domine, quo vadis? (O Lord, where are you going?)

English does not have a vocative case. The name 'John' remains unchanged whether or not we speak to him or about him:

John, can you help me, please?

Have you seen John?

The information that is carried in Latin by means of a case ending is carried in English by using a name, by its position in a sentence or by intonation.

See also CASE, GRAMMAR

evoke, invoke

These verbs are occasionally confused, partly because they both derive from Latin *vocare*, 'to call'. *Evoke* can mean 'call up a memory':

The melody evoked wonderfully happy memories.

and 'produce':

Their insubordination evoked her anger.

Invoke can mean 'call upon God, spirits or an outside authority':

They invoked God's help on their enterprise.

Faustus invoked Mephistopheles in an attempt to gain greater knowledge.

She invoked the anti-discrimination laws.

ex-

The PREFIX *ex-* can mean 'out of', 'from' and, more recently, 'former':

exhume (dig a body out of the ground)

expel (send away from)

ex-wife (former wife).

This prefix is very widely used in English and is frequently paralleled by an IN- form:

exclude, include

exhale, inhale

exhibit, inhibit.

ex gratia

This Latin expression meaning 'out of kindness' is normally, though not always, italicized. In English, it usually occurs in the collocation:

an *ex gratia* payment

meaning a payment where there is no legal obligation to provide one:

We have decided to make you an *ex gratia* payment of £50.

exacerbate, exasperate

These verbs are occasionally misused. *Exacerbate* means 'make something worse':

The medication seems to have exacerbated his condition.

Exasperate means 'cause great irritation', 'infuriate':

I have never known any other person capable of exasperating me the way you can!

exaggerate

This verb, which means 'represent as being bigger or better or greater than is actually the case', is frequently misspelled:

Why do they feel the need to exaggerate their wealth?

See also HYPERBOLE

exalt, exult

These verbs are occasionally confused. *Exalt* means 'raise', 'elevate'

Now that he has such an exalted position, he has little time for his friends.

Exult means 'to delight in':

They exulted in their victory.

exceed

This verb, which means 'go beyond the limits', is sometimes misspelled, especially in the past tense:

Micawber often exceeded his income.

The verb is not spelled like 'recede'.

See also SPELLING

excel

Excel is a regular verb meaning 'be excellent at, surpass':

They excelled at tennis.

This verb doubles the 'l' before '-ed' and '-ing' endings in both British and American English:

excel(s), excelled, excelling.

Other derived forms such as 'excellent' and 'Excellency' also have '-ll-'.

except, excepted, excepting, save

The preposition *except* means 'other than, apart from':

All the children came except John.

In such a context *except for* is not necessary:

All the children came except (for) John.

although it is necessary when the exclusion comes at the beginning of the sentence:

Except for John, all the children came.

Except, like all prepositions, takes the object form of the pronoun:

Everyone was there except me. (*except I)

Everyone has heard except him. (*except he)

In certain regions of Britain, *except* can occur with the meaning of 'unless':

Except you do as I say, you'll lose your job.

but in most places this use of *except* as a conjunction is archaic, old-fashioned or unacceptable.

Excepted and *excepting* are used to imply exclusion in relatively formal structures involving 'not', 'without' and 'always' as in:

We all went, the children not excepted.

We all went, not excepting the children.

Excepting precedes the noun phrase and *excepted* follows it. The uses above are grammatical but would be avoided by many speakers. *Excepting* is used colloquially in such sentences as:

Everyone was there excepting me.

The preposition *save* meaning 'except' is now archaic, although it is still occasionally found in such sentences as:

They were all dead, save one.

This *save* derives from French *sauf*, and not from the verb *save* meaning 'rescue', 'preserve'.

See also PROVIDED/PROVIDING

exceptional, exceptionable

These adjectives are frequently confused although their meanings should be clearly differentiated. *Exceptional* means 'out of the ordinary':

The 1997 vintage has been exceptional in terms of both quality and quantity.

Today has not been exceptional in any way.

In British English *exceptional* usually means 'uncommonly good':

She's an exceptional student, the best we've had in five years.

but in American English it can also be used of something that is out of the ordinary, whether good or bad:

She's an exceptional student, one of the poorest we've had in five years.

Exceptionable means 'objectionable':

I find his behaviour exceptionable. I can tolerate casualness and eccentricity but not open discourtesy.

excessive

Excessive is an adjective meaning 'exceeding the norm, immoderate':

This bill is excessive. We'll have to challenge it.

exchangeable

This adjective needs an 'e' before '-able':

If this desk doesn't fit, is it exchangeable for another?

exclamation

The noun *exclamation* derives from Latin *ex + clamare*, 'to cry out', 'to utter loudly', and implies a type of emphasis that is signalled by intonation in speech, by the exclamation mark in writing, by specific words, such as 'how' or by changes in word order.

Statement: It was awful.
Exclamation: How awful!

A statement may be converted into an exclamation simply by a change of intonation or by the use of an exclamation mark:

You cannot be serious.
You cannot be serious!

'How' and 'what' are frequently used in exclamations:

How terrible!
What a treat!

Wishes expressed with 'if only' are often exclamatory:

If only you'd asked!

Conventionally, a sentence that is syntactically incomplete is acceptable if it ends with an exclamation mark:

No!
Really!
She did!

In fiction, the heavy use of exclamation marks in the language used to describe a character may suggest to a reader that the character is young, shallow, emotional or given to exaggeration.

See also INTERJECTION, PUNCTUATION, SENTENCE, STILE/STYLE

executioner, executor

These two nouns should be clearly distinguished. An *executioner* is a person who puts a criminal to death:

The last executioner in Britain had his memoirs serialized in a Sunday newspaper.

An *executor* (with the spelling '-or') is a person who is appointed by someone who makes a will to ensure that his or her instructions are carried out. The female form of *executor* is 'executrix' but, generally, the same word is used for both sexes:

I've asked Mary to be the executor for my will.

exemplary

The adjective *exemplary* is related to 'example' and is applied to a person whose behaviour is suitable for imitation:

John behaved with exemplary courtesy throughout this trying period.

The adjective is occasionally used with the meaning of 'illustrative' as in:

Here is an exemplary sentence.

exempt

Exempt can function as an adjective and as a regular verb meaning '(be) not liable', '(be) free from an obligation, duty or payment':

These goods are exempt from VAT because they can be purchased only by people who are taking them out of the country.
Men with flat feet used to be exempted from military service.

exercise, exorcize

These words are occasionally confused. *Exercise* can function as a noun and a verb meaning 'train', 'improve one's muscles':

He worked out a special exercise for us before the big game.
I try to exercise for an hour a day.

Exercise is also used to refer to tasks set for students:

I haven't finished my Latin exercise yet but we don't have to hand it in until Monday.

Exorcize is a verb meaning 'expel or attempt to expel spirits:

There is something really strange about that house. I'm sure it's haunted. If I lived there I'd ask a priest to exorcise its spirits.

exhausting, exhaustive

These adjectives are sometimes confused. *Exhausting* means 'tiring, causing one to be drained of energy':

The three-mile walk from the station to the house was exhausting.

Exhaustive means 'thorough, comprehensive in scope':

We've carried out an exhaustive study of the books and we still cannot find how or where the money was taken.

exhibit, exhibition

Until recently in British English, *exhibit* was used exclusively as a verb meaning 'display to the public', and *exhibition* was the associated noun:

Have you heard that Ben has been invited to exhibit his paintings in Brussels? If the exhibition is well attended, it could make a big difference to his standing in the art world.

In America and increasingly now in Britain, *exhibit* is used as a noun with two main meanings: as a legal document or object produced in court:

The gun was produced as Exhibit A.

and as an art display:

There is a sculpture exhibit in the Brotherton Gallery this month.

exhilarate

The regular verb *exhilarate* and its derivatives 'exhilarating' and 'exhilaration' are frequently misspelled. Often the 'h' is omitted because people forget that it is related to the noun 'hilarity'. *Exhilarate* means 'gladden, elate':

We were exhilarated by the view.

existential

This adjective has become widely used with the meaning of 'based on personal experience', 'empirical' rather than theoretical:

Describe and comment on Simone de Beauvoir's existential theories.

exorbitant

The adjective *exorbitant* means 'extremely high, excessive':

Their prices are exorbitant. I enjoy looking at their clothes but I'd never buy them.

Exorbitant is frequently misspelled. It derives from Latin *exorbitare*, 'to deviate'.

exorcize

See EXERCISE/EXORCIZE

exotic

Exotic comes from Latin *exoticus*, 'foreign', and used to mean 'from a foreign country':

These sculptures are exotic. They are probably from West Africa.

The more usual meaning of *exotic* now is 'alluring', 'excitingly different' although it still carries overtones of 'foreign':

Would you like to try some really exotic food?

I'd enjoy a holiday in somewhere exotic like Mauritius.

expatriate

An *expatriate* is an exile:

Paris is full of expatriate Americans.

The word can also be used as an adjective referring to someone who works in a country that is not his or her own:

There are sixteen expatriate teachers working in the college.

expect

See ANTICIPATE/EXPECT

expectorate

Expectorate comes from Latin *expectore*, 'expel from the breast', and means 'spit':

If you need to expectorate, please use the spittoons.

expedient, expeditious

These adjectives are sometimes misused. *Expedient* means 'appropriate', 'suitable in the circumstances':

It is expedient that one man dies for the people.

Expeditious comes from Latin *expedire*, 'free the feet as from a snare', and means 'prompt', 'quick', 'speedy':

First-class post is not always as expeditious as we might hope.

We all wish you an expeditious recovery.

expel

This regular verb, meaning 'drive out by force' is spelled the same way in both British and American English:

expel(s), expelled, expelling.

explicable

Many verbs have related adjectives ending in '-able':

Verb	Adjective
describe	describable
wash	washable

The adjective that means 'capable of being explained' is *explicable*, not *explainable:

Every care was taken to ensure that every delegate was contacted so our failure to contact you is not explicable.

See also -ABLE/-IBLE

explicate

The verb *explicate* is more comprehensive than 'explain'. It suggests 'explain and analyse in detail':

He did not merely explain the contract to us; he explicated every detail and nuance.

explicit, implicit

These adjectives derive from Latin *explicitus*, 'unfolded', and *implicitus*, 'interwoven'. The adjective *explicit* is occasionally misused. It means 'fully stated', 'clearly and overtly described':

Your instructions were explicit.

I don't want innuendoes; I want a straightforward, explicit account of what you think I've done wrong.

It is also used to mean 'with nothing hidden':

Some viewers may find the explicit sex scenes offensive.

Implicit means 'implied, indirect':

There was an implicit criticism in his comments.

explosion, implosion

These two nouns both involve 'bursting'. With an *explosion*, the bursting is outwards:

The explosion scattered debris for hundreds of metres.

With *implosion*, the bursting is inwards:

Electric light bulbs can implode because there is a vacuum inside them.

export

Export can function as both a noun and a verb:

Our exports to Europe have gone down this year but they still exceed our imports.

They export 200,000 cars to Europe every year.

expose

See DISCLOSE/EXPOSE

exposition

An *exposition* is usually associated with clear, detailed explanations:

Her exposition on language change was so clear and cogent than even the children understood.

Occasionally, this noun is also used for a large exhibition:

I visited the Science Exposition in Brussels. It was extremely interesting and covered almost every aspect of the subject.

expropriate

Expropriate is sometimes used when 'misappropriate' would be more accurate. *Expropriate* traditionally meant 'take away someone's property, normally without paying the owner and normally for the benefit of the public':

Governments sometimes find it both rewarding and popular to expropriate the lands of the wealthy.

Careful users dislike the use of *expropriate* when it is used as a euphemism for 'steal', 'misappropriate':

She expropriated the takings from the till.

extant

The adjective *extant* means 'still in existence', 'surviving' and is applied to inanimate objects, most frequently to documents:

I believe that this is the only extant manuscript from the fifth century.

extempore

The adverb *extempore* derives from Latin *ex tempore*, 'out of time', and is used to mean 'spontaneous, without premeditation, without notes':

He spoke extempore for fifteen minutes without hesitation or false start.

The same form is used adjectivally:

He made an extempore speech.

extended, extensive

These adjectives are occasionally misused. *Extended* means 'stretched, enlarged':

We made an extended tour of Zimbabwe.

The extended family is a source of considerable social stability.

Extensive means 'large in area, wide-ranging':

I'd never before seen such extensive gardens.

Their knowledge of Middle English is extensive.

extol

Extol is a regular verb meaning 'praise lavishly':

I wish someone would extol my virtues in public!

The verb has 'll' in American English:

UK. extol(s), extolled, extolling
US: extoll(s), extolled, extolling.

See also SPELLING, UK AND US ENGLISH

extrinsic, intrinsic

The adjective *intrinsic* derives from Latin, *intra + secus*, 'within + alongside', and means 'inherent'. Its opposite, *extrinsic*, is approximately synonymous with 'extraneous'. *Intrinsic* has been popularized by the media:

The results of 'blue-sky' research may not be immediately obvious, but its intrinsic value should be recognized.

whereas *extrinsic* is less widely used:

The intrinsic value of three-hour examinations is open to question but their extrinsic value in preparing students to work under pressure should not be overlooked.

extrovert, introvert

The noun *extrovert* means a person who is more interested in external reality than in introspection. It has come to be used to mean someone who is cheerful and optimistic.

The noun *introvert* is quite widely used for a person who has a tendency to be introspective:

He's something of an introvert, much more interested in his own thoughts and feelings than in trying to be sociable.

The form *intravert does not exist.

exult

See EXALT/EXULT

eyrie

See AERIE/EYRIE

F

f

F is a consonant. It is used as an abbreviation for Latin *forte*, an instruction to a musician to play loudly.

face, face up to

The word *face* can be used as a regular verb meaning 'accept, confront':

He faced all adversities with courage and good humour.

Some people object to the phrasal verb *face up to*, claiming that the 'up to' is as unnecessary here as the 'up with' in 'meet up with'. Yet *face up to* can introduce the meaning of 'face with courage', 'finally acknowledge':

He faced up to his responsibilities.
He faced up to his limitations.

facetious

The adjective *facetious* comes from Old French *facetie*, 'witty saying', and means 'flippant', 'jocular but often inappropriate'. It is often misspelled:

I think that some of your facetious remarks are an attempt to hide your feelings.

facia, fascia

These nouns are variant spellings and derive from Latin *fascis*, 'bundle'. They both refer to flat bands or surfaces:

'Fa(s)cia is another word for 'dashboard'.
The fa(s)cia underneath the eaves needs to be replaced.

facile

The adjective *facile* has undergone semantic change. It derives from Latin *facilis*, 'easy', but it is now frequently used to mean 'superficial', 'glib':

Do we have to listen to such facile arguments?

See also SEMANTIC CHANGE

facility

The noun *facility* comes from Latin *facilis*, 'easy'. It can be used in two different contexts. It can mean 'the skill and ease with which something is done':

He learns languages with a facility that the rest of us can only admire or envy.

When it is used in the plural it means 'the buildings and equipment necessary to perform certain tasks':

We lack the facilities to develop first-class tennis players.

facsimile, fax

A *facsimile* means 'an exact copy or reproduction':

Few artists make facsimiles of their work although they may produce variations on a theme.

The noun was extended to mean 'a system by which a document could be scanned and transmitted electronically':

We've just telegraphed you a facsimile of the plans.

This usage was abbreviated to *fax* and the word is used as both a noun and a verb:

Send me another fax of your report.
Why don't you fax the report?
I faxed it yesterday.

fact

The noun *fact* is overused. Sometimes it is modified by 'true' although the adjective is redundant:

We shall reveal the true facts.

Often, *fact* is used in a phrase as a FILLER or discourse marker, included more for emphasis or linkage than for its meaning:

As a matter of fact, I don't think I know her.
In fact, I can't be sure who said it.

The phrase *the fact* can be obligatory in sentences where a noun phrase is required between a preposition and the conjunction 'that':

We ought to take account of the fact that Joan is leaving.

In other contexts, however, the phrase is often redundant:

I hope you understand the fact that we are right.

See also DISCOURSE

faction

The word *faction* as used in:

Tomorrow's programme is faction but the events could be happening now, in your neighbourhood.

is a blend of 'fact' and 'fiction' and is a coinage popularized by television.

Similar coinages are:

dramadoc (drama + documentary)
edutainment (education + entertainment).

There is another word *faction* that derives from Latin *facere*, 'to make'. It is overused in the media to mean 'group within a group':

The influence of the Eurosceptic faction seems to be growing.

factor

The noun *factor* is widely used to mean 'contributory cause':

The drop in the cost of natural gas was the main factor in their reduced profits.

The noun is frequently used in such sentences as:

The safety factor has been threatened.

Student numbers have increased by a factor of eight.

faculty

The noun *faculty* comes from Latin *facultas*, 'capability', and is related to 'facility'. It can mean 'a mental power or ability':

She has lost her sight but her mental faculties are as sharp as ever.

'a group of related departments in higher education':

Are you in the Faculty of Arts or the Faculty of Science?

and 'the teachers in an institute of learning':

Faculty are asked to report at 7:30.

The third meaning is more likely to occur in America than in Britain.

fad word

Fad words are a feature of most ages and of many groups. They come into prominence and either fade as they are overused or become integrated into mainstream usage. Some of the vogue words over the last twenty years are:

aspiration, baseline, charisma, dimension, escalation, framework, grassroots, grey area, hopefully, interface, situation.

See also CLICHÉ, JARGON

fahrenheit

See CELSIUS/CENTIGRADE/FAHRENHEIT

faint, feint

These homophones can both function as adjectives and nouns, and *faint* can also be a verb. *Faint* comes from Old French *faindre*, 'to be idle', and has a range of meanings. As an adjective, it can mean 'not clear':

Listen. There's a faint noise in the background.

'lacking conviction':

Damn with faint praise.

and 'dizzy':

I feel faint. Could I have some water, please?

The related noun and verb are associated with losing consciousness:

Has she recovered from her faint?

He fainted when he heard the news.

Feint comes from Old French *feindre*, 'to feign'. The adjective *feint* is sometimes used to mean that the lines in an exercise book are not sharply drawn but 'ruled feint'. The noun is more widely used and can mean 'a mock attack':

The soldiers were not misled by their feint.

The noun *feint* is also used in whiskey making to describe the residue left as whiskey is distilled. The etymology of this word is unclear.

fair, fairly

Fair can function as an adjective meaning 'light in colour':

He has blue eyes and fair hair.

'lovely':

And she is fair, and fairer than that word ...

and 'just':

That decision was not fair.

It can also function as an adverb, especially with the verbs 'act', 'fight' and 'play':

You weren't acting fair.

He didn't fight fair.

They are instructed to play fair.

The noun homophone *fair*, as in:

a world fair

comes from a different source.

Fairly is an adverb meaning 'justly':

You were not fairly treated.

and 'moderately':

He's fairly bright.

See also KINDLY

fakir

Fakir derives ultimately from Arabic *faqir*, 'poor', and is a term applied to an Indian ascetic mendicant or holy man. It is also occasionally used of an Indian snake charmer or man who performs certain tricks:

I cannot explain it but I have seen a fakir lie on a bed of nails.

The noun *fakir* is not to be confused with 'faker', that is, 'one who fakes':

He was the greatest faker of all time. His counterfeit notes were so good that even the authorities thought they were genuine.

Falkland Islands

An inhabitant of the islands in the south Atlantic is a 'Falkland Islander'; the adjective is 'Falkland' or 'Falkland Island'. The capital is Port Stanley.

false etymology

See ETYMOLOGY

familiar

The word *familiar* derives from Latin *familiaris*, 'domestic', and is related to 'family'. As an adjective, it means 'well-known', 'acquainted with' and also 'friendly', 'intimate, 'informal':

You are rehearsing a familiar argument.

I am familiar with this argument.

I don't expect people to be quite so familiar when I meet them for the first time.

The noun *familiar* is not widely used but it can refer to a supernatural spirit that is said to assume an animal form to help a witch:

Many old women whose only crime was to be old were burnt at the stake as witches, and their cats were thought to be their familiars.

family relationship

The terms for describing *family relationships* in any language reflect the structure of the society. For example, mother-tongue speakers of English use only a limited number of terms, which are differentiated according to generation and also according to gender:

Generation	Female	Male	Both F and M
2 removed	grandmother	grandfather	grandparent
1 removed	mother	father	parent
1 removed	aunt	uncle	
same	sister	brother	cousin
1 removed	daughter	son	
1 removed	niece	nephew	
2 removed	grand-daughter	grandson	grandchild

Relationships created by marriage derive from the same terms:

Generation	Female	Male	Both F and M
1 removed	mother-in-law	father-in-law	parents-in-law
same	sister-in-law	brother-in-law	
1 removed	daughter-in-law	son-in-law	

The idea of the nuclear family is often an idealization, taking little account of changes such as divorce and remarriage.

family tree

The metaphor of the *family tree* is often applied to languages, so that it is commonplace to refer to French and English as 'related' or 'sister languages' or to Indo-European as the 'parent language' of both. This metaphor is then often illustrated by means of rigid relationships such as the one illustrated under INDO-EUROPEAN.

famous, infamous, notorious

The adjectives *famous* and *infamous* are both derived from 'fame' and imply 'well known'. *Famous* now implies 'renowned for positive achievements':

We are fortunate indeed to have as our main speaker such a famous writer.

Infamous implies 'renowned for negative reasons', 'having a bad reputation':

Richard III was, for centuries, accused of such infamous conduct as murder and treason. Recent studies of the period suggest that he does not deserve his bad reputation.

Are you referring to that infamous highwayman?

The derived noun is 'infamy.'

Notorious comes from Latin *notorius*, 'well-known', but now implies 'well known for some unfavourable quality or action':

He was notorious for turning up uninvited.

They were notorious for their tall tales.

fantastic

The adjective *fantastic* derives from 'fantasy' and used to mean 'strange, exotic, bizarre':

Some of these fantastic tales have travelled around the world and children of all cultures have enjoyed their creativity and flights of fancy.

It has been widely used recently to mean 'excellent':

It was a fantastic film, so realistic and down to earth.

Many careful users object to this type of semantic BLEACHING but it is a feature of language change.

fantasy, phantasy

These are variant forms of a word borrowed directly from Latin *phantasia* and via French in the form *fantasie*. The *fantasy* spelling is more widespread but they are both acceptable. *Fantasy* functions as a noun meaning 'imaginary creativity':

Fantasy fiction is popular now but it has been popular for hundreds of years. Even the staid Victorians enjoyed stories of vampires and wizards.

farther, further

These words can both function as adjectives and adverbs, and when they describe distance they are in free variation, although *farther* is becoming less common:

It's on the farther/further side of the hill.

How much farther/further have we to go?

Some careful users suggest that *farther* should be used for literal distances:

Mars is farther away than the moon.

and *further* for figurative usage:

He travelled further in the mind than any other writer.

A study of current usage, however, suggests that very few users of English adhere to this distinction.

In the expressions 'until further notice' or 'any further help', *farther* is not acceptable.

A simple rule is, if in doubt about which one to use, choose *further*.

fascia
See FACIA/FASCIA

fascination
The noun *fascination* is overused and occasionally misused. It means 'irresistible attraction' and can occur in the structure:

Numbers hold a fascination for me.

It is not correct to say:

*I have a fascination for numbers.

The associated verb 'fascinate' is also overused. We should remember that we are 'fascinated by' a person and 'fascinated with' a thing:

I've always been fascinated by the Brontës.
I was fascinated with history and especially the Tudor period.

fast
Fast provides an excellent example of POLYSEMY and multi-functionality. *Fast* has five main meanings. It can be the equivalent of 'quick' and 'quickly':

The new fast service takes two hours to reach London.
Don't drive so fast.

'fully, completely' in the fixed phrase 'fast asleep':

I was fast asleep by the time you arrived.

'sexually promiscuous':

He has a reputation for being fast.

'very tightly' in the collocations 'hold fast' and 'stuck fast':

Hold fast! We're putting the plane into a nose-dive.
Help me, please. My car is stuck fast.

and 'abstinence from food, abstain from food':

It's only a twenty-four hour fast.
During Ramadan people fast for thirty days.

The multi-functionality of *fast* is clear from these sentences, where it functions as an adjective, an adverb, a noun and a verb.

See also ADJECTIVE, ADVERB, MULTI-FUNCTIONAL

fat
Fat comes from an Old English verb *fætan*, 'to cram' and it can function as an adjective:

I've never seen such fat lambs!

and as a noun:

Some people worry about their fat intake and about the effect certain fats have on cholesterol levels.

The normal verb form is 'fatten':

Hansel was very thin and the witch thought that he should be fattened.

Fat as both an adjective and a noun has suffered from what linguists call 'semantic degradation' or 'pejoration'. In other words, it has developed negative connotations. A nineteenth-century compliment such as 'a fat child' might be considered an insult today.

Many people have tried to find acceptable synonyms for 'fat' such as 'big', 'Junoesque' or 'well built'.

See also POLITICAL CORRECTNESS, SEMANTIC CHANGE

fatal, fateful
These adjectives are occasionally confused. *Fatal* involves 'death' whereas *fateful* involves 'fate':

There has been a fatal accident on the Inner Ring Road.
I'll always remember that fateful day when I lost my purse and found a friend.

fault
Fault derives ultimately from Latin *fallere*, 'to fail'. It can function as a noun or verb meaning 'failure, flaw, blame':

I suppose my main fault is pride.
I couldn't fault his performance. It was truly flawless.

The derived adjective is 'fallible':

I'm fallible. I'm like everyone else. I make mistakes.

faun, fawn
These words are homophones. A *faun* is a Roman deity represented as part man and part goat:

Was the god Pan a faun?

Fawn can function as an adjective:

I must buy some greyish-brown shoes to go with my fawn coat.

a noun:

A fawn is a young deer of either sex.

and a verb meaning 'seek attention by flattering':

I wouldn't mind a little more attention but I don't want anyone fawning on me.

fauna
The noun *fauna* is really the feminine form of Latin *faunus*, from which 'faun' derives. It is used in English in the fixed phrase:

flora and fauna

to refer to animal life.

See also FLORA

favour, favor
These words can function as nouns and as regular verbs, the former being the preferred form in Britain, the latter in America:

UK: Will you do me a favour, please?
US: Will you do me a favor, please?
UK: favour(s), favoured, favouring (He has always favoured his youngest child.)
US: favor(s), favored, favoring (He has always favored his youngest child.)

The derived adjectives are 'favourite' and 'favorite':

UK: Green is my favourite colour.
US: Green is my favorite color.

See also SPELLING, UK AND US ENGLISH

fax
See FACSIMILE/FAX

feasible
This adjective meaning 'able to be done' is often misspelled. It ends in '-ible':

It is simply not feasible to write a complete chapter in twenty-four hours.

Like many popular words, *feasible* is being bleached of meaning and is sometimes used to mean 'possible':

Will John come to the party? It's feasible.

See also BLEACHING

feature article
A *feature article* in a newspaper or magazine is usually in a prominent position and on an issue of current interest. Topical news stories are very often ephemeral, whereas a *feature article* is a well-written essay on a topic of lasting significance.

February
The second month of the year comes from Latin *Februarius mensis*, 'the month of purification'. It is often mispronounced as if it were *Febuary.

feed
Feed can function as a noun:

The suspect cattle feed was banned in 1988.

but it is most frequently used as a verb:

feed(s), fed, feeding
Have you fed the chickens yet?

feedback
The noun *feedback* has been overused in the media. Originally, it had a technical meaning:

Feedback involves the return of part of the output of an electronic circuit to its input, in such a way that the input is modified.

but it has come to be used as a loose synonym for 'reaction', 'response':

We sent questionnaires to fifty academics and we are still waiting for feedback from forty of them.

See also BLEACHING, FAD WORD

feel
Feel is an irregular verb:

feel(s), felt, feeling
We felt tired but very happy.

It can take a direct object or a complement:

I felt *the surface of the road* = object.
I felt *weak* = complement.

This accounts for the fact that *feel* is often followed by an adjective:

I feel bad about it.

whereas verbs that do not take complements are followed by adverbs:

I drove badly.

Many people dislike the use of the noun *feel* to mean 'quality', 'sensation':

I haven't yet got the feel of the village.
I can't explain it, but it's got a strange feel.

The cliché 'the feel-good factor' may be useful shorthand for journalists and politicians but should be avoided in formal usage.

See also BE, COMPLEMENT, COPULA

feint
See FAINT/FEINT

female, male; feminine, masculine
The terms *female* and *male* refer to the sexual classification of a person or animal and, occasionally, a plant:

The female spider is normally larger than the male.
The male seahorse gives birth to the young.
The stamen is the male reproductive organ of a flower.

The terms *feminine* and *masculine* refer to linguistic gender and need not have any direct link with sex. In French, for example, all nouns, whether animate or inanimate, have a gender:

Feminine: *la baie* (bay), *la cage* (cage), *la dame* (lady)
Masculine: *le bal* (ball), *le café* (coffee), *le monsieur* (gentleman).

See also GENDER, FEMININE FORM/MASCULINE FORM, SEXIST LANGUAGE

female, lady, woman
There is a lot of confusion about what terms to use to and about adult females. In theory, the nouns *lady* and *woman* are synonyms in that both words refer to adult females. In practice, however, there are times when one term is preferred. In the past, *lady* was a courtesy term, but nowadays a young *woman* may prefer to be referred to as a *woman* or a 'young *woman*'. An older woman might well prefer to be called 'an old *lady*' rather than 'an old *woman*'. There are, of course, individual, regional and age differences, but the easiest rules are these:

■ Use *women* in very much the same way as you would use 'men', for general references to adults:

There were three women in the queue.

■ If it is necessary to specify the gender of a doctor or a constable, use *woman*:

Can you tell me if there is a woman doctor in the practice?

■ If the woman being talked about is present, it is acceptable to use *lady*:

This lady has lost her purse.

■ If you need a term to include females of different ages, it is advisable to use *female*:

Joe is surrounded by females: a grandmother, a mother, a wife and four daughters.

■ Use the following terms whenever possible:

cleaner (rather than cleaning lady)
constable (rather than policeman/woman)
doctor (rather than lady doctor)
person (rather than man or woman).

The most general rules are to be courteous in all contexts; to use gender designations only if necessary; and to use the following patterns:

girl, for minors
female, where 'male' would be appropriate for a man
woman, for general references to adults
lady, where 'gentleman' would be appropriate for a man.

See also POLITICAL CORRECTNESS, SEXIST LANGUAGE

feminine form, masculine form

Some English nouns include a gender reference. The gender may be overt as in:

Feminine: actress, poetess, widow
Masculine: actor, poet, widower

or covert as in:

Feminine: girl, goose, mare, woman
Masculine: boy, gander, stallion, man.

The feminine forms that add a suffix to a male form, as with:

author + -ess = authoress

are not popular with many people and are better avoided.

See also GENDER, POLITICAL CORRECTNESS, SEXIST LANGUAGE

ferment, foment

These verbs are not synonymous but they can be used in similar contexts. *Ferment* means 'undergo fermentation':

The apple juice is fermenting. What did you put in it?

It also means 'stir up':

The mercenaries tried to ferment trouble.

The second meaning of *ferment* overlaps the primary meaning of *foment*, 'instigate trouble':

I will not tolerate anyone here trying to foment discord or disharmony.

fetch

Fetch is a regular verb meaning 'go to get something and bring it back':

fetch(es), fetched, fetching
Will you run home and fetch my list for me, please?

This verb is less widely used today than in the past and the adjective 'fetching' meaning 'attractive' is obsolescent:

She was a charming girl wearing a very fetching gown.

fête

Fête comes from French *fête*, 'feast', and is used as both a noun and a verb:

Our fête is like a gala bazaar held out of doors, and all our takings go to charity.
Jonathan was fêted by the entire country when he broke the world record.

Fête may be pronounced to rhyme with 'late' or with 'let'.

fetid, foetid

These are alternative spellings of the adjective that comes from Latin *fetere*, 'to stink'. The *fetid* form is now more widespread:

What five-letter word means 'having a stale, nauseating smell'? Fetid.

fetus, foetus

These are variant spellings for an unborn baby. *Foetus* is the usual form in Britain; *fetus* is preferred in America.

few, a few

Few can function as a determiner and a noun meaning 'only a small number, hardly any':

I live a simple life. I have few needs but many good friends.
Many are called but few are chosen.

A few means 'a small number':

I think I'll buy a few plants. There are none in the flat.

The main distinction between *few* and *a few* can best be explained by saying that *few* contrasts with 'many' whereas *a few* contrasts with 'none', 'not any'.

fewer, less, lesser

Fewer and *less* can both function as comparatives but they should be used differently. *Fewer* is the comparative form of 'few'. It modifies countable nouns:

There are fewer cars on this road now.

The distinction between *fewer* and *less* is an easy one to make. *Less* is used as an adjective:

People eat less meat now.

an adverb:

That injection hurt less than I expected.
He is less attractive than he used to be.

and as a noun:

The less I see you, the more I want to see you.

Less always involves a comparison between two. When it is used adjectivally, it should modify only uncountable or mass nouns:

less milk, less sugar, less tea.

It is wrong to use *less* to modify countable nouns:

*less men, *less students, *less towels

although many people do so. The BBC frequently transmits phrases such as:

*less coins in circulation
*less policemen on the beat
*less teachers.

Lesser can function as an attributive adjective, meaning 'not as great in quantity, size or worth':

A lesser person would not have admitted her guilt.
*He is lesser.
I'd love to visit the Lesser Antilles.

It occurs adverbially in such constructions as:

We are selling off some of our lesser-used products.

and is found in the fixed phrases:

the lesser of two evils
to a lesser extent.

See also ADJECTIVE, COUNTABLE AND UNCOUNTABLE, LEAST

fiancé, fiancée

These nouns are the male and female forms of a person who is engaged to be married:

My fiancé's name is Jeremy.
My fiancée's name is Josephine.

They are pronounced identically and are always written with the acute accent.

fibre, fiber

These are alternative spellings of the noun that comes from Latin *fibra*, 'a filament'. The preferred British spelling is *fibre*, whereas *fiber* is more widespread in America:

UK: This material is made from a natural fibre.
US: This material is made from a natural fiber.
UK: We need someone with moral fibre.
US: We need someone with moral fiber.

See also SPELLING, UK AND US ENGLISH

fictional, fictitious

These adjectives both derive from the noun 'fiction' meaning 'invented story'. *Fictional* is normally used in the sense of 'found in fiction':

Some fictional characters live in the memory a lot longer that real people.

Fictitious means 'made up, assumed':

Why did you give the police a fictitious name and address?

fidget

Fidget is a regular verb meaning 'twitch', 'move restlessly':

fidget(s), fidgeted, fidgeting
Please stop fidgeting. It's getting on my nerves.

fifth

The numeral *fifth* is sometimes pronounced *fith in colloquial speech. Care should be taken to pronounce the second 'f'.

figure of speech

There are many *figures of speech*, each of them involving a non-literal use of language. The *figures of speech* that are widely used are:

■ Antithesis – balanced opposition:

Marry in haste and repent at leisure.

■ Apostrophe – formal address:

Death be not proud, though some have called thee Mighty and dreadful, for, thou art not so.
John Donne, 'Holy Sonnet 10'

■ Bathos – anticlimax:

Here Thou, great Anna, whom three realms obey
Dost sometimes counsel take and sometimes tea.
Alexander Pope

■ Hyperbole – exaggeration:

There must have been thousands of black cats there.

■ Irony – language that implies two meanings, one literal:

And Brutus is an honourable man ...

■ Metaphor – covert comparison:

John roared his defiance.

■ Metonymy – substitution of one item for something closely related:

She swore allegiance to the throne.

■ Oxymoron – contradiction in terms:

a cruel kindness

■ Personification – attributing human qualities to things:

The clouds cried and the winds sighed.

■ Simile – overt comparison usually involving 'like' or 'as':

She was like a force of nature.
He was as tall as a tree.

■ Synecdoche – a part represents a whole:

They sold one hundred head of cattle.

Fiji

A Polynesian inhabitant of the nation in the south-central Pacific is a 'Fijian'; the derived adjective is the same. The capital is Suva.

Filipino

Many of the inhabitants of the Philippines refer to themselves as *Filipino* or 'Pilipino'. The noun *Filipino* is also sometimes used to refer to Tagalog, an official language of the Philippines.

fill in, fill out, fill up

These phrasal verbs are all used in connection with completing a form. In Britain, *fill in* is preferred:

Fill in Form AFD/T and send it to the Administrator.

In America, *fill out* is more widely used:

Why do we have to fill out so many forms?

Many British speakers do not like the use of *fill out* to mean 'complete' since it can mean 'enlarge, extend':

John has begun to fill out. He was thin for a long time.

The phrasal verb *fill up* can mean 'complete' but it is less widely used than *fill in* or *fill out*:

I'm hopeless at filling up application forms.

filler

Unrehearsed speech often contains *fillers*, that is, words and phrases that are unnecessary semantically but useful from the point of view of discourse. They may help to preserve the rhythm or to avoid uncomfortable silences. Some of the most frequently used fillers are:

actually, as it were, as you know, by and large, from where I stand, here and now, in my opinion, kind of, sort of, you know, you see.

Many stylists condemn fillers as being unnecessary, clumsy or imprecise, but there is evidence that fillers contribute to the fluency of speech.

fillet

When *fillet* is used as a verb, the 't' is not doubled:

fillet(s), filleted, filleting
Who filleted this plaice? It's full of bones.

filter, philter, philtre

These homophones have different origins and meanings. *Filter* comes from Latin *filtrum*, 'felt or other substance used for separating liquids and solids':

I've got grains of sand in this water. Has anyone got a filter?

The two nouns beginning with 'ph-' derive from Greek *philtron*, 'love potion'. *Philtre* is the British form and *philter* is preferred in America:

UK: Ginseng is used in love philtres.
US: Ginseng is used in love philters.

find

Find is an irregular verb and it is associated with loss:

find(s), found, finding
I've found the ring that I lost.
I've found a ring. Someone must have lost it.

In colloquial varieties of English, *find* can occur as a noun:

She's a real find. We don't know what we'd do without her.

See also DISCOVER/INVENT

finite

The term *finite* is applied to a verb or a verb phrase that can take a subject:

you (= subject) wrote

show contrasts in tense:

you write
you wrote

show agreement:

you write
she writes

and occur alone in an independent sentence or main clause:

She writes. I'm not sure whether she writes prose or poetry.

The non-finite parts of the verb are the infinitive:

to write

the present participle:

writing

and the past participle:

written.

See also VERB

Finland

An inhabitant of the northeastern Europe republic is a 'Finn'; the adjective is 'Finnish'. The capital is Helsinki.

fiord, fjord

These are variant spellings for a deep, narrow inlet of the sea. The word comes from Old Norse *fjörthr*, 'narrow inlet of the sea', and is related to 'firth' and 'ford'. Either spelling is acceptable:

We spent a week on the Norwegian fiords.

first, firstly

First can function as an adjective and an adverb; *firstly* is not widely used but is always an adverb:

Her first car was a lovely blue Peugeot.
When I first arrived I knew nobody.
Firstly, I read my mail.

Some stylists and publishing houses used to insist that *firstly* should not be used in such lists as:

I want you to do the following. Firstly, tidy your bedroom. Secondly, throw away your old football boots …

The prescriptive attitude was summed up by Eric Partridge's claim:

'*Firstly* is inferior to *first*, even when *secondly, thirdly* follow it.'

Usage and Abusage, 1982

and the logical argument was that since *first* means 'preceding all others in time, order or significance' it is unnecessary to use the '-ly' form. However, *firstly* has been used in lists since the sixteenth century, is widely used today and is as acceptable as 'secondly' or 'fourthly' in all styles.

first name

The phrase *first name* is more appropriate than CHRISTIAN NAME in a multicultural society.

fish

The normal plural of *fish* is *fish*:

It was a green and gold fish.

Fish are aquatic vertebrates with jaws and gills.

The plural can also be 'fishes' but this plural is found mainly in religious and technical writing:

Tell me the story about the five fishes and two loaves.

Sharks belong to the class Chondrichthytes, that is, cartilaginous fishes.

fit

The verb fit is treated differently in Britain and America. In Britain, it is a regular verb, like 'bat':

fit(s), fitted, fitting

The dress doesn't fit.

He fitted a new handle on the door.

In America, *fit* is usually an irregular verb, like 'hit':

fit(s), fit, fitting

He fit a new handle on the door.

Many verbs that end in 't' and 'd' do not add '-ed' endings to indicate the past tense:

He cut his hair yesterday.

He spread butter on the bread yesterday.

See also -ED/-T

fix, repair

These verbs can be synonyms when they mean 'mend':

I'll need to fix the dishwasher.

I'll need to repair the dishwasher.

Fix has a wider range of meanings than *repair*. It can mean 'attach', 'agree on' and, colloquially, 'provide' and 'influence':

I've fixed the cupboard to the wall.

We must fix a date for the party.

How are we fixed for food?

That was not a fair contest. It was fixed.

Repair is a regular verb:

repair(s), repaired, repairing

I don't think the television can be repaired.

The adjectives 'repairable' and 'reparable' both derive from 'repair'. 'Repairable' means 'capable of being mended'. It takes its main stress on the second syllable and is usually applied to objects such as bags, shoes and watches:

I'm afraid these shoes just aren't repairable.

'Reparable' has its main stress on the first syllable and is applied mainly to abstractions:

The damage that has been done to your reputation is reparable.

The negative form of 'reparable' is more frequently used than the positive and frequently co-occurs with 'damage':

You've done irreparable damage to the good name of the club.

See also IRREPARABLE

fjord
See FIORD/FJORD

flaccid, placid

These adjectives are occasionally confused. *Flaccid* means 'limp', 'floppy':

This doll won't stand up without support. It's too flaccid.

The word has two acceptable pronunciations. It may rhyme with 'back Sid' or 'crass Sid'.

Placid means 'calm':

When they went out the lake was placid. No one expected such a sudden storm.

flagrant
See BLATANT/FLAGRANT

flair, flare

These words are homophones. *Flair* functions as a noun meaning 'talent, natural ability':

She has a flair for interior decorating.

Flare can function as a noun or a regular verb meaning 'blaze of light':

flare(s), flared, flarings

They sent up a flare, which was seen and reported to the coastguard.

The rocket flared against the black sky.

Since a *flare* normally spreads out from a narrow point to a wider shape, *flare* can also be used in connection with fashion to refer to a shape that widens:

The skirt is cut with a flare.

flak

Flak is an acronym meaning 'anti-aircraft fire'. It comes from German:

Fliegerabwerkanone (aircraft defence gun).

Occasionally, the word is spelled 'flack'.

flammable, inflammable, non-flammable

Many users of English have trouble distinguishing *flammable* and *inflammable*. Both adjectives mean 'combustible', 'liable to catch fire', but there is a tendency for 'inflammable' to be used of emotions and *flammable* of volatile substances:

Petrol is highly flammable.

Don't tease him. He's got a highly inflammable temper.

Difficulties arose with 'inflammable' because the 'in-' prefix in English is often used to negate words:

sensitive, insensitive

fertile, infertile

and so, for many speakers, 'inflammable' suggested 'not combustible'.

The normal warning now used to mark chemicals and substances that can be easily ignited is *flammable*, and *non-flammable*, which means 'incapable of burning', 'not easily set alight', is preferred for the negative.

flannel

The noun *flannel* tends to be used in Britain to refer to a soft, light woollen fabric or a pair of trousers made from such material:

Has anyone seen my flannels?

Occasionally, *flannel* is used to refer to a face cloth or 'wash cloth' as Americans prefer.

The verb *flannel*, which can mean 'flatter' in British English, doubles the 'l' in Britain but not in America:

UK: flannel(s), flannelled, flannelling
US: flannel(s), flanneled, flanneled.

See also UK AND US ENGLISH

flare

See FLAIR/FLARE

flaunt, flout

These verbs are frequently misused. *Flaunt* possibly comes from Scandinavian *flanta*, 'wander about'. It has two related meanings in contemporary English, 'display oneself in public':

What was it Mae West said? If you've got it, flaunt it.

and 'wave or display something or someone ostentatiously or impudently':

What was he flaunting at us? I couldn't see it.

Many people also use *flaunt* to mean 'treat rules with contempt' but the correct verb in this context is *flout*, which means 'show contempt for', 'scoff at':

She seems to take pleasure in flouting the rules.

The etymology of *flout* is uncertain but it may be derived from Old French *flauter*, 'play the flute'.

flautist, flutist

These nouns both refer to a person who plays the flute. *Flautist* is the correct term in Britain; *flutist* is preferred in America:

UK: She's a flautist in the orchestra.
US: She's a flutist in the orchestra.

flavour, flavor

Both forms derive from Old French *flaour* and are variants found respectively in Britain and America. The noun means 'distinctive taste or quality':

I can't describe this flavour but it is wonderful.

The regular verb means 'impart a flavour to':

UK: flavour(s), flavoured, flavouring
US: flavor(s), flavored, flavoring
You've flavo(u)red this with cinnamon.

flea, flee

These homophones are occasionally misspelled. *Flea* refers to a small insect; *flee* means 'run away, escape'. Their meanings are played with in the children's rhyme:

Once a flea and a fly were caught in a flue.
Said the flea: 'Let us fly.'
Said the fly: 'Let us flee.'
So together they flew through a flaw in the flue.

See also FLEE/FLOW/FLY

fledgeling, fledgling

These are variant forms of a noun that means 'young bird just able to fly':

Take heed, young fledgeling, till your wings
Have feathers fit to soar.
     'The Castle of Dromore', trad. Irish folksong

See also JUDGEMENT/JUDGMENT

flee, flow, fly

These three verbs all relate to movement. *Flee* means 'escape' and is an irregular verb:

flee(s), fled, fleeing, fled
They fled for their lives.

Flow is a regular verb and refers to the movement of a liquid:

flow(s), flowed, flowing
The river once flowed through this valley.

Fly means 'move through the air' and is also an irregular verb:

fly (flies), flew, flying, flown
I have flown 25,000 miles this year.

See also FLEA/FLEE

flier, flyer

These are both acceptable forms of a noun meaning 'person who flies, pilot'.

fling

Fling is an irregular verb:

fling(s), flung, flinging
He flung the book across the table.

floe

The noun *floe* meaning 'piece of floating ice' is often misspelled:

An ice floe is a sheet of ice floating on the water. It differs from an iceberg in that only the tip of an iceberg appears above the water.

floor

In British English, buildings of more than one storey are described as having a ground floor, then a first floor and second floor. In American English, the British 'ground floor' is called the 'first floor'. Thus, in a three-storeyed building, the terminology would be as follows:

UK	US
ground floor	first floor
first floor	second floor
second floor	third floor

See also STOREY/STORY, UK AND US ENGLISH

floppy disk

A *floppy disk* is a storage device used with computers. It is a plastic disk that fits into a disk drive. The term 'floppy' is also used:

Has anyone seen my floppies? I'll die if I've lost them.

flora

The phrase *flora and fauna* means 'plant and animal life, especially in a given area or region':

He's fascinated by the flora and fauna of Australia.

Flora was the Roman goddess of flowers.

See also FAUNA

flotation

The noun *flotation* meaning 'the launching and/or financing of a commercial enterprise' is normally spelled *flot-* but it derives from the verb 'float' and is, occasionally, spelled 'floatation':

Many small investors bought shares in the big privatization flotations.

flounder, founder

Apart from rhyming and an association with water, these regular verbs have little in common and yet they are confused. *Flounder* is thought to be a blend of *founder* and 'blunder'. It may also have developed from the flatfish of the same name. It means 'struggle', 'behave awkwardly':

I tried to offer my sympathy but I floundered about and couldn't find the right words.

Founder comes from Old French *fondrer*, 'to submerge' and means 'sink, collapse':

The ship foundered off the coast of Newfoundland.

flout

See FLAUNT/FLOUT

flow

See FLEE/FLOW/FLY

flu, influenza

The viral infection is normally referred to as *flu*. Often, in speech, the definite article is optional:

I've got flu.
I've got the flu.

Influenza is from Italian *influenza*, 'influence', 'epidemic'. It came into English in the mid-eighteenth century and replaced 'grippe'.

The influenza epidemic of 1919 probably killed as many people as the First World War.

fluorescent

The adjective *fluorescent* is often misspelled. It is most frequently used to refer to a particular type of light:

I find these fluorescent lights quite hard on my eyes.

flutist

See FLAUTIST/FLUTIST

fly

See FLEE/FLOW/FLY

flyover, underpass

A *flyover* is a section of elevated road that passes over another road:

Flyovers are less expensive than subways but they are probably less environmentally friendly.

An *underpass* is a section of road that passes under another road. It is gradually being replaced by 'subway':

Look for the first intersection after the underpass and take the second exit.

focus

Focus comes from Latin *focus*, 'hearth'. It can function as a noun meaning either 'point of convergence of light' or, more frequently now, 'a point upon which attention is concentrated':

Ensuring that people know about our product must be our main marketing focus for the next three months.

Focus has two plurals, 'focuses' and 'foci', the former being more frequently used. The usual pronunciation of 'foci' rhymes it with 'oh sigh'.

The regular verb *focus* means 'fix attention on,

concentrate'. The 's' is not doubled before '-ed' and '-ing':

They focused attention on us.

The popular use of 'focused' as an adjective to describe a person is becoming a cliché:

He's very focused and ambitious.

foetid
See FETID/FOETID

foetus
See FETUS/FOETUS

foggy, fog(e)y
These words are occasionally misspelled or misused. *Foggy* derives from 'fog' and rhymes with 'doggie':

The conditions are foggy with visibility down to 50 metres.

Fogy or *fogey* are alternative spellings of a noun meaning 'fussy, old-fashioned person' and it is usually preceded by 'old'. Nobody knows what it comes from but it rhymes with 'yogi':

I don't know why you thought you'd get good advice about clothes from that old fogey.

folk
The use of *folk* to mean 'people' is less common in Britain than in America:

I've always got on well with country folk.

Folk can be either singular or plural but 'folks' is also found and is acceptable:

I'm not sure how my folks will react to my choice of career.

Folk frequently functions as a modifier:

folk dance, folk medicine, folk memory, folk music

and the compound 'folklore' is widely used to refer to the unwritten literature of people and may include folk tales, history, proverbs, riddles and songs.

folk etymology
Folk etymology is the term applied to two semantic phenomena: the alteration of a learned or unfamiliar word by ordinary users of a language:

Gruss Gott (Great God) = Great Scott!
verloren hoop (lost troop) = forlorn hope
vin blanc (white wine) = plonk

and a popular but incorrect interpretation of a word:

asparagus from sparrow grass
cucumber from cow cumber
Ypres from Wipers.

Folk etymology can provide productive affixes. The compound 'Hamburger steak' was clipped to 'hamburger'. 'Hamburger' was reinterpreted as 'ham' + 'burger', giving rise to such forms as:

cheeseburger, chickenburger.

foment
See FERMENT/FOMENT

fontanel, fontanelle
These are variant spellings for the soft membranes between the bones of the skull in a baby:

Fontanel comes from a French word meaning 'little spring'.

food and drink
There are considerable differences in the terminology used for *food and drink* in many parts of the English-using world. Some of the best-known differences in such terminology in Britain and America are included under the headword UK AND US ENGLISH.

See also MEALS

foot
Foot is an irregular noun but regular verb:

He has small feet.
He footed the bill.

Many people are uncertain when to use *foot* and when to use *feet* when dealing with measurements. If it is part of a compound adjective, use *foot*:

a twelve-foot squid
a nine-foot python.

If one is expressing height colloquially, use *foot*:

She's five foot three.
He's six foot four.

But, if the word 'inches' is also used, 'feet' is often preferred:

She's five feet three inches tall.
He's six feet four inches tall.

Figures are often used with measurements:

He's 6 feet 4 inches tall.

The hyphen occurs in compounds before a noun.

See also MEASUREMENT

for
For is sometimes used as a conjunction meaning 'because':

I wanted to leave for I knew I'd stand a better chance in a city.

Many people dislike this usage.

See also AS/BECAUSE/FOR/SINCE

for-, fore-
Many people are uncertain when to use the prefixes *for-* and *fore-*. The best guide is this. *For-* can imply abstention:

forbearing
neglect:
forsake
and prohibition:
forbid.

Fore- is related to 'before' and implies before in time:
forebears
higher in rank:
foreman
and at or near the front:
forehead.

See also PREFIX

for ever, forever
Some British people use *forever* (one word) as a noun only:
Forever is a long time.
He took forever to get here.
and *for ever* (two words) as the adverb:
I don't want to live here for ever.
People would stay there for ever and ever.
In American English *forever* is widely used in all contexts and this usage is spreading in Britain.

forbid
Forbid is an irregular verb meaning 'ban', 'prohibit':
forbid(s), forbad(e), forbidding, forbidden
He forbade me to go alone.
The past tense may be either 'forbade' or 'forbad' and the pronunciation of the second syllable may rhyme with 'made' or 'mad'. The 'forbade' spelling is more widespread, as is the pronunciation that rhymes with 'mad'.

forceps
Forceps is a singular noun derived from Latin *formus* + *capere*, 'hot + to seize'. It is a surgical instrument often used in the delivery of babies:
a forceps baby.
Although 'a' *forceps* is acceptable, many people prefer to treat *forceps* as they do 'scissors' and use the expression:
a pair of forceps.

fore-
See FOR-/FORE-

forecast
Forecast meaning 'predict' used to be regular:
forecast(s), forecasted, forecasting
but the '-ed' ending is now rare and *forecast* is treated like 'cast':
forecast(s), forecast, forecasting

Who forecast the weather last night?

See also -ED/-T

foregrounding
When the normal word order of a sentence is changed, the word, phrase or clause moved to the front is described as being foregrounded. *Foregrounding* is a form of emphasis:

Normal word order	Foregrounding
We must see that.	That we must see.
I saw her on Friday.	On Friday I saw her.
She saw me when I arrived.	When I arrived, she saw me.

Often, foregrounded information is introduced by 'It's' and 'It was':
I saw John last week.
It was John I saw last week.
I saw John last week.
It was last week (that) I saw John.

forehead
Many people worry about the pronunciation of *forehead*. The usual pronunciation rhymes with 'horrid' as in the rhyme:
There was a little girl who had a little curl
Right in the middle of her forehead;
And when she was good, she was very very good
And when she was bad, she was horrid.

The spelling pronunciation that rhymes *forehead* with 'for dead' is acceptable.

foreign loan-words
English speakers have always borrowed words from other languages and an examination of the foreign words found in English provides insights into the contacts made by speakers of English. It can also indicate their attitudes to the people and items contacted. Greek, Latin and French borrowings, for example, are likely to be taken from written sources and are usually regarded as prestigious; borrowings from African, Amerindian, Australian or Celtic languages are usually taken from spoken sources and are often less accurately transcribed as well as having less prestige.

The process of anglicizing the pronunciation or the spelling of a borrowed word is erratic. Words in popular usage, such as:
anorak, café, éclair
are easily absorbed, whereas those limited in use may retain their non-English spelling and pronunciation:
angst, sotto voce, tête-à-tête.

In the written medium, words that are still regarded as foreign are italicized:
ad hominem, au courant.

Pronunciation is a useful guide to what is, and what is not, regarded as foreign although it is not infallible. There are two acceptable pronunciations for such words as:

garage, margarine, trait.

Below is a selection of the words borrowed from various parts of the world and absorbed into the vocabulary of world English. The list is meant to be illustrative only:

African: banjo, cola, okra, safari, zebra
Amerindian: coyote, hickory, moccasin, skunk, squaw
Arabic: admiral, algebra, cipher, sugar, zero
Australian: boomerang, dingo, kangaroo, koala, wombat
Celtic: bard, brock, slogan, trousers, whiskey
Chinese: chop suey, ketchup, pekinese, silk, tea
Dutch: boorm, easel, landscape, skipper, yacht
French: café, essay, government, language, police
German: hamster, pretzel, quartz, shale, zinc
Greek: bathos, coma, cosmos, larynx, phlox
Hebrew: cherubim, kibbutz, seraph, shibboleth, teraph
Indian: bungalow, guru, juggernaut, mango, purdah
Italian: fresco, grotto, mezzanine, oratorio, soprano
Japanese: kimono, mikado, saki, sushi, tycoon
Malay: bantam, cockatoo, kaok, (rice)paddy, orangutan
Scandinavian: husband, keg, sky, smug, troll
Spanish: aficionado, bravado, cockroach, guitar, junta, sombrero.

See also ACCENT MARK, BORROWING, ITALICIZATION

forensic

The adjective *forensic* derives from Latin *forensis*, 'public, of the forum', and means 'relating to or used in a court of law':

forensic science.

It has been popularized by the media but it is a prestigious word and lends an aura of scientific rigour to some things that are, by their very nature, variable:

forensic linguistics.

foreword, preface

These words are used to refer to statements that occur at the beginning of a book. They are sometimes used loosely to mean the same thing but careful users distinguish them.

A *foreword* is an introductory essay or statement at the beginning of a book and is normally written by someone other than the main author of the work:

John has asked his former tutor to write the foreword to his book.

A *preface* is usually an introduction to a book, article or thesis written by the author. It may include the author's aims, comment on any assistance received, and acknowledge permission to reprint anything in the copyright of another author.

She took ages to write the short preface to her first book.

forget

Forget is an irregular verb:

forget(s), forgot, forgetting, forgotten
I've forgotten my list again!

forgive

Forgive is an irregular verb meaning 'grant pardon':

forgive(s), forgave, forgiving, forgiven
I didn't ask to be forgiven because I didn't do anything wrong.

The derived forms are 'forgivable' and 'forgivably' (no 'e') and 'forgiveness':

You needn't ask for my forgiveness.

forgo, forego

These are variant spellings of an irregular verb meaning 'do without', 'give up':

forgo(es), forwent, forgoing, forgone
forego(es), forewent, foregoing, foregone
Workers have been asked to forgo their annual increment in the hope of preserving jobs.

The verb *for(e)go* is mostly used in its infinitive and present tense forms. A sentence such as:

I forewent my increment.

is grammatically correct but unlikely to occur.

'Foregoing' and 'foregone' are used adjectivally with the meanings of 'preceding' and 'finished, accepted':

The foregoing reference to 'diaspora' requires an explanation.
It was a foregone conclusion that they would get married and live happily ever after.

formal English

In the spectrum of English styles, *formal English* is far removed from intimate interaction or slang. It is characterized by particular choices and may include some or all of the following:

■ Slow speech

■ Less assimilation and vowel reduction:

two pence
rather than:
tuppence

■ Choice of appropriate words:

I received your letter.
rather than:
I got your note.

■ Full forms rather than reduced forms:

I am afraid I must inform you that I have not yet
received your essay.

rather than:

I'm sorry to tell you that haven't got your essay yet.

Formal English, which is suitable for academic
writing, business letters, job applications,
speeches and in impersonal contacts and contexts, is not superior to informal English. Each is
appropriate to a particular situation and the use
of formal English in a context where it is not
required is as inappropriate as wearing wellington
boots going to a ball.

See also REGISTER, STILE/STYLE

formality

There are various degrees of formality in any
language. Martin Joos once divided English into
five levels of formality – frozen, formal, consultative, casual and intimate – and, although these
divisions are arbitrary, they are helpful. Each level
of formality is marked by grammar and vocabulary. A sentence such as:

It would appear to be correct.

is formal, whereas:

It seems to be okay.

is casual.

See also COLLOQUIAL ENGLISH

former, latter

These words can function as adjectives and
nouns. As an adjective, *former* can refer to an
earlier time:

These are the relics of former glory.

and, as a noun, it refers to the first of two:

I met Bill and Ben ten years ago. The former (i.e.,
Bill) was cheerful and outgoing; the latter (i.e., Ben)
was cheerful but quiet.

If the list is longer than two, then 'first' and 'last'
should be used, not *former* and *latter*:

I met Bill, Bob and Ben ten years ago. The first was
cheerful and outgoing; the last-named was cheerful
and quiet.

As well as functioning to mean 'the second of a
pair', the adjective *latter* can mean 'near the end':

There was a breakthrough in the latter part of the
discussion.

See also LAST

formidable

The adjective *formidable* comes from Latin
formidare, 'to dread', and, like a lot of adjectives
associated with fear and terror, it has been
bleached of some of its meaning. Today,
formidable tends to mean 'extremely difficult':

I know I face formidable problems.

or, with certain nouns 'considerable', 'extraordinary':

These men [a group appearing in the BBC
programme, *The World's Strongest Man*] have
formidable powers of recuperation.

Formidable is normally stressed on the first
syllable and many users dislike the growing
tendency to stress the second syllable.

formula

The word *formula* has two plurals: 'formulae' in
scientific or formal English and 'formulas' in other
contexts:

Do you remember the formulae for nitrous oxide
and sulphuric acid?

Every culture has a number of storytelling formulas.

This noun is often mispronounced and misspelled
as *formular.

See also PHATIC COMMUNION

forsake

Forsake is an irregular verb:

forsake(s), forsook, forsaking, forsaken

Will you forsake all others?

forte

The noun *forte* derives from Latin and is used to
mean someone's 'strong point':

Singing is just not her forte.

The word rhymes with 'for May'.

fortuitous

The adjective *fortuitous* comes from Latin
fortuitus, 'happening by chance', and means
'accidental, unplanned':

Ours was a fortuitous meeting, the result of an
unscheduled stop in Derby.

Because the adjective is so frequently used to
describe a 'lucky happening', *fortuitous* is sometimes used when 'fortunate' or 'lucky' would be
more appropriate:

It was fortunate that I stopped because I avoided a
very serious accident.

*It was fortuitous that I stopped because I avoided a
very serious accident.

forty

Forty is frequently misspelled as *fourty. It can
function as an adjective:

There are forty children in her classroom.

and as a noun:

If you divide forty by five, what do you get?

forward, forwards

The normal rule is that *forward* can function as
both an adjective and an adverb but *forwards* can
be used only as an adverb:

He kicks the ball ... a forward movement ... oh dear oh dear oh dear straight into his own net.

Move forward please.

*a forwards movement

We seem to have been moving forwards all day.

There is a tendency for *forward* to be used more frequently than *forwards*, especially when the reference is to time and not space.

We'll have to bring the next committee meeting forward.

but *forwards* is retained in the fixed phrase 'backwards and *forwards*'.

See also -WARD/-WARDS

founder
See FLOUNDER/FOUNDER

foyer
The noun *foyer* is used to refer to a large hall or lobby used as a meeting place in a hotel, cinema or theatre:

I'll meet you in the foyer at 7:30.

Some people pronounce *foyer* in an approximation to French, to rhyme with 'boy + yey'; others rhyme it with 'boy + yer'.

fracas
The noun *fracas* comes from French *fracasser*, 'to shatter', and refers to a noisy quarrel:

There was a terrible fracas outside my room last night.

Fracas has the same form for both singular and plural but the second syllable of the singular noun rhymes with 'hah' and the plural noun with 'vase'.

fraction
A *fraction* is a part of a whole:

$1/2 = 50\% = 0.5$

$1/4 = 25\% = 0.25$.

Some people use *fraction* to mean 'small part of':

Oh that's much too big. Just give me a fraction of that.

but a fraction can be any size.

France
An inhabitant of the European republic is a 'Frenchman' or a 'Frenchwoman'; the adjective is 'French'. The capital is Paris.

See also FRENCH

fraught
Fraught, in the sense of 'filled', 'charged', has virtually died out of the language:

It was fraught with danger.

It is related to 'freight'.

-free
The adjective *free* is now widely used as a SUFFIX in such words as:

additive-free

duty-free.

free, freely
The normal rule is that *free* is an adjective and *freely* an adverb and this rule applies in most cases:

a free meal

We moved freely for the first time in months.

However, *free* is generally used as an adverb when the meaning is 'without having to pay' and 'without restrictions', especially in the phrase 'run free':

Do you think they'll let us in free?

Why did they let him run free?

See also ADJECTIVE, ADVERB

freeze
Freeze is an irregular verb:

freeze(s), froze, freezing, frozen

I almost froze to death waiting for you!

French
English has borrowed more words from and via French than from any other language. The borrowing began in the eleventh century, largely due to the Norman Conquest (1066) and included words for culture, food, government, trades and professions:

lyric, poem, sonnet

beef, mutton, veal

castle, count, law

carpenter, mason, plumber

dean, judge, surgeon.

The French language affected the pronunciation and the spelling of English, providing the sound 'zh' as in the middle of 'pleasure' and the spelling 'qu' instead of 'cw'. It also introduced such well-known suffixes as '-ation', '-our/-or' and '-ous':

derivation, favour, disastrous

and most of the fixed phrases where the adjective follows the noun it modifies:

attorney general

heir apparent

Princess Royal.

See also BORROWING, FOREIGN LOAN-WORDS

friable, fryable
These spellings are sometimes used to distinguish between *friable* as in:

friable soil (soil that crumbles easily)

and *fryable* as in:

fryable steak (steak that can be fried).

The adjective from 'fry' may, however, be spelled with 'i' or 'y'.

See also -ABLE/-IBLE

friar, frier, fryer

A *friar* is a member of a religious order. The word derives from French *frère*, 'brother':

He is a friar in the Franciscan Order.

Frier and *fryer* are variant spellings meaning 'a person or thing that fries':

He bought me a deep-fat fryer.

friend

The noun *friend* is frequently misspelled although it follows the traditional rule that 'i' goes before 'e' except after 'c'.

-friendly

The form *-friendly* has been widely used as an affix in such compounds as:

eco-friendly (friendly to our ecosystem)
environmentally friendly practices
ozone-friendly chemicals
skin-friendly deodorant
user-friendly software.

See also USER-FRIENDLY

frightful

Frightful is an adjective that used to mean 'full of fright' or 'capable of frightening'. The word has been bleached and can often function merely as an intensifier:

I've had a frightful day.

See also BLEACHING

frolic

When *frolic* functions as a verb, it needs 'k' before '-ed' and '-ing':

frolic(s), frolicked, frolicking
Look at the lambs frolicking in the fields.

fryable

See FRIABLE/FRYABLE

fryer

See FRIAR/FRIER/FRYER

fuchsia

The plant *fuchsia* is often misspelled. It is named after the German botanist Leonhard Fuchs (1501–66).

fuel

The word *fuel* comes from medieval French and is related to *feu*, 'fire'. It can refer to any substance used as a source of heat or power:

The main fuel in some nuclear reactors is uranium-235.

When *fuel* functions as a verb, the 'l' is doubled in British English, but left single in America:

UK: fuel(s), fuelled, fuelling
US: fuel(s), fueled, fueling
What do they use to fuel the Ariane rocket?

-ful

The SUFFIX *-ful* is etymologically the same word as 'full' and is used to form adjectives and nouns:

frightful, painful
a mouthful, a spoonful.

There is a difference between 'mouthful' and 'mouth full', as can be shown by the following sentences:

I took a mouthful of food.
I had my mouth full of food.

The second sentence can be transformed into:

My mouth was full of food.

showing that 'mouth' and 'full' are separate.

The plural of nouns ending in *-ful* can be marked by putting the '-s' after or before *-ful*:

three spoonfuls of sugar
three spoonsful of sugar.

The first method is the more widespread.

fulfil, fulfill

The infinitive and present tense of the verb meaning 'carry out, bring about the completion of' is spelled *fulfil* in Britain and *fulfill* in America:

UK: fulfil(s), fulfilled, fulfilling (I tried to fulfil my promise.)
US: fulfill(s), fulfilled, fulfilling (I tried to fulfill my promise.)

full stop

A *full stop* or 'period' (.) is used for several purposes in English, the main one being to mark the end of a sentence that is not a question or an exclamation:

Come here.
I saw him yesterday.

The other uses of a *full stop* are:

■ To mark some abbreviations:

Gk. (Greek)

■ To mark well-known utterances, even if they are not complete sentences:

One person, one vote.

■ To divide dollars and cents, pounds and pence:

$4.50
£3.45.

See also ABBREVIATION, PUNCTUATION

fullness, fulness

Both forms are acceptable. *Fullness* is preferred in Britain; *fulness* is widely used in America:

UK: in the fullness of time
US: in the fulness of time.

fulsome

The adjective *fulsome* originally meant 'abundant' but now often means 'excessive, exaggerated', even 'insincere':

His colleagues have been fulsome in their praise.
Such fulsome compliments do not sound genuine.

function

Words in English grammar may be described in terms of their 'form' or their *function*. A verb such as 'take', for example, has the forms:

take, takes, took, taking, taken, to take

and it can *function* as a verb in:

I'll take that one.

and as a noun in:

That's a take.

functional shift

The phrase *functional shift* describes the movement of a word from one class to another. A noun such as 'sandwich' can be used adjectivally in:

a sandwich course

and as a verb in:

I was sandwiched between them.

Many words can be involved in *functional shifts*:

Walk <u>tall</u>. (adjective used as adverb)
They <u>upped</u> the price. (adverb used as verb)

See also MULTI-FUNCTIONAL, WORD FORMATION

fundamental

The adjective *fundamental* comes from Latin *fundamentum*, 'foundation', and means 'basic, primary':

You fail to make the fundamental distinction between a word's 'form' and its 'function'.

Fundamental has suffered from being overused and bleached of meaning in phrases such as:

There has been a fundamental improvement in relations.

where an adjective such as 'marked' would be more appropriate.

See also BLEACHING, FAD WORD

fungus

The usual plural of *fungus* is 'fungi' but 'funguses' is also found:

Fungi are plants that usually lack leaves, stems and roots. They include mildew, rust and mushrooms.

Fungi may be pronounced to rhyme with 'rung guy' or 'gunge eye' or, less frequently, 'bungee'.

funnel

The word *funnel* can function as a noun and a verb:

A funnel has a wide mouth and tapers to a small hole.
We funnelled petrol from my car into John's.

The spelling of the verb differs in Britain and America:

UK: funnel(s), funnelled, funnelling
US: funnel(s), funneled, funneling.

furore, furor

The noun *furore* has three syllables and rhymes with 'glory' in British English, but has two syllables and is spelled *furor* in America. It derives from Latin *furere*, 'to rave':

UK: I have never in all my life heard such a furore, such a public outburst.
US: I have never in all my life heard such a furor, such a public outburst.

further

See FARTHER/FURTHER

fused sentence

The term *fused sentence* is applied to a structure that is really two sentences:

*Please place your essay in my pigeon hole, the late ones will not be marked.

This structure should be either:

Please place your essay in my pigeon hole. The late ones will not be marked.

or:

Please place your essay in my pigeon hole; the late ones will not be marked.

Fused sentences are an example of poor style and should be avoided.

See also ANACOLUTHON, DANGLING PHRASE OR CLAUSE

future

English has no *future* tense although it can refer to the future by using auxiliaries and/or adverbs:

She will go.
She leaves tomorrow.

In French, for example, we have:

elle va = she goes, she is going
elle ira = she will go

but in English the future is carried not by a change in verb form (i.e., tense) but by means of an auxiliary.

See also TENSE

G

g

G is a consonant that has two main pronunciations as in 'gas' and 'sage'. The letter is sometimes used as an abbreviation of 'gallon(s)', 'gram(s)', and 'gravity':

The rocket thrust is the equivalent of 7g.

gabardine, gaberdine

This word is used for both a thick, durable fabric and for a long, loose cloak or coat. The spelling *gabardine* is usually used for the cloth and *gaberdine* for the garment.

John needs a new gaberdine for school.

Gabon

An inhabitant of the west-central African republic is a 'Gabonese'; the derived adjective is the same. The capital is Libreville.

gage, gauge

Gauge rhymes with 'wage' and can function as a noun and a regular verb:

A 'gauge' is a standard measurement or an instrument to check measures.

gauge(s), gauged, gauging

We haven't been able to gauge its value yet but we'll give you our report next week.

Gauge is widely misspelled, a fact that has contributed to the acceptability of the variant spelling 'gage'.

gallop

Gallop is a regular verb. The 'p' is not doubled before '-ed' and '-ing':

gallop(s), galloped, galloping

They galloped off into the night.

gallows

The noun *gallows* meaning 'wooden structure used for hanging people' can be both singular and plural:

I've never seen a gallows.

Gallows were often sited at crossroads.

Gambia, The

An inhabitant of the West African nation is a 'Gambian'; the derived adjective is the same. The capital is Banjul.

gamble, gambol

These verbs are homophones. *Gamble* means 'bet':

gamble(s), gambled, gambling

I have never gambled in my life although I have enjoyed watching horse-racing.

Gambol is often used in connection with lambs that jump and skip:

The lambs gambolled playfully.

In British English, the 'l' is doubled before '-ed' and '-ing' but it is left single in American English:

UK: gambol(s), gambolled, gambolling

US: gambol(s), gamboled, gamboling.

gaol, jail

These words, which are pronounced in exactly the same way, are variant forms of the Old French word *jaiole*, 'a cage'. The form *gaol* is not used in America and is becoming rare in Britain:

The population in British jails almost doubled between 1986 and 1996.

The name of the person who looks after prisoners is 'jailer' but the variants 'jailor' and 'gaoler' are also found. The simplest rule is to use *jail* and 'jailer'.

garage

The word *garage* was borrowed from French and has several acceptable pronunciations. The BBC tends to stress the first syllable and rhyme it with 'carriage' but many Americans and an increasing number of British speakers stress the second syllable and pronounce the ending as in 'mirage'.

Garage can function as a noun:

The car is too big for the garage.

and as a regular verb:

garage(s), garaged, garaging

We garaged the car at the airport for two weeks.

gas

A *gas* is a substance that is neither liquid nor solid. The word can function as a noun with two acceptable plurals:

gas, gases/gasses

The word 'gas' was coined by a Flemish chemist.

Gas can also function as a regular verb:

gas(gases/gasses), gassed, gassing

They were gassed because the water heater had not been properly maintained.

The verb, like the plural noun, may be 'gases' or 'gasses'. The form 'gases' is more likely to be a plural noun and the form 'gasses' is widely used as a verb.

Gas is used as an abbreviation for 'gasoline', an American word for 'petrol'.

gaseous, gassy

Gaseous is an adjective deriving from 'gas'. It means 'having the characteristics of a gas':

Oxygen is a colourless, odourless, tasteless, gaseous element.

The adjective *gassy* means 'containing gas':

It's a gassy drink.

gasoline, gasolene

The noun *gasoline* has two acceptable spellings, although the '-ine' variant is more widespread:

We're looking for the nearest gasoline station. Can you help us, please?

gâteau, gateau

Gâteau is the French word for 'cake' and it is pronounced to rhyme with 'plateau'. The word is used in English to refer to a rich cake. The plural is, as in French, 'gâteaux':

We'll have six chocolate gâteaux.

The spelling without the circumflex is now more widespread.

gauge

See GAGE/GAUGE

gay

The word *gay* derives from French *gai*, 'carefree, merry', and it has traditionally been used as an adjective with this meaning:

Gone are the days when my heart was young and gay ...

Stephen Foster

In the recent past, it has been widely used as a noun or an adjective meaning 'homosexual':

Such legislation would not be in the interests of gays and lesbians.

See also POLITICAL CORRECTNESS

gelatin, gelatine

These are acceptable variants of the noun meaning 'soluble protein used in food and glues':

Jelly-babies are sweetened, flavoured gelatin.

Gelatin rhymes with 'sin' and *gelatine* with 'seen'.

gender

The noun *gender* comes from Latin *genus*, 'kind', 'type', and it is used in linguistics as a means of classifying nouns into the categories masculine, feminine and neuter. There are two types of *gender*: natural gender and grammatical gender.

Natural gender means that the sex of the item in the real world determines its classification in a language. Thus, in English, 'cow' and 'girl' are female and classified as being 'feminine'; 'bull' and 'boy' are male and are classified as being 'masculine'; 'table' and 'chair' are inanimate and classified as being 'neuter'.

Grammatical gender means that words in a language are classified with little or no relation to sex. Thus in French the term 'feminine' is applied to *boîte* (box) and *lune* (moon) whereas the term 'masculine' is applied to *bois* (wood) and *luxe* (luxury). There is no neuter in French.

Natural gender and grammatical gender can overlap, as when French treats *femme* (woman) as feminine and *homme* (man) as masculine, but there is no guarantee of this. Even related languages can classify the same item in different ways. *Flos* (flower), for example, is masculine in Latin but *fleur* is feminine in French.

English makes little use of grammatical gender. Nouns are either masculine, feminine or neuter and they take the appropriate pronominal referent:

Feminine	Masculine	Neuter
girl	boy	coat
she	he	it

There are a few exceptions to this pattern. Some nouns refer to animate beings of indeterminate sex:

baby, cat, child, member, parent, pet, student.

The pronouns used for these nouns can lead to awkwardness, since there is no singular pronoun serving for 'female' or 'male' or 'non-human'. Increasingly, 'they' is being used as a singular for this purpose:

Will each student see that they have submitted their dossier by 1 June.

A number of nouns in English have both male and female forms. These include:

abbot/abbess
actor/actress
blond/blonde
comedian/comedienne
deacon/deaconess
fiancé/fiancée
hero/heroine
masseur/masseuse
usher/usherette
waiter/waitress.

In all these examples, the female form is derived from the male form and many users of the language feel that the female profession is regarded, consciously or unconsciously, as of less importance. Sociologically, the attitude relates to the place of women in society. Linguistically, we can show a similarity between the above list and the creation of diminutives:

cigar/cigarette

duck/duckling
star/starlet.

Many women prefer to be referred to as 'actor', 'author' or 'poet', believing that they should be judged by the quality of their work rather than by their gender. Sometimes, however, the gender distinction has persisted because it is socially significant, as in the sets:

bridegroom/bride
king/queen
monk/nun
widower/widow.

See also FEMALE/MALE/FEMININE/MASCULINE, FEMININE FORM/MASCULINE FORM, SEXIST LANGUAGE

genealogy

This noun meaning 'direct descent of an individual or family from an ancestor' is often misspelled. It ends in '-alogy', not the more usual '-ology', because the word derives from Greek *genea*, 'race':

I'm trying to plot my family's genealogy. It's easy enough for a few generations but difficult when we get back to the 1800s.

genera

See GENUS/GENERA

genial

See CONGENIAL/CONGENITAL/GENIAL

genitive

The grammatical term *genitive* is normally applied to a case ending that is attached to nouns and pronouns to indicate possession:

Kate has a cat. Kate's cat. It is hers.
She has a cat. Her cat. It is hers.

In English, there are two methods of indicating possession: modification of the noun:

the cat's back

and the use of a phrase involving 'the noun of (the) noun'. This is sometimes called the 'periphrastic genitive':

the back of the cat.

It is the first method that is referred to as the genitive case. This method of indicating possession is more likely to be used with animate nouns:

Mary's cat
the cat's back
the leg of the chair.

The genitive marker is apostrophe + s ('s) for singular possession and s + apostrophe (s') for plural:

the cat's back
the cats' backs.

The genitive can be attached to phrases:

the star of the show's appeal

although this phenomenon is more likely to occur in speech, especially where complex phrases are concerned.

The apostrophe + s marker is frequently attached to temporal nouns to indicate relationships such as duration:

an hour's time
a day's journey
a week's work.

See also APOSTROPHE, CASE, POSSESSION

genteel, gentle, Gentile

These words all derive ultimately from Latin *gentilis*, 'belonging to the same family or tribe', but they have acquired different meanings. *Genteel* means 'respectable, well-bred' but it has taken on pejorative overtones and can suggest 'affected':

He's a genteel old man. He has never in his life been rude to anyone.
I hate it when you try to be so genteel. It's so artificial.

Gentle suggests 'mildness and moderation':

Gentle Jesus, meek and mild ...

and it can be applied, metaphorically, to inanimate nouns:

Come on. It's a gentle slope. We'll be able to ride up very easily.

Gentile is a noun meaning 'non-Jewish' or, more recently, 'non-Mormon':

Jew or Gentile, male or female, we're all capable of doing and saying things that would be better left unsaid.

genuflect

Genuflect means 'bend the knee as a sign of reverence':

Why did they refuse to genuflect before the main altar?

The derived noun may be either 'genuflection' or 'genuflexion', with the latter spelling being more widespread in Britain.

See also -CT-/-X-, SPELLING

genus, genera

These nouns are limited to biology. A *genus* is a group into which a family is divided and that contains one or more species. *Genera* is the usual plural of *genus*:

Vulpes (fox) is a genus of the dog family.

Occasionally, the plural 'genuses' is also found but normally only when the word is used loosely to refer to groups with common characteristics.

gerbil, jerbil

The forms *gerbil*, 'gerbille' and *jerbil* are all variant spellings for a burrowing rodent that is sometimes kept as a pet. *Gerbil* is the most usual spelling.

geriatric

The adjective *geriatric* comes from Greek *geras*, 'old age', and is often misused as a synonym for 'elderly' or, less kindly, 'over the hill':

*These drivers are all geriatric.

The adjective means 'relating to the branch of medicine that is concerned with the diagnosis and treatment of illnesses associated with old age':

Geriatric medicine is poorly funded.

The noun *geriatric* is used to mean 'elderly person'.

Germanic

The word *Germanic* can function as an adjective meaning 'characteristic of a group of related Indo-European languages':

The Germanic sub-group includes Dutch, English, German and the Scandinavian languages.

The noun refers to this branch of the Indo-European languages:

Germanic split into East Germanic and West Germanic.

Germany

An inhabitant of the European country is a 'German'; the derived adjective is the same. The capital is Berlin.

gerontocracy, gerontology

These nouns both derive from Greek *geras*, 'old age'. *Gerontocracy* means 'government by old men':

The Soviet Union used to be headed by a gerontocracy. Nobody in the government seemed to be under seventy.

Gerontology means 'the scientific study of ageing':

Everyone should be interested in the development of gerontology because, if we are lucky, we'll all be old one day.

gerrymander

The verb *gerrymander*, meaning 'divide voting areas so as to give unfair advantage to one person or group', is an example of a blend. The word derives from Elbridge *Gerry* (a US politician) plus 'sala*mander*' from the shape of an 1812 electoral district.

gerund

The word *gerund* comes from Latin *gerundum*, 'something to be carried on', and is applied to

-ING FORMS that come from verbs and can function as nouns:

Loving you is easy; liking you is more difficult.

Gerunds function like nouns in that they can be the subject (S), object (O) or complement (C) of a sentence:

Dancing (S) is a wonderful form of exercise.
I love dancing (O).
He is exasperating (C).

but they retain some of their verbal qualities in that they can take an object. In the sentence:

Smoking cigarettes can seriously damage your health.

'cigarettes' are the object of the *gerund* 'smoking'. Gerunds can also be modified by an adverb:

I love dancing vigorously.

When a *gerund* occurs in such structures as:

She does not approve of his smoking.
She does not approve of Mike's smoking.

the possessive adjective is frequently replaced in colloquial speech by an object pronoun or the unmarked noun:

She does not approve of him smoking.
She does not approve of Mike smoking.

The possessive form of the adjective and noun are more acceptable in formal contexts.

See also NOUN, VERB

get

Get is an irregular verb:

UK: get(s), got, getting, got
US: get(s), got, getting, got/gotten

and one of the most overused verbs in the language:

I got up at six. I got washed and dressed and got some breakfast before I got the bus to town. I got to my office by 7:30 and got quite a lot of work done before I got the daily post and got the bad news that I'd got the sack.

Because it can function as an omnipurpose verb in this way, generations of teachers have criticized its use.

In America and increasingly in other parts of the world, such as Australia, 'gotten' can be used as a past participle, especially when *get* means 'acquire':

I'd just gotten a new car.

but 'gotten' is only acceptable in Britain in such phrases as:

ill-gotten gains.

See also UK AND US ENGLISH, VERB

Ghana

An inhabitant of the West African republic, formerly the Gold Coast, is a 'Ghanaian'; the derived adjective is the same. The capital is Accra.

Ghana should be clearly distinguished from Guyana in South America.

ghastly, ghostly

These adjectives were originally variants and meant 'ghost-like'. Now they have distinct meanings. *Ghastly* tends to be more widely used in Britain than elsewhere and means 'unhealthy' or 'horrible':

She's a ghastly colour.
I feel ghastly this morning.

Ghostly means 'spectral', 'like a ghost':

And there in the mirror was a ghostly face, grinning at him.

ghetto

The noun *ghetto* is often misspelled, in spite of its recent media popularity. It comes from Italian, possibly from *borghetto*, a diminutive of *borgo* 'city', and was used to refer to 'a settlement outside a walled city', where Jews were sometimes required to live. It now means 'a slum area' and the plural may be either 'ghettoes' or 'ghettos':

Many new immigrants are forced by circumstances to live in ghettoes.

Derived forms such as 'ghettoization' have also been popularized:

Such ethnic cleansing can lead to ghettoization.

gibe, gybe, jibe

The forms *jibe* and *gibe* are variant spellings of a colloquial word of uncertain origin meaning 'jeer', 'taunt', 'scoff':

jibe(s), jibed, jibing
I couldn't stand being gibed at.
Don't listen to their jibes.
Such jibes are often more painful than physical suffering.
They jibed him because of his unusual appearance.

The verb *gybe*, also spelled *gibe* or *jibe*, meaning 'move a sail from one side to the other', is also of uncertain origin although it may be related to 'gibbet'.

Gibraltar

An inhabitant of the British dependency is a 'Gibraltarian'; the derived adjective is usually 'Gibraltar'.

giga-

The prefix *giga* comes from Greek *gigas*, 'giant', and denotes the number 10^9 or 1,000,000,000. It has been popularized by computerization:

I'll need hard disk storage of at least a gigabyte.

A 'gigabyte' is actually 1,073,741,824 bytes or units of data.

gild, guild

These words are homophones. *Gild* is normally used as a regular verb meaning 'cover with a layer of gold':

gild(s), gilded, gilding
I think I might gild the clouds in my picture.

Guild is a noun and refers to an association of people, linked by position or occupation:

I was able to trace my ancestors because they belonged to a guild of craftsmen.

Sometime *gild* is used as an alternative spelling for *guild* but this is not widespread and should be avoided.

gilt, guilt

These words are homophones. *Gilt* can function as an adjective or noun meaning 'gold' or 'substance looking like gold':

The gilt edging was wearing thin.
It's worthless. It's only gilt.

Guilt is a noun meaning 'remorse', 'state of having done wrong':

He is full of guilt because of having left his family.
The defendant's guilt was never in doubt.

Gipsy

See GYPSY/GIPSY

give

Give is an irregular verb:

give(s), gave, giving, given
They were given the same opportunity as the other children.

gladiolus

The usual plural of the sword lily or *gladiolus* is 'gladioli' although 'gladioluses' is also acceptable. The last syllable of 'gladioli' rhymes with 'tie':

I've never been very fond of gladioli.

This noun is derived from Latin *gladius*, 'a sword', the word that also gave us 'gladiator', a soldier with a sword.

glamour, glamor

Glamour is a noun and a variant form of 'grammar'. It used to mean 'magic spell' or 'charm' but now refers to 'beauty and allure':

Glamour is often only make-up deep.

The usual American spelling is *glamor* and the derived forms do not usually have a 'u', even in Britain:

glamorize, glamorization, glamorous, glamorously
although the spelling 'glamorise' is acceptable.

glycerin, glycerine, glycerol

These are all variant names for an odourless,

sweet, syrupy liquid. *Glycerol* is the technical term and the other two are the non-technical equivalents.

GMT

This ABBREVIATION stands for Greenwich Mean Time.

gnomic utterance

A *gnomic utterance*, derived from Greek *gnosis*, 'knowledge', is not related to the 'gnome' of folklore (from Latin *gnomus*, 'dwarf'). A *gnomic utterance* is a saying, aphorism, maxim or moral comment that expresses a widely-accepted truth. Gnomic verses in Greek go back to the sixth century BC and are found again in Old English as a means of preserving such traditional wisdom as the utterance attributed to King Alfred:

It is in vain to argue with a fool or vie in yawning with an oven.

Gnomic utterances have much in common with proverbs but usually deal with less everyday subjects.

See also PROVERB

gnu

The noun *gnu* refers to a type of antelope. The 'gn' should be pronounced 'n' as with 'gnat', 'gnaw' and 'gnome'. Partly because of a comic song and a series of advertisements where *gnu* was pronounced 'g+nu' (two syllables), many speakers in Britain now pronounce the 'g'. The correct pronunciation is still /nu/. The plural may be *gnu* or 'gnus':

Are there many gnu(s) in South Africa?

go

Go is an irregular verb:

go(es), went, going, gone
They've gone for a walk.

Go is used as a noun meaning 'chance, turn':

Let me have a go.

and as an adjective in the expression:

It's all systems go.

'Going' can be used as an adjective meaning 'current':

What's the going rate now?

and as a noun meaning 'way' as in the adage:

When the *going* gets tough, the tough get going.

gobbledegook

The noun *gobbledegook* was coined by a Texan congressman, Maury Maverick, to describe the verbose, pompous language of official communications. Such language is often characterized by obscure words and pompous phraseology:

But something happened of unearthly import last week: the Inland Revenue quietly admitted that the language of tax is incomprehensible gobbledegook.
Sunday Times, 4 August 1996

In many countries the Plain English Campaign has tried to counter the worst effects of *gobbledegook* by writing 'translations' of the more confusing official forms and documents and by offering advice on how such forms should be written. It is also sometimes spelled 'gobbledygook'.

See also CIRCUMLOCUTION, JARGON

god, God

A *god* is any supernatural being:

The gods in these stories seem just as fallible as we are.

God with a capital G refers to the supreme being:

I believe in God, the father, the almighty ...

gofer, gopher

The noun *gofer* and its variant *gopher* derive from 'go for' and refers to someone who runs errands:

We really need a bright student who can act as a gofer.

This word became popular in US English because it filled a gap and because it sounds the same as 'gopher' (a small burrowing animal).

See also COINAGE, WORD FORMATION

good, well

In Standard English, *good* is always an adjective:

She's a good singer.
She was very good.

and *well* is its adverbial equivalent:

She sings well.
She behaved well.

Well can also function as an adjective meaning 'healthy' or 'satisfactory':

You're looking very well.

The adage:

All's well that ends well.

shows *well* functioning as both an adjective and an adverb.

See also WELL

gorilla, guerrilla

These words may be homophones, but a *gorilla* is a large anthropoid ape while a *guerrilla* is a member of an unofficial but politically motivated army. *Gorilla* is a modified form of Greek *gorillai*, 'hirsute tribe'. *Guerrilla* is a diminutive form of Spanish *guerra*, 'war', and the spelling with one 'r' should be avoided.

gossip

Gossip can function as a noun meaning 'casual chat' or 'person who frequently talks about other people':

We often meet for a coffee and a gossip.

and as a regular verb:

gossip(s), gossiped, gossiping
We were gossiping about the children.

Gossip is an interesting example of SEMANTIC CHANGE. It started off in Old English times as *godsibb*, 'godparent of either sex', changed to female godparent and thence to a person who talked a great deal, often maliciously.

See also POLITICAL CORRECTNESS, SEXIST LANGUAGE

got, gotten

See GET

gourmand, gourmet

These nouns are occasionally confused. *Gourmand* comes from Old French *gourmant* and refers to a person who is devoted to eating and drinking, often to excess:

He's a gourmand: he doesn't mind what he eats and drinks as long as there is plenty of it.

Gourmet comes from Old French *gromet*, 'serving boy', 'vintner's assistant', but has undergone a semantic transformation in that it now refers to a person with a discriminating palate:

The food was wonderful enough for even the most critical of gourmets.

The second syllable of *gourmet* rhymes with 'day'.

government

Like a lot of words that are singular in form but plural in meaning, *government* is sometimes used as a plural noun:

The government have invariably tried to strengthen the laws against criminals. They have done this by enacting new laws and by strengthening old ones.

Careful users would prefer singular agreement as in:

The government has invariably tried to strengthen the laws against criminals. It has done this by enacting new laws and by strengthening old ones.

See also COUNTABLE AND UNCOUNTABLE, NOUN

graceful, gracious

These adjectives both derive from the noun 'grace', but they have developed distinct meanings. *Graceful* is applied to movement and means 'characterized by beauty of movement':

I've never in my life seen such a graceful dancer.

Gracious is applied to character and means 'characterized by courtesy':

She's kind and infinitely courteous. She is, by any standards, a gracious lady.

gradable

The adjective *gradable* is used in two main ways in language descriptions. Adjectives and adverbs are said to be *gradable* when they can occur in positive, comparative and superlative forms:

Positive	Comparative	Superlative
big	bigger/less big	biggest/least big
dark	darker/less dark	darkest/least dark
intelligent	more/less intelligent	most/least intelligent
quickly	more/less quickly	most/least quickly

Adjectives such as 'big/small', 'good/bad', 'long/short' or 'soft/hard' are often described as 'implicitly graded' because they have no absolute values. A 'big fly' is smaller than a 'small pig', for example. Adjectives such as 'dead/alive' or 'male/female', on the other hand, have absolute values and are not, logically, gradable. We cannot normally talk about one corpse being 'more dead' than another.

See also ADJECTIVE, ADVERB, ANTONYM, SEMANTICS

graduate

The noun *graduate* is sometimes used differently in Britain and the United States. In both countries it refers to a holder of an academic degree, but in Britain a *graduate* who is studying for a higher degree is normally referred to as a 'postgraduate' whereas *graduate* suffices in the United States:

UK: I'm a postgraduate (student).

US: I'm a graduate student.

The terminology for undergraduates is also different, and some of these differences are described at the entry UK AND US ENGLISH.

The verb *graduate* rhymes with 'gate' and tends to be used intransitively:

My son will graduate next year.

In the United States, however, the verb can also be used transitively to mean 'grant an academic degree' and 'award a particular grade':

They regularly graduate 90 per cent of their student intake.

graffiti

Graffiti is a plural noun but the singular 'graffito' is almost never used. The word comes from Italian meaning 'little scratches' but is used in English to mean inscriptions and drawings, often obscene, that are usually put on walls:

Some people regard the graffiti on the underground as a modern art form.

gram, gramme

These are variant spellings for the metric measurement equal to one thousandth of a kilogram. In the past, *gramme* was quite common but *gram* or the abbreviation 'g' are now more widespread:

There are approximately 440 grams in a pound.

See also WEIGH

grammar

The noun *grammar* is not easy to define because it has been used to describe many different aspects of, and approaches to, language. The word derives ultimately from Greek *gramma*, 'a letter', and originally meant 'the art of writing'. All definitions of *grammar* have one common denominator: they all deal with the ways in which larger units of language, such as sentences, are constructed from smaller units, such as words. The main modern approaches to grammar are summarized below.

Normative or prescriptive grammar

This approach describes language so that it might be used 'correctly'. Such grammars did not describe actual usage, but rather they prescribed what was socially acceptable. Normative grammars insisted, for example, that it was wrong:

to end a sentence with a preposition

to split an infinitive

to use 'aggravate' to mean 'annoy'.

Many normative grammars relied on Greek and Latin-based models and assumed that if something was not acceptable in them, it should not be acceptable in English.

Descriptive grammar

This type of grammar is based on a corpus of spoken or written language, or both. It does not recommend any particular usage but offers generalizations about tendencies and trends.

Comparative or contrastive grammar

This approach tends to compare and contrast two languages so as to help speakers of one acquire the other. Such grammars point out the areas of potential difficulty likely to be met by speakers of A as they learn language B.

Pedagogic grammar

This is designed specifically for teaching purposes and so may grade the language in terms of what is easy to learn. A grammar that concentrates on teaching a particular section of English, for example, to a special group of people such as bankers, geographers or scientists is often described as ESP (English for Special/Specific Purposes) or TESOL (Teaching English as a Second or Other Language).

Intuitive grammar

This is the innate knowledge of a language possessed by a native speaker, a knowledge that enables a speaker, in the words of Noam Chomsky, 'to make infinite use of finite means' by producing and understanding an infinite number of acceptable utterances. Native speakers also have an innate ability to evaluate degrees of acceptability. They know, for example, that:

a powdered wig

is more acceptable than:

a powdered keg

or:

*a powdwigered.

Theoretical grammar

This attempts to theorize about the nature of language as a human ability as well as about individual languages. Such grammars often deal with linguistic universals, the common denominators that are found in all human languages.

Transformational generative grammars

These postulate two levels of language – a surface structure and a deep structure – and they attempt to relate the levels systematically. Such grammars suggest, for example, that the structures:

John broke the window with a stone.

The window was broken by John.

The window was broken with a stone.

The window broke.

are all surface manifestations of the same underlying deep structure.

In Britain the term *grammar* tends to refer to one level of language only, namely 'syntax' (i.e., all that is not sound or meaning). In America *grammar* tends to comprehend all levels of language, including sound, words, phrases, clauses and meanings.

grand-, great-

These prefixes are both used in kinship terms to describe relationships that are two generations apart:

My son's daughter is my granddaughter.

My father's father is my grandfather.

My niece's daughter is my great-niece.

My aunt's mother is my great-aunt.

The prefix *grand-* is always used for the direct line of descent:

grandfather, grandmother, grandchildren, grandparents.

The prefix *great-* is more usual for aunts, uncles, nephews and nieces and for relationships further removed than two generations:

My grandmother was called 'Wallace'. Her mother, my great-grandmother, was called 'Campbell'.

See also FAMILY RELATIONSHIP

grapefruit

The noun *grapefruit*, like 'fruit', does not change in the plural:

I bought six grapefruit this morning.

grateful, gratified

These adjectives both derive from Latin *gratus*, 'grateful'. *Grateful* suggests 'thankful for a favour':

I was very grateful for your thoughtfulness.

Gratified suggests 'pleased', 'satisfied':

I was gratified to see that you did, after all, accept my ideas.

gratis, gratuitous

These adjectives derive from the Latin *gratis*, 'free', a meaning that *gratis* retains:

We were allowed in *gratis*. That's what I said. We got in free, *gratis* and for nothing.

Gratuitous originally meant 'given free' but is now used most frequently to mean 'unnecessary', 'unwarranted':

There is far too much gratuitous violence in films.

grave

A *grave* accent rhymes with 'halve' and is found over the 'a' in *à propos*. When it occurs over '-ed' it indicates that the syllable should be pronounced separately:

She blessed the children. (blessed = 1 syllable)
She is blessèd among women. (blessèd = 2 syllables)

See also ACCENT MARK

great-

See GRAND-/GREAT-

Great Britain

Great Britain consists of England, Scotland and Wales whereas the 'United Kingdom' includes Northern Ireland.

See also BRITAIN

Greek, Grecian

Both these words relate to Greece but they are differentiated. *Greek* means 'relating to Greece, its language, its people':

These are Greek coins.
Quite a number of Greek men are called 'George'.
I learnt a little Greek at school.

Grecian implies 'elegant' and refers to Classical Greece:

Can you remember the opening line of Keats's 'Ode on a Grecian Urn'?

Gradually, *Greek* is replacing *Grecian*, even in its references to classical Greek art and culture.

Greenland

An inhabitant of the self-governing Danish island is a 'Greenlander'; the derived adjective is 'Greenlandic'. The capital is Godthaab.

Grenada

An inhabitant of the West Indian nation is a 'Grenadian'; the derived adjective is the same. The capital is St George's.

grey, gray

In Britain, the colour that is intermediate between black and white is spelled *grey*, whereas *gray* is preferred in America:

UK: Grey clothes are thought to be conservative and dull.
US: Gray clothes are thought to be conservative and dull.

The phrase 'grey area' has been overused to refer to a topic or part of a discussion where the categories are unclear or controversial:

The problem of stalking is not easy to deal with. It is a grey area in legal terms in that it is often hard to draw a sharp line between one individual's right to privacy and another's right to freedom of movement.

grief, grieve, grievous

These words are frequently misspelled. The noun *grief* means 'great sadness':

I should like to express our sympathy in your time of grief.

The regular verb *grieve* means 'mourn, sadden':

She grieved all her life for her lost child.

The adjective *grievous* means 'very serious':

It was a grievous fault.

Grievous ends in '-ous' not '-ious'.

grill, grille

The British tend to *grill* meat when they cook it by direct heat. Americans prefer 'broil' for this method of cooking. *Grill* can function as a noun:

I'd prefer a grill, if that's possible.
Cook it under the grill.

and as a regular verb:

grill(s), grilled, grilling
Your father grills the meat to charcoal when we have a barbecue.

The noun *grille* is a homophone of *grill* and refers to 'metal framework':

We need a new grille for the fireplace.

Increasingly, this word is spelled *grill*, especially when it refers to the 'radiator grill' of a vehicle.

grind

Grind is an irregular verb meaning 'reduce to small particles':

grind(s), ground, grinding
They ground the corn with a pestle.

grisly, grizzly

These adjectives are homophones but their

meanings are distinct. *Grisly* comes from Old English *grislic* and means 'gruesome':

He told us some really grisly stories. They were absolutely horrible and totally unforgettable.

There is vacillation in the use of comparative and superlative forms. People often say 'grislier' and 'grisliest' and write 'more' and 'most grisly'.

Grizzly comes from French *gris*, 'grey', and means 'grey' or 'streaked with grey':

A grizzly bear is a greyish-brown variety of the brown bear.

grotto

A *grotto* is a small cave and it has two acceptable plurals, 'grottoes' and 'grottos':

Many grottoes have a religious significance.

grovel

The verb *grovel* means 'humble or abase oneself'. It doubles the 'l' before '-ed' and '-ing' in British English:

UK: grovel(s), grovelled, grovelling

US: grovel(s), groveled, groveling

I don't want to grovel to him but if I have to I will.

grow

Grow is an irregular verb meaning 'increase in size, develop':

grows, grew, growing, grown

The children have grown such a lot since last year.

The derived noun 'growth' has been widely used in the media as an adjective in such clichés as:

a growth industry.

Its use as in:

Since Henman's victories, tennis has become a growth sport.

should be avoided in both formal speech and writing.

Guadeloupe

An inhabitant of the overseas region of France in the Lesser Antilles is a 'Guadeloupan'; the derived adjective is the same. The capital is Basse-Terre.

Guam

An inhabitant of the US territory in the north Pacific is a 'Guamanian'. The adjectival form is 'Guam' or 'Guamanian'. The capital is Agaña.

guarantee, warranty

The nouns *warranty* and *guarantee* are sometimes used interchangeably. Although their meanings overlap, they are not identical. A *guarantee* is a promise to stand surety for another's debts or a promise that faulty goods will be replaced. The word, meaning 'assurance',

'warranty' 'assure', can function as a noun or a regular verb. It is often misspelled:

guarantee(s), guaranteed, guaranteeing

We have a three-year guarantee for our camcorder.

A small deposit will guarantee the product at this price.

Occasionally, especially in America in business and legal contexts, the variant 'guaranty' is used:

She works for the Guaranty Trust Company.

A *warranty*, in property law, means a covenant by which the vendor vouches for the security of the title being conveyed. In insurance law, it means an undertaking that the facts given are correct.

Guatemala

An inhabitant of the Central American republic is a 'Guatemalan'; the derived adjective is the same. The capital is Guatemala City.

guerrilla

See GORILLA/GUERRILLA

guess

The word *guess* can function as a noun and a verb meaning 'estimate':

My best guess is that she's in Brittany.

I can't guess what you've got in this parcel.

The expression 'I guess', meaning 'I think, suspect', is a colloquialism popularized by speakers of American English. It serves to make an assertion less dogmatic:

I guess he's gone.

He's about nineteen, I guess.

'I guess' used to be confined to Americans but it has been popularized by the media and is regularly used by non-American speakers.

See also SHIBBOLETH

guest

Many users of English dislike the use of *guest* as a verb in such constructions as:

Cher guested on the Lottery show.

The use of nouns as verbs is extremely widespread in English, as in:

There should always be someone in the office to man the telephone.

but all overused words should be avoided.

See also HOST

guild

See GILD/GUILD

guilt

See GILT/GUILT

Guinea

An inhabitant of the West African republic is a 'Guinean'; the derived adjective is the same. The capital is Conakry.

Guinea-Bissau

An inhabitant of the West African republic is a 'Guinean'; the derived adjective is the same. The capital is Bissau.

gut

The use of *gut* as an adjective meaning 'instinctive' is overdone:

My gut reaction is to cut my losses.

guttural

The adjective *guttural* meaning 'relating to the throat' is frequently misspelled. It does not have an '-er' in it but derives from Latin *gutturalis*, 'concerning the throat':

Velar and uvular sounds are often described as 'guttural'.

Guyana

An inhabitant of the republic in South America is a 'Guyanese'; the derived adjective is the same. The capital is Georgetown.

gybe

See GIBE/GYBE/JIBE

gymkhana

Gymkhana is often misspelled. It comes from Hindi *gend-khana*, 'ball house', and refers to an event in which riders and horses show their skills, sometimes in competition:

Miranda won a prize for jumping at the gymkhana.

gynaecology, gynecology

These variants, meaning 'the branch of medicine concerned with the illnesses of women', are often misspelled. The '-ae-' spelling occurs mostly in Britain; *gynecology* is the preferred form in America.

See also -AE-/-E-, SPELLING

Gypsy, Gipsy

The word *Gypsy* comes from 'Egyptian', because it was widely believed that the Romani people came from Egypt. In fact, they came from India, and the Romani language still has a great deal in common with other Indic languages such as Hindi and Sanskrit.

When the word is used to refer to a Romani, then an upper case 'G' should be used, just as it is when we refer to an African, an Indian, a Catholic or a Jew, because the word *Gypsy* can refer to a Romani's race or culture:

Because Gypsies have often been treated as social outcasts, they have not received the respect that they deserve.

See also POLITICAL CORRECTNESS, RACIST LANGUAGE

H

h
H is a consonant. The letter is pronounced 'aitch' but some speakers write and say 'haitch'.

See also HYPERCORRECTION

'h' silent and dropped
The initial 'h' is often silent in words originally borrowed from French:

heir (héritier)
honest (honnête)
hour (heure).

This non-pronunciation of 'h' is perfectly standard and is different from the tendency in many regions to drop the 'h' in such words as:

hand, heart, home.

There is some vacillation in the pronunciation of 'historic' and 'hotel', both from French. Webster's dictionary recommends 'an historic occasion' but not 'an hotel', while Collins's dictionary prefers 'a historic decision'. Formerly, the rule was that 'an' should be used before a word beginning with 'h' when the initial syllable was unstressed:

an habitual criminal
an hereditary title
an historical account
an hotel
an hysterical act.

This rule is gradually disappearing and 'h' is being treated in the same way as other consonants.

The social stigma attached to dropping initial 'h' has resulted in HYPERCORRECTIONS where an 'h' is prefixed to words that should not have them, as in 'haitch' for 'aitch'.

habitable, inhabitable, uninhabitable
These adjectives are sometimes confused. They all derive from Latin *habitare*, 'to dwell'. *Habitable* and *inhabitable* both mean 'capable of being lived in' although the first is more likely to be applied to houses and the latter to areas of the world:

His house is no longer habitable. It is damp and cold.
Human beings have made even desert regions inhabitable.

Uninhabitable negates both *habitable* and *inhabitable*:

His house is uninhabitable.
The South Pole is uninhabitable.

habitual
The adjective *habitual* derives from 'habit' and means 'done or experienced regularly and repeatedly':

a habitual liar
my habitual comment.

Many speakers and writers still use 'an' with *habitual*:

an habitual drinker

but this usage is not as widespread as it used to be.

The term 'habitual aspect' is sometimes applied to phrases, such as 'keep on', that indicate the habitual nature of an action:

He kept on trying.
She used to visit us every Thursday.

See also 'H' SILENT AND DROPPED

hadj, hajj
The noun *hadj* or *hajj* comes from Arabic *hajj*, 'pilgrimage', and is used to refer to a pilgrimage to Mecca:

All Muslims try to go on a hadj at least once in their lives.

A Muslim who has made the pilgrimage is called a 'hadji', 'haji' or 'hajji':

These hadjis have all made the pilgrimage three times.

Neither 'hadj' nor 'hadji' is italicized.

The female equivalent, 'hadjira', 'hajira' or hajjira', occurs less frequently.

haemo-, hemo-
This prefix is used in a variety of words relating to blood. *Haem-* is still preferred in Britain but the influence of American *hem-* is growing. The prefix comes from Greek *haima*, 'blood'.

haemophilia, hemophilia
This word is frequently misspelled. It refers to a disease where normal blood clotting does not occur:

UK: Haemophilia can be successfully treated with Factor-8.
US: Hemophilia can be successfully treated with Factor-8.

haemorrhage, hemorrhage
This word is frequently misspelled. It can function as a noun or verb and indicates profuse bleeding:

UK: It's a brain haemorrhage.
US: It's a brain hemorrhage.
UK: The blood vessel has ruptured. He's haemorrhaging badly.
US: The blood vessel has ruptured. He's hemorrhaging badly.

hail, hale

These words are homophones. The noun *hail* refers to frozen rain:

We can expect hail and snow.

The verb *hail* means 'greet enthusiastically', 'acclaim':

The fans hailed the singer.

The adjective *hale* meant 'healthy' but now only occurs in the fixed phrase:

hale and hearty.

Haiti

An inhabitant of the republic in the western part of the island of Hispaniola is a 'Haitian'; the derived adjective is the same. The capital is Port-au-Prince.

hajj

See HADJ/HAJJ

half

Half can function as an adjective:

a half sovereign

and as a noun:

We divided the cakes into halves.

Half can occur in two sets of equally acceptable constructions:

half the money, half of the money
half a dozen, a half dozen
a kilo and a half, one and a half kilos.

Verbal agreement depends on whether *half* precedes a singular or a plural noun:

Half (of) the word was blotted out.
Half (of) the words were blotted out.

Before a noun, there is a choice between *half* and *half of*, although the latter is marginally more formal. When followed by a pronoun, *half of* is essential:

I want half of you to weed the garden.
*I want half you to weed the garden.

half-

Half- is widely used as a prefix. It can combine with adjectives:

half-serious

with adverbs:

half-heartedly

with nouns:

half-French, half-human

and with verb participles:

half-eaten, half-protesting.

A *half*-sister is a blood relative. The term is sometimes confused with 'step-sister'.

See also FAMILY RELATIONSHIP

hallo, hello, hullo

These greetings are all widely used in Britain. The spellings differ but they all tend to be stressed on the second syllable and have an unstressed vowel in the first. The spelling *hello* is probably the most widely used. The use of *hello* as an exclamation of surprise as in:

Hello! What on earth is this!

is now old-fashioned.

halo

A *halo* is a circle of light, usually around the head of a saint. The plural is 'haloes':

These haloes have faded badly. We should touch them up.

Hamitic, Semitic

Semitic and *Hamitic* can both function as nouns and adjectives. *Semitic* is a branch of the Afro-Asiatic family of languages that includes Arabic, Aramaic, Amharic and Hebrew. *Hamitic* is a group of North African languages related to Semitic. The *Hamitic* branch includes Berber, Chadic, Cushitic and Egyptian.

The adjective *Semitic* can be used to denote a language:

Phoenician was a Semitic language.

or it is sometimes used as a synonym of 'Jewish':

Traces of Semitic culture can be found in African communities as far south as Zimbabwe.

The adjective *Hamitic* is applied to languages:

Is Hausa a Hamitic language?

Semitic and *Hamitic* derive ultimately from 'Sem' and 'Ham', two of the sons of Noah.

handful

Some people have argued that the correct plural of *handful* should be 'handsful', but the acceptable form is 'handfuls':

If each of us added a few handfuls of grain, there would soon be enough for everyone.

handicap

Handicap is a regular verb:

handicap(s), handicapped, handicapping
He felt he was handicapped by living in the provinces.

It can also function as a noun:

Some of the children in the school have severe handicaps.

Some people dislike the use of terms such as 'handicapped', preferring 'disabled' or a phrase that does not define a person in terms of a disability.

See also POLITICAL CORRECTNESS

hands-on

The compound *hands-on* is overused by the media in such phrases as:

hands-on experience

a hands-on activity.

It means 'practical' or 'useful' or refers to an activity that needs close attention:

We need a director with hands-on experience, not simply a theorist.

hang, hanged, hung

The verb *hang* has two past tense and past participles, depending on its meaning. When *hang* means 'fasten', 'suspend', it is irregular:

hang(s), hung, hanging

They've hung that picture in the wrong place.

When *hang* means 'suspend by the neck until dead', it is a regular verb:

hang(s), hanged, hanging

Until the 1950s, murderers were frequently hanged in this country.

The compound 'hang-up' is widely used as a colloquial synonym for a mental or emotional inhibition:

She's a brilliant student but she has hang-ups about her written work.

Occasionally, in American English, 'hangup' is not hyphenated.

hangar, hanger

These homophones are occasionally misspelled. A *hangar* (ending in '-ar') is a place where aircraft are stored and maintained:

We were shown over the new hangar at Heathrow.

A *hanger* (ending in '-er') is a support on which something is hung:

We'll need to buy some more coat hangers.

haplography, dittography

These words are antonyms. *Haplography* refers to the accidental omission of a repeated letter or syllable in a word:

plasterer: *plaster

remember: *rember.

Dittography involves the unintentional repetition of letters, syllables or words:

determination: *determinatation

on the desk: *on the the desk.

haplology

Haplology is the omission of a repeated sound or syllable in a word. This often occurs in rapid speech and in part accounts for some misspelled words:

library: *libary

veterinary: *vetinry.

hara-kiri

Hara-kiri comes from Japanese *hara*, 'cut', *kiri*, 'belly', and refers strictly to ritual suicide by means of falling on one's sword. The meaning is sometimes widened in English to any form of ritual suicide:

They committed *hara-kiri* by crashing their planes on the decks of enemy warships.

Sometimes, the form *hari-kari* is used, but this is an anglicization of the Japanese form and should be avoided.

harass

The regular verb *harass* means 'give persistent trouble to'. It is often misspelled:

harass(es), harassed, harassing

He is harassed by naughty boys who ring his doorbell and run away.

In Britain, *harass* tends to be stressed on the first syllable, whereas it is regularly stressed on the second in America. The American pronunciation seems to be gaining ground in Britain with the verb and also with the noun 'harassment'.

When we use 'harassed' as an adjective as in:

You look harassed, John.

its meaning is often equivalent to 'troubled'.

harbour, harbor

Harbour can function as a noun or verb. The '-our' ending is standard in Britain and the '-or' in America:

UK: The new ship is anchored in the harbour.

US: The new ship is anchored in the harbor.

UK: harbour(s), harboured, harbouring (I don't harbour any resentment.)

US: harbor(s), harbored, harboring (I don't harbor any resentment.)

See also SPELLING

hard, hardly

Hard can function both as an adjective with a range of meanings from 'not soft' to 'trying' and as an adverb:

This pencil is too hard. I need something softer for sketching.

It's been a hard day.

You'll have to work hard.

They robbed me of my hard-earned cash.

Hardly is an adverb whose meaning is no longer related to *hard*. Rather, it is the equivalent of 'barely' or 'scarcely':

I can hardly hear you.

See also BARELY/HARDLY/SCARCELY

hassock

See CASSOCK/HASSOCK

hauler, haulier

The derived noun from 'haul' is *haulier*, but 'hauler' is occasionally found, mainly in US English. Some people even use both, with *hauler* meaning someone or something that carries a load:

We need to borrow a hauler because our van has broken down.

and *haulier* meaning a person whose job it is to carry goods:

He works as a haulier between London, Birmingham and Leeds.

haute couture

The French phrase literally means 'high dress-making' and is used in English to mean 'high fashion':

She felt that she represented *haute couture* in this country.

French phrases are prestigious in fashion and cookery and *haute cuisine*, 'high cookery', is used to refer to 'high-class cooking':

I've never understood the appeal of *haute cuisine*.

In both phrases, the 'h' is dropped and *haute* is pronounced like 'oat'.

have

Have is an irregular verb:

have (has), had, having, had.

It can function as a main verb and as an AUXILIARY:

I have a wonderful collection of stamps. (main verb)
I have saved stamps since I was a child. (auxiliary verb)

There are some differences between British and American speakers in the use of *have* as main verb. British speakers are less likely to use 'do' with *have* when asking questions:

UK: Have you any children?
UK: Has she a printer?
US: Do you have any children?
US: Does she have a printer?

In colloquial speech in Britain, 'got' is usually combined with *have*:

Have you got any children?
Has she got a printer?

As an auxiliary, *have* is used to form what linguists call 'perfective aspect':

I have bought your book.
He has written home at last.

Have combines with 'got' in British English and with both 'got' and 'gotten' in American English:

UK/US: I've got a cold.
UK: I've got a new job.
US: I've gotten a new job.

See also GET, UK AND US ENGLISH

have (got) to

Have got to is used as a colloquial equivalent of 'must, ought to':

I must go.
I ought to go.
I've got to go.

See also MODALITY

he or she

In the past, it was usual to use *he*, *him* and *his* as the pronouns of 'common gender' – that is, where the gender was either not known or not regarded as significant:

Every child must do his best.
Everyone here has been instructed that he must accept the rules or leave the club.

Many people have objected to the use of *he*, *him* and *his* to represent both women and men, considering such usage sexist. There are four main ways of dealing with this problem:

■ Use *she* or *her* rather than *he* as the common gender pronoun:

Every child must do her best.
Everyone here has been instructed that she must accept the rules or leave the club.

This solution is, however, just as sexist as the use of *he*.

■ Use *she* and *he* randomly:

Every student must register with her tutor. He should do this by Friday, 7 October at the latest.

This solution is potentially ambiguous. Does the 'he' refer to the student, to the tutor, to both or to neither?

■ Use *he or she* or *she or he* in each instance:

Every student must register with his or her tutor. He or she should do this by Friday, 7 October at the latest.
Every student must register with her or his tutor. She or he should do this by Friday, 7 October at the latest.

This solution is clumsy and not altogether satisfactory. Should *she* precede or follow *he*?

■ Use 's/he':

S/he must register before Friday.

This solution is not altogether satisfactory. It works well for the subject pronoun but does not work for 'her/him' or 'hers/his'.

■ Use the plural:

Students must register with their tutors. They should do this by Friday, 7 October at the latest.

This solution is least likely to give offence but it does not solve all problems:

Everyone should do her/his/their best.

See also EVERY, EVERYBODY/EVERYONE, GENDER, SEXIST LANGUAGE

head

Head combines readily in English to form adjectives:

She has always been a headstrong child.

adverbs:

He went headlong into the river.

nouns:

I've got a headache.

and verbs:

He has headlined this issue.

As with many compounds, there is no absolute rule about when they should be written with a hyphen, as one word or as two:

head-first, headlight, head teacher.

See also COMPOUND, HYPHEN

headlines

The language of *headlines* has become a popular art form, revealing many of the features associated with both poetry and advertising. *Headlines* are meant to catch the attention of the reader and so they exploit the use of abbreviations:

Far-Out Trekkers [Star Trek enthusiasts]

of acronyms:

KO for NATO?

of alliteration:

Blazing Busman Horror

of ambiguity:

Giant Waves Down Tunnel

of rhyming:

Dearer Shearer for North

of puns:

Bonfire of the Inanities [Bonfire of the Vanities]

and of short, simple, often predictable vocabulary such as:

ban, curb, cuts, freeze, fury, horror, mole, orgy, probe, rap, row, snag, switch.

The grammar of *headlines* also results from the combined desire to be brief and yet make a strong impact. Thus, we may find omissions of subjects, auxiliaries, articles and copulas:

[This is the] Day of Reckoning

FA [is/are/have been] all at Sea over Mariner

[Our athletes have been] Pushed to 35th.

We also regularly find headlines that consist of a string of nouns:

Research Rankings

Trunk Road Jumbo Trap.

If a verb occurs in a *headline*, it is likely to be either the infinitive:

Tories to Change Chairman

or a present tense form:

Russians Attack Grozny.

See also JOURNALESE, TELEGRAPHESE

hear, listen

These verbs are related. *Hear* implies perceiving sounds automatically, whereas *listen* implies making a conscious effort to hear:

I was reading when I heard a noise.

I listened intently but I could hear nothing.

We usually *hear* a talk or a recital, but we *listen* to music when we play records. The distinction is similar to the one between 'see' and 'look', 'look at'.

Hear is an irregular verb:

hear(s), heard, hearing.

The use of the simple present verb implies ability:

I hear something. = I can hear something.

Although it applies mainly to the auditory sense, it is also used as an approximate synonym for 'believe':

I hear you've got top grades at A-level.

Verbs of perception such as *hear* rarely occur with the progressive:

*?I am hearing him.

Listen frequently occurs with the progressive:

You didn't hear because you weren't listening.

I didn't hear you although I was listening for you.

See also ASPECT, LOOK/SEE/WATCH

heave

In all but a few nautical instances, *heave* is a regular verb:

heave(s), heaved, heaving

I heaved at the rock but could not move it.

He heaved a sigh when he thought of them.

When *heave* is used of a vessel, especially in the fixed phrase '*heave* into view', the past tense and past participle may be 'hove':

The yacht hove into view.

Heaven, heaven(s)

When *Heaven* refers to the place where God lives, it has a capital letter:

People used to think that Heaven was in the sky, but the truth is, we do not know where God and the angels are.

When the word *heaven(s)* is used to refer to the sky, it does not have a capital:

Look up into the heavens and see the marvels of creation.

Hebrew

English has borrowed *Hebrew* words for religious phenomena. It has also borrowed from YIDDISH and from Israel.

See also FOREIGN LOAN-WORDS

hectic
Hectic was originally used in English to describe someone who had a fever. It is now used to mean 'very busy', 'rushed' and implies that the action is characterized by feverish energy:

I don't know how you manage such a hectic schedule.

height
This noun is related to 'high' and is often misspelled. It rhymes with 'might' but is spelled like 'eight':

What height is she?

heinous
This formal word is often misspelled. It ends in '-ous', not '-ious':

It was a heinous crime.

The first syllable may be pronounced to rhyme with 'mane' or with 'mean'.

heir, heiress
The noun *heir* is a homophone of 'air' and is often misspelled:

John is her heir.

Heiress is the female equivalent:

Did you see the film called *The Heiress*? It starred Olivia de Havilland and Montgomery Clift. He only wanted to marry her for her money.

The related abstract noun is 'inheritance'.

See also GENDER

hello
See HALLO/HELLO/HULLO

help
Help is a regular verb meaning 'aid, assist':

help(s), helped, helping.

It may be followed by an infinitive verb with or without the 'to', although some people dislike the omission of 'to':

He helped her to reach her car.
He helped her reach her car.

Both usages are acceptable, but in Britain the infinitive with 'to' tends to be more usual in writing.

hemi-
Hemi- is a prefix deriving from Greek *hemi-*, 'half'. It occurs in a number of words including:

hemisphere (half a sphere)

and:

hemistich (half a line of verse).

See also DEMI-, SEMI-

hemo-
See HAEMO-/HEMO-

hemophilia
See HAEMOPHILIA/HEMOPHILIA

hemorrhage
See HAEMORRHAGE/HEMORRHAGE

hence
Hence can function as an adverb meaning 'from this time':

A few years hence, no one will remember or care about this.

Its use in the sense of 'for this reason' is not widely used:

We failed to achieve our targets and hence we have had to let some staff go.

and its use as a verb meaning 'go away' is now obsolete:

*Hence and quit my sight!

hendiadys
Hendiadys derives from Greek *hen dia duoin*, 'one through two'. The main stress is on the second syllable, which is pronounced 'die'. *Hendiadys* is a rhetorical device in which two words are joined by 'and' and carry the same meaning as the modified second word:

nice and comfortable = extremely comfortable.

The first word comes from a limited set of positive words including 'good', 'lovely' and 'nice':

good and ready = absolutely ready
lovely and smooth = extremely smooth
nice and warm = comfortably warm.

hepta-
Hepta- is a prefix deriving from Greek and meaning 'seven'. It is the equivalent of Latin *septa*. It is found in such words as:

heptagon (7-sided figure)

and:

Heptateuch (first seven books of the Bible)
heptathlon (competition with seven events).

hereditary, heredity
These words derive from Latin *hereditas*, 'inheritance'. *Hereditary* is an adjective and denotes characteristics or titles that can be passed from one generation to another:

Certain medical conditions are known to be hereditary.
Tony gave up his hereditary title.

Traditionally, and in conservative varieties of English, 'an' was used before *hereditary*:

Was it an hereditary title?

Heredity is a noun that refers to the transmission

of genetic factors as well as to the totality of inherited characteristics:

Her height and colouring can be accounted for by her heredity.

It's impossible for any of us to be aware of all the factors in our heredity.

See also 'H' SILENT AND DROPPED

hero

The plural of *hero* is 'heroes':

A hero must have exceptional courage or nobility.

heroic

Heroic is an adjective meaning 'courageous':

That was the most heroic act I have ever seen.

Traditionally, 'an' was used before *heroic*:

That was an heroic achievement.

See also 'H' SILENT AND DROPPED

heroin, heroine

These words are homophones. *Heroin* is an addictive drug derived from morphine:

Heroin is another name for diacetylmorphine.

Heroine is the female form of 'hero'. It can refer to a woman possessing a high degree of courage or to the main female character in a piece of literature or a film:

Grace Darling was a heroine. She rescued people from a sinking ship.

Maggie is the heroine in *The Mill on the Floss*.

hers

The pronoun *hers* never takes an apostrophe:

The book is hers.

Hers is the greatest novel ever written.

hesitancy, hesitation

These nouns both derive from Latin *haesitare*, 'to cling to'. *Hesitancy* suggests the state of mind in which one is irresolute:

This hesitancy you show is characteristic of you. It suggests timidity and irresolution.

Hesitation suggests a pause, a reluctance to act on the spot:

I did it without a moment's hesitation.

hew

Hew means 'chop', 'cut with an axe', and it is much less widely used now than in the past. It is usually treated like a regular verb:

hew(s), hewed, hewing

but 'hewn' is occasionally used as a past participle:

He has hewn all the wood.

hexa-, sex-

Hex(a)- is a prefix deriving from Greek *hex*, 'six', and corresponding to Latin *sex*. It is found in such words as:

hexagon (six-sided figure)

hexameter (line of verse with six strong stresses).

Sex- is found in such words as:

sextet (a work for six musicians)

sexagenarian (a person in their sixties)

Sexagesima Sunday (the second Sunday before Lent in the Christian calendar).

It is found in the form *ses*- in such words as:

sestet (the last six lines of a sonnet).

hiatus

The noun *hiatus* comes from Latin *hiare*, 'to gape'. It may be pluralized by adding '-es' or the singular form may function also as a plural.

When two vowels are juxtaposed and both are clearly enunciated, a break occurs between them that is known as *hiatus*. There is, for example, a hiatus after 'pre-' in 'preempt' and after 're-' in 'reassess'. The word *hiatus* can be somewhat misleading in that it suggests a gap or silence between two vowels, whereas in normal speech we usually introduce a glide from one to the other.

Different regions deal with hiatus in individual ways. Occasionally the hiatus is reinforced by a glottal stop or, in certain contexts, such as:

awe-inspiring

people from the south of England introduce an intrusive 'r':

awe (+ r) inspiring.

In formal speech, it is advisable to employ hiatus between juxtaposed vowels.

See also ELISION, INTRUSIVE 'R', RHOTIC

Hiberno-English

This term is sometimes applied to the English spoken by people whose ancestral mother tongue was Irish Gaelic. Many speakers prefer it to the more ambiguous 'Anglo-Irish'.

Words like 'begorrah' do not occur in Hiberno-English.

See also ANGLO-

hiccup, hiccough

We are not certain of the etymology of either of these nouns; they are first recorded in the sixteenth century. Both spellings are acceptable for noun and verb and they both often occur in the plural:

I've got hiccups.

He's had hiccoughs for over an hour.

Hiccup is more widely used, especially in the metaphorical sense of 'small problem':

We've been experiencing a few hiccups with our computerization programme.

hide

Hide is an irregular verb:

hide(s), hid, hiding, hidden
Where have they hidden the clues?

high, tall

These adjectives both mean 'of greater than average height' but *high* is usually applied to inanimate nouns:

I'd never seen such high mountains.
The wall was two metres high.

The meaning of *tall* has changed over the centuries. In the fourteenth century, its meaning was close to 'valiant'. It now describes someone or an animal, or less commonly, something that is of higher stature than average.

I'd never seen such a tall man/elephant/tree.
He was two metres tall.
He's very tall for his age.
Older houses often have this type of tall chimney.

The adjective is used to describe an object in the compound word 'tallboy' meaning 'a high chest of drawers'.

highjack, hijack

These are variant spellings of the word meaning 'seize or divert a vehicle while it is in transit'. The origin of the word is unknown and *hijack* is the more widely-used form for both noun and verb:

They think it's a hijack.
The plane has been hijacked and we are still not certain where it will be allowed to land.

Hindi

Hindi is an official language in India and it is a member of the Indo-European family. Sometimes people confuse the name of the language with 'Hindu', which is the name of a follower of Hinduism or the Hindu religion.

See also BORROWING, FOREIGN LOAN-WORDS

hippopotamus

The noun *hippopotamus* comes from Greek *hippos* (horse) + *potamus* (river). It has two acceptable plurals, the more widely-used ending in '-es', the other in '-i'. 'Hippopotamuses' rhymes with 'fusses', and 'hippopotami' rhymes with 'my', or less frequently, 'ah me'.

hire, lease, let, rent

There is some overlap and a certain amount of confusion on the part of English speakers with regard to the precise use of these verbs.

Hire is most commonly used to mean 'pay for the temporary use of something':

We hired the hall for our anniversary celebration.

It also occurs, especially with 'out', to mean 'permit the temporary use of something for payment':

We hired out our marquee for the fête.

In the United States, *hire* is most frequently used to mean 'give a job to someone':

We weren't able to hire her because she didn't have a green card.

Lease is a regular verb:

lease(s), leased, leasing

which means 'pay for the use of something for a specified time' or 'permit the paid use of something for a specified time':

We leased our house for twelve months.
They leased our house from us for twelve months.

Let can mean 'provide accommodation for an agreed payment', a usage that is common in Britain:

I hope to let the basement flat to two quiet students.

Rent, like *hire*, can mean both 'pay for the temporary use of something' and 'permit the temporary use of something for payment':

I rented a house until I could afford to buy one.
They rented me their house until I could afford to buy my own.

In Britain, *rent* implies a longer period of time than *hire*:

I hired a van for the weekend.
I rented a cottage for the summer.

In America *rent* is common for both short- and long-term contracts.

The main differences between *rent* and *hire* are in usage. Houses and accommodation tend to be 'rented'; clothes for a wedding tend to be 'hired'; electrical goods tend to be 'hired'.

We *rent* something from someone:

We rented the house from John's parents.

We can *hire* to as well as from:

I hired my computer to them.
I hired a car from them.

Rent and *rent out* are also used with 'to':

They rented their cottage (out) to us for the holidays.

historic, historical

These adjectives both derive from 'history' but have developed distinct meanings. *Historic* means 'significant, momentous':

The first flight by the Wright brothers stayed in the air for only a brief time but it was one of the most historic events in the twentieth century.

Historical means 'pertaining to history':

The signing of the Magna Carta was a historical fact.

Traditionally, 'an' was used before *historic* and *historical*:

an historic achievement

an historical event.

See also 'H' SILENT AND DROPPED

hither

Over the last 400 years, English has lost a number of spatial words such as *hither*, 'thither', 'yon' and 'yonder'. These words now tend to be limited to the dialects or to fixed phrases. *Hither* means 'to here':

Come hither.

and its related form 'hitherto' means 'up to now':

I have been patient hitherto but I am no longer willing to wait.

See also THITHER, YONDER

hoard, horde

These nouns are homophones. A *hoard* is an accumulated store that is usually hidden away:

He found a hoard of silver coins that had remained hidden since Roman times.

A *horde* is a large throng. The word comes ultimately from Turkish *ordu*, 'camp', and is related to the language 'Urdu':

Rome was attacked many times by barbarian hordes.

hoi polloi

The phrase *hoi polloi*, where both words rhyme with 'toy', comes from Greek and means 'the many'. Purists say that the introductory 'the' should not be used. The phrase has been applied correctly to 'the masses':

He did not share his brother's love for democracy and the rights of the *hoi polloi*.

and incorrectly to mean 'the elite':

He enjoys hobnobbing with the *hoi polloi*.

Any phrase that is capable of being misunderstood and misused should be avoided.

hold

Hold is an irregular verb:

hold(s), held, holding

I was held against my will.

See also VERB

holey, holy, wholly

These three words are usually homophones. If something is *holey*, it has holes in it:

I can't wear these holey old socks.

If a person or thing is *holy*, he, she or it is sacred:

It was a privilege to be in the presence of such a holy woman.

Wholly is the adverb derived from 'whole'. It means 'completely', 'entirely', 'without exception':

Were you wholly convinced by their argument?

Your actions were wholly inappropriate.

Many adverbs are formed by adding '-ly' to the adjective:

fine, finely

live, lively

sole, solely.

Wholly is irregular in that the final 'e' of 'whole' is dropped.

In very careful speech, *wholly* is pronounced as 'whole lea', but for most people it is a homophone of *holy*.

holistic

The adjective *holistic* does not predate the twentieth century and it has been popularized by the media. It refers to the concept that the whole is greater than the sum of its parts and is widely used in the phrase:

holistic medicine

to refer to a medical approach that considers the individual as a whole rather than concentrating on an illness or a weakness.

Holland

See NETHERLANDS, THE

holocaust, Holocaust

The noun *holocaust* derives ultimately from Greek *holos*, 'whole', + *kaiein*, 'to burn', and referred to an offering to God of a burnt sacrifice. When used with a capital letter, the *Holocaust* refers to the genocide of Jews and Gypsies during the Second World War.

homely

The adjective *homely* usually means 'unpretentious'. In Britain it has overtones of warmth:

It was such a homely meal that I felt like one of the family.

In America, when *homely* is applied to people, it can mean 'plain, ugly':

I don't want to look homely!

homicide, manslaughter, murder

These nouns all relate to killing, but they differ in the degree of intention that they imply. *Homicide* means 'the killing of another person'. It does not mark intention:

He's certainly guilty of homicide but is he also guilty of murder?

Manslaughter means the unintentional killing of another person:

The verdict has to be one of manslaughter. She killed him, but the death was an accident.

The second and third syllables rhyme with 'daughter'.

Murder means the deliberate killing of another person:

It was murder. He stalked his victim for weeks before killing him.

homo-

The prefix *homo-* is borrowed from Greek *homo-*, 'same', a meaning it preserves in English:

homocentric (having the same centre)
homogeneous (of a uniform nature).

In a word such as 'homosexual', the *homo-* means 'same' but because the Latin word *homo* means 'man', this word is sometimes thought to refer to 'man'.

See also ETYMOLOGY

homoeopathy, homeopathy

These spellings are both acceptable but the second is now more widespread:

Homeopathy treats a disease by using small doses of drugs that, in a healthy person, produce symptoms similar to those being treated in the patient.

homogeneous, homogenous

These adjectives are variant but acceptable forms of the Greek word *homogenes*, 'of the same kind'. They mean 'similar, uniform in nature':

This liquid is no longer homogeneous. The fats have separated out.

Homogeneous is usually pronounced with the main stress on the third syllable and with the first syllable rhyming with 'Rome'. *Homogenous* tends to be stressed on the second syllable and the first syllable rhymes with 'Tom'.

Related forms such as 'homogenize' and 'homogeny' tend to be stressed on the second syllable.

homograph, homonym, homophone

All three of these words use the Greek prefix *homo-*, meaning 'same'. *Homographs* are words that have the same spelling but differ in meaning, origin or pronunciation:

I want you to *read* this book.
I *read* it yesterday.
She shed a *tear.*
Don't *tear* your clothes.

Homonyms are words that have the same spelling and pronunciation but different meanings and origins:

The brown bear is related to the grizzly.
I could hardly bear the pain.

What has she left you in her will?
He will be available tomorrow morning.

Homophones are words that are pronounced the same way but have different meanings, spellings and origins:

boar (male pig), bore (dull person)
loan (borrowing), lone (solitary).

Honduras

An inhabitant of the Central American republic is a 'Honduran'; the derived adjective is the same. The capital is Tegucigalpa.

Hong Kong

An inhabitant of Hong Kong is referred to as a 'citizen of Hong Kong'; the adjective is Hong Kong.

honorary, honourable

These adjectives both derive from Latin *honor*, 'esteem', but they now have distinct meanings. *Honorary* refers to something that is held or given as a mark of esteem:

The post is honorary and will therefore carry no remuneration.
She has been awarded two honorary degrees.

Honourable means 'highly principled, worthy of esteem':

He is utterly honourable. His entire life has been moulded by his high principles.

honour, honor

These words are regional variants, *honour* being preferred in Britain. They can function as a noun or a regular verb:

UK: It was an honour to meet him.

US: It was an honor to meet him.

UK: honour(s), honoured, honouring (He was honoured by his country.)

US: honor(s), honored, honoring (He was honored by his country.)

hoofs, hooves

The noun 'hoof', meaning 'the horny covering on the foot of some animals', has two acceptable plurals, *hoofs* and *hooves*.

hookah, hooka

These forms are both acceptable. They derive from Arabic *huqqah*, 'pipe connected to a container of water'. *Hookah* is the more widely-used of the two variants:

Hookahs were popular in Britain in Victorian times.

hopefully

Hopefully can function as an adverb modifying a verb and meaning 'in a hopeful manner':

We waited hopefully for the results.
Is it really better to travel hopefully than to arrive?

It is also used as a sentence modifier meaning 'It is to be hoped that' in such sentences as:

Hopefully, we'll all pass our examinations.

Many people dislike this second usage, regarding it as either clumsy or an Americanism. It is now well established in the language but, because it is so strongly disliked, it is better to avoid it in formal contexts.

See also ADVERB, MODIFIER

horrible, horrid

These adjectives are both widely used with the meaning 'unpleasant':

I've had a horrible day.
He was horrid to us.

Horrible comes from Latin *horrere*, 'to tremble with fear', and *horrid* from Latin *horridus*, 'bristling, shaggy'. They have undergone considerable semantic change and should not be used in formal contexts.

See also BLEACHING, SEMANTIC CHANGE

horror

The noun *horror* comes from Latin *horrere*, 'to tremble with fear'. It can still be used in the sense of 'extreme fear, terror':

No words can describe the horror of finding yourself totally alone, totally rejected.

but it has been so widely used as a buzz word in headlines that it has lost much of its impact:

Holiday Horror.

hospice

The noun *hospice* used to refer to places of shelter for travellers. Such *hospices* were run by monks, and the word gradually faded from the language until it was reintroduced to mean a 'hospital for the terminally ill':

I used to think that a hospice must be a very sad place until I visited one, and found that the people in it were treated with warmth and respect.

hospitalize

Some people dislike the use of '-ize' to create verbs from nouns and adjectives. *Hospitalize* has been criticized much more than others, such as 'idealize' or 'idolize', but it is a perfectly serviceable coinage:

I hope I won't have to be hospitalized.

host

Although nouns have been transformed into verbs for many centuries, some users of language show a particular distaste for the transformation of *host* from a noun to a verb as in:

Bob Monkhouse hosted the show for two years.

See also GUEST

hotel

The noun *hotel* comes from French *hôtel*, a word that is related to 'hostel'. Traditionally, people put 'an' in front of *hotel*:

We'll have to spend the night in an hotel.

but 'a hotel' is now more widespread.

See also 'H' SILENT AND DROPPED

household

Many of the words used for household items differ in Britain and the United States although American usage is gaining ground world-wide.

See also AMERICANISM, UK AND US ENGLISH

how

How functions as an adverb meaning 'in what manner':

How did he do that?
I wondered how he had done it.

Colloquially, *how* is sometimes used where 'that' would be more appropriate:

She told me how she studied English at college.

'As how' is also quite widely used, but it is not acceptable even in colloquial speech:

*She told me as how she studied English at college.

how ever, however

When *how ever* is written as two words, it is a question and the 'ever' is an emphasizer:

How ever did you manage to get extra leave?

However means 'in whichever way'. It is written as one word and used as a sentence modifier:

However, I have not received your bill.
I have not, however, received your bill.
I have not received your bill, however.

See also EVER/-EVER

hullo

See HALLO/HELLO/HULLO

human

Although most dictionaries record *human* as both an adjective and a noun, many careful users dislike its nominal use as in:

Do you think machines will ever replace humans?

In view of this dislike, however illogical, it is advisable in formal contexts to use 'human being', rather than *human*:

Human beings are often accused of destroying the planet.

humour, humor

Humour is the preferred British spelling and *humor* is the usual American form. They can both function as nouns and regular verbs. The noun means 'comedy' and 'temper, mood':

UK: I don't really like his sense of humour.
US: I don't really like his sense of humor.
UK: She was in good humour today.
US: She was in good humor today.

The verb is used to mean 'attempt to gratify, indulge':

UK: humour(s), humoured, humouring (You shouldn't humour him this way. He must learn that he cannot always have what he wants.)
US: humor(s), humored, humoring (You shouldn't humor him this way. He must learn that he cannot always have what he wants.)

The forms 'humorist' and 'humorous' are the same throughout the English-speaking world.

See also WIT

humus, humous, hummus

These words are occasionally confused. *Humus* is a noun and comes from Latin *humus*, 'mould', 'ground', 'soil'. It refers to rich, organic material formed by the decay of dead vegetaion.

Humus is essential to the fertility of the soil.

The derived adjective from *humus* is *humous*, and it means 'rich in humus':

The problem with much soil can be traced to the presence of free humous acids.

The noun *hummus*, which is also spelled 'houmous', derives from Arabic and refers to a creamy dip originally made from 'tahina' (a sesame seed paste) or from chickpeas.

I had never eaten hummus before my visit to the Middle East.

hung

See HANG/HANGED/HUNG

Hungary

An inhabitant of the central European country is a 'Hungarian'; the derived adjective is the same. The capital is Budapest.

hybrid

A *hybrid* word is a word composed of elements from more than one language:

Ireland = Eire (Irish Gaelic) + land (English)
microwave = micro (Greek) + wave (English)
refill = re- (Latin) + fill (English)
television = tele (Greek) + vision (Latin).

hygiene

This noun is frequently misspelled:

Hygiene is concerned with the maintenance of health and not simply with clean practices.

hypallage

Hypallage is a rhetorical device in which the attributes of one element in a statement are applied to another. In a sentence such as:

She gave me a reluctant kiss.

the kiss is not 'reluctant'; she is.

See also FIGURE OF SPEECH

hype

The verb *hype*, means 'promote or advertise something extravagantly', as in:

They hype the top songs on the radio.

The word *hype* has recently become very popular throughout the English-speaking world, although its etymology is not certain. It may derive from 'hypodermic' or from 'hyper' in such words as 'hyperbole' and 'hypermarket', or even from a blend of 'high' and 'pressure' as in :

high pressure sales.

See also ETYMOLOGY, FAD WORD, JARGON

hyper-, hypo-

These prefixes derive from Greek *huper-*, 'over', and *hupo-*, 'under', and they can occasionally cause confusion, as words such as 'hyperglycaemic', 'an abnormally high level of sugar in the blood' sound like 'hypoglycaemic', 'an abnormally low level of sugar in the blood'. Other pairs that might cause confusion are:

hyperpituitarism (overactivity in the pituitary gland)
hypopituitarism (underactivity in the pituitary gland)
hypertension (abnormally high blood pressure)
hypotension (abnormally low blood pressure).

hyperbole

The noun *hyperbole* is a figure of speech involving deliberate exaggeration for effect. It derives from Greek *huper*, 'over', and *bole*, 'a throw'. It is widely used in speech:

There must have been millions of fans there.

hypercorrection

In speech communities where non-standard variants exist, certain forms may be stigmatized. The stigmatized forms may relate to pronunciation:

'boid' for 'bird'
'otter' for 'hotter'
'lyin" for 'lying'

to choice of words:

'appen' for 'perhaps'
'nowt' for 'nothing'

to structures:

'for to go' for 'to go'
'I done it' for 'I did it'
'she might of' for 'she might have'.

Often, in modifying towards the standard, a speaker will overcompensate and produce hypercorrections such as:

*'garding' for 'garden

*'hold' for 'old'

*'I have did it' for 'I have done it'

*'She invited John and I.' for 'She invited John and me.'

See also 'H' SILENT AND DROPPED, IMPORTANT

hyphen

A *hyphen* is the punctuation mark (-). It comes from Greek *huphon*, 'together', and is used to separate the parts of a compound word:

forget-me-not, mother-in-law

to link words that are being used adjectivally:

It affects the foot and mouth.

foot-and-mouth disease

It was off the cuff.

an off-the cuff remark

and to mark the breaking of a word at the end of a line of print.

See also COMPOUND, PUNCTUATION

hypothetical

The adjective 'hypothetical' is overused, especially in the phrase:

a hypothetical situation.

Hypothetical questions and statements often involve the use of an 'if' clause and the modal 'should' or 'would' in the main clause:

If you won the Lottery, would you stop working?

If he could put himself in my position, he would not be so critical.

'Were' rather than 'was' is used in the 'if' clause, especially when the hypothesis is improbable:

If I were the President, I'd change a few things.

If she were me, she'd do the same.

See also MODALITY, SUBJUNCTIVE

hysterical

The adjective *hysterical* derives from *hustera*, 'the womb'. It is used to mean 'highly emotional', is more frequently applied to a woman than a man and often implies criticism:

Take a deep breath. Don't be hysterical. Tell us quietly what happened.

Traditionally, 'an' was used before *hysterical* as in:

an hysterical student

but 'a' is now more widespread:

a hysterical outburst.

See also 'H' SILENT AND DROPPED

I

i

I is a vowel. The letter is used to represent a range of sounds in English as is clearly illustrated by the words 'shin', 'shine', 'machine'.

I, me

I and *me* are first-person pronouns. *I* is the subject form; *me* is the object form. We use *I* when the pronoun is the subject of a sentence or clause:

I saw John [when I arrived this morning].

and when the pronoun is part of a compound subject:

Mary and I saw John.

My parents, teachers and I saw John.

We use *me* when the pronoun is the object of a sentence or clause:

John saw me [when he passed me in his car].

when the pronoun is part of a compound object:

John saw Mary and me.

John saw Mary, the children and me.

and when the pronoun follows a preposition:

John gave it to me.

beside me

with me.

There are three uses involving pronouns that cause people trouble:

■ When to use 'John and I' and when to use 'John and me'. The solution is easy. When the phrase can be replaced by 'we', use 'John and I'; when the phrase can be replaced by 'us', use 'John and me':

John and I went home. = We went home.

He invited John and me. = He invited us.

It was between John and me. = It was between us.

■ Whether to use *I* or *me* in comparisons. Traditionalists insist that the correct form is:

John is taller than I.

whereas most people say:

John is taller than me.

Because so many people have such strong feelings about this construction, it is safer to use:

John is taller than I am.

■ Whether to use 'It's I' or 'It's me'. Again, there is a difference between what people actually say and write and what many traditionalists tell us to say. In answer to the question 'Who's there?', most people would say 'Me.' or 'It's me.' but COPULA verbs, such as 'be', do not take objects

and, therefore, 'It's I' is theoretically correct. We can explain this point of view by examining two sentences:

I was a student.

I saw a student.

In the first sentence, which contains the copula verb, 'I' and 'a student' refer to the same person, whereas in the second sentence 'I' and 'a student' refer to two different people. However, in spite of the logic of the above argument, 'It's me' is acceptable in all contexts.

See also ME/MY, MYSELF, PRONOUN, WE/US

I mean

Most speakers use fillers in spontaneous speech. Sometimes the fillers are noises such as 'er' or 'um', sometimes words such as 'like' and sometimes clauses such as *I mean* or 'you know':

I like him. I mean, who doesn't like him?

I mean is acceptable, even in formal speech, when it used to clarify what one has said:

He's out on a limb. I mean, he's taking an enormous risk.

See also FILLER

-ian

See -AN/-EAN/-IAN

ibid.

The abbreviation *ibid.* comes from the Latin word *ibidem*, 'in the same place', and is used in older scholarly writings to avoid the necessity of repeating bibliographical details that have already been cited.

-ible

See -ABLE/-IBLE

-ic, -ical

The suffixes *-ic* and *-ical* are both used to form adjectives and there is no absolutely fixed rule as to why one has been chosen rather than the other. Sometimes, when the noun ends in *-ic*, the adjective ends in *-ical*:

critic, critical

lyric, lyrical

but we can have *-ic* and *-ical* forms that are both adjectives and nouns:

chemical, comic.

Occasionally, we have two adjectives, one ending in *-ic* and another in *-ical*, that are interchangeable:

metric, metrical

satiric, satirical

but the pairs are usually differentiated either in meaning:

classic, classical (a classic car, a classical education)

economic, economical (an economic solution, economical habits)

or in frequency of usage:

electric, electrical

magic, magical.

See also AFFIX, SUFFIX

Iceland

An inhabitant of the island republic in the North Atlantic is an 'Icelander'; the derived adjective is 'Icelandic'. The capital is Reykjavik.

-ics

The SUFFIX *-ics* is widely used in the naming of academic disciplines:

linguistics, mathematics, phonetics.

Such nouns are singular:

Linguistics is the scientific study of language.

Often, when an *-ics* noun is used in a general rather than an academic context, it is treated as a plural:

Politics is part of my first degree.

His politics are not always easy to understand.

Statistics is not an absolute science.

These statistics are capable of several interpretations.

See also COUNTABLE AND UNCOUNTABLE, MASS NOUN, NOUN

ideal

The word *ideal* can function as both an adjective and a noun:

an ideal husband

Such ideals are well worth striving for.

This form has given rise to 'idealism', 'ideate' and 'idealize'. The related words 'ideologist' and 'ideology' have '-eo-' and not '-ea-'.

See also IDEOLOGY

idée fixe

This phrase comes from French and is used to mean 'fixed idea', 'obsession'. The plural is *idées fixes*:

With James, it is one *idée fixe* after another.

identical to, identical with

The adjective *identical* means 'similar in all respects':

Equilateral triangles are identical.

Although, *identical* is an absolute, people often modify it when they imply that two people or objects are similar in most respects:

She and her sister are almost identical.

It's almost identical to the suggestion I put forward last week.

Some careful users distinguish meanings depending on whether *identical* is followed by 'to' or 'with'. *Identical to* is used to suggest close similarity:

Her dress is almost identical to mine.

Identical with suggests they are the same:

Her symptoms are identical with those of malaria.

For most speakers, however, the phrases are interchangeable.

identify (with)

Identify is a very popular media verb and can be used to mean 'determine the identity of':

She was asked if she could identify the body.

'find':

We plan to identify new markets for our product.

and 'share the ideas and aspirations of':

We all identify with the new thinking of the chairman.

Some people dislike the BLEACHING of meaning that *identify* is undergoing, but it is a natural process with words that are popular.

identifying relative clause

Identifying relative clause is another name for a 'defining relative clause' – that is, a clause that limits the scope of the noun it modifies. The sentence:

The men who smoked were given healthchecks.

means that the healthchecks were given only to the men who smoked.

See also DEFINING RELATIVE CLAUSE

ideology

The noun *ideology* involves the use of the Greek prefix *idea*, meaning 'idea'. An *ideology* is a collection of ideas that reflect the beliefs and aspirations of a group. The word now carries suggestions of 'false ideas':

He was totally caught up in the ideology of the cult.

See also IDEAL

idiolect

The noun *idiolect* is widely used in sociolinguistics to describe the variety of a language used by one individual. The word is a blend of Greek *idio-*, 'private', 'separate', and *-lect* from 'dialect':

All idiolects are unique but people of the same age, background and education often sound alike.

idiom

An *idiom* is a phrase whose meaning cannot be deduced from an understanding of the individual words in the phrase. There are, for example, many idioms for 'die', including:

kick the bucket

pass on
pop your clogs
although a knowledge of the meanings of 'kick',
'bucket', 'pass', 'on', 'pop' or 'clogs' would not
help us to deduce their composite meaning.

Idioms can reflect different degrees of opacity.
They can be:

■ Totally opaque. This means there is no link
whatsoever between the meaning of the *idiom*
and the meaning of the individual words. Unless
one knows that 'a hat trick' means 'taking three
wickets with successive balls' or 'scoring three
goals in a match', one could not work out its
meaning.

■ Semi-opaque. This means that part of the
phrase is used literally. The *idiom*, 'hit someone
for six' comes from cricket and uses the literal
meaning of 'hit'.

■ Almost transparent. This means that one can
usually see the metaphorical nature of an *idiom*
like 'burn the candle at both ends'.

See also METAPHOR, SIMILE

idiosyncrasy
This is one of the most frequently misspelled
words in English. It ends in '-asy' not '-acy'.

See also SPELLING

idle, idol, idyll
The adjective *idle* and the noun *idol* are
homophones. *Idle* means 'not working, inactive,
lazy' and can be applied to both people and
machines:

He he has become increasingly idle recently.
It is expensive to leave machinery idle for two weeks.

Idle can also function as a regular verb meaning
'loiter' or 'turn over without doing anything
useful':

idle(s), idled, idling
He'll happily idle his life away.
The engine was idling.

The noun *idol* refers to an object or person
worshipped as a god:

There's a one-eyed yellow idol to the north of
   Khatmandu,
There's a little broken cross below the town;
There's a broken-hearted woman tends the grave of
   Mad Carew,
And the Yellow God forever gazes down.
         J.M. Hayes, 'The Green Eye of the Yellow God'

The noun *idyll* rhymes with 'fiddle' and is often
spelled *idyl* in America. It means an idealized
picture of rural life:

This description of a charming pastoral scene is far
from reality. It is an idyll, an idealization, a dream.

i.e.
See E.G./I.E.

-ie-, -ei-
There are no absolutely definitive rules about
spelling but there are two useful guidelines with
regard to the use of *-ie-* and *-ei-*.

■ When the vowel sound in the word rhymes
with 'he', we use 'i' before 'e' except after 'c':
achieve, field, thief
ceiling, deceit, receive

■ When the vowel sound in the word rhymes
with 'hay', we use '-ei-':
abseil, eight, weight.

There are, however, a number of exceptions.
There are *-ei-* words that are pronounced like 'he'
but do not follow 'c':

protein, plebeian, seize, Sheila, weird
and 'species' breaks the rule in having '-ie-' after
'c'.

Words such as 'either', 'neither' have two
acceptable pronunciations.

See also -EI-, EITHER/NEITHER, SPELLING

-ie, -y
Often, the suffixes *-ie* and *-y* are in free variation,
although *-ie* is more widely used:
Billie, Billy.
They can indicate diminutives and often affection:
doggie, pussy
imply informality in connection with a person's
place of origin:
Aussie, townie
be used as a (mild) form of abuse:
commie, leftie
and be used as a generic reference:
Paddy (= from Ireland)
Tommy (= from England).

See also SUFFIX

if
If is a subordinating conjunction used to indicate
condition.

If you work hard, you will do well.

Sometimes, when *if* is used instead of '(al)though'
or 'whether' it can be ambiguous. Such sentences
as:

The programme was poor, if not appalling.
Tell him if it is sunny.

could mean:

The programme was poor and perhaps even
appalling.
Tell him about the weather.

or:

The programme was poor although it was not appalling.

Tell him about something only if the weather is good.

See also CONJUNCTION

if and when

Careful users of language tend to dislike the use of *if and when* in such sentences as:

I'll come to see you if and when I'm in Texas.

They point out that the sentence would be more precise with only one conjunction:

I'll come to see you if I'm in Texas.
I'll come to see you when I'm in Texas.

However, the combined conjunction is well established and serves a purpose in that it can be the equivalent of:

It is possible that I'll be in Texas and, if I am, that is when I'll come to see you.

il-

Il- is a prefix, the equivalent of 'in-'. It is used before 'l':

legitimate, illegitimate
literate, illiterate
logical, illogical.

See also IM-, IN-, IR-, PREFIX

ilk

Ilk derives from Old English *ilca*, 'the same family', and it is used with a similar meaning in the Scottish expression:

Dunbar of that ilk

meaning 'Dunbar, the laird of the place called Dunbar'.

Ilk is sometimes used in English in the phrase 'of his/that ilk' meaning 'of his/that type':

We don't want people of that ilk in the club.

Many people dislike the phrase and, since it is capable of being misunderstood, it is better to avoid it.

ill, sick

In the idiolects of many speakers, these adjectives are synonymous, although ill tends to be more formal. Both adjectives relate to poor health, but they can have different implications in different parts of the world.

Ill can refer to a temporary state of discomfort or nausea:

I felt ill when I realized what I had done.

In Britain it can also refer to longer term or serious illnesses:

The patient is seriously ill and can see no one except his immediate family.

In British usage, *sick* has two main implications. It can imply vomiting:

Stop the car. I'm going to be sick.

and it can be used to imply a long-term or chronic illness:

He tended his sick wife for the last months of her life.
Your father is a sick man. It is unlikely that he will be mobile again.

Ill is the preferred usage in Britain and can cover both temporary and chronic bad health. *Sick* is used, however, in such fixed phrases as:

to be off sick
to be on sick leave
to tell a sick joke.

Sick can function as both an attributive and a predicative adjective:

a sick child
The child is sick.

Ill is normally used after a copula verb rather than before a noun:

John was ill.
He suddenly became ill.

Ill does not usually occur attributively:

The phrases:

?an ill man
?*an ill child

are not acceptable to all speakers.

The child is ill.

In American English, *sick* can cover a wider range of illness than in Britain:

My tutor is sick.
He was sick to his stomach.
The children are both very sick.

Sick has also been extended metaphorically to mean 'tired of':

I'm sick of being a couch potato.

illegal, unlawful

Illegal means 'against the law of the land':

It is illegal to do a U-turn here.

Unlawful means 'against the law' and the law referred to can be both human and divine:

It is unlawful to drive at more than 70mph on the motorway.
It is unlawful to tell lies about your neighbour.

illegible

See ELIGIBLE/ILLEGIBLE/UNREADABLE

illicit

See ELICIT/ILLICIT

illusion

See ALLUSION/DELUSION/ILLUSION

im-

Im- is a prefix with two different meanings. It can imply 'not' or 'into' and it is a phonological variant of IN-. When 'in-' was prefixed to a word beginning with 'b', 'm' or 'p', the 'n' was changed to an 'm'.

It is used to mean 'not' in such constructions as:

balance, imbalance
mobile, immobile
possible, impossible.

It is used to mean 'into' in such constructions as:

bed, imbed/embed
migrate, immigrate
peril, imperil.

See also IL-, IR-, PREFIX

imagery

The noun *imagery* is widely used in literary criticism, where it covers the descriptive language in a literary text, especially when it relates to the senses:

Discuss the imagery in Yeats's poem 'The Second Coming'.

and the use of images, especially as these are used in similes, metaphors and symbols:

Discuss the imagery of war in *Othello*.

See also FIGURE OF SPEECH, METAPHOR, SIMILE

imaginary, imaginative

Both these adjectives derive from 'image'. *Imaginary* suggests 'unreal, existing only in the mind':

When she was a child, she had an imaginary twin.

Imaginative means 'creative, capable of making the most of one's imagination':

She is the most imaginative storyteller I've ever met. We all see the same things but she can weave them into something magical.

imbue, instil, instill

These regular verbs are occasionally confused and misused. *Imbue* means 'permeate, fill' and there is a strong suggestion of 'inspiration':

imbue(s), imbued, imbuing
Her talks were imbued with her love of Africa.

Instil and *instill* are variant spellings of a regular verb meaning 'implant', 'infuse' that collocates with 'in(to)'. *Instil* is more widespread in Britain and *instill* in America.

UK: instil(s), instilled, instilling (It is impossible to instil such a complex idea in the mind of a child.)
US: instill(s), instilled, instilled (He instilled in us respect for human rights.)

imitate

See EMULATE/IMITATE

immanent

See EMINENT/IMMANENT/IMMINENT

immaterial

The adjective *immaterial* used to mean 'spiritual', 'incorporeal', but this meaning is now carried by 'non-material' or 'unmaterial', whereas *immaterial* has come to mean 'of little or no significance':

It's immaterial to me whether we eat in or go out for a meal.

See also BLEACHING

immeasurable

This adjective should, logically, be applied to things that cannot be measured, but like many overused words its meaning has been weakened in casual speech:

Commercial travellers cover immeasurable distances.

It is often used metaphorically to mean 'incalculable':

She has made an immeasurable difference to my life.

immigrant

See EMIGRANT/IMMIGRANT/MIGRANT

imminent

See EMINENT/IMMANENT/IMMINENT

immoral

See AMORAL/IMMORAL

immovable, irremovable

These adjectives are occasionally confused. *Immovable* is sometimes spelled with an extra 'e' – 'immoveable' – but this form is less common and should be avoided. It means 'fixed, unable to be moved':

What happens when an irresistible force meets an immovable object?

The adjective *irremovable* means 'unable to be removed':

The jacket is ruined. I've tried everything on the stain but it is simply irremovable.

The noun 'immoveables' always has '-eable' and means 'tangible property'; it is often used in a legal sense:

All his assets and immoveables have been seized.

immunity, impunity

These nouns both include the meaning of 'freedom'. *Immunity* means 'freedom from an obligation or duty', 'resistant to a certain disease':

I'm seeking immunity from such taxes on the grounds that I am not normally resident in this country.

An inoculation cannot guarantee immunity from a particular disease but it will enable you to produce antibodies and so resist the disease.

Impunity means 'freedom or exemption from punishment':

No one should be able to walk away from such a crime with impunity.

impassable, impassible, impassive

These adjectives look and sound alike but they have distinct meanings. *Impassable* means 'incapable of being passed':

The storms have brought down hundreds of trees and all the minor roads are impassable.

Impassible is an unusual adjective that is quite likely to become obsolete. It means 'incapable of feeling pain':

There were no drugs or anaesthetics available, yet he seemed absolutely impassible as they cut out the bullet.

This adjective has been superseded by *impassive*, meaning 'not revealing or affected by emotion', 'unemotional':

Is it possible for anyone to be as imperturbable and impassive as she seems?

Many students have argued about the Mona Lisa's impassive expression.

impassioned

See DISPASSIONATE/IMPASSIONED

impeccable

The adjective *impeccable* is often misspelled. It comes from Latin *impeccabilis*, 'sinless', and means 'flawless', 'faultless':

His behaviour is, and always has been, impeccable.

imperative

In grammatical descriptions, the term *imperative* is used for structures that give commands:

Come here.

Don't do it.

Please sit down.

The form of the verb used in imperatives is identical to the infinitive without 'to'. In negative imperatives, the verb is usually preceded by 'don't'.

Occasionally, imperatives do not involve verbs:

Here!

In!

Paw!

Such imperatives are more likely to be used to animals or children. They are indicated by intonation in speech and by an exclamation mark in writing.

The imperative does not show contrasts of persons because it always implies a second person subject. Nor does it show tense changes, referring always to a future, which may be immediate, proximate or remote:

Come and see us now.

Come and see us next week.

Come and see us next summer.

See also AUXILIARY, INDICATIVE, SUBJUNCTIVE

imperial, imperious

These adjectives both derive from Latin *imperare*, 'to give orders', but they are differentiated in meaning. *Imperial* means 'relating to an empire':

Many people no longer remember Britain's imperial past.

Imperious means 'domineering', 'arrogant', 'bossy':

Of course, he has to give orders. One understands that, but there is no necessity for him to behave in such an imperious and aggressive fashion.

imperil

This regular verb means 'endanger':

My life was imperilled by your thoughtless action.

The 'l' is doubled before '-ed' and '-ing' in Britain but not in America:

UK: imperil(s), imperilled, imperilling

US: imperil(s), imperiled, imperiling.

impious

The adjective *impious* derives from Latin *im* + *pius*, 'not holy', and means 'lacking respect for God or society'. The first two syllables rhyme with 'wimpy':

Such behaviour is not just irreverent; it is impious.

implement

The verb *implement* has been overused by the media. It used to mean 'supply with tools' but that meaning has now become obsolete, although the noun *implement* can still mean 'tool', 'piece of equipment':

I'd need to replace some of my gardening implements.

The verb now means 'carry out', 'fulfil':

I want you to implement these instructions.

implicit

See EXPLICIT/IMPLICIT

implosion

See EXPLOSION/IMPLOSION

imply, infer, insinuate

These three verbs are often confused. They are related in meaning in that they are all associated with the processes by which meaning is conveyed. *Imply* and *insinuate* both relate to production, whereas *infer* is related to reception.

Imply comes from the Latin verb *implicare*, 'to involve'. It is a regular verb and means 'hint' or 'suggest something indirectly without actually saying it':

imply(implies), implied, implying
I didn't imply that you were lazy. I merely said that you showed no signs of stress.

Infer comes from Latin *in + ferre*, 'to bring in'. It is a regular verb and means 'deduce' or 'work out what is implied by someone's words or actions':

infer(s), inferred, inferring
I inferred from your statements that you think I'm lazy.

Infer is frequently misused for 'imply':

*You inferred that I was lazy.

Insinuate comes from Latin *in + sinuare*, 'to curve'. It is a regular verb and means 'suggest by hints or innuendo'. *Insinuate* normally carries unpleasant, derogatory connotations:

You insinuated that I was dishonest.
She insinuated that he needed a bath.

important

Important is a buzz word that has been used so often it has been bleached of much of its meaning:

an important meeting
an important person
an important point.

There is nothing intrinsically wrong with *important* but, like 'nice', it suffers from overuse.

See also BLEACHING

(more) importantly

The use of *importantly* instead of 'important' as a sentence modifier has attracted quite a lot of hostile criticism. Many claim that we should say and write:

More important, we are losing our reputation for fair play.

and not:

*More importantly, we are losing our reputation for fair play.

It is not surprising that people use *importantly* as a sentence modifier: they are analogizing from such examples as:

We've got a cash-flow problem, or more accurately, we're broke!
More precisely, our exports are being affected.

See also HOPEFULLY, MODIFIER

impossible, improbable

These adjectives refer to different degrees of likelihood. If something is *impossible* it is incapable of being done or of happening:

It would be impossible for us to walk on the surface of Jupiter.

Improbable suggests that an action is unlikely but not impossible:

It is improbable that I'll ever walk on the moon.

imposter, impostor

These are variant spellings for a person who deceives people by taking on a false identity. The '-or' ending is more widely used:

It is hard to believe that she was an impostor. She seemed to know all sorts of details about the Russian royal family.

impracticable, impractical

These adjectives should be distinguished. *Impracticable* means 'not feasible, incapable of being put into practice':

Your scheme is utterly impracticable. Even if we had the money to fund it, we do not have the personnel to put it into effect.

Impractical means 'not workable, theoretically sound but incapable of being put into action':

People thought he was an impractical dreamer but society would never advance without such visionaries.

impresario

An *impresario* is a producer or sponsor of public, usually musical, entertainment. The noun comes from Italian and means 'one who undertakes':

He likes to refer to himself as an 'impresario' but he has never produced anything bigger than an amateur musical.

The noun has been widened in meaning and was frequently applied to the host of a popular television talent competition.

improbable

See IMPOSSIBLE/IMPROBABLE

improvident, imprudent

These adjectives are occasionally confused. *Improvident* means 'not taking care to provide for the future, thriftless':

Do you know the story of the ant and the grasshopper? The ant worked hard all spring and summer but the grasshopper was improvident and spent his time singing and dancing and not preparing for winter.

Imprudent is one degree less provident than *improvident*. It means 'rash, heedless':

We warned him that his actions were imprudent, but he refused to be cautious and has lost everything.

improvise

Improvise derives from Italian *improvvisare*, 'unforeseen', and means 'do something without previous planning' or 'make do with what is available':

The comedians who improvise well have a great deal of experience. As the adage suggests: 'Everything seems easy that is practised to perfection.'

Improvise is never spelled with '-ize'.

impunity
See IMMUNITY/IMPUNITY

in
In can function as an adjective:

It's the in thing at the moment.

as an adverb:

He walked in.

as a noun:

I don't understand the ins and outs of the problem.

but its chief function is as a preposition indicating 'inside':

She is in the bath.

Some careful users of language dislike the use of *in* where *within* would be less ambiguous:

Please return these proofs in a week. = after a week
Please return these proofs within a week. = any time during the next week

See also AT, IN TO/INTO, WITHIN

in-
The PREFIX *in-* is among the most widely-used in the language. It has two main uses and two origins: *in-*, meaning 'not', derives from Latin:

active, inactive
audible, inaudible

and *in-* meaning 'in, within' derives from English *in*:

born, inborn
breed, inbreed.

The prefix *in-* has also been used to carry an intensive or causative function:

flame, inflame
peril, imperil.

The 'n' of the prefix *in-* is realized as 'l' before 'l', as 'm' before 'p, b, m', and as 'r' before 'r':

illegal
imbibe, immobile, impart
irregular.

See also EN-/IN-, EX-, IL-, IM-, IR-

in fact
The phrase *in fact* is used as a sentence modifier meaning 'actually':

I have not, in fact, written to the director.

The phrase should always be written as two words:

*I have not, infact, written to the director.

Many people object strongly to the use of 'in actual fact' because it is redundant.

See also ACTUALLY, FILLER

-in-law
The hyphenated suffix *-in-law* is added to familial terms to indicate relationships produced by marriage:

My sister's husband is my brother-in-law.
I have two brothers-in-law.

The plural 'brothers-in-law' is preferred to 'brother-in-laws' although the latter is acceptable in informal contexts.

Some people dislike the use of *in-law* as a noun:

How are you getting on with your in-laws?

but such usage is firmly established in colloquial speech.

See also FAMILY RELATIONSHIP

in lieu of
The phrase *in lieu of*, is an ELEGANT VARIATION of 'instead of'. It is disliked by many people, and so although there is nothing intrinsically wrong with it, it should be avoided in formal contexts:

He took my ring in lieu of my debt.

in order
The phrase *in order* may be followed by a clause or an infinitive:

He did it in order that he might win his freedom.
He did it in order to win his freedom.

The choice of 'that' results in a formal structure but is essential when the subject of the clause after *in order* is not the same as the subject in the main clause.

He did it so that she might win her freedom.

The alternative:

He did it in order to win her freedom.

is ambiguous and could mean:

He did it in order that he might win her freedom.

Often the phrase *in order* is redundant:

I did it (in order) to get even.

in so far as
This phrase should not be written as *'insofar as'.

See also INASMUCH AS

in spite of
See DESPITE/IN SPITE OF

in that
The phrase *in that*, meaning 'because', is disliked by many:

She won't ask for help in that she feels the help will be refused.

Where the phrase means 'to the extent that', it is perfectly acceptable:

Both tenders are acceptable in that they offer us all that we require within the limits of our budget.

in the circumstances, under the circumstances

Some people are uncertain about when to use *under the circumstances* and when to prefer *in the circumstances*. The simplest rule is to use the latter:

The train strike will make it difficult for people to get to work. In the circumstances, arrangements will be made to provide alternative transport.

in to, into

Although *in to* and *into* are identical in origin, they are now used differently. *In to* can mean 'inside, in order to':

I went in to get my book.

and it can be used to mean 'inside to':

They went in to tea.

Into is a preposition that can mean 'to the inner part of':

I delved into the mystery.

and 'against':

I drove into the garage door.

It can indicate a change:

He turned into a pussycat.

It is used in mathematics:

Six into five won't go.

in toto

The Latin phrase *in toto* means 'totally', 'entirely':

We have not agreed *in toto* but we have managed to reduce the number of our disagreements.

Sometimes the phrase is used, incorrectly, to mean 'in total':

*We have spent fifty pounds *in toto*.

inadmissible

This adjective is frequently misspelled. It ends in '-ible':

The new evidence was judged to be inadmissible.

inadvisable, unadvisable

These adjectives are both negations of 'advisable' but they have clearly differentiated meanings. *Inadvisable* means 'not to be recommended':

In view of the weather conditions, we think that your planned climb is inadvisable.

Her large investment was inadvisable. It is always best to spread one's assets and one's risks.

Unadvisable is less frequently used but means 'unwilling to take advice':

You can try talking to them if you wish but I have found them unadvisable. They have made up their minds and they are unlikely to change them.

He's at the age when he is unadvisable. He feels he knows best what is right for him.

inapt, inept

These adjectives both derive from Latin *aptus*, 'fitting', 'suitable', but they now have clearly differentiated meanings. *Inapt* means 'inappropriate', 'not fitting':

His long sermon was totally inapt when he knew that so many people had nowhere to sit.

Inept suggests 'clumsy, incompetent':

I've never seen such inept workmanship.

inasmuch as

It is difficult to offer rules about why some compounds are acceptable and others are not. *Inasmuch as* is normally written with 'in', 'as' and 'much' joined:

We are not certain how to proceed inasmuch as our experiment was inconclusive.

See also IN SO FAR AS

incapable, unable

These two adjectives are often, incorrectly, used as synonyms. They share an overlap of meaning, but *unable* suggests a temporary inability; *incapable* a more permanent one:

I am unable to walk far because I have broken my leg.
I am incapable of walking far since my serious heart attack.

Notice that *unable* is followed by the infinitive whereas *incapable* is followed by 'of + V-ing'.

incident

The noun *incident* meaning 'a distinct occurrence' has been weakened by overuse:

He was involved in an incident outside a pub.
The latest terrorist incident occurred last night.
It was an incident of no significance.

The associated adverb 'incidentally' is often misspelled. It needs '-ally' after the noun and not '-ly'.

See also BLEACHING, SPELLING

incomparable

The pronunciation of this adjective, which means 'unequalled', 'matchless', is in the process of being changed. The usual pronunciation puts the stress on the second syllable. Many speakers now stress the third syllable and rhyme it with 'bare'.

inconceivable

This adjective, which used to mean 'incapable of being imagined', has been weakened by overuse and is often used to mean 'hard to imagine':

It is inconceivable that anyone would be angry with you.

See also BLEACHING

incorrect, uncorrected

These words are occasionally misused. *Incorrect* means 'wrong, not correct':

The answer is incorrect. Try again.

Uncorrected means 'not corrected':

I have 30 uncorrected essays on my desk.

incredible, incredulous

These adjectives both derive from Latin *credere*, 'to believe', but they have markedly different meanings. *Incredible* is normally applied to actions, things or events and means 'beyond belief':

Some of the gadgets we take for granted today would have been regarded as incredible or even magical a hundred years ago.

In popular speech *incredible* has been weakened to mean 'amazing', 'surprising':

It's incredible how quickly some people can eat!

Incredulous is applied to people. It means 'unwilling to believe something':

I know it sounds strange but you shouldn't be so incredulous. Look at the evidence before you decide that it didn't happen.

incur

Incur is a regular verb that derives from Latin *incurrere*, 'to run into'. It means 'bring something unpleasant upon oneself':

incur(s), incurred, incurring

He has not only incurred my wrath; he has incurred a heavy fine.

indefinite article

The *indefinite article* has two forms: 'a' before consonants and 'an' before vowels:

a banana, an orange.

See also A/AN, ARTICLE

indefinitely

This adverb is often misspelled. It does not end in '-ately'.

independence

This noun and its associated adjective are often misspelled. The word ends in '-ence' and the associated adjective is 'independent'.

See also -ANT/-ENT

index

Index comes from Latin *index*, 'pointer', 'forefinger'. It has two main meanings and two plurals in English. It means an alphabetical arrangement of people, places or topics, and in this sense is usually pluralized as 'indexes':

I have divided the concordance into four indexes: one for people, one for places, one for topics and one for bibliographical references.

It also means a number placed as a superscript of another number and indicating such relationships as the square or the cube of a number:

$8^2 = 64$

$10^3 = 1000$.

This meaning is usually pluralized as 'indices'.

Recently, *index* has been used to refer to a scale that indicates changes in inflation or the cost of living:

The cost of living index rose sharply in November.

This meaning is pluralized as both 'indices' and 'indexes'.

India

An inhabitant of the country India is an 'Indian'; and the derived adjective is the same as the word 'Indian' can be used as both an adjective and a noun:

The Indian population is approaching one billion.

Many Indians speak their mother tongue, Hindi, and English.

The capital is New Delhi.

The term *Indian* used to occur as the name of the original inhabitants of the Americas, but 'Amerindian' or 'Native American' is now preferred.

indicative

The term *indicative* is an alternative of 'declarative'. It is used in grammatical descriptions to refer to statements:

I walked home this morning.

I won't do that again.

Indicative contrasts with IMPERATIVE, INTERROGATIVE and SUBJUNCTIVE:

Indicative: This is madness.

Imperative: Be sensible.

Interrogative: Is this madness?

Subjunctive: If this be madness, we should all be mad!

indict, indite

These regular verbs both derive from Latin *indicere*, 'to declare'. They are homophones and rhyme with 'site'. *Indict* means 'charge formally with a crime':

indict(s), indicted, indicting

They have been indicted for murder.

Indite is a formal word meaning 'write down':

indite(s), indited, inditing

Their names have been indited and will appear in future registers.

indifferent

The adjective *indifferent* looks as if it should mean 'not different' but, in fact, it does not. It derives from Latin *indifferens*, 'making no distinction' and means 'showing no care for':

He is completely indifferent to the sufferings of others.

and 'only average', 'not good':

She may be an indifferent student but she is a brilliant dancer.

indigestible, undigested

These adjectives are both derived from 'digest'. *Indigestible* means 'incapable of being digested, difficult to absorb':

I've chewed and chewed this meat but it is simply indigestible.

He can't deal with so many figures. He finds them indigestible.

Undigested means 'not digested':

The stomach contains evidence of an undigested meal.

indirect speech

Indirect speech is another name for 'reported speech'. It is the phrase used to describe a set of conventions by which we express in the written medium what someone is supposed to have said or thought.

Direct speech	Indirect speech
'I love you,' he said.	He said that he loved her.
'Come to me,' she said.	She asked him to go to her.
'Will you come?' he asked.	He asked if she would go.

Indirect speech usually differs from live speech in: the choice of pronouns, the degree of formality employed, word order and the words used to refer to time and space. There is rarely a one-to-one correlation between direct and indirect speech:

Direct speech	Indirect speech
'I love you,' she said.	She said that she loved him/her/them.
'Don't do it,' he cried.	He urged him/her/them not to do it.
'Hell! What's happened here?'	He swore and asked what had happened there.

See also DIRECT SPEECH, INVERTED COMMAS

indiscreet, indiscrete

These homophones are not related semantically. *Indiscreet* means 'tactless, not discreet':

It was utterly indiscreet of you to talk about my new job before it was official.

Indiscrete means 'not divisible or divided into parts':

Prime numbers are indiscrete.

indiscriminate, undiscriminating

These adjectives are almost synonymous although careful users distinguish them. *Indiscriminate* can mean 'lacking discrimination, random':

The indiscriminate privatizations have deprived everyone of shared assets.

The violence was mindless and indiscriminate.

Undiscriminating means 'lacking in judgement':

They are undiscriminating in the films they watch.

indispensable

This adjective, which means 'essential', is often misspelled:

I don't know how we managed without a xerox machine. It has now become an indispensable part of the office.

indite

See INDICT/INDITE

individual

Individual derives from Latin *individuus*, 'indivisible', and it can function as an adjective and a noun:

The individual pages are attractive enough but the binding and cover are unacceptable.

A democracy should uphold the rights of the individual.

Many writers have criticized the use of *individual* as a synonym for 'person' but the usage is acceptable when a single person is being discussed and contrasted with a group.

See also COMMON/MUTUAL

Indo-European

Indo-European is used as a label for a family of related languages, all of which are thought to be descended from Proto-Indo-European:

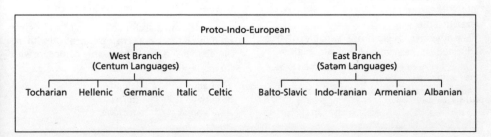

Not all languages in Europe are Indo-European. Basque and Finnish, for example, are non-Indo-European. Equally, not all the languages of India are Indo-European. Many of the southern Indian languages, such as Telugu, are actually Dravidian.

The term *Indo-European* can function as an adjective and a noun:

Welsh is an Indo-European language.

Information from many languages is used in the reconstruction of Proto-Indo-European.

Indonesia

An inhabitant of the republic in southeast Asia is an 'Indonesian'; the derived adjective is the same. The capital is Djakarta.

indoor, indoors

The usual distinction made is that *indoor* functions as a prenominal adjective:

indoor sports

an indoor swimming pool

whereas *indoors* functions mainly as an adverb, as in the sentence:

When it rained, we went indoors.

See also OUTDOOR/OUTDOORS

indorse

This is a little-used variant spelling of the verb 'endorse'.

See APPROVE/ENDORSE

inedible, uneatable

Inedible comes from the Latin verb *edere*, 'to eat'. It is an adjective meaning 'not fit to eat':

The food was condemned as inedible.

Uneatable comes from the English verb 'eat'. It is an adjective meaning 'not suitable for eating':

The food was presented in such a way as to be uneatable.

There is a subtle distinction between these adjectives but the distinction is unlikely to be preserved as most speakers regard the adjectives as being interchangeable.

ineducable

This adjective means 'not capable of being educated'. It does not have an '-at-' in it:

Autism, in extreme cases, may cause a child to be ineducable.

*Autism, in extreme cases, may cause a child to be ineducatable.

See also BARBARISM

inept

See INAPT/INEPT

inequity, iniquity

These nouns are occasionally confused, and they are etymologically related. *Inequity* is related to 'equal' and means 'lack of justice':

There is already inequity in the legal system. If we remove the right to legal aid, we shall make a bad situation worse.

Iniquity meant 'inequality', and now means 'wickedness':

It is hard for ordinary people to guard against such iniquity.

inestimable

See ESTIMABLE/ESTIMATABLE/INESTIMABLE

infamous

See FAMOUS/INFAMOUS/NOTORIOUS

infectious

See CONTAGIOUS/INFECTIOUS

infer

See IMPLY/INFER/INSINUATE

inferior

Inferior means 'lower in quality or rank':

So-called 'copy watches' are normally of inferior quality and construction.

The rank of major is inferior to that of general.

See also SUPERIOR

inferno

An *inferno* used to refer to 'hell' but now means 'conflagration'. It forms its plural by adding 's':

Towering Inferno was the name of a film about a burning tower block.

infinitive

The word *infinitive* is applied to the non-finite part of the verb. Infinitives in English are often preceded by 'to':

Infinitive with 'to'	Infinitive without 'to'
I advised him to wait	I listened to her play
he asked me to go	he watched me go

and so the most useful definition of an English infinitive is that it is a verb form, identical with the imperative and that it frequently co-occurs with 'to':

Imperative	Infinitive
Be good	(to) be
Have a break	(to) have
Drive carefully	(to) drive

The infinitive is capable of functioning as a noun or a noun phrase:

To do anything else would have seemed churlish.
Matt is human. To err is human.
I want coffee. I want to dance.

Infinitives are negated by being preceded by 'not':

To be or not to be …
I asked her not to come.

In many languages, the infinitive is a single word:

French	Latin	English
aller	ire	to go
être	esse	to be
venir	venire	to come

and such forms could not be split. Because Latin could not have a SPLIT INFINITIVE, traditional grammarians taught that it is unacceptable to split an infinitive as in such a sentence as:

I asked him to never do such a thing again.

See also VERB

infix

Infixes are MORPHEMES that can be fitted into a word. In English PREFIXES and SUFFIXES are used in every style whereas infixes are rare. They are limited to a number of disyllabic words, like 'bloody', 'blooming' and their taboo equivalents. These words are occasionally inserted into poly-syllabic words directly in front of the main stress:

abso + bloody + lutely = absobloodylutely
inter + bloomin' + ference = interbloominference.

inflammable
See FLAMMABLE/INFLAMMABLE/NON-FLAMMABLE

inflammatory

The adjective *inflammatory* ends in '-ory' and means 'tending to arouse violence':

Such inflammatory speeches will not be tolerated.

The earlier meaning of 'characterized by inflam-mation' is now rarely found outside medical texts.

inflation

The noun *inflation* has been so closely associated with the meaning of 'a progressive increase in the level of prices' that it is rarely used in the sense of 'putting air into something':

Inflation is at its lowest level for six years.

inflection, inflexion

These are variant spellings for 'modulation of the voice' and 'a change in the form of a word':

I love listening to her. Her inflection is, to me, as perfect as human speech can be.
Grammatical inflection can signal such changes as tense and number.

inflict
See AFFLICT/INFLICT

influenza
See FLU/INFLUENZA

informant, informer

These nouns both derive from the verb 'inform', meaning 'tell', 'give information'. An *informant* is a person who gives information about a subject, often an academic subject:

My informant has provided me with linguistic and sociolinguistic data on Kiswahili.

An *informer* provides information to the police or security forces about activities that have occurred or are about to occur:

According to the television programme The Bill, a police informer is called a 'snout'.

infrequent, unfrequented

These adjectives both derive from 'frequent', but they are not synonymous. *Infrequent* is an adjective meaning 'occasional', 'rare', and it is the negative equivalent of 'frequent':

These birds are infrequent visitors to our shores.
They depend on an infrequent bus service for transport into the nearest town.

Unfrequented is the negative of 'frequented' and means 'not visited often':

This last unfrequented wilderness on the planet is not immune from pollution.
They lived on a lonely, unfrequented stretch of moorland.

-ing form

Traditional grammarians subdivided *-ing forms* such as 'coming' and 'going' into three types:

■ Present participles, which occur with auxiliary verbs and indicate on-going activities:

I'm singing in the rain.
They have been working all morning.

■ Adjectives:

advancing years
a warbling bird

■ Gerunds, which function as nouns:

Smoking can seriously damage your health.
I love dancing.

In Standard English, the verb 'want' is usually followed by the past participle:

Does she want her car collected?

but in many regions the *-ing form* is used:

Does she want her car collecting?

Many people object to this usage and so it is better to avoid it in formal contexts.

There are uncertainties about spelling when *-ing*

is added to certain verbs. When verbs end with a silent 'e', the 'e' is deleted before '-ing':

dodge, dodging

ensue, ensuing

hide, hiding

love, loving.

There are exceptions to this rule, the main ones being verbs that end in 'ee', 'inge', 'oe' and 'ye':

agree, agreeing

singe, singeing

shoe, shoeing

dye, dyeing.

Where the loss of an 'e' would result in ambiguity, as between 'dying' and 'dyeing', the 'e' is retained. Where the loss of the 'e' would not cause confusion, as in 'aging', the form without 'e' is permitted. When verbs end in 'ie', the 'ie' is replaced by 'y' before '-ing':

die, dying

lie, lying.

The phrase *-ing form* is neutral as to function and is now used instead of such words as 'gerund' and 'participle'.

See also ASPECT, GERUND, PARTICIPLE, SPELLING, VERB

ingenious, ingenuous

These adjectives are occasionally confused. *Ingenious* means 'clever', 'skilful':

It was an ingenious plot and would have succeeded if one of the conspirators had not revealed the details to his brother-in-law.

Ingenuous means 'simple', 'naïve', 'lacking in artifice':

It is not easy to decide whether she is ingenuous or whether she cultivates an innocent frankness.

inhabitable

See HABITABLE/INHABITABLE/UNINHABITABLE

inherent, inherited

These adjectives are sometimes confused. *Inherent* derives from Latin *inhaerere*, 'cling to', 'be attached to', and means 'intrinsic', 'not separable':

Every human being has inherent rights: the right to freedom, justice and the pursuit of happiness.

This adjective has two pronunciations. The first and by far the most widespread pronounces the first two syllables as in 'inherit'; the second pronounces it like 'in here'.

Inherited comes from Latin *inhereditare*, 'appoint an heir', and means 'derived from a predecessor':

We shall soon be able to screen for certain inherited illnesses.

inhuman, inhumane

These adjectives both derive from Latin *humanus*, 'human', and they have developed different meanings. *Inhuman* means to lack all human characteristics:

Wars often produce inhuman behaviour.

Inhumane is normally used to mean 'cruel, lacking in humanity':

Many people regard hunting as an inhumane method of culling animals.

iniquity

See INEQUITY/INIQUITY

initial

Initial is a regular verb that doubles the 'l' before '-ed' and '-ing' in British English:

UK: initial(s), initialled, initialling (He initialled the contract yesterday.)

US: initial(s), initialed, initialing (The President initialed the treaty.)

injury

See DAMAGE/INJURY

innings, inning

In British English, *innings* (a portion of a game played by one person or a side), is both singular and plural:

This is his second innings.

Both his innings were inspirational.

In American English, *inning* is singular and *innings* plural:

What does a baseball inning entail?

What do baseball innings entail?

innuendo

Innuendo derives from Latin *innuere*, 'to convey by a nod', and the plural is 'innuendoes'. It is a type of irony consisting of oblique or indirect allusions that are often malicious or unkind:

You managed to sing in tune once or twice today.

See also IRONY, SARCASM

innumerable

See ENUMERABLE/INNUMERABLE

inoculation

The noun *inoculation* and the related verb 'inoculate' are often misspelled. They have one 'n' and one 'c' and come from Latin *inoculare*, 'to implant':

I had a smallpox inoculation when I was a child.

input

Input can function as both a noun and a verb:

Her input cannot be exaggerated. She has turned the company round almost single-handed.

We need someone with keyboard skills to input the data. I'm not sufficiently computer literate to do it myself.

inquiry

Inquiry is a variant of 'enquiry'. It has two acceptable pronunciations, one with the stress on the second syllable and one with the stress on the first.

See also ENQUIRE/INQUIRE

inside (of)

Inside can function as an adjective, an adverb, a noun and a preposition:

He passed me on the inside lane.

She went inside.

Have you seen the inside of their home?

It was strange being inside a palace.

Sometimes *inside of* is used as a compound preposition, with the meaning of 'within':

I'll be back inside of an hour.

but careful writers avoid this kind of construction, and its use as an equivalent of 'in':

It was inside of the smaller box.

is regarded as colloquial and should be avoided in formal contexts.

insinuate

See IMPLY/INFER/INSINUATE

instal, install

These are acceptable variants of the regular verb meaning 'put in position':

Have you installed the machinery yet?

The form *install* is more usual and the 'll' is used before '-ed' and '-ing' in both Britain and America:

instal(l)(s), installed, installing.

The derived noun is spelled 'instalment' in Britain but 'installment' in America.

instantaneously, instantly

These adverbs both derive from 'instant' and can both be used to mean 'immediately'. *Instantaneously* can also mean 'very quickly', 'almost at the same time':

She fell from the tree and died almost instantaneously.

instil, instill

See IMBUE/INSTIL/INSTILL

instrumental (in)

The phrase *instrumental in* is sometimes used in

the popular press as a roundabout way of indicating involvement:

He was instrumental in changing society. = He helped to change society.

insurance

See ASSURANCE/INSURANCE

insure

See ASSURE/ENSURE/INSURE

integral

The adjective *integral* has been overused, especially in the phrase:

an integral part.

Integral means 'intrinsic to', 'an essential part of' and so the phrase 'an integral part' is tautological:

A back-to-front baseball cap has become an integral part of every teenager's wardrobe.

The word is usually stressed on the first syllable, like 'integer', to which it is related, but some people stress the second syllable.

integrate

Integrate comes from Latin *integrare*, 'to make into a whole'. It is overused to mean 'incorporate' and 'desegregate':

We should integrate these suggestions into our corporate plan.

From September all state schools will be integrated.

intense, intensive

These adjectives both derive from Latin *intensus*, 'stretched'. *Intense* means 'characterized by extreme force, strength or degree':

I was suffering from the intense heat.

I want a quiet, relaxed life. I don't go in for intense relationships.

Intensive means 'concentrated', 'unremitting':

We had an intensive Spanish course with six months' work packed into two weeks.

Intensive is often used after the noun in such fixed phrases as:

The venture is capital-intensive.

The work is labour-intensive.

intensifier

The term *intensifier* is normally applied to a set of adverbs such as:

really, too, very

that add emphasis to the meaning of an adjective or adverb:

She was really/very/too beautiful.

He drove really/very/too fast.

The simplest test for an *intensifier* is to see if it can replace 'very'.

In British usage, a number of *intensifiers* such as:

awfully, dreadfully, frightfully

are marked for class and age in that they tend to be used by people who were socially mobile upwards.

See also ADJECTIVE, ADVERB

inter, intern

These verbs are occasionally confused. *Inter* means 'bury the dead':

He was interred after the church ceremony.

Intern means 'imprison without a trial':

He was interned for five years during the war.

In the United States and increasingly in Britain, *intern* is used as a noun to mean a recently trained doctor who is working in a hospital as an assistant to a senior physician or surgeon. By extension, *intern* is used as a verb to mean 'train as an intern or houseman':

I interned at Guy's Hospital.

inter-, intra-

These prefixes are frequently used. *Inter-* comes from Latin *inter*, 'between', and is used to mean 'between', 'among', 'reciprocal':

We are having an inter-denominational service with Christians, Hindus, Jews and Muslims all represented.

Intra- comes from Latin *intra*, 'within, on the inside', and means 'within'. It is frequently used in medical contexts:

He's been having intramuscular injections.

She's on an intravenous drip.

There prefixes both occur before 'national' and are sometimes misunderstood. *International* means 'between nations' and *intranational* means 'within the one nation'.

inter alia

The Latin phrase *inter alia* means 'among other things':

He spoke *inter alia* about linguistic change.

Many people do not like the use of Latin phrases. They can be seen as unnecessarily complex. In general, any expression that is likely to be misunderstood should be avoided.

interface

The noun *interface* means a 'common boundary', and it has become overused, partly because of its link with computers:

An interface is an electrical circuit linking one computer with another.

It is widely used now as both a noun and a verb to mean 'link', 'point of contact':

This painting illustrates the interface between the naturalistic and the baroque.

The groups planned to interface before the last part of the climb.

interjection

An *interjection* is a sound or word expressing sudden pain, pleasure or surprise. Such expressions are usually given an exclamation mark in the written medium:

Ow!

Wow!

Gosh!

Some writers use the term *interjection* to describe phrases such as:

Heavens above!

My goodness gracious me!

and expletives such as:

Blast!

Damn!

but these are probably better dealt with as EXCLAMATIONS.

internecine

The adjective *internecine* derives ultimately from Latin *necare*, 'to kill', and means 'mutually destructive'. It occurs most frequently in the phrase 'internecine war':

The world has closed its eyes to the internecine wars that are still raging.

interrogative

The term *interrogative* is applied to sentences that ask questions:

Did she take it?

Haven't they arrived yet?

There are several types of *interrogative*:

■ Those that expect a 'yes' or 'no' answer:

Are you happy?

■ Those that begin with a question word, such as How?, When?, Who?, Why? and that cannot receive a 'yes/no' answer:

What time is it?

■ Those that use intonation to suggest a question:

You're going?

■ Those involving *interrogative* pronouns:

Which should I read?

■ Those involving *interrogative* adjectives:

What books have you read?

■ Tag questions:

He's a lovely person, isn't he?

She didn't sing well tonight, did she?

'Yes/no' questions involve the inversion of the subject and predicate when the predicate is 'be', 'have' or the modals:

Statement	Interrogative
She's lovely.	Is she lovely?
They have arrived.	Have they arrived?
You can't swim.	Can't you swim?/
	Can you not swim?

'Do' is required to form questions with other verbs when there is no other auxiliary verb present:

Statement	Interrogative
She loves coffee.	Does she love coffee?
We hate litter.	Do we hate litter?

See also INVERSION, QUESTION, SENTENCE

intolerable, intolerant

These adjectives derive from 'tolerate'. *Intolerable* means 'unbearable':

The heat and humidity were almost intolerable.

Intolerant describes a person who lacks respect for the opinions of others:

She is intolerant of other people's views.

See also TOLERANCE/TOLERATION

intonation

Intonation is a technical term to describe the melody of speech utterances. In British English a falling melody usually signals statements or questions using question words, and a rising melody tends to indicate a yes/no question. *Intonation* can be of significance in interpreting speech because our *intonation* can indicate our attitude to a topic or to our listener, and it can be used to imply respect, admiration, insolence, sarcasm, disbelief or enthusiasm.

See also PARALINGUISTICS

intra-

See INTER-/INTRA-

intransitive

The term *intransitive* is applied to verbs that do not take an object:

John arrived.

It disappeared.

Many verbs in English, especially those involving change or movement, can occur in both transitive and intransitive constructions:

I boiled the water.

The water boiled.

I opened the door.

The door opened.

See also ACTIVE VOICE/PASSIVE VOICE, ERGATIVE, TRANSITIVE, VERB

intreat

See ENTREAT/INTREAT

intrinsic

See EXTRINSIC/INTRINSIC

introvert

See EXTROVERT/INTROVERT

intrusive 'r'

Many varieties of British English are non-rhotic – that is, they do not pronounce the 'r' in words such as:

air, farm, sure.

They do, however, use a linking 'r' in phrases such as:

here and away

war and peace.

There is a tendency among some speakers to use an *intrusive 'r'* in phrases where one word ends with an 'aw' sound and the next begins with a vowel as in:

law and order = law (+ r) and order

saw a house = saw (+ r) a house.

Such usage should be avoided in careful speech.

See also -R-, RHOTIC

intrust

See ENTRUST/INTRUST

Inuit

See ESKIMO/INUIT

invalid

The spelling *invalid* represents two pronunciations and two meanings. The adjective *invalid*, which is pronounced with the main stress on the second syllable so that it sounds like 'in + valid' means 'not valid or legal':

Your visa is invalid. It expired last year.

The noun *invalid* means 'a person suffering from a chronic illness'. It has the main stress on the first syllable and may rhyme the third syllable with either 'deed' or 'did':

She's been an invalid for three years and totally housebound for two.

invaluable, priceless, valuable, valueless

There are many words in English that can be prefixed by 'in-' to form a word that is opposite in meaning:

audible, inaudible; edible, inedible; sensitive, insensitive

but this is not the case with *valuable* and *invaluable*.

Valuable means 'of considerable worth', 'precious':

She has a valuable collection of dictionaries.

His information proved valuable.

The adjective *invaluable* means 'exceptionally valuable', 'of such a high value it is priceless':

Her service to the company has been invaluable.
I don't know how to thank you for your invaluable help and advice.

The opposite of *valuable* is *valueless*, which means 'worthless':

It looks like gold but it is only a trinket and practically valueless.

We do not tend to apply the adjective *invaluable* to objects that are worth a lot of money. A suggestion might be *invaluable*, but a Dali painting, for example, might be *priceless*, that is, 'of inestimable worth':

How can you put a price tag on a work of art that has survived for over two thousand years? It is priceless.

An item may be valued for its associations rather than for any intrinsic worth. Such items are often said to be 'of sentimental value':

She was heartbroken by the loss of her photographs. They were of sentimental value only but to her they were priceless.

'Valuables' is a noun meaning 'precious personal items' and is used in the plural form:

Were any of your valuables stolen?

In colloquial British English *priceless* can be used to mean 'extremely funny':

Did you see the talent competition? The comedian was priceless.

inveigh, inveigle

These regular verbs are not widely used and so, when they are, they are often misspelled or misused. *Inveigh* rhymes with 'in hay' and means 'speak out loudly against':

inveigh(s), inveighed, inveighing
The MP inveighed against greed and then voted himself a large increase in salary.

Inveigle has two pronunciations. It can rhyme with 'bagel' or with 'beagle' and means 'cajole someone into doing something':

inveigle(s), inveigled, inveigling
I don't know how I could have been inveigled into joining. He is the most persuasive talker I have met.

invent
See DISCOVER/INVENT

inversion

Inversion involves reversing the order of a series or part of a series:

A + B + C = C + B + A
He said so. = So said he.

We find inversion in English:

- When we ask questions:

He is sad. = Is he sad?

She will. = Will she?

- When we use tagged clauses involving 'neither', 'nor' and 'so':

I don't like tea and neither do you.
He cannot drink milk; nor can his children.
I like coffee and so does he.

- When we begin a conditional clause with 'had':

Had I only known then what I know now!

- And after 'hardly' and 'scarcely':

Hardly had I sat down when he knocked at the door!
Scarcely had I sat down when he knocked at the door!

See also INTERROGATIVE

inverted commas

Inverted commas are another name for 'quotation marks'. They may be either single, '...', or double, "... ", and they are used to indicate DIRECT SPEECH:

UK: 'Come in,' he called. 'Just open the door and come in.'
US: "Come in," he called. "Just open the door and come in."

for the titles of book chapters, short poems and stories:

My favourite poem is 'Easter, 1916'.

and for drawing attention to a word or phrase:

I wasn't sure how to spell 'separate' until Tony told me that there is 'a rat' in 'separate'.

See also PUNCTUATION, QUOTATION, QUOTATION MARKS

invite

Invite is a regular verb meaning 'ask someone to attend a gathering or to do something':

invite(s), invited, inviting
I was invited to give a talk.

Many people dislike the use of *invite* as a noun:

I received an invite to the party.

since 'invitation' already exists.

Printed invitations are often formal, using the third person and titles. A typical format for such an invitation is:

The Management and Staff of the Inland Mission
request the pleasure of the company of
Michael Jones and partner
at a reception to mark the Silver Jubilee
of their foundation
on Friday, March 17, at 12:00 noon
at their premises, 'The Port', Dockland Road.
RSVP: B. Martin Pickles, Manager
Refreshments will be served 12 noon – 2 p.m.

RSVP stands for *Répondez s'il vous plaît* (i.e., 'Please reply').

invoke
See EVOKE/INVOKE

involve

The regular verb *involve*, meaning 'engage, entail, occupy', has been overused in the media and so bleached of some of its meaning:

involve(s), involved, involving

They are involved in crime detection.

The trial involved claim and counter-claim.

He was involved in an accident.

The pressures involved in teaching are underestimated.

There is nothing intrinsically wrong with *involve* or with other words such as 'get', 'important' or 'nice', but overused words tend to be imprecise and should be avoided in technical or formal contexts.

inward, inwards

In British English, *inward* is an adjective:

inward emotions

and *inwards* an adverb:

They moved inwards.

but *inward* can function as both adjective and adverb in American English.

See also -WARD/-WARDS

ipso facto

The Latin phrase *ipso facto*, 'by that fact', is often used as the equivalent of 'thus':

Only part of the relevant evidence was laid before the court and, *ipso facto*, the court ruling is invalid.

IQ

The abbreviation *IQ* stands for 'intelligence quotient'.

ir-

The prefix *ir-* occurs before words beginning with 'r' and is a phonological variant of IN-:

radiate, irradiate

reverent, irreverent.

See also IL-, IM-, PREFIX

Iran

The preferred adjective and noun are now 'Iranian' rather than 'Persian', although the Persian Gulf is still so called in America. The capital is Teh(e)ran.

Iraq

The derived adjective and noun are Iraqi; there is no 'u' after the 'q'. The capital is Baghdad.

Irish English

English is one of the two official languages in Eire and the only official language of Northern Ireland. *Irish English* comprehends the various types of English current on the island. These types include: Standard English with a variety of Irish accents; regional dialects such as Hiberno-English; the English used by some people whose ancestral mother tongue was Irish Gaelic; and Ulster Scots, the Scottish-influenced English of some speakers whose ancestors came from Scotland.

ironic, sarcastic

These adjectives are often used as synonyms, but careful users differentiate them. *Ironic* means 'expressing irony':

It is ironic that the person chosen to be her successor should undo virtually every change that she made.

Ironical is a variant form of *ironic*.

Sarcastic means 'characterized by mockery or scorn':

Even when such sarcastic comments are untrue, they can hurt and offend.

irony

The noun *irony* derives ultimately from Greek *eiron*, 'to dissemble'. The term is given to a figure of speech where there are at least two levels of interpretation. There are several forms of *irony*:

■ The use of words to imply the opposite of what is actually said:

This is just wonderful! (= awful)

Many people would disclaim this as *irony*, believing that *irony* should involve wit.

■ Dramatic irony occurs when a character in literature says something that is meaningful at one level to the character and at another level to the audience. In Shakespeare's *Othello*, the use of the adjective 'honest' in relation to Iago is intentionally ironic.

■ Tragic irony or irony of fate is a literary convention involving a cruel reversal of fortunes at the very moment when the hero's expectations seem likely to be fulfilled.

■ Socratic irony is a method of argument favoured in some philosophical discussions. It pretends ignorance in order to question an opponent closely and so reveal any inconsistencies or false assumptions in the opponent's position.

See also FIGURE OF SPEECH, INNUENDO, SARCASM

irrefutable

The adjective *irrefutable* means 'incontrovertible', 'impossible to deny or refute'. It is so overused in phrases such as:

irrefutable evidence

that its meaning is being weakened. *Irrefutable* may be stressed either on the second or the third syllable. The stress on the third syllable is growing in popularity.

irregardless

Irregardless can sometimes be used as an emphatic variant of 'regardless':

*You should apply for the post, irregardless of the outcome.

This usage should be avoided. It is unnecessary and also potentially ambiguous because of the use of IR- as a negative PREFIX.

irregular verb

Most verbs in English are regular, that is, they form their past tense by adding '-ed' in the written medium and 'id', 'd' or 't' in speech:

bolt, bolted
bray, brayed
cook, cooked.

They mark the present tense of verbs with third-person singular subjects by adding '-s' in the written medium and 'iz', 'z', 's' in speech:

rage, rages
bay, bays
cook, cooks.

All verbs that do not follow this rule are *irregular*. Some of the most frequently used verbs in the language, such as 'be' and 'have', are very irregular; others, like 'say', are only slightly irregular. All newly coined verbs are regular, and many irregular verbs are in the process of being regularized.

A significant number of verbs have different forms in Britain and America, the most widely-used of which are:

UK and UK-influenced	US and US-influenced
dive, dived	dive, dove
fit, fitted	fit, fit
get, got	get, got, gotten
wake, woke, woken	wake, waked

See also -ED FORM, -ED/-T, VERB

irrelevant

This adjective meaning 'not pertinent' is often misspelled:

Such information is irrelevant. It has no bearing on our current discussion.

irremovable

See IMMOVABLE/IRREMOVABLE

irreparable

Irreparable means 'incapable of being put right':

You have done irreparable damage to your own cause.

The stress falls on the second syllable.

See also FIX/REPAIR

irrespective of, regardless

Irrespective of is a compound preposition used in job advertisements as a synonym for *regardless*:

Applications are sought from well-qualified people irrespective of race, creed or gender.

Regardless can function as an adjective, usually followed by 'of' and meaning 'heedless':

He ran forward, regardless of his own safety.

It can also function adverbially, especially in the cliché:

Carry on regardless

meaning 'disregard drawbacks and problems'.

irresponsible, unresponsible

The distinction between these words is potentially a useful one, but *unresponsible* is rarely used. *Irresponsible* means 'reckless', 'unreliable', 'unwilling or unable to accept the duties of one's position':

Your behaviour has been thoughtless and irresponsible. It could have endangered the lives of your colleagues.

He's a delight to talk to but a nightmare to work with because of his irresponsible attitude. The buck never stops with him.

Unresponsible means 'not to be held accountable':

We are unresponsible for the difficulties encountered. Please take the matter up with the Service Manager of the Company where the car was bought.

irruption

See ERUPTION/IRRUPTION

-ise

See -IZE/-ISE

Islam

The religion of Muslims is *Islam*. The derived adjectives are 'Islamic' and, less often, 'Islamist':

Islamic law is enshrined in the constitution.
This Islamist group is not strictly fundamentalist.

isle

See AISLE/ISLE

Isle of Man

Inhabitants of the island in the Irish Sea are 'Manxman/men' and 'Manxwoman/women'; the derived adjective is 'Manx'. The capital is Douglas.

-ism

The suffix *-ism* has traditionally been used to form nouns from personal names to suggest 'the views of X' or 'the doctrines associated with X':

Lenin, Leninism
Thatcher, Thatcherism.

It is currently also used as a shorthand method of indicating 'discrimination':

ageism: discrimination according to age

racism: discrimination according to race

sexism: discrimination according to gender

and even:

heightism: discrimination against short people.

See also POLITICAL CORRECTNESS

Israel

An inhabitant of the Middle Eastern country is an 'Israeli'; the derived adjective is the same. The capital is Jerusalem.

issue

The verb *issue* takes different prepositions depending on the structure:

A five-digit number is issued to each student.

Each student is issued with a five-digit number.

-ist, -ite

The suffixes *-ist* and *-ite* can both be used to create new nouns. The SUFFIX *-ist* is much more frequently used and can indicate a person who performs a certain action:

cycle, cyclist

motor, motorist

a person who practises a certain discipline:

physics, physicist

science, scientist

and a person characterized by a certain quality:

pragmatic, pragmatist

pure, purist.

The suffix *-ite* can indicate a supporter of a person or policy:

Blair, Blairite

Thatcher, Thatcherite

a mineral or salt:

krypton, kryptonite

sulphur, sulphite

and, in the past, an inhabitant:

Israel, Israelite.

The *-ite* suffix is often used in a derogatory sense:

Such Labourites (i.e., supporters of the Labour Party) fail to point out that inflation and taxes have always risen under a Labour government.

See also -AN/-EAN/-IAN

isthmus

An *isthmus* is a narrow strip of land connecting two larger land masses:

The Panama Canal was dug through the narrowest part of the isthmus of Panama joining Central and South America.

Isthmus has two acceptable plurals, 'isthmuses' and 'isthmi', the former being more usual. The 'th'

is not pronounced and so *isthmus* rhymes with a rapid pronunciation of 'Christmas'.

italicization

Italics are used for several purposes, including the titles of published books, films, journals, magazines, plays, long poems, operas, ballets and long musical compositions:

When was *The English Language Today* published?

Gone with the Wind was one of the most financially successful films of all time.

Have you read all of *Paradise Lost*?

the names of ships, aircraft and spacecraft:

the *Golden Hind*

the *Enterprise*

and foreign words and phrases that are used in English but are not fully assimilated:

de jure

ipso facto.

See also FOREIGN LOAN-WORDS

Italy

An inhabitant of the European country is an 'Italian'; the derived adjective is the same. The capital is Rome.

Many words associated with food, music and painting have been borrowed into English from Italian.

See also FOREIGN LOAN-WORDS

-ite

See -IST/-ITE

its, it's

There is considerable confusion about when to use *its* and *it's*, and yet the rules are extremely simple. *Its*, without an apostrophe, can function only as a possessive meaning 'belonging to it':

Where did you take the book from? I can't find its space.

Austin airport is renowned for its swift throughput of passengers.

It's is always an abbreviation for either 'it is' or 'it has':

It's raining. = It is raining.

It's ruined my day. = It has ruined my day.

See also APOSTROPHE

it's I, it's me

Although it is regarded as correct to say:

It's I.

most people use:

It's me.

The use of *it's me* is perfectly acceptable in casual contexts.

See also AGREEMENT, COPULA, I/ME

Ivory Coast

An inhabitant of the West African republic is an 'Ivorian'; the derived adjective is the same. The capital is Yamoussoukro.

-ize, -ise

The SUFFIX -*ize* or -*ise* can be added to adjectives and nouns to form verbs. The -*ize*/-*ise* ending is Greek in origin but it is not restricted to words of Greek origin. The form -*ise* is widely used in Britain, whereas -*ize* is preferred in the United States. There is, however, a growing tendency to prefer the -*ize* ending in Britain, and it is the preferred style of most UK publishing houses.

Adjective + ize	Verb
legal	legalize
modern	modernize
tranquil	tranquillize

Noun + ize	Verb
computer	computerize
hospital	hospitalize
vandal	vandalize

The following verbs can occur only with -*ise*:

advertise, advise, apprise, arise, chastise, circumcise, comprise, compromise, despise, devise, disguise, excise, exercise, improvise, incise, merchandise, promise, revise, supervise, surmise, surprise, televise.

Words ending with '-yse', although usually spelled with a 'z' in the United States, are always spelled with an 's' in Britain:

UK: analyse, paralyse

US: analyze, paralyze.

Many writers have objected to some of the more recently coined -*ize*/-*ise* verbs because they duplicate the meanings of other verbs:

finalize: conclude, end, settle

or because they are associated with jargon:

modularize, politicize, semesterize.

J

j

J is a consonant pronounced like 'jay'. The letter was introduced into English by Norman scribes after the Norman Conquest of 1066.

jacket

Jacket is most frequently used as a noun. Americans can use *jacket* for a folder for documents or a 'dust cover'. When *jacket* is used as a verb, the 't' is not doubled:

jacket(s), jacketed, jacketing
These discs should be jacketed to protect them from the dust.

jail

See GAOL/JAIL

jalousie, jealousy

See ENVY/JALOUSIE/JEALOUSY

jam, jamb

These words are homophones. *Jam*, in the sense of 'fruit preserve', is usually called 'jelly' in America. The unrelated sense of *jam* meaning 'crowd' or 'congestion' can function as a noun or regular verb:

jam(s), jammed, jamming
Avoid the road ahead if you want to avoid a traffic jam.
The road was jammed.

Jam can also mean 'block a transmission':

They've jammed our broadcasts by transmitting other signals on the same wavelength.

and 'play rock music together':

Louis Armstrong was one of the first to be recorded taking part in jam sessions.

Jamb or occasionally 'jambe' is from Old French *jambe*, 'leg', and refers to the vertical side frame of a door or window:

The door will have to be replaced and the jamb strengthened.

Jamaica

An inhabitant of the island in the West Indies is a 'Jamaican'; the derived adjective is the same. The capital is Kingston.

Jamaican (English)

This term is sometimes applied to the English of speakers whose parents came from Jamaica and settled in Britain:

I was born in Brixton but I can speak Jamaican.

The *Jamaican* of Britain is not identical to the variety spoken on the Caribbean island.

See also PIDGIN AND CREOLE

Japan

An inhabitant of the island nation of the Far East is a 'Japanese' man or woman; the derived adjective is 'Japanese'. The captial is Tokyo.

jargon

No one is certain of the origin of the noun *jargon* but it has a range of meanings today, most of which are pejorative. It can refer to: gibberish; a simplified, hybrid language such as a pidgin; a specialized, technical language of a particular group; or a pretentious language involving circumlocutions, polysyllabic words and complex syntax.

The common denominator in all of these uses is that jargon is not intelligible to an outsider or to the uninitiated. Yet technical vocabularies, whether used by tinkers, tailors, soldiers, sailors or doctors, may permit very precise communication exchanges, and insofar as they perform such a role they are of value.

See also ARGOT, CANT, CIRCUMLOCUTION, CLICHÉ, GOBBLEDEGOOK, PIDGIN AND CREOLE, SLANG

Java

An inhabitant of the most important island of Indonesia is a 'Javanese'; the derived adjective is the same. The capital, also the capital of Indonesia, is Djakarta.

jealous

See ENVIABLE/ENVIOUS/JEALOUS

jejune

The adjective *jejune* comes from Latin *jejunus*, 'fasting', and it usually implies 'meagre', 'lacking in substance', 'devoid of interest'. Recently, possibly because users have been influenced by French *jeune*, meaning 'young', it has also been used as a synonym for 'naïve', 'puerile', 'unsophisticated'. Many purists object to this change in meaning, but such mobility is natural in language and not necessarily a sign of decay.

See also SEMANTIC CHANGE

jeopardize, jeopardy

The noun *jeopardy* derives from French *jeu parti*, 'divided game', and the first syllable rhymes with 'pep'. The noun means 'danger of loss or death':

Your life may be in jeopardy if you undertake this mission.

The regular verb *jeopardize* means 'risk':

jeopardize(s), jeopardized. jeopardizing
You should not jeopardize your capital although you might like to invest some of your income.

These words are frequently misspelled because there are no other words in English beginning 'jeop-'.

jerbil
See GERBIL/JERBIL

Jew
The noun *Jew* derives from Hebrew *Jehudah*, 'Judah', and refers to a member of a Semitic group that is directly descended from the biblical Israelites. The derived adjective is *Jewish*:

The Jewish religion is Judaism.

The feminine form, *Jewess*, is not widely used.

See also HAMITIC/SEMITIC, POLITICAL CORRECTNESS

jewellery, jewelry
These forms are used in Britain and America respectively:

UK: Her jewellery is insured for £50 million.
US: Her jewelry is insured for $50 million.

The related words have double 'l' in Britain but only one 'l' in America:

UK: jewelled, jeweller, jewelling, bejewelled
US: jeweled, jeweler, jeweling, bejeweled.

jibe
See GIBE/GYBE/JIBE

jingoism
The noun *jingoism* derives from the exclamation 'By jingo!', a modified form of 'Jesus', and it has come to mean 'bellicose form of chauvinism':

I wish to dissociate myself and my country from the unacceptable jingoism that turned a game of football into belligerent racism.

jodhpurs
The noun *jodhpurs*, meaning 'riding breeches', comes from the name of the Indian town *Jodhpur*, which is in Rajasthan.

Jordan
An inhabitant of the Middle Eastern kingdom is a 'Jordanian'; the derived adjective is the same. The capital is Amman.

journalese
The noun *journalese* is applied to the language of newspapers, and it has been extended to cover the journalistic traits found in some radio and television programmes. *Journalese* has derogatory connotations and cannot be accurately applied to all newspaper language. It refers to characteristics of style that are occasioned by limitations of time and space and are also intended to attract and retain a reader's attention. The commonest features of journalese are found in headlines and include the use of abbreviations, initials and acronyms:

New Lib-Lab Pact on the Cards

alliteration:

Baking Britain Beats Bermuda

ambiguity, both intentional and unintentional:

Paul Plays the Field (footballer)
Fierce Dogs Act Under Pressure

emotional language intended to play on a reader's emotions:

Children Battered and Abused

first names and surnames:

Tony in Climbdown over School
Dole Draws Sympathy Vote

omission of articles and auxiliary verbs:

Teachers appalled by arson outrage

pre-noun modification:

65-year-old-pedalling pensioners, Bert and Millie ...

puns:

John Majors On

rhyming:

Frills and Spills

stock words:

ace, axe, ban, bid, clash, curb, cuts, fury, hit, horror, jinx, mystery, outrage, quit, rap, riddle, shock, slam, stampede, storm

and the present tense

Live-in Lover Loses Lou.

See also HEADLINES, TELEGRAPHESE

judge
See ADJUDGE/JUDGE

judgement, judgment
These are variant spellings. *Judgement* is probably more common in Britain and *judgment* in America and in legal work in Britain, but both spellings are found in both countries:

She will give her judg(e)ment on Monday.

Whichever spelling is selected, consistency is recommended.

See also ACKNOWLEDGEMENT/ ACKNOWLEDGMENT, SPELLING

judicial, judicious
These adjectives both derive ultimately from Latin *judex*, 'a judge', but they are clearly differentiated

in meaning and usage. *Judicial* means 'relating to judges, justice and the administration of justice':

There is to be a judicial review of the rights of minors in such cases.

Judicious means 'showing good judgement', 'wise', 'prudent':

What this group needs is a judicious dose of common sense.

jujube

The noun *jujube*, meaning 'chewy sweet', comes from Latin *jujuba*, 'tree of the genus *Ziziphus*':

Jujubes are made of flavoured gelatine. They are often medicated to soothe sore throats.

Many speakers incorrectly use a reduplicated form 'jubejube'.

See also REDUPLICATION

juncture

In the past *juncture* was used as a synonym of 'junction', meaning 'a coming together of roads, railway lines or events'. *Juncture* has been popularized and overused to mean 'critical point in time':

At this juncture, it seems likely that he will lose the election.

The phrase 'at this juncture' is often simply an ELEGANT VARIATION of 'now'.

See also BLEACHING

junta

The noun *junta* derives from Spanish *junta*, 'council', and is used to mean 'a group of army officers holding power in a country, often after a coup':

The military juntas of the 1970s have been replaced by elected governments.

In British English, *junta* is normally pronounced to rhyme with 'Bunter' and the 'j' is pronounced as in 'jump'; in American English, an approximation to the Spanish pronunciation is also heard where 'j' is pronounced 'h' and where 'u' is pronounced 'oo'.

just

The word *just* is multifunctional:

a just person (adjective)
He has just finished (adverb)
the just and the righteous (noun).

The adverb *just* has little constant semantic content but can be used with different intonation patterns to suggest different attitudes. For example, a sentence such as:

The talk was just brilliant.

can mean:

The talk was absolutely brilliant.

whereas:

The food was just edible.

is likely to mean:

The food was barely edible.

Just can occur in a number of sentence positions, and position can affect meaning:

Just wait till I get you home! (just = only)
Just a minute! (just = please wait)
I just didn't know what to say. (just = simply)
I usually know just what to say. (just = exactly)
It was just perfect. (just = absolutely)
It was just adequate. (just = barely)
They've just left. (just = very recently)
We made it — just! (just = with nothing to spare)

In theory, adverbs cannot be used to modify adjectives, such as 'perfect' or 'unique', that are absolutes. *Just*, however, is used colloquially with such absolutes to imply the speaker's attitude:

His performance was just perfect.
She is just unique.

In Britain, *just* can occur with inversion in emphatic agreement:

They played brilliantly.
Didn't they just! (= they certainly did)

In British usage, when *just* means 'very recently', it usually occurs with the present perfect, that is, 'have' + past participle:

She has just heard the news.
You've missed them. They have just left.

In American English, *just* frequently occurs with the simple past:

She just heard the news.
You've missed them. They just left.

See also ADVERB, INTONATION

justify, rectify

These regular verbs are sometimes confused. *Justify* means 'offer an excuse or explanation for':

It is not the mistake that we object to; it is your attempt to justify it. Mistakes should be acknowledged and, where possible, rectified.

Rectify means 'correct, put right, remedy':

I can rectify my factual errors but how can I rectify the suffering that I must have caused?

K

k

K is a consonant. The letter *k* is one of the least used letters in the alphabet. Old English used 'c' for the initial sound in both 'king' and 'queen':

cyning (king), cwen (queen)

but 'k' and 'q' were introduced after the Norman Conquest in 1066.

The sound /k/ is represented in English by:

'c' as in 'call'
'ch' as in 'chemistry'
'ck' as in 'duck'
'k' as in 'kite'.

The capital letter is used as an abbreviation for 'thousand':

The salary will be in the region of £50K.

kaleidoscope

This word is widely used and widely misspelled:

My toy kaleidoscope introduced me to complex patterns of changing colours and shapes.

The stress is in the second syllable, which rhymes with 'my'.

Kazakhstan

An inhabitant of the republic, formerly part of the USSR, is a 'Kazakh'; the derived adjective is the same. The capital is Almaty, which is sometimes spelled Alma-Ata.

keep

Keep is an irregular verb:

keep(s), kept, keeping

and one of the most frequently used verbs in the language. *Keep* has a wide semantic range. It can function as an equivalent of 'be faithful to':

I was unable to keep my promise.

'control':

You should learn to keep your temper in check.

'preserve':

Miss Foolish used Brand X and kept her teeth white.
Miss Wise used Brand Y and kept her white teeth.

and 'retain':

They kept all the profits for themselves.

Keep also occurs with the preposition 'at' to indicate persistence:

He'll keep at that problem until he solves it.

with 'on + a present participle' to mark repetition:

She'll keep on trying until she succeeds.

and with 'up' to suggest competition:

Keeping up with the Joneses is not always easy or sensible.

See also VERBS

ken

Ken meaning 'knowledge' is now obsolete except for the phrase:

beyond our ken.

As a verb, it is quite widely used in Scottish dialects:

A dinnae ken. (I don't know.)

and is frequently used by writers as an indicator of Scots.

Kenya

The name of this East African country used to be pronounced with the first syllable rhyming with 'teen'. It is now regularly pronounced to rhyme with 'ten'. The derived adjective and noun are 'Kenyan'. The capital is Nairobi.

kerb

See CURB/KERB

kerosene, paraffin

Kerosene is the name given in America, Canada, Australia and New Zealand to the liquid fuel that is usually called 'paraffin' in Britain:

When we go on safari, we'll need two drums of kerosene for the lamps and refrigerator.

ketchup

The noun *ketchup* derives from Chinese *koe*, 'seafood', + *tsiap*, 'sauce'. It has been spelled *ketchup*, 'catchup' and also 'catsup':

Ketchup is any one of a variety of piquant sauces but most British people associate it with 'tomato ketchup'.

key

The noun *key* is polysemous and can refer to:

a door key
a piano key
a key to a mystery.

It is now regularly used as a verb meaning 'put on a computer':

We'll need someone to key in the text.

Key has been used in compounds:

keyboard, keyhole, key-ring

but many people dislike its current adjectival use as a synonym for 'crucial, essential':

The key question is this.
making key decisions.

khaki

This word is frequently mispronounced and misspelled. English borrowed the word from Urdu *khak*, 'dust'. The first syllable of the word rhymes with the notes 'fah' and 'lah'. *Khaki* can refer to a yellowish-brown colour:

Of all the colours in the world, you had to choose khaki.

or to a hard-wearing fabric often favoured by the military:

I've had this khaki jacket since I left the army.

See also FOREIGN LOAN-WORDS

kibbutz

A *kibbutz* is a collective agricultural settlement in Israel. The plural is 'kibbutzim' and a person who lives on a *kibbutz* is sometimes called a 'kibbutznik':

They stayed on a kibbutz called Sarid.

kid

In colloquial speech, *kid* is often used to mean 'child':

Things weren't like this when I was a kid.

The usage is perfectly acceptable colloquially but it would be inappropriate in formal styles.

See also FORMAL ENGLISH, STILE/STYLE

kidnap

This word originally meant 'steal a kid'. It is a regular verb but the spelling differs in Britain and America:

UK: kidnap(s), kidnapped, kidnapping
US: kidnap(s), kidnaped, kidnaping (They kidnaped people and held them for ransom.)

kilo

The noun *kilo* is used as an abbreviation for 'kilogram':

You are allowed to carry 22 kilos only.

Kilo comes from Greek *khilioi*, '1000', and it rhymes with 'fee low'.

kilometre, kilometer

A *kilometre* is a measurement equal to 1000 metres. There are approximately eight kilometres in five miles. In Britain, the French spelling, ending in '-metre' is used, but the '-meter' spelling is preferred in America. There are two widely-used pronunciations. In Britain the main stress is on the first syllable; in America it tends to fall on the second, which rhymes with 'Tom'.

The abbreviation 'k' is regularly used:

I cycled 10k today.

kimono

The noun *kimono*, meaning 'a loose, sashed, ankle-length garment', comes from Japanese *ki*, 'wear', and *mono*, 'thing':

I bought a lovely silk kimono yesterday.

The plural is 'kimonos'.

kin

The noun *kin* comes from Old English *cyn*, 'family', a meaning it partially retains in the phrase:

kith and kin (relatives)

and in such compounds as:

kinsman, kinship.

The word, like 'kith', which meant 'people who were well known', is virtually obsolete.

kind, sort, type

These words should be used with singular forms of verbs and demonstrative adjectives:

What kind/sort/type of behaviour is this?
This type of bulldog has been bred for centuries.
That kind of behaviour is unacceptable.
This sort of activity is popular.

Often, in colloquial speech, *kind*, *sort* and *type* are used with 'these' and 'those' instead of 'this' and 'that' when they modify plural nouns:

*I don't like these type of stories.
*these kind of things
*those sort of activities

The acceptable forms are:

this kind of thing
these kinds of thing
this sort of activity
these sorts of activity.

kind of, sort of

The colloquialisms *kind of* and *sort of*, often written 'kinda' and 'sorta', are frequently used as fillers:

I've kind of lost my way.
I feel sort of funny.

Such usage is acceptable in everyday, casual speech, but not in writing. It is occasionally seen in Britain as a working-class variant of 'as it were' and 'rather':

He's happy now, sort of.
He's happy now, as it were.
She's sort of intelligent.
She's rather intelligent.

See also FILLER

kindly

Kindly looks like an adverb but it can function as both an adjective and an adverb:

a kindly smile

He behaved kindly.

Kindly is also used as an adverb in such requests as:

Will the owner of the vehicle parked outside the terminal kindly remove it at once.

See also FAIR/FAIRLY

King's English, Queen's English

The term *King's English* or *Queen's English* is determined by the sex of the ruling British monarch and is sometimes used, in Britain, to refer to Standard English. Both terms are a relic of the influence of the English court in establishing the prestigious variety of English that subsequently developed into the standard language. The power of the monarchy in affecting attitudes to language is still strong in parts of Britain.

See also ACCENT, NETWORK NORM, STANDARD ENGLISH

Kirghizia

An inhabitant of the republic, formerly part of the USSR, is a 'Kirghiz'; the derived adjective is the same. The capital is Frunze (formerly Pishpek). The republic is also spelled Kyrgyzstan.

Kiribati

An inhabitant of the island republic in the south-central Pacific is a 'Kiribati'; the derived adjective is 'Kiribatan'. The capital is Tarawa.

kneel

Kneel may be treated as a regular verb, as it is in America:

kneel(s), kneeled, kneeling
I kneeled down to thank God for my escape.

In Britain the past tense and the past participle are usually 'knelt':

I knelt quietly at the back of the chapel where I had knelt many times as a child.

See also -ED/-T

knit

Knit is usually treated as a regular verb when it means 'create a garment by using yarn and long, eyeless needles':

knit(s), knitted, knitting
My mother knitted me this beautiful Aran sweater.

When *knit* is used metaphorically to mean 'join closely together', it is now often irregular:

knit(s), knit, knitting, knit
The football team has knit the whole community together.

Knit also occurs in such phrases as:

a close-knit family.

It seems likely that *knit* in all its meanings will soon be treated like 'put' and 'set'.

See also -ED FORM

knock-on

The compound *knock-on* is widely used in the phrase:

knock-on effect
meaning an effect that has been triggered:

The knock-on effect of such mergers is redundancies.

Like all clichés, *knock-on* should be avoided in formal contexts.

knot

The noun *knot* is used as a unit of speed in connection with sailing and flying:

He is travelling at about 18 knots.

A *knot* is approximately 1.5 miles or 1.85 kilometres.

The phrase:

at a rate of knots
is used to mean 'very fast':

He was running at a rate of knots!

know

Know is an irregular verb:

know(s), knew, knowing, known
I knew his father well and I have known John since he was a baby.

knowledgable, knowledgeable

These are both acceptable spellings:

They are both knowledg(e)able about grapes.

See also -ABLE/-IBLE, SPELLING

Korea

Inhabitants of both North and South Korea are 'Koreans'; the derived adjective is the same. The capital of North Korea is Pyongyang. The capital of South Korea is Seoul.

kudos

Kudos is a singular noun meaning 'acclaim, prestige'. It comes from Greek *kudos*, 'acclaim' and has been overused recently:

I don't see why I should do all the work if you get all the kudos.

Kuwait

An inhabitant of the emirate is a 'Kuwaiti'; the derived adjective is the same. The capital is Kuwait City.

L

l

L is a consonant that has two main pronunciations. When it occurs before a vowel as in 'like', it is called a 'clear l', and when it occurs at the end of a syllable, as in 'full', it is called a 'dark l'.

The capital letter *L* is occasionally used to represent the £ (pound) symbol.

-l-, -ll-

It is not always easy to know when to use a single 'l' and when to double it, and the rules often differ in Britain and America. As far as British usage is concerned, the following rules apply in the majority of cases:

■ Verbs that end in a single vowel + 'l' double the 'l' before the suffixes beginning with a vowel, including '-able/-ible', '-ation', '-ed', '-er/-or':

distillable, distillation, distilled, distilling, distiller.

Such verbs do not double the 'l' before '-ment':

fulfilled, fulfilling, fulfilment.

■ Most words ending in 'll' drop an 'l' before suffixes that begin with a consonant, including '-ful', '-ly', '-ment', '-some':

fulsome, fully, instalment, wilful.

Such words retain their 'll' before '-ness':

fullness, illness.

See also SPELLING, UK AND US ENGLISH

laager, lager

These words are homophones. A *laager* is an Afrikaans word that derives from German *legar*, 'bed', 'lair'. It is used to refer to a camp, especially a circular formation of wagons. The word was popularized in the phrase:

the laager mentality

often applied to people who felt their culture and way of life were threatened or under siege.

Lager is a type of beer.

label

The word *label* can function as both a noun and a regular verb:

Will you put a label on each of the bags, please?
UK: label(s), labelled, labelling (You've labelled this packet incorrectly.)
US: label(s), labeled, labeling (You've labeled this packet incorrectly.)

laboratory

All users of English spell *laboratory* the same way:

Some of the most significant scientific research of the twentieth century was carried out in this laboratory.

In Britain, *laboratory* is pronounced as if it had four syllables with the main stress occurring on '-bor-'; in America, the five syllables are usually pronounced with 'la-' and '-to-' receiving greater stress than the other syllables.

labour, labor

These spellings are found in Britain and America respectively. The word is a synonym of 'work' and can function as a noun and a verb:

UK: the labour market
(He laboured for years to provide for his children.)
US: the labor market
(He labored for years.)

The derived words are spelled:

UK: labourer, labourism
US: laborer, laborism.

'Laborious' and 'laboriously' are spelled thus in both Britain and America.

lace

Lace derives ultimately from Latin *laqueus*, 'noose'. As a noun, it refers both to a delicate fabric and to the cord with which shoes are fastened:

The bride's dress was trimmed with cream lace.
I need some new laces for my trainers.

The verb *lace* can refer to fastening corsets or shoes, or to adding spirits to a drink:

Women used to be laced into their corsets.
He laced the coffee with brandy.

lackadaisical, lacksadaisical

Lackadaisical is a modified version of the obsolete interjection 'lackaday', meaning 'alas'. *Lackadaisical* means 'lazy, idle, purposeless':

This warm weather encourages me to be lackadaisical.

The regional variant *lacksadaisical* has probably been influenced by the adjective 'lax'.

laden, loaded

The verb *load* is now regular:

load(s), loaded, loading

but the old past participle *laden* survives, especially in the phrase:

heavily laden

which tends to be applied to animals rather than vehicles:

That donkey is too heavily laden.
That lorry is too heavily loaded/overloaded.

lady
See FEMALE/LADY/WOMAN

lama, llama
For most speakers these words are homophones. A *lama* is a Tibetan priest:

Lama comes from the Tibetan word *blama*, 'a priest'.

A *llama*, pronounced either 'lama' or 'hlama', is a South American animal that resembles a humpless camel:

Llamas are beasts of burden in many parts of the Andes.

lamentable
The adjective *lamentable* is stressed on the first syllable in Britain but often on the second syllable in America and other parts of the world:

Their plight was lamentable. They were being treated like slaves and yet we could do nothing to help.

landscape, portrait
These terms have been taken over from art and are applied to the shape of a page. A *portrait* page is one where the length is greater than the width. A *landscape* page is greater in width:

Most books have a portrait format but we've chosen landscape for our book of cartoons.

language change
As long as a language is spoken, it will change. Standard English has changed less in vocabulary and syntax over the last 300 years than in any other comparable period, but even during the last fifty years there have been changes. These have affected pronunciation:

the 't' in 'often' is now often pronounced

meaning:

'direct' can mean 'by phone', as in 'Lombard Direct'

usage:

'women' is now often preferred to 'ladies'

and grammar:

verbs such as 'knit' are being simplified.

langue and parole
The terms *langue* and *parole* were introduced into linguistics by the Swiss linguist, Ferdinand de Saussure. *Langue* means the total language knowledge of a speech community, whereas *parole* refers to actual instances of speech uttered by an individual on a specific occasion.

Parole is similar to the Chomskyan term 'performance', that is, 'actual speech samples', but *langue* differs from 'competence' in that *langue* is the language knowledge of a speech community, whereas 'competence' is the idealized knowledge of a language possessed by an ideal speaker-hearer.

See also COMPETENCE AND PERFORMANCE, TRANSFORMATIONAL GRAMMAR

languid, languor, languorous
Languid is one of the adjectives derived from *languor*. It means 'lacking in energy, spirit or enthusiasm':

I knew that the heat and humidity would affect the team but I didn't expect everyone to be quite so languid.

Languor is often misspelled. The '-uor' ending comes directly from Latin spelling. The word means 'physical or mental weariness':

Tennyson describes the languor that gradually saps the energy of the travellers in 'The Lotus Eaters'.

The adjective *languorous* is similar to *languid* but is perhaps a little stronger in its suggestion of weariness and lack of energy.

lanolin, lanoline
These are alternative spellings for a substance originally abstracted from wool. It comes ultimately from Latin *lana*, 'wool', + *oleum*, 'oil'.

Lanolin is used in certain medicinal ointments.

The last syllable may rhyme with 'tin' or with 'teen'.

Laos
An inhabitant of the southeast Asian country is a 'Laotian'; the derived adjective is the same. The capital is Vientiane.

lapse
See ELAPSE/LAPSE

largess, largesse
These spellings are both acceptable for 'exceptional generosity' or 'the favours received from exceptional generosity':

The family is renowned for its largess. The father left one-third of his fortune to found a museum and both sons have contributed generously to its upkeep.

I don't know how to thank you for such largesse. I was expecting a present but not such a generous one.

Largess may be pronounced like 'large', the word from which it derives, or the 'g' pronounced as it would be in French, the language from which the word was borrowed.

larva
The noun *larva* comes from Latin *larva*, 'ghost'. Its plural is 'larvae', which rhymes with 'Harvey':

A larva is an immature form of insect that develops into a different adult form by metamorphosis.

last

The adjective *last* can be ambiguous in that it can mean 'final':

This is the last piece of bread in the house.

and 'most recent':

I can't find John's last letter. I've found the one I got last week, but not the one I got yesterday.

Often, the context helps to clarify our meaning but a sentence such as:

I posted John's last cheque.

is ambiguous.

Last can also function as an adverb:

His horse came in last.

and as a noun in:

Last shall be first and first shall be last.

The phrase:

last but one

means 'next to final, penultimate':

He was on the last bus but one.

With short nouns such as 'bus', people often say:

He was on the last but one bus.

but with longer words or phrases such as 'ferry crossing', it is more acceptable to say and write:

the last ferry crossing but one.

See also FORMER/LATTER

late

Late can mean 'coming after the expected time':

My bus was late this morning.

'not early':

He goes to bed late and thinks everyone else should be wide awake at midnight.

and 'recently dead':

He is the son of the late Michael Smith.

A television advertisement urging people not to drive fast punned on the first and third meaning of *late* in the slogan:

Better late than the late.

lath, lathe

These nouns can be confused. A *lath* rhymes with 'bath' and means 'a narrow strip of wood':

We'll need about twenty laths to provide a support for the tiles.

Lathe rhymes with 'bathe' and is a machine for shaping wood or metal:

You can hire a lathe for the weekend.

Latin

English has borrowed heavily from *Latin*. The borrowings have affected three main groups:

■ Affixes: many of our most frequently used affixes are from Latin. These include the prefixes 'anti-', 'de-', 're-' and the suffixes '-able', '-ate', '-ation'.

■ Words: these may be identical to the originals, as with 'alias', 'apex', 'alibi', or modified as with 'bishop', 'formulas', 'virile'.

■ Phrases: many of these have no precise English equivalents. Among the most frequently cited are *ad hoc*, *ad infinitum* and *ad nauseam*.

The vocabularies of commerce, cooking, education, the law, warfare and spirituality rely heavily on Latin borrowings. The borrowings may be directly from Latin or via French or Italian. The previous sentence, for example, has ten words, five of which ('the', 'may', 'be', 'from' and 'of') are from Old English. The others are, either directly or indirectly, from Latin.

See also BORROWING

Latinate models of grammar

Until the twentieth century, many grammars of English were based on descriptions of Latin. Nouns were declined, following the Latin model, as if they had six cases and two numbers (singular and plural):

	Singular	Plural
Nominative	lord	lords
Vocative	O lord	O lords
Accusative	lord	lords
Genitive	lord's, of a lord	lords', of lords
Dative	to, for a lord	to, for lords
Ablative	by, with, from a lord	by, with, from lords

In English, however, only two case differences occur:

lord, lord's
lords, lords'

in that the genitive or possessive is different from the nominative. The difference is marked for the plural in the written medium but not in speech. For example, the genitive, 'the lords" in:

the lords' decision

sounds exactly like the nominative plural in:

The lords decided.

Verbs were conjugated as in Latin:

	Present	Past	Future
Singular			
1st person			
	I walk	I walked	I shall walk
2nd person			
	you walk	you walked	you will walk
3rd person (m)			
	he walks	he walked	he will walk
3rd person (f)			
	she walks	she walked	she will walk
3rd person (n)			
	it walks	it walked	it will walk

	Present	Past	Future
Plural			
1st person			
	we walk	we walked	we shall walk
2nd person			
	you walk	you walked	you will walk
3rd person			
	they walk	they walked	they will walk

(m = masculine, f = feminine, n = neuter)

and described in terms of four moods:

■ Indicative mood for statements:

I walked   I did not walk

■ Imperative mood for commands:

Walk!   Don't walk!

■ Interrogative mood for questions:

Did you walk?   Did you not walk?

■ Subjunctive mood for subordinate clauses, hypotheses and wishes:

I heard that you walked.
If you walked ...
May you walk far!

Latin could not end a sentence with a preposition:

A preposition is a word you can't end a sentence with.

or take an accusative pronoun after the COPULA verb:

It was him.

or split an infinitive:

to boldly go

and so such structures were condemned in Latinate models of English grammar.

The value of Latinate models was their clarity – it was easy to know what was right and what was wrong – and their ability to suggest the underlying similarities in all languages.

Their main weaknesses were that they failed to stress that each language is unique and must be described in its own terms, and that they were prescriptive and therefore did not fully allow for the changes that occur in all living languages.

See GRAMMAR

latinism

The term *latinism* is used for three features of language:

■ A word, phrase or idiom borrowed from Latin:

This is called a *parabola*.
I don't like such *ad hoc* arrangements.
Hamlet's 'To be or not to be' speech is a variation on the theme of *Timor mortis conturbat me*.

■ A preference for a polysyllabic style using Latin-derived words:

She proceeded to incise the protuberance.

rather than:

She went on to cut the bump.

■ A use of constructions based on Latin models:

Having fulfilled our expectations, she left.
On hearing the news, he slept peacefully.
Of arms and the man I sing.

Latinisms involve the conscious use of learned language. They are a feature of formal prose and can be pretentious in speech or informal writing.

See also ELEGANT VARIATION

latter
See FORMER/LATTER

Latvia

An inhabitant of the republic, formerly in the USSR, is a 'Latvian'; the derived adjective is the same. The capital is Riga. The language of Latvia is Lettish.

laudable, laudatory

These words both derive from Latin *laudare*, 'to praise'. *Laudable* is an adjective meaning 'praiseworthy':

I'd like to commend the laudable efforts you have made to improve your driving.

Laudatory is an adjective meaning 'eulogistic, expressing praise':

It's a shame he kept such laudatory comments for her obituary.

launch (window)

The word 'launch' is now widely used to mean 'start', 'set in motion':

They launched their new product yesterday.
I attended the launch of her new book.

Like all over-used words, *launch* should be avoided in formal usage.

The phrase *launch window* is derived from 'weather window' and refers to the limited period during which a space vehicle may be launched on a particular mission. Like much space and computer terminology, it has been borrowed by the media and used to mean 'limited time for a particular effect':

The launch window for this venture is likely to be shorter than the three weeks mentioned by the firm. As soon as sufficient funds have been raised, the issue will close.

launder

The verb *launder* has recently been given a

metaphorical extension. It can now refer to putting illegally earned money into legitimate businesses:

The drug barons have been able to launder billions of pounds.

lavatory, toilet, washroom

Lavatory should be used with care because it is a taboo word for some speakers and it can also have different meanings in Britain and America. In Britain, a *lavatory* is a water closet or a room containing a WC. In America, it is a place where one can wash one's hands. There are many synonyms for *lavatory* in English, including BATHROOM, 'loo', 'powder room', 'toilet' and, more recently, 'comfort station'. Each word carries connotations that may relate to age, class or gender.

The word *toilet* to mean 'lavatory' is often regarded as a lower-class marker in British English although it is often used in signs in public places. The usual American equivalent is 'bathroom'. This can, however, be ambiguous in British English, where a bathroom may not necessarily have a *toilet*. The most widely-used informal word in Britain is 'loo':

The loo is upstairs, first on the right.

The most widely-used term internationally at present is 'washroom'.

See also UK AND US ENGLISH

lawful, legal, legitimate

These adjectives are all associated with the law but they are differentiated. *Lawful* means 'permitted by law':

When is it lawful to drive a car in the bus lane?
Mary is his lawful wife.

Legal can usually be substituted for *lawful*, but it has the additional meaning of 'relating to law':

He's in the legal profession.
*He's in the lawful profession.

Legitimate is most frequently applied to children born inside a marriage:

Charles II had no legitimate children.

It can also mean 'genuine, valid':

They have no legitimate reason for being here.

lay, lie

These irregular verbs are sometimes misused because their forms and their meanings overlap.

Lay is often used instead of *lie* in informal speech, but the verbs should be kept separate:

lay(s), laid, laying
We shall lay him to rest in the family vault.
I lay down and slept peacefully.

Lay means 'put someone or something down', and 'produce an egg'. It takes an object:

We were told to lay the babies on their backs.
John laid the bricks and I did the plastering.
This is the goose that laid a golden egg.

Lie means 'be supine or recumbent', 'be in a horizontal position'. It is an irregular verb and it does not take an object:

lie(s), lay, lying, lain.
Don't lie on the floor. Sit up.

The most frequent confusion of these verbs involves the use of 'laying' for 'lying':

I was lying in the shade.
He was lying on the bed.
*He was just laying there, doing nothing.
*He was laying on the bed.

Both *lay* and *lie* have homophones. *Lay* can function as an adjective meaning 'not a cleric' and, more recently, 'not a specialist':

This church appeal is aimed at our lay people.
The book is written for linguists and lay people alike.

Lie can be a noun or a verb related to telling untruths:

That's a lie! I know that John didn't do it because I did!
He lied to me once so how can I ever trust him?
You should not have been put in a position where you felt you had to lie.

These verbs come from different Old English verbs, *leogan*, 'to speak untruthfully', and *licgan*, 'to be supine'.

See also LIAR

lb

The abbreviation for 'pound' is lb. This is an abbreviation of Latin *libra*, 'scales'. The Latin weight was equal to about 12 ounces, whereas an English 'pound' contains 16 ounces:

20kg = 44lb.

The plural is lb, not *lbs.

lead

The English verb *lead* meaning 'go before, take someone or something to a place' is irregular:

lead(s), led, leading
He used to lead the team onto the field.
She led the team for four years.

The English noun *lead* looks like the verb but rhymes with 'dead':

The chemical name for lead is plumbum.

It also rhymes with the past tense form 'led'. The related adjective 'leaden' rhymes with 'redden' and means 'dull, heavy':

Look at the leaden sky. We'll have rain soon.

leading question

The phrase *leading question* has been popularized by the media. It was originally limited to the law courts and referred to questions that seek to influence the witness's answer or to insert information that is not acceptable. A question such as:

Do you know the accused to be a violent man, capable of attacking his neighbour?

could be regarded as *leading*.

The phrase is now often used to refer to a question that might prove embarrassing to answer:

I felt that it was wrong of him to ask such a leading question when her morals were not the issue in the case.

leak

This word has been overused by the media to refer to unofficial disclosures:

The party manifesto has been leaked to the press.

The Prime Minister plans to stop these harmful leaks and to find the mole or moles responsible for them.

lean

The verb *lean* has two past tense forms and two past participles:

lean(s), leaned, leaning, leaned
lean (s), leant, leaning, leant
I leaned/leant on the wall for support.

In Britain, 'leant' is perfectly acceptable and it is pronounced to rhyme with 'bent'; in America, 'leaned' is more widespread and it rhymes with 'gleaned'.

See also -ED/-T

leap

Leap, like *lean*, has two acceptable past tense and past participle forms:

leap(s), leaped, leaping, leaped
leap(s), leapt, leaping, leapt
She leaped/leapt for joy when she heard the news.

Even when speakers use 'leaped', they often rhyme it with 'swept', although the pronunciation that rhymes with 'peeped' is also heard.

leap-frog

Leap-frog can function as the name of a children's game and as verb meaning 'advance in leaps':

I don't think I could play leap-frog any more. I doubt that I'd be able to put my hands on someone's back and leap over them.

Our breakthrough in technology means that we have leap-frogged over our competitors.

The verb is regular and doubles the 'g' in both British and American English:

leap-frog(s), leap-frogged, leap-frogging.

learn, teach

These two verbs are associated with imparting and acquiring knowledge. Standard English uses *learn* when the meaning intended is 'study', 'receive instruction', and *teach* when the meaning intended is 'instruct', 'cause someone to learn'. The verbs are sometimes called 'reciprocal verbs' because they can be complementary:

I am teaching him Greek.
He is learning Greek from me.

Teach is an irregular verb:

teach(es), taught, teaching
She has taught here for twenty years.

It can be followed by a pronoun, noun, reflexive pronoun, noun phrase and subordinate clause:

She taught me (French).
She taught Henry (French).
She taught herself (French).
She taught the Sixth Form twice a week.
She taught (us) that we achieved most when we worked together.

Learn has two acceptable past tense and past participle forms:

learn(s), learned, learning, learned
learn(s), learnt, learning, learnt.

In many nonstandard varieties of English, *learn* is over-applied and used for both the productive and the receptive activities:

*She was learning me to draw.

but *learn* cannot be followed by a personal pronoun other than 'it', by a reflexive pronoun or a human object:

I learned it at school.
*I learned him French.
*He learned himself Greek.
*He learned John.

lease

See HIRE/LEASE/LET/RENT

least

Least can function as a superlative adjective. It is always used in comparisons of three or more:

I have a little knowledge.
I have less knowledge than John.
I have least knowledge.

It can also function as a superlative adverb:

I like it a little.
I like this less.
I like this least.

Least can also function as a noun:

That is the least I can expect.

The adverbs 'leastways' and 'leastwise' are often stigmatized and so it is preferable to use the phrase 'at least':

*Leastways, I'll have my freedom.

At least I'll have my freedom.

See also FEWER/LESS/LESSER, LITTLE

leave

Leave is an irregular verb:

leave(s), left, leaving

John left school when he was sixteen.

Leave is sometimes used where 'let' would be more appropriate:

?*Leave me be.

Let me be.

The expression:

Leave me alone.

is, however, more likely to occur.

See also LET

Lebanon

An inhabitant of the Middle Eastern republic is a 'Lebanese'; the derived adjective is the same. The capital is Beirut.

legal

See LAWFUL/LEGAL/LEGITIMATE

legendary

Legendary used to mean 'associated with legend':

King Arthur is a legendary hero.

Recently, it has been widely used to mean 'famous':

This is one of the best recordings made by the legendary Bob Dylan.

legible, readable

These adjectives both relate to reading, but they are occasionally misused. *Legible* means 'able to be deciphered and read':

Her handwriting is barely legible.

I cannot give this script a mark. It is simply not legible.

Readable often means 'able to be read with enjoyment' or 'easy to read':

It is the most readable novel that I have come across.

Her book is the most readable introduction to the subject of language acquisition.

See also ELIGIBLE/ILLEGIBLE/UNREADABLE

legitimate

See LAWFUL/LEGAL/LEGITIMATE

leisure

The noun *leisure* is often misspelled. It comes via French *leisir* 'permission', 'freedom' from Latin *licere*, 'to be allowed', and means 'time or opportunity for relaxation':

I'm on holiday and entitled to a little leisure.

In Britain, *leisure* rhymes with 'pleasure'; in America, it tends to rhyme with 'seizure'.

lend

See BORROW/LEND/LOAN

lengthways, lengthwise

In Britain, *lengthwise* is preferred in adjectival usage:

It should be a lengthwise cut.

and it is the preferred form for both the adjective and adverb in America. The words are equally acceptable as adverbs in British English:

Place the shelf lengthways and carefully position each bracket.

The material should be cut lengthwise.

See also -WAYS/-WISE

lengthy

Lengthy means 'extremely long' and it is often a temporal rather than a spatial adjective:

a lengthy meeting.

It has overtones of boredom:

We had to sit through his lengthy address at two graduation ceremonies.

It should not be used where 'long' is sufficient:

*She had lovely, lengthy hair.

Careful users pronounce the 'ng', however, in casual speech, most people rhyme 'length' with 'tenth'.

lenience, leniency

These forms are both acceptable in all contexts:

The judge is expected to show lenience.

The judge is expected to show leniency.

although some speakers prefer *leniency*.

lens

Lens is a singular noun deriving from Latin *lens*, 'lentil', because of its shape:

I have a lens that can converge transmitted light.

The plural is 'lenses':

Although we promise to make 99 per cent of our lenses within an hour, your lenses will take about one week to make.

leopard

The word *leopard* is often misspelled, partly because the 'o' is not pronounced. It comes from Latin *leopardus*, 'lion + pard':

There are very few leopards left in the forests now.

Lesotho

An inhabitant of the southern African country, formerly Basutoland, is a 'Sotho'; the derived adjective is the same. The capital is Maseru.

less, lesser
See FEWER/LESS/LESSER

lest

Lest is an obsolescent conjunction meaning 'so as to prevent any possibility that':

I shall strive to do well lest I fail in my endeavours.

If *lest* is used, it requires one of two structures. It must be followed by 'should':

I'll save these books lest I should need them one day.

or by the unmarked form of the verb, that is, the infinitive without 'to':

He ran out of the burning building lest he perish.

Notice that we do not say 'perished' or 'perishes'. This usage goes back to a time when English had a subjunctive. We have a few relics of this in contemporary English:

Long live the queen! (not 'lives')
If this be true ... (not 'is')
... lest she fail (not 'fails').

See also SUBJUNCTIVE

let

Let is an irregular verb meaning 'allow, permit':

let(s), let, letting, let
They won't let him go to France.

It is often used as an auxiliary verb to express a request, proposal or warning:

Please let me go to France.
Let's try again.
Let me catch you doing that again and I'll have your guts for garters.

When *let* is used in this way, it always takes the object pronoun, 'me', 'her', 'him', 'us', 'them':

Let her go.*Let she go.

Sometimes people misuse *let* when it is followed by a plural construction:

*Let Mary and I do it.
Let Mary and me do it.
Let us do it.

The negative form of 'Let's' is 'Let's not':

Let's go to town. No, let's not (bother).

Often, in colloquial speech, people say:

UK: Don't let's do it.
US: Let's don't do it.

but neither of these usages is regarded as fully acceptable.

See also HIRE/LEASE/LET/RENT, LEAVE

letters

Letters can range from intimate to extremely formal. Their style should take the following elements into account: the purpose (for example, congratulations, gossip, job application, sympathy) and the addressee (for example, a close contemporary, a parent, the manager of a firm, a bereaved friend or acquaintance).

The two main types of letter are personal and official and the conventions differ slightly in Britain and America.

The writer's address is usually given at the top right-hand corner of the first page. The lines of the address start either directly below each other or each line starts two letter spaces to the right of the line above. The date comes immediately below this address. A small margin is left at the right-hand side of the page.

When writing a business or official letter, the addressee's name and address are given close to the left-hand margin and two spaces lower than the date. The margin on the left-hand side is conventionally wider than that on the right. Men's names may be given as:

Mr Jones
Mr J. Jones
Mr James Jones.

Forms of women's names include:

Ms Jones
Mrs Jones
Miss/Ms/Mrs A. Jones
Miss/Mrs/Ms Anne Jones

with 'Ms' being the preferred form for younger women.

Professional titles take the place of 'Miss', 'Mr', 'Mrs' and 'Ms':

Dr A. Jones
Professor J. Jones.

A space of one or more lines is left between the recipient's address and the salutation 'Dear X', which occurs close to the left-hand margin. Formal business letters begin 'Dear Sir' or 'Dear Madam'; less formal letters imply varying degrees of intimacy by such uses as 'Dear Ms Jones', 'My dear James'. The main differences between salutation conventions in the UK and the United States are as follows:

UK	US
Dear Ms Jones	Dear Anne Jones
Dear Sirs	Gentlemen
Dear Anne,	Dear Anne:

The first sentence of the letter begins with a capital letter and starts underneath the end of the salutation. Subsequent paragraphs are indicated by indenting five spaces. If indentation is not used, double spaces are left between paragraphs.

Letters opening with the formal greetings 'Dear Sir(s)', 'Dear Madam' or 'Gentlemen' close as follows:

UK	US
Yours faithfully	Yours sincerely

Letters with less formal greetings may use a range of endings 'Sincerely', 'Yours', 'Best wishes', 'Love' or an individual conclusion. Each of these endings conforms to the spacing for paragraphs and may be followed by a comma.

The writer's name is typed or printed below the signature in formal letters and, if the writer has a special function, this is given either after or directly under the name:

Anne Jones, Head of Department
James Jones
Club Secretary.

leukaemia, leukemia
Both spellings are acceptable for this chronic blood disease. The second is the norm in America and is growing in use in Britain.

level
Level can function as an adjective meaning 'having a surface of equal height':
The table must be absolutely level for snooker.
as a noun, especially in the phrase:
on the level
and as a regular verb. The 'l' is doubled before '-ed' and '-ing' in British English:
UK: level(s), levelled, levelling (This win has levelled the series.)
US: level(s), leveled, leveling (This win has leveled the series.)

lexical verb
In verb phrases, one to five verbs may co-occur as a unit:
(she) trained
(she) may have been being trained.
The final verb in the sequence is known as the 'head verb' or *lexical verb*. The others are known as 'auxiliaries'.

See also AUXILIARY, VERB

lexicography, lexicology
These nouns are often confused because their meanings overlap and they both derive from Greek *lexis*, 'word'. *Lexicography* refers to the compiling of dictionaries and the principles involved in such compilation:
Samuel Johnson and Noah Webster were eminent lexicographers.

Lexicology refers to the study of vocabulary and includes the history, development and organization of words. The study may or may not be in alphabetical order and may include an examination of antonyms, collocations, hyponyms, idioms, synonyms, toponyms and polysemy.

See also LEXICON/LEXIS, VOCABULARY

lexicon, lexis
The noun *lexicon* derives from Greek *lexikon*, 'pertaining to words'. It can mean: the alphabetically arranged inventory of the words of a language together with their definitions; the vocabulary of a language (spoken or written); the vocabulary of a speaker or a group of speakers; and the vocabulary employed in a text.

The word *lexis*, which derives from Greek *lexis*, 'speech', 'word', is used as a synonym for 'vocabulary', especially a subset of the entire vocabulary of a language:
The lexis employed in his poetry is mainly of Germanic origin.

See also VOCABULARY

liable to, likely to
These phrases both imply probability:
Hurricanes are liable to occur in the Caribbean in August.
I'm not likely to be an astronaut, am I?
Liable to suggests regularity of occurrence; *likely to* suggests only that the occurrence is possible. In addition, *liable to* is normally associated with unpleasant occurrences:
He's liable to walk out on the team.
It is also used to mean 'subject to' or to refer to habitual probability:
He's liable to lose his temper if things don't run smoothly.
She is liable to blackouts, triggered occasionally by flickering lights.

Likely to, however, can be associated with pleasant and unpleasant occurrences:
The weather's likely to be fine tomorrow.
The weather's likely to be dull tomorrow.

See also APT/LIABLE

liaise, liaison
These words are frequently misspelled. They come from French *lier*, 'to bind', and mean 'communicate and retain contact with':
We've asked Patrick to liaise with the other boards.

Liaison means 'close contact' and it can sometimes have sexual connotations:
I'm not certain that their liaison is as innocent as he suggests.
Liaise is a BACK FORMATION from *liaison*.

liar
The noun *liar* derives from the verb 'lie', meaning 'tell untruths'. It is frequently misspelled because it ends in '-ar', not '-er':
LIAR AND CHEAT (headline)
Nobody likes to be called a liar.

See also LAY/LIE

libel, slander

Libel and *slander* both involve false accusations about a person. *Libel* tends to occur in the written medium:

Such libel cannot and will not go unchallenged.

When *libel* occurs as a verb, the 'l' is doubled before '-ed' and '-ing' in Britain but not in America:

UK: libel(s), libelled, libelling (The minister was libelled in her book.)

US: libel(s), libeled, libeling (The minister was libeled in her book.)

Slander, like 'libel', involves statements that are calculated to injure a person's character. *Slander* is normally spoken whereas 'libel' is written, although this distinction tends to be blurred in popular usage. *Slander* can occur as a noun or a regular verb:

It is hard to prove slander unless there are uninvolved witnesses.

slander(s), slandered, slandering

I was prepared to overlook the early innuendoes but it is impossible to overlook an insult when one is slandered in public.

liberalism, liberality

Liberalism comes from Latin *liber*, 'free', and refers to broadmindedness or freedom from prejudice:

The family has always been renowned for its liberalism and total lack of prejudice.

Liberality comes from the same Latin word but means 'generosity':

I've never known such liberality. They have put their home and all that they have at our disposal.

Liberia

An inhabitant of the West African country is a 'Liberian'; the derived adjective is the same. The capital is Monrovia.

libido

The noun *libido*, a Latin borrowing meaning 'lust, desire', is used in psychoanalysis:

The libido is the psychic energy emanating from the id.

In the media, it is often used as a synonym for 'sexual desire':

Hollywood emphasized his libido by photographing him with a series of beautiful girls.

library

Careful speakers pronounce both 'r's in *library*, but in rapid speech many omit the first 'r'.

See also HAPLOGRAPHY/DITTOGRAPHY

libretto

Libretto is an Italian diminutive of *libro*, 'book'.

In English, it means 'a text written for and set to music in an opera' and it has two acceptable plurals, 'librettos' and 'libretti':

These librettos were written for operas.

Libya

An inhabitant of the North African country is a 'Libyan'; the derived adjective is the same. The capital is Tripoli.

licence, license

In Britain, the noun *licence* is spelled with '-ence' and the verb is spelled with '-ense':

I seem to have lost my driving licence.

Have you licensed the television yet?

In America, the '-ense' ending is used for both noun and verb:

It is not easy to get a gun license.

I am licensed to carry a gun.

lichen

Lichen is a kind of moss that can grow on rock, trees or on the ground. It has two acceptable pronunciations. It may be a homophone of 'liken' or it may rhyme with 'kitchen'.

licorice

See also LIQUORICE/LICORICE

lie

See LAY/LIE

Liechtenstein

An inhabitant of the European principality is a 'Liechtensteiner'; the derived adjective is 'Liechtenstein'. The capital is Vaduz.

lieu

Lieu comes from French *lieu*, 'place', and is widely used in the phrase:

in lieu of

I'll gladly take that computer in lieu of the money you owe me.

Lieu is often pronounced 'loo' but careful speakers prefer to say 'lyoo'.

lieutenant

A *lieutenant* is an officer. In British English the first syllable is pronounced to rhyme with 'deaf', but in American English it rhymes with 'do'. The situation is further complicated by the fact that in the British navy the first syllable is pronounced like 'le' in French.

lifelong, livelong

Lifelong is an adjective meaning 'throughout one's life':

I have just lost a lifelong friend. He and I started school together and were close friends for fifty years.

Certain elements of the press use *lifelong* as a euphemism for 'homosexual':

He now lives in Scotland with his lifelong partner.

Livelong is an obsolescent word meaning 'entire'. It rarely occurs outside the phrase 'the *livelong* day':

They sang and danced the livelong day.

The 'live' in *livelong* is pronounced like 'give', not 'dive'.

lifestyle

Lifestyle, meaning 'way of life', has been overused in the media:

What is required is a fundamental rethink of our lifestyle.

lift

See ELEVATOR/LIFT

light, lighted, lit

The verb *light* has two acceptable past tense and past participle forms:

light(s), lit, lighting, lit
He struck a match and lit his pipe.

light(s), lighted, lighting
He lighted the Christmas tree.

In Britain, *lit* is used much more frequently than *lighted*, which is the preferred American term.

British and Americans speakers both use *lighted* as an adjective:

You must never let children play with lighted matches.

light year

A *light year* is a measurement used in astronomy. It refers to the distance that light can travel in a year, that is:

186,000 x 60 x 60 x 24 x 365 miles
The nearest solar system is many light years from earth.

lightening, lightning

These words are occasionally confused. *Lightening* is the present participle of 'lighten', meaning 'make less dark or less heavy':

The doors were very dark so we've been stripping the dark varnish and lightening them.
Your help is lightening my load.

Lightning is a flash of electricity in the sky. It is normally preceded by 'thunder':

It is rare to get thunder and lightning in winter.

like

Like can function as an adjective meaning 'similar':

Like minds are attracted to this subject.

as a noun:

I have little time for soap operas and the like.

and as a preposition:

He looks like me.

It is also used as a FILLER:

He was staring at us, like, really staring.

Like is acceptable as a conjunction in such American-influenced sentences as:

She spent money like it was going out of style.

and such usage may oust 'as if' in casual styles:

It looks like it could rain.
She doesn't love you like I do.

However, in formal contexts, *like* is not acceptable as a conjunction:

* She sang well, like she always does.
She sang well, as she always does.

See also CONJUNCTION

like, as

Like functions as a preposition in comparisons:

This kitchen looks like a bomb site!
It's like a balloon.

As also functions in similes:

It is as round as a hoop.

and this similarity in usage may have helped the spread of *like* as a conjunction.

See also AS, CONJUNCTION, LIKE, SIMILE

like, love

These verbs both imply affection, enjoyment and desire:

He likes Mary but he loves Triona.
I like tea but I love coffee.
She'd like a car but she'd really love a boat.

Love is often stronger than *like* and is used to describe the feeling one has for family and country:

I love my children.
I love my country.

Love is not normally modified by 'quite':

*He quite loves her.
He quite likes her.

Like tends to be used to indicate approval and choice:

I like your way with words.
Go wherever you like.

Both words can be used as nouns:

Give us a list of your likes and dislikes.
My love for you is as strong as ever.

Like is occasionally used as a noun meaning 'equal':

Where will we ever find her like?

but this usage is no longer common.

-like

The suffix *-like* is added to nouns to form adjectives:

childlike = resembling a child
lifelike = resembling life.

Usually, these adjectives are not hyphenated unless they are unusual:

dinosaur-like

or could cause misunderstanding:

mussel-like.

likeable, likable

These spellings are both acceptable but *likeable* is more widely used:

She is pleasant, friendly and one of the most likeable people I have ever met.

likely to

See LIABLE TO/LIKELY TO

lineage, linage

These words are rarely used in the same context, but *lineage* is sometimes used for both. *Lineage* has three syllables and the first two rhyme with 'finny'. It refers to the direct descent from an ancestor:

They can trace their lineage to Robert the Bruce.

Linage or *lineage* has two syllables and the first part of the word is pronounced 'line'. It refers to the number of lines in a written or printed text:

Our linage requires that you delete three lines from this page.

lineament, liniment

These nouns are occasionally confused. *Lineament* is often pluralized and means 'a distinctive feature or characteristic':

Facial lineaments are most clearly revealed when one is asleep or relaxed.

Liniment is a medicated liquid used as a rub:

I'm very stiff. Do you think that liniment would help?

lingerie

The noun *lingerie* was borrowed from French *lingerie*, 'linen undergarments' and is used to mean 'women's underwear and nightwear' and it often suggests garments that are frilly, lacy and expensive:

Our new Department has a range of imported lingerie of the highest quality.

The first syllable of *lingerie* is usually pronounced like the first syllable in 'longevity'.

lingo

The noun *lingo* probably comes from Portuguese *lingoa*, 'language', 'tongue'. It tends to be used for:

■ Non-native varieties of languages, such as pidgins, which have often been disparagingly described as 'bastard lingos'

■ Foreign languages, especially ones that are non-prestigious:

Can you make out her lingo?
I'm afraid I don't speak the lingo.

■ The language of a particular group of people:

The lingo of many of the professions is deliberately designed to fool the lay person.

See also CANT, JARGON, PIDGIN AND CREOLE

Lingua Franca, lingua franca

The name *Lingua Franca* comes from Italian and means 'Frankish Tongue'. When it is written with capital letters, it refers to a simplified language that was used as a trade language in the Mediterranean from the time of the Crusades. Although it probably predates the Crusades the multilingual Crusaders helped to spread *Lingua Franca*.

The vocabulary of *Lingua Franca* was Romance, inflections were dropped and the syntax was simple, regular and fixed, thus making *Lingua Franca* one of the earliest known pidgins as well as one of the most viable intergroup contact languages in history.

The term *lingua franca* with lower case letters has been extended to any language that facilitates communication between people with different mother tongues:

English may now be regarded as the world's lingua franca.

Since the phrase is Italian, its correct plural is 'lingue franche', but increasingly its plural is being anglicized to 'lingu francas'.

See also PIDGIN AND CREOLE

linguist, polyglot

The noun *linguist* is used with two distinct meanings: a person who makes a scientific study of language:

Mary wants to be a linguist and is concentrating on grammar.

and a *polyglot* – that is, a person who is has skills in several languages:

She's a gifted linguist and speaks several languages fluently.

linguistics

Linguistics is usually defined as the scientific study of language. Linguists study all aspects of language, including:

- Phonology (the study of sounds and sound patterns)

- Morphology (the study of morphemes, that is, meaningful combinations of sounds)

- Lexicology (the study of words)

- Syntax (the study of meaningful combinations of words)

- Semantics (the study of meaning).

Among the hybrid disciplines studied by linguists are:

- Psycholinguistics (the relationship between language and the mind)

- Sociolinguistics (the uses of language in society)

- Stylistics (the study of style and styles).

See also GRAMMAR

liniment

See LINEAMENT/LINIMENT

linkage

Linkage is defined as the patterns that give cohesion to a text. It involves any techniques that link one part of a text with another and may include alliteration, assonance, intonation, rhyme and rhythm. The commonest items of linkage are units that:

- Substitute for nouns or noun phrases, including pronouns and phrases such as 'the former', 'the latter'

- Substitute for verbs, including auxiliaries and phrases such as 'to do so'

- Imply addition, including conjunctions such as 'and', 'and so' and adverbs such as 'furthermore'

- Imply alternatives, including 'either', 'or', 'otherwise'

- Imply a sequence, including numbers, 'first', 'second' and adverbs such as 'then', 'finally'

- Imply cause and effect, including 'because', 'therefore'

- Imply conditions, including 'if', 'unless'

- Imply time, including 'after', 'before', 'later'.

See also COHERENCE/COHESION, PARALLELISM

liquefy, liquify

These spellings are both acceptable. They derive from Latin *liquefacere*, 'cause something to become a liquid'. The following alternative spellings for the derived words are also acceptable:

liquefactive, liquifactive
liquefaction, liquifaction
liquefiable, liquifiable
liquefier, liquifier.

The form ending in '-efy' is often given first in dictionaries but, because of the influence of 'liquid', the '-ify' is more widely used:

liquefy(ies), liquefied, liquefying
liquify(ies), liquified, liquifying
What should we do to liquefy this gas?

See also PUTREFY

liqueur, liquor

These nouns both come from Latin *liquere*, 'to be liquid', but they have developed distinct meanings. A *liqueur* is a highly flavoured, sweetened spirit or, more recently, a hollow chocolate containing *liqueur*:

Drambuie is a Scottish liqueur.

In Britain, *liquor* is often misspelled. It ends in '-or', not '-our'. It refers collectively to alcoholic drinks, especially spirits:

The supermarket has closed its liquor section but it will continue to sell wines.

liquorice, licorice

These spellings are used in Britain and America respectively. The name has nothing to do with 'liquor' but comes from Greek *glukus + rhiza*, 'sweet + root':

Let's have some Liquorice Allsorts.

The last syllable may rhyme with 'kiss' or 'wish', and in Britain this second pronunciation has given rise to the spellings 'lickerish' and 'liquorish'.

listen

See HEAR/LISTEN

lit

See LIGHT/LIGHTED/LIT

liter, litre

These spellings are standard in America and Britain respectively. A *litre* is equivalent to 1.76 UK pints and 2.11 US pints:

I still haven't got used to buying petrol in litres. I wish that petrol stations would quote the price in gallons.

literally

Literally means 'actually', 'truly' as opposed to 'metaphorically':

This is not a story. It may sound far-fetched, but these events literally took place here in this village, exactly as we shall recount.

Because of overuse, it has been bleached of much of its meaning and is often used as an intensifier, with little meaning:

I was literally dying of cold.

She was literally swept off her feet.

See also BLEACHING

literature

Literature derives from Latin *litteratura*, 'writing', but its meaning has been widened. It can refer to any type of written material:

I've got some literature somewhere on pesticides.

but it is most frequently applied to works of imagination, whether oral or written:

Every society in the world has a language and a literature.

The phrase 'literary genre' is used to describe a subdivision of literature according to purpose and structure. The three basic literary genres are poetry, drama and prose fiction or the novel.

See also STILE/STYLE

Lithuania

An inhabitant of the republic, formerly in the USSR, is a 'Lithanian'; the derived adjective is the same. The capital is Vilnius.

litotes

Litotes comes from Greek *litos*, 'small', and is a figure of speech involving understatement:

It was nothing.

How can you call a heart attack 'nothing'?

The first syllable of *litotes* rhymes with 'high' and the third with 'bees', and the same form is used for both singular and plural:

These litotes are clichés.

Litotes often features a negative or double negative construction that is used to emphasize a positive:

The Sultan is certainly not poor. (He's the wealthiest person in the world.)

Flash floods are not uncommon in these parts. (They are very common.)

Litotes often depends on intonation for its full effect and so is frequently found in speech.

See also FIGURE OF SPEECH, MEIOSIS, UNDERSTATEMENT

little

Little can function as an adjective:

a little girl

as an adverb:

She little knew what that future would hold.

and as a noun:

He gave away the little that he had.

It can be used with countable nouns to refer to size:

A little elephant is bigger than a big flea.

With uncountable nouns, it refers to quantity:

There is little beauty left in our cities.

When *little* occurs as an adjective, it is frequently used attributively:

I saw a little cottage in the Dales.

?The cottage is little.

and it can imply affection or disdain:

It's a lovely little place!

It's a horrible little place!

In Britain, *little* is occasionally used to indicate dislike and social condescension rather than size:

I don't know why she went and married that awful little man.

Little is not normally graded as a modifier of countable nouns:

the little cottage/the small cottage

the smaller cottage

the smallest cottage.

Occasionally, children use the forms 'littler' and 'littlest' and a number of television programmes, such as *The Littlest Hobo*, have adopted their usage.

The comparative and superlative forms of *little* as a modifier of uncountable nouns and as an adverb are 'less' and 'least':

little money

less money

least money

She said little to me.

She said less to me.

She said least to me.

When *little* is used without a determiner before an uncountable noun, it has negative implications:

I have little respect for his behaviour.

There is little news from the war zone.

Similar implications apply when *little* is used adverbially:

I heard little that I did not already know.

See also COUNTABLE AND UNCOUNTABLE, FEWER/LESS/LESSER, GRADABLE, LEAST

live

When *live* functions as a verb, it rhymes with 'give'; when it functions as an adjective, it rhymes with 'hive':

Was the concert live or recorded?

livelong

See LIFELONG/LIVELONG

livid

The adjective *livid* comes from Latin *lividus*, 'black and blue', a meaning that it could still have in the sentence:

His wound was livid.

Livid has been used so often as a synonym for 'angry' that it is often associated with 'red':

I was livid with John. I could feel my face redden as I told him what I thought of his poor behaviour.

living room

There are many different words for the room in the house where people relax. For some, it is *living room*, for others 'sitting room' or LOUNGE. One's choice may indicate class or region:

We had to take the TV out of the living room because the children always wanted to watch it when we had visitors.

loaded

See LADEN/LOADED

loadstar, lodestar

These spellings are both acceptable equivalents for the Pole star:

Mariners in the northern hemisphere navigated by means of the lodestar.

loadstone, lodestone

These are variant spellings for a piece of rock that is naturally magnetic. The second spelling is more widespread:

A lodestone means a guiding stone.

Like LODESTAR, this word is virtually obsolete.

loaf

The plural of *loaf* is always 'loaves':

They had five loaves.

loan

See BORROW/LEND/LOAN

loath, loathe, loth

Loath and *loth* are alternative spellings for the adjective that rhymes with 'both' and means 'extremely reluctant':

They were loth to leave their comfortable home but they had no choice in the matter.

Loathe is a verb that rhymes with 'clothe' and means 'detest':

He loathed the very idea of having to sing in public.

local, locale

Local is most frequently used as an adjective meaning 'nearby', 'close at hand':

The children go to the local school.

Local is also used as a noun in Britain meaning 'nearby pub':

The men play snooker at their local.

Locale is stressed on the second syllable and rhymes with 'Carl'. It means 'place or area, often one where something significant occurred':

The original 'Boot Hill' graveyard is reputed to have been in this locale.

location, locality

These nouns both derive from Latin *locus*, 'place', but they have developed distinct meanings. *Location* means 'exact position':

We are trying to find the location of the Battle of Stamford Bridge.

Locality means 'general area' or 'approximate position':

I don't know exactly where the battle took place but it was certainly in this locality.

locum

The noun *locum* meaning 'temporary replacement for a doctor', comes from the Latin phrase *locum tenens*, 'holding the place':

Dr Edwards is not available today but we could give you an appointment with her locum.

The usual plural is 'locums':

It is not unusual to find that all night visits are made by locums.

lodestar

See LOADSTAR/LODESTAR

lodestone

See LOADSTONE/LODESTONE

logo

A *logo* is a trademark or emblem of a firm or company. It is an abbreviation of 'logotype':

Some companies spend millions of pounds on their logos because a well-designed logo is immediately recognizable.

lone

See ALONE/LONE

lonely, lonesome

The adjective *lonely* means 'isolated' or 'without company':

Don't you find this place lonely in winter?
I feel lonely even when I am surrounded by people.

Lonesome is more widely used in America than in Britain and means 'feeling alone and isolated':

Are you lonesome tonight? Do you miss me tonight?

See also ALONE/LONE

longevity

Longevity is a noun meaning 'long life':

Longevity runs in his family. His parents were both in their nineties when they died and his aunt is 102.

The 'g' is pronounced like the 'g' in 'gentle'.

longitude

This word contrasts with 'latitude' and refers to distance in degrees east or west of the prime meridian O°, which is at Greenwich:

Your location is: Latitude 59°N, Longitude 5°W.

Longitude is frequently misspelled. It does not end in '-titude' or '-ditude' The 'g' is sometimes pronounced like the 'g' in 'orange', but a spelling pronunciation where the first syllable rhymes with 'song' is gaining in popularity.

loo

See LAVATORY/TOILET/WASHROOM

look, see, watch

These verbs have much in common but their individuality should be recognized. The verb *look* implies making an effort to see; *see* implies perceiving something with the eyes; *watch* implies both making an effort to see and to observe an action or process for a purpose:

I looked for you at the concert but I couldn't see you.
I saw you at the concert last night.
I watched *Neighbours* on television.

When there is any emphasis on a conscious effort, *look* or *watch* should be selected. Thus, we may *see* a person, a play or a performance; but we *look at* a book because we are in control; and *watch* television because we are in control and also because a process is taking place.

See is an irregular verb:

see(s), saw, seeing, seen

which can be used in the simple present to imply a wider range of perceptions, such as 'appreciate', 'understand':

I admit that I can see his point of view.

It does not normally occur in progressive structures with reference to the present:

I am watching him now.

but not:

*I am seeing him now.

but it is perfectly acceptable in references to the future:

I'm seeing him at 10:00 tomorrow.

and in structures where 'see' means 'attend to':

I am seeing a patient at the moment.

'Hear' is similar to *see* in that it has a related verb 'listen (to)' that implies conscious effort.

See also ASPECT, HEAR/LISTEN, VERB

look(-)alike

A *look(-)alike* means a 'double' and it is often hyphenated:

I've never seen so many Elvis Presley lookalikes!

loose, loosen, lose

Loose is an adjective meaning 'not fixed, not tight':

This screw is loose. You should tighten it or you'll lose it.

Loose rhymes with 'goose' and can be used attributively and predicatively:

a loose tile
The tile is loose.

The phrase 'let loose' is used to mean 'release':

He let loose the arrow.
I'll let the dog loose now.

Loose is sometimes used as a verb meaning 'set free' or 'release' usually from an obligation:

I will loose you from your promise.

This usage has an old-fashioned, biblical quality reminiscent of:

And whomsoever you shall loose from his sins shall be loosed.

Loosen is a regular verb meaning 'cause to become less tight, untie':

loosen(s), loosened, loosening
I can't loosen this cap. Can you get it off for me?

The verb *lose* rhymes with 'ooze' and means 'mislay, part with', usually by means of carelessness or theft:

I've lost my mother's brooch. I can't remember when I last saw it.

lot, lots

The noun *lots* is widely used in casual speech to mean 'a large quantity' and 'very much':

I saw lots of herons today.
I'm lots quicker on the computer now.

Such usage, particularly the adverbial use of *lots*, is not, however, totally acceptable in the written medium.

The singular form *lot* is more acceptable:

I saw a lot of herons today.
I'm a lot quicker on the computer now.

but in formal contexts it is better to use such expressions as 'a large number' and 'very much':

I saw a large number of herons today.
I'm very much quicker on the computer now.

loth

See LOATH/LOATHE/LOTH

loud, loudly

Loud functions as an adjective meaning 'noisy':

I hate loud noises.

Loud is the only acceptable form in the phrase 'out loud':

We were supposed to whisper, but she spoke out loud.

but, generally, *loudly* should be used as the adverb:

I'd never play the piano as loudly as that.

See also ADJECTIVE, ADVERB

lounge

The noun *lounge* can refer to a room in a private house or apartment:

We try to keep all office work out of the lounge because that's where we relax.

Some people regard the use of *lounge* as pretentious.

It can also refer to a large public room in a hotel or at an airport:

Let's put our cases in our rooms and then meet in the lounge for coffee.

The departure lounge is crowded because several planes have been delayed by bad weather.

See also LIVING ROOM

lour, lower

These words are occasionally confused. *Lour* rhymes with 'our' and is a regular verb meaning 'frown, scowl, look overcast':

lour(s), loured, louring

When she describes the 'louring sky', she means that it is dark and menacing.

This word is occasionally spelled *lower* but pronounced as *lour*.

Lower rhymes with 'rower'. It can function as a comparative adjective:

She sat on the lower chair.

and as a regular verb meaning 'cause to go down':

lower(s), lowered, lowering

We had to wait while they lowered the bridge.

He was told to lower his voice when preaching.

lovable, loveable

These are variant spellings for the adjective meaning 'easy to love':

She is the most lovable person I've ever met.

The 'e' is normally dropped before '-able' but *loveable* is acceptable.

See also -ABLE/-BILE

low-key

Low-key or, less frequently, 'low-keyed', means 'having a low intensity or tone':

The photograph is low-key because it has a predominance of dark grey tones.

Recently, *low-key* has been overused in the media to mean 'modest, restrained':

The conference was a very low-key affair. We had no invited speakers and we simply sat around and talked about the meaning of 'Meaning'.

low profile

Low profile and its opposite 'high profile' are both overused in the media. *Low profile* means 'unobtrusive', 'inconspicuous':

I don't want any fuss so I'm keeping a low profile.

It's a low budget, low-profile collection.

See also PROFILE

lower case, upper case

These phrases were originally printer's terms, but they are now used more widely. *Lower case* refers to small letters, as opposed to 'capital letters' or *upper case*. Most headlines in the popular press use upper-case letters as a means of catching the reader's attention. Broadsheets use more lower-case letters in their headlines.

See also CAPITALIZATION

lumbar, lumber

Lumbar, like 'lumbago' derives from Latin *lumbus*, 'loin', and refers to the part of the body between the lowest ribs and the hip-bone:

She needed a lumbar puncture when she had meningitis.

Etymologists are not certain of the origins of *lumber*. In America, it refers to logs:

They turned the forests into lumber yards.

In Britain, *lumber* can also mean 'useless household articles' or 'to burden':

We'd need a lorry to carry away the lumber that has been stored in the attic.

I wish they wouldn't try to lumber us with their problems.

lunch, luncheon

Both these nouns refer to a midday meal. *Lunch* tends to be light and informal:

We often meet for a sandwich lunch.

Luncheon refers to a much more formal social occasion:

The guest of honour at the luncheon spoke about her latest novel.

See also DINNER, MEALS, TEA

lustre, luster

This is a relatively formal noun meaning 'sheen, gloss'. It is spelled *lustre* in Britain and *luster* in America:

He loves that car. He's not content with a shine; he wants the brightest lustre he can manage.

See also SPELLING

Luxembourg

An inhabitant of the European grand duchy is a 'Luxembourger'; the derived adjective is 'Luxembourg'. The capital is Luxembourg.

luxuriant, luxurious

These adjectives both derive from Latin *luxuria*, 'excess'. *Luxuriant* means 'rich, abundant, lush' and is often applied to vegetation:

It was the most luxuriant garden I'd ever seen. Every centimetre had been used and every bush, every plant seemed to be bursting with life.

Luxurious suggests 'extremely comfortable' and often 'very expensive':

I had no idea we were booking such a luxurious hotel, but let's enjoy it now that we're here.

-ly

The suffix *-ly* derives from Old English *lic* and *lice*, '-like', and it could be used to form adjectives and adverbs. When *lic* was added to nouns, it formed an adjective meaning 'with the qualities of X', 'like X':

brother + ly (like a brother)
god + ly (like God)
friend + ly (like a friend).

When *lice* was added to an adjective or a noun, it could form adverbs meaning 'in the manner of', 'to a certain degree':

bad + ly
chief + ly
quick + ly.

lynch

Lynch is an example of a personal name becoming a verb. Charles Lynch (1736–96) was a judge and a vigilante in Virginia. His name came to be associated with 'killing by taking the law into one's own hands':

That wasn't a fair trial. The man may well have been innocent, but the mob lynched him.

See also EPONYM

M

m
M is a nasal consonant. The lower-case letter is used as an abbreviation for 'metre'.

Ma'am, Madam, Madame
These terms of address and reference all derive from French *ma dame*, 'my lady'. *Madam* is the English spelling. It is formal and is used mainly to members of the nobility and to the clientele of certain stores:

Would Madam like us to deliver?

Ma'am, rhyming with 'balm', is a term of address, again mainly to high-ranking women:

Thank you, Ma'am.

but a more colloquial pronunciation rhyming with 'Sam' is used as a respectful term of address, especially in America.

Madame is used as the French equivalent of 'Mrs':

Madame G. Bédé, teacher of French.

All of these forms are less widely used in English now than in the past.

Mac, Mc, Mc
These forms derive from Gaelic *mac*, 'son', and are used to mean 'son of':

MacDonald (son of Donald)
McEwan (son of Ewan)
McMichael (son of Michael).

Most directories treat them as variants of *Mac* and alphabetize them accordingly.

Macao
An inhabitant of the Portuguese colony on the southeast coast of China (which reverts to China in 1999), is a 'Macaoan'; the derived adjective is the same. The capital is Macao. The spellings 'Macau' and 'Macauan' are also acceptable.

Macedonia
An inhabitant of the Balkan country is a 'Macedonian'; the derived adjective is the same. The capital is Skopje.

machination
The noun *machination* derives from Latin *machinare*, 'to plan', and is used to mean 'intrigue, plot, scheme', often one that is devious:

Othello was totally unaware of Iago's machinations.

The first syllable of *machinations* is normally pronounced to rhyme with 'back' but the spelling pronunciation that rhymes it with 'bash' is growing in popularity.

macho
The adjective *macho* comes from Mexican Spanish *macho*, 'male', and is used in English to mean 'aggressively male':

As Zsa Zsa Gabor said: 'A man who is too macho is not mucho.' (mucho = much of a man)

The first syllable of *macho* is identical with 'match'. The related noun *machismo* is pronounced like 'mack *is* mo', with the stress on the second syllable.

mackintosh
The person after whom the *mackintosh* raincoat was named was Charles Macintosh (1760–1843). It is acceptable to use the spelling without the 'k' but the spelling with 'k' is now widespread:

Floor 2: Mackintoshes, Umbrellas, Rainwear.

See also EPONYM

macro-, micro-
The prefixes *macro-* and *micro-* come from Greek *makros*, 'large', and *mikros*, 'small'. They are used mainly in scientific language and they are often contrasted:

macrocosm (complex structure – e.g., the universe)
microcosm (miniature representation of something large)

Nature replicates itself infinitely. The atom with its revolving electrons is a microcosm of the solar system, which is a miniaturization of the macrocosm, our expanding universe.

Hyphens are often used when the prefix precedes a vowel:

macro-economics
macro-evolution.

mad
See ANGRY/MAD

Madagascar
An inhabitant of the island republic off the southeast coast of Africa is a 'Madagscan'; the derived adjective is the same. The capital is Antananarivo.

Madam, Madame
See MA'AM/MADAM/MADAME

magic, magical
Magic can function as a noun:

It can't be a trick and so it must be magic!

and as an adjective, meaning 'relating to an art that supposedly transcends the natural':

Would you like to see a magic pencil?

Magical is also an adjective. Its meaning is wider than *magic* and can suggest 'entertaining' 'romantic' and 'mysterious':

We had a magical evening. It went perfectly from beginning to end.

The night was magical, dark and warm.

See also -IC/-ICAL

magnitude

Magnitude is overly used to mean 'size', 'extent':

The hospital was surprised by the magnitude of the problem.

It is a problem of the first magnitude.

This BLEACHING of meaning is a feature of media language, which often puts novelty before precision. The metaphor 'of the first *magnitude*' is taken from astronomy, where it describes the apparent brightness of stars as they are seen from earth.

maharaja(h)

This term for an Indian prince comes from Hindi *maha*, 'great', + *raja*, 'king'. Either spelling is acceptable. The female equivalent is 'maharani' or 'maharanee', both pronounced to rhyme with 'tree':

The maharajahs introduced the British to an affluence and an elegance that they had never known.

main clause

A *main clause* is the clause that is most like a sentence in being able to occur in isolation. There is only one clause, a *main clause*, in a simple sentence:

[I saw John.]

[Go away!]

In sentences that contain more than one main verb, we have one *main clause* (MC) and one or more subordinate clauses (SC):

MC	SC	SC
I heard	that you are leaving.	
I heard	that you are leaving	when John comes.

See also CLAUSE, SUBORDINATE CLAUSE

main verb

A *main verb* is a synonym for 'head verb' and 'lexical verb'. A *main verb* may be modified by up to four auxiliaries. In the following sentences, 'watch' is the main verb:

I watched.

I may watch.

I may have been being watched.

See also AUXILIARY, VERB

mainly

Mainly is an adverb meaning 'principally, for the most part'. To avoid ambiguity, it is important to position *mainly* as close as possible to the word or words it modifies. A sentence such as:

I mainly do the housework on Monday.

means:

I set aside Mondays for the housework.

whereas:

I do the housework mainly on Monday.

means that some of the housework may spill over into other days.

maize

See CORN/MAIZE

major

The adjective *major* is overused in the contemporary press, where it has become a synonym for 'great', 'chief', 'serious':

a major influence on Blair

the major contributors to party funds

*The break-up of the nuclear family is the most major difficulty facing society today.

and the phrase:

the major part

means no more than 'most'.

There is nothing wrong with using *major* as an adjective meaning 'chief', but no adjective should be used to excess or dredged of so much meaning that it becomes semantically useless.

majority, minority

These nouns mean, respectively, 'the greater number or part of something' and 'the smaller number or part of something'. Both words are used to excess in the media and are losing much of their meaning. In the following sentences, for example:

The majority of the garden is given over to flowers.

Only a minority of the money went to the charity.

the speakers should have used 'most of' and 'only a small part of' or they might have been more precise:

Only 2 per cent of the money went to the charity.

Majority and *minority* are singular nouns and so should be used with the appropriate form of the verb:

The majority of the population is female.

As with many collective nouns, however, some people use plural agreement especially if *majority* or *minority* is followed by a phrase such as 'of people':

A minority of people are beginning to realize that cars will have to be banned from city centres.

However, care with agreement should be exercised, especially in formal writing:

*The majority of these workers have traditionally voted for Labour.

The noun *majority* is also frequently used to refer to the number of votes an elected member gained over rivals:

Her majority was 22,000, an increase of 3.7 per cent.

Minority is also widely used in the phrase:

ethnic minority.

See also COLLECTIVE NOUN, NOUN

make

Make is an irregular verb and one of the most frequently occurring verbs in the language:

make(s), made, making.

It has two main functions: as the semantic equivalent of 'create, construct':

He makes all his own furniture.

and as a causative auxiliary verb:

You made me do it.

She made me laugh.

Make occurs in a range of idioms, including:

Make a mountain out of a molehill (exaggerate)

Make believe (pretend)

Make (both) ends meet (manage on little)

Make fun of (mock)

Make good (succeed)

Make waves (create a stir).

See also CAUSATIVE

malapropism

The term *malapropism* denotes the incorrect use of a word, usually a learned word. It comes directly from the name of a character 'Mrs Malaprop', in R.B. Sheridan's play, *The Rivals* (1775), and her name is an anglicization of French *mal à propos* (in an inappropriate manner). Mrs Malaprop confuses such words as 'allegory' and 'alligator' and 'allusion' and 'illusion', and she is outraged when her usage is criticized:

Sure, if I reprehend [comprehend] anything in this world, it is the use of my oracular [vernacular] tongue and a nice derangement [arrangement] of epitaphs [epithets].

        Act III, Scene iii

Mrs Malaprop was not the first literary character to use malapropisms. Shakespeare's common characters often delight in polysyllabic words that sound impressive but are inappropriate.

Malapropisms occur frequently in speech:

I was always afraid of the fire and broomsticks [brimstone].

See also ELEGANT VARIATION, FOLK ETYMOLOGY

Malawi

An inhabitant of the republic in southern Africa is a 'Malawian'; the derived adjective is the same. The capital is Lilongwe.

Malaysia

An inhabitant of the southeast Asian federation is a 'Malay', a 'Malaysian' or, less frequently, a 'Malayan'. The usual adjective is Malayan. The capital is Kuala Lumpur. Malay, the language, has provided English with a number of words.

See also FOREIGN LOAN-WORDS

Maldives, The

An inhabitant of the island republic is a 'Maldivan'; the derived adjective is 'Maldivian'. The capital is Malé.

male, man, masculine

Male can function as both an adjective and a noun:

The male chickens are usually not kept.

The males and females have separate societies.

The adjective *masculine*, like its counterpart 'feminine', refers to GENDER. In languages such as French, nouns are either *masculine* or 'feminine':

Masculine	Feminine
le mur (wall)	*la fenêtre* (window)
le plafond (ceiling)	*la porte* (door)

The terms *masculine*, 'feminine' and 'neuter' are applied to nouns in English according to whether they are male, female or inanimate:

Masculine	Feminine	Neuter
boy	girl	book
bull	cow	cake

In the past, *man* was often used to mean 'people':

Man cannot live by bread alone.

One man, one vote.

and many nouns were coined using -*man* as a suffix:

chairman, mailman, policeman.

Recently, it has been pointed out that such usage may contribute to an undervaluing of women in society. It is usually possible to avoid insulting anyone by using well-chosen synonyms, such as:

ancestors for 'forefathers'

humanity for 'mankind'.

See also FEMININE FORM/MASCULINE FORM, POLITICAL CORRECTNESS, SEXIST LANGUAGE

malevolent, malicious, malign, malignant

These adjectives all derive from Latin *male*, 'ill', and they all incorporate the meaning of wishing ill to someone, although they vary in intensity. *Malevolent* is the opposite of 'benevolent':

He is not a malevolent person. He's quiet and likes to be left alone but he does not intend to hurt anyone.

Malicious suggests 'evil, vicious intentions':

The stories that were circulated were malicious in the extreme. They were evil and intended to hurt.

Malign means 'destructive', 'injurious', 'negative':

I'm glad he has left that office. His character changed when he came under the malign influence of Jay.

Malignant is perhaps the strongest of the four. It suggests a desire for evil when applied to a person and 'cancerous' when applied to a tumour:

Iago's actions were described as 'motiveless malignity'. His behaviour was malignant because it was motivated by the desire to destroy. And he succeeded. The deaths of Desdemona and Othello can be attributed to him.

We are delighted that the tumour is not malignant.

malfunction
See DYSFUNCTION/MALFUNCTION

Mali
An inhabitant of the northwest African country is a 'Mali'; the adjective is 'Malian'. The capital is Bamako.

malnourished, undernourished
These adjectives are occasionally used as synonyms, but their meanings are different. *Malnourished* means that one lacks certain things that are essential in a balanced diet:

Many of the children were overweight and malnourished.

Undernourished suggests that one lacks enough food:

The children are undernourished because they are not getting their daily dietary requirements. They eat when there is food, but often there is not enough for everyone.

malnutrition
Malnutrition is sometimes used as a euphemistic equivalent of 'starvation':

In the famine zone, all of the children are suffering from malnutrition.

See also EUPHEMISM

Malta
An inhabitant of the Mediterranean island is a 'Maltese'; the derived adjective is the same. The capital is Valletta.

mamba, mambo
These nouns both derive from African languages.

Mamba comes from the Zulu *imamba*, 'venomous snake':

The green mamba is not as dangerous as the black mamba but it is much harder to see.

The etymology of *mambo* is not certain but it came into English from Spanish to refer to a South American dance like the 'rumba':

There are several different mambos in Venezuela.

man-
The prefix *man-* can come from two different sources, English *man*, 'adult male' and Latin *manus*, 'hand':

manhole (hole through which a person could enter)
manhood (state of being manly)
manpower (power supplied by people)
manacle (handcuff)
manage (control by hand)
mandate (given by hand).

There are, of course, many words in English, such as 'mango', where the syllable 'man-' does not come from English *man* or Latin *manus*.

See MALE/MAN/MASCULINE

manakin, manikin, mannequin
These nouns all derive from Dutch *manneken*, 'little man', but their meanings are now distinct. A *manakin*, sometimes spelled *manikin*, is a small South American bird. A *manikin*, sometimes spelled *mannikin*, is a little man, puppet or medical model. A *mannequin* is a woman who models clothes at a fashion show. The words are all pronounced alike but the last syllable of *mannequin* is sometimes pronounced 'quin' rather than 'kin'.

mandatory
Both the meaning and the pronunciation of *mandatory* have been undergoing change. *Mandatory* means 'obligatory', 'compulsory' and comes from Latin *mandatum*, 'command'. The usual pronunciation stresses the first syllable, but the word is now frequently stressed on the second syllable, which is pronounced 'date'. It is also being used to mean 'essential':

It is not mandatory to have Latin, but it may help.

mania, manic
Manic means 'characterized by a chronic mental disorder':

Her manic behaviour became too much for her brother who had her committed to a mental hospital.

It is gradually being bleached of meaning and used to mean 'extremely funny':

I've never laughed so much in my life. The comedian was just manic.

Such a meaning may eventually become acceptable but is not standard now.

A similar BLEACHING of *mania* is apparent in the popular press, where 'mania' means 'strong interest in':

Her golfing mania is well known.

mankind

Many people now object to the use of *mankind* where 'humanity' or 'people' would be more appropriate:

When you look at the state of the world, you are forced to admit that mankind has not evolved very far.

See also MALE/MAN/MASCULINE, POLITICAL CORRECTNESS, SEXIST LANGUAGE

manoeuvre, maneuver

These spellings are acceptable in Britain and America respectively:

UK: I have never been able to manoeuvre a car the way she can.

US: I have never been able to maneuver a car the way she can.

manslaughter

See HOMICIDE/MANSLAUGHTER/MURDER

mantel, mantle

These words are homophones. *Mantel* or 'mantelpiece' is the usual spelling for a shelf over a fireplace:

I remember there were china dogs on the mantel.

Mantle is the only acceptable spelling for a cloak:

Mary puts round him her mantle of blue.

The spelling *mantle* is occasionally, but wrongly, used for 'shelf'.

many

Many can function as a determiner:

I have seen many places.

a pronoun:

Many are called but few are chosen.

and as a noun:

The many are exploited by the few.

It is used with countable nouns to denote a large number:

I saw many things that I'd rather forget.

and, when it occurs as part of the subject, it requires a plural verb:

Many lives have been saved by the use of lifebelts.

In colloquial speech, people often use 'many a' and 'many's the' before singular nouns and verbs:

Many a child has studied here.

Many's the child has played here.

Such usage is perfectly acceptable in casual or colloquial contexts.

See also DETERMINER, FEWER/LESS/LESSER, PRONOUN

Maori

The *Maori* are a Polynesian people living mostly in New Zealand. English has borrowed words from *Maori*, including:

kia ora (good health)

kiwi (flightless bird).

The plural of *Maori* may be either 'Maori' or 'Maoris'.

margarine

Margarine, like the name 'Margaret', comes from Greek *margaron*, 'pearl'. It was used as a name for a butter substitute because it contained margaric acid. Originally, the 'g' in *margarine* was pronounced like the 'g' in 'Margaret', but it is now more usual to pronounce it like the 'g' in 'merger'.

marginal

Marginal is related to the noun 'margin' and has come to mean 'close to the limit'. In theory, the limit could be either upper or lower, but *marginal* is now most frequently used with regard to the lower limit:

We must allow for marginal profits when disposing of these goods.

Many people object to the use of *marginal* as a synonym for 'small', 'slight':

There was a marginal improvement in his health.

It is acceptable, however, in the collocations:

marginal land (unproductive land)

a marginal seat (one where the MP has a small majority).

marijuana, marihuana

Both spellings are acceptable as the name of a narcotic also called 'cannabis' and 'hemp'. The 'j' spelling is more widespread and is pronounced as a 'y'.

marshal, martial

These homophones are occasionally misspelled and confused. *Marshal* can function as a noun meaning 'officer':

In America, a marshal is like a sheriff.

and as a regular verb meaning 'arrange in order':

You should marshal your facts before you try to present them.

UK: marshal(s), marshalled, marshalling

US: marshal(s), marshaled, marshaling.

Martial is an adjective meaning 'characteristic of war':

It's easy to see that he's a military man: he has a martial air.

marten, martin

These different spellings refer to different animals. A *marten* is an arboreal mammal; a *martin* is a bird:

Martens are found in Europe, Asia and North America.

Martins were called after St Martin because they were believed to migrate on his feast day, 11 November.

Martinique

An inhabitant of the French island in the Lesser Antilles is a 'Martinican'; the derived adjective is the same. The capital is Fort-de-France.

marvel

Marvel can function as a noun meaning 'something or someone causing wonder':

My computer is a marvel! It can even wake me up in the morning!

and as a regular verb meaning 'to be filled with wonder':

We marvelled at the beauty of the desert.

UK: marvel(s), marvelled, marvelling

US: marvel(s), marveled, marveling.

The related adjective has 'll' in British English and 'l' in America:

UK: It's marvellous.

US: It's marvelous.

See also SPELLING

masculine form

See FEMININE FORM/MASCULINE FORM

mask, masque

These were originally variants but are now differentiated. They were taken into English from Italian but derive ultimately from Arabic *maskharah*, 'clown'. (The cosmetic 'mascara' has a similar source.) A *mask* is a covering for the face:

We used to wear masks on Hallowe'en and we thought nobody would recognize us.

A *masque* is an entertainment that was popular in the sixteenth and seventeenth centuries:

Masques usually included dancing, dialogue and music.

mass noun

Nouns in English can be subdivided into 'countable' nouns such as 'pen':

one pen, ten pens

and *mass* nouns or 'uncountable' nouns that cannot usually be counted:

*one sand, *ten sands.

Mass nouns may take the definite article:

The sand stretched for miles.

or no article, especially when the reference is generic:

Sand often contains rounded grains of quartz.

an indefinite quantifier such as 'some':

We'll need some sand for the play area.

but not, in normal circumstances, an indefinite article:

*a sand.

See also COUNTABLE AND UNCOUNTABLE, NOUN

masterful, masterly

These adjectives both derive from 'master', originally from Latin *magister*, 'master', 'teacher'. *Masterful* suggests 'imperious', 'fond of being in control':

From the moment Iago appeared on the stage, his masterful manipulation of the other characters was established.

Masterly means 'skilful':

It was a masterly performance! How can a child have become such a skilled pianist?

material, materiel

These words have different meanings and, usually, different pronunciations. *Material* is stressed on the second syllable and can refer to a substance from which something is made:

We'll need to order building materials.

Materiel or *matériel* is stressed on the last syllable, which rhymes with 'bell', and refers to the equipment of a military force:

The United States provides its allies with materiel during times of conflict.

materialize

Materialize used to mean 'take material form':

The spirit of his father materialized before his eyes.

Recently, it has been used as a synonym of 'happen', 'occur':

I hope the airline workers' strike doesn't materialize. My holiday starts on the 5th.

Mauritania

An inhabitant of the republic in northwestern African is a 'Mauritanian'; the derived adjective is the same. The capital is Nouakchott.

Mauritius

An inhabitant of the island nation in the Indian Ocean is a 'Mauritian'; the derived adjective is the same. The capital is Port Louis.

maxim

A *maxim* is a pithy statement, originally intended to improve moral conduct:

Wilful waste makes woeful want.

The term *maxim* is often used loosely to describe an APHORISM or PROVERB.

maximal

Maximal is an adjective deriving from 'maximum':

We are aiming at maximal impact.

It is not widely used because 'maximum' can also be used as an adjective:

What is the maximum load it can carry?

may, might

May and *might* are modals, and they can both be used to suggest possibility:

He may come today.

He might come today.

The main difference between these sentences is that 'might' is a little less likely than 'may'.

They can also be used in asking for something:

May I have the salt, please?

Might I have the salt, please?

Again, the meanings here are similar, but the question is perhaps less open with 'might'. In other words, it suggests an element of criticism by the speaker.

May and *might*, like all modals, can be followed by the auxiliaries verbs 'be' and 'have':

I may be wrong.

He might have gone.

I may have been wrong.

When they precede 'have', their meanings are different. If we look at the sentences:

She may have died.

She might have died.

the first is uncertain as to whether or not 'she' is dead, whereas the second makes clear that, although 'she' was in danger, she did not die.

See also CAN/MAY, MODALITY

may be, maybe

May be, written as two words, are verbs:

She may be late.

Maybe, written as one word, is an adverb meaning 'perhaps':

Maybe I'll go. I'm not sure.

May Day, Mayday

The noun *Mayday* or *mayday*, written as one word, is an international radiotelephone distress call:

Mayday! Mayday! This is mayday!

It comes from French *m'aider*, 'to help me'.

May Day, as two separate words, refers to 1 May, originally celebrated as the first day of spring, and it is now usually a holiday in honour of working people:

The May Day celebrations have started.

maybe, perhaps

These two words are virtually synonymous, but *maybe* tends to be more widely used in informal, colloquial speech:

Maybe he didn't hear us.

whereas *perhaps* tends to occur in more formal contexts:

It is, perhaps, possible but I doubt it.

See also ADVERB

mayonnaise

The noun *mayonnaise*, 'a thick, creamy sauce' is often misspelled. It has '-nn-' not '-n-'.

me

See I/ME

me, my

Me is an object pronoun and *my* is a possessive adjective:

Pass me my bag, please.

In colloquial speech, people often use *me* before a gerund but *my* is preferred in formal usage:

He wanted to see me riding a bike.

He wanted to see my riding.

See also GERUND, -ING FORM

mead, meed

These homophones are now both virtually obsolete but are sometimes encountered in literature. *Mead* could refer to an alcoholic drink and to a meadow:

Perhaps you'd like a glass of my mead?

The knight's son was described as being as colourful as a spring mead.

Meed meant 'recompense, reward':

So this is my meed for all my efforts?

meagre, meager

This adjective means 'deficient in quantity'. It ends in '-re' in British English and '-er' in America:

How could anyone live on such a meagre amount?

meals

The words used for *meals* and the times at which they are eaten often provide information on a person's social or regional origins. The middle-class usage in Britain is:

breakfast (the first meal of the day)

lunch (often a light meal in the middle of the day)

tea (optional snack around 4pm)

dinner (full evening meal).

In working-class communities, the meals are likely to be:

breakfast (the first meal of the day)

dinner (biggest meal of the day, eaten around midday)

tea (meal eaten around 6pm)

supper (optional meal around 9–10pm).

In other parts of the world, different customs prevail. In Guyana, for example, 'tea' is often the first meal of the day.

Because most people now eat the sort of meals that fit in with their lifestyles, some of these terms are becoming ambiguous. The sentence:

I saw her at teatime.

could mean 'around 4pm or around 6pm' and:

I'll meet you after dinner.

could mean 'after 1pm or after 9pm'.

See also DINNER, FOOD AND DRINK,
LUNCH/LUNCHEON, TEA, UK AND US ENGLISH

mean

Mean frequently occurs with 'I' as a filler or hesitation feature:

He did it ... I mean, I think he did it.

See also FILLER

meaningful

Meaningful is an adjective equivalent to 'having meaning':

'What ho!' is not a very meaningful expression, is it?

Recently, it has been overused by the media to mean 'important', 'serious', 'significant':

Both sides report that they've had meaningful discussions.

We also find *meaningful* used to mean 'affectionate', 'warm' in:

meaningful relationship, meaningful smile.

means

The noun *means* is singular when it refers to 'method':

This means of cheap transport is not yet universally available.

When it refers to money or resources, it is plural:

Our means were not adequate to the needs of three children.

meantime, meanwhile

These words both relate to an 'intervening period of time'. *Meantime* is most frequently used as a noun, in the phrase 'in the meantime':

In the meantime, you should wait in my office.

Meanwhile is used as an adverb:

He rushed outside to get help. Meanwhile, I tried to phone for an ambulance.

measles

Measles derives from Old English *mesel*, 'leper', and is a singular noun:

Is German measles contagious?

measurement

Although most English-speaking countries now use metric units of measurement, some features of the old Imperial measurements have been retained, especially in America and in popular speech, for distances, height, length and weight:

Leeds is 200 miles from London.

He's just under 6 feet 6 inches tall.

I need about a yard of cotton.

She's 112 pounds.

or, in Britain:

She's 8 stone.

Petrol is often discussed in terms of gallons although it is sold in litres.

media, medium

The *media* is the collective name for modern mass communications, including newspapers, radio, television and, occasionally, film. It is the plural of Latin *medium*, the neuter singular of 'middle', and should be used with plural agreement:

These media are best suited to advertising.

However, it is increasingly being used as a singular:

The media is not responsible for the world's crime.

Media is also used adjectivally in such phrases as:

a media circus, a media event.

In addition to referring to one element of the *media*:

I think television is the most influential medium of our time.

Radio was the most influential medium of the 1930s and 1940s.

the noun *medium* can, with the plural 'mediums', refer to a 'spiritual intermediary':

I'd never had much interest in mediums until I saw her performance.

and to the system by which language is transmitted, usually by speech and writing:

The mediums of speech and writing differ in terms of transmission, reception and acquisition.

mediaeval, medieval

These spellings are both acceptable but the second is standard in America and increasingly used in Britain:

I'm interested in medieval literature.

The word was traditionally pronounced as having four syllables, like 'medi + evil'. The simpler spelling is leading to a pronunciation with three syllables, 'med + evil'.

See also -AE-/-E-

mediate
See ARBITRATE/MEDIATE

mediocre
The adjective *mediocre*, meaning 'of average or ordinary quality', is spelled with '-re' in both Britain and America:

It's a mediocre book. I finished it because I had nothing else to read.

The related noun is 'mediocrity':

I like to be good at things. I could never be satisfied with being a mediocrity.

Mediterranean
The word *Mediterranean* is widely misspelled. It comes from Latin *mediterraneus*, 'middle + land':

The Mediterranean is virtually landlocked.

medium
See MEDIA/MEDIUM

meed
See MEAD/MEED

meet with
In Britain, *meet with* tends to be limited in meaning to 'experience':

Our venture has already met with some success.

The use of *meet with* to mean 'encounter' is thought of as American:

We met with her family yesterday.

but there is a difference between 'meet', which is accidental, and *meet with*, which is planned:

I met John in the street yesterday and I hadn't seen him for ten years.

I met with John at ten o'clock yesterday to discuss his firm's requirements.

mega-
Mega- is a prefix deriving from Greek *megas*, 'huge, powerful'. It was originally used to mean 10^6 but is now frequently used to mean 'great, large':

It was a mega media event.

UB40 was a mega-successful group.

See also SEMANTIC CHANGE

meiosis
Meiosis comes from Greek *meion*, 'less'. It has two main meanings in English. It can be a figure of speech involving understatement:

He's not unintelligent.

or a term in biology for cell division:

Meiosis is a type of cell division in which a nucleus divides into four daughter nuclei.

See also FIGURE OF SPEECH, LITOTES, UNDERSTATEMENT

melt, molten
Melt is now a regular verb:

melt(s), melted, melting.

Its original, irregular past participle *molten* is now used to modify words for materials that do not melt easily:

molten lava, molten steel.

'Melted' is used for items that can melt easily:

melted cheese, melted chocolate.

mend
See AMEND/EMEND/MEND

mendacity, mendicity
Mendacity comes from Latin *mendax*, 'untruthful' and relates to telling lies:

Mendacity is never acceptable. You will find that veracity is not just a virtue: it is a form of self-preservation.

The derived adjective is 'mendacious'.

Mendicity is rarely used. It comes from Latin *mendicare*, 'to beg' and relates to begging:

Mendicity is now widely practised on the streets of all major cities.

-ment
The SUFFIX *-ment* comes from Latin *-mentum* and is primarily used to create nouns:

amaze, amazement
enjoy, enjoyment
manage, management.

mental
Mental derives from Latin *mens*, 'mind', and is an adjective meaning 'involving the mind':

It took enormous mental effort.

The colloquial tendency to use *mental* to mean 'foolish' as in:

You'd have to be mental to want that job.

should be avoided.

mentalism
Mentalism is a branch of psychology that is popularly invoked in discussions of acquisition of language. Mentalists claim that children are born with a predisposition to acquire language and that the speed of acquisition can in part be accounted for by the child's inherent linguistic abilities.

meretricious, meritorious
These adjectives are occasionally confused. *Meretricious* comes from Latin *meretrix*, 'prostitute', and means 'superficially attractive', 'insincere':

It has a certain amount of meretricious appeal but it is fundamentally unsound.

Meritorious comes from Latin *meritum*, 'reward', and means 'praiseworthy', 'showing merit':

It was a thoroughly praiseworthy action, all the more meritorious for being virtually unseen.

meta-

Meta- is a Greek prefix indicating 'change':

metamorphosis (complete change of physical form)

'alteration':

metabolism (chemical processes occurring in a living organism)

and 'beyond':

metapsychology (studies going beyond laws of experimental psychology).

Recently, *meta-* has been used as a prefix meaning 'better', 'of a higher order':

These new writers are creating a metafiction that is not yet fully appreciated.

It is also used in the coinage 'metalanguage', which is the specific variety of language used to describe language. Many of the descriptions in this book involve metalanguage. The study of metalanguage is 'metalinguistics'.

metal, mettle

Metal comes from Latin *metallum*, 'mine, product of a mine', and is the general term for such chemical elements as:

copper, gold, iron.

The homophone *mettle* was originally a variant spelling of *metal*, but it came to mean 'courage, spirit':

I like this horse's mettle.

metaphor

The noun *metaphor* derives ultimately from Greek *metapherein*, 'to transfer'. It is a figure of speech in which one item is covertly identified with another. In a sentence such as:

They bleated.

the underlying identification is:

Sheep bleat. The children sounded like sheep. They bleated.

A *metaphor* may be expressed with adjectives:

She gave me a *warm* smile. (A 'smile' cannot be 'warm'.)

with adverbs:

He replied *acidly*.

with nouns:

They got in *touch* with us.

with verbs:

The engine *purred*.

and with phrases:

They *blew up* the bank.

Many *metaphors* are 'dead' in that we are no longer conscious of their figurative nature when we use them:

the *mouth* of a river

a *boiling* kettle.

There are many different kinds of *metaphor*, including those:

■ That give animate qualities to inanimate nouns:

the *laughing* brook

The film *ran* for three hours.

■ That give physical substance to abstractions:

a *fleshed-out* plan

the plot *thickens*

■ That give non-human attributes to people:

She *crowed* with pleasure.

He's *pigeon-toed*.

■ That give divine qualities to people:

her *eternal* smile

He *created* this department.

■ That give human qualities to non-human nouns:

a *brave* effort

the *dying* day

■ In which the qualities associated with one sense are applied to another. These are called 'synaesthetic' metaphors:

a *hard* look

a *loud* purple.

See also FIGURE OF SPEECH, IDIOM, SIMILE, SYNAESTHESIA

metathesis

The noun *metathesis* comes from Greek *meta-tithenai*, 'to transpose'. *Metathesis* involves the transposition of sounds in a word, usually to break up a consonant cluster or to analogize with other words. Many speakers, for example, incorrectly say 'nucular ' and 'vunerable' for 'nuclear' and 'vulnerable'. In this way, they avoid the clusters '-cl-' and '-ln-' and analogize with such words as 'secular' and 'venerable'.

Metathesis has occurred throughout the known history of English. Words such as 'horse' and 'bird' were once 'hros' and 'bridd'.

See also CONSONANT CLUSTER

meter, metre

In Britain, these different spellings represent different things. A *meter* is an instrument for measuring:

My electricity meter is in the kitchen but my gas meter is outside.

and a *metre* is a measurement equal to 39.36 inches:

I need 6 metres of silk brocade.

In America, *meter* is used for both.

The noun *metre* (*meter* in America) is also used for regulated rhythm. In English poetry, the number of stressed syllables is often regulated (below, stressed syllables are represented by /, unstressed syllables by x):

Humpty Dumpty sat on a wall. = / x / x / x x /
Humpty Dumpty had a great fall. = / x / x / x x /
All the king's horses = / x / / x
And all the king's men = x / x / /
Couldn't put Humpty = / x / / x
Together again. = x / x x /

Latin verse could be subdivided into feet, and so four types of poetic foot were used to describe English verse:

anapest: x x / (two unstressed + one stressed syllable)
dactyl: / x x (one stressed + two unstressed syllables)
iamb: x / (one unstressed + one stressed syllable)
trochee: / x (one stressed + one unstressed syllable).

English verse does not fit easily into Romance patterns because English is a stress-timed language, whereas the Romance languages are syllable-timed. In stress-timed languages, stressed syllables are produced at regular intervals of time and the number of unstressed syllables may vary. In syllable-timed languages, however, the syllables are produced at equal intervals of time with the number of stresses being random.

See also PARALLELISM, RHYTHM, STRESS, SYLLABLE

meticulous

The adjective *meticulous* means 'painstaking', 'scrupulously careful', as in:

She pays meticulous attention to detail.

The word seems to be undergoing a semantic change and is now occasionally used to mean 'fussy':

It certainly wasn't necessary to be so meticulous about every detail of the form.

See also SEMANTIC CHANGE

metonymy

The noun *metonymy* comes from Greek *meta* + *onyma*, 'change + name'. It is a figure of speech in which someone or something is referred to by an associated item:

He addressed the bench (i.e., the judge).
She chose the stage (i.e., to be an actor).

Metonymy is distinct from SYNECDOCHE, where a part represents a whole, thus:

She employs twenty hands (i.e., workers).

See also FIGURE OF SPEECH

metre
See METER/METRE

mettle
See METAL/METTLE

Mexico

An inhabitant of the North American republic is a 'Mexican'; the derived adjective is the same. The capital is Mexico City.

micro-
See MACRO-/MICRO-

mid-

Mid- is a prefix deriving from Old English *midel*, 'middle'. It can indicate a middle part or time:

midday, mid-June, the Midlands (counties in the middle of England), midway.

The hyphen tends to occur before a proper noun as in 'mid-June' or in the less frequently used expressions.

See also HYPHEN

middle
See CENTRE/MIDDLE

Middle English

Middle English refers to the variety of English spoken and written in England from about the twelfth to the fifteenth century. During this period, English changed from an inflected Germanic language to a relatively uninflected language with extensive borrowings from Latin and French.

See also OLD ENGLISH

might
See COULD/MIGHT, MAY/MIGHT

migraine

Migraine has two acceptable pronunciations. The first syllable may rhyme with 'tea' or with 'tie':

The new medication should bring some relief for sufferers of migraine. It relieves the headache and the nausea.

migrant
See EMIGRANT/IMMIGRANT/MIGRANT

mileage, milage

According to many dictionaries, these spellings are both acceptable for 'distance expressed in miles'. However, *mileage* is much more frequently used and *milage* seems to be obsolescent:

Do you think the mileage on this car is correct? It seems a remarkably low mileage for a five-year-old vehicle.

milieu

The French word *milieu*, 'place', is sometimes used in English for 'location, setting':

We've selected this milieu because this village has changed less than most over the last century.

The pronunciation approximates to French and the plural may be formed by adding 'x', as in French, or 's' as for other English plurals.

militate, mitigate

These verbs are occasionally confused. *Militate* comes from Latin *militare*, 'to be a soldier'. It frequently co-occurs with 'against' or 'for' and means 'have a strong influence':

In spite of laws against ageism, I feel certain that my age militated against my getting the position.

Mitigate comes from Latin *mitigare*, 'to be milder', and means 'moderate, lessen the severity':

We have taken your youth into consideration and feel that your sentence should be mitigated because of it.

millennium

A *millennium* means '1000 years'. It comes from Latin *mille* + *annus*, '1000 + year', and is frequently misspelled. Like its Latin source, it has double 'l' and double 'n':

Many projects have received large grants from the Millennium Fund.

million, millionaire

A *million* is 1,000,000. It should be spelled out:

There are almost 60 million people in this country.

The word *millionaire* is often misspelled. It has only one 'n'. It can be preceded by a unit of currency to indicate how wealthy an individual is:

She's a millionaire. (She has over £1 million.)
He's a dollar millionaire. (He has over $1 million.)
This cat has been left a fortune. It's a Swiss franc millionaire.

See also BILLION/MILLION/THOUSAND

mimic

Mimic can function as a noun or verb:

Sally's a wonderful mimic. She can imitate all the female singers.
mimic(s), mimicked, mimicking
I don't like being mimicked.

The art of being a *mimic* is 'mimicry'. It does not have a 'k'.

mina, myna, mynah

These spellings are all acceptable variants for an Asian starling. The name comes from Hindi *maina*, 'starling':

Mina birds had religious significance in parts of Asia.

miner, minor

These homophones are occasionally misused. A *miner* is a person who works in a mine:

He's worked as a miner all his life. His father worked in the pits and his grandfather too.

Minor can function as an adjective meaning 'not significant':

He was a minor poet in the seventeenth century.

and as a noun meaning 'a person who has not reached a particular age':

Cigarettes cannot be sold to minors.

minimize

See DIMINISH/MINIMIZE

minority

See MAJORITY/MINORITY

minus, plus

Minus is occasionally used to mean 'without':

I'm afraid I've come minus my chequebook.

Plus is represented by the symbol +. It is increasingly used as an emphatic form of 'and' or 'also':

I've got a mortgage to pay. Plus, my job is not secure.

Many people dislike this usage but it is growing among the young.

minuscule

Minuscule means 'very small'. It is often misspelled but the correct spelling will be used if we remember that *minuscule* begins with 'minus':

The forensic scientist had to work with minuscule amounts of fabric.

minutiae

Minutiae is a relatively formal word meaning 'very small details':

I haven't yet been able to study the minutiae but I've got a good idea of the general terms of the agreement.

The word is pronounced as 'min + yoosh + ee + ee' with the strongest stress on the second syllable.

misanthropy, misogamy, misogyny

These abstract nouns all include the Greek suffix *miso*, 'hatred of'. *Misogamy* means 'hatred of marriage'; *misogyny* 'hatred of women'; and *misanthropy* 'hatred of people'.

miscellaneous

This adjective, meaning 'mixed', 'varied', is often misspelled. The three areas of difficulty are the '-sc-', the '-ll-' and the ending in '-eous':

They had a miscellaneous collection of clothes, books and shoes.

mischievous

The adjective *mischievous* meaning 'naughty', is often misspelled and mispronounced. It ends in '-ous' not '-ious' and thus has three syllables, not four. The second syllable rhymes with 'give', not 'eve':

They're not bad children, just mischievous.

misogamy, misogyny

See MISANTHROPY/MISOGAMY/MISOGYNY

Miss

Miss is an abbreviation of 'Mistress' and was, until the 1960s, the usual term of address and reference for an unmarried woman:

Miss Smith, may I please leave the room?
I saw Miss Smith last Thursday.

Many people now prefer a term that is unmarked for marital status and so use 'Ms'.

See also MS/MS

misspell

The verb *misspell* has two acceptable past tense and past participle forms in Britain. Americans prefer to used 'misspelled':

misspell(s), misspelt/misspelled, misspelling, misspelt/misspelled
You have misspelled 'accommodation' three times.

In Britain, 'misspelled' may rhyme with 'felt' or 'felled'. The 'felled' pronunciation is the norm in America.

mistakable, mistakeable

This adjective is not widely used. It can be spelled with or without the 'e':

I suppose it is mistakable for an 's'. My handwriting is not very clear.

mistrust

See DISTRUST/MISTRUST

misuse

See ABUSE/MISUSE

misused

See DISUSED/MISUSED/UNUSED

miter, mitre

A *mitre* is the liturgical head-dress of a bishop or abbot:

Why are mitres so high and pointed and why do they have two ribbons at the back?

In America, the usual spelling is *miter*.

mitigate

See MILITATE/MITIGATE

mix

Mix is a regular verb:

mix(es), mixed, mixing
Mix together the flour, sugar and salt.

Mix is occasionally used instead of 'mixture':

Put the muffin mix into twelve muffin cases and bake for twenty minutes.

It is also being used as a noun meaning 'range':

We have a wide mix of abilities at the school.

Many people dislike this usage.

mixed language

The term *mixed language* has frequently been applied to pidgins and creoles. Such languages are 'mixed' in the sense that their vocabulary may be from a variety of languages and their grammar from yet another. Mixing is not, however, limited to pidgins and creoles. It is found in all communities where two or more languages are in use. If we look at the previous sentence, 'It is … use', we find fourteen words, eleven from English and three from French ('communities, languages, use').

See also BORROWING, PIDGIN AND CREOLE

mnemonic, pneumonic

These adjectives are sometimes confused. The adjective *mnemonic* comes from Greek *mnemon*, 'mindful', and means 'something to help one's memory':

pale gas (Pride, Avarice, Lust, Envy, Greed, Anger, Sloth = seven deadly sins)
wysiwyg (what you see is what you get)
vibgyor (violet, indigo, blue, green, yellow, orange and red = colours of the rainbow).

The initial 'm' in *mnemonic* is silent.

There are many *mnemonic* devices in the language, the most obvious being:

- Alliteration:

Warm, wet, westerly winds in winter

- Assonance:

Did you see father pass the dark path?

- Rhyme:

The rain in Spain
Stays mainly on the plain.

- Parallelism:

Have a break.
Have a Kit Kat.

Pneumonic means 'relating to the lungs':

In such pneumonic conditions, one or both of the air sacs are filled with liquid.

moat, mote

These homophones have quite distinct meanings. A *moat* is a water-filled trench round a castle:

Castles had drawbridges that could be lowered across part of the moat.

A *mote* is a speck of dust:

We often see the mote in someone else's eye but not the plank that is in our own.

mobile

Mobile is most frequently used as an adjective meaning 'capable of moving':

She's gradually becoming more mobile but she's still got a problem with stairs.

Mobile can also be a name for a sculpture that is suspended and moves with currents of air and for a mobile phone:

Colin has a mobile over his cot. It plays nursery rhymes when it moves.
You can get her on her mobile.

moccasin

Moccasin comes from Algonquian *mocussin*, 'soft leather shoe':

I find moccasins a little too flat. I need a heel on my shoe.

It is often misspelled.

modality

Modality refers to the attitudes expressed by a speaker towards the statement or proposition being made. This is sometimes indicated in novels by means of such verbs of attribution as 'implied', 'simpered', 'suggested', 'urged'. The attitudes expressed include ability, compulsion, desire, insistence, intention, obligation, permission, possibility, willingness and uncertainty.

In English, *modality* can be signalled in a variety of ways, the most important of which are:

■ The use of modal verbs. The nine modal verbs are: 'can', 'could', 'may', 'might', 'must', 'shall', 'should', 'will', 'would'.

I can swim. = I have the ability to swim.
I must go. = I am compelled to go.

■ The use of verbs such as 'dare', 'need', 'ought to', 'used to', which share some of the syntactic characteristics of modals:

I daren't trust myself.
I ought to stay.

■ The use of verbs that share much of the meaning of modals. These include 'be able to', 'be about to', 'have to':

He's not able to swim.
She had to go.

■ The use of intonation. By varying our intonation, we can modify meaning as in the sentence:

That's just great!

which can mean 'That's really great' and 'That's just awful'.

■ The use of modifiers such as 'hopefully', 'maybe', 'perhaps':

Hopefully she'll have what we need.
Perhaps he'll go.

See also AUXILIARY, MOOD, VERB

(à la) mode

See À LA

model

Model comes from Latin *modulus*, 'little way', 'mode'. It can function as an adjective:

This model ship is built to scale.

as a noun:

Most female models are at least 5 foot 8 inches.

and as a regular verb:

UK: model(s), modelled, modelling (Their social system was modelled on ours.)
US: model(s), modeled, modeling.

modest

Modest comes from Latin *modestus*, 'moderate', and normally means 'shy', 'bashful', 'retiring':

How could anyone say such a thing about this gentle, modest girl?

Recently, it has been used to mean 'middling', 'not large':

He has a modest income.
They live in a modest house in a quiet, residential area.

modicum

Modicum means 'a small amount':

If he had even a modicum of humility, I might be able to overlook his behaviour.

modifier

A *modifier* is a word, phrase or clause that is structurally dependent on, and qualifies the meaning of, other units, especially nouns, verbs, adjectives, adverbs and sentences. The most widely-used *modifiers* are adjectives, which qualify nouns:

a *tall* girl

adverbs, which qualify verbs, adjectives, other adverbs and sentences:

She sang *well*.
She's a *very* tall girl.
She sang *very* well.
However, we must not lose sight of our goal.

and preposition phrases:

a man *of steel*
He sat *in the corner*.

In traditional grammars, adjectives were said to 'qualify' nouns and adverbs to 'modify' verbs, adjectives, sentences and other adverbs. Today, the nouns 'modifier' and 'qualifier' and the verbs 'modify' and 'qualify' are used interchangeably, with 'modifier' and 'modify' being the preferred terms.

See also ADJECTIVE, ADVERB, PART OF SPEECH

modus

The Latin word *modus*, meaning 'way', 'method', 'manner', 'mode', occurs in two well-known phrases:

modus operandi (method of working, way of doing things)
I don't like his *modus operandi*.

modus vivendi (working arrangement – i.e., way of living])
Can we establish a *modus vivendi* that will keep things moving until we can find a permanent solution?

Mohamet, Mohammed, Muhammad, Muhammed

There are several English versions of the name of the founder of Islam. The form *Mohamet* is regarded as old-fashioned, and at the moment, *Muhammad* is the most frequently used:

The prophet Muhammad lived from about 570 to 632.

mold, mould

These words can be used as nouns and verbs. *Mould* is the preferred form in Britain; *mold* is American. The noun has two meanings. It can be a fungus or a shaped cavity used for producing particular forms. The verb means 'shape', 'form':

UK: mould(s), moulded, moulding (I've tried moulding this child's behaviour.)
US: mold(s), molded, molding (I've tried molding this child's behavior.)

Moldova

An inhabitant of the former republic of the USSR is a 'Moldovan'; the derived adjective is 'Moldavian'. The capital is Kishinev.

mollusc, mollusk

A *mollusc* is an invertebrate:

Slugs and snails are molluscs.

The word derives ultimately from Latin *mollis*, 'soft'. The spelling *mollusk* is preferred in America.

molt, moult

The verb *moult* means 'shed skin, hair or feathers'. The preferred American form is *molt*:

UK: moult(s), moulted, moulting (My dog is moulting.)
US: molt(s), molted, molting (My dog is molting.)

molten

See MELT/MOLTEN

moment

Moment comes from Latin *momentum*, 'movement', and has a number of meanings. It can refer to a short period of time:

In a moment, it was gone.

It can also mean 'significance', but this usage is obsolescent:

I don't know if this information is of any moment.

Moment and 'minute' are used in different regions:

I haven't any at the moment.
I haven't any at the minute.

The cliché 'at this *moment* in time' is widely disliked. 'Now' is preferred.

momentarily

The adverb *momentarily* has different meanings and different pronunciations in Britain and America. In Britain, it usually means 'just for a moment':

I was momentarily stunned.

In America, it can be used like this but it can also mean 'straightaway':

I'll do it momentarily.

In Britain, the first syllable rhymes with 'home' whereas it tends to rhyme with 'Mom' in America.

momentary, momentous

Momentary and *momentous* are adjectives whose meanings reflect the two main meanings of MOMENT. *Momentary* means 'fleeting', 'transitory':

A momentary lapse in concentration can be enough to lose the game.

Momentous means 'significant, of considerable consequence':

It was the most momentous decision of her life.

Monaco

An inhabitant of the European principality is a 'Monegasque'; the derived adjective is the same. The capital is Monaco-Ville.

money

Precise sums of *money* are given in figures and symbols:

63¢ (sixty-three cents)
25p (twenty-five pence)
$1.20 (one dollar twenty cents)
£2.35 (two pounds thirty-five pence).

For sums involving larger amounts, the usual conventions are:

$2 billion (two billion dollars)
£6 million (six million pounds).

Britain originally used 'billion' to mean 'one million million' but the term is now used with its US meaning of 'one thousand million'.

Sums of money are often treated as singular:

£10 billion is now being spent on health.

£6,000 is urgently needed for repairs.

When a sum is used as a modifier, it is sometimes spelled out:

a ten million pound health bill

a six thousand pound repair bill.

See also BILLION/MILLION/THOUSAND, NUMBERS

Mongolia

An inhabitant of the republic in northern Asia is a 'Mongolian' or, less frequently, a 'Mongol'; the derived adjectives are the same. The capital is Ulan Bator.

mongoose

A *mongoose* is a small predatory mammal. The word comes from Marathi *mangus* and the spelling has been influenced by 'goose'. The plural of *mongoose* is 'mongooses', not *mongeese:

Mongooses have a long tail and a brindled coat.

monogram, monograph

These nouns are occasionally confused. A *monogram* is a design, often of initials:

He wanted an embroidered monogram on his shirts.

A *monograph* is a long essay on a particular subject:

Have you read her monograph on Milton's early poems?

monologue

A *monologue* is a speech made by one person. The dramatic monologue or 'soliloquy' is a literary convention that allows characters to communicate their thoughts directly to an audience. Colloquially, *monologue* is applied to the speech of a person who talks at, rather than with a listener.

mood

In normal usage, *mood* refers to a state of mind:

Is he in a good mood today?

In language studies, *mood* is closely related to MODALITY. Traditionally, *mood* was applied to verbs to distinguish between statements (INDIC-ATIVE mood), orders (IMPERATIVE mood) and subordinate clauses or wishes (SUBJUNCTIVE mood).

moose
See ELK/MOOSE

moot

The adjective *moot* comes from Old English *gemot*, 'meeting', and now means 'debatable, open to question' in the fixed phrase:

a moot point.

The regular verb *moot* means 'suggest', 'raise for debate':

I mooted the possibility that she could be wrong.

I believe that possibility was mooted at the meeting.

moped

The spelling *moped* can be the past tense or past participle of the regular verb *mope*:

mope(s), moped, moping

I think he's moping because he and his girlfriend have split up.

This *moped* rhymes with 'hoped'.

Moped can also be a light motorcycle, a blend of '*mo*tor + *ped*al':

I had a moped when I was a teenager.

This *moped* is a disyllabic noun and rhymes with 'so said'.

moral, morale, morals

These words all derive from Latin *moralis*, 'relating to morals or customs'. *Moral* can be an adjective:

a moral victory

or a noun meaning 'lesson to be derived':

The moral of the story is: We can achieve great things if we cooperate.

Moral is stressed on the first syllable and rhymes with 'coral'.

Morale refers to the positive spirit of a person or group:

We'll have to raise his morale if we want him to win.

Our morale was sky-high after our successful run.

Morale is stressed on the second syllable and rhymes with 'corral'.

The noun *morals* refers to principles and modes of behaviour:

Without morals, how would any of us know what is right and what is wrong?

more, most

These adverbs are used to form the comparative and superlative forms of adjectives and adverbs:

more intriguing, most intriguing

more intriguingly, most intriguingly.

More is used when comparing two items; *most* is used for more than two:

History is more interesting than Geography.

Chemistry is the most interesting subject.

Often, in colloquial speech, *most* is used where *more* is required:

*Of the two, I find History most interesting.
Of the two, I find History more interesting.

More can function as a determiner, the comparative equivalent of 'many' or 'much':

many lovely days, more lovely days
much happiness , more happiness

as a pronoun, both singular and plural:

We have a lot of food, but more is needed.
We have a lot of workers, but more are needed.

and as a noun:

I can't take more.
The more, the merrier.

Most can function as a determiner meaning 'nearly all':

Most children are attractive.

as a pronoun, both singular and plural:

Most of the work is finished.
Most of the workers are tired.

and as a noun:

The most I can afford is £50.

Occasionally, the adverb *most* can occur in a similar position to the adverb 'mostly', but their meanings are different:

I was most interested in the computers.
I was mostly interested in the computers.

Most is an absolute adverb in this context, whereas 'mostly' suggests that I was also interested in something else.

more or less

The phrase *more or less* means 'approximately'. It should not be hyphenated:

We are more or less ready.

more than, over

Colloquially, people often use *over* in references to numbers when *more than* would be more appropriate:

He wrote over thirty plays.
He wrote more than thirty plays.

Although *over* is a positional preposition:

They flew over the house.

its use as a shorter equivalent of *more than* is growing. Many careful users dislike the use of *over* to mean 'more than':

He has over ten employees.

preferring:

He has more than ten employees.

See also OVER

mores

Mores is a Latin plural noun meaning 'customs'. It has been used in sociology and, like SIBLING, it has been extended beyond the discipline:

She went to New Guinea and studied the language and mores of the Enga people.

Mores is pronounced to rhyme with 'more rays'.

Morocco

An inhabitant of the northeast African monarchy is a 'Moroccan'; the derived adjective is the same. The capital is Rabat.

morpheme

A *morpheme* is defined as the smallest unit of meaning in a language. There are two types of morpheme in English: bound morphemes and free morphemes. A bound morpheme is a form such as 're-', which has meaning but cannot occur in isolation:

re + lease = release

and a free morpheme is a form such as 'lease', which is equivalent to a word.

morphology

Morphology is the study of the structure of words and MORPHEMES. It covers inflection:

book, books
go, goes, went, gone
soon, sooner, soonest

and word formation:

attract + ive + ness = attractiveness
motor + pedal = moped
tiger + lily = tigerlily.

See also AFFIX, DERIVATION, WORD FORMATION

mortgage

The 't' in *mortgage* is silent and this means that the word is often misspelled. The word comes from Old French *mort* + *gage*, 'dead + pledge or security', and it is used as a noun and a regular verb:

They have finally paid off the mortgage on their home.
mortgage(s), mortgaged, mortgaging
They mortgaged their home to help support their business.

The person who borrows money is called a 'mortgagor' or a 'mortgager'; the lender is called a 'mortgagee'.

Moslem, Muslim

The name for a follower of Islam has been spelled in a variety of ways in English. *Muslim* is currently the most acceptable form although the older variant *Moslem* is still used. There are two pronunciations of *Muslim*. The '-u-' is normally pronounced as in 'put' but it is sometimes pronounced as in 'but'. The term 'Mohammedan' is outdated and unacceptable.

mosquito

Mosquito is the diminutive form of Spanish *mosca*, 'fly'. It may be pluralized by adding '-s' or, more often, '-es':

Mosquitoes are instrumental in spreading malaria.

most

See MORE/MOST

mote

See MOAT/MOTE

motif, motive

These words both derive ultimately from Latin *motivus*, 'moving', but they were borrowed at different times and have distinct meanings. A *motif* is a theme established in a work of art:

Many of her designs have a floral motif.
The metaphor of decay is a motif that runs through Shakespeare's final plays.

Motive means 'reason':

What was Iago's motive for deceiving Othello?

motivation

Motivation means 'incentive', 'inducement', but it is increasingly being used to mean 'reason':

We have examined her motivation for behaving in this way.

Such usage serves no useful purpose but weakens the meaning of *motivation*.

mould

See MOLD/MOULD

moult

See MOLT/MOULT

moustache, mustache

This noun comes from Italian *mostaccio* and is frequently misspelled in both Britain and America. The commonest error is to omit the final 'e'. In Britain the '-o-' is compulsory, but it is omitted in American English:

Kipling said that a kiss from a man without a moustache was like eating an egg without salt.

In Britain the stress occurs on the second syllable; in America, it occurs on the first, which rhymes with 'bus'.

mouth

Mouth can function as a noun and as a regular verb:

I've never been any good at drawing mouths.
mouth(s), mouthed, mouthing.

The verb is not used in formal or courteous English.

movable, moveable

These alternative spellings are both acceptable:

Is this desk moveable/movable?

Some removal firms now use the word as a noun:

Please ensure that moveables and breakables are clearly marked.

The version without 'e' is used in legal work.

mow

Mow is now usually a regular verb:

mow(s), mowed, mowing, mowed

but 'mown' is still occasionally used as the past participle:

Have you mown the grass yet?

'Mown' is now used almost exclusively as an adjective, especially in the fixed phrase:

the new-mown hay.

Mozambique

An inhabitant of the republic in south-eastern Africa is a 'Mozambican'; the derived adjective is the same. The capital is Maputo.

Mr, Mrs

The courtesy titles in the past were:

Miss (for a single woman)
Mr (for a single or married man)
Mrs (for a married woman)
Master (for a boy).

Mr and *Mrs* are still used, but many women prefer the term 'Ms' because it is unmarked for marriage. In general, the term of address and reference should be in keeping with the wishes of the person who is being addressed or referred to.

Ms, MS

Ms is pronounced to rhyme with 'fizz' and is the unmarked title for a woman. *MS* is the abbreviation for 'manuscript' and the plural is MSS:

Has Ms Smith submitted her MS yet?

See also MISS

much

Much can function as an adverb:

I feel much better now.

as a determiner, usually in negative sentences:

I haven't much money.

and as a pronoun:

Much remains to be done.

The use of *much* as an adjective in negative constructions, as in:

It's not much but it's all mine.
They haven't much land.

is acceptable, but *much* in positive sentences such as:

They have much land.

is rarely used. Most people prefer:

They have a great deal of land.

or

They have a lot of land.

---

mucous, mucus

These words are often misused. *Mucous* or, less frequently, *mucose* is an adjective, whereas *mucus* is a noun.

Mucous membranes secrete mucus.

Muhammad, Muhammed

See MOHAMET/MOHAMMED/MUHAMMAD/
MUHAMMED

---

multi-

Multi- is a frequently used prefix. It derives from Latin *multus*, 'much, many', a meaning it still has:

multicultural (possessing many cultures)
multilingual (able to speak many languages).

---

multi-functional

Many words in English are *multi-functional*, that is, they can function in a variety of roles:

a round table (adjective)
He'll come round this evening. (adverb)
Let's go for a round of golf. (noun)
I walked round the garden. (preposition)
She rounded the bend as we spoke. (verb)

Multi-functionality is a feature of uninflected languages.

See also PIDGIN AND CREOLE

---

murder

See HOMICIDE/MANSLAUGHTER/MURDER

Muslim

See MOSLEM

---

must

Must is a modal verb that can express obligation:

I must do what I can to help.

resolution:

I must work harder.

or certainty:

It must be true!

Must is often replaced by 'have to', especially when a past time reference is necessary:

We must go now.
We had to go then.

When *must* is negated, it expresses prohibition:

You must not walk on the grass.

Must is now widely used in colloquial speech and the popular press as a noun:

Haven't you seen this show? Believe me, it's a must.

See also MODALITY

---

mustache

See MOUSTACHE/MUSTACHE

---

mutation

The noun *mutation* derives from Latin *mutare*, 'change'. It is applied to the vowel changes that mark some plurals:

goose, geese
mouse, mice

and some verbal distinctions:

shoot, shot
sing, sang, sung.

---

mutual

See COMMON/MUTUAL

---

my

See ME/MY

Myanmar

See BURMA/MYANMAR

---

myna, mynah

See MINA/MYNA/MYNAH

---

myself

Myself is a reflexive pronoun:

I wasn't able to wash myself this morning because there was no water.

It is increasingly being used as an emphasizer:

I myself do not indulge in politics.

This is perfectly acceptable in speech. The tendency to use *myself* rather than 'me', as in:

He invited John and myself to dinner.

is less acceptable.

See also I/ME

N

n
N is a nasal consonant.

naive, naïve
The word *naïve* was borrowed from French *naif*, *naïve*, 'natural'. The meaning changed from 'natural' to 'ingenuous', 'innocent', 'artless', 'unsophisticated':

She seems naive but it is hard to decide whether her innocence is real or contrived.

I did not expect such a naive argument from such an eminent critic.

Many users continue to use the dieresis to indicate that the word is disyllabic. The derived noun has four acceptable forms, namely 'naiveté', 'naïveté, 'naïvety' and 'naivety'. As these words are now firmly established in English, it seems reasonable to use 'naive', 'naively' and 'naivety'. The forms that are chosen should be used consistently.

See also ACCENT MARK, BORROWING

naked, nude
These words can occasionally function as synonyms:

a naked man

a nude man

but they have different origins and uses. *Naked* comes from Old English *nacod*, 'uncovered', 'bare'. It can mean 'totally uncovered' and can apply to people or things:

Her naked body was found a short distance from her home.

I hadn't realized that a naked flame could be so dangerous.

It can also be used metaphorically to mean 'unaided, unsupported':

How far can you see with the naked eye?

In its metaphorical senses *naked* cannot be replaced by *nude*.

Nude comes from Latin *nudus*, 'bare', and means 'totally uncovered'. It frequently occurs in the phrase:

in the nude

It is regularly used as a noun to describe a model who poses for a painting or sculpture or for the work of art:

Paintings of nudes make you appreciate how beautiful the human body can be.

name
In most societies, naming is highly significant. Among English speakers, it is usual for people to have at least one given *name* and a family *name*:

Amanda Jane Smith

Ahmed Jibril.

In parts of Africa and Asia, the family name is often put first:

Djou Dun Ren

Kripilani Bablu

Mokolo Donatus

even when signing one's name.

In the United States it is not uncommon to find that generations are indicated:

Michael Green

Michael Green Jr

Michael O'Shea III

The titles 'Senior/Sen/Sr' and 'Junior/Jr' are occasionally found in Britain and Australia, but they tend to suggest American influence. The use of an initial before a given name as in:

P. Michael Green

is also thought of as Americanized.

Double-barrelled names may arise in three main ways. A woman may add her husband's surname to her own. Thus Joanne Ingham may marry a Sam Brown and become:

Joanne Ingham-Brown.

Less frequently, Sam Brown may become:

Sam Brown-Ingham.

A child may take on a mother's maiden name. Thus, the children of Anne Fitzgerald and Michael Green may become:

Annette Fitzgerald-Green

Brian Fitzgerald Green.

When surnames are common, as with Brown, Jones and Smith, double-barrelled names are chosen as a way of distinguishing among families. Usually, the wife's name precedes the husband's. Thus Mary Taylor and Owen Brown may become Mary and Owen Taylor-Brown.

See also CHRISTIAN NAME

Namibia
An inhabitant of the country in southern Africa is a 'Namibian'; the derived adjective is the same. The capital is Windhoek.

nano-
Nano- is a prefix deriving from Greek *nanos*, 'dwarf'. It is used in such technical words as:

nanometre (one thousand-millionth of a metre)

nanosecond (one thousand-millionth of a second).

naphtha

Naphtha comes originally from Persian *neft*, 'naphtha, a distillation from coal tar'. It is frequently misspelled, as are the related forms 'naphthalin(e)' and 'naphthene':

Naphtha is an obsolete name for 'petrol'.

naphthalene, naphthaline, naphthalin

These are all acceptable spellings for the volatile crystalline solid used in mothballs:

Naphthalene is used in the manufacture of explosives.

napkin

Napkin comes from Old French *nape*, 'tablecloth'. It used to refer to a square piece of cloth used as a 'serviette':

Have you seen the table napkins?

Its meaning was extended to 'a diaper':

Napkins used to be made of towelling but now nappies are usually made of disposable material.

The choice of *napkin* or 'serviette' is often seen as a class marker. 'Serviette' is regarded by some people as indicating a desire for upward social mobility.

narcissus

The plural of *narcissus* is usually 'narcissi', although 'narcissuses' is occasionally found. The '-i' at the end of 'narcissi' is usually pronounced to rhyme with 'my'. The *narcissus* gets its name from a Greek myth in which a beautiful young man, Narcissus, fell in love with his own reflection.

narration, narrative

The nouns *narration* and *narrative* come from Latin *narrare*, 'to tell a story'. They now have a number of distinct uses, but the meanings all involve an account of a sequence of events. *Narration* means 'the act or process of giving an account, often a traditional account':

The narration lasted for almost an hour but we still had not heard more than an outline of the events.

A *narrative* can comprehend both a continuous chronological account in speech or writing and portions of a novel or story that are not conversation:

David Copperfield is a first-person narrative.

The narrative, speech and thought processes are often blended in a stream-of-consciousness novel.

See also DIRECT SPEECH

nationalize, naturalize

These verbs are occasionally misused. The verb *nationalize* is used when a government puts resources or a private company under state control:

The coal industry was nationalized after the war because it was felt that such a vital resource should not be in private hands.

Naturalize means 'give citizenship to a person of foreign birth':

People who are not born in a country are often naturalized after a period of residence there. Some countries, however, do not give citizenship to immigrants, no matter how long they have lived in the country.

native

The word *native* comes from Latin *nasci*, 'to be born'. As an adjective, it means 'belonging to a person by virtue of birth and upbringing', 'innate':

He never works but he can get by on his native wit.

Daffodils are not native to Australia.

The noun *native* means 'a person born in a particular place':

I live in London now but I'm a native of Aberdeen.

The older meaning of *native* as 'indigenous, non-white person as opposed to a settler' is no longer acceptable, although the phrase:

Native American

is used for Amerindians.

See also POLITICAL CORRECTNESS

Native American

The phrase *Native American*, with capital letters, is used for the Amerindian people who lived in America before the continent was colonized.

Native Americans are struggling to preserve their languages and customs.

The phrase 'Native Australian' is sometimes used as a synonym for Australian Aborigines.

nature

The noun *nature* often occurs in circumlocutions such as:

books of that nature (such books)
It is in the nature of advertisers to exaggerate. (Advertisers exaggerate.)

There is nothing intrinsically wrong with the word *nature*, but clichés involving it should be avoided.

Two nouns deriving from *nature* are occasionally confused. These are 'naturalist' and 'naturist'. A 'naturalist' studies animals and plants:

What renowned naturalist introduced 'Wildlife on One'?

'Naturist' is a synonym for 'nudist':

There are not many naturist beaches in Britain.

naught, nought

These words are homophones and rhyme with 'bought'. *Naught* used to mean 'nothing':

Your plans will come to naught.
There is naught to fear in death.

It rarely occurs in the standard language but is still found in British dialects:

He said naught to me.

The regional form in the north of England rhymes with 'out' and is regularly spelled 'nowt':

It cost me nowt.

Nought is another word for 'zero':

There are six noughts in a million.

In America *naught* is the usual spelling for zero:

US: There are six naughts in a million.

Nauru

An inhabitant of the island republic in the Pacific is a 'Nauruan'; the derived adjective is the same. The capital is Nauru.

nauseous

Nauseous is the adjective from 'nausea', 'a feeling of sickness':

This drug may make you nauseous.

In the past, the expression:

I felt nauseous (sick).

was almost exclusively American but it is now widely used in Britain.

Nauseous has two acceptable pronunciations: the middle 's' may be pronounced 's' or 'z'.

naval, navel

These homophones have different origins and meanings. *Naval* is an adjective and comes from Latin *navis*, 'a ship', and describes something related to the navy:

a naval destroyer
a naval uniform.

Navel is a noun and comes from Old English *nafela*, 'the hole in the centre of the stomach':

A child is attached by an umbilical cord from its navel.

NB, N.B., n.b.

These are all acceptable abbreviations for Latin *nota bene*, 'note well'. It is sometimes used as a method of reminding the reader of the significance of a point:

NB This critic has the same name as the author but they are not related.

See also ABBREVIATION

near by, nearby

Careful users distinguish between the single-word adjective and the two-word phrase. *Nearby* is an adjective meaning 'close':

We visited a nearby church.

Near by is an adverbial phrase:

The vicar lived near by.

Many writers use *nearby* for both.

nebula

The noun *nebula* has two acceptable plurals, 'nebulae' and 'nebulas':

A nebula is a diffuse cloud of gases and particles.

necessary, necessarily

The adjective *necessary* is one of the most frequently misspelled words in the language. It has one 'c' and double 's'.

Computer skills are necessary in most jobs.

The traditional pronunciation of *necessarily* puts the main stress on the first syllable, but most speakers now stress the third syllable.

née

The French past participle of the verb *naître*, 'to be born' is *né(e)*:

Elle est née ... (She was born)
Il est né ... (He was born).

Née is sometimes used to provide a woman's maiden name:

Mary Morgan, née Magee, is my aunt.

It rhymes with 'hay'.

The *né* form is never used of a man, even if he has changed his name:

William Carlton, born Liam O'Carollan, was a writer.

The acronym and abbreviation 'aka' (also known as) is widely used in the press, but more often as a reference to a person's pseudonym than to a maiden name:

Chris Grieve, aka Hugh MacDiarmid.

See also ALIAS

need

Need can function as a regular verb:

need(s), needed, needing
He needs to broaden his mind.
Do you need any help?

It can also function as an auxiliary verb in negative and interrogative constructions:

He need never worry about money again!
Need she reply?

and in such constructions it does not show agreement:

*He needs never worry ...
*Needs she reply?

There is a growing tendency for *need* to be treated like a regular verb:

He doesn't ever need to worry about money again!
Does she need to reply?

needless to say

The cliché *needless to say* is like 'It goes without saying (that) …' and they are both often used in speech:

Needless to say, they didn't take my advice and I wasn't surprised. We all have the right to make up our own minds.

Many people claim that *needless to say* is redundant, but it is acceptable as an emphasizer or as a FILLER in casual speech.

negation

Negation involves the contradiction or denial of an affirmative statement:

I like you: I don't like you.

It is normally conveyed by the negative adverb 'not/n't' either alone or in combination with the negative response 'no':

Do you like me? No, I don't.

Negation can be marked in several ways, including by the use of negative affixes:

cheerful: uncheerful, cheerless
fearful: fearless
legal: illegal
mutable: immutable
trust: distrust, mistrust

by the use of negative words beginning with 'n':

either: neither
ever: never
one: none
or: nor

by the use of such negative verbs as:

deny, doubt, negate

by the use of such adverbs as 'hardly', 'seldom', 'rarely':

He hardly ever comes here.
He very seldom comes here.

and by the use of an intonation that refuses permission:

Can I go to Paris this weekend?
Of course. Why don't you stay at the Georges V Hotel!

Until the seventeenth century, double or multiple *negation* was widely used. Then grammarians introduced the rule that 'two negatives make an affirmative' and so the Shakespearean-type emphasis became nonstandard. In spite of the rule, however, multiple negation is widely used in dialects:

I never go nowhere these days.
They didn't give them nothing.

In colloquial speech, people frequently make use of transferred negation with verbs of thinking:

I don't think they'll go. = I think they won't go.
I don't believe she said it. = I believe she didn't say it.

In balanced structures, 'neither' must be used with 'nor':

He'll neither work nor want.

It is increasingly being used with 'or', but this is not acceptable:

*He said he would neither give us the money or lend it to us.

See also BARELY/HARDLY/SCARCELY, EITHER/NEITHER, OR

negative
See AFFIRMATIVE/NEGATIVE

negative prefix

The main negative prefixes in English are:

dis- + appear = disappear
in- + decisive = indecisive
non- + sense = nonsense.

In- is realized as 'il-', 'im-' and 'ir-' before words beginning with 'l', 'm' and 'r':

legible: illegible
mobile: immobile
rational: irrational.

See also IL-, IM-, IN-, IR-

neglectful, negligent

These adjectives can both mean 'careless in fulfilling a duty' but *negligent* suggests habitual neglect:

I was neglectful of my duty on just one occasion.
I know I should try not to be negligent.

Negligent is the more widely-used adjective. *Neglectful* is less likely than the verb 'neglect':

I've neglected the garden this year.

negligible

Negligible is an adjective meaning 'so small as to be insignificant':

The discrepancy is negligible but I hate not being able to make the books balance perfectly.

Negro

The adjective and noun *Negro* come from Spanish and Portuguese *negro*, 'black'. The adjective is found in such phrases as:

Negro spirituals

and the noun is sometimes used as a technical term for 'black-skinned people of Africa' or their descendants:

The Negroes and Caucasians have learned to live in harmony.

Many black people prefer to be called 'Africans', 'African-Americans', 'Blacks' or to be designated by the country they come from rather than by the colour of their skin:

I'm a Nigerian.

See also AFRO-, BLACK, POLITICAL CORRECTNESS

neighbour, neighbor

These are alternative spellings for people who live nearby. *Neighbour* is the British spelling and *neighbor* is favoured in America:

UK: My neighbour is all mankind ...

US: My neighbor is all mankind ...

The same distinction applies to the related noun 'neighbo(u)rhood':

UK: This is a quiet neighbourhood.

US: This is a quiet neighborhood.

neither

See EITHER/NEITHER

neologism

A *neologism* is a newly coined word or phrase, or a familiar word used with a new meaning. The word comes from Greek *neos* + *logos*, 'new + word':

chocoholic (chocolate + alcoholic)

chortle (chuckle + snort)

stagflation (stagnation + inflation)

unisex (uni- + sex).

People sometimes express disapproval of neologisms, but such new words either disappear or are accepted into the language.

The terminology associated with computers contains many neologisms that are being absorbed into English:

format, menu, windows.

See also COINAGE, NONCE, WORD FORMATION

Nepal

An inhabitant of the Asian monarchy is a 'Nepali'; the derived adjective is 'Nepalese'. The capital is Kathmandu.

nephew

A *nephew* is the son of a brother or a sister. It has two acceptable pronunciations in that the central consonant may be pronounced '-v-' or '-f-'. The 'v' pronunciation is widespread in Britain but the 'f' pronunciation is preferred in America.

net

Net can function as a noun:

a fishing net

or as a regular verb:

net(s), netted, netting

They netted a huge profit from the sale.

There are two acceptable spellings for the adjective meaning 'remaining after all deductions':

Their net(t) profit after tax was £15,000.

The phrase:

surf(ing) the Net

is widely used by people who like computers to mean 'enjoying the World Wide Web':

Some of the students surf the Net instead of doing their computer assignments.

Netherlands, The

The Netherlands is the preferred form for Holland. The derived noun and adjective are 'Dutch', a term that some people from the Netherlands dislike. The capital is Amsterdam.

network

A *network* is an interconnected group:

Each of us has a network of friends and relations.

In computer terminology, a *network* is a set of terminals linked to a central computer. *Network* is also used as a regular verb:

network(s), networked, networking

We were networked ten years ago. Every student can input or access data simultaneously.

network norm

Although standard written English is almost identical throughout the English-speaking world, there are numerous regional pronunciations. Some pronunciations are more prestigious than others and these tend to be the ones used by newscasters on radio and television. Such *network norms* are based on the educated speech of a country.

See also ACCENT, RADIO, STANDARD ENGLISH

neurotic

The adjective *neurotic* originally meant 'suffering from an obsessive kind of mental disorder'. Because of overuse, it has come to mean 'anxious', 'highly strung':

She's neurotic! She worries that people won't like her.

never

Never is a negative adverb deriving from Old English *ne* + *æfre*, 'not + ever':

I have never heard such nonsense!

It is often applied, incorrectly, to a single occasion as an emphatic negative:

Did you hear the bell? *No, I never heard it.

It would, however, be correct to say:

The bell was rung for hours on a Sunday but I never heard it because I switched off my hearing aid.

The exclamation:

Well I never!

is now as old-fashioned as:

My goodness gracious me!

never-

Never- can function as a prefix in a number of words, such as:

never-ending, nevertheless

The expression 'never-never' is used as an adjective in the phrase:

never-never land (imaginary place)

and as a noun in the British colloquialism:

buy something on the never-never (on hire purchase).

nevertheless

Nevertheless is an adverbial meaning 'in spite of that'. It is not hyphenated:

You have made a number of serious mistakes. Nevertheless, we feel you deserve another chance.

new, novel

New means 'recently made', 'unused':

I've got a lovely new dress.

The adjective *novel* comes from Latin *novellus*, a diminutive of *nova*, 'new'. It is used to describe something that is 'fresh, original':

That's a novel idea!

New Zealand

An inhabitant of this country is called a 'New Zealander' and the adjective is 'New Zealand'. The colloquial use of 'Kiwi' to refer to New Zealanders or their produce should be avoided if it would cause offence. The capital is Wellington.

new-

New- is a widely used prefix, helping to form adjectives:

new-born

and nouns:

newcomer.

news

The noun *news* is singular and uncountable:

This is the news.

Isn't there any good news today?

News has given rise to a number of compounds, including:

newsagent, newscaster, newsletter, newsprint.

See also COUNTABLE AND UNCOUNTABLE, NOUN

Newspeak

The noun *Newspeak* was coined by George Orwell in *Nineteen Eighty-Four* (1948) to describe a variety of language designed to control people's minds. This noun has given rise to other coinages, such as:

airspeak, mediaspeak, seaspeak

for varieties of language associated with a particular group or job.

See also DOUBLESPEAK

next

Next comes from an Old English superlative *nehst*, 'nearest'. It can be used as an adjective meaning 'immediately following':

She's on the next train.

as an adverb, especially in instructions involving several steps:

Next, place the screws in the drilled holes …

'Next to' can mean 'adjacent to' or 'almost':

He sat next to me in class.

I have next to nothing left.

There are regional differences in the meanings people give to temporal phrases involving *next* and 'this'. If A tells B on Monday:

I'll see you next Wednesday.

it can, in different regions mean:

I'll see you the day after tomorrow.

or:

I'll see you in nine days' time.

Some speakers use 'this Wednesday' to mean the one that is close and 'next Wednesday' to mean the one that is over a week away. Care should be exercised in the use of these phrases to avoid misunderstanding.

Next occurs in a number of fixed phrases including:

next-door neighbour

next of kin

next-to-new (hardly used).

Nicaragua

An inhabitant of the Central American country is a 'Nicaraguan'; the derived adjective is the same. The capital is Managua. In Britain, the 'agua' of *Nicaragua* is pronounced like 'jaguar' but in America there is a tendency to pronounce it like 'ah gwa'.

nice

The adjective *nice* is a clear example of the semantic changes undergone by many English words. *Nice* comes from Latin *nescius*, 'ignorant', and it came into English in the fourteenth century with the meanings of 'foolish,' 'silly'. Later, *nice* developed the meaning of 'wanton' and 'lascivious'. Later still, it meant 'shy' and then 'precise', as in:

a nice distinction.

By the eighteenth century it signified approval and it can now be used in such phrases as:

a nice evening (I liked it.)

nice food (I enjoyed it.)
a nice person (I like her.)
Have a nice day! (I wish you well.)

Because of its overuse and imprecise meaning, *nice* is often condemned by teachers and stylists in much the same way as 'get' is.

See also CLICHÉ, PHATIC COMMUNION, SEMANTIC CHANGE

nicety

Nicety is a noun derived from 'nice' and meaning 'subtle point of distinction':

I did not expect you to draw attention to such niceties. I thought you would concentrate on the broad sweep of the novel.

niche

Niche was borrowed from French *nichier*, to nest', and applied to a wall recess:

It is customary to find statues in eighteenth-century niches.

He spotted the gap in the market and is now a niche publisher of books about local history.

The word has been extended metaphorically to mean 'very suitable position':

I wish he could find his niche in life.

Niche has two pronunciations. The older one rhymes with 'itch' and the more recent one approximates to the French pronunciation and rhymes with 'leash'.

nickname

Nickname comes from Middle English *an eke name*, 'an additional name'. The phrase was incorrectly divided, or we would now have 'icknames'. A *nickname* can be given to a person or place, and it can be familiar, complimentary or derisory:

We call her 'Trixie' because 'Beatrix' seems very formal.

They called her 'Jane the Brain' because she was so clever.

They called me 'Four-Eyes' because I wore spectacles.

Niger

An inhabitant of the north-central African country is 'Nigerien', to distinguish from an inhabitant of NIGERIA. The derived adjective is the same. The capital is Niamey.

Nigeria

An inhabitant of the West African country is a 'Nigerian'; the derived adjective is the same. The capital is now Abuja (which has replaced Lagos).

nigh

Nigh is an obsolescent word for 'near'. It is now only found in literature and the dialects:

He's nigh on a hundred.

The compound 'well nigh' meaning 'almost' is also archaic:

It is well nigh midnight.

night

Night occurs in a wide range of compounds, some hyphenated, some not:

night-clothes, night-light, night-time
nightclub, nightfall, nightmare
night blindness, night nurse, night owl.

See also DAY, HYPHEN

no one, nobody, none

No one may be either hyphenated or not, with the non-hyphenated form being more widely used. *Nobody* means 'no person, no one'. It is singular and, like its synonym *no one*, takes a singular verb:

Nobody is to blame.
No one was listening.

When *nobody* or *no one* occur in sentences that have tag questions, there are problems of agreement:

Nobody knows the answer, does he/she/do they?
No one used your name, did he/she/they?

The normal rules of agreement imply that, since *nobody* and *no one* are singular, the tag should be either:

Nobody knows the answer, does she?
Nobody knows the answer, does he?

To prevent confusion or sexism, many writers suggest that we should adopt the colloquial usage with 'they', as in:

Nobody knows the answer, do they?

None comes from Old English *ne + an*, 'not + one'. It is also singular and should be followed by a singular verb:

None was wasted.

None is often followed by the construction 'of + plural noun':

None of the children is at school yet.

In these circumstances the plural form of the verb occurs in colloquial speech and increasingly in the written medium:

None of the children are at school yet.

but, since *none* means 'not one', logic suggests the use of the singular form of the verb.

Nobody, *no one* and *none* can occur as objects as well as subjects:

I saw nobody.
I heard no one.
I liked none (of them).

but most people prefer to negate the verb and say:

I didn't see anybody.

I didn't hear any one.
I didn't like any of them.

See also CONCORD, EVERY, GENDER, HE OR SHE,
NUMBER

no sooner
No sooner functions adverbially:

No sooner had he arrived than he asked for tea.

See also BARELY/HARDLY/SCARCELY

no thing, nothing
The phrase *no thing* is rare, but when it is used,
the 'no' is stressed and rhymes with 'go':

Do you think I'm afraid of ghosts? No 'thing' is going
to drive me from this house.

Nothing can function as an indefinite pronoun:

Nothing will disturb her equilibrium.

noblesse oblige
The French phrase *noblesse oblige*, 'nobility
obliges', means 'nobility imposes obligations of
courtesy and honour':

It was a question of noblesse oblige. He felt it was
his privilege to honour his father's promise even
though he was under no legal obligation to do so.

Often, the phrase is used ironically:

When Marie Antoinette was told that the peasants
had no bread, she suggested that they should eat
cake. *Noblesse oblige*, I suppose.

nobody
See NO ONE/NOBODY/NONE

noisome
Noisome is occasionally misused. It looks as if it
related to 'noise', but it derives from English
(an)noy + *some*, 'offensive', 'dangerous', and it is
becoming obsolete:

There's a noisome odour coming from somewhere.

nominal, nominalization
The term *nominal* is used in grammar to refer to
a noun, a pronoun, a noun phrase or a structure
that can function as a subject, object or noun
complement. The underlined items in the
following sentences are all *nominals*:

The child in the pram was crying. She had lost her
rattle.
They wanted to protect the poor and the hungry.
What you did was foolish.

A *nominalization* is a term used in grammar for
the process of forming nouns from other word
classes. Often the process involves the addition
of a suffix:

bad (adj) + ness = badness
nice (adj) + ty = nicety
putt (verb) + -er = putter

but sometimes only the function of the word
changes:

We all have our ups and downs.

See also NOUN

non-
Non- is one of the most frequently used negative
prefixes in the language:

non-alcoholic, non-fiction, non-swimmer.

Most compounds involving *non-* are hyphenated.
The best known exceptions are:

nondescript, nonentity, nonsense.

See also NEGATION

non compos mentis
This Latin phrase means 'not in control of one's
mind' and is frequently used as an adjective
meaning 'mentally unsound', 'incapable of
looking after one's own affairs':

His behaviour suggests that he's *non compos mentis*,
but we are all capable of behaving erratically at
times.

non-defining clause, non-restrictive clause
These are relative clauses.

See DEFINING RELATIVE CLAUSE, THAT/WHICH

non-flammable
See FLAMMABLE/INFLAMMABLE/NON-FLAMMABLE

non sequitur
This phrase is Latin for 'it does not follow' and it
is often italicized. It is used in English of a
statement that seems to have little or no
connection with what preceded it:

Surely that claim about heredity is a *non sequitur*, or
did I miss something?

non-U
This adjective is occasionally used in Britain to
refer to pronunciations and words that are not
characteristic of the upper classes:

It's non-U to say 'cutlery'. You should say 'knives and
forks'.

There is no logical reason why some structures
should be preferred to others but snobbery is
rarely based on logic.

See also U AND NON-U

nonce
Nonce words are created 'for the nonce', that is,
on or for a particular occasion. The word comes
from an incorrect segmentation of Middle English
for then anes, 'for the once'. *Nonce* words look
and sound like English words in that they do not

break the rules of the language, but they are often ephemeral.

Nonce words can result from blends:

smog (smoke + fog)

false analogy:

I'm hoping to be incommunicated. (compare 'excommunicated')

humour:

BA's hostesses are flylingual.

and slips of the tongue:

low fying log (low-lying fog).

Often, advertisers use nonce-type words:

Every bubble's passed its fizzical.

If a *nonce* word ceases to be ephemeral, it ceases to be a *nonce* word. Words such as 'chortle' and 'pandemonium' started as *nonce* words but are now integrated into the vocabulary.

See also COINAGE, NEOLOGISM, WORD FORMATION

none
See NO ONE/NOBODY/NONE

none the less
None the less is frequently used adverbially:

He's good. None the less, I think we should interview some other candidates before making up our minds.

It is usually written as three words because 'none the' can be followed by other comparative adjectives:

She is none the wiser for her experience.

He's none the worse for his fall.

However, it can also be written as one word, on analogy with 'nevertheless'.

See also NEVERTHELESS

nonplus
Nonplus comes from Latin *non plus*, 'no further', and is used as a regular verb meaning 'be at a loss, confound':

UK: nonplus(ses), nonplussed, nonplussing (I was nonplussed by such totally unexpected behaviour.)

US: nonpluses, nonplused, nonplusing (I was nonplused by such totally unexpected behaviour.)

nonstandard English
There is a written standard language that is accepted (with minor differences) throughout the English-speaking world. It is the language of education, politics and international transactions. In addition to this, there are several types of nonstandard English in existence.

See also DIALECT, RECEIVED PRONUNCIATION, STANDARD ENGLISH

nor
Nor is part of a coordinating conjunction joining alternatives:

She neither came nor sent an apology.

Nor goes with 'neither' just as 'or' goes with 'either'.

See also EITHER/NEITHER

norm
A *norm* may be regarded as the habitual language use of a group. The group may be as small as a family or as large as a country. A *norm* is useful in providing a fixed point from which a series of comparisons may be made. For example, the norm of Received Pronunciation (RP) in Britain provides a basis for pronunciation comparisons between speech in Leeds and in Liverpool, as well as between either of these and RP. Although all language norms are arbitrary, there is a tendency for a *norm* to become prestigious and for variations to be regarded not simply as different but as inferior.

See also NETWORK NORM

north, North, northern
The word *north* is written with a lower case 'n' unless it is part of a geographical name:

We drove north.

He lives in North America.

Northern is written with a capital letter only when it is part of a name:

I was born in Northern Ireland.

He's an example of northern grit.

Norway
An inhabitant of the north European country is a 'Norwegian'; the derived adjective is the same. The capital is Oslo.

nostalgia
Nostalgia comes from Greek *nostros*, 'return home' + '-*algia*', and it was originally used as the equivalent of homesickness. It is now used with the meaning of 'wistful yearning' for the past:

We all felt the same sense of nostalgia when we remembered the plans we had made in this very room so many years ago.

There is even a tendency now for *nostalgia* to imply sentimentality:

The nostalgia that was novel in her early books is now cloying.

not
Not is a variant of NAUGHT and derives from Old English *na* + *wiht*, 'no whit'. It is now an adverb that negates utterances:

I am not happy with this.

It is often combined with auxiliaries and reduced to 'n't':

I cannot/can't find it.

It can combine with 'that' to form a conjunction:

I did my best, not that I expect any favours for my efforts!

and it often occurs with an adverb such as 'certainly' or 'definitely' to deny a claim:

Have you ever cheated the taxman? Certainly not.

The position of 'not' in a sentence can affect the meaning:

She is not hoping to go out tonight.

is, for example, in contrast to:

She is hoping not to go out tonight.

The first sentence suggests that it is unlikely she will go out. The second suggests that it is unlikely she will be able to stay in.

not only ... but also

These conjunctions introduce balanced phrases or clauses:

He is not only handsome and intelligent but also honest and kind.

She won not only the prize for best athlete but also the prize for top student.

nota bene

Nota bene is a Latin phrase meaning 'note well' and used mostly in its abbreviated form to direct a reader to take note of some point.

See also NB/N.B./n.b.

notable, noticeable

These adjectives are occasionally misused and misspelled. *Notable* (no 'e' before '-able') means 'worthy of being noted, remarkable':

The tally of medals in the paralympics was notable.

Noticeable (an 'e' before '-able') means 'easily seen':

Is this mark on my jacket very noticeable?

nothing

See NO THING/NOTHING

notorious

See FAMOUS/INFAMOUS/NOTORIOUS

notwithstanding

Notwithstanding is always written as one word and means 'in spite of':

Notwithstanding their limited budget, they educated all of the children.

nougat

Nougat derives ultimately from Latin *nux*, 'nut', and is used for a chewy sweet containing nuts.

The normal spelling is an approximation to the French in that the first syllable rhymes with 'who' and the second with 'fah'. The less prestigious pronunciation has *nougat* and 'nugget' as homophones.

nought

See NAUGHT/NOUGHT

noun

In traditional grammars, a *noun* was defined as a 'naming word' or 'the name of a person, animal, place or thing'. Recent definitions of nouns tend to concentrate on their form and their function.

Form

As far as form goes, it can be shown that most nouns change to indicate plurality and possession:

Singular	Possessive	Plural	Possessive
bat	bat's	bats	bats'
boy	boy's	boys	boys'
horse	horse's	horses	horses'

In speech, there is no difference between plurality and possession in regular nouns, both of which are signalled by the addition of 's', 'z' or 'iz' to the word. In the written medium, '-s' or es' indicate plurality, an apostrophe + 's' indicates singular possession, and 's' + an apostrophe indicates plural possession.

Nouns in English can be subdivided in a number of ways. They can be feminine, masculine or neuter:

a widow, a widower, a window.

They can be common:

child, country, language

or proper:

Charlie, China, Greek.

Common nouns begin with a small letter and proper nouns begin with a capital.

Nouns can be abstract:

duty, intelligence, love

or concrete:

door, ivy, lemon.

They can be either countable or uncountable/mass. A countable noun can be preceded by 'a', can have both a singular and a plural form and can, as its name suggests, be counted:

a banana, six bananas

a tree, six trees.

Whereas singular countable nouns can be preceded by 'a', uncountable nouns tend to be preceded by 'some' and they cannot normally be pluralized or counted:

*two butters (two kinds of butter)

*two woods (two pieces of wood).

Occasionally, uncountable nouns can be treated as countable. This occurs when a word such as 'butter' is interpreted to mean 'type of butter':

Two of the French butters are unsalted.

In English, there are many collective nouns, such as 'committee', 'family' or 'team'. These nouns are singular in form but refer to a number of people, animals or things. Collective nouns should occur with singular forms of the verb and should be replaced by singular pronouns:

My family is the most important thing in my life. It supports me in good times and in bad.

Function

Nouns can function as subjects:

Books are expensive.

as objects:

I bought books.

and as complements:

These are books.

They can follow prepositions:

near Manchester

and be replaced by pronouns:

George Washington was a general.
He was the first president of the USA.

See also ABSTRACT NOUN, COLLECTIVE NOUN, COUNTABLE AND UNCOUNTABLE

nova

A *nova* is a faint variable star. The word comes from Latin *nova stella*, 'new star'. It has two acceptable plurals, 'novas' and 'novae':

With novas you can see a huge increase in luminosity as they explode.

novel

See NEW/NOVEL

nowadays

Nowadays is written as one word and is an adverb meaning 'in these times':

Nowadays there is not enough respect for people and property.

nubile

The adjective *nubile* comes from Latin *nubilis*, 'suitable for marriage'. It did not mean 'sexy' or, necessarily, 'sexually attractive', meanings that are now sometimes attached to it:

In her day, she must have been a nubile young woman.

Nubile is applied only to young women and so may be regarded as sexist.

nuciferous, nucivorous

The pronunciation of these words differs only in terms of one sound. They are therefore capable of

being misunderstood. *Nuciferous* means 'nut-bearing':

Nuciferous plants should be cultivated because many nuts are a rich source of protein.

Nucivorous means 'nut-eating':

Squirrels are nucivorous animals; foxes, on the other hand, are not.

nuclear

The adjective *nuclear* is often mispronounced. It should be pronounced 'nuke + leer' and not *nucular. The common mispronunciation is partly due to the tendency to break up consonant clusters and partly due to analogizing with such words as:

insular, singular, vehicular.

nude

See NAKED/NUDE

number

Number is used technically in the classification of words that can display a contrast between singular and plural:

Singular	Plural
mouse	mice
A mouse squeaks.	Mice squeak.
It squeaks.	They squeak.

Thus, grammatical *number* can apply to nouns, pronouns and to the present tense of verbs.

Usually, grammatical *number* corresponds to life:

Michael/he	likes	books.
Norma/she	likes	books.
He + she/they	like	them.

There are, however, nouns that are singular in form but plural in meaning:

family, team

or plural in form but singular in meaning:

linguistics, physics.

In addition, uncountable nouns such as 'beef' refer to quantities rather than specific entities:

a kilo of beef
*two beefs.

Personal pronouns have been subdivided into first, second and third persons singular and plural:

Person	Singular	Plural
1st	I/me/my/mine	we/us/our/ours
2nd	you/your/yours	you/your/yours
feminine	she/her/hers	3rd they/them/their/theirs
3rd masculine	he/him/his	they/them/their/theirs
3rd neuter	it/its	they/them/their/theirs

Although 'we' is regarded as 'first person plural', it does not mean 'I + I + I' but rather 'I + (you) + (he/she/it/they)'.

Most verbs exhibit number contrasts only in the present tense and only with third person subjects:

Present	Past
I sing	I sang
he sings	he sang

The verb 'be' shows some contrasts in both present and past and with different subjects:

Present	Past
I am	I was
you/we/they are	you/we/they were
he/she/it is	he/she/it was.

See also COLLECTIVE NOUN, CONCORD, COUNTABLE AND UNCOUNTABLE

a number of, the number of

These phrases can sometimes cause problems with agreement. *A number of* means 'several' and should be treated as a plural:

A number of men were arrested and are being questioned by the police. Their identities have not been released.

The number of means 'the total' and should be treated as singular:

The number of students is increasing each year. It now stands at just over 20,000.

numbers

There are two types of number in English: cardinal *numbers*, such as 'one', 'two' and 'three', and ordinal *numbers*, such as 'first', 'second' and 'third'. There are a number of conventions associated with *numbers*. These can be summarized as follows:

■ Words not figures should be used for the numbers 'one' to 'ten' (or sometimes 'twelve'):

I bought six loaves and eleven tins of beans.

Figures, not words, should be used for numbers from 11 (or 13) upwards and before abbreviations:

17 metres, 3kg, 4pm

■ When numbers above twenty are spelled out, they should be hyphenated:

She is a thirty-five-year-old cyclist.

However, it is simpler to write:

She is a 35-year-old cyclist.

a 35-year-old cyclist.

■ Round figures, such as 'a thousand' or 'five million' should be written as words.

■ Percentages should be written either as:

sixteen per cent

or:

16 per cent.

The form 16% should be used in tables and lists. The American preference is 'percent'.

■ When numbers occur at the beginning of a sentence, they should be written out whenever possible.

Sixteen per cent of the workers voted to strike.

■ Figures should be used for dates, in addresses and for exact sums of money:

21 August 1923
11 Blenheim Terrace
£35.25.

The figure '0' is normally called 'nought' in Britain and 'zero' in the United States. It is also referred to as '0' (pronounced 'oh'), especially in a sequence of numbers, as 'zero' in temperature measurements, as 'nil' in football matches and as 'love' in tennis matches.

See also AGE, BILLION/MILLION/THOUSAND, MEASUREMENT, MONEY, PUNCTUATION

O

o

O is a vowel that is used to represent a range of vowel sounds including those in 'go', 'got' and 'son'.

O, oh

O is always written with a capital letter. It is used to attract attention, often in poetry:

O, my luve is like a red red rose
O wild West Wind, thou breath of Autumn's being.

Oh is an exclamation that has a capital 'O' when it occurs at the beginning of a sentence and a lower-case 'o' in other positions:

Oh dear! Oh dear! Oh dear!
I feel oh so tired!

-o plurals

There is no fixed rule for pluralizing words that end in -*o*. Some take '-es', more take '-s', a few may take either '-es' or '-s' and a declining number take '-i':

-es	-s-	es/-s	-i
dominoes	egos	haloes/halos	scherzo/scherzi
echoes	kilos	ghettoes/ghettos	virtuoso/virtuosi

The best advice is to check in a dictionary.

OAP

This abbreviation for 'Old Age Pensioner' is often seen as politically incorrect. It is undesirable to describe a person simply in terms of either age or the money they earn or have earned.

See also POLITICAL CORRECTNESS

oasis

An *oasis* is a fertile area in a desert. The plural form is 'oases':

Nomads in the Sahara can die if too many oases go dry.

object

The word *object* can function as a noun or a verb. In speech, the noun is stressed on the first syllable and the verb is stressed on the second:

What is your object in life?
Why do you object to him?

The noun *object* is used in grammar to refer to nouns, noun phrases and pronouns that follow transitive verbs:

I like music. (music = object)
I like classical music. (classical music = object)
I like it. (it = object)

Some verbs, such as 'build', 'give' and 'write', can occur with two objects, a direct object and indirect object:

	Indirect	Direct
I built	them	a garage.
I gave	her	a hug.
I wrote	him	a letter.

There is no difference in form between a subject noun an object noun:

Trees are beautiful.
I love trees.

but there is a difference between subject and object pronouns:

Subject	Object
I	me
you	you
he	him
she	her
it	it
we	us
they	them
who	whom

See also COPULA, NOUN, PRONOUN, VERB

objective, subjective

These adjectives are often used as opposites. *Objective* suggests 'scientific', 'unbiased', 'not influenced by personal opinion' whereas *subjective* means 'unscientific', 'influenced by personal views and opinions':

It's never easy to be objective about literature.
My opinion is a subjective one.

Objective is also widely used as a noun meaning 'aim', 'purpose', 'goal':

My main objective is to rid the garden of dandelions.

obliged, obligated

These two adjectives come from Latin *obligare*, 'to bind together'. They can both be used to mean 'constrained morally or legally':

I felt obliged to make up the deficit.
I felt obligated to make up the deficit.

but the second sentence is more emphatic and more formal.

Obliged can be used in two ways that would be impossible for *obligated*. It can mean 'physically constrained':

They were obliged to remain in their car.

and it can be used in an active construction to mean 'do someone a favour':

He obliged us with a song.

This last usage is becoming obsolescent.

oblivious

Oblivious derives from Latin *oblivio*, 'forgetful-ness', and its original meaning was 'forgetful':

While I listened to the music, I was oblivious of all my worries and problems.

It is now most frequently used to mean 'unaware' and is followed by 'of':

When you're in love, you're oblivious of the weather.

In the past, it was considered poor usage to follow *oblivious* with 'to', especially where 'blind to' can be substituted as in:

He was oblivious to (blind to) the dangers ahead of him.

Although some careful users still prefer 'of' in all circumstances, '*oblivious* to' is now fully acceptable.

observance, observation

These two nouns are both derived from the verb 'observe', but their meanings have been differentiated. *Observance* means 'recognition of or compliance with a law or practice'. Often, the practice is a religious one:

Apart from trying to keep the commandments, I follow no strict religious observances.

Observation can mean 'the act of watching' or 'a remark':

We don't know whether he's seriously ill or not. He's under observation at the moment.

She doesn't say much but when she does she is capable of stunningly acute observations.

obsolescent, obsolete

These adjectives are occasionally misused and *obsolescent* is frequently misspelled. They both come from Latin *obsolescere*, 'to wear out'. *Obsolescent* means 'dying out', 'going out of date':

Dialect words such as 'ginnel' are becoming obsolescent because people no longer have ginnels between rows of houses.

Obsolete means 'no longer current', 'out of use':

Why did the penny-farthing bicycle become obsolete?

obverse

The noun *obverse* has two main meanings. It can refer to the side of the coin that bears the main design:

The date is on the obverse.

or to the logical counterpart to a proposition:

The obverse of 'Every piece is correct' is 'No piece is incorrect'.

occasion

The noun *occasion* is frequently misspelled and misused. It means 'the time of a particular happening':

On royal occasions there are more security measures.

Some people dislike the use of the verb *occasion* to mean 'cause', 'bring about':

My financial problems were occasioned by poor judgement.

occur

Occur is a regular verb meaning 'happen':

occur(s), occurred, occurring

Slight tremors occur on a regular basis.

occurrence

The noun *occurrence* is regularly misspelled. It has double 'c' and 'double 'r' and ends in '-ence':

Shooting stars are a regular occurrence at certain times of the year.

octa-, octo-

These variant forms of the prefix meaning 'eight' cause some spelling problems. English uses both, and care should be used to select the correct form. The most widely-used words with these prefixes are:

octagon (eight-sided figure)
octameter (eight-foot verse) ·
octogenarian (person over eighty)
octopus (eight-tentacled mollusc).

oculist, ophthalmologist, optician, optometrist

These nouns all relate to eye specialists. The 'op-' words derive from Greek *ops*, 'eye'. *Oculist* comes from Latin *oculus*, 'eye' and was used for what is now called an 'ophthalmologist'.

An *ophthalmologist* is a doctor who specializes in the diagnosis and treatment of eye diseases:

Her ophthalmologist has recommended surgery to correct her chronic short-sightedness.

Optician is the most widely-used term and refers to a person who makes or sells spectacles:

I've just had a reminder from my optician. It's two years since my last eye examination.

An *optometrist* is a person who tests eyes and prescribes corrective lenses. The word is less widely used in Britain than in America:

Many opticians are optometrists. Those who are not qualified employ optometrists to offer eye tests.

-odd

The suffix *-odd* is added to numbers to suggest an indefinite number that is close to the round number used:

There were forty-odd policemen on duty.

It is vitally important to use the hyphen to distinguish:

forty-odd policemen (approximately forty policemen)

from:

forty odd (i.e., unusual) policemen.

odour, odor

The noun *odour* comes from Latin *odor*, 'smell', and is used to mean 'a characteristic smell':

It has an odour of sandalwood.

The *odour* spelling is British. Americans prefer *odor*, but the adjective 'odorous' is spelled '-or-' in both countries.

-oe-

See -E-/-OE-

oedema

See EDEMA/OEDEMA

of, off

The words *of* and *off* come from the same Old English word *of* and they were not fully differentiated until the seventeenth century. They are now clearly distinguished in the standard language.

Of is a preposition that can be used to indicate:

■ Attributes:

a woman of substance

■ Cause:

She died of grief.

■ Contents:

a bucket of water

■ Location:

the foot of the hill

■ Material used:

a cover of leather

■ Part of a whole:

a piece of bread

■ Possession:

the wealth of Croesus

■ Relationships:

an aunt of my mother's first husband

■ Time, especially in the United States:

a quarter of two (1:45)

■ Weights and measurements:

a kilo of sugar
10 litres of petrol.

When *of* occurs as an indicator of possession, it can often be replaced by a structure involving an apostrophe + 's':

the daughter of a count = a count's daughter.

The structure with *of* is preferred when the nouns involved are inanimate:

the leaves of the tree

or when the phrase is idiomatic:

the brow of the hill.

Off occurs most frequently as an adverb:

She walked off without saying a word.

but it can also function as an adjective:

I'm having an off day.

and as a preposition:

I jumped off the cliff.

Both words are sometimes used incorrectly. *Of* is occasionally misused in structures such as:

*I should of gone.

The reason for such misuse is that the unstressed forms of *of* and the auxiliary 'have' can sound identical:

a pound of apples
I should've asked.

Off is incorrectly used instead of 'from' in such sentences as:

*I bought it off a trader.

although:

I bought it off a market stall.

is acceptable. The widespread use of *off* + a person is gradually legitimizing structures like the first.

The combined use of *off* + *of* as in:

*He fell off of the roof.

is widely used in dialects but is not acceptable in the standard language.

of course

The phrase *of course* is so useful, especially in speech, that it is in danger of being overused. It can function as an emphatic answer to a question:

Did you remember the paper? Of course I did.

Different intonation can make the *of course* suggest certainty, courtesy or impatience.

It can also be used as a sentence modifier meaning 'admittedly':

He was, of course, an old man at the time.

but this usage can be ambiguous in the written medium where a sentence such as:

Of course, you ought to have turned right.

can imply comprehension, an apology or a criticism.

offence, offense

These spellings are the preferred forms in Britain

and America respectively. *Offence* can mean 'an illegal act':

It is an offence to walk on the road.

When used with 'give' or 'take', it can mean 'anger, displeasure':

I didn't mean to give offence. I just didn't think about what I was saying.

Why did he take offence when I asked him where he lived?

The adjective is 'offensive' in both Britain and America.

official, officious

These adjectives both come from Latin *officium*, 'duty, service', but their meanings are now totally distinct. *Official* means 'related to an office', 'authorized', 'sanctioned':

The Palace issued an official denial.

It's not official yet, but the colleges are hoping to merge.

Officious used to mean 'attentive', 'obliging', but the meaning has changed to 'bossy, interfering':

She should try not to be so officious. She's only been here a week but she's already telling everyone how things should be done.

officialese

Many words have been coined recently using the '-ese' suffix:

headline + ese = the language of headlines

journal + ese = the language of journalists

mother + ese = the language used by caregivers to children.

Officialese means 'the language of official documents' and it has strong implications of 'pedantic' and 'verbose':

All documents are to be written simply and clearly. The officialese currently used is wasteful and unhelpful.

often

Often has several acceptable pronunciations. The 'of-' may rhyme with the first part of 'awful' or 'offal', and the 't' may be pronounced. The most frequently used pronunciation rhymes with 'soften', but the spelling pronunciation with 't' is growing.

There are also two acceptable comparative and superlative forms:

oftener, more often

oftenest, most often.

The forms with 'more' and 'most' are preferred in formal contexts.

okay, OK

The word *okay* is also found as *ok*, *OK* and *O.K.* It signals approval and can be used as an informal equivalent of 'yes':

Will you do it? Okay, I will.

as an adjective:

He's okay now.

an adverb:

He ran okay.

a noun:

Did you get the okay from head office?

and as a regular verb:

okay(s), okayed, okaying

The changeover is about to be okayed.

In spite of its widespread use and multi-functionality today, no one is certain of the etymology of *okay*. It may derive from the 'O.K. Club' founded in America in 1840; it may be an abbreviation of 'oll korrect', a variant of 'all correct'; it may be a modified form of the Scottish expression 'Och aye'; or it may be from West African languages, where several have *oki* or *oka* as an expression of agreement.

See also ETYMOLOGY

Old English

Old English is the name given to the varieties of English used in parts of England from about AD450 to 1100. It is also sometimes referred to as 'Anglo-Saxon'. *Old English* was a Germanic language, closely related to earlier forms of Dutch and Danish. All the *Old English* dialects were highly inflected: nouns, both animate and inanimate, had grammatical gender; adjectives agreed with the nouns they modified; predicates agreed with subjects; and case endings permitted freedom of word order.

See also INFLECTION/INFLEXION, MIDDLE ENGLISH

olden

Olden is an obsolescent word meaning 'former':

In olden days, children often worked sixteen-hour days.

It rarely occurs outside the fixed phrases:

in olden days

in olden times.

older

See ELDER/OLDER

Oman

An inhabitant of the sultanate in the Arabian peninsula is an 'Omani'; the derived adjective is the same. The capital is Muscat.

omelette, omelet

This noun is spelled *omelette* in Britain and *omelet* in America. It is pronounced like 'om + lit':

UK: Omelettes may be sweet or savoury.
US: Omelets may be sweet or savory.

omit

Omit is a regular verb that is often misspelled. It comes from Latin *omittere*, 'send away', and means 'leave out, fail or neglect to do':

omit(s), omitted, omitting
I omitted the crucial section.
Mike has been omitted from the team.

The derived noun is 'omission', with one 'm' and double 's'.

omnibus

The noun *omnibus* comes from Latin *omnis*, 'all', *omnibus*, 'for all'. As a term for a vehicle, it has been replaced by its abbreviated form 'bus'. The full term is now used mainly for a book that either presents a writer's work in one volume or presents several works on a similar topic in one volume:

I bought an omnibus volume of Jane Austen. It was wonderful value but the print was small.

omnipotent, omniscient

These adjectives are occasionally misused and the second one is often misspelled. *Omnipotent* means 'all-powerful' and was originally reserved for God. Like many adjectives, its meaning has been weakened by usage and it now often means 'having virtually unlimited power':

The first visitors seemed omnipotent. They could travel on the sea without waiting for favourable winds and they could carry boxes of fire sticks in their pockets.

Omniscient means 'all-knowing' and it was also an epithet applied to God:

Goldsmith's village schoolmaster seemed omniscient:
And still they gaz'd, and still the wonder grew,
That one small head could carry all he knew.
Oliver Goldsmith, 'The Deserted Village'

on, up on, upon

Many writers are uncertain when to use *on* and *upon* and also when to use *upon* and *up on*. The rules are relatively clear.

Upon and *on* are syntactically synonymous in that they are both prepositions meaning 'in contact with', 'attached to', 'in the vicinity of':

Climb upon my knee, Sonny Boy.
Climb on my knee, Sonny Boy.

In contemporary English, *on* is more usual than *upon*, which has literary and archaic connotations. *Upon* still occurs, however, in such fixed collocations as:

Once upon a time …

but the eccentricity of such a phrase was illustrated by Dylan Thomas's:

Once below a time …

In almost every case, *on* can be substituted for *upon*:

She put it upon/on the pillow.

There is a clear distinction, however, between *upon* and *up on*. The former is a compound preposition, the latter a sequence of adverb + preposition. Let us examine two sentences:

She came upon a train.
She came up on a train.

The first sentence means that she unexpectedly saw a train; the second means that she got on a train and travelled on it to a particular destination. These sentences are distinguished in the spoken medium by the pause after *up* in the second.

A further example may help the clarification. In the sentence:

She went up on the escalator.

we can show that the *up* is more closely associated with the verb than with the preposition by substituting 'ascended' for 'went up':

She ascended on the escalator.

See also IN TO/INTO, ON TO/ONTO, PREPOSITION

on-line

The computer compound *on-line* is now often used to mean 'connected directly':

You are now on-line to the manager.

Like many computer terms that have been taken up by the public, *on-line* should be used with care.

See also COMPUTERESE

on-stream

On-stream is a frequently used adjective meaning 'in operation' or 'about to go into operation':

We are expecting our new syllabus to come on-stream within one year.

on to, onto

Many users are uncertain about when to use *on to* and when to use the compound word *onto*. The compound form, *onto*, can only be used as a preposition and it can be replaced by another preposition, usually 'on':

I ran onto the grass.
I ran on/over/across the grass.

The two-word form may be a combination of the adverb 'on' and the infinitive of a verb:

He ran on to win the race.

This means 'He continued to run and he won the race.' In the spoken medium, there can be a pause after 'on'.

The two-word form may be a combination of the adverb 'on' and the preposition 'to':

He ran on to Huddersfield.

In such sentences, the adverb 'on' can be replaced by the adverb 'onwards':

He ran onwards to Huddersfield.

The final piece of advice is simple: if in doubt, use *on to* because this is also acceptable for the combined prepositions.

See also ON/UP ON/UPON

one

One can function as a numeral:

Five times one is five.
One man and his dog went to mow a meadow.

as a pronoun meaning 'someone unique':

She's one in a million.

and as an indefinite personal pronoun equivalent to 'we' or 'they' or 'I':

One should also do one's best.

The use of *one* to mean 'I' is acceptable in small doses, but it can sound pompous or foolish:

One washed one's hair and one can't do a thing with it.

If we use *one*, we must be consistent:

One would be foolish to think that one is infallible.

The use of 'he/she' for the second 'one' is widespread but unacceptable in the written medium:

One would be foolish to think that he/she is infallible.

from the points of view of agreement and meaning. The 'he/she' may refer to another person.

There are a number of compound pronouns involving -*one*:

anyone, everyone, no one, someone.

One combines with '-self' to form 'oneself', a reflexive that is no longer widely used. It is still grammatically correct in such sentences as:

One doesn't do oneself any harm by working hard.
One talks to oneself because no one else listens properly.

but such structures are highly unlikely in American English and are regarded as class-marked in Britain. Most people would prefer to use 'you':

You don't do yourself any harm by working hard.

See also EACH OTHER/ONE ANOTHER, ONE'S, YOU

one's

One's can function as a reduced form of 'one is':

One's always in a hurry these days.

but it is normally the possessive form of 'one':

Where does one put one's coat?

This is the only possessive adjective that takes an apostrophe:

Where does he put his coat?
Where did you put its basket?

See also APOSTROPHE

onerous

The adjective *onerous* comes from Latin *onus*, 'a burden, load', and means 'laborious':

You are taking on an onerous task, with no guarantee of success.

The word has two acceptable pronunciations. The first syllable may be pronounced like 'own' or 'on'.

ongoing

Ongoing, which is sometimes spelled with a hyphen, *on-going*, is used as an adjective meaning 'actually in progress' or 'still developing':

The department has two ongoing projects, one of which will be completed early next year.

This adjective is overused and so is disliked by many stylists, especially in the cliché:

ongoing situation.

only

The adverb *only* often causes ambiguity if it is not properly placed in the written medium. In speech, the sentence:

I only bought a book.

may, depending on intonation, mean:

I bought a book, not a library!

or:

I bought a book. I didn't write it.

In the written medium, we do not have intonation to disambiguate and so *only* must be positioned as close to the word it modifies as possible. In a sentence such as:

Mary was appointed last week.

the *only* may occur in different positions, each with a different meaning:

Only Mary was appointed last week. (None of the others were.)
Mary was only appointed last week. (not promoted)
Mary was appointed only last week. (not last year)

Other adverbial limiters that need to be treated with similar care include 'even', 'exactly', 'just', 'merely', and 'simply'.

onomatopoeia

Onomatopoeia is the creation or use of words that denote an action or object by suggesting a sound associated with the action or object:

bang, buzz, crash, hiss, hoot, galump, moo, neigh, whoosh.

For most words in a language, the link between sounds and meaning is usually completely arbitrary. Water, for example, is still H_2O whether it is called 'agua', 'eau', 'wasser' or 'uisce'. With onomatopoeic words like 'cuckoo', however, the name is derived from the sound reputedly made by the bird.

A number of scholars have pointed out that certain sounds in English regularly occur with a particular meaning. Thus, words beginning with 'sl-' tend to have unpleasant connotations, as in:

slam, slick, slime, slither, slouch, slush.

and words beginning with 'fl-', and 'gl-' are regularly connected with movement and light:

flame, flicker, flitter, flow
gleam, glimmer, glitter, glow.

When sounds or combinations of sounds frequently occur with a specific meaning, the phenomenon is referred to as SOUND SYMBOLISM.

The final -*poeia* is pronounced like 'pea a'.

onward, onwards

In Britain, *onward* tends to be used as an adjective and *onwards* as an adverb:

Nothing can withstand the onward march of progress.

We walked onwards, ever onwards.

In American English, *onward* can function as both adjective and adverb.

See also -WARD/-WARDS

operative

Operative for 'worker' is a type of verbal inflation. It is meant to give status to manual workers:

We employ fifty operatives.

See also POLITICAL CORRECTNESS

ophthalmologist, optician, optometrist

See OCULIST/OPHTHALMOLOGIST/OPTICIAN/ OPTOMETRIST

opossum, possum

The noun *possum* is a shortened form of *opossum*, an arboreal marsupial. The word is most frequently heard in the phrase:

play possum

meaning 'pretend to be dead or dormant so as to deceive an enemy':

'Possum' and 'opossum' are used in Australia and New Zealand for a group of marsupials otherwise known as 'phalangers'.

opposite

See APPOSITE/OPPOSITE

optimal, optimum

These words both come from Latin *optimus*, 'best'. *Optimal* is an adjective meaning 'most favourable':

This is the optimal time for investing.

Optimum can function as an adjective, identical in meaning to *optimal* and more widely used:

This is the optimum time for investing.

and as a noun meaning 'condition or circumstance to produce the best results':

Experiments conducted in zero gravity are thought to be the optimum.

The noun has two plurals, 'optima' and 'optimums'. Neither is widely used.

Optimal and *optimum* are sometimes bleached of their meaning in advertising and the popular press and suggest little more than 'best':

For optimal whiteness, use Brand X.

The derived verb is 'optimize', which means 'make the most of':

We must optimize our resources.

It, too, is overused.

optimistic

The adjective *optimistic* refers to a tendency to expect the best and to see the best in everything:

An optimist sees that the glass is half full; a pessimist sees it as half empty.

The word is increasingly being used, however, to mean 'cheerful' or 'hopeful':

She's always optimistic, always smiling.

She's optimistic about finding her lost luggage.

or

Or is a coordinating conjunction that offers alternatives. It can join words:

John or Paul
fruit or vegetables

phrases:

It's on the bed or in the wardrobe.

or clauses:

I gave it to him or he borrowed it from me. I can't remember which.

Occasionally there are questions about agreement. In a sentence such as:

John or Paul is next in line.

the verb is singular. When the contrasted items differ in number, the verb agrees with the noun closest to it:

Two boys or one man is required.
One man or two boys are required.

If the sentence seems strained as in:

Is she or I the one you've selected?

it is preferable to rephrase it:

Have you selected her or me?

Or often occurs as the second part of the conjunction:

either ... or.

See also AND, CONJUNCTION, EITHER/NEITHER

-or
See -EE/-ER/-OR

oral
See AURAL/ORAL

oral tradition
Every community in the world has a language and a literature. With many societies, the literature is not written but spoken. All literatures derive from *oral traditions* and many still make use of mnemonic devices that are no longer strictly necessary. Among such devices are alliteration, antithesis, assonance, parallelism, rhyme, regulated rhythm and formulaic openings and conclusions:

Once upon a time …
And they lived happily ever after.

See also LITERATURE

orature
Orature is a blend of *or*al liter*ature*, and it refers to the oral traditions of a people: their songs and riddles, their stories and proverbs, and their stored wisdom.

A related blend is 'oracy', meaning 'the capacity to express oneself fluently': *or*al + liter*acy*.

orbit
Orbit derives from Latin *orbis*, 'circle'. It can be used as a noun meaning 'the path of a planet, satellite or comet around another heavenly body':

The moon is in orbit around the earth.

Orbit can also be used as a regular verb:

orbit(s), orbited, orbiting
The satellite is at present orbiting Mars.

orchestrate, organize
Orchestrate and *organize* are used in ostensibly similar contexts. They both imply 'arrange events in an effective way', but in media reports *orchestrate* tends to be unfavourable whereas *organize* is favourable:

It was an orchestrated demonstration against government policy.
It was an organized event and passed off very peacefully.

Loaded language of this kind can have a strong but unchallenged effect on popular opinion.

See also CONNOTATION, PROPAGANDA

ordinal
Ordinal numbers are 'first', 'second', 'forty-ninth' and so on. They should be spelled out in full.

See also NUMBERS

ordinance, ordnance
Neither of these words is widely used and they are often confused or misspelled. They were originally variants and both derive ultimately from Latin *ordinare*, 'to set in order'. An *ordinance* is a rule or regulation:

This booklet contains the ordinances affecting local government.

Ordnance is a military word and can include 'artillery' as well as military supplies:

The Ordnance Survey is the official map-making body. Good maps are essential to military success.

orient, orientate, orienteering
The verb *orient* originally meant 'face east':

The graves were oriented so that the dead could face the rising sun.

Now it is used to mean 'adjust or align oneself':

I cannot seem to orient myself. The sky is overcast and my compass needle seems to have stuck.

Orient is the preferred form in America but *orientate*, which is probably a back formation from 'orientation', is widely used in Britain.

The recently created sport of *orienteering* requires contestants to run over a course with the aid of a map. The sport has given rise to the verb 'orienteer', meaning 'navigate between checkpoints by means of a map'.

orthography
Orthography refers to two related aspects of language: the spelling principles in a language and the study of writing systems. The word derives ultimately from Greek *orthos + graphos*, 'straight + writing'.

See also PUNCTUATION, SPELLING

orthopaedic, orthopedic
The adjective *orthopaedic* refers to the branch of medicine associated with bones and joints:

He's an orthopaedic surgeon and has performed hundreds of hip replacement operations.

The preferred American spelling is *orthopedic*.

ostensible, ostentatious
These adjectives both derive from Latin *ostendere*, 'to show', but they have quite distinct meanings and applications. *Ostensible* means 'shown outwardly' and it has taken on the meaning of 'apparent', 'pretended':

The ostensible reason for her departure is clear enough but there must be some reason other than the need for a break.

Ostentatious means 'showy', 'pretentious' and it carries with it the suggestion of 'vulgar':

Tom thought that the furnishings were ostentatious. I thought they were lovely.

other

Other can function as a determiner:

Other people think differently.

and as a noun:

Show me some others please.

See also ANOTHER

other than

Other than can function with the meaning of 'apart from':

There was no way in other than the hole in the wall.

There was no way in other than by climbing through the window.

Some careful speakers dislike the usage of *other than* before a verb, preferring 'apart from'.

Occasionally the *other* and *than* are split:

What other choice than that did he have?

otherwise

Otherwise can function as an adverb meaning 'or else':

Do your best. Otherwise, you'll be sorry.

'differently':

I've always thought otherwise.

and 'in other respects':

We must operate to have any hope. We're in an otherwise hopeless position.

Otherwise is now widely used as part of a phrase linked by 'or':

The money was lost, accidentally or otherwise.

Hand in the reports, completed or otherwise, by Friday.

Many speakers dislike this usage, especially since it seems to encourage the use of 'or' with *otherwise* when *otherwise* means 'or else':

*You must do it or otherwise you'll get into trouble.

ought to

Ought to functions like a modal verb and expresses 'duty', 'obligation' or 'expectation'. It forms negatives and questions without 'do':

You oughtn't to go there so often.

Ought I to have gone?

In speech, many people use 'do' to form negatives and questions but this is not acceptable in formal contexts:

*You didn't ought to go there so often.

*Did I ought to have gone?

If the structure sounds strained, it is better to replace *ought to* with 'should':

You shouldn't go there so often.

Should I have gone?

See also AUXILIARY, MODALITY

our, ours

Our is a first person plural possessive adjective:

They have just bought our house.

Ours is a possessive pronoun. It never takes an apostrophe:

It's not ours.

Our and *ours*, like 'we', can be either inclusive or exclusive. That means it can include or exclude the listener:

This is our job. (i.e., yours and mine but not theirs)

This is our job. (i.e., mine and theirs but not yours)

This is our job. (i.e., yours and theirs and mine)

our, us

In formal contexts *our* is preferred before the gerund:

They didn't like our suggesting that.

although *us* is widely used in colloquial speech:

They didn't like us suggesting that.

See also GERUND, -ING FORM

out, out of

In Britain, the compound preposition *out of* is used, especially with such verbs as 'look', 'run' and 'walk', where most Americans prefer *out*:

UK: She spent hours looking out of the window.

US: She spent hours looking out the window.

American usage is spreading in Britain, but in formal styles it is still advisable to use *out of*.

With idioms, both communities use *out of*:

Are you out of your mind?

He's out of his depth in the business world.

out-, -out

Out- occurs very frequently as a PREFIX. The most widely-used words tend not to be hyphenated:

outback, outbreak, outcast.

Newer words and phrases tend to be hyphenated:

out-patient, out-sell, out-and-out, out-of-touch.

A number of phrasal verbs such as 'sell out' have given rise to compound nouns involving '-out':

a sell-out (sellout)

a wash-out (washout)

a white-out (whiteout).

See also HYPHEN

outdoor, outdoors

Outdoor is an adjective:

They held a successful outdoor party.

Outdoors is an adverb, but many people prefer the phrase 'out of doors':

She prefers being outdoors.

It can also function as a noun, especially in the phrase 'the great outdoors':

They spent months planning their adventure in the great outdoors.

See also INDOOR/INDOORS

outlet

The noun *outlet* used to mean a 'vent or opening':

The gas outlet is at the top of the machine.
The silt is building up near the outlet.

Recently, it has been widely used to mean 'shop':

Poor trading conditions have caused the closure of 180 outlets.

See also SEMANTIC CHANGE

output, productivity

These words are occasionally used as synonyms in the context of manufacturing industry, but they can and should be differentiated. *Productivity* relates to efficiency of production whereas *output* implies the amount produced:

The AUT's claim hinges on the fact that lecturers have not been paid for their increased productivity. The staff–student ratio has changed from 10:1 to 23:1 over five years.
The output of noxious gases has increased over the past eight months.

outrageous

This adjective is often misspelled. The 'e' from 'outrage' is retained:

That was the most outrageous behaviour I have ever seen.

outside, outside of

The preposition *outside* meaning 'beyond the environs of' is sometimes replaced by *outside of* in American speech:

UK: I used to live outside Leeds.
US: I used to live outside (of) Austin.

Outside of can be used to mean 'apart from':

Outside of that I have no problems.

but, although this is heard in Britain, it still suggests American influence.

outstanding

The adjective *outstanding* can be ambiguous and should be used with care. It can mean 'excellent', 'conspicuous' and also 'unsettled, unpaid, overdue':

She has had an outstanding career in the diplomatic corps.
The most outstanding feature is the density of woodland.
The bill is still outstanding.

Sentences where two meanings of *outstanding* could apply should be avoided:

Two of this student's essays are outstanding.

outward, outwards

In Britain, *outward* is an adjective and *outwards* an adverb:

The outward journey took an hour longer than we expected.

The paint spread slowly outwards until the entire canvas had a blue tint.

Outward is preferred for both adjectival and adverbial usage in America.

See also -WARD/-WARDS

outwit

The verb *outwit* is regular and means 'get the better of by ingenuity':

outwit(s), outwitted, outwitting
I told them the story about how the tortoise outwitted the elephant.

outwith

The preposition *outwith* is used for 'outside' in Scottish English and parallels the use of 'within':

Such courses may be taken outwith the university.
These matters are outwith my control.

over

Over is multi-functional. It can be an adverb:

He was run over.

a noun:

There are three overs left. (as in cricket)

and a preposition:

A cuckoo flew over the house.

See also ABOVE/OVER, MORE THAN/OVER

over-, -over

Over- occurs frequently as a PREFIX. The more frequently used words are generally not hyphenated:

overawe, overbalance, overcast

but some of the longer or newer compounds continue to use a hyphen:

over-apprehensiveness, over-confident, over-react.

A number of phrasal verbs such as 'take over' have given rise to compound nouns involving '-over':

a hangover, left-overs, a stop-over.

See also HYPHEN

overall

Overall is an adjective meaning 'from one end to the other':

The overall length of the garden is 16 metres.

Overall is used as an adjective to mean 'complete, total', and as an adverb to mean 'altogether':

Her overall appearance was attractive.
It will take three weeks to finish overall.

In Britain, the noun 'overalls' means a 'protective overgarment':

I bought some overalls for working on the car.

overkill

Overkill is a favourite noun of reporters and is used to mean 'overuse', 'over-exposure', 'excess':

The media coverage of sport has resulted in overkill.

overly

Overly is an adverb meaning 'excessively':

She is overly protective of her children.
It is frequently overused.

overview

Overview is a popular word and should not be overused to mean 'review, survey, summary':

I'd like an overview of the sales figures by five.

owing to

See DUE TO/OWING TO

oxymoron

Oxymoron comes from Greek *oxus*, 'sharp' + *moros*, 'stupid'. It is a figure of speech involving two semantically exclusive or contradictory terms:

false truth
happy misery
sweet sorrow
victorious defeat.

Oxymoron is stressed on the third syllable. It has a plural 'oxymora', but this is not widely used.

See also FIGURE OF SPEECH

P

p

P is a consonant. The letter *p* is used as an abbreviation of 'penny'.

-p-, -pp-

The normal rules for doubling 'p' are summarized below.

Monosyllabic words

When a monosyllabic word ends in a single vowel + p, the 'p' is doubled before the suffixes '-ed', '-ing', '-y', '-er' but not before '-ful':

cap, capped, capping
cup, cupped, cupping, cupful
flop, flopped, flopping, floppy.

It is not doubled if the monosyllabic word has two vowels + 'p':

sheep, sheepish
soap, soaped, soaping, soapy.

Polysyllabic words

When the word is polysyllabic and the stress falls on the first syllable, the 'p' is doubled before suffixes:

kidnap, kidnapped, kidnapping, kidnapper
worship, worshipped, worshipping, worshipper.

When the main stress falls on the last syllable of a polysyllabic word ending in 'p', the 'p' is doubled before suffixes, except for '-ful' and '-ment':

equip, equipped, equipping, equipment.

See also SPELLING, SUFFIX

package, packet, parcel

These nouns are virtually synonymous when they refer to a wrapped or boxed item:

There's a package/parcel for you in the office.

Americans tend to use *packet* where British people use *package*:

There's a packet for you in the office.

and this usage is gradually ousting *package* in its literal sense.

Package is used metaphorically to mean 'set of proposals' or 'set of items that are offered together':

The unions are expected to accept the latest package.
Package holidays are often very good value.

The verbs can be synonymous when they have the literal meaning of 'wrap something up':

I'll package/parcel the presents for you.

but their metaphorical meanings differ. *Package* can mean 'group items or proposals together', 'present':

The political parties are being packaged like detergents.

Parcel is a regular verb, parts of which are spelled differently in Britain and America:

UK: parcel(s), parcelled, parcelling
US: parcel(s), parceled, parceling.

It can mean 'divide up into portions':

They parcelled out the spoils.

paed-, ped-

The prefix *paed-* comes from Greek *pais*, *paid*, 'child', and is used in such words as:

paediatrics (branch of medicine concerned with children and children's diseases)
paedophile (adult who is sexually attracted to children).

The *ped-* form is preferred in America.

See also -AE-/-E-

page, paginate

These two verbs have overlapping meanings. *Page* can mean 'leaf through printed material':

I paged through the book, unable to concentrate.

Paginate means 'number the pages of a written document':

I forgot to paginate the chapter.

pagoda

The noun *pagoda* is often misused. It is a temple, usually shaped like a tower that narrows towards the top. It comes from Sanskrit *bhagavati*, 'divine':

There are pagodas in many countries in Asia.

pail, pale

These words are homophones. *Pail* is a noun meaning 'bucket':

Jack and Jill went up a hill
To fetch a pail of water.

Pale usually functions as an adjective or a verb meaning 'lacking strong colour', 'lose colour':

She looked pale but it may have been the result of the pale colours she was wearing.
He paled at the thought of what lay ahead.

Less frequently, *pale* can function as a noun meaning 'upright slat in fence'. This *pale* comes from Latin *palus*, 'stake', whereas the others come from Latin *pallere*, 'to look wan'. The noun *pale* is now used almost exclusively in the metaphorical phrase:

beyond the pale

meaning 'outside the limits of acceptable behaviour'. The literal meaning is 'outside the fenced enclosure'.

pair, pare

These words are homophones. *Pair* can mean 'two' or 'put two together':

That pair is up to no good.

We have decided to pair John with Janet and Dick with Dora.

Pare is a verb meaning 'cut a thin layer off':

I was peeling the potatoes but I pared my thumb instead.

pair of

There are many nouns in English that can be prefixed by 'a pair of'. These nouns have two symmetrical parts, are plural and end in '-s'. The best known of these are:

binoculars, glasses, gloves, jeans, knickers, pants, pyjamas/pajamas, scissors, shoes, shorts, socks, stockings, trousers, tweezers.

When used with 'pair of', these nouns take singular agreement:

This pair of scissors is lethal.

These scissors are lethal.

pajamas, pyjamas

The night attire consisting of a jacket and pair of trousers is spelled *pyjamas* in Britain and *pajamas* in America. The singular form is used adjectivally in such phrases as:

a pyjama party.

Pakistan

Pakistan is a republic in Asia. The derived adjective and noun are 'Pakistani', and the capital is Islamabad.

palaeo-, paleo-

These are variant forms of a prefix deriving from Greek *palaios*, 'old'. The '-aeo-' form is still quite common in Britain but the preferred American form with '-eo-' is sometimes found. It means 'old', 'prehistoric' and occurs in such words as:

pal(a)eoanthropology (branch of anthropology dealing with early humans and hominids)

pal(a)eography (study of handwriting of the past)

pal(a)eolithic (period of time about 2.5–3 million years ago).

Most speakers pronounce the first syllable to rhyme with 'pal' but many, especially in America, rhyme it with 'pale'.

palatal, palatial

These adjectives are occasionally confused. *Palatal* relates to the palate:

Palatal sounds are made on or near the roof of the mouth. They may be made either on the hard palate or on the soft palate.

Palatial derives from 'palace':

They have bought a palatial apartment near Hyde Park.

palate, palette

The *palate* is another word for the roof of the mouth. It can also be used metaphorically to mean 'sense of taste':

Wine tasters pride themselves on their fine palates.

The noun should not be confused with its homophone *palette*, which is the flat piece of wood on which painters mix their colours:

I've always wanted a palette with a hole for my thumb so that I could pretend to be a better painter than I am.

This noun can also be spelled 'pallet', which, in turn, can also refer to a straw-filled or makeshift bed.

pale

See PAIL/PALE

palindrome

The noun *palindrome* derives from Greek *palindromos*, 'running back again'. It involves an arrangement of letters and words so as to give the same message backwards and forwards:

Hannah, Malayalam, level, pip

Able was I ere I saw Elba.

pall

The noun *pall* comes from Latin *pallium*, 'cloak, cover'. It refers literally to a cloth, often black, that covers a coffin:

The bishop's pall was richly embroidered.

and metaphorically to a dark covering:

The dark clouds were like a pall over the city.

The verb *pall*, meaning 'become insipid, tiresome', is not related to the noun although they are both homophones of 'Paul'. It derives from 'appal':

I used to enjoy that soap opera but it has started to pall.

palpable

The adjective *palpable* has undergone a semantic change. It derives from Latin *palpare*, 'to stroke, touch', and was originally applied to something that could be felt or touched:

a palpable knock

palpable heat.

Now it tends to mean 'easily seen' or 'obvious':

How did he expect to get away with such a palpable lie?

palpate, palpitate

These verbs are occasionally confused, partly because they can both occur in medical contexts. *Palpate* comes from Latin *palpare*, 'to stroke', 'to touch', and means 'examine part of the body by touch':

We haven't even got a stethoscope, so all chest patients are palpated.

Palpitate comes from Latin *palpitare*, 'to throb', and means 'flutter', 'tremble', 'beat at a fast rate':

My heart seems to palpitate even after gentle exercise.

pamphlet

The word *pamphlet* comes ultimately from a Greek proper name *Pamphilos*. It is used to refer to a booklet or small publication, usually with a paper cover. It is often misspelled, with '-n-' substituted for '-m-':

We've published a pamphlet to help new students through the maze of modularization.

pan-

The prefix *pan-* comes from Greek *pan*, 'all'. It is used to mean 'all' in such words as:

panacea (remedy for all ills)

panchromatic (sensitive to all colours)

and 'relating to all parts':

Pan-African, Pan-American.

panacea

The noun *panacea* comes from Greek *pan + akes*, 'all + remedy', and has the literal meaning of 'a remedy for all illnesses':

The aspirin is the closest we come to a panacea.

It is increasingly being used metaphorically to mean 'cure':

So many 'solutions' to the world's problems have turned out to be a source of trouble rather than a panacea.

Panama

An inhabitant of the Central American country is a 'Panamanian'; the derived adjective is the same. The capital is Panama City. A 'panama hat' is spelled with a lower-case 'p'.

pancake

The noun *pancake* can have different meanings in different parts of the world:

All pancakes are thin and flat but a 'Scotch pancake' is another word for a 'drop scone' or 'griddle cake'.

Words for food items are often specific to a region.

pandit, pundit

These variant forms of Hindi *pandit*, 'learned', are now used with different meanings. *Pandit* is a title of respect:

No one will ever forget the work of Pandit Nehru.

whereas *pundit* means 'a self-appointed expert':

He's the office pundit. He has an answer to every problem, usually not the right answer, but an answer.

panel

The word *panel* can function as a noun meaning 'a flat section' or 'team':

I'll need another two panels to finish covering the walls.

She's been asked to be part of the local educational panel.

and as a regular verb meaning 'to decorate with panels':

UK: panel(s), panelled, panelled

US: panel(s), paneled, paneled.

Related words such as 'panel(l)ing' and 'panel(l)ist' have double 'l' in British English and 'l' in America.

panic

Panic means 'feeling of terror or anxiety':

I was in a panic when I realized that I didn't know where I had parked the car.

The regular verb adds 'k' before '-ed' and '-ing':

panic(s), panicked, panicking

and the adjective 'panicky' also has a 'k'.

See also SPELLING

papaw, papaya

This fruit, which has a sweet yellow edible pulp, is also called a 'custard apple'. The name *papaya* is a Spanish version of an Amerindian name:

I'd like a slice of papaya for breakfast.

The form *papaw* or 'pawpaw' is preferred in Britain:

I had never tasted a papaw until I was well over twenty.

Papua New Guinea

An inhabitant of the country in the southwest Pacific is a 'Papua New Guinean'; the derived adjective is the same. The capital is Port Moresby.

par excellence

The phrase *par excellence* comes from French and means 'by way of excellence'. In English, it is normally written in italics and means 'beyond comparison, without equal':

He was Hamlet *par excellence*. No one has ever given a finer interpretation of the character.

para-

There are two *para-* prefixes, one from Greek *para*, 'alongside', 'beyond':

paragraph, paranormal

and one from Italian *para-* indicating an object that acts as a protection against something:

parachute, parasol.

paradigm

Paradigm rhymes with 'dime' and means 'a pattern or model':

This period of benign government should act as a paradigm for all future parliaments.

or 'a set of all the inflected forms of a word':

All Latin nouns were set out in a paradigm of six cases and two numbers.

paradox

Paradox comes from Greek *para* + *doxa*, 'beyond + opinion'. It is a figure of speech involving an apparent contradiction:

First shall be last and last shall be first.

Paradox is often used in religious language because it is impossible to express divine attributes in human terms.

Recently, *paradox* has been applied to a person who is not easy to understand:

I simply don't understand you. You're a paradox.

See also FIGURE OF SPEECH

paraffin
See KEROSENE/PARAFFIN

paragraph

The noun *paragraph* comes from Greek *para* + *graphein*, 'to write beside'. It is applied to the blocks into which a prose text is divided. Paragraphs developed in prose in much the same way as stanzas developed in verse: to represent a stage in the development of an argument, or to indicate a sequence.

Each *paragraph* starts on a new line and may be signalled by indenting the first word five letter spaces from the left-hand margin or by leaving a double space between paragraphs, but not both.

Paraguay

An inhabitant of the South American country is a 'Paraguayan'; the derived adjective is the same. The capital is Asunción.

paralinguistics

Paralinguistics is the study of 'paralanguage' – that is, features other than sounds, letters, words and structures that can affect meaning. They can be divided into:

■ Features of speech such as breathiness, giggling, lisping, loudness and tenseness. These are meaningful but are not as integrally involved in linguistic messages as words.

■ Gestures and the use of space. These include eye contact, posture and body movements. Often these bodily accompaniments to speech are referred to as 'kinesics' or 'body language'.

parallel

This word is frequently misspelled. It can function as an adjective meaning 'separated by an equal distance at every point':

Parallel lines can never meet.

as a noun:

The safe area lies between parallels 36 and 39.

and as a regular verb:

parallel(s), paralleled, paralleling

My 'near-death experience' paralleled those already recorded, except that I wasn't ill or dying.

parallelism

The term *parallelism* is given to the repetition of linguistic elements for stylistic effect. *Parallelism* can apply to sounds, vocabulary, grammar or meaning, or to a combination of some or all of these. It is regularly employed in poetry, oratory and persuasive language:

P–p–pick up a penguin.

Think once. Think twice. Think bike.

See also ALLITERATION, ASSONANCE, METER/ METRE, REPETITION

paralyse, paralyze

This verb is regularly spelled '-yse' in Britain and '-yze' in America:

UK: He is paralysed from the waist down.

US: He is paralyzed from the waist down.

The derived noun is 'paralysis' and it can be used literally or metaphorically:

It is too early to know whether or not the paralysis is permanent.

The paralysis from which the entire company seems to be suffering is hard to understand.

See also SPELLING

paramedic

The noun *paramedic* designated a person like a laboratory technician who helped in the work of the medical profession. Recently, it has been used of a medically-trained person who goes to the scene of an accident and who can provide care before the patient is transferred to hospital:

Many accident victims owe their lives to paramedics.

parameter, perimeter

The noun *parameter* has a particular meaning in mathematics:

A parameter is an arbitrary constant that determines the form of a mathematical equation.

It is now popularly used to mean 'limiting factor':

Let's establish some parameters before we discuss this issue.

Perimeter means 'outer boundary':

They have electrified the perimeter fence.

paranoia

Paranoia is a serious mental illness, characterized by delusions. The word is widely and inaccurately used to refer to 'largely unfounded fear or suspicion':

*She has a paranoia about being followed.

The adjective 'paranoid' is also being weakened by overuse:

*I'm paranoid about Tony. Every time I see him I start worrying about what will go wrong!

See also PHOBIA

paraphrase

Paraphrase comes from Greek *paraphrazein*, 'to recount', and refers to an alternative version of a text – that is, to a version that changes the form but not the content. For example:

And all my worldly goods I thee endow.

may be paraphrased as:

And share all that I have with you.

parasite

A *parasite* is an animal or plant that lives on another. It is often misspelled. It ends in '-site', not '-cite':

Parasites can sometimes perform a useful function for the host animal.

John is a parasite: he lives at our expense.

parcel

See PACKAGE/PACKET/PARCEL

pardon

Pardon can function as a noun meaning 'forgiveness':

He begged for a pardon but was sent to the gas chamber.

and as a regular verb:

pardon(s), pardoned, pardoning

He has no authority to pardon you or anyone else.

In Britain, it can also be used as an interjection that can mean 'I'm sorry', 'Excuse me' or 'I didn't hear what you said'. Many English people insist that one should say 'I beg your pardon' rather than 'Pardon' or 'Pardon me' if one is apologizing. The American expression 'Excuse me?' for 'What did you say?' is increasingly being used in other parts of the world.

pare

See PAIR/PARE

parent

A *parent* is either a mother or a father. The noun 'parenting' is a recent development and stresses the fact that both parents are or ought to be involved in the upbringing of children:

We've both been attending classes on parenting.

Occasionally, 'parenting' is extended to adults who may not be the biological parents but who treat a child as their own:

Parenting is what is important, not biology.

parenthesis

The noun *parenthesis* comes from Greek *parentithenai*, 'to put beside'. It is used to describe an explanatory phrase, inserted into a passage and marked off by brackets, commas or dashes; and the pair of brackets used to enclose such a phrase. If something is 'in parenthesis', it is highlighted.

See also BRACKETS, PUNCTUATION

parliament, Parliament

A *parliament* is a political assembly. It is written with a lower case 'p' when it refers to any legislative assembly and with an upper case 'P' when it refers to a specific governing body:

It is rare for Parliament (i.e., the British House of Commons) to be recalled during the summer vacation.

The vowels '-ia-' are normally unstressed and realized as the same vowel sound as an unstressed 'a' in 'visa'. The spelling pronunciation that pronounces the '-ia-' is widely used but is still only marginally acceptable.

parlour, parlor

The noun *parlour* used to refer to a ground-floor reception room. This usage is now old-fashioned, but the word is occasionally used in such phrases as:

an ice-cream parlour

to refer to a business establishment where ice-cream may be bought. The American spelling is *parlor* and the word is more widely used in America for a room or shop where a particular business is conducted:

a pool parlor.

See also LIVING ROOM, LOUNGE

parlous, perilous

These words are variants and both mean

'hazardous, dangerous'. *Parlous* is now virtually obsolete except for the phrase:

a parlous state
They knew that their journey was perilous.
Mountain-climbing has always been dangerous.

parody

The noun *parody* derives ultimately from Greek *para* + *oide*, 'near + song', and refers to a composition that imitates the style of a serious work for comic effect:

Have you read his parody of *Paradise Lost*? I find it impossible to read the original without thinking about the parody.

See also IRONY, SATIRE/SATYR

part from, part with

These phrasal verbs have different meanings. *Part from* means 'separate, leave':

We parted from each other without bitterness.

Part with means 'give up':

He doesn't want to part with his train set.

part of speech

Traditional grammars were based on Greek and Latin models and they usually identified nine *parts of speech*, that is, words that functioned in a particular way in the language. These were:

- Adjectives such as 'good':

a good girl, She is good.

- Adverbs such as 'fairly':

fairly good, He judged fairly.

- Articles such as 'a/an', 'the':

an apple, the new book

- Conjunctions such as 'and':

a song and dance

- Interjections such as 'Hey!':

Hey! That's mine.

- Nouns such as 'child, children':

The children are bright.

- Prepositions such as 'in':

in the woods

- Pronouns such as 'she, her':

She saw her yesterday.

- Verbs such as 'go, goes, going, gone, went':

He's gone.

Modern grammars tend to concentrate on the forms and the functions of words. Thus 'man' is a noun in:

That man is very tall.

but a verb in:

We need someone to man the telephone.

partially, partly

These adverbs both mean 'to some extent', 'not completely' and they can be used interchangeably when they modify a single adjective:

The course was cancelled because it was only partially/partly full.

When the adverb occurs in two balanced phrases, *partly* is usually preferred:

The collection is partly audio-visual material and partly text.

and *partly* can almost always be used where the meaning is 'not completely', even when referring to the human body, where *partially* is widely used:

He's partially sighted./He's partly sighted.

Partially cannot be substituted for *partly* when the adverb precedes 'because':

Partly because of her background, she went quickly to the top.
*Partially because of her background, she went quickly to the top.

Partly cannot be substituted for *partially* when *partially* means 'in a biased manner':

It is hard for a father not to behave partially when his children's futures are involved.

participle

All verbs have two parts that are referred to as the 'present participle' and the 'past participle'. The present participle always ends in '-ing' and usually follows a part of the 'be' verb:

I am watching you.
They have been studying hard.

The past participle is the part of the verb that follows 'have':

I had already written to your parents.
They may have walked home.

The past participle of regular verbs is identical in form with the past tense:

I watched the match.
I have watched the match.

but the past participle of irregular verbs often differs from the past tense form:

I wrote to your parents.
I have written to your parents.

Participles can be used adjectivally:

I was always aware of the watching eyes.
A watched kettle never boils.

The word *participle* is normally stressed on the first syllable but the pronunciation that stresses the second syllable is acceptable, although not so frequent.

See also AUXILIARY, GERUND, -ING FORM, VERB

partly
See PARTIALLY/PARTLY

passable, passible
The adjective *passable* is sometimes misspelled.
It comes from the verb 'pass':

This essay is just about passable.

There used to be an adjective *passible* related to
'passion' and meaning 'able to feel, susceptible to
feeling' as in:

He's not exactly sensitive; passible would be a better
description.

but this adjective is now obsolete.

passé
The adjective *passé* comes from French and is
used to mean 'out of date, jaded, past its prime':

Exclamations like 'fab' are passé now.

The feminine form is 'passée', but it is very rarely
used:

Are you suggesting that she's passé?

passed, past
These words are homophones but they have
different meanings and uses. *Passed* is the past
tense and the past participle of the verb 'pass' in
all its meanings, from 'go by' to 'gain a required
mark':

I passed the house where I used to live.
Has he really passed all his examinations?

Past can function as an adjective meaning
'completed':

Judging by past experience, this species is probably
doomed.

an adverb meaning 'on':

Who was that who just walked past?

as a noun, referring to a period of time that is over:

My past is an open book.

and as a preposition:

She walked quickly past us.

Past can never function as a verb:

*He past by.

The word *past* occurs in three widely-used
colloquialisms:

He's past it. (He's no longer able to do what he could
once do.)
Don't put it past me. (Consider me for that task.)
I wouldn't put it past them ... (They are quite
capable of doing ...)

passim
The adverb *passim* is usually italicized and means
'here and there throughout this text':

The word 'creole' occurs passim with the following
meaning.

passive
Passive has two main uses in English. It can
function as an adjective with the meaning 'not
active':

Children's passive knowledge of the language is
much greater than their active knowledge at this
stage.

It can also be used in grammatical descriptions to
refer to sentences of the form:

Jay was followed (by his younger brother).

See also ACTIVE VOICE/PASSIVE VOICE

past
See PASSED/PAST

pastel, pastille
These words should not be confused. *Pastel* is a
noun meaning 'type of crayon':

I didn't know that 'pastel' was another name for
'woad'.

and an adjective meaning 'pale, delicate in
colour':

They have decorated the house in lovely light pastel
shades.

A *pastille* is a 'flavoured lozenge':

Have you got any throat pastilles, please?

In many pronunciations, these words are homophones, however, some speakers put the stress on
the second syllable in *pastille* and rhyme it with
'feel'.

pate, pâté
These nouns provide a clear example of the
difference that accent marks can make to pronunciation and meaning. *Pate* is an obsolescent
word meaning 'head'. It survives largely in the
fixed expression 'bald pate':

I used to have a fine head of hair. Now just look at
my bald pate!

The noun *pâté* comes from French and refers to
a spread of finely minced meat:

I find the idea of pâté de foie gras off-putting.

The words *pâté*, 'pasta', 'paste' and 'pasty' are all
variants of the same Latin word *pasta*, 'dough'.

patent
The word *patent* has different meanings, pronunciations and uses. When used as an adjective,
as in:

patent leather, patent falsehood

the first syllable usually rhymes with 'pate' in
British English but with 'pat' in America.

The noun *patent* meaning 'a document conveying
certain rights and privileges':

His patent for his wind-up radio has finally been
granted.

is usually pronounced the same way as the

adjective, but some people in Britain now use the 'pat-' pronunciation.

The verb *patent* is regular and means 'obtain a patent for':

patent(s), patented, patenting
They've patented their game and hope to make some money from its sale.

pathetic

The adjective *pathetic* is currently undergoing semantic change. It derives from the noun 'pathos' and means 'evoking or expressing sympathy':

The 'Pathetic Fallacy' was the romantic belief that Nature shares in our pains.

Colloquially, it is now used to mean 'hopeless, inadequate':

That performance was just pathetic! How could he stand in front of an audience and sing so badly!

patio

This word is borrowed from Spanish *patio*, 'a courtyard' and means 'paved area adjoining a house':

We've decided to build a conservatory where the patio is.

The plural is *patios*.

See also FOREIGN LOAN-WORDS

patois

The noun *patois*, pronounced 'patwa', originally referred to rustic French speech. Currently, it can mean a non-standard dialect of French; a French creole; or any creole. Many Jamaicans refer to their English-related creole as 'patois'. It can also mean a special language of an occupation or group. A *patois*, like a 'dialect', differs from the standard language in sounds, words and structures.

See also ARGOT, CANT, DIALECT, PIDGIN AND CREOLE

patriot

The noun *patriot* comes from Latin *patria*, 'fatherland', and describes a person who loves and supports his or her country and its culture and customs:

True patriots are not jingoists. They love their country enough to die for it.

In Britain, the usual pronunciation rhymes the first syllable with 'mate'; in America, it usually rhymes with 'mat'.

patrol

Patrol can function as a noun meaning 'security action' or 'group carrying out a security watch':

Have you taken part in the neighbourhood patrol?

patrol(s), patrolled, patrolling
They were attacked while patrolling the perimeter fence.

pay

Pay can function as a noun meaning 'recompense for work' or as an irregular verb:

Her pay is only 45 per cent of the national average.
pay(s), paid, paying, paid
We paid cash for the house.

peaceable, peaceful

These adjectives both derive from 'peace' but their meanings are quite distinct. *Peaceable* means 'calm', 'tranquil', 'peace-loving' and it is used of people:

I thought he was a peaceable man but I suppose we all have our breaking point, and his came when they tried to cut down his trees.

Peaceful means 'quiet', 'calm' and tends to be used of things:

It would be wonderful to find peaceful uses for all these engines of war.

ped-

See PAED- / PED-

pedal, peddle

These words are homophones. *Pedal* can be a noun meaning 'a foot-operated lever or device' or its associated regular verb:

My foot slipped off the pedal.
UK: pedal(s), pedalled, pedalling (We pedalled all the way home.)
US: pedal(s), pedaled, pedaling.

Peddle is becoming obsolescent. It means 'go from place to place selling small items':

Why don't you peddle your goods somewhere else?

The related noun is 'pedlar' or 'peddler' in Britain but 'ped(d)ler' in America.

pejorative

The adjective *pejorative* comes from Latin *pejorare*, 'to make worse', and means 'having unpleasant connotations':

A word like 'régime' always has pejorative overtones now. Journalists describe governments of which they disapprove as 'régimes'.

Pejorative is not widely used and so it is often misspelled. It begins with 'pej-' and not 'perj-'. The first syllable is usually pronounced like the first syllable in 'pedestrian', but some speakers stress the first syllable and pronounce it like 'pea'.

pence

Pence is the irregular plural of 'penny'. Before 1971 in the UK, there were twelve *pence* in a shilling, but after decimalization the only terms

in widespread use became 'penny', 'pence' and 'pound'. Colloquially, 25 pence is written and often referred to as:

25p ('twenty-five pee').

pencil

The word *pencil* can function as a noun and a regular verb:

Has anyone seen my green pencil?

UK: pencil(s), pencilled, pencilling

US: pencil(s), penciled, penciling (Please pencil in any suggested changes.)

pendant, pendent

These words both derive from Latin *pendere*, 'to hang', and were originally variants. Today, the word ending in '-ant' is a noun that refers to a necklace:

He gently placed the pendant round her neck.

Pendent is an adjective, often regarded as poetic:

The pendent dewdrop hung for a moment and dropped.

It is sometimes replaced by *pendant*. This is acceptable, but it is never acceptable to use *pendent* as a noun.

See also -ANT/-ENT

peninsula, peninsular

In British English these forms are confused, partly because many people do not pronounce postvocalic 'r' and partly through hypercorrection. The form without the 'r' is a noun, referring to a piece of land almost entirely surrounded by water:

There is a spur of land that juts into the sea. The books call it 'Tern Peninsula' but we knew it as 'Eagle's Toe'.

Peninsular is an adjective:

The Peninsular War was fought between 1808 and 1814. Wellington referred to it as 'Napoleon's running sore'.

pensioner

A *pensioner* is someone who receives a pension. Therefore, a twenty-year-old widow who receives a widow's pension could be called a *pensioner*. However, the word is generally applied to a person receiving an old-age pension from the state. Many people object to its use in describing people of a certain age, partly because it suggests they are dependent on the state and partly because it is ageist.

See also POLITICAL CORRECTNESS

people

See PERSON/PERSONS/PEOPLE

per

Per can function to mean 'for every':

25p per pound

Allow two servings per person.

Often, *per* can be replaced by 'a':

25p a pound.

It cannot be replaced in such Latin phrases as *per annum*, 'for each year':

The basic salary is £30,000 per annum.

and *per capita*, 'according to heads':

How is a country's per capita income calculated?

In trade letters associated with building, the phrase 'as per specification' is sometimes used, but this should not be carried across into speech.

per-

Per- is a frequently used prefix in words of Latin origin, where it meant 'through', 'throughout', 'away':

percolate (cause a liquid to pass through)

perdition (ruin)

perfume (impart smell to).

per cent, percentage

Per cent comes from Latin *per centum*, 'in or for every hundred', and it is used adverbially in English:

We asked for 10 per cent of the profits.

In American English, *percent* is written as one word and this usage is spreading in Britain.

Percentage is a noun that originally meant 'proportion or rate per hundred parts'. It is now most frequently used to mean 'proportion':

What percentage of your grant is spent on books?

Many people dislike the use of 'a percentage' to mean 'a tiny part':

We could not draw any firm conclusions because only a percentage of the students returned the questionnaires.

per se

The Latin expression *per se*, 'in or by itself, himself, herself, themselves', is used in English with the meaning of 'intrinsically' and is often replaced by 'as such':

I have nothing against streaming per se.

Both *per se* and 'as such' should be avoided. They are usually redundant.

perceptible, perceptive, percipient

These adjectives have overlapping meanings and they all derive from Latin *percipere*, 'to perceive, comprehend'. *Perceptible* means 'noticeable', 'recognizable':

There has been a perceptible rise in the temperature since the insulation was completed.

Perceptive and *percipient* are normally applied

to people and both suggest 'observant', 'sensitive'. The main difference is one of formality. *Percipient* is rarely used in speech:

That was a very perceptive comment, John.

Much of his prose is turgid but occasionally we are rewarded by a percipient observation.

percolator

This noun is often misspelled. It ends in '-or' and does not have a '-u-' in the middle:

I gave them a percolator because they love coffee but didn't have a coffee-pot.

perennial

See ANNUAL/PERENNIAL

perestroika

Perestroika is a Russian word meaning 'restructuring'. It is one of a number of Russian words such as *glasnost*, 'openness', and *sputnik* to have entered English since the 1950s.

perfect

Traditional grammarians used the term *perfect* to describe structures using 'have' + the past participle:

she has gone

you have written

and the term 'pluperfect' to describe one stage further back:

she had gone

you had written.

The term *perfect* in this context means 'achieved', 'carried out' because the action involved has occurred. Most modern linguists refer to the structure using 'have' + the past participle as 'perfect aspect' rather than 'perfect tense', because 'tense' relates strictly to time whereas 'aspect' refers to the continuity of an action or to its completion.

The adjective *perfect* meaning 'faultless', 'unblemished' is an absolute, like 'unique'. It should not, therefore, be modified by 'absolutely' or 'quite':

*I've found a house that's absolutely perfect.

However, adjectives in English are frequently bleached of some of their meaning and thus absolutes can become restricted in meaning.

See also ASPECT, BLEACHING, SEMANTIC CHANGE, TENSE

perhaps

See MAYBE/PERHAPS

perilous

See PARLOUS/PERILOUS

perimeter

See PARAMETER/PERIMETER

period

The *period* is the preferred term in America for what British people call a 'full stop'. It is also sometimes used in speech to mark overtly the end of a discussion:

And that's my last word on the subject. Period.

A 'periodic sentence' is a complex, formal structure that reserves an essential piece of information for the end of the sentence.

See also FULL STOP, PUNCTUATION

periphrasis

Periphrasis comes from Greek *peri* + *phrazien*, 'around + to declare'. Like circumlocution, it is a method of expressing something in a roundabout way:

She refused to give us a definitive response.

for:

She wouldn't say yes or no.

See also CIRCUMLOCUTION, ELEGANT VARIATION, GOBBLEDEGOOK

perk

The noun *perk* as in:

This lovely office is one of the perks of the job.

is an abbreviation of 'perquisite' and goes back to the early nineteenth century.

The phrasal verb 'to perk up' is a widely-used colloquialism:

She perked up considerably when she heard that we had won a prize in the lottery.

See also PERQUISITE/PRE(-)REQUISITE

permanent

In theory, *permanent* means 'lasting until the end':

We need to put a permanent stop to crime.

In practice, it often means 'long-lasting' as on a description for a hair colorant:

Permanent colour: will last for up to eight washes.

See also BLEACHING

permissible, permissive

These adjectives are occasionally confused. They both derive from the word 'permission'. *Permissible* means 'allowable':

It is permissible to take dictionaries into the examination.

Permissive has come to mean 'indulgent in matters concerning sex':

Sexual taboos are not the only rules broken in a permissive society.

permit

Permit can function as a noun and a regular verb. The stress is on the first syllable for the noun and on the second for the verb:

You'll need a permit if you want to fish here.

permit(s), permitted, permitting

Is the wearing of casual clothes permitted?

See also ALLOW/ALLOW OF

perpetrate, perpetuate

These regular verbs are occasionally confused. *Perpetrate* derives from Latin *perpetrare*, 'to perform thoroughly', and means 'carry out or be responsible for a serious crime':

He has perpetrated a crime against humanity.

Perpetuate comes from Latin *perpetuare*, 'to continue without interruption', and means 'continue, preserve':

We do not want to perpetuate these sadistic initiation rites.

perquisite, pre(-)requisite

These nouns are both formal and are occasionally confused. A *perquisite* is an incidental benefit:

I would not have accepted the post if I had known that the perquisites were to be discontinued.

In informal contexts it is often abbreviated to 'perk':

Free health insurance is one of the perks of working there.

A *pre(-)requisite* is something that is required as a precondition:

The essential pre-requisite is an A in A-level English.

The HYPHEN is becoming less common.

See also PERK

persecute, prosecute

These regular verbs are occasionally confused. *Persecute* means 'oppress or harass, often because of race or religion':

We have been persecuted for centuries because of our religion.

Prosecute means 'bring criminal action against':

The notices 'Trespassers will be prosecuted' are not always legally enforceable.

Persia

Until the mid-1930s *Persia* was the name used for what became Iran. The derived adjective and noun were 'Persian':

Did Persian cats originally come from Persia?

The Persian Cyrus the Great established his empire in the sixth century BC.

persistent

See CONSISTENT/PERSISTENT

person

When *person* is used in a grammatical context it refers to a system of references between participants in discourse. First person refers to 'I' or 'we', second person to 'you' and third person to 'he, she, it, they'.

All 'persons' have both singular and plural forms, except 'you', which can be used for both:

Tom, can you come in at six?

Tom and Peter, can you come in at six?

Many dialects of English distinguish between 'you' singular and 'you' plural by using such plural forms as 'youse', 'yiz', 'ye', 'you all'.

English indicates *person* in the verb only in the present tense, where the first and second persons singular and the first, second and third persons plural take the base form of the verb:

I/you/we/they like music.

and a third person singular subject takes '-s/-es':

He/she/it likes milk.

He/she/it rushes to meet me.

See also PRONOUN, VERB

person, persons, people

Contemporary usage prefers *person* in some contexts where 'man' was used in the past:

No one can take total responsibility for another person's actions.

but the substitution of *-person* in compounds is often strained:

chairperson, salesperson, a four-person crew.

Care must be taken to avoid giving offence without producing stilted language. Often, there is a word such as 'constable' that can be used instead of either 'policeman' or 'policeperson'.

A *person* means an 'individual human being' and the normal plural is *people*, not *persons*:

A person has rights, you know.

People have rights, you know.

Person can also be used in the fixed phrases:

in person (actually present)

about one's person (on one).

The plural *persons* is rare outside formal written prose or descriptions of certain police procedures:

Police sources reveal that three persons are now being interviewed.

The noun *people* derives from Latin *populus*, 'populace'. It is generally a plural noun:

These people are in need of our help.

but it can be used as a singular when it refers to a group sharing the same country or language:

We are a people who do not take at all kindly to injustice.

All the nomadic peoples of the world are under pressure from developers.

Generally, *people* is the preferred plural of 'person':

I met a lovely person at the party.

I met some lovely people at the party.

persona non grata

The Latin phrase *persona non grata*, 'unacceptable person', is italicized and used mainly to describe unacceptable or unwelcome guests:

Why is he regarded as a *persona non grata*?

The phrase was originally used in the diplomatic service to describe a diplomat who was unacceptable to the country to which he or she had been accredited.

personable

The adjective *personable* is sometimes misused or misunderstood. It means 'attractive in appearance and personality':

She's an extremely personable young woman.

personal

The adjective *personal* has a number of meanings. It can refer to the private aspects of a person's life:

They have no right to ask such personal questions.

the care or appearance of one's body:

It would be impossible to overemphasize the importance of personal hygiene.

something carried on one's person:

I've got a personal CD and a personal stereo.

and a home computer, usually abbreviated to a PC:

Personal computers are now found in 68 per cent of British homes.

personal name

The term *personal name* is sometimes used instead of CHRISTIAN NAME, 'first name' or 'given name'. It is also occasionally used when a person's name, often a surname, is given to a discovery or product:

curie (from Marie Curie) = unit of radioactivity
joule (from James Joule) = unit of energy.

personally

The emphatic modifier *personally* as in:

Personally, I think it's rubbish.

is avoided by careful users of the language who point out that it is often redundant.

personification

Personification is the attribution of human characteristics to non-human nouns, usually for artistic effect:

the weeping willow tree.

See also METAPHOR

personnel

The noun *personnel* is often misspelled. It has double 'n' but a single 'l'. It refers to the people employed in an organization:

Every company relies on the goodwill of its personnel.

perspective, prospective

These words are occasionally confused. *Perspective* is a noun and refers to a way of looking at objects or facts:

The perspective in this painting is wrong. The people on the far side of the river should look much smaller.

I was working so hard that I got everything out of perspective.

Prospective is an adjective meaning 'likely', 'expected':

He is the prospective parliamentary candidate for the new constituency.

persuadable, persuasive

Persuadable is an adjective that means 'capable of having one's opinion altered':

I'm not certain that Jo is persuadable, but it may be worth a try.

Persuasive means 'having the ability to influence another':

I still don't know why I bought this! That door-to-door salesman was extremely persuasive.

persuade

See CONVINCE/PERSUADE

perturb

See DISTURB/PERTURB

Peru

An inhabitant of the South American country is a 'Peruvian'; the derived adjective is the same. The capital is Lima.

peruse, pursue

These verbs are occasionally confused because of their similar spelling. *Peruse* means 'read and examine with care':

I asked you to peruse the document, not to skim it!

Pursue is a formal word meaning 'follow':

I've pursued a dream for most of my life.

perverse, perverted

These adjectives come from the same Latin word *pervertere*, 'to turn the wrong way', but their meanings are now sharply differentiated. *Perverse* means 'wayward', 'contrary':

Who would have thought that such a perverse child would have grown into such a considerate adult?

Perverted means 'deviating from what is normal', and it is often applied to sexual behaviour:

The torture and abuse of children is perverted behaviour.

petrol

Petrol is an abbreviation of 'petroleum', and it is the usual word in Britain for the fuel used in cars. Many Americans use the abbreviation 'gas' from 'gasoline' or 'gasolene'.

See also UK AND US ENGLISH

phantasy

See FANTASY/PHANTASY

pharaoh

This word is often misspelled. It derives ultimately from an Egyptian word for 'great house' but is the title of the ancient Egyptian kings. A lower-case 'p' is used in referring generally to such kings:

How many pharaohs were there?

phatic communion

Bronislaw Malinowski coined the term *phatic communion* to describe the language that people use in order to establish bonds. In *phatic communion*, what we say is less important than the need to communicate friendliness:

Saying 'good morning' is an example of phatic communion.

phenomenon, phenomenal

The noun *phenomenon* comes from Greek *phainomenon*, 'appearance', and means 'something that can be perceived by the senses':

The topic of our discussion today is the phenomenon of dark holes.

The plural is 'phenomena':

These phenomena are not easy to study.

This noun has been overused by the media and has taken on the meaning of 'someone or something outstanding':

She's a phenomenon. I've never known anyone who can go for so long without sleep.

The adjective *phenomenal* has also come to mean 'extraordinary', 'remarkable':

How can we explain the phenomenal growth in line dancing?

See also BLEACHING, SEMANTIC CHANGE

Philippines

An inhabitant of the Philippines is a FILIPINO. The capital is Manila.

philology

The noun *philology* comes from Greek *philos + logia*, 'love + word'. It is used now to mean the scientific study of language and the changes undergone by a language over time. Its older meanings of the study of literature of an earlier period and of the language used in the literature are no longer current.

philter, philtre

See FILTER/PHILTER/PHILTRE

phlegm

Phlegm is frequently misspelled. It derives from Greek *phlegein*, 'to burn, inflame', and has two distinct meanings. It can refer to mucus secreted in the respiratory tract:

Phlegm is a characteristic of this particular virus.

and apathy, imperturbability:

He likes to be admired for his phlegm, his *sang froid*.

The second meaning is now becoming less common.

phobia

The noun *phobia* comes from Greek *phobos*, 'fear'. It means 'morbid or obsessive fear'. Its meaning has been weakened by overuse so that it is often used as a synonym for 'fear' or 'dislike':

I have a phobia about walking under ladders.

It can combine to create a range of words indicating prejudices or mental disorders linked to fear or dislike:

acrophobia (fear of heights)
arachnaphobia (fear of spiders)
anglophobia (dislike of English people)
homophobia (dislike of homosexuals).

See also PARANOIA

phone, -phone

Phone is an abbreviation of 'telephone' and can function as a noun or regular verb:

I've just bought a cordless phone.

phone(s), phoned, phoning

Have you phoned for an ambulance?

In very formal circumstances 'telephone' may still be used but *phone* is more likely in speech and casual writing.

The suffix *-phone* from Greek *phone*, 'sound, voice', usually refers to an instrument or sound system:

xylophone, gramophone.

Recently, it has been used to refer to people who speak certain languages, often not their first language:

anglophone (speaker of English)
francophone (speaker of French)

In Cameroon, about 65 per cent of the population are francophones and the rest are anglophones.

phoneme

A *phoneme* is a sound that serves to distinguish one word from another. In English, 'p' and 'b' are phonemes because they distinguish one set of words from another:

pat, bat
pang, bang
pay, bay
pin, bin.

See also PRONUNCIATION

phonetics

Phonetics is the scientific study of speech sounds:

It is impossible to study speech accurately if you are not well trained in phonetics.

phoney, phony

These are variant spellings of the adjective meaning 'fake, insincere'. No one is certain of the etymology of *phoney* and its use is limited to colloquial styles:

His manner seems so phoney.

When the word is used as a noun, it has two acceptable plurals, 'phonies' and 'phoneys':

I'm sure he's a phoney.

phrasal verb

A *phrasal verb* is a group of words involving a verb and one or more prepositions or adverbs. Phrasal verbs often have idiomatic meanings:

be in on (know about): He was in on the burglary.
give up (surrender): They refused to give up.
put down (kill): I had to have the cat put down.

See also IDIOM

phrase

A *phrase* is a group of words that function as a unit. In English, there are five types of phrase:

■ Adjective phrases:

It was a truly unforgettable experience.

■ Adverb phrases:

He ran away unbelievably quickly.

■ Noun phrases:

The young man ran away.

■ Preposition phrases:

I put it under my pillow.

■ Verb phrases:

I may be arriving late.

physician, physicist

These nouns are occasionally misused. A *physician* is a doctor, often one who does not specialize in surgery:

My physician thinks I need a minor operation and has recommended a very good surgeon.

A *physicist* is a scientist who specializes in physics:

He's a famous physicist and has been honoured for his work on wave mechanics.

physiognomy

This noun is frequently misspelled. It comes from Greek *phusis* + *gnomon*, 'nature + judge', and means 'a person's features or characteristic expression as an indicator of personality':

Many old people are adept at judging a person's likely behaviour from their physiognomy.

The '-g-' is not pronounced and the word rhymes with 'astronomy'.

piano

Piano is an abbreviation of 'pianoforte'. The plural is 'pianos':

They have two pianos in their house.

picaresque, picturesque

These adjectives are occasionally confused. *Picaresque* comes from Spanish *picaresco*, 'rogue', and is applied to a type of fiction in which the hero goes through a series of adventures:

Tom Jones is one of the earliest picaresque novels in English.

Picturesque means 'visually pleasing'. It comes from Italian *pittoresco*:

They live in a picturesque little village in Cornwall.

Both words rhyme with 'desk'.

piccolo

A *piccolo* is a small flute. The word is frequently misspelled:

The notes of most piccolos are an octave above the flute.

picket

Picket can function as a noun meaning 'a pointed stake used in a fence':

Our fence needs to have some of its pickets replaced.

It is also used for a group of people on strike:

We refused to cross the picket.

The position they occupy is called the 'picket line':

Only a handful of workers crossed the picket line.

Picket can also function as a regular verb meaning 'post a group of people outside a workplace':

picket(s), picketed, picketing
Why is the Post Office being picketed?

picnic

Picnic can function as a noun meaning 'informal meal eaten outside':

I love picnics but I hate the insects they attract.

and as a regular verb:

picnic(s), picnicked, picnicking
They've been picnicking in the park.

The derived noun 'picnicker' also needs a 'k' after the second 'c'.

picturesque

See PICARESQUE/PICTURESQUE

pidgin, pigeon

These nouns are homophones but their meanings are totally distinct. A *pidgin* is a simple spoken language that develops in ports or along trade routes to permit communication between people who do not share a mother tongue:

Pidgin languages are known to have existed for at least a thousand years.

A *pigeon* is a bird of the dove family:

There were so many pigeons in the city that the council decided to feed them birth control pills.

pidgin and creole

Pidginization is a process of simplification that occurs in languages when people who do not share the same language come into contact. It has played its part in the development of Old English into Modern English. Pidginized versions of Dutch, French, English, Italian, Portuguese and Spanish developed in the wake of European colonial expansion from the fifteenth century.

A *pidgin* is a simple spoken language that develops so as to permit communication between people who do not share a common language. Pidgins are nobody's mother tongue, and they are characterized by: the exploitation of linguistic common denominators; a small vocabulary drawn almost exclusively from the socially dominant language; a fixed word order; a simple grammar; and reinforcement by signs and body language.

The essential difference between a *pidgin* and a *creole* is sociological rather than linguistic: a pidgin is not a mother tongue; a creole is. Because it is a mother tongue, a *creole* is expanded so that it can fulfil all the linguistic needs of its speakers.

pigmy, pygmy

These are variant spellings. The 'py-' spelling is more widespread. The word comes from Greek *pugmaios*, 'undersized'. The noun is given a capital 'P' when it refers to specific people:

The Pygmies of Cameroon live in the equatorial forests.

but a small 'p' when used adjectivally as in:

pygmy nuts.

pilot

When *pilot* is used as a verb meaning 'to control a craft', it does not double the 't' before '-ed' and '-ing':

pilot(s), piloted, piloting
They piloted the cargo ships into port.

pincers, pinch

The words *pincers* and *pinch* both derive from an Old French verb *pincier*, 'to pinch'. Nowadays, except for some regional dialects, they are differentiated. A pair of *pincers* is a gripping tool:

Pass me the pincers, please. I'll have to pull out these nails.

Pinch can function as a noun or verb meaning 'nip':

He pinched me and it hurt!
These shoes pinch my toes.

and it is also a slang term for 'steal':

Somebody has pinched my bag.

piteous, pitiable, pitiful

These three adjectives are derived from *pity*, which comes ultimately from Latin *pietas*, 'duty'. They can all mean 'arousing or deserving pity' but only *pitiful* is widely used. *Piteous* usually describes something inanimate like a 'cry, sob':

I couldn't resist her piteous cry.

Pitiable regularly describes a figure or object. It suggests 'deserving our sympathy':

He was a pitiable figure, standing there with no possessions and hardly any clothes.

Pitiful often collocates with 'sight'. It suggests that the speaker feels sympathy:

It was a pitiful sight.

It is also used to mean 'capable of arousing contempt':

We collected a pitiful amount of money.

pity

Pity can function as a regular verb meaning 'feel sympathy or sorrow':

pity(ies), pitied, pitying
It's no good pitying these people if you don't do anything to help.

pivot

Pivot can function as a noun meaning a 'supporting pin on which something turns'. It is most frequently used metaphorically, especially with reference to a person:

He is the pivot on which the entire project depends.

It can also be a regular verb:

pivot(s), pivoted, pivoting.

The adjective 'pivotal' has become a vogue word meaning 'of crucial importance':

She's pivotal to the operation.

Like all overused words, 'pivotal' should be treated with care and avoided in formal contexts.

pixie, pixy

These are both acceptable spellings for an 'elf'. The plural of both is 'pixies':

They look like little pixies in their new uniforms.

pizza

Pizza is borrowed from Italian and is pronounced like 'Pete's a':

I'd like a pizza with lots of extra cheese.

place-names

Place-names can be used to explain the history of a region because they often reveal the origins of early settlers. Northeast England, for example, has many Norse-derived place-names, such as:

Brigg, Grimsby, Heckmondwike

indicating the extent of Viking settlements. We also find the city of 'Leeds', however, which reveals a Celtic past.

Place-names are sometimes extended into general use and are referred to as 'toponyms'. Among the best known are:

blarney (Blarney, Co. Cork, Ireland)

canary (Canary Islands)

denim (de Nimes, France).

See also ETYMOLOGY, WORD FORMATION

placebo

The noun *placebo* comes from Latin and means 'I shall please'. It is used medically to mean 'an innocuous substance given as a medicine to someone who feels they need medication' or 'to half of the patients in a drug test', and thus something that may give mental rather than medical relief:

The patients receiving the new drug have had 75 per cent fewer attacks than those on the placebo.

Placebo has two acceptable plurals, 'placebos' and 'placeboes'. The form ending in '-os' is more usual.

placid

See FLACCID/PLACID

plagiarism

Plagiarism comes from Latin *plagiarius*, 'plunderer', and involves the theft and use of another person's ideas, words or inventions. It is not always easy to draw a sharp dividing line between plagiarism and research that depends on the work of others, and so there are legally binding guidelines about how much of a writer's material can be borrowed without permission.

plague

Plague is occasionally misspelled. It can function as a noun meaning 'widespread, contagious disease':

Plagues regularly wiped out entire communities.

As a verb, *plague* means 'afflict', 'harass':

plague(s), plagued, plaguing

Can you stop these children plaguing me?

plaid, plait

These words rhyme with 'bad' and 'bat':

I wear the Stuart plaid. It's my favourite tartan.

Why were plaits called pigtails?

plain, plane

These homophones are occasionally confused because they both have many meanings. *Plain* can function as an adjective meaning 'unadorned', 'unattractive', 'simple', 'clear':

I've told you the plain truth.

As a noun, it means 'a level tract':

The plains stretch out for miles in all directions.

and as an intensifying adverb:

That's just plain stupid.

A *plane* can be a tool for levelling or smoothing wood and a verb meaning 'level', 'smooth':

I'll need to buy a plane to get rid of these bumps.

I've planed most of the woodwork.

Plane is also an abbreviation of 'aeroplane':

We were lucky because, although we were late, the plane had been delayed for technical reasons.

plaintiff, plaintive

These words are occasionally confused. They both derive from Old French *plaintif*, 'grieving'. *Plaintiff* is a noun and ends in '-ff'. It means 'a person who brings a legal action':

The plaintiff has accused his partner of theft.

Plaintive is an adjective meaning 'mournful':

Irish folk music can also be plaintive, expressing clearly the melancholy of the people.

plateau

A *plateau* is 'a piece of flat, high ground'. It is usually pluralized in the French way by adding '-x', but 'plateaus' is also acceptable:

There are many plateaux in the subtropical regions.

The word has been popularized by the media with the meaning of 'levelling off':

Inflation has now reached a plateau. Prices are expected to stay at this level for about three months before falling.

plateful

The normal plural of *plateful* is 'platefuls':

There were several platefuls of sandwiches left.

See also -FUL

platform

The noun *platform* has been widely used in the media as a shorthand expression for the 'policies of a political candidate or party':

His stated platform suggests that he is the most right-wing candidate running for office since Governor Wallace.

platypus

The noun *platypus* comes from Greek *platus + pous*, 'flat + foot'. It is often misspelled. The plural is 'platypuses':

The duck-billed platypus lays eggs but suckles its young.

playwright

See DRAMATIST/PLAYWRIGHT

plead

In Britain, *plead* is usually a regular verb meaning 'appeal earnestly':

plead(s), pleaded, pleading
I pleaded with him for hours but he refused to change his mind.

In America, *plead* may be regular or irregular. When it is treated as an irregular verb, 'pled' may be used for the past tense and past participle forms:

I have pled such cases before the Supreme Court.

Occasionally, 'plead' is used for the past tense and past participle but is pronounced to rhyme with 'led'. In other words, the verb *plead* is treated like 'read':

plead(s), plead, pleading, plead
read(s), read, reading, read.

plectrum

A *plectrum* has two acceptable plurals, namely 'plectra' and 'plectrums'. A *plectrum* is sometimes called a 'plectron'. *Plectrum* comes from Latin and means 'quill'; 'plectron' comes from Greek *plektron* and means 'something to strike with'.

plenty

Plenty can function as a noun:

There is plenty for everyone.
There are plenty of seats.

It is also used colloquially as an intensifying adverb:

*I was plenty mad when I heard the news.

but this usage is not standard.

pleonasm

Pleonasm comes from Greek *pleonazein*, 'to be excessive'. It is a term for the use of superfluous words:

In this day and age = now.

The related adjective 'apleonastic' is occasionally used by stylisticians to describe a style where redundancy is minimized.

See also CIRCUMLOCUTION, PERIPHRASIS, REDUNDANCY, TAUTOLOGY

plimsole, plimsoll

For a long time these spellings were acceptable variants in Britain for a light canvas sports shoe, but this word has now been replaced by 'trainers':

Please wear your plimsolls when you are in the gym.
I need new trainers for sports.

The expression 'Plimsoll line' is the name for the line on a ship to indicate how low the ship may be in the water when it is fully loaded. This usage is always *Plimsoll* because the safety line was called after an English Member of Parliament, Samuel Plimsoll.

plough, plow

In Britain, *plough* is the spelling for the agricultural implement, for its associated verb and also for the constellation 'The Plough':

Few people now use horse-drawn ploughs.
plough(s), ploughed, ploughing
You have ploughed your furrow and you will reap the consequences.

In America, *plow* is the preferred form in all instances, including compounds:

UK: ploughman, ploughshare
US: plowman, plowshare.

See also UK AND US ENGLISH

plum, plumb

These words are homophones. A *plum* is a fruit:

Plums are usually dark red or purple.

Plumb comes from Latin *plumbum*, 'lead', and is mainly used in the fixed expressions:

plumb line (string with metal weight)
to plumb the depths (suffer from depression).

plural

Most nouns in English form their plural by adding '-s' or '-es':

bat, bats

bridge, bridges
latch, latches.

There are many variations to this rule. Below, we provide some useful generalizations.

- Nouns ending in a vowel + y normally form their plurals regularly:

day, days
donkey, donkeys

but we have:

money, moneys/monies (as a technical term)
storey, storeys (UK), stories (US).

- Nouns ending in a vowel + o normally form their plurals by adding '-s':

cameo, cameos
video, videos.

- Nouns ending in a consonant + o usually form their plurals by adding '-es':

hero, heroes
potato, potatoes.

The main exceptions to this rule are:

dynamo, dynamos
Eskimo, Eskimos
Filipino, Filipinos
photo, photos
piano, pianos
solo, solos
soprano, sopranos.

There are also many nouns with two acceptable plurals:

banjo, banjos/banjoes
cargo, cargos/cargoes
domino, dominos/dominoes.

- Nouns ending in 'ch', 's', 'sh', 'ss', 'tch', 'x' or 'z' form their plurals by adding '-es':

bunch, bunches
bus, buses
crash, crashes
loss, losses
match, matches
flex, flexes
fez, fezzes.

- Nouns ending in a consonant + y usually form their plurals with '-ies':

berry, berries
caddy, caddies.

- Many nouns ending in 'f' form their plurals with '-ves':

loaf, loaves
thief, thieves
wolf, wolves.

- Some words ending in 'f' have two acceptable plurals:

dwarf, dwarves/dwarfs
hoof, hooves/hoofs.

'Knife', 'life' and 'wife' end in '-fe' but have the plurals 'knives', 'lives', and 'wives'.

There are many irregular nouns in the language, the most frequently used of which are:

brother, brethren (in religious language)
child, children
foot, feet
goose, geese
louse, lice
man, men
ox, oxen
tooth, teeth
woman, women.

Some irregular plurals are adopted from other languages. Latin has provided:

datum, data
index, indices

Greek has provided:

criterion, criteria
phenomenon, phenomena

Hebrew has provided:

cherub, cherubim
seraph, seraphim

and French has provided:

bureau, bureaux
plateau, plateaux.

Because of the process of regularizing borrowed words, some words have two plurals:

antenna, antennae/antennas
formula, formulae/formulas
index, indices/indexes.

Some nouns do not change their form in the plural. The most widespread in this category are words for people:

Chinese, Japanese

and words for animals, fish and game:

buck, deer, fowl, grouse, salmon, sheep.

Plurals of compound words usually add '-s' at the end:

armchair, armchairs
mouthful, mouthfuls.

Occasionally, however, the first element is pluralized as with:

brothers-in-law, passers-by

or both parts are:

lords justices, trades unions.

See also COUNTABLE AND UNCOUNTABLE, NOUN, SINGULAR AND PLURAL

plus
See MINUS/PLUS

p.m.
See A.M./P.M.

pneumatic

English words that begin with 'pneum-' derive from Greek *pneuma*, 'breath, spirit, wind'. The 'p' is not pronounced and the syllable is a homophone of 'new'. *Pneumatic* means 'concerned with air':

pneumatic brakes (brakes operated by compressed air)

pneumatic drill (drill using compressed air)

pneumatic tyre (tyre filled with air under pressure).

pneumonic

See MNEMONIC/PNEUMONIC

poetess

Most female poets prefer to be called 'poets' because *poetess* sounds less serious:

The poetess Elizabeth Barrett married Robert Browning.

See also FEMININE FORM/MASCULINE FORM, GENDER, NOUN, POLITICAL CORRECTNESS, SEXIST LANGUAGE

poetic diction

Poetic diction is a term applied to vocabulary that was regarded as being suitable for poetry. It includes words such as:

beauteous, comely, dryad, ere

as well as archaisms such as:

thou art, 'twill.

See also DICTION

pokey, poky

The informal adjective meaning 'small and cramped' may be spelled with or without an 'e':

These pokey little rooms are often stuffy.

Poland

An inhabitant of the east European country is a 'Pole'; the derived adjective is 'Polish'. The capital is Warsaw.

polemic, polemical

A *polemic* is a controversial dispute, usually involving religious or social issues. It may take the form of an unsupported attack on a person or principle or a closely reasoned argument. *Polemic* can also function as an adjective where it is in free variation with *polemical*. It should not be used as a synonym for 'controversial':

It will be a polemic debate because they disagree profoundly on matters of principle.

*We should invite a polemical speaker. We don't always need to support the status quo.

politic, political

These adjectives are occasionally confused. They both derive from Greek *politikos*, 'concerning civil administration'. *Politic* means 'appropriate, prudent, shrewd,' and can have undertones of 'crafty'. It is stressed on the first syllable:

We decided that it would be politic not to mention our departure until we had received our annual bonus.

It also occurs in the fixed phrase:

the body politic

meaning 'the state' or 'the people of a nation considered as a political entity'.

Political is more widely used than *politic* and means 'concerning politics'. It is stressed on the second syllable:

She was the most extraordinary political figure of the twentieth century.

political correctness

Political correctness or *PC* refers to a set of views on such issues as gender, race, sexual orientation or disability:

PC or not PC ... that was 1993's burning question.
          Sunday Times headline

The phrase may be used positively:

Political correctness assumes the equality of all human beings, irrespective of colour, creed, class or condition.

or it may be used critically:

Political correctness is more of a virus than a movement.

Advocates of *PC* concentrate on language use because they believe that, if we change the language, we will be able to change the prejudices that often underlie language choice. They argue particularly against:

Ageism

We can compare the different implications of such words as

Ageist	Non-ageist	Extreme PC
old	mature	chronologically gifted
pensioner	senior citizen	experientially enhanced

Racism

Many idiomatic uses of 'black' are negative and have nothing to do with the colour:

black fish (fish caught illegally)

blackmail

black market

black sheep.

The names used for people can cause offence. Native Americans object to being called 'Red Indians', and many Inuits dislike the term 'Eskimo', which means 'eater of raw meat'.

Sexism

Women should not be excluded or depicted as dependent on males. We are told about 'forefathers', but 'foremothers' is not an acceptable coinage. In addition, many women dislike the use of sets such as:

actor, actress

poet, poetess

and point out the different implications of words that are, theoretically, equivalent:

bachelor, spinster

governor, governess

master, mistress

old man, old woman.

Sizeism

Large people often feel discriminated against. We can compare such sets as:

fat, Junoesque, horizontally challenged

short, petite, vertically challenged.

Many PC coinages, such as:

differently interesting (boring)

differently pleasured (sadist)

domestic engineer (housewife)

follicularly challenged (bald)

rodent operative (rat catcher)

may for different reasons be unacceptable, but the original aim of political correctness was to accord courtesy and respect to everyone.

See also AFRO-, BLACK, RACIST LANGUAGE, SEXIST LANGUAGE

polyglot

See LINGUIST/POLYGLOT

polyp

The noun *polyp* meaning 'a small growth' is often misspelled:

The polyps are benign but they will have to be removed.

polysemy

Polysemy comes from Greek *poly + sema*, 'many + sign'. It is the term used to denote that a word, phrase or AFFIX can have several meanings. The word 'duck', for example, has many meanings, including:

an aquatic bird

a heavy cotton fabric

an amphibious vehicle

to swerve to escape

to submerge.

Many phrases can also be polysemous:

blow up = inflate, explode

put down = lower, kill

and so can affixes. The PREFIX 'un-' can mean 'reverse the action':

do, undo

pack, unpack

and 'not':

happy, unhappy

likely, unlikely.

See also MULTI-FUNCTIONAL, SEMANTICS

pommel, pummel

These words are occasionally misspelled or misused, and it is likely that they are variants, although their etymology is unclear. A *pommel* is a noun meaning 'raised part at the front of a saddle' or the 'knob on a sword':

The pommel has come off in my hand. Is there any way of putting it on again?

Pummel is a verb meaning 'hit hard and repeatedly':

UK: pummel(s), pummelled, pummelling

US: pummel(s), pummeled, pummeling

Stop pummel(l)ing that child!

Neither word is widely used and so people are uncertain of spelling.

pompom, pompon

These words are frequently confused and misused, but their meanings are quite different. A *pompom* or *pom-pom* is a type of quick-firing gun, often found on a ship.

Pompon or *pom-pon*, which means a 'tufted ball', can be used as the noun:

I bought some pompons for our cheerleaders.

and as an adjective:

They're called pompon chrysanthemums.

The spelling *pompom* can be used with this second sense, so if you are in any doubt, the advice is to use *pompom*. Careful writers, however, distinguish between the spellings.

See also REDUPLICATION

pore, pour

These words are homophones. *Pore* can function as a noun meaning 'small opening on the skin':

Spots are often caused by clogged pores.

As a verb, *pore* means 'make a close examination of'. It is related to 'peer':

I've pored over this manuscript until I've got spots in front of my eyes.

Pour means 'cause to flow':

Please pour the tea for us.

In some accents, 'paw' and 'poor' are also homophones of *pore* and *pour*.

portmanteau

Portmanteau comes from French *porter + manteau*, 'carry + mantle'. It refers to a large travelling bag and can form its plural by adding either '-x' or '-s'. The expression 'portmanteau word' is an older term for a blend:

fly + bilingual = flylingual (adjective used in British Airways advertisement) stagnation + inflation = stagflation.

See also BLEND

portrait
See LANDSCAPE/PORTRAIT

Portugal
An inhabitant of the European country is a 'Portuguese'; the derived adjective is the same. The capital is Lisbon.

possession
Possession is indicated in six main ways.

■ Using the genitive form of the noun – that is, noun + 's for the singular and noun + s' for the plural:

Peter's cat
the cat's tail
the cats' tails

■ Using 'of':
the bark of the tree
the roofs of the houses

■ Juxtaposing nouns:
the table leg (the leg of the table)
the treetop (the top of the tree)

■ Using verbs that indicate ownership:
He has a Persian cat.
She got all the prizes.
They don't own all the houses.

■ Using possessive adjectives:
his cat
her dog

■ Using possessive pronouns:
It's theirs.
That's mine.

See also APOSTROPHE, CASE, GENITIVE, GERUND, OF/OFF

possum
See OPOSSUM/POSSUM

post-
Post- is a frequently used PREFIX. It derives from Latin *post*, 'after', 'behind', and creates such words as:

post-hypnotic, post-traumatic.
The older coinages are written as one word:
postdate, postscript
whereas the relatively more recent creations are hyphenated:
post-colonial, post-millennial.

posthumous
The adjective *posthumous* comes from Latin

postumus, 'last', but the spelling reflects an incorrect etymology. It is based on Latin *post* + *humus*, 'after + earth', and thought to mean 'after the burial'. *Posthumous* means 'happening after one's death':

The posthumous performance of Potter's last play was broadcast both by BBC1 and Channel 4.

The word is often misspelled and mispronounced. The first two syllables rhyme with 'costume'.

potato
The plural of the noun *potato* is 'potatoes':

The word 'potato' is a modified form of Spanish *patata*, which was itself borrowed from *batata*, the name of the root vegetable in the Amerindian language, Taina.

pour
See PORE/POUR

practicable, practical
These adjectives are often confused. *Practicable* applies to something that is possible, something that can be practised, performed or used:

It's not practicable to have drivers working seven days a week.

A *practicable* proposal is one that seems feasible but has not already been tested. The adjective 'practicable' is most commonly used in negative constructions:

The scheme was so expensive that it was not practicable.

Practical applies to people and to things that are sensible, useful and that have a proven reliability:

It was such a practical proposal that we put it into effect immediately.
She's more practical than theoretical in her interests and so she has decided to study nursing.

practically
Practically is an adverb that is derived from 'practical':

He doesn't always behave very practically but then he's very young.

It has been used so frequently as an intensifier, however, that it now means 'almost' or 'nearly':

I've practically finished all the food in the house.

See also BLEACHING, SEMANTIC CHANGE

practice, practise
In British English, the noun and the verb are distinguished by spelling. The noun ends in '-ice' and the verb in '-ise':

She has an inner-city practice.
I've practised for years and I'm still not a good pianist.

In American English, *practice* is used as both a noun and a verb:

US: I've practiced for years.

practitioner
The noun *practitioner* is no longer widely used. It refers to a person who practises an art or profession:

a medical practitioner.

In certain contexts a *practitioner* is a person who is authorized to carry out spiritual healing.

pray, prey
These homophones can both function as regular verbs. *Pray* means 'elevate the soul to God':

St Monica prayed for forty years for the conversion of her son.

Pray had a weaker meaning in English. It could mean 'beg, plead':

Let me go, I pray you.

but this usage is old fashioned and virtually obsolete.

Prey can be a noun meaning 'animal that is hunted' or a verb meaning 'behave in a predatory way':

He preyed on people who were in weak positions.

pre-
Pre- is a widely-used PREFIX deriving from Latin *prae*, 'before', 'in front':

pre-arrange, pre-chill.

Older compounds tend not to have a HYPHEN:

precaution, precognition, predate, prefix.

pre(-)requisite
See PERQUISITE/PRE(-)REQUISITE

precede, proceed
These verbs are occasionally confused and often misspelled. *Precede* means 'go before' and can refer to place or time:

She preceded him into the hallway.
Shakespeare preceded Milton.

Proceed means 'go forward, continue with':

She proceeded to win three gold medals.
Do you intend to proceed with your application?

The noun derived from proceed is 'procedure':

We followed the installation procedure to the letter but the software still doesn't work properly.

precedence, precedent
These nouns both derive from 'precede'. *Precedence* (or, less frequently, 'precedency') means 'priority in order or rank':

Does a duchess take precedence over a countess?

A *precedent* is an example that serves to justify a later ruling:

This award for damages will set a precedent for others.

precipitate(ly), precipitous(ly)
These adjectives and adverbs are often confused. *Precipitate* means 'rash, sudden':

What on earth caused such precipitate action?
It was foolish to behave so precipitately.

Precipitous means 'very steep':

I found the climb much more precipitous than I had expected.
The mountain rose precipitously to a height of 4000 metres.

précis
A *précis* is a condensed paraphrase. It provides a summary of a text without omitting any significant point:

How could anyone write a précis of Paradise Lost in 300 words?

Often, the word is written without an acute accent.

See also PARAPHRASE

predicate
The noun *predicate* rhymes with 'delicate'. It is a term used by grammarians to refer to the part of a sentence that asserts something about a subject:

Subject	Predicate
The cat	jumped.
The cat	is beautiful.
The cat	chased the mouse.
The cat	ran away.
The cat	did not like that.

The term 'predicator' is sometimes reserved for the verb in the predicate, that is, for 'jumped', 'is', 'chased', 'ran' and 'did ... like' in the sentences above.

predicate, predict
These verbs are occasionally confused. *Predict* means 'foretell':

Is it ever possible to predict the future?

Predicate means 'affirm', 'declare':

They predicated that their firm was financially viable.

Predicate can also be used passively to mean 'be based on':

Her success was predicated on hard work and natural talent.

The verb *predicate* rhymes with 'date'.

preface
See FOREWORD/PREFACE

prefer

Prefer is a regular verb meaning 'like better':
prefer(s), preferred, preferring.

Prefer is followed by 'to' not 'than':
I prefer rice to pasta.
*I prefer rice than pasta.

The derived forms 'preferable' and 'preference' are stressed on the first syllable and do not double the 'r'. 'Preferable' is followed by 'to' and 'preference' by 'for':
Anything would be preferable to toast again.
Has she shown a preference for any particular painting?

prefix

A *prefix* is a meaningful unit, or AFFIX, sometimes referred to as a MORPHEME. It can be attached to the beginning of a word:
dis + taste = distaste
in + sight = insight
re + place = replace
un + happy = unhappy.

Prefixes are morphemes like:
anti-, de-, dis-, ex-, in-, il-, im-, ir-, pre-, pro-, re-, un-
which can precede words, modifying their meaning. Most prefixes derive from Latin and they can affect the meaning of the root word in terms of:

■ Direction:
anti + clockwise = anticlockwise
contra + flow = contraflow

■ Negation:
in + definite = indefinite
un + happily = unhappily.

The 'in-' prefix can appear as 'il-' or 'im-' or 'ir-', as the 'n' is assimilated to the following consonant:
in + legal = illegal
in + mobile = immobile
in + reparable = irreparable.

■ Number:
bi + cycle = 2 wheels
giga + byte = 1,000,000, 000 bits
mega + byte = 1,000,000 bits.

Unlike suffixes, prefixes tend not to change the class of a word:

Prefix + adjective	Adjective
in + fertile	infertile
un + fit	unfit

Prefix + noun	Noun
ante + chamber	antechamber
ex + husband	ex-husband

Prefix + verb	Verb
re + do	redo
pro + create	procreate

Words can have two or more prefixes:
re + de + ploy + ment = redeployment
un + pre + possess + ing = unprepossessing
and occasionally two or more prefixes and suffixes as in:
anti + dis + establish + ment + ar + ian + ism.

See also DERIVATION, SUFFIX, WORD FORMATION

prehensile

This adjective comes from Latin *prehendere*, 'to grasp'. *Prehensile* means 'adapted for grasping' and it is applied often to hands, feet and tails:
Spider monkeys have prehensile tails.

prejudice

Prejudice is frequently misspelled by people who are unaware of its etymology. It comes from Latin *praejudicium*, 'a prior judgement', and means 'an opinion formed beforehand'. In the eighteenth century *prejudice* was commendable because it implied that people had thought about a certain issue before making up their minds. Now, the noun suggests irrational attitudes formed without sufficient evidence or knowledge:
We all probably have a certain amount of prejudice but we should not allow it to cloud our judgement.

Many people have pointed out that certain prejudices are ingrained in the English language. Certain professions usually imply a gender unless prefaced by a gender marker:
a male nurse
a woman solicitor
and the word 'man' is used when 'person' or 'human being' is implied:
The Ascent of Man
One man, one vote.
Colour, race and religion are denigrated in such expressions as:
to black (a factory, ship, etc.)
to gyp
to jew
and in such nouns as:
wog, wop.

See also BLACK, POLITICAL CORRECTNESS, PROPAGANDA, RACIST LANGUAGE, SEXIST LANGUAGE

prelude

Prelude is often used to mean 'a piece of music that precedes a fugue'. Recently, it has been overused by the media to mean 'introduction' or 'forerunner':
Truanting is often a prelude to crime.

Like all overworked words, *prelude* in this sense should be avoided in formal contexts.

premier, première

These words are both borrowed from French. *Premier* is the masculine and *première* the feminine form of 'first'. In English, *premier* is often overused as an adjective meaning 'foremost':

Premier sportsman's £15 million tag.

It is also occasionally used instead of 'Prime Minister':

Premier Thatcher was a close friend and ally of President Reagan.

Première is used as a noun meaning 'first public performance':

Simultaneous premières will be held in London and New York.

and occasionally as a verb meaning 'put on for the first time':

Friel's latest play was premièred in New York.

premise, premises

These words both derive from Latin *praemittere*, 'to send in advance', but they have developed distinct meanings. *Premise* may be used as a noun or a verb meaning 'statement that is assumed to be true and from which a logical conclusion may be drawn'. The noun may also be spelled 'premiss':

Let us begin with the premise that all human beings are equal ...
The equality of all human beings is premised.

The noun *premises* means 'piece of land with its buildings' or simply 'buildings':

Are these premises licensed to sell food?

preposition

A *preposition* is a linking word such as 'at' or 'in'. Prepositions precede nouns, noun phrases and pronouns to form a unit:

I went to John for advice.
I went to the woods. (I went there.)
He went on his own. (He went alone.)

The word *preposition* comes from Latin *praeponere*, 'to put in front of', and prepositions in Latin always preceded and governed a noun phrase:

ad infinitum (to eternity)
in hoc signo (in this sign).

Latin sentences could not end with a preposition and so seventeenth-century scholars claimed that English sentences should not end with prepositions. This belief continues to influence structures and so, in the written medium, many people prefer:

To whom will I send it?

rather than the more colloquial:

Who will I send it to?

Sentences ending in prepositions are perfectly acceptable in most contexts. The only reason for avoiding such usage is that purists continue to stigmatize it.

The most widely-used prepositions in the language are:

at, by, for, from, in, of, on, to, with

but prepositions may consist of two or three words:

according to, in accordance with.

When prepositions are followed by pronouns, the pronoun is always in the accusative form:

between you and me (*between you and I)
to me
with her.

This rule applies even when a noun or noun phrase goes before the pronoun:

He sent it to John and me.
*He sent it to John and I.
We went with her parents and her.
*We went with her parents and she.

See also AMONG/AMONGST/BETWEEN, I/ME, PART OF SPEECH, WE/US

prescribe, proscribe

These regular verbs are occasionally confused. *Prescribe* means 'lay down a rule', 'order':

We should prescribe a methodology for inducting new staff.
This medication was prescribed by my doctor.

Proscribe means 'ban', 'condemn', prohibit':

Meetings of more than ten people were proscribed.

prescriptive grammar

A *prescriptive grammar* provides rules about how English should be used. In the past, such grammars were the norm and inculcated beliefs such as 'me' cannot follow a copula verb:

It was I.
*It was me.

and prepositions cannot come at the end of a sentence:

That was a rule up with which I could not put.
*That was a rule I could not put up with.

A grammar made up entirely of prohibitions is called a 'proscriptive' grammar. Contemporary grammarians often claim that a scholar's task is to describe and not to prescribe. Many speakers are uncertain about usage and therefore value guidance.

See also GRAMMAR

present-day

The adjective *present-day* means 'contemporary, current':

This course concentrates on present-day English.

It is currently overused.

presently

In Britain, *presently* means 'soon, in a little while':

We'll have tea presently.

However, it is increasingly being used with the meaning of 'at present', mainly because of influence from America:

She is presently on tour.

Because of the potential for ambiguity, care should be used to make sure that the meaning of *presently* is clear.

See also HOPEFULLY

press

The *press* is a term for newspapers and their staff:

He has had no peace since the press got hold of the story.

pressure, pressurize

Pressure is most frequently used as a noun meaning 'the exertion of force'. The force may be literal or metaphorical:

This boiler is under considerable pressure.

I've been under pressure to change my vote.

The verb *pressure* tends to be used only in the metaphorical sense of 'coerce':

It is not acceptable for people to be pressured in this way.

Pressurize means 'increase the pressure in an enclosure':

The aircraft is pressurized to maintain atmospheric pressure throughout the passenger cabins.

In the metaphoric sense, *pressurize* also means 'coerce':

I don't want you to feel pressurized, but it would help us if we could have your decision by tomorrow.

prestige

Prestige is stressed on the second syllable, which rhymes with 'liege'. It derives ultimately from a Latin noun *praestigiae*, 'feats of juggling', and is a good example of a word whose meaning has been elevated. *Prestige* now means 'high status or reputation':

He is more interested in the loss of prestige than in whether or not he has done something wrong.

Many speakers dislike the adjectival use of *prestige* as in:

a prestige car, a prestige job.

See also SEMANTIC CHANGE

prestigious

The adjective *prestigious* is derived from 'prestige'

and rhymes with 'religious'. It means 'having or conferring status':

Too much Lottery money has been spent on prestigious projects, such as theatres, and not enough on such necessary tasks as housing the homeless.

presume

See ASSUME/PRESUME

presumptive, presumptuous

These adjectives are occasionally misused and the second is frequently misspelled. *Presumptive* means 'based on probability' and often co-occurs with 'evidence':

They'll need more than presumptive evidence if they are to secure a conviction.

The phrase 'heir presumptive', meaning an heir who may not inherit if someone more closely related to the monarch is born, is rarely used now. It should be distinguished from 'heir apparent'.

Presumptuous is often pronounced as if it ended in '-ious' and this tendency has affected the spelling. It means 'forward', 'impudent':

I don't like the way mature people are called by their first names when they are in hospital. It seems presumptuous and lacking in respect.

pretence, pretense

Pretence means 'a false display':

It's all pretence. They live in a world of their own and don't distinguish between fact and make-believe.

This noun ends in '-ence' in Britain but usually in '-ense' in America.

prevaricate

Prevaricate is a regular verb meaning 'speak or act evasively with the intention of deceiving':

They prevaricated for a few days until they managed to sort our their cashflow problems.

The word is often used as a formal equivalent of 'tell lies' but the two are not identical. One can prevaricate by telling the truth but not all of the truth.

Courts try to guard against prevarication by insisting that people tell 'the truth, the whole truth, and nothing but the truth'.

prevent

The regular verb *prevent* now means 'hinder, impede, stop something happening':

Why did they prevent you from attending?

Prevent may be followed by 'from' + a present participle:

She prevented me from going.

possessive adjective + present participle:

She prevented my going.

possessive noun + present participle:

She prevented John's going.

She prevented her children's going.

and the object form of the pronoun + present participle:

She prevented me going.

She prevented them going.

In casual speech, the last option is the most likely, although the construction with 'from':

She prevented me from going.

is preferred.

See also GERUND

preventive, preventative

These adjectives are both used to mean 'tending to hinder or impede':

She is specializing in preventive medicine.

She is specializing in preventative medicine.

Careful speakers dislike *preventative* because it is unnecessary, but if we judge by current media usage, it is perhaps more widely used than the etymologically more correct *preventive*.

prey

See PRAY/PREY

priceless

See INVALUABLE/PRICELESS/VALUABLE/VALUELESS

prima facie

The Latin phrase *prima facie* is normally italicized and means 'at first sight':

First, we must see if there is a *prima facie* case for promotion; then we must find external referees.

The phrase is usually pronounced to rhyme with 'time a geisha'.

primeval

The adjective *primeval* is also spelled 'primaeval' and means 'belonging to the first age':

There is a primeval dread of darkness in most of us.

primitive

Primitive is an adjective meaning 'characteristic of an early stage, crude':

People dream of travelling to outer space and encountering advanced or primitive life forms.

In the past the adjective was sometimes applied to people who lived in non-industrial, non-literate societies. Such usage is no longer acceptable.

principal, principle

Principal can function as an adjective meaning 'primary, most important':

The principal reason for agreeing to the merger is the hope of avoiding redundancies.

As a noun, *principal* has three main meanings. It can refer to the head of a school or college:

Who was principal when you were at school?

a person for whom someone else acts as representative:

She was in telephone contact with her principal throughout the auction.

and an invested sum of money:

They can no longer live on their interest and so they have had to use part of the principal.

The homophone *principle* functions as a noun and means 'rule, fundamental truth, basis of reasoning':

She explained the principle of the hovercraft.

The 'Peter Principle' claims that we promote people to the point of their incompetence.

prior to

Prior to is frequently used as a compound preposition meaning 'before':

We need to discuss strategies prior to our meeting with the Principal.

In general, the preposition 'before' is to be preferred. It is simpler and clearer.

prioritize

Prioritize or *prioritise* is a regular verb formed from 'priority'. It means 'put in order of importance':

Few of us learn to prioritize. We tend to give equal time and effort to the insignificant and to the vital.

prise, prize

These homophones can both be used as regular verbs. In British English, *prise* means 'force apart by levering':

I've lost the key so we'll have to prise open the door.

In America, the form *prize* is preferred:

I've lost the key so we'll have to prize open the door.

In both Britain and America, *prize* can be a noun meaning 'reward for winning':

She won the Booker Prize for the best novel of the year.

and also a verb meaning 'treasure, value highly':

He prized your letters and re-read them often.

pristine

The adjective *pristine* comes from Latin *pristinus*, 'primitive'. It means 'original', 'dating from an early period':

All religions, in their pristine forms, make strong demands on their followers.

Recently, the adjective has been used with the meaning of 'new, unblemished':

Everything in the house looked pristine and new. It was as if nothing had ever been used or washed.

Pristine rhymes with 'Christine'.

privacy

In Britain the first syllable of the word *privacy* normally rhymes with 'give'; in America, it rhymes with 'hive':

The Press Commission believes that tougher privacy laws are not necessary.

pro rata

The phrase *pro rata* comes from Latin and means 'in proportion':

They deserve a pro rata increase in pay for their greater productivity.

pro-

Pro- is a frequently used prefix. English borrowed one *pro-* from Greek meaning 'before in time or place':

prognosis (knowledge beforehand)

progress (move forward)

and one from Latin meaning 'in favour of':

pro-Catholic

pro-Japanese.

probable

This adjective is occasionally misspelled. *Probable* means 'likely':

The probable outcome is that we will put off a decision until next month.

The word 'probeable' exists but is rarely used. It means 'capable of being probed, examined':

Only certain parts of the body are probeable even with flexible instruments.

probe

Probe is a buzz word popularized by the press. It is short and therefore more useful in headlines than words such as 'enquiry or 'investigation':

Police Force Sexism Probe.

proceed

See PRECEDE/PROCEED

procrastinate

Procrastinate incorporates the Latin word *cras*, meaning 'tomorrow', and means 'put off until a future time something that could be done now':

It is tempting to procrastinate and put difficult decisions off, but, as the proverb suggests, 'Procrastination is the thief of time'.

prodigy, protégé

These nouns are occasionally confused. A *prodigy* is a person, often a child, who has unusual and exceptional talents. The word comes from Latin *prodigium*, 'unnatural happening':

He was a musical prodigy. At three he was playing the piano and at seven he was composing music.

Protégé comes from French *protéger*, 'to protect', and is used of a person who receives help and patronage from another person:

He was a protégé of the Earl of Southampton.

The female form is 'protégée':

She was their most successful protégée.

Both male and female forms are pronounced the same and are approximated to French pronunciation in that the final syllable rhymes with 'may'.

productivity

See OUTPUT/PRODUCTIVITY

profession, professional

The noun *profession* used to refer to the occupation of people who were educated to a certain level and who earned salaries:

a profession in medicine

the legal profession.

The term has been widened:

His chosen profession of football provided him with fame, fortune and opportunities for misbehaving.

Less frequently, the noun *profession* can mean a 'declaration':

His open profession of faith was as inspiring as it was unexpected.

The adjective *professional* has a range of meanings. It can still refer to a subset of salaried occupations:

His professional responsibilities to his practice left little time for a home life.

or to any gainful occupation:

Professional cricketers earn more than professional darts players.

As a noun, it can be used of someone who is exceptionally competent:

She's a professional and will do a first-class job.

proficient

The adjective *proficient* is often misused and equated with 'efficient'. *Proficient* means 'skilled':

I used to be quite a proficient bowler.

profile

The noun *profile* means 'outline' and it is used both literally and metaphorically:

The photographer tends to concentrate on her profile.

Let us have a short profile of five employees. We don't want too much detail, just a short biographical sketch.

Recently, the noun has been overused in the fixed phrases:

high profile (conspicuous, in the public eye)

low profile (unobtrusive, avoiding publicity)

and *profile* has come to be used as a synonym for 'status, perceived importance':

Part of your job will be to raise the profile of the college.

prognosis
See DIAGNOSIS/PROGNOSIS

programme, program
British people use *programme* and Americans *program* for 'a list of events':

UK: Theatre programmes are available in the foyer.

US: Theater programs are available in the foyer.

When the word means 'computer instructions' or 'provide a computer with instructions' it is spelled *program* in both countries:

Which computer program are you using?

We'll need to find someone to re-program our cluster.

In both Britain and America, it is usual to double the 'm' before '-ed' and '-ing':

program(s), programmed, programming

but Americans also use:

program(s), programed, programing.

progressive
In English, speakers distinguish between:

I work (i.e., for a living)

and:

I am working now.

The first example has traditionally been called the 'simple present' and the second example 'the present continuous' or 'the present *progressive*'.

See also ASPECT

project
The noun *project* meaning 'plan, scheme' is stressed on the first syllable. The vowel in the first syllable may be the same as the vowel sound in 'dodge' or 'dough'. Both pronunciations are acceptable. When *project* is used as a verb meaning 'plan' or 'protrude, stick out', the stress is on the second syllable.

proliferate, prolific
The verb *proliferate* derives ultimately from Latin *proles* + *ferre*, 'to bear offspring'. It means 'grow or reproduce rapidly':

Greenfly proliferate at a speed that gardeners prefer not to think about.

Recently, the verb has been widely used as a polysyllabic variant of 'grow':

These perennials will proliferate for years.

The adjective *prolific* means 'producing in abundance', 'fruitful'. In the past it was applied to the producer only:

a prolific plant

a prolific writer.

Careful users do not like the fact that it is now sometimes applied to the product as well as to the producer:

*The output was prolific.

but it seems likely that this usage will continue.

prone, prostrate, supine
These adjectives all mean 'lying down' but careful users distinguish their usage. *Prone* comes from Latin *pronus*, 'bent forward', and means 'lying flat or face downwards':

We didn't know whether or not he had actually hurt himself. We just saw him lying prone on the kitchen floor.

Prostrate comes from Latin *prosternere*, 'to throw to the ground', and means 'lying with the face downwards as in submission or prayer':

The acolytes prostrated themselves before the altar.

It can also suggest 'defenceless', 'emotionally or physically exhausted':

We could see immediately that something was wrong. He was lying prostrate and helpless on the kitchen floor.

Supine comes from Latin *supinare* 'to lay on the back', and means 'lying flat with the face upwards':

They found him supine on the grass looking at the sky and the clouds.

prone to
The phrase *prone to* means 'having an inclination to':

People who have lived in the tropics are less prone to malarial infection than visitors.

Careful users dislike the use of *prone to* where 'susceptible' might be used as in:

She is prone to colds.

but this usage is growing and is acceptable.

pronoun
The word *pronoun* comes from Latin *pro + nomen*, 'acting as a substitute for a noun'. It thus resembles such words as 'proconsul' (acting for the consul). Pronouns can replace nouns, noun phrases and noun clauses:

John was right. He was right.

The young man was right. He was right.

What you did was right. That was right.

Pronouns can reflect gender:

Jack is tall. He is tall.

Jean is tall. She is tall.

The building is tall. It is tall.

They can also reflect case. The nominative occurs as the subject of a sentence; the possessive indicates ownership; and the accusative occurs after a preposition and as the object of a sentence:

She is tall.
The book is hers.
I gave it to her.
I saw her yesterday.

There are several types of pronoun:

■ Personal pronouns:

Person		Singular		Plural	
		Nom	Acc	Nom	Acc
First		I	me	we	us
Second		you	you	you	you
Third	feminine	she	her	they	them
	masculine	he	him	they	them
	neuter	it	it	they	them

■ Possessive pronouns:

Person		Singular	Plural
First		mine	ours
Second		yours	yours
Third	feminine	hers	theirs
	masculine	his	theirs

■ Reflexive pronouns:

Person		Singular	Plural
First		myself	ourselves
Second		yourself	yourselves
Third	feminine	herself	themselves
	masculine	himself	themselves
	neuter	itself	themselves

■ Demonstrative pronouns:

Singular	Plural
this	these
that	those

■ Interrogative pronouns:

Nominative	Accusative	Possessive
who?	whom?	whose?
what?	what?	
which?	which?	

■ Relative pronouns:

Nominative	Accusative	Possessive
that	that	
which	which	
who	whom	whose

■ Distributive pronouns:

all: All (of the children) are here.
both: Both (of them) are here.
each: Each (of them) won a prize.
either: Either (of the children) would do.
neither: Neither (of us) would go.

■ Indefinite pronouns:

any: I don't want any.
one: One cannot be too careful.
some: Some thought it was excellent.

See also ANTECEDENT, COMPLEMENT, OBJECT, PART OF SPEECH, SUBJECT

pronounce

Pronounce is a regular verb meaning 'articulate sounds':

pronounce(s), pronounced, pronouncing
She always pronounces borrowed French words as if they were still French.

The derived adjective is 'pronounceable', ending in '-eable' and the nouns are 'pronouncement' and PRONUNCIATION, with '-nunc-' not '-nounc-':

We are expecting an official pronouncement from the Vatican within minutes.
Her pronunciation of words like 'park' suggests she's an Australian.

pronunciation

The word *pronunciation* is itself frequently misspelled and mispronounced. The second syllable is '-nun-', not '-noun-'. Pronunciation means 'a method of articulating sounds'. When it relates to a person's normal pronunciation, it can mean 'an accent'.

There has never been one acceptable system of pronunciation for English, although some pronunciations have been more prestigious than others. Most educated speakers approximate to the standard grammar and vocabulary of the written language in their speech and pronounce the language according to the accepted norms of their region. Increasingly, these norms are set by regional radio and television announcers, but, since these media are international, it seems likely that people throughout the world are beginning to sound more alike.

Speakers of English throughout the world agree more closely on the pronunciation of consonants than on that of vowels. One of the major differences between varieties of English relates to the pronunciation of 'r' in words such as:

far, farm.

So-called RHOTIC speakers pronounce the 'r' in such words; non-rhotic speakers do not.

See also ACCENT, UK AND US ENGLISH

propaganda

Propaganda is an example of a word where the meaning has been changed. It is treated as a singular noun and does not have a plural form. It was originally a religious term derived from *Congregatio de Propaganda Fidei* ('Congregation for the Spread of the Faith'), and it referred to the dissemination of Christian beliefs. Today, the word often has negative implications and suggests spreading information for the purpose of hurting a cause, person or organization, or less commonly, spreading information with the intention of helping a cause, person or organization; or the information transmitted in a paper or news medium:

He never reads a broadsheet. He prefers to take his propaganda from a tabloid.

Propaganda transmits attitudes and values with its information. It makes use of such techniques as emotive vocabulary; playing on feelings of insecurity, pride and envy; emphasizing the prestige of the speaker; and non-linguistic devices, including music and colour, to influence the opinions of the audience.

propel
Propel is a regular verb deriving from Latin *propellere*, 'to drive forward':

propel(s), propelled, propelling

This song has propelled the group to the number one position in Britain.

propellant, propellent
These words are related to 'propel'. The form ending in '-ant' is the noun and means 'something that pushes forward':

What sort of propellant is used on the Ariane rocket?

Propellent is an adjective and is sometimes used to describe fuels:

Car manufacturers are experimenting with using hydrogen as a propellent gas because the only waste product would be water.

See also -ANT/-ENT

propeller, propellor
A *propeller* is a device with blades. It rotates to create a thrust:

The blades in the ship's propeller were badly bent and corroded.

An alternative spelling with '-or' is occasionally used in America.

proper noun
A *proper noun* is the name of a particular person, place or language.

See also NOUN

prophecy, prophesy
These words are related and they both derive from Greek *prophetes*, 'prophet'. *Prophecy* is a noun meaning 'message of divine truth'. It is stressed on the first syllable and rhymes with 'legacy':

Many prophecies have indeed come true.

Prophesy is a verb meaning 'foretell'. It has a secondary stress on the third syllable, which rhymes with 'sigh':

prophesy(sies), prophesied, prophesying

Nostradamus is supposed to have prophesied the use of nuclear weapons.

proportion
In certain journalistic styles, *proportion* is used where 'some' might be more appropriate:

A proportion of your time will be devoted to interviewing.

Proportion means 'ratio, the relationship between different things':

The area increases in direct proportion to any increase in length or breadth.

proposal, proposition
These nouns both come from Latin *proponere*, 'to display' and their meanings are distinct. A *proposal* is usually an offer of marriage:

Why did she not accept his proposal?

although it can also mean a plan:

Her proposal was that we should camp out for the night.

A *proposition* is often more mercenary than a *proposal*. It is usually a topic or enterprise presented for discussion:

The proposition put forward by the Council is that the bill for home helps for the elderly should be reduced by 10 per cent.

proprietary, propriety
These words are occasionally misused and misspelled. *Proprietary* is an adjective suggesting 'privately owned or controlled':

They take their proprietary interest in the block of flats very seriously.

The adjective also describes a drug that is manufactured and sold under a trade name:

Doctors are encouraged not to prescribe proprietary drugs as generic ones are cheaper.

Propriety is a noun meaning 'having correct standards of behaviour':

He would never have done such a thing. He is the last person in the world to offend against propriety.

proscribe
See PRESCRIBE/PROSCRIBE

prosecute
See PERSECUTE/PROSECUTE

prosody
Prosody derives ultimately from Greek *prosoidia*, 'song sung to musical accompaniment'. Today, it is applied to the study of verse, with particular regard to such features as rhyme, rhythm and stanza pattern. In linguistics, *prosody* refers to the patterns of stress, rhythm, pitch and intonation in a spoken language.

prospective
See PERSPECTIVE/PROSPECTIVE

prostrate
See PRONE/PROSTRATE/SUPINE

protagonist
A *protagonist* is the principal character in a play. The word comes from Greek *protagonistes*, 'first actor':

The heroic protagonist normally has a single human weakness, but circumstances conspire to exploit such a weakness and bring about his downfall.

The noun is also used to mean 'champion, strong supporter':

Some people see him as the chief protagonist of New Labour; others dismiss him as a spin-doctor.

Some people dislike this usage on two grounds. They argue that the word includes the meaning of 'great', 'principal' and they dislike the semantic shift away from the theatre.

See also SEMANTIC CHANGE

protégé
See PRODIGY/PROTÉGÉ

protest (against)
Protest comes from Latin *protestari*, 'to make a formal declaration'. When it functions as a noun, it is stressed on the first syllable and means 'public dissent':

They're organizing a protest against the export of live animals.

When it is used as a verb, it is stressed on the second syllable and means 'object strongly to'. In British English, this use of the verb requires the preposition 'against', but the preposition is not required in America:

UK: We're protesting against the loss of grants.
US: We're protesting the loss of grants.

The use of the verb to mean 'strongly affirm' does not require a preposition:

We protested our innocence.

protozoon, protozoa
These words come from Greek *protos + zoion*, 'first animal'. The singular form is *protozoon* or *protozoan* and refers to any minute invertebrate. The form *protozoa* is the normal plural:

We had to study such protozoa as ciliates, sporozoans and amoebae.

prove
The verb *prove* may be treated as regular:

prove(s), proved, proving, proved

or it may have 'proven' as its past participle:

prove(s), proved, proving, proven

although this usage is dying out.

In Scotland, there are three possible legal verdicts,

'guilty', 'not guilty' and 'not proven', and 'proven' is the normal form of the adjective:

I've learnt to stick to proven methods.

The first syllable of 'proven' may rhyme with either 'dough' or 'do'.

See also VERB

proverb
A *proverb* is a mnemonically concise saying that expresses a generally recognized truth:

A bird in the hand is worth two in the bush.
Too many cooks spoil the broth.

Proverbs are most frequently found in rural, often pre-literate societies.

Many people dislike the use of *proverb* or its adjectival form 'proverbial' to mean 'clear example' or 'famous':

She's a proverb for kindness and courtesy.
Her courtesy is proverbial.

but such changes in meaning are widespread in English.

See also APHORISM, MAXIM, SEMANTIC CHANGE

provided, providing
Provided and *providing* can both be used as conjunctions meaning 'on condition that':

He promised to be here at ten provided/providing that his plane was not delayed.

In formal contexts, it is preferable to use *provided*.

See also EXCEPT/EXCEPTED/EXCEPTING/SAVE

provident, providential
These adjectives are occasionally confused. They both come from Latin *providere*, 'to foresee', but their meanings should be differentiated. *Provident* means 'thrifty', 'providing for the future':

He's unexpectedly provident for such a young man.

Providential means 'unexpectedly lucky', 'the result of divine providence':

It was providential that I bought a lottery ticket!

proviso
A *proviso* is a condition or stipulation. It may be pluralized by adding '-es' or '-s':

How many more provisos will she dream up before she signs the contract?

provocative
See EVOCATIVE/PROVOCATIVE/VOCATIVE

prowess
Prowess used to mean 'bravery', 'fearlessness in battle', but it has been bleached of some of its

meaning and now suggests 'exceptional ability, skill':

You should see her prowess on the tennis court!

See also BLEACHING

pry

The verb *pry* is regular and means 'enquire', 'peer':

pry(pries), pried, prying

We don't want you prying into our private affairs.

PS

PS is an abbreviation of Latin *post scriptum*, 'written after'. It is used mainly to highlight a message added to the end of a letter as an afterthought after the letter has been signed:

PS I love you.

psyche

In Greek mythology Psyche was a beautiful girl who was loved by Eros. She became the personification of the soul. (Her name derives from Greek *psukhein*, 'to breathe'.) In English *psyche* is used to mean 'human soul or mind' and the word is pronounced like 'my key', with the main stress on 'sigh':

It's much more serious than that. She's suffering from a sickness of the psyche.

psyche-, psycho-

Psyche- or *psycho-* occurs as a PREFIX in a range of English words relating to the mind or to altered perceptions:

psychedelia (vivid dress, music, objects)

psychoanalysis (studying the mind so as to cure mental disorders)

psychopath (person afflicted with antisocial personality disorder).

psychedelic

The adjective *psychedelic* or, less often, 'psychodelic' comes from 'psyche' + Greek *delos*, 'visible'. It relates to altered sensory perceptions sometimes brought about by hallucinogenic drugs:

The mid-sixties were associated with psychedelic clothes, music and painting.

psycholinguistics

Psycholinguists is a subdivision of linguistics. It studies the mental processes underlying our acquisition, use and loss of language.

publicly

Publicly is often misspelled. It does not end in '-ally' and does not have a 'k' after the 'c':

She admitted publicly that she had removed a page from a medieval manuscript.

puerile

The adjective *puerile* comes from Latin *puer*, 'boy'. It means 'immature', 'silly', 'trivial' and is pronounced like 'pure isle':

Do we have to listen to such puerile conversation?

Puerto Rico

An inhabitant of the US self-governing island in the Caribbean is a 'Puerto Rican'; the derived adjective is the same. The capital is San Juan.

pummel

See POMMEL/PUMMEL

pun

The word *pun* was first used with its current meaning in the seventeenth century. It refers to a humorous or witty use of a word or phrase so as to exploit ambiguity or innuendo:

He clipped the hedge as well as his speech.

What two letters do dentists hate? D.K. (decay).

See also AMBIGUITY, POLYSEMY, SYLLEPSIS, ZEUGMA

punctilious, punctual

These two adjectives derive from Latin *punctum*, 'point', but they have developed distinct meanings. *Punctilious* means 'overly attentive to detail' and is often applied to manners:

We need proofreaders who are observant and meticulous. Indeed, if possible, we'd like them to be punctilious.

She is punctilious about writing thank-you letters.

Punctual means 'prompt'. It is a characteristic of people who try to keep to arranged times:

My father used to remind me that it is as unpunctual to be early as to be late. Being punctual means arriving on time.

punctuation

Punctuation is the use of a set of written symbols to indicate aspects of meaning not otherwise apparent. In English, the following thirteen punctuation marks are in widespread use:

Apostrophe

The apostrophe is represented by ['] and is used to indicate possession, contractions and omissions:

a child's book

won't (will not)

the '45 Rebellion (the rebellion of 1745).

Brackets

There are several types of brackets:

angle <...>

brace {...}

parentheses (...)

square [...].

They tend to isolate information that is regarded as supplementary. Only paren-theses and square brackets are regularly used:

She was born in 1891 (although she always insisted it was 1894).

Moneys [sic] is the root of all evil.

Colon

The colon is represented by [:]. It is used mainly to introduce illustrations or the rephrasing of a previous statement:

She is perhaps the greatest dancer in the world: the non-pareil of dancers.

Comma

The comma is represented by [,] and is the most widely-used punctuation mark. It tends to mark off logical subdivisions that are shorter than a sentence:

When they arrived, they were told what had happened and quickly ushered into the meeting.

Dash

The dash is represented by [–] and is used in pairs as an alternative to parentheses:

I am – if I may say so – the best player here.

and singly to indicate fragmented speech:

I am – or I hope I am – I mean – I think.

Ellipsis

Ellipsis consists of three dots [...] and indicates that something has been omitted from an original text or statement:

Fair daffodils, we weep to see
You haste away so soon:
... the early-rising sun
Has not attain'd his noon.
                              Robert Herrick

Exclamation mark

The exclamation mark or exclamation point is represented by [!] and is used to signal exclamations or emphatic utterances:

You what! You contradicted him!

Full stop or period

The full stop or period is represented by [.]. The term *full stop* is preferred in Britain and *period* in America. It is used mainly to mark the end of a sentence that is not an exclamation or a question:

Once upon a time, there was a large wood. The wood was near the top of a high hill.

Hyphen

The hyphen is represented by [-] and is used mainly in compound words:

brother-in-law

an off-the-cuff remark.

It is also used to break words at the end of a line, to show that such words are not normally broken.

Oblique or slash

The term *oblique* tends to be used in Britain

whereas *slash* can occur in America. This punctuation mark is represented by [/] and it is used mainly to separate alternatives:

Each student is asked to collect his/her form and take it to his/her personal tutor to be signed.

Question mark

The question mark is represented by [?] and is used mainly to indicate a direct question:

Will you come over for a meal tomorrow?

Quotation marks

Quotation marks may be either single ['...'] or double ["..."]. Single quotation marks or 'inverted commas' are more commonly used in Britain and double quotation marks are the norm in America. They are used mainly to mark out direct quotations:

UK: 'Come in, my child,' she whispered. 'Come in.'

US: "Come in, my child," she whispered. "Come in."

Semicolon

The semicolon is represented by [;]. It is used mainly to mark off parts of a sentence that are syntactically complete but semantically linked:

She was our representative; she was our teacher; she was our friend.

See also ABBREVIATION, APOSTROPHE, BRACKETS, COLON, COMMA, DASH, ELLIPSIS, EXCLAMATION, FULL STOP, HYPHEN, QUESTION, QUOTATION, SEMICOLON

pundit
See PANDIT/PUNDIT

pupa

A *pupa* is an insect at the intermediate stage between larva and adult. The usual plural is 'pupae' but the anglicized plural 'pupas' is also found.

pupil, student

In Britain in the past there was a clear distinction between *pupil* and *student* based on age and the place of education. A *pupil* was a child at school and a *student* was a person receiving tertiary education:

She has forty-three five-year-old pupils in her class.

The staff-student ratio in this university is 12 to 1.

Mainly because of influence from America, *student* is now the more widely-used term and is often applied to schoolchildren:

The strike was the result of the special treatment given to a disruptive ten-year-old student.

See also SEMANTIC CHANGE

purée

The word *purée* derives from French *purer*, 'to purify' and has been taken over from French to mean 'smooth paste made from sieved vegetables or fruit'. It can be used as a noun or a regular verb:

We had to feed her purées because she could not swallow anything that had not been strained and sieved.

purée(s), puréed, puréeing

I don't want you to purée my food any more. I like to recognize what I'm eating.

purist

The term *purist* is often applied to a person who is punctilious about correct usage or who objects to the inclusion of foreign words in English. Many purists dislike SEMANTIC CHANGE, arguing that words borrowed from Latin, for example, should retain their Latin meanings. The idea of linguistic 'purity' is a myth. English contains words from the languages of virtually all the people with whom English speakers have been in contact. Purists are right to point out that rapid and uncontrolled change can lead to ambiguity and lack of precision.

purposely, purposefully

These adverbs both derive from 'purpose' but their meanings should be distinguished. *Purposely* means 'for a specific reason, on purpose':

You purposely asked that question because you knew I couldn't answer it.

Purposefully means 'with strong determination':

Robert the Bruce watched the spider as it tried purposefully to weave a web that crossed the chasm.

putrefy

The verb *putrefy* is often misspelled. It ends in '-efy' and means 'decompose, often with a bad smell':

putrefy(refies), putrefied, putrefying.

What caused these bodies to putrefy so quickly?

The derived noun is 'putrefaction'.

See also LIQUEFY/LIQUIFY

putsch

See COUP/PUTSCH

pygmy

See PIGMY/PYGMY

pyjamas

See PAJAMAS/PYJAMAS

Q

q

Q is a consonant that was introduced into English after the Norman Conquest. It is invariably followed by 'u' except in such place-names as 'Qatar'.

Qatar

An inhabitant of the emirate in the Persian Gulf is a 'Qatari'; the derived adjective is the same. The capital is Doha.

qualifier

The noun *qualifier* is sometimes applied to both adjectives and adverbs:

In the sentence 'The tall girl sang superbly', we have two qualifiers, 'tall' and 'superbly'.

In traditional grammars an adjective was said to 'qualify' a noun whereas an adverb was said to 'modify' a verb. Today, the terms are used interchangeably, with 'modifier' being in wider use.

See also ADJECTIVE, ADVERB, MODIFIER

qualitative, quantitative

Qualitative is an adjective relating to the quality or to the composition of something:

A-level Chemistry students are required to perform a qualitative analysis of a salt. This reveals the constituents present in the salt.

Quantitative is an adjective relating to number:

After the qualitative analysis, they are then required to perform a quantitative analysis in order to determine the amount of each constituent present.

quality

Quality is sometimes used adjectivally to mean 'first class, excellent':

quality goods.

quandary

This noun, which means 'dilemma', 'predicament', is frequently misspelled, probably because it is usually pronounced as two syllables.

quango

A *quango* is an acronym for 'quasi-autonomous non-governmental organization':

She makes a living by serving on quangos that discuss all sorts of problems from the teaching of reading to the preservation of the rural wetlands.

quantitative

See QUALITATIVE/QUANTITATIVE

quantum leap

This phrase has been popularized by the press and television to mean 'enormous change', 'advance':

John has made a quantum leap in his studies this year.

The phrase derives from 'quantum theory', a theory concerning the behaviour of physical systems.

quarrel

Quarrel can function as a noun or regular verb meaning 'dispute, serious disagreement':

I didn't pick a quarrel but I didn't run away from it.

In British English the 'l' is doubled before '-ed' and '-ing' but it remains single in American English:

UK: quarrel(s), quarrelled, quarrelling
US: quarrel(s), quarreled, quarreling.

quarry

The noun *quarry* has two distinct meanings. A *quarry* can mean an open-cast mine for the extraction of such rocks as stone, slate and marble:

The slate quarry closed down when a cheap substitute for Portland Blue was found.

This *quarry* comes from Old French *quarrière*, 'a place for making four-sided or square-shaped stones'.

The other meaning of *quarry* is 'prey':

They chased the animal but the quarry escaped.

This word also derives from a French form, *quirre*, 'the entrails given to hounds'.

quarto

The noun *quarto* is related to 'quarter' and was used of a book where the pages were made by folding a sheet of paper into four. The plural is 'quartos':

When was Shakespeare's first quarto published?

quasi

The word *quasi* comes from Latin and meant 'as if'. It tends to be used now as a prefix meaning 'seemingly', 'almost but not quite':

He's a quasi-scholar: all of the jargon and none of the substance.

Quasi has two main pronunciations. It can rhyme with 'fah + zee' or 'Fay's eye'.

quasi-modal

As well as the nine modal verbs,

can, could; may, might; must; shall, should; will, would

there are two sets of verbs that share some of the characteristics of modal verbs and that can therefore be described as *quasi-modals*. The first set of quasi-modals is:

ought to, dare, need, used to

and these share some of the formal properties of modals.

The second set of quasi-modals shares meanings with the modals and can express attitudes concerning ability, compulsion, insistence, intention, obligation, permission, possibility and willingness. Below we list the most frequently occurring verbs in this set, together with exemplary sentences and parallel sentences involving modals:

■ Be to:

I am to leave tomorrow.
I shall leave tomorrow.

■ Be able to:

She is able to stand now.
She can stand now.

■ Be about to:

He's about to start soon.
He will start soon.

■ Be going to:

We are going to get it right.
We shall get it right.

■ Have to:

They have to go home.
They must go home.

■ Have got to:

You've got to do better.
You must do better.

■ Let:

Let me go to the dance.
May I go to the dance?

See also MODALITY

quatercentenary

This noun is frequently misspelled. The first part is 'quater', borrowed from Latin and meaning 'four times'. *Quatercentenary* means 'four times its centenary' or '400th anniversary':

Oxford University Press celebrated its quatercentenary several years ago .

quay

The noun *quay* is a homophone of 'key' but refers to a 'wharf that is built parallel to the shoreline' and was probably borrowed from Old French *kai*, 'a wharf':

We bought a house near the quays.

The 'Florida Keys' are a chain of small islands off the coast of Florida. This word 'Keys' is borrowed from Spanish *cayo*, 'a low reef'.

See also FOREIGN LOAN-WORDS

Queen's English

See KING'S ENGLISH/QUEEN'S ENGLISH

queer

This word can be used as an adjective meaning 'odd', 'strange', a meaning it has had since the sixteenth century:

It's a queer old world!

Queer can also be used as a verb meaning 'spoil':

He has queered the pitch for the rest of us.

The noun *queer* meaning 'homosexual' should be used with sensitivity. For some homosexuals, it is a term of abuse; for others, a word that is used with pride.

See also POLITICAL CORRECTNESS, SEXIST LANGUAGE

query

Query can function as both a noun and a verb. As a noun, it is used to mean 'question':

I have only two queries for you.

As a verb *query* means 'raise doubts about':

She queried my statements in a most insensitive way.

It is also sometimes used to mean 'ask':

She queried me about John's whereabouts.

Many stylists dislike this usage, claiming that a distinctive meaning of *query* is being lost.

question

Questions are utterances that explicitly ask for information and that are signalled in the written medium by a question mark. Questions normally differ from statements in their word order:

Statement	Question
You can go there.	Can you go there?
You can't sing well.	Can't you sing well?

Where there is no auxiliary in the verb phrase, the dummy auxiliary is used:

Statement	Question
John likes cheese.	Does John like cheese?
John played well.	Did John play well?

There are five main types of question in English:

■ Yes/no questions. These require the answer 'yes' or 'no':

Is he coming?
Weren't you listening?

■ Wh-questions. These involve the question words 'how, what, when, where, which, why':

How can I get to the bottom of this?
Which door leads to the garden?

Why was she angry?

■ Tag questions:

He lost it, didn't he?

She didn't say that, did she?

■ Intonational questions. These do not involve inversion of the subject and the predicate. Rather, they use the rising intonation of questions:

You're going? Really?

It's not still working?

■ Loaded or leading questions. These are questions that either suggest the answer they require:

Would you claim that this degree of quotation is equivalent to plagiarism?

or that include unwarranted claims:

When did you stop stealing?

So-called 'rhetorical questions' are questions in form but not in meaning. A RHETORICAL QUESTION is usually the equivalent of an emphatic or ironic statement and they are frequently signalled by an exclamation mark:

Could she sing! (She could sing extremely well.)

Was I stupid! (I was extremely stupid.)

See also AUXILIARY, INTERROGATIVE, INVERSION, SENTENCE, YES/NO QUESTION

question mark

A question *mark* is the symbol [?]. It is used at the end of an interrogative:

Will you be able to go?

questionnaire

The noun *questionnaire* refers to lists of questions designed for a specific purpose. It is frequently misspelled:

The courses are regularly changed in the light of student questionnaires.

queue

See CUE/QUEUE

qui vive

The phrase *qui vive* comes from French and literally means 'who lives'. It usually occurs only in the fixed phrase 'on the qui vive', meaning 'on the alert':

We'll have to be on the qui vive to spot him as he leaves the train.

The phrase comes from a sentry's challenge and was the approximate equivalent of 'Who do you support?' It is not italicized.

quiche

A *quiche* is a savoury flan:

I often make an asparagus quiche.

The word rhymes with 'leash' and probably comes via French from German *Küchen*, 'a small cake'.

quick, quickly

Quick normally functions as an adjective meaning 'fast':

a quick reply

a quick train

and *quickly* as the adverbial equivalent:

She replied quickly.

The train moved quickly.

In informal speech, however, 'quick' is often used adverbially:

Go as quick as you can.

and 'quicker' and 'quickest' are preferred in casual speech to 'more quickly' and 'most quickly':

Hill covered the circuit quicker than his rivals.

She works quickest when she is under pressure.

In formal contexts, however, it is appropriate to distinguish between adjectival and adverbial forms.

Quick can occur as a noun meaning 'living' in the religious collocation:

the quick and the dead

and in the compound:

quicksilver

meaning 'living silver' and referring to mercury.

See also ADJECTIVE, ADVERB

quiescent

The adjective *quiescent* is often misspelled and misused. It means 'inactive, motionless, passive':

This volcano has been quiescent for well over 500 years but it would be rash to say that it will never again erupt.

Quiescent has two acceptable pronunciations. The more frequently heard of the two rhymes the first syllable with 'see'; the alternative pronunciation rhymes it with 'sigh'.

quiet, quieten

Quiet can function as an adjective meaning 'hushed, with little or no sound':

She was as quiet as a little mouse.

Quiet please! Talking is not permitted in the library.

It also occurs, especially in American English, as a regular verb:

quiet(s), quieted, quieting

How can I quiet the baby? I don't know what to do to make her stop crying.

In British English the regular verb *quieten* is often preferred:

quieten(s), quietened, quietening

How can I quieten the baby?

quire
See CHOIR/QUIRE

quit, quitted
Quit is a verb meaning 'leave, depart'. It can be treated as regular or irregular:

quit(s), quitted, quitting, quitted
quit(s), quit, quitting, quit.

Both *quit* and *quitted* are acceptable as past tense and past participle forms but the *quit* form is more widespread, especially in America.

quite
The adverb *quite* is often used with two different meanings. Its traditional meaning is 'completely':

I've quite finished the cereal. We'll have to get some more.

More recently, it has been widely used to mean 'partially':

I'm quite happy with the painting but it still needs a lot of work.

quiz
Quiz can be used as a noun meaning 'competition' and as a regular verb meaning 'ask questions':

quiz(zes), quizzed, quizzing
Shall we organize a quiz?
He quizzed me for over an hour.

quota
Quota is a noun meaning 'allocation':

We've got our full quota of students for the year.

It is also widely used to mean 'maximum amount' or 'maximum number of people':

There are strict quotas on the number of cars imported into Britain.

quotation
The noun *quotation* is used to indicate any phrase, verse, sentence or paragraph taken from another writer. A quotation should normally be an exact copy of the original, any alterations being clearly indicated and explained. The normal conventions for presenting quotations are summarized below.

Single or double quotation marks
Quotation marks (or inverted commas) are usually single in Britain and double in the United States:

UK: 'I'm sorry,' he said.
US: "I'm sorry," he said.

Quotations within quotations are signalled by the reverse of the above, thus double within single in the UK and single within double in the US:

UK: 'My favourite song on the album *Abbey Road* is "Come Together".'

US: "My favorite song on the album *Abbey Road* is 'Come Together'."

Additions and interpolations
Alterations to a quotation must be clearly indicated in an academic text. Additions are marked by square brackets, omissions by ellipsis:

We wrote compositions in Greek ...
We marched, [and] countermarched ...
Louis MacNeice

If the original has an inaccurate or unusual spelling, an unexpected feature of vocabulary, unconventional syntax or a wrong date, the interpolation [sic] may be used to confirm that the quotation is accurate:

The mountain roads ends [sic] here ...
Kenneth Rexroth

... fullstoppers and semicolonials [sic] ...
James Joyce

Punctuation marks
Punctuation marks belonging to the passage are normally placed inside the quotation marks and those belonging to the writer are placed outside:

I hate the exclamation 'Jolly hockeysticks!' It seems so false.

When a sentence ends with a quotation that ends with a full stop, the one full stop is sufficient.

I replied, 'That's right.'

Titles
Quotation marks are used for the titles of short poems, articles, stories and chapters in books. They are also used for words cited as items rather than for their meaning:

There are six uses of 'important' in this paragraph.
What is the English equivalent of 'tête-à-tête'?

Extracts
Quotations of a single line or a few words of poetry should be within quotation marks and incorporated in the text. In theses and dissertations it is sometimes preferred that prose quotations of up to ten typed lines or 100 words should be given within quotation marks and incorporated in the text. In books, lengthy extracts are more often set with a line space above and below and indented at one or both sides. Lengthy extracts may also be set in a small typesize. In such cases quotation marks are not necessary.

See also ELLIPSIS, PLAGIARISM, PUNCTUATION

quotation marks
Quotation marks are also called 'inverted commas' and 'quotes'. Many people dislike the use of 'quotes' in this way but it is becoming established practice:

Please use single quotes throughout your text.

quote

Often, when reading a quotation aloud, a person may begin with the word *quote* and end with 'unquote':

She has written in her diary quote Tuesday at 10:00 unquote.

qwerty

Qwerty is used as an adjective to describe a keyboard that is set out in the traditional typewriter style with the letters q, w, e, r, t, y occurring as the first six letters on the top left-hand section.

R

-r-

R is a consonant that is pronounced differently in many parts of the English-speaking world. It may be rolled, as in parts of Scotland, or retroflex, as in parts of India, or at the end of words and before consonants, as in southeast England. In rapid speech, some people use an INTRUSIVE R to separate vowels in expressions such as:

law (+ r) and order.

See also RHOTIC

-r-, -rr-

Many people are confused about when to double the 'r' in spelling. The following rules should help.

Monosyllabic words

When a monosyllabic word ends in a single vowel + r as in 'bar', 'fur' or 'stir', the 'r' is doubled before '-ed', '-ing' or '-y' and other affixes beginning with a vowel:

bar(s), barred, barring, barrage

fur(s), furred, furring, furry

stir(s), stirred, stirring, stirrable.

When a monosyllabic word ends in two vowels + r as in 'bear', 'floor' or 'lour', the 'r' is not doubled:

bear(s), bearing, bearable

floor(s), floored, flooring

lour(s), louring, loured.

Polysyllabic words

When a polysyllabic word ends in 'r', the 'r' is doubled if the main stress is on the last syllable:

occur(s), occurred, occurring, occurrence

reinter(s), reinterred, reinterring.

When a polysyllabic word ends in 'r', the 'r' is not doubled if the main stress does not fall on the last syllable:

canter(s), cantered, cantering

enter(s), entered, entering

suffer(s), suffered, suffering.

See also -ABLE/-IBLE, SPELLING

rabbi

A *rabbi* is a Jewish cleric. The word rhymes with 'dab eye' and the plural 'rabbis' with 'dab eyes'.

rabbit

Rabbit can be used as a noun and a verb:

There were hundreds of rabbits in the fields behind our house.

The verb traditionally meant 'catch rabbits' but is occasionally used, especially with 'on', to mean 'talk a lot':

He was rabbiting on about his life at sea.

Such usage is informal.

race

Words such as *race* and its derivatives 'racism' and 'racist' have been used by so many people, often in a prejudiced way, that they are now hard to use without evoking subjective responses. In theory, *race* means 'a group of people of common ancestry, often sharing physical characteristics such as colour and hair type':

The main races are Caucasoid, Mongoloid and Negroid.

Unless the noun is being used in this way, it is better to use a synonym:

the Bantu group

the Japanese people.

The word 'nation' is preferred by many Amerindians:

the Navaho nation.

racialism, racism

These nouns are generally interchangeable, although some careful speakers try to distinguish between them. The words are used to mean the belief that each race has distinctive cultural and physical characteristics that are determined by hereditary factors; the belief that such characteristics endow a race with an intrinsic superiority over others; and abusive, aggressive, discriminatory or prejudiced behaviour towards people of a different race.

Careful speakers try to use *racialism* for the first meaning, which recognizes difference but not intrinsic superiority of one race over another. They use *racism* for beliefs that claim or suggest the inherent superiority of a race. This distinction is a useful one but is not adhered to by the majority of speakers.

racist language

Attitudes towards race and sex were, for centuries, relatively fixed in Western society and these attitudes are reflected in English. For at least four centuries the attitudinal norm was a white, Anglo-Saxon, Protestant male, and anyone deviating from that norm was, at best, 'different', at worst 'inferior'. Wherever differences exist in terms of class, money, race, religion or sex, prejudices have arisen and these prejudices find expression in language and in racial stereotypes.

See also BLACK, POLITICAL CORRECTNESS, SEXIST LANGUAGE

rack, wrack

These homophones are occasionally confused:

*The house has gone to wrack and ruin.

The simplest way to avoid problems is to use *wrack* for 'seaweed' only and to use rack for a framework:

I've bought a little spice rack.

an instrument or the cause of torture:

He was cruelly tortured on the rack.
I have been on the rack all day wondering what was happening.

and the neck or rib section of mutton, pork or veal:

He described how they used to buy a rack of mutton.

---

racket, racquet

These nouns are homophones. A racket is a noisy disturbance:

There was a terrible racket from across the street last night; the loud music and the noise went on for hours.

The same noun *racket* is also used to refer to an illegal enterprise:

Money from such rackets as extortion and drug dealing is often laundered through major banks.

Racquet, which derives ultimately from Arabic *rahat*, 'palm of the hand', is the normal spelling for the bat that has a network of strings:

Has anyone seen my tennis racquet?

Increasingly, the spelling *racket* is used also for such bats.

---

radical, radicle

These homophones have markedly different meanings. *Radical* can be an adjective meaning 'fundamental':

This is not just a trifling disagreement: it's a radical difference of opinion.

It can also be used as a noun meaning a person who favours fundamental reforms of existing institutions:

He is as much a radical now as he was in his student days.

and the root of a word:

The radical is the part of the word that is left when all affixes have been removed – e.g., 'man' is the radical in the word un + man + ful + ly.

A *radicle* is a very small root. This word is also spelled 'radicel':

All the radicles must be removed if the spread of dandelions is to be stopped.

---

radio

Many people are uncertain about the spellings associated with *radio*. The plural is 'radios' and the regular verb is:

radio(s), radioed, radioing.

Until the middle of the 1920s, few people were exposed to any form of language other than that of the school, of their church, their neighbours and books. The cinema was initially silent.

Increasingly from the 1920s radio affected the lives of English speakers. At first, only the rich could afford sets, but from the early 1940s the radio became as normal an item of household furniture as a clock. Radio speech has affected society in many ways. Most listeners assumed that the people broadcasting the news were speaking English the way it should be spoken, with the result that the pronunciation of newsreaders became equated with 'standard' pronunciation. Radio pronunciation was imitated, both consciously and unconsciously, so that regional differences in speech began to diminish, and the influence of the radio on language has been reinforced by television. People have become familiar with other varieties of world English.

The popularity of radio and television programmes in English has helped to spread English throughout the world.

See also NETWORK NORM

---

radius

A *radius* is a straight line drawn from the centre of a circle to the circumference. The normal plural is 'radii' but 'radiuses' is also found. The word *radius* is often used metaphorically to mean a circular area:

The police are combing an area within a radius of one mile from the child's home.

---

railway, railroad

Both these words refer to the network on which trains run. *Railway* is the usual term in Britain and *railroad* is more widespread in America:

UK: The railway revolutionized travel in the country.
US: The railroad revolutionized travel in the country.

---

rain-

Rain occurs in a wide range of compounds, some written as one word, some hyphenated and some written as two words:

rainbow, raincoat
rain-cloud, rain-gauge
rain forest, rain shadow.

See also HYPHEN

---

raise, raze

These homophonic verbs can have opposite meanings. *Raise* can mean 'lift up':

They raised a new city from the wreck of the old.

Raze means 'completely destroy' and often occurs in the collocation '*raze* to the ground':

Rome was almost razed to the ground.

This regular verb is occasionally spelled 'rase', especially in America.

raise, rear, rise

These words are used in both Britain and America but they have different distributions. *Raise* is a regular transitive verb:

raise(s), raised, raising

It can mean 'lift', 'set or put in an upright position', 'bring up', 'increase':

He raised his hat.

He raised the height of the bridge.

He raised chickens.

He raised his prices.

He raised his voice.

Raise as a noun in the United States means an increase in pay; the preferred British term is *rise*:

US: She richly deserved her raise. She is now one of the highest earners in the firm.

UK: She richly deserved her rise. She is now one of the highest earners in the company.

Rear is used as a regular transitive verb, mainly in Britain, to mean 'bring up', 'foster':

rear(s), reared, rearing

She reared a large family and then helped rear her grandchildren.

See also ARISE/AROUSE/RISE

raison d'être

The phrase *raison d'être* literally means 'reason for being':

My main raison d'être now is my children.

RAM

The acronym *RAM* means 'random access memory'. It is distinguished from ROM, 'read only memory'. The acronyms are so frequently used in computer magazines that they are sometimes written with lower-case letters:

If you want to use Windows 95, you'll need at least eight megs of RAM.

rancour, rancor

Rancour is the usual British spelling for 'resentful spite', 'malice':

Rancour comes from the Latin word *rancor* meaning 'stink'. People who cannot accept defeat gracefully are often said to react with rancour.

Rancor is the usual spelling in America, but the derived forms 'rancorous', 'rancorously' and 'rancorousness' are spelled the same way throughout the English-speaking world.

rap, wrap

The verb *rap* means 'knock', 'hit', 'tap':

I rapped but nobody came to the door.

The idiom 'rap someone over the knuckles' means 'chastise', 'criticize':

I was rapped over the knuckles for borrowing the chairs without permission.

This verb is totally distinct from *wrap*, which means 'cover, enfold':

She wrapped my sandwich in plastic film.

He wrapped a towel around her.

rapped, rapt, wrapped

These homophones are occasionally confused. *Rapped* is the past tense and past participle form of the verb 'rap', meaning 'knock, strike something against something else':

She rapped gently at the door.

I was rapped across my knuckles with a pen.

Rap(ped) can also be applied to a type of rapid, rhythmic speech:

They rapped out the mathematical tables using the rhythmic patterns they had heard at home.

Rapt comes from Latin *raptus*, 'carried away' and is used to mean 'totally absorbed, spellbound'. It is related to 'rapture':

The painting captures her serenity, her rapt smile ...

Wrapped is part of the regular verb 'wrap' and means 'cover, wind something round as a cover':

He who is wrapped in purple robes
With planets in His care ...
    W.B. Yeats

rarefy

Rarefy, ending in '-efy' and not '-ify', is a regular verb meaning 'make or become rarer, thin out':

rarefy(ies), rarefied, rarefying

The air begins to rarefy at this altitude.

The verb is seldom used, but the adjective 'rarefied' occurs with the meaning of 'exalted', 'esoteric' in such collocations as:

a rarefied atmosphere.

rarely

Rarely is an adverb meaning 'seldom':

I rarely visit the country now.

Rarely often occurs in the fixed phrases:

rarely if ever

rarely or never

and in the less acceptable expression *'rarely ever'.

See also BARELY/HARDLY/SCARCELY

rarity

The noun *rarity* meaning 'a rare person or thing' is sometimes misspelled. The plural is 'rarities':

Once-common fish like plaice and snoek have become rarities.

ratchet

Ratchet can be used as a noun or regular verb. It refers to a device with teeth that permits motion in one direction only:

The ratchet is useless because it has lost several of its teeth.

ratchet(s), ratcheted, ratcheting

Could you ratchet it up another notch, please?

rateable, ratable

This adjective means 'able to be evaluated'. It is often spelled with an 'e' in British English, although the form *ratable* is also acceptable. The phrase '*rat(e)able* value' is used in Britain to refer to a fixed value assigned to a property by a local authority:

The rateable value far exceeds the actual value of my home.

rather

The adverb *rather* can be used with the modal verb 'would' to mean 'prefer':

I would rather walk than take a bus.

Occasionally the structure 'had rather' is used with a similar meaning:

I had rather die than accept charity.

but this usage is now regarded as extremely formal. The form:

I'd rather

can be seen as an abbreviation of either 'I would' or 'I had'.

Many people criticize the use of *rather* before the indefinite article + an adjective as in:

?I've had a rather frightening experience.

preferring:

I've had rather a frightening experience.

If there is no adjective, *rather* must precede 'a':

He's rather an idiot!

ratio

The plural of *ratio* is 'ratios':

The women outnumber male students by a ratio of two to one.

I can't work out these ratios: there are too many variables.

rational, rationale

Rational is an adjective meaning 'logical, reasonable, sane':

She tries to persuade us by rational means.

Rationale is a noun and the main stress falls on the third syllable, which is pronounced to rhyme with 'Carl' or, for some speakers, with 'Al'. It means 'reasoned exposition':

We have been asked to listen to his rationale.

ravage, ravish

The regular verbs *ravage* and *ravish* are sometimes misused and confused:

ravage(s), ravaged, ravaging

ravish(es), ravished, ravishing.

Ravage always has negative connotations. It can mean 'devastate, cause considerable destruction':

Cambodia has been ravaged by war.

Ravage can also be used as a noun:

The ravages of time take their toll on even the most beautiful!

Ravish has two main meanings, one positive, the other negative. It can mean 'delight', 'enthral':

He was clearly ravished by her beauty.

It can also mean 'rape':

Lovelace ravished Clarissa both mentally and physically. He destroyed her trust in people as well as raping her.

The adjective 'ravishing' is often used as a synonym for 'extremely beautiful, enchanting':

Where else can one find such ravishing, such unspoiled beauty?

raze

See RAISE/RAZE

re

The preposition *re*, meaning 'about' used to occur in business letters:

Re your request of the 24th ult ...

It is now rarely found in either speech or writing but has been preserved by players of Scrabble because of its usefulness.

re-

Re- is a frequently used prefix. It can indicate a return to a previous state:

rebuild, redecorate, renew

or a repetition:

readmit, redo, remarry.

Occasionally, the prefix can be doubled, as in the Radio 1 announcement:

This is a re-release of an old classic.

Because most *re-* verbs involve the meaning of restoration or repetition, it is usually unnecessary to use the adverbs 'back' or 'again':

He returned home.

not:

*He returned back home.

She readmitted the patient.

not:

*She readmitted the patient again.

Re- usually takes a hyphen when the word to which it is attached begins with a vowel, especially 'e':

re-adopt, re-edit

or to distinguish two meanings:

recollect (remember), re-collect (collect again)
release (set free), re-lease (lease again).

See also HYPHEN, RE-COUNT/RECOUNT,
RE-COVER/RECOVER, RE-CREATION/RECREATION,
RE-FORM/REFORM, RE-PRESENT/REPRESENT,
RE-PRESS/REPRESS, RE-SORT/RESORT

read

The irregular verb *read* is pronounced 'reed'. Its past tense form is also spelled *read* but pronounced 'red':

read(s), read, reading, read
I read this paper regularly.
I read this paper yesterday.

readable

See LEGIBLE/READABLE

reafforestation, reforestation

These nouns are variants and both are used to mean the replanting of an area that was formerly a forest:

Several countries in the equatorial belt are involved in reforestation schemes.

Many people prefer *reforestation* but the alternative form is also widely used in ecological journals.

real

Real is an adjective meaning 'actual', 'existing':

Fictional dialogue should never be equated with real speech.

Real has been overused recently to mean 'important', 'serious':

The real issue here is: do we still have a democracy?

Real is sometimes used in colloquial speech, especially in America, where 'really' is required:

She's a real smart lady!

realistic

The adjective *realistic* is often used to mean 'sensible' or 'reasonable':

We would like you to come up with a more realistic proposal.

Such shifts of meaning are inevitable in a living language but care should be exercised when *realistic* is used.

realize

Realize is a regular verb, which may be spelled with '-ise'.

realize(s), realized, realizing.

The form *realise* is becoming less widely used, even in Britain.

really

The adverb *really*, like other adverbs such as 'actually', is often used in speech when it is unnecessary:

I'm really quite hungry.
She's really good fun to be with.

There is nothing intrinsically wrong with *really* as an intensifier but it has been so overused that its meaning is often unclear.

See also BLEACHING

rear

See RAISE/REAR/RISE

reason

Many careful users of English dislike the use of 'because' or 'why' with *reason* as in:

?*The reason he left was because he wanted to work on his own.

?*The reason why he left was to work on his own.

They dislike such uses because they are tautological. The meaning of 'cause' is included in *reason*:

The reason he left was to work on his own.

See also TAUTOLOGY

rebel

Rebel can function as an adjective, a noun or a regular verb:

a rebel army
He's a rebel without a cause.
She rebelled against all authority.

The 'l' is doubled before suffixes beginning with a vowel:

rebel(s), rebelled, rebelling
rebellion, rebellious.

rebuff, rebuke, rebut

These regular verbs are not as widely used as they once were and so their meanings are occasionally confused. *Rebuff* means 'snub, reject an offer of help' or 'beat back an enemy':

rebuff(s), rebuffed, rebuffing
All my offers of help were rebuffed.
It is not so easy to rebuff the enemies that we cannot see.

Rebuke means 'scold or reprimand':

rebuke(s), rebuked, rebuking
I was sternly rebuked for my thoughtless action.

Rebut means 'refute by offering a contrary point of view':

rebut(s), rebutted, rebutting
He rebutted their theory on the basis of his own research.

rebus

Rebus rhymes with 'see bus' and refers to a puzzle involving letters and pictures. For example, the word 'spin' could be represented by the letter 's' + a picture of a pin. *Rebus* derives from the Latin tag *Non verbis sed rebus* meaning 'Not by words but by things'. The plural is 'rebuses'.

recall

Recall is similar in meaning to 'recollect' in that they both involve remembering, but *recall* normally implies a conscious effort:

I have tried to recall his name but all that I can recollect is that it begins with 'T'.

receipt

The noun *receipt* is frequently misspelled. It means 'a written acknowledgement that money or goods have been received':

I've lost the receipt for the television set. Will the 12-month guarantee be honoured?

Received Pronunciation

Received Pronunciation, which is usually referred to as *RP*, is a prestigious British accent that was and is associated with Oxford, Cambridge, the court, public schools and with educated speakers whose regional origins are not apparent in their speech. In the mid-1920s the BBC specifically chose *RP* speakers as radio announcers, because *RP* was regionally neutral and likely to be easily understood nationally and internationally.

RP is still a prestigious accent both in England and abroad. It continues to have prestige beyond its number of speakers because it is one of the most comprehensively described speech varieties in the world.

See also ACCENT, PRONUNCIATION

recherché

The adjective *recherché* means 'rare, known only to connoisseurs' or even 'affected, pretentious'. It is sometimes misspelled and frequently misused:

Her writings are somewhat recherché but they are well worth the effort you will have to make to find them.

reciprocal

The adjective *reciprocal* is frequently misused. It involves an action or feeling given by each of two people, groups or countries. It derives from Latin *reciprocus*, 'alternating', and so, in theory, involves only two:

Britain and Japan have reciprocal tax arrangements for expatriates who work in each other's country for more than two years.

See also COMMON/MUTUAL

reckless, ruthless

These adjectives are occasionally confused. *Reckless* means 'rash', 'heedless':

His reckless driving could have caused a serious accident.

Ruthless means 'without mercy, unscrupulous':

This ruthless killer must not be approached by members of the public.

reckon

The regular verb *reckon*:

reckon(s), reckoned, reckoning

is frequently used to mean 'estimate' and 'regard':

She reckoned their costs without taking the tax into account.

She is reckoned to be one of our most successful agents.

The use of *reckon* meaning 'guess, think':

Is it broken? I reckon so.

is regarded as an Americanism while its use in such sentences as:

I reckon we're all in for a surprise.

is colloquial.

recognize

Both forms of this verb, *recognize* and *recognise*, are used and are acceptable, but the form with '-ize' is more widely used, even in Britain. The derived forms such as 'recognizable' are also equally acceptable with an '-s-' or '-z-' but the '-z-' forms are more common.

See also SPELLING

recommend

This regular verb is often misspelled. Many people incorrectly double the 'c':

recommend(s), recommended, recommending.

reconcile

Reconcile is a regular verb that is often used passively:

reconcile(s), reconciled, reconciling.

She is now reconciled to her illness.

The adjective is 'reconcilable':

These views are just not reconcilable.

See also -ABLE/-IBLE

reconnaissance

Reconnaissance is a noun from 'reconnoitre' and means 'exploratory inspection':

The earlier reconnaissance did not provide us with as much information as we need on the position, activities and resources of the enemy.

Although many dictionaries give 'reconnoissance' as an alternative spelling, it is now virtually obsolete and should not be used.

reconnoitre, reconnoiter

The word *reconnoitre* is used mainly as a verb meaning 'survey or inspect a piece of land or an enemy position and bring back information':

I was sent to reconnoitre the course to ensure that it wasn't too difficult for twelve-year-olds.

The British spelling ends in '-re' and the American equivalent in '-er':

UK: reconnoitre(s), reconnoitred, reconnoitring
US: reconnoiter(s), reconnoitered, reconnoitering.

re-count, recount

These regular verbs have different meanings. *Re-count* with a hyphen, with the first syllable rhyming with 'me' and with the main stress usually on the first syllable, means 'count again':

We re-counted the votes.

Re-count is often used as a noun:

The Labour candidate asked for a re-count.

Recount without a hyphen and with the stress on the second syllable means 'narrate, tell a story':

They quietly recounted the harrowing details of their captivity.

See also HYPHEN, RE-

recourse

Recourse functions as a noun meaning 'course of action, especially when one is in a difficult position':

What other recourse was open to her? She had tried everything else.

re-cover, recover

The meanings of these verbs are distinguished by the use or non-use of the hyphen in the written medium and by the pronunciation of 're-' in speech. *Re-cover*, where the 're-' rhymes with 'me', means 'cover again':

We should re-cover these old armchairs.
We should re-cover the area, this time interviewing one in ten householders.

Recover means 'regain':

He seems to have recovered his good humour.

See also HYPHEN, RE-

re-creation, recreation

In the written medium, the hyphen is necessary to distinguish the meanings of these nouns. *Re-creation* is, theoretically, an impossible form in that something can be 'created' only once. However, the noun is used to mean 'reproduction':

The film company's re-creation of eighteenth-century Bath was inaccurate in many details.

Recreation means 'leisure', 'pastime':

My main recreations are reading and horse-riding.

See also HYPHEN, RE-

rectify

See JUSTIFY/RECTIFY

recur

Recur is a regular verb meaning 'happen again':

recur(s), recurred, recurring.

The derived forms 'recurrence', 'recurrent' and 'recurrently' also double the 'r' in both British and American English. The related noun 'recursion', meaning 'the act of turning back', does not, however, double the 'r'.

red

Red can be used as an adjective or a noun:

red, redder, reddest
That is the reddest tomato I've ever seen.
Red is a primary colour.

Red occurs in a number of idioms:

in the red (owing money)
see red (become angry)

as well as in a wide range of compounds, some hyphenated:

redbrick, redhead
Red Cross, red herring
red-blooded, red-letter.

See also HYPHEN, IDIOM

redolent

The adjective *redolent* means 'exuding a pleasant smell'. It is followed by 'of':

I walked into a house redolent of country freshness and home-made bread.

The adjective is occasionally used to mean 'reminiscent of':

The woman and the kitchen were redolent of Dutch paintings.

Many careful users dislike this secondary meaning, pointing out that *redolent* comes from *re* + *olere*, 'to smell again'. Such criticism, however, overlooks the metaphorical nature of language and the fact that 'smell' can be used with abstract nouns as in:

the sweet smell of success.

They also dislike the use of *redolent* followed by 'with':

It was redolent with memories of my childhood.

However, this usage is widespread, especially when *redolent* is used with abstract nouns such as 'nostalgia'.

reduce

See DEPLETE/REDUCE

redundancy

Redundancy involves the use of unnecessary words or phrases:

an added bonus
climb up
in actual fact
mix together.

The term 'pleonasm' is used in rhetoric to describe the use of redundant vocabulary.

See also CIRCUMLOCUTION, TAUTOLOGY

reduplication

Reduplication involves partial or complete repetition:

abracadabra, bow wow, choo choo, knick knack, puff puff.

Reduplication is used in some languages, including many pidgins, to indicate a degree of intensity:

luk (look), lukluk (stare)

plurality:

ston (stone), ston ston (stony, stones everywhere)

and class change:

ben (bend), benben (crooked).

In English, we find the following types of reduplication:

■ Complete reduplications such as:

baba, bye-bye, goody goody, (on the) never-never

■ Complete reduplications with additional elements inserted:

day by day, hand in hand, one by one

■ Rhyming reduplications:

itsy bitsy, lovey dovey, nitty gritty

■ Reduplications with a vowel change:

ping-pong, tick-tack, wishy-washy.

See also PIDGIN AND CREOLE

refer (back)

The regular verb *refer* means 'to allude to':

refer(s), referred, referring.

The related forms 'referee', 'reference', 'referendum' and 'referent' do not double the 'r'.

Many people unnecessarily add *back* to *refer* as in:

He referred back to an earlier part of the talk.

The 'back' is unnecessary here and reduces its value in the perfectly acceptable:

We referred her paper back to Jean so that she might make minor adjustments to it.

where *refer back* means 'return a document or question to the person from whom it was received for further attention'.

referendum

A *referendum* is the testing of an important issue by asking the electorate to vote on it:

There was a referendum on decimalization in 1974.

There are two acceptable plurals, the etymologically correct Latin 'referenda' and the more widely-used 'referendums'.

reflect

The regular verb *reflect* can be used literally as in:

Mirrors distort the images they reflect.

and metaphorically as in:

We reflected on our actions.

The noun 'reflection' or, less commonly, 'reflexion', also has both meanings.

reflexive

A *reflexive* pronoun has the ending '-self' for singular pronouns and '-selves' for plurals:

myself, yourself, himself, herself, oneself, ourselves, yourselves, themselves.

In English, reflexive pronouns are used as the object of a transitive verb when the object is the same person as the subject:

I'll suit myself.
They washed themselves.

as a pronoun that follows a preposition when the pronoun refers to the subject of the sentence:

She thinks very well of herself.
You brought this trouble on yourselves.

and for emphasis:

He himself has never studied the language but he feels no qualms about teaching it.
They asked Sam to the party themselves.

reforestation

See REAFFORESTATION/REFORESTATION

re-form, reform

In the written medium, the hyphen is used to distinguish *reform*, meaning 'improve':

There is little evidence that incarceration helps people to reform.

from *re-form* meaning 'form anew':

Do you think we should try to re-form the Mermaid Society?

The meanings are distinguished in speech because the 're-' in *re-form* rhymes with 'me'. In addition, the stress is on the first syllable of *re-form* and on the second syllable of *reform*.

See also HYPHEN, RE-

refraction

See DIFFRACTION/REFRACTION

refute

See DENY/REFUTE

regalia

The noun *regalia* comes from Latin *regalis* and originally referred to royal privileges. Nowadays, *regalia* refers to the ceremonial emblems and clothes associated with high office:

The Queen appeared in the regalia appropriate to the state opening of Parliament.

In theory *regalia* is plural and needs plural agreement:

The royal regalia are no longer kept in the Tower.

In practice and especially when people use the word humorously to mean 'finery', it is treated as a singular:

My regalia is only taken out for weddings.

regard(s)

Many people misuse this word when it combines with prepositions. The rules are as follows.

The singular form is used only in the phrases 'in regard to' and 'with regard to' where *regard* means 'reference':

We have examined your statement in regard to your claims concerning unfair treatment.

With regard to your claims of unfair treatment, the panel would be grateful for additional information.

Both these phrases are formal and are more likely to occur in writing than in speech.

The plural form *regards* is used mainly in the phrases 'as regards':

As regards your suggestion that you were unfairly treated ...

and in 'with kind(est) regards', a phrase that is often used to end a friendly letter.

regardless

See IRRESPECTIVE OF/REGARDLESS

regime, regimen

The noun *regime* is a French borrowing; it is sometimes spelled *régime* and refers to a system of government, often one that the writer disapproves of:

a fascist regime
the former regime.

The noun *regimen* tends to be confined to medical documents and refers to 'a course of therapy' or 'a diet':

I'd like to recommend a particular regimen, but if you agree to it you must follow it to the letter.

Often, in modern medical textbooks, *regime* is used where previously *regimen* would have been required.

register

A *register* normally refers to an official list recording names, events or transactions:

Some of their registers go back to 1760.

The noun has three other well-known uses in the study of sound and language. In music, it refers to the range of a voice or an instrument:

Dame Janet Baker's voice had an especially unique quality in its lower register.

In phonetics, it has a related meaning and refers to the voice quality, which is affected by the length, tension and thickness of the vocal cords. A woman's vocal cords are usually shorter and tenser than a man's.

In SOCIOLINGUISTICS the term *register* is often used to refer to varieties of language used in specific contexts rather than by specific individuals. We can, for example, often distinguish between religious and scientific registers. A religious *register* might be characterized by the use of such archaisms as 'Thou knowest' and such abstract nouns as 'faith', 'grace' and 'redemption'.

regret

Regret is a regular verb meaning 'feel sorry or upset about':

regret(s), regretted, regretting
I deeply regret any offence that I may have given.

The derived forms 'regrettable' and 'regrettably' have '-tt-' but the forms taking a suffix that begins with a consonant do not double the 't':

regretful, regretfully, regretfulness.

regretfully

The adverb *regretfully* is sometimes misused. *Regretfully* means 'with regret':

I look back regretfully at the time I wasted.

Many careful speakers dislike the use of *regretfully* as a sentence initiator meaning 'I am sorry that':

Regretfully, we have no vacancies for the nights you have requested.

and prefer:

Unfortunately, we have no vacancies for the nights you have requested.

or:

We regret that we have no vacancies.

See also ADVERB, HOPEFULLY

reign, rein

These homophones, which can function as both nouns and verbs, are occasionally confused. *Reign* is associated with kings and queens:

He was born in the reign of Queen Elizabeth I.
King James I reigned from 1603 to 1625.

Rein is associated with controls:

The horse's reins were wearing thin near the bit.
I had to rein him in hard because he was still not used to being ridden.

The collocation 'the reins of power' as in:

She held the reins of power for thirteen years.

is the phrase where the incorrect spelling is most likely to occur.

reiterate

This regular verb means 'say again'. It is not necessary, therefore, to use 'again' with it:

*I have said it once and I will reiterate it again.

There is a tendency for words to be bleached of some of their meaning and for a reinforcer to be used. 'Iterate', for example, comes from Latin *iterare*, 'say again' and so, in theory, even the 're-' is unnecessary.

See also BLEACHING

relations, relatives

Both these nouns can be used to refer to people connected by blood or marriage:

I have no blood relations in New Zealand but I have some good friends there that I often call 'aunt' and 'uncle'.

I have a huge number of relatives. We now tend to meet only at weddings and funerals.

Contemporary English is limited in its number of kinship terms and many of the items available derive from French. Below, we show the main ones, using small capitals for native English terms and normal print for terms borrowed from French:

GREAT-grandparents: GREAT-grandMOTHER, GREAT-grandFATHER

GREAT-GREAT aunt, GREAT-GREAT uncle

grandparents: grandMOTHER, grandFATHER

GREAT-aunt, GREAT-uncle

MOTHER, FATHER, aunt, uncle

BROTHER, SISTER, cousin

CHILD, SON, DAUGHTER, niece, nephew

grandCHILDREN: grandDAUGHTER, grandSON

grandniece, grandnephew.

In-law terms are based on family terms and include:

parents-in-law: mother-in-law, father-in-law

in-laws: sister-in-law, brother-in-law

children-in-law: daughter-in-law, son-in-law.

See also FAMILY RELATIONSHIP

relative

The term *relative* is used in grammar to refer to *relative* clauses and *relative* pronouns such as 'that', 'which', 'who', 'whom' and 'whose' as in:

the book that I bought
the task, which I faced
the man who came in
the man whom I saw
the man whose book I read.

See also RELATIVE CLAUSE

relative clause

A *relative clause* is an adjective clause that

occurs within a noun phrase. It is called a 'relative clause' because it is often introduced by a relative pronoun or a preposition + relative pronoun:

(The book [that I read]) was by Dumas.
(The people [whom we met]) were from Italy.
(The girls [who won the prizes]) are from my school.
(Banks [on which we rely]) should not close at 3:30.

In speech and informal writing, object relative pronouns that introduce clauses can be omitted:

(The book [I read]) was by Dumas.
(The people [we met]) were from Italy.

See also CLAUSE, DEFINING RELATIVE CLAUSE, RESTRICTIVE CLAUSE/NON-RESTRICTIVE CLAUSE

relevant

The adjective *relevant*, meaning 'pertinent', and its related noun 'relevance' are sometimes misspelled and overused:

Do you think that last point was relevant?
What was the relevance of that particular comment?

relic

A *relic* is an object of religious or, more recently, historical interest:

In the past, Mass was said on an altar stone containing the relics of three saints.
This tapestry is one of the few remaining relics of fourteenth-century handiwork.

relocate

The regular verb *relocate* is often used by estate agents as a synonym for 'move':

Thinking of relocating? We have the most extensive range of prestige homes in Headingley.

See also EUPHEMISM, SYNONYM

reluctant, reticent

These adjectives are occasionally confused. *Reluctant* means 'disinclined or unwilling to do something':

I'm extremely reluctant to switch off the engine. If I switch it off, it may never start again.

Reticent means 'reserved', 'shy', 'unwilling to say much':

She was always reticent in company but her reticence disappeared when she was with close friends.

remedial, remediable

These adjectives are occasionally confused because they both derive from, and are related to, 'remedy'. *Remedial* means 'intended as a cure'. The word is almost invariably used in connection with special teaching needs:

The children need remedial English classes. Their reading skills are more than 6 months lower than expected for their age group.

Remediable means 'capable of being cured':

The damage is severe but remediable. You'll have to leave your car with us for a week.

reminiscent

This adjective is used predicatively and followed by 'of':

It was reminiscent of a painting I saw in Madrid.

*a reminiscent painting.

Reminiscent is frequently misspelled.

remit

Remit is a regular verb meaning 'send payment by post for goods or services':

remit(s), remitted, remitting

You have not yet remitted the payment agreed on 9 July.

It tends to have formal and legal overtones, as does the derived noun 'remittance':

Your remittance is now due.

Increasingly, people use *remit*, where the first syllable rhymes with 'see', as a noun meaning 'brief', 'task', 'terms of reference':

Your remit will be to promote and reward productivity.

remove

Remove is most frequently used as a regular verb meaning 'take from and put elsewhere':

remove(s), removed, removing

He removed my car without my permission.

The noun *remove* is pronounced in the same way as the verb and is often used to mean 'the degree of difference separating one person or thing from another' especially in the phrase:

at one remove

She's at one remove from the top job.

The phrase 'once removed' is often used in kinship terms. The sentence:

She's my first cousin once removed.

means:

She's the daughter of my first cousin = My grandparents are her great-grandparents.

See also RELATIONS/RELATIVES

remunerate

The regular verb *remunerate* means 'pay someone for a service':

remunerate(s), remunerated, remunerating

I have been well remunerated for the work I did.

rend

Rend is an irregular verb that is becoming obsolete, although it is still found in biblical language. It means 'tear':

rend(s), rent, rending, rent

Rend your hearts and not your garments.

The adjective 'heart-rending' meaning 'extremely sad' has been overused, especially in the blurbs of popular romances:

Read of her heart-rending struggle against ...

render

Render is a regular verb that is becoming obsolescent. It means 'submit':

Render to Caesar the things that are Caesar's.

'show':

This version renders Hamlet as a scheming coward.

'deliver':

The court is expected to render its verdict today.

'cover with plaster':

The walls haven't been rendered yet.

and 'melt down (fat)':

We haven't yet managed to render down all the fat.

rendezvous

Rendezvous can function as a singular or plural noun meaning 'meeting, assignation':

Where is your rendezvous this afternoon?

They had been having secret rendezvous for months.

The singular noun rhymes with 'shoe', the plural with 'shoes'. *Rendezvous* can also be used as a verb meaning 'meet at a specified place':

We will rendezvous at the club at 16:00.

renege, renegue

The regular verb *reneg(u)e* means 'go back on a promise':

reneg(u)e(s), reneg(u)ed, reneg(u)ing

They have consistently reneg(u)ed on their promises.

The verb rhymes with 'plague' and derives from Latin *renegare*, 'to renounce', the source also of 'renegade'. The '-ege' spelling is more widely used in England but the '-egue' ending is still the preferred form in Ireland and parts of America.

renounce

Renounce is a regular verb meaning 'formally give up':

renounce(s), renounced, renouncing

He renounced his claim to the throne but, since he was sixteenth in line, it wasn't much of a sacrifice.

The derived noun is 'renunciation'.

rent

See HIRE/LEASE/LET/RENT

reorganize, reorganise

Both spellings are acceptable for this regular verb. The derived noun is 'reorganization' or 'reorganisation'.

repair
See FIX/REPAIR

repast
Repast is an obsolescent word for 'meal' although it continues to be used humorously and as an ELEGANT VARIATION:

We stopped at noon for a light repast.

repel, repulse
Both these verbs are regular:

repel(s), repelled, repelling
repulse(s), repulsed, repulsing.

The derived noun 'repellent' is often misspelled. It is frequently used in compounds such as:

insect-repellent, stain repellent.

repercussions
The noun *repercussions* is overused in journalism as a synonym for 'results' or 'effects':

Banning cars from the centre of the city will have serious repercussions.

The word comes from Latin *repercutere*, 'to strike back', and was originally used to mean 'rebound' or 'reverberations' in a literal sense. The more recent usage can be seen as a metaphorical extension.

repertoire, repertory
These words both derive ultimately from Latin *repertorium*, 'storehouse', but they were borrowed into the language at different times, *repertory* in the sixteenth century and *repertoire* in the nineteenth century. Their meanings are usually differentiated. *Repertoire* means 'the entire collection':

This company has an extensive repertoire. They are equally at home with serious opera and with twentieth-century musicals.

Repertory is usually reserved for a company of actors that presents a series of plays, musicals or other entertainments in the course of a season:

a repertory company
a repertory theatre.

repetition
Repetition is a stylistic device that may occur at all levels of a language:

■ Sounds, consonants and vowels:

Coca Cola
Good Food Guide

■ Syllables and words:

Row us out from Desenzano, to your Sirmione row!
So they rowed, and there we landed – 'O venusta Sirmio!'
There to me thro' all the groves of olive in the summer glow,

There beneath the Roman ruin where the purple flowers grow ...

Tennyson, 'Frater Ave Atque Vale'

■ Structure:

If you drive carefully and if you avoid accidents you can get cheaper insurance.

Like to the falling of a star;
Or as the flights of eagle are;
Or like the fresh spring's gaudy hue;
Or silver drops of morning dew;
Or like the wind that chafes the flood;
Or bubbles which on water stood ...

Henry King, 'Sic Vita'

Repetition can be both effective and impressive when it is used skilfully, but when it is the result of carelessness it can contribute to poor style. English can avoid nominal repetition by the use of pronouns and possessive adjectives, and verbal repetition by the use of auxiliaries and adverbs like 'too' and 'so':

Mike works hard for his (i.e., Mike's) wife and family and he (i.e., Mike) does it (i.e., works hard) because he (i.e., Mike) loves them (i.e., his wife and family).

See also ELEGANT VARIATION, PARALLELISM, REDUPLICATION, TAUTOLOGY

repetitious, repetitive
These adjectives are frequently confused, partly because they both derive from 'repeat' and are associated with saying or doing something over and over again. The main difference is that *repetitious* means unnecessary or tedious repetition:

He went on and on, supplying us with the most repetitious description imaginable. We were told about every word and every action and we were told everything at least twice!

Repetitive need not be unnecessary:

The poem is characterized by a repetitive rhythm.

replace, substitute
Replace is often used as a synonym of 'substitute' although careful speakers and writers distinguish between them. *Replace* means 'take the place of' and a person or thing is replaced by 'by' not 'with':

A good secretary could never be replaced by a computer.

Substitute means 'be put in place of another' and it is followed by 'for':

John was substituted for Michael at the last moment.

replaceable
The adjective *replaceable* is sometimes misspelled. It keeps the 'e' before the suffix '-able':

Everyone of us is replaceable. It's folly to assume that we are indispensable.

The antonym 'irreplaceable' is used much more frequently:

I broke the Greek vase and have never been allowed to forget that it was irreplaceable.

replica

A *replica* is an exact copy of an original, often on a smaller scale:

The artist usually made a scaled replica of his best sculptures.

The noun has been overused, especially in the popular press, to mean any copy or clone or duplicate:

The political parties are now replicas of each other on all major issues.

reply, retort, riposte

These three nouns are related but each incorporates an additional piece of information. A *reply* is an answer:

I should be grateful if we could have your reply within 72 hours.

A *retort* is a sharp answer:

I asked her why she hadn't told me and she retorted that it was not my business.

A *riposte* is a witty answer:

When Oscar Wilde was asked if he had anything to declare, his riposte was 'Only my genius!'

Riposte is the least widely used of the three. All three words can also function as regular verbs but *riposte* is the rarest:

reply(ies), replied, replying

retort(s), retorted, retorting

reposte(s), riposted, riposting.

report

The word *report* can function as a noun or as a regular verb meaning '(give) a spoken or written account':

I was asked to write a report on the teaching of English in schools.

I reported on English teaching in schools.

Both noun and verb occur with 'on', as in the above examples, but increasingly newspaper and television reporters are using 'into':

He was asked to report into higher education.

Although the usage with 'into' is disliked by some, it is now acceptable.

reported speech

See INDIRECT SPEECH

reprehensible

This adjective is often misspelled and misused. It means 'blameworthy, open to criticism':

His behaviour was foolish and thoughtless rather than evil, but it was reprehensible nonetheless.

re-present, represent

The hyphen acts to distinguish these words in the written medium and the 're-' in *re-present* rhymes with 'me' in speech. *Re-present* means 'to put something forward again':

We have been given the opportunity to re-present our case because there were certain council irregularities when we first presented it.

Represent means 'correspond to, act as a substitute for, act as a delegate for':

Let's assume that this box represents a block of flats.

John represented his father at the ceremony.

The local doctor now represents this constituency in parliament.

re-press, repress

The meanings of these words are distinguished in writing by the hyphen and in speech by pronunciation. *Re-press* rhymes with 'sea stress' and is frequently used to mean 'make additional copies of a disk':

The song was so popular that it sold out in a week and the company has had to re-press it.

Repress means 'suppress or restrain feelings':

Self-control is an excellent quality but it is unhealthy to repress all our urges.

reproof, reprove

Reproof can function as a noun meaning 'rebuke':

I know I was wrong but I wasn't expecting such a public reproof.

The verb *re-proof*, with a hyphen, means 'retexture a coat so as to make it waterproof':

My raincoat is useless at the moment. I must get it re-proofed if I'm to wear it in the rain again.

Reprove is the regular verb meaning 'rebuke':

reprove(s), reproved, reproving

I know I was wrong but I wasn't expecting to be reproved in public.

repulse

See REPEL/REPULSE

repute

Repute can function as a regular verb normally used in the passive to mean 'considered to be':

She is reputed to be the best cellist in the world.

Repute is also used as a noun meaning 'public estimation':

I know her by repute.

She is a scholar of considerable repute.

It is gradually being ousted by 'reputation' except in such fixed phrases as:

by repute

a house of ill repute.

require

Require is a regular verb often used in formal language to mean 'need, want':

We may require your services at a later date.

requisite, requisition

These words both derive from 'require'. *Requisite* can function as an adjective meaning 'absolutely essential':

He may not have the requisite experience but he is young and very willing to learn.

It can also function as a noun meaning 'necessity':

Being computer literate is a requisite of the post.

The noun 'prerequisite' is often used in such a context and implies 'required as a prior condition'. Often the use of 'pre-' is tautological but 'prerequisite' is the more widely-used noun.

A *requisition* is an authoritative or official request or the form on which such a request is made:

We cannot supply your order unless we receive an official requisition or advance payment.

See also PERQUISITE/PRE(-)REQUISITE

reredos

The noun *reredos* comes ultimately from Old French *arere* + *dos*, 'behind back', and refers to a screen or wall covering in a church at the back of an altar:

The reredos has been replaced by a painting of Christ in what looks like a night-gown.

The noun, which has 'reredoses' as a plural, is pronounced to rhyme with 'deer moss'. Its use is limited to liturgical contexts.

research

The word *research* can function as a noun and as a regular verb:

I'm doing research on the use of 'else' in contemporary English.

She researched the language used in maritime logs of the seventeenth century.

The word *research* has two main pronunciations. It can be stressed on the second syllable and the vowel in 're-' is unstressed as it is in 'refer'. Some people prefer to stress the first syllable, producing 'ree + search'. There is a third pronunciation that pronounces the 's' in *research* as if it were 'z'. This pronunciation is not as widespread as the others, but it seems to be gaining ground.

reserve

Reserve, where the 's' is pronounced as if it were 'z', can function as an adjective, noun and regular verb. The adjective means 'withheld':

I have several reserve strategies if this one fails.

The noun *reserve* means 'something set aside for future use':

I don't want to dip into our reserves unless there is no other way of meeting this unexpected expense.

The verb *reserve* means 'set aside, withhold':

I have reserved two seats in Row 'E' for you.

resin

Resin is a type of gum used in medicines and varnishes. The alternative spelling *rosin* is almost exclusively reserved for the substance used to treat bow strings:

Many resins are now synthetic although they were originally made from plant exudations.

resolve

This word usually functions as a regular verb but it can occur as a noun meaning 'strong determination':

In spite of all the problems, his resolve remains unshaken.

As a verb, *resolve* is stressed on the second syllable and the 's' is pronounced 'z'. It means 'firmly determine':

I have resolved to give up driving. This sacrifice will be my small contribution to the green revolution.

re-sort, resort

Both these forms can function as nouns and regular verbs. *Re-sort*, where the 're-' rhymes with 'me' and the 's' is pronounced as an 's', means 'sort again':

Don't tell me we have to re-sort all those examination scripts?

We've already had a re-sort. Surely it won't be necessary to sort them a third time?

Resort as a noun means 'place of recreation':

Blackpool is one of the most popular resorts in the country.

As a verb, it means 'to have recourse to':

He invariably resorts to mockery when he feels he is under attack.

The 's' in both the noun and the verb is pronounced as if it were 'z'.

respect

The phrases 'in respect of' and 'with respect to' are used in formal, usually written language:

Employees will receive 1/80th of their salary in respect of each pensionable year that they have worked.

We have now discussed your suggested modifications with respect to the contract we offered.

In less formal language, it is preferable to use 'for' instead of 'in respect of' and 'about' instead of 'with respect to'.

respective

The adjective *respective* and its related adverbial

form 'respectively' mean 'related separately to two or more people':

We followed our respective routes and did not meet again until we reached the checkpoint.

Often, these words are redundant:

Put the disks in their respective slots.

I visited each of the farms respectively.

but they are useful in distinguishing between:

I visited John and Mary (one visit).

and:

I visited John and Mary respectively (two visits).

respite

The noun *respite* may rhyme with 'bit' or 'bite', unlike 'despite', which always rhymes with 'bite'. It means 'pause or rest from exertion', 'relief', 'delay':

It was a welcome respite from our efforts in the garden.

responsible

The adjective *responsible* is frequently misspelled. It can also be ambiguous in that it can mean both 'accountable':

I don't want to be responsible for her actions.

and 'the cause of':

I admit that I was responsible for the accident.

restaurateur, restauranteur

The name of a person who owns a restaurant is *restaurateur*. There is traditionally no 'n' in the word in British English or in French, the source of the borrowing. The form *restauranteur* (from 'restaurant + eur') is acceptable in American English and is now being increasingly used in Britain:

UK: John is a restaurateur and owns a chain of restaurants.

US: John is a restauranteur and owns a chain of restaurants.

restive, restless

These adjectives are occasionally misused, partly because they can both be applied to someone who is anxious. *Restive* can be applied to animals or people and suggests 'anxious, impatient, uneasy':

The animals are restive: they know that something terrible is going to happen tomorrow.

I'm feeling restive: I'm very worried about John's health.

Restless can mean 'fidgety, unable to stay still':

I had a restless night: I twisted and turned and could not get comfortable.

restrain
See CONSTRAIN/RESTRAIN

restrictive clause, non-restrictive clause

Restrictive and *non-restrictive* clauses are alternative names for 'defining' and 'non-defining' clauses. A *restrictive* or defining clause limits the scope of the noun phrase it modifies:

The antiques [that I bought] are fakes.

This sentence implies that I bought only some of the antiques and that the ones I bought are fakes. A *non-restrictive* or non-defining clause provides additional information:

The antiques, [which I bought], are fakes.

This sentence implies that I bought all the antiques and they are all fakes. In speech, intonation helps to disambiguate these clauses. In writing, punctuation and the selection of either 'that' or 'which' fulfils the same function.

See also DEFINING RELATIVE CLAUSE

resume, résumé

Resume with no accents is a regular verb meaning 'begin again, go on with':

resume(s), resumed, resuming

He resumed his talk as soon as the heckler had been ejected.

Résumé with two acute accents is a noun meaning 'short summary':

Provide a résumé of the passage in not more than 75 words. Do not use any of the words or phrasing of the original passage.

In America, *résumé* is the usual term for 'curriculum vitae':

I've sent in my résumé and copies of my certificates.

resuscitate

The verb *resuscitate* means 'restore to consciousness'. It is frequently misspelled:

They tried desperately to resuscitate him but their efforts were in vain.

reticent
See RELUCTANT/RETICENT

retina

The *retina* is the light-sensitive membrane of the eyeball. It has two acceptable plurals 'retinas' and 'retinae'. The former is now much more widely used:

Has she had operations on both retinas?

retort
See REPLY/RETORT/RIPOSTE

retro-

Retro- is a prefix meaning 'back, backwards':

retroflex (curved backwards)

retrogress (go back).

In the mid-1990s, *retro* began to be used as a near synonym of 'nostalgia', as in the BBC1 reporter's comment on Vespas in May, 1996:

There's very much a retro feel to it [a Vespa]. It's part of the 90s nostalgia.

retroactive, retrospective

These adjectives are occasionally confused. *Retroactive* means 'effective from a date prior to enactment, applying to the past':

The government has introduced retroactive legislation meaning that a person can be tried for a crime not committed in this country.

Retrospective means 'looking back':

It is easy to be wise when we have retrospective knowledge.

Retrospective can occur as a noun meaning 'an exhibition of past work':

It was an interesting retrospective of Joan Eardley's paintings.

Réunion

An inhabitant of the French Indian Ocean island is a 'Réunion'; the derived adjective is the same. The capital is St Denis.

reveille

Reveille, which means 'a signal given to awaken service personnel', is normally stressed on the second syllable and pronounced to rhyme with 'tally'. An alternative pronunciation rhymes it with 'jelly':

Reveille is at 5:30 in this camp.

revel

Revel can function as a noun, usually in the plural, meaning 'noisy celebrations' and as a regular verb:

Did you hear the student revels last night? Exams are over, I assume.

UK: revel(s), revelled, revelling
US: revel(s), reveled, reveling

She is revelling in her new job. It might almost have been designed with her in mind.

revenge

See AVENGE/REVENGE

reverend, reverent

These two words are often confused. *Reverend*, with a 'd', tends to be written with a capital letter and to be used in titles or as an address term of respect:

I'd like to introduce the Reverend David Jones.
Dear Reverend Mother.

Reverent means 'feeling of reverence or religious respect':

They approached the building with a sense of reverent awe; thousands of pilgrims had been here before, all seeking spiritual fulfilment.

reversal, reversion

These nouns have similar meanings although they derive from different verbs and their uses should be distinguished. *Reversal* comes from 'reverse'. Its meanings are 'the act of turning round' and 'a change for the worse':

Everyone approved of the court's reversal of its earlier decision.

The business has suffered a reversal of fortune. The profit margins are down by 80 per cent.

Reversion comes from 'revert' and means 'return to an earlier condition':

A severe stroke is sometimes characterized by a loss of speech or by a reversion to a type of speech characteristic of an earlier maturational state.

review, revue

A *review* is an examination of a film, play, text:

His film reviews are classics.

It can also be an examination to see how well a course or person is working:

We've been offering these courses for five years. It's time we carried out an in-depth review to check on their relevance.

Review can also function as a regular verb:

He reviewed films for ten years.
We shall be reviewing our intake procedures soon.

A *revue* is a theatrical entertainment, often consisting of sketches, songs and dances:

The revue was televised and shortened. Many of the comedy sketches were cut.

revoke

Revoke is a regular verb meaning 'cancel, rescind':

revoke(s), revoked, revoking
That particular licensing law has been revoked.

The derived forms use 'c', not 'k':

revocable, revocation.

The adjective 'irrevocable' is stressed on the second syllable and not on the third.

revolt, revolution

The main difference between these nouns is size. A *revolt* is normally a local rebellion or uprising against an authority. It is usually unsuccessful:

One can understand their revolt against machinery. Many weavers thought they would lose their jobs.

The Peasants' Revolt was ruthlessly suppressed.

A *revolution* is a widespread uprising against a government. It is often successful:

The French Revolution led to changes in government throughout Europe.

revue

See REVIEW/REVUE

rhetoric

The noun *rhetoric* has two related meanings. First, it can refer to the rules of *Rhetoric* practised and described in Classical Greek. This *rhetoric* was prescriptive, defining formulas for effective public speaking (and later, writing) in the form of such devices as repetition or such figures of speech as 'hyperbole'. Aristotle claimed that rhetorical prose appealed to reason, whereas poetry appealed to the senses. Prescriptive *rhetoric* was popular in England and, from the sixteenth century, specific styles and figures of speech were taught in schools and widely used in literature. Today, examples of prescriptive *rhetoric* can be found in the teaching of effective public speaking or in some courses of instruction in composition and creative writing. Usually, they are not referred to as *rhetoric*. Second, it can be applied to patterned devices used in literary language. Stylisticians examine rhetoric in their analysis and description of literary texts.

We do not have to be trained in *rhetoric* to use rhetorical devices. Every effective speaker, most proverbs and virtually every advertisement uses parallelism and repetition, often in twos and threes:

I have come not to inform you, not to appeal to you, not to plead with you. I have come to demand your support.

> Trade Unionist speech

Look before you leap.

A Mars a day helps you work, rest and play.

The study of *rhetoric* helps to describe and clarify the techniques that can contribute to a skilful use of language.

See also FIGURE OF SPEECH

rhetorical question

A *rhetorical question* does not expect an answer. It is often used as the equivalent of an emphatic statement:

Was I tired? = I was extremely tired.

or as a dramatic comment on events:

What could anybody do?

What on earth is happening to the weather?

See also QUESTION

rheumatism

Rheumatism is a painful disorder of the joints. The word is frequently misspelled. It derives from *rheum*, 'a discharge from the eyes or nose', and is related to the noun 'humour' in the sense of a bodily fluid that can affect health and personality.

rhinoceros

The noun *rhinoceros* is often misspelled. The plural may be the same as the singular or have '-es' added:

Did you know that white rhinoceros(es) have three toes on each foot?

rhombus

A *rhombus* is a four-sided equilateral parallelogram with opposite angles equal. Two of the angles are under 90° and two are over 90°. There are two acceptable plurals, 'rhombi' and 'rhombuses'. The latter is more frequently used.

The adjective 'rhomboid' means 'rhombus-like' but it is applied to a figure where adjacent sides are of unequal length:

This parallelogram is rhomboid: opposite sides are equal but adjacent sides are unequal.

rhotic

The adjective *rhotic* (occasionally 'rotic') is used by phoneticians to describe accents in which the 'r' is pronounced in words like 'hear' and 'heart'. The degree of rhoticity can vary: in some accents of English, such as those of Georgia or southern England, post-vocalic 'r' is not pronounced at all; occasionally, in regionally modified Irish accents, it is barely perceptible; and in some Scottish accents, the 'r' may be rolled in all positions. Rhotic accents are prestigious in the United States and Canada and non-prestigious in England, Australia and India.

Some non-rhotic accents in the south of England use a linking 'r' to join two vowels as in:

law (+ r) and order

potato (+ r) and cheese.

See also ACCENT, INTRUSIVE 'R'

rhyme, rime

Both *rhyme* and *rime* are used to identify the chiming terminal sounds in lines of verse:

Humpty Dumpty sat on a wall,
Humpty Dumpty had a great fall.

The *rhyme* form is preferred, although the word was borrowed from French *rime* and owes the 'h' to the influence of the unrelated *rhythm*.

Rhyming is popular with speakers of English from early childhood and indeed much reduplication dates from this age:

bow-wow, choo-choo, ta ta.

Skipping rhymes, chants and recitation games are widespread throughout the English-speaking world and seem to play a part in a child's acquisition of language. As a literary device, *rhyme* was not an integral feature of English poetry until after the Norman Conquest, when it gradually supplanted alliteration as the characteristic feature of English verse.

Rhyme is a form of parallelism in which there is sound correspondence between syllables. The likeness may depend on similar vowels:

knee, me, sea

or similar vowels plus following consonant(s):

lamb, ram, Sam
band, land, strand.

Because *rhyme* depends on sound, similarity of spelling is not essential. 'Lamb' is a perfect rhyme for 'Sam'.

The following types of rhyme are often distinguished:

- Masculine *rhyme* is usually referred to simply as *rhyme*. In this we find correspondence between single stressed syllables:

hand and sand
hind and rind
hive and derive

- Feminine or 'rich' *rhyme* has two consecutive rhyming syllables, the first being stressed, the second being unstressed and final:

breaking and shaking
braving and shaving
brawling and trawling

- Triple *rhyme* has three consecutive rhyming syllables:

clamouring and hammering
caringly and sharingly
rightfully and frightfully.

In English verse, the categories of feminine and triple rhymes are often combined. This type of rich *rhyme* tends to be limited to light or humorous verse.

- End rhyme occurs when the corresponding syllables occur at the end of the line. The rhyming lines may be adjacent, as in W.B. Yeats's 'The Secret Rose':

Far off, most secret, and inviolate Rose,
Enfold me in my hour of hours; where those
Who sought thee in the Holy Sepulchre
Or in the wine-vat, dwell beyond the stir
And tumult of defeated dreams; and deep
Among pale eyelids, heavy with the sleep ...

or alternate, as in the first four lines of Shakespeare's sonnet 106:

When in the chronicle of wasted time
I see descriptions of the fairest wights,
And beauty making beautiful old rhyme,
In praise of ladies dead and lovely knights ...

or fit into a more unusual pattern, such as that used by Donne in 'A Valediction: of Weeping':

    Let me pour forth
My tears before thy face, whilst I stay here,

For thy face coins them, and thy stamp they bear,
And by this mintage they are something worth,
For thus they be
Pregnant of thee;
Fruits of much grief they are, emblems of more:
When a tear falls, that thou fall'st which it bore,
So thou and I are nothing then, when on a diverse
    shore.

- Internal rhyme is where the rhyming syllables occur within a line as in the sonnet 'Carrion Comfort' by G.M. Hopkins:

O in turns of tempest, me heaped there; me frantic
    to avoid thee and flee?

- Eye rhyme bases its parallelism not on sound but on spelling:

are and bare
cove and move
gas and was

- Half rhyme depends on a likeness (such as a short vowel + the same consonant) rather than on perfect correspondence:

bit and bet
cad and cud
hat and hot

- Consonance is when only the end consonants match:

bread and bid
cling and song
while and will.

The term 'rhyme scheme' is given to the sequence of end rhymes in a poem and is represented by a letter of the alphabet for each rhyme. Thus the rhyme scheme for a Petrarchan sonnet is abba abba cde cde (or cd cd cd) and the rhyme scheme for most traditional ballad stanzas is abab.

See also PARALLELISM

rhyming slang

Rhyming slang involves using a word that rhymes with the intended word rather than the word itself. Thus 'bone' is rhyming slang for 'phone'. The best-known form of *rhyming slang* is associated with Cockney:

apples and pears (stairs)
plates of meat (feet).

Often the slang expression is reduced so that 'apples' and 'plates' imply 'stairs' and 'feet'.

See also SLANG

rhythm

The word *rhythm* is frequently misspelled and misunderstood. It derives from Greek *rhuthmos* from the verb *rehein*, 'to flow'. *Rhythm* refers to regular auditory patterns of stresses in speech. In English, these patterns are associated with the length and degree of stress given to a particular syllable. In a word like 'predicate', for example, the first syllable receives more stress than the other two, whereas it is the second syllable that receives the greatest stress in 'predicament'. Speech rhythms play a considerable part in intelligibility.

When the rhythm is systematically regulated, as it is in verse, it is known as 'metre'. In the following three lines from Milton's sonnet on his blindness, each line has five strong stresses in a pattern of x = unstressed and / = stressed:

    x / x / x / x / x /
    When I consider how my light is spent

    x / x / x / x / x /
    Ere half my days in this dark world and wide,

    x / x / x / x / x /
    And that one talent which is death to hide ...

See also METRE, PARALLELISM, STRESS

riches

The noun *riches* is patterned on French *richesse*, which is singular in form. The English word refers to 'wealth' but is treated as if it were plural:

His riches are of little use to him now.

ricochet

The verb *ricochet*, which means 'rebound from a surface', has two acceptable spellings, the former of which is more usual:

ricochet(s), ricocheted, ricocheting
ricochet(s), ricochetted, ricochetting.

The usual pronunciations rhyme with 'play', 'played' and 'playing', but the spelling pronunciations rhyming with 'net', netted' and 'netting' are no longer unusual.

rid

Rid is an irregular verb:

rid(s), rid, ridding
She rid the house of every trace of his presence.

In the past it was quite normal to use 'ridded' as the past tense form:

We ridded the country of leprosy.

This is still acceptable but seems a little old-fashioned.

The derived noun is 'riddance', a word that is often used in the phrase:

Good riddance!

meaning 'It's good to be free of something that was unwelcome'.

ride

Ride is an irregular verb:

ride(s), rode, riding, ridden.

rider

See CODICIL/COROLLARY/RIDER

right, rightly

Right can function as an adjective:

a right turn

an adverb:

Do it right.

a noun:

It's on my right.

and a regular verb:

She righted the vase.

Rightly can function as a pre-verbal adverbial, meaning 'correctly':

It has been rightly said that love of money is the root of all evil.
*It has been (right) said (right) that love of money is the root of all evil.

Rightly can only be used after the verb when it is used in parenthesis, as in:

It has been said, rightly, that love of money is the root of all evil.

right-

Right occurs in a large number of compounds:

right-angled, right-handedness
right angle, right winger.

See also HYPHEN

rigor, rigour

When the word means 'strictness', it is spelled '-our' in British English and '-or' in America:

UK: He approached the task with the rigour and discipline we have come to expect.
US: He approached the task with the rigor and discipline we have come to expect.

When *rigor* is used in the phrase *rigor mortis*, 'the stiffening of the body after death', it is spelled '-or' by both communities. The derived adjective 'rigorous' also has '-or-' in both Britain and America.

rime

See RHYME/RIME

ring

The verb *ring* can have two different meanings. When *ring* means 'make a ring around, encircle', it is regular:

ring(s), ringed, ringing
I ringed all the A answers.

When *ring* means 'makes a bell-like noise' or 'make a telephone call', it is irregular:

ring(s), rang, ringing, rung
I rang his doorbell but he could not have heard me.
I'll be ringing my mother tonight.

riot

Riot can function as a noun or verb:

Many houses were burnt down, two people were killed and eighty were injured in the urban riots.

Riot is a regular verb:

riot(s), rioted, rioting

What are they rioting for? Aren't there any peaceful forms of protest open to them?

riposte

See REPLY/RETORT/RIPOSTE

rise

See ARISE/AROUSE/RISE, RAISE/REAR/RISE

risible

This adjective comes from Latin *ridere*, 'to laugh', and means 'having a tendency to laugh or cause laughter' and, more recently, 'silly, ridiculous'. The first syllable rhymes with 'fizz':

Their attempts were both puerile and risible.

risky, risqué

These adjectives are not closely related in meaning although they both derive from French *risquer*, 'to hazard'. *Risky* means 'dangerous', 'perilous':

Only volunteers will be allowed to go on this very risky venture.

Risky investments tend to offer bigger returns than safe ones.

Risqué means 'bordering on impropriety or indecency':

His jokes are always slightly risqué.

The first syllable of *risqué* rhymes with 'fleece' whereas the first syllable of *risky* rhymes with 'miss'.

ritual

Ritual can function as an adjective and a noun and relates to 'rites' that have religious, social or psychological significance:

Ritual bathing is practised in the Ganges.

A compulsive personality disorder is sometimes characterized by obsessive, repetitive behaviour such as a ritual of checking and rechecking that all doors are locked and lights off.

rival

Rival can function as an adjective:

a rival company

a noun and a verb. As a noun, it means a person or organization that is in competition with another:

They are rivals in love, but one of them will have to lose.

As a verb, *rival* means 'be the equal of, compete with':

His genius rivals Einstein's.

In British English the 'l' is doubled before '-ed' and '-ing':

UK: rival(s), rivalled, rivalling
US: rival(s), rivaled, rivaling.

rivet

A *rivet* is a short metal pin:

We need a rivet to fasten these pieces of metal together.

The regular verb *rivet* means 'hold together' or 'hold firmly':

rivet(s), riveted, riveting

I was riveted to the spot, too terrified to move.

road, street

In theory, it is easy to distinguish between a *road* and a *street*. A *road* is bigger and tends to denote an open thoroughfare between towns, cities and other settlements:

This road runs from Leeds to Huddersfield.

A *street* is usually a thoroughfare within a town or city:

I live at 21 Church Street. It's off the Otley Road.

In Britain, however, the terms are not always as easily distinguishable as this.

rob

See BURGLE/BURGLARIZE/ROB/STEAL

rodeo

The noun *rodeo* was borrowed from Spanish *rodear*, 'to go around', and is used in American English mainly for a display of such skills as bare-back horse-riding, throwing and tying steers. The word has two main pronunciations. In the first, the main stress falls on the first syllable, which is pronounced 'road'; in the second, the main stress falls on the second syllable, which rhymes with 'hay':

In the big rodeos, you can still see skills that were popularized by cowboy films.

role, roll

These homophones are occasionally misused. The noun *role* is sometimes spelled with a circumflex *rôle* and is often used to refer to a part in a play or film:

He played the role of Hamlet's father.

Recently, it has been used with the meaning of 'function':

Describe the role of the IPA script in phonetics.

A *roll* is either a small loaf:

I'd like six bread rolls, please.

or something that has been rolled up:

We need a new roll of paper for the fax machine.

roman

Roman is used to describe typesetting and typewritten characters, and is distinguished from *italic* or **bold**. It was the term used by printers to indicate ordinary type.

Roman numerals are based on letters:

i = 1
ii = 2
v = 5
ix = 9
L = 50
C = 100
M = 1000.

Arabic numerals such as 1 and 2 are preferred for most purposes, but *roman* numerals are still used for the numbers associated with a ruler's name:

Charles V
Pope John Paul II

books of the Bible:

I Samuel
II Chronicles

and, sometimes, world wars:

World War I.

See also ARABIC INFLUENCE, BIBLE, NUMBERS

Romania

An inhabitant of the European country is a 'Romanian'; the derived adjective is the same. The capital is Bucharest.

roof

The plural of *roof* is 'roofs':

I wouldn't like to have to mend roofs for a living: I'm scared of heights.

Some people, analogizing from 'hoof', 'hooves', say and write *rooves, but this is not the standard form.

See also SPELLING

rosary

The noun *rosary* is often misspelled. It ends in '-ary', not '-ery'. A *rosary* is a series of prayers counted on a string of beads:

The Catholic rosary has beads to indicate the Lord's Prayer, the Hail Mary and the Gloria.

There is a noun *rosery*, meaning 'garden or bed of roses' but this word is virtually obsolete. Both words derive from Latin *rosarium*, 'a rose garden'.

rosé

Rosé functions in English as the name for a pink wine:

A good rosé is made by removing the skins of red grapes after only a little of the colour has been extracted.

The word is disyllabic and rhymes with 'nosegay'.

roster, rota

A *rota* is another name for a *roster*. It refers to a list or register, especially one showing the order of people listed for particular tasks or duties. *Rota* is less common than *roster* in America:

Have you drawn up the rota/roster for taking the bottles to the bottle bank?

Rota is used only as a noun but *roster* can also function as a regular verb:

roster(s), rostered, rostered
You've been rostered for the last shift.

rostrum

A *rostrum* is a platform or dais for public speaking or conducting. It has two acceptable plurals, 'rostrums' and 'rostra'. The former is the more widely-used form.

rotund

Rotund is an adjective meaning 'rounded or spherical'. It is also used as a synonym for 'plump'. It is occasionally used instead of 'orotund' to mean 'sonorous'. Careful speakers keep these meanings separate:

He is a rotund tenor with an orotund voice.

round

See AROUND/ROUND

round about, roundabout

The form *round about* can be used as a preposition or adverb:

We met round about two o'clock.
A crowd had gathered round about.

A *roundabout* is used in Britain for both a 'merry-go-round' and a 'traffic circle':

The children loved their rides on the roundabout.
We just avoided the accident at the roundabout. A juggernaut failed to stop at the junction.

rouse

See ARISE/AROUSE/RISE

rout, route

These words can both function as nouns and regular verbs. *Rout* rhymes with 'out' and means 'overwhelming defeat, cause an enemy to flee':

It was not merely defeat; it was a rout.
The Scots may have been routed at Flodden but their spirit remained strong.

Route rhymes with 'boot' in Britain and with 'out' in America. It means 'choice of roads', 'plan the choice of roads' or 'send by a particular way':

We've worked out the most direct route between here and Washington.
The traffic is being routed via Meanwood Road because of the accident on the Otley Road.

rubbish

Rubbish has been used as a noun since the fourteenth century. It means 'worthless or unwanted material, refuse':

We are taking our household rubbish to the recycling centre. They can recycle almost everything.

In the late twentieth century it has begun to be used as a verb meaning 'criticize and make little of'. The use is still informal but it has been used in the House of Commons:

I do not appreciate being rubbished by the honourable member for X.

In some varieties of English it is also used as an adjective:

rubbish man = useless man.

This usage, however, is not mainstream.

rue

Rue can function as a noun or a regular verb. The noun can refer to an aromatic plant:

Rue is an aromatic Eurasian shrub with small yellow flowers and evergreen leaves.

Rue meaning 'sorrow, pity' is now almost obsolete but the verb continues to be used:

You'll rue the day you crossed swords with me!

rumour, rumor

A *rumour* is a piece of gossip or information that may or may not be true. The British noun is *rumour* whereas Americans prefer *rumor*:

UK: There's a rumour that he is about to resign.
US: There's a rumor that he is about to resign.

See also SPELLING

run

Run is an irregular verb:

run(s), ran, running, run
John has run in four marathons.

It has a wide range of meanings from 'rapid movement' to 'control':

The film has been running for thirty minutes.
My eyes are running.
Mary runs the office most efficiently.

The noun also has a range of meanings from 'exercise' to a 'score' in a ball game:

I like a gentle run in the morning.
He has scored 15 runs so far.

Run occurs in a wide range of compounds and idioms:

runaway
run-of-the-mill
in the long run
I'll give him a good run for his money.
She is badly run down.
He's giving you the run-around.

Some people object to the use of such expressions as 'run-around' or the use of 'run-up' as in:

the run-up to the election

but they are part of current colloquial speech.

See also VERB

running head

Running head is a term used in printing. It refers to a heading printed at the top of every page. Sometimes it incorporates page numbers and it is conventional for the book title to appear on the left-hand pages and the chapter title to appear on the right-hand pages.

rural, rustic

These adjectives both derive from Latin *rus, ruris*, 'the country', but they have developed different connotations. *Rural* is the more neutral adjective. It is often used in contrast to 'urban' and relates to the countryside:

We have chosen a rural setting for the play.

Rustic also means 'characteristic of the countryside' but it has overtones of 'unsophisticated', 'quaint', 'awkward':

The house is so simple, so unpretentious, so rustic.

See also CONNOTATION

Russia

Russia is not and was not a synonym for the Soviet Union. These names should be used with care. The Soviet Union did not exist prior to 1917 and the partial break-up of the union in the 1990s means that countries formerly part of the union are now independent.

ruthless

See RECKLESS/RUTHLESS

Rwanda

An inhabitant of the republic in east-central Africa is a 'Rwandan'; the derived adjective is the same. The capital is Kigali. The spelling 'Ruanda' should be avoided.

S

s

S is a consonant. Its pronunciation varies depending on the sound it follows. It is pronounced 's' in words such as 'raps', 'rats' and 'racks' but is pronounced 'z' in words such as 'hobs', 'hods' and 'hogs'. Less frequently, it is pronounced 'sh' in a word such as 'sugar'.

's, s'

The apostrophe is used before 's' for two main purposes. It marks possession in a regular singular noun:

the cat's paw
Yeats's poetry

and it indicates the omission of one or more letters:

She is tall. = She's tall.
She has gone. = She's gone.
Let us go. = Let's go.

The apostrophe is used after 's' to mark possession in a plural noun:

the boys' beds
the cats' home.

See also APOSTROPHE, ITS/IT'S, PUNCTUATION

Sabbath

Sabbath comes from Hebrew *shabbath*, meaning 'day of rest'. It is a day dedicated to the service of God. For Muslims, Friday is the *Sabbath*, for Jews it is Saturday and for Christians it is Sunday.

sabre, saber

The noun *sabre* often occurs in adventure stories. It is the name of a broad sword with a curved blade. The American spelling is *saber*:

The noun sabre/saber comes via French from *szablya*, a Magyar word for a weapon.

See also FOREIGN LOAN-WORDS

saccharin, saccharine

These words are often confused. *Saccharin*, without an 'e', is a noun meaning 'non-fattening sugar substitute':

I prefer to put sugar in my tea. I always think that saccharin leaves an after-taste.

Saccharine, with an 'e', is an adjective frequently used to mean 'excessively sweet':

Have you seen his saccharine smile?

sacred, sacrosanct

These words both derive from Latin. *Sacred* comes from *sacrare*, 'to set aside as holy', and is used to mean 'regarded with reverence and respect':

She considered it a sacred duty to follow her father's wishes to the letter.

Sacrosanct derives from *sacrosanctus*, 'made holy by sacred rite', and is currently used to mean 'inviolable':

John's private life is sacrosanct. He does not want anyone to intrude.

sacrilegious

Sacrilegious is an adjective, related to 'sacred'. It means 'impious or guilty of desecrating something holy':

Respect for places of worship has diminished in our society. In the past, stealing from a church would have been regarded as sacrilegious.

This adjective is often misspelled in that people incorrectly pattern it on 'religious'.

saga

A *saga* has both a technical and a popular meaning. Technically, *sagas* refer to medieval heroic prose narratives written in Iceland or to similar narratives. Popularly, *saga* is applied to a story stretching over a long period:

We study the sagas as part of our course in Icelandic.
Catherine Cookson's greatest saga: the struggles of three generations.

sailer, sailor

These nouns are occasionally confused. *Sailer*, ending in '-er', is a vessel:

There was a time when Bristol and Liverpool were filled with sailers.
It may look like a great boat but it's a lousy sailer.

Sailor, ending in '-or', is a person who sails, a member of a ship's crew:

Why did sailors wear bell-bottom trousers?

Saint

Saint derives from Latin *sanctus*, 'holy', and is a title given, after death, to a person of exceptional goodness and holiness. It can also be used informally:

Saints can be canonized centuries after they died.
She's a living saint.

The normal abbreviation of *Saint* is 'St'.

The church is dedicated to St Patrick.
The feast of St Brigid is 1 February.

The normal abbreviation of *Saints* is SS:

The church is dedicated to SS Peter and Paul.

but, since this is also the abbreviation for 'a paramilitary organization within the Nazi party' and for 'steamships', some people prefer to use 'Sts':

The church is dedicated to Sts Peter and Paul.

sake

The noun *sake*, meaning 'benefit', 'interest', normally occurs after a possessive adjective:

for my sake

or after a noun marked for possession. The noun may be animate or inanimate:

for Mary's sake
for heaven's sake
for pity's sake.

There are two problems with *sake*. Often, when the preceding noun ends with an 's' or an 's' sound, an 's is not added:

for goodness sake not *for goodness's sake
for conscience sake not *for conscience's sake

although some writers like to use an apostrophe:

for goodness' sake
for conscience' sake.

It is not uncommon for an apostrophe + s to be lost, especially in compounds. A place-name like 'Andersonstown', for example, is derived from:

Anderson's + town.

Many writers dislike the use of *sakes* as in:

for all our sakes

preferring:

for the sake of all of us.

The noun *sake* is the acceptable spelling of the Japanese drink made from fermented rice. Other spellings, 'saké' and 'saki', should be avoided.

salary, wage

The terms *salary* and *wage* both refer to money paid to employees. Payment to professional workers is normally referred to as a *salary*, which is generally paid monthly:

Salary to include generous resettlement package.
My salary is paid monthly in arrears.

A *wage* is usually paid to manual workers either weekly, fortnightly or monthly. The singular form *wage* is less common than *wages*. It tends to be used more generally:

All employees should be paid a living wage.

The plural tends to be used for payment to an individual, normally for manual work:

Wages will be paid fortnightly in arrears.

See also POLITICAL CORRECTNESS

salivary

The adjective *salivary* derives from 'saliva' and is most frequently used in the phrase '*salivary* gland', referring to the glands such as the parotid that secrete saliva. *Salivary* is often misspelled. It

ends in '-ary' not '-ery'. It has two acceptable pronunciations. The stress may fall on the second syllable, causing the ending to sound like 'ivory'. Less commonly, the stress may fall on the first syllable and the last three syllables rhyme with 'livery'.

salmonella

Salmonella is a bacterium that may cause food poisoning. It is often misspelled and mispronounced. The 'l' is pronounced because *salmonella* has nothing to do with the fish 'salmon' but derives its name from Daniel E. Salmon, a veterinary surgeon.

salubrious

Salubrious means 'wholesome', 'favourable to health':

We shall have to find a more salubrious place to live.
The city is very convenient but the pollution is bad.

salutary, salutatory

These adjectives are occasionally confused. *Salutary* is used much more frequently; it derives from Latin *salus*, 'health', but has been extended to mean 'beneficial':

Working for his fees was a salutary experience for John. It taught him to appreciate how hard some people have to work for their money.

Salutatory is now rare; it derives from 'salutation' and means 'friendly', 'welcoming':

Their salutatory gesture was so welcome after weeks of being alone.

salvage, selvage

These nouns are occasionally confused and the second is frequently misspelled. *Salvage* refers to the act of rescuing property, especially at sea:

The salvage operation cannot begin until the boat is officially declared a wreck.

Selvage derives from 'self edge' and refers to the non-fraying edge of a piece of material:

There is no need to hem it up if you use the selvage as the edging.

An alternative spelling is 'selvedge' and, although some people dislike it, 'selvedge' is perfectly acceptable. What is unacceptable is the blend *selvege.

salve

The word *salve* can function as a noun and a verb. It is an old-fashioned word for 'ointment':

They applied salve to the open wound.

The noun tends to rhyme with 'halve'. In other words, the 'l' is not pronounced. The regular verb tends to rhyme with 'valve' and means 'comfort, soothe':

He's only doing it to salve his conscience.

salvo

A *salvo* is a simultaneous discharge of weapons, especially on a ceremonial occasion. The plural may be 'salvos' or 'salvoes':

The salvo was in honour of the Queen's jubilee.

same

The word *same* means 'identical' and should not be confused with 'similar'. *Same* can function as an adjective and a noun:

They have both applied for the same job.

I did exactly the same when I was young.

The tendency in correspondence to use *same* as in:

We have received your order for stationery and we will despatch same forthwith.

is now regarded as outmoded.

San Marino

An inhabitant of the European republic is a 'San Marinese' or a 'Sammarinese'; the derived adjective is the same. The capital is San Marino.

sanatorium, sanitarium

These variants refer to a medical institution usually caring for people who are chronically ill. The normal plurals are 'sanatoriums' and 'sanitariums' but plurals ending in '-ia' are also acceptable:

UK: She's in a sanatorium in Switzerland.

US: She's in a sanitarium in Switzerland.

sanction

Sanction derives from Latin *sancire*, 'to decree', and can be used as a noun meaning 'permission', 'authorization' and as a verb meaning 'permit, give authority to':

I have asked the department to sanction my leave of absence.

Since the 1960s, the plural form of *sanction* has increasingly been used to mean 'ban', 'embargo':

The oil sanctions have hurt the very people they were intended to help. The rich can still drive around in cars but public transport has stopped.

sank

See SINK/SANK/SUNK

Sanskrit

Sanskrit is still an official language of India even though it is used almost exclusively for religious purposes. It has the oldest written literature of any Indo-European language and is the language of the Vedas. *Sanskrit* was vitally important in the study of Indo-European languages and has contributed a number of words to English:

Brahman/Brahmin (member of the priestly caste)

mantra (sacred word or phrase used to help concentration)

yoga (state of tranquillity induced by mental and physical exercise).

Sarawak

An inhabitant of the state of Malaysia is a 'Sarawakan'; the derived adjective is the same. The capital is Kuching.

sarcasm

Sarcasm often involves mockery or contempt. Because it is often used by someone in a superior position, it is regarded as 'the lowest form of wit'.

See also INNUENDO, IRONY, WIT

sarcastic

See IRONIC/SARCASTIC

sari

The plural of *sari* is 'saris':

I bought some beautiful saris in Bombay but I find it difficult to drape them artistically.

sat

See SIT/SAT/SITTING

satire, satyr

These nouns are occasionally confused. *Satire* is any form of speech or writing in which someone or something is held up to ridicule or scorn:

Politics is often the subject matter of satire.

The rhetorical devices commonly used in satire are BATHOS, caricature, IRONY, ridicule, SARCASM and WIT.

A *satyr* was a Greek woodland god, often represented as a goat and associated with drinking and sexual indulgence:

Did satyrs always have tails or have the representations of satyrs and devils been confused?

See also PARODY

Saudi Arabia

An inhabitant of the Middle Eastern kingdom is a 'Saudi'; the derived adjective is 'Saudi Arabian'. The capital is Riyadh.

sauté

Sauté derives from French and was used as an adjective referring to food that has been fried quickly in a little fat. The word is now used in English as a regular verb:

sauté(s), sautéd or sautéed, sautéing or sautéeing

We've sautéed the potatoes so now we're ready to eat.

savanna

A *savanna* or *savannah* is an open grassland, characteristic of high regions of tropical Africa:

The climate in the savanna areas of Cameroon and Nigeria is as healthy as Switzerland.

In the past, the form *savannah* was more usual and indeed the American port is called after the *Savannah*, which was the first steamship to travel from Liverpool to Georgia in 1819.

There are fashions in the use or non-use of 'h' at the end of personal names including:

Debora(h), Sara(h).

save

See EXCEPT/EXCEPTED/EXCEPTING/SAVE

saviour, savior

These are variant forms of the noun, meaning 'one who rescues another from danger or harm'. The form *saviour* is British and the Americans prefer *savior*. The form with a capital letter refers to Jesus Christ:

UK: He is our Saviour.
US: He is our Savior.

savour, savor

The noun *savour* and its American equivalent *savor* refers to the taste or smell of a substance:

UK: It had the savour of sandalwood.
US: It had the savor of sandalwood.

In Britain especially, *savour* and its related *adjective* 'savoury' refer to meaty rather than sweet smells:

There is nothing in the world quite like the savour of a barbecued chicken.
And for the savoury course, we'll have lamb.

The American form of the adjective is 'savory'.

Savour is often used metaphorically as a verb meaning 'suggest':

It savours of nepotism.

saw

Saw was an irregular verb meaning 'cut with a saw':

saw(s), sawed, sawing, sawn.

Recently, it has begun to be regularized and the past participle 'sawed' is now acceptable even on the BBC:

He claimed to have sawed through the floor by mistake.

Many careful users still prefer 'sawn' and this is the form that occurs in the phrase:

sawn-off shotgun

although that, too, is being changed to:

sawed-off shotgun.

The noun *saw* meaning 'wise saying', 'proverb' is related to 'say' and is virtually extinct, found only in quotations such as:

wise saws and modern instances.

say

Say is an irregular verb:

say(s), said, saying, said
You said I could go.

In RECEIVED PRONUNCIATION 'said' rhymes with 'bed' and not with 'bayed'.

scallop

A *scallop* is a shellfish. The word is normally pronounced to rhyme with 'dollop' although a spelling pronunciation that rhymes *scallop* with 'gallop' is increasingly common.

scan

Scan is used with two different, almost contradictory, meanings. It can mean 'examine closely':

I scanned the piece of paper over and over again, hoping that a close reading would reveal another meaning.

It can also mean 'glance over':

I haven't had a chance to read it properly but I've scanned it.

Many careful users dislike the second meaning.

scarcely

See BARELY/HARDLY/SCARCELY

scare

Scare is a regular verb meaning 'fill with fear':

scare(s), scared, scaring
You really scared me when you pretended to be dead!

Some careful users of language dislike 'scared of' as a synonym for 'afraid of', preferring:

I'm afraid of spiders.

to the colloquially acceptable:

I'm scared of spiders.

In America, *scare* is sometimes used informally with 'up' to mean 'produce' a meal:

I'll try to scare up a light snack.

scarf

Scarf has two acceptable plurals, 'scarves' and 'scarfs'. The first plural is older and parallels 'hooves' but the second is now more widespread and parallels 'roofs' and 'dwarfs'.

scenario

Scenario was traditionally used to mean 'summary of the plot of a play' but recently it has been used – possibly overused – to mean 'projected state of affairs':

The worst-case scenario would see our department in so much debt that one in four members of staff would be required to resign.

Like all overused words, it is best to avoid *scenario* in careful speech or writing.

The usual pronunciation rhymes this word with 'Mario' but there is a growing tendency to pronounce it to rhyme with 'airy-o'.

sceptic, skeptic, septic
A *sceptic* is a person who challenges and refuses to accept traditional beliefs:

He's the oddest sceptic I've ever met: he attends church regularly and insists on his children receiving religious education.

Americans prefer the spelling *skeptic* but both American and British speakers pronounce the initial cluster as in 'scalpel'.

The words *sceptic* and *septic* are occasionally confused. *Sceptic* is a noun and *septic* is an adjective meaning 'related to or caused by sepsis or putrefaction':

The wound is septic.

See also CYNICAL/SCEPTICAL

sceptre, scepter
These are variant spellings of the noun meaning 'ceremonial staff used as a symbol of authority'. *Sceptre* is the preferred form in Britain and *scepter* is used in America.

See also SPELLING

schedule
A *schedule* is a list of times or duties or programmes:

My schedule is very tight. Is there any chance that I could take an extra day in Newark?

In America the initial cluster is pronounced like 'sch-' in 'school' and this pronunciation is growing in popularity in Britain, where the older pronunciation of 'sh-' is also found.

schism
The noun *schism* comes from liturgical Latin *schisma*, meaning 'a split in the church':

The most serious schism in church history was the Reformation.

Traditionally, the 'sch-' of *schism* was pronounced 's'. More recently, the spelling pronunciation of 'sk-' has occurred and is also acceptable. The pronunciation beginning with 'sh-' is not standard.

schizophrenic
A *schizophrenic* is a person with a severe psychotic disorder:

Schizophrenics may suffer from delusions, emotional instability and hallucinations if their disorder is not treated.

Schizo- derives from Greek *skhizein*, 'to split', and it is now regularly pronounced like 'skits'.

school
The word *school* can function as a noun or verb:

I went to school when I was four.

We were schooled in the art of self-defence.

It is frequently misspelled.

scientific English
During the last fifty years, over 400,000 scientific words have been invented and accepted internationally. Many of these words, such as 'dichromaticism' or 'dieldrine', tend to be used only by scientists, doctors or students, but others, like DNA (deoxyribonucleic acid) or PVC (polyvinylchloride), have been popularized by the media.

English has become an international language for scientists but, while scientists need to know the registers associated with their own calling, they may not need to know the technical vocabularies necessary for dealing with other trades or professions. Many teachers of English have evolved courses of English for Specific Purposes, including Science, and these attempt to give the learners competence in the skills that they will need to function adequately in their profession.

Scientific English tends to be characterized by a precise vocabulary, often polysyllabic and based on Greek and Latin roots:

dimercaprol

dimethylsulphoxide

by formulae that are interpretable throughout the world:

$CH_2(SH)(CH)(SH)CH_2OH$

$(CH_3)_2SO$

and by complex premodification:

highly concentrated dye solution.

It also exhibits a preference for simple or compound sentences, the frequent introduction of subordinate clauses by 'if', 'when', 'that' and 'which', and by the use of the passive voice:

The solution is added.

There is a preference for the present tense and for statements and an avoidance of questions and exclamations; of the modals 'may', 'might', 'must', 'shall', 'should', 'would'; and of personal references.

Scientists can, of course, write as parents and poets as well as scientists. When they write as scientists, however, their aim is to communicate unequivocally and unemotionally with other scientists and, over the centuries, scientific discourse has evolved its own style.

See also JARGON

scissors

Scissors is a plural noun:

The scissors are in the drawer.

Often, the word is used with 'a pair of':

I bought a pair of scissors yesterday.

scone

There is regional variation about what exactly a *scone* is and whether or not it should contain sugar. There is also debate about the pronunciation. Many people rhyme *scone* with 'stone'; others rhyme it with 'gone'. Both pronunciations are acceptable.

Scotch, Scots, Scottish

The word *Scotch* should be used as an adjective only in the fixed collocations:

butterscotch (sweet, candy)

hopscotch (children's hopping game)

scotch egg (boiled egg covered with sausage meat)

scotch whisky (often referred to as scotch).

In all other contexts, *Scots* or *Scottish* should be used.

Scots can be used as a noun referring to both the people:

The Scots are a peace-loving people.

and the language:

Apart from Standard English, Scots is one of the few varieties of English to have its own official orthography.

Scots occurs as an adjective, especially before 'English', 'man', 'woman' or their equivalents:

Scots English (the language)

a Scots girl

a Scotsman.

Scottish is used as an adjective and is probably more popular than *Scots*:

the Scottish economy

Scottish industry.

Scottish and *Scots* are acceptable alternatives.

Scottish English, Scots

When the Germanic tribes invaded Britain in the fifth century, some of the Angles settled in southern Scotland. Their language was a Germanic dialect, closely related to the dialects spoken by the Saxons and the Jutes. It was described as 'Inglis' until 1494, when Adam Loutful referred to it as both 'Inglis' and 'Scottis'.

In Scotland today, as in many English-speaking regions, we find a number of class, urban and regional dialects, but the following features are recognizably Scots: the use of such spelling pronunciations as:

ain (own), hame (home), sae (so), stane (stone)

and:

aboot (about), hoos (house), toon (town)

the use of such words as:

bairn (child), bonny (fine), burn (small river), wee (small)

and the use of 'nae', 'no' or 'ny' as a negator:

She canny dance.

See also DIALECT, RECEIVED PRONUNCIATION

scrimmage, scrummage

These words are variants of each other and both are related to 'skirmish'. Today, their meanings are distinct. A *scrimmage* is a rough and disorderly struggle:

Their behaviour was unacceptable. Many fans spilled over into the pitch and joined the scrimmage.

Scrimmage is also a technical term in American football:

Scrimmage is the period between the time when the ball goes into play and when it is declared dead.

A *scrummage* is a technical term in rugby, now more frequently referred to as a 'scrum':

When the referee calls a scrummage, it is a 'set scrum(mage)'; when it forms spontaneously, it is a 'loose scrum(mage)'.

scull, skull

These homophones are occasionally confused. A *scull* is a single oar that propels a boat from the stern. The term is also applied to a lightweight boat with one oarsman who uses two oars:

He won silver in the single sculls.

A *skull* is the bony skeleton of a head:

He picked up the skull and said: 'Alas, poor Yorick!'

sculpt, sculptor, sculpture

These words are all related but they are occasionally misused. *Sculpt* is a verb meaning 'carve or cast an image in stone, wood or metal':

'David' was sculpted from local marble.

A *sculptor* is a person who creates a *sculpture*:

Women sculptors often prefer not to be called 'sculptresses'.

Barbara Hepworth was a famous British sculptor.

Sculpture is both the art of creating figures by carving or casting and the artefacts:

He spends his time studying sculpture.

This is my favourite sculpture.

Sculpture is also used as a regular verb with the same meaning as *sculpt*:

I'd love to sculpture George's head.

sea

When people use the phrase 'the sea', they are referring to the mass of salt water on the surface of the earth:

I love to watch the sea on a stormy day.

The basic difference between *sea* and 'ocean' is size:

The Irish Sea is part of the Atlantic Ocean.

séance

A *séance* (occasionally *seance*) is a meeting at which attempts are made to make contact with, or get messages from, the dead:

I'd be too frightened to take part in a séance.

sear, seer

These homophones are occasionally confused. *Sear* is a verb meaning 'scorch, burn the surface':

I could feel the heat searing my skin.

The word *seer* is a noun and is the English equivalent of 'prophet'. It is used, on occasion, for a person who can foretell the future:

She was more than just a wise woman. I'm convinced she was a seer. She certainly seemed to know what was going to happen to me.

seasonable, seasonal

These adjectives both derive from 'season' but their meanings are different. *Seasonable* means 'suitable to the season':

It is not seasonable to have fog and frost in May but that's what we got in 1996.

Seasonal means 'relating to a certain season or occurring during a particular season':

Apple-picking is seasonal work.

seasons

The four *seasons*, spring, summer, autumn (fall) and winter are not normally given a capital letter:

Why does summer pass more quickly than winter?

seaspeak

Seaspeak is a term coined by analogy with NEWSPEAK to refer to a variety of English created to facilitate communication among all people involved in sailing and navigation. English is the most widely-used maritime language in the world and considerable confusion can arise if, for example, a Thai captain wants to berth in a Japanese port. In 1980, a group of mariners and linguists in Britain decided to analyse tape recordings of conversations between ships' officers and to isolate the words and structures necessary for unambiguous communication. *Seaspeak* was the result.

See also DOUBLESPEAK

secateurs

Secateurs are small shears used for pruning:

Has anyone seen my secateurs? I had them yesterday when I was pruning the roses.

There are two frequently used pronunciations of this word. The first approximates to French, does not pronounce the final 's' and rhymes with 'chauffeur'. The second rhymes the last syllable with 'hers'.

second floor

In Britain the ground-level floor of a building is called 'the ground floor' and the one above is called 'the first floor'. In America, the ground-floor level is called 'the first floor' and the level above is 'the second floor'.

See also FLOOR, STOREY/STORY

secret, secrete

Secret functions as an adjective and a noun:

It's our secret garden.
Don't tell anyone else. It's a secret.

Secrete rhymes with 'discrete' and has two unrelated meanings:

'hide':

He tried to secrete the drugs in the lining of his case.

and 'release a secretion':

This plant secretes a milky substance that becomes rubbery after exposure to the air.

see

See LOOK/SEE/WATCH

seeing

Seeing can function as a conjunction meaning 'in the light of, because, since'. It is often followed by 'that':

Seeing that you're here, you may as well help out.

In certain varieties of colloquial speech, *seeing* is followed by 'as' or 'as how':

*Seeing as you're here, you may as well help out.
*Seeing as how you're here, you may as well help out.

but these structures are not acceptable in Standard English.

seek

Seek is an irregular verb:

seek(s), sought, seeking
I did not seek you out. You offered your services.

A common mistake is to use 'for' with *seek*:

He sought fame in America.
*He sought for fame in America.

seer

See SEAR/SEER

seize

This verb is frequently misspelled. It is one of the words that does not follow the rule 'i' before 'e' except after 'c':

Seize your opportunities when you are young. They may not come again!

seldom

Seldom is an adverb meaning 'not often', 'rarely':

We seldom go for a drive now. The roads are too congested.

It sometimes co-occurs with 'or never':

We seldom or never go out.

The use with 'or ever' is unacceptable:

*We seldom or ever go out.

self, -self

Self can occur as a noun whose plural is 'selves' but only in very restricted circumstances:

her usual self

your good selves

The 'self' is our distinct identity or character.

Self- is a widely-used combining form, found in adjectives:

self-addressed envelope

adverbs:

self-centredly

nouns:

self-defence

and pronouns:

myself.

See also PRONOUN, REFLEXIVE

sell

Sell is an irregular verb:

sell(s), sold, selling

We didn't move because we couldn't sell the house.

selvage

See SALVAGE/SELVAGE

semantic change

The phrase *semantic change* refers to a process by which word meanings alter with time. Thus 'fiend' used to mean 'enemy', 'someone you did not love', and 'lord' used to mean 'giver of bread'. Both words have undergone major semantic changes. There are several types of semantic change the most common are summarized below.

Amelioration

This is when the associations of a word improve. 'Minister', for example, meant 'one who served or ministered to someone else' but now implies 'one in orders' or 'a high-ranking government official'.

Deterioration or pejoration

This is when the meanings become less pleasant or lose some of their former glory. 'Lust' used to mean 'pleasure' and not 'sexual desire'; 'knave' referred to a non-aristocratic boy who was set a task; and 'villain' simply meant 'peasant'.

Generalization

This is when the meaning of a word moves from the specific to the general. Thus 'bead' changed from a 'prayer' to a 'bead' on a rosary to a 'bauble' and 'disk' was extended in meaning from 'something round' to 'floppy disks', which are neither floppy nor round.

Narrowing

This is when a meaning becomes more specific. 'Girl' originally meant 'a young person, either male or female' and 'gentle' referred to 'one of noble birth'.

Polysemy

This is where a number of meanings develop from one central meaning. 'Key', for example, can refer to an object that opens a door, as well as the 'levers' on a piano, typewriter or computer, and it can also mean the 'solution' to a mystery or 'explanations' on a map.

As well as these five categories, there are other, less frequently occurring types of semantic change, such as:

Concretization

This is where an abstraction is concretized, as when words such as 'grace', 'holiness', 'majesty' or 'worship' are used as terms of address or reference in connection with bishops, popes, monarchs and judges.

Euphemism

This is when words for death, disease, size or bodily functions are avoided and replaced by idioms that are either pleasant circumlocutions:

to pass away

to go to heaven

or supposedly humorous as with:

to kick the bucket

to pop your clogs.

Folk etymology

This is where a false understanding can cause a shift of meaning. 'Pantry', for example, is derived from Latin *panis* meaning 'bread' but was associated with 'pans' and so thought of as a place where pans were kept. This process can also occur when people try to make sense of a word they do not understand, as with 'asparagus' becoming 'sparrow grass' or 'Purgatoire' becoming 'Picketwire'.

Semantic change is inevitable in a language, and

attempts to halt change in a living language are doomed to failure.

See also ETYMOLOGY, PROPAGANDA, PURIST

semantics

Semantics is the branch of linguistics devoted to the study of meaning. Among the problems that semanticists attempt to explain are the following.

Antonymy

Certain words appear to be opposite in meaning to others:

badness/goodness
heal/hurt
high/low
quickly/slowly.

Hyponymy

Certain words seem to comprehend others:

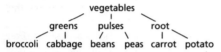

Idiom

Often, combinations of words have meanings that differ from the combination of their individual elements. Thus 'put down' meaning 'kill' cannot be deduced from the meanings of 'put' + 'down'.

Polysemy

Words can have more than one meaning. A 'bull', for example can be a male animal, but a 'papal bull' is a proclamation.

Semantic features

Linguists also often deal with the phenomenon of semantic features. Thus 'man' and 'woman' share more features with each other than they do with 'filly':

man	woman	filly
+ noun	+ noun	+ noun
+ animate	+ animate	+ animate
+ human	+ human	− human
+ adult	+ adult	− adult
+ male	+ female	+ female

Synonymy

Different words appear to have essentially the same meaning:

beautiful/lovely
exterminate/kill
looking glass/mirror.

See also ANTONYM, IDIOM, SYNONYM

semi-

Semi- occurs very frequently as a PREFIX meaning 'half' or 'partially':

semicircle, semi-retired.

See also DEMI-, HEMI-

semicolon

A *semicolon* is a punctuation mark represented by a full stop over a comma (;). It is used to indicate a pause intermediate in length between a comma and a full stop.

He was tall and very strong; he was gentle and utterly reliable; he was the nicest human being I've ever met.

See also PUNCTUATION

Semitic

See HAMITIC/SEMITIC

send

Send is an irregular verb:

send(s), sent, sending
She sent me a postcard from Turkey.

Senegal

An inhabitant of the West African republic is a 'Senegalese'; the derived adjective is the same. The capital is Dakar.

senhor, señor, signor

These words all derive from Latin *senior*, 'an older man'. They are used as terms of address equivalent to 'Mr' in Portugal, Spain and Italy. The female terms are derived:

Portugal	Spain	Italy
senhora	señora	signora
senhorita	señorita	signorina

senior citizen

In an age when both common courtesy and POLITICAL CORRECTNESS demand that people of all ages, races and creeds should be treated with respect, some people worry about classifying a large section of the community on the grounds of whether or not they have retired from work.

In the past, this group of people was referred to as 'old-age pensioners' or 'pensioners' but these titles defined a large section of the community as people receiving money. In an attempt to give more respect, 'old-age pensioner' has partially given way to *senior citizen* and to other terms such as 'golden oldie' or 'woopy' (well off older person).

See also OAP

sensible, sensitive

These adjectives are occasionally confused. *Sensible* means 'gifted with common sense', 'practical':

We should put Mary in charge. She is the most sensible person in the group.

If we are going out walking then I'd better put on some sensible shoes.

Sensitive has a range of meanings from 'easily hurt':

Children's skins are particularly sensitive so they must not be exposed to direct sunlight.

through 'easily offended':

He's very sensitive about his accent. He feels it marks him out as a southerner.

and 'being perceptive':

Your essay shows a sensitive response to the language of Keats.

to 'needing to be treated with secrecy':

These documents are extremely sensitive. It would be disastrous if they were to fall into the wrong hands.

sensual, sensuous

These words both relate to the physical senses but they are markedly different in implication. *Sensual* applies to the pursuit of physical gratification, with particular reference to the sexual appetites. It contrasts with intellectual or spiritual pursuits and it is often carries an element of censure:

His sensual appetites, once aroused, gradually overcame his innate inhibitions.

Sensuous applies to qualities that appeal to the senses, particularly aesthetic qualities. It implies no censure:

The appeal of Keats's odes is often sensuous rather than intellectual.

sentence

No one has, as yet, provided, a completely satisfactory definition of a *sentence*. The simplest definition is that it is a structure that begins with a capital letter and ends with a full stop:

Yes.
On the contrary.
That's the one.

Linguists have spent a great deal of time and energy trying to offer a comprehensive description of *sentence* and have offered such definitions as:

A sentence is a grammatically independent unit that can express a statement, a command, a wish, an exclamation or a question.

Sentences can be subdivided in various ways. A major *sentence* contains a finite verb:

I'm going home.
Come over here, please.

whereas a minor *sentence* does not:

Going home.
Over here.

Minor sentences are common in advertising and are spoken with the same intonation pattern as major sentences. Minor sentences are sometimes called 'elliptical' or 'incomplete' because we can usually supply a word or group of words to convert it into a major sentence:

[I'm] Going home.
[Come] Over here.

Sentences can be used in statements:

I can drive now.
That's not very nice.

in questions:

Can you drive?
Is he not nice?

commands or imperatives:

Do your best.
Don't break my best cups.

and exclamations:

What a treasure!
You haven't lost again!

Sentences can be considered in terms of their syntactic simplicity. A simple sentence is one that contains only one verb phrase:

I like the country.
I have not been feeling well recently.

A compound sentence consists of two or more simple sentences joined by coordinating conjunctions such as 'and', 'but', 'or':

I like the country and I have always loved the food.
I have not been feeling well recently but I seem to be much better today.

A complex sentence consists of two or more clauses, one of which is syntactically more important that the other(s). In other words, in a complex sentence we have one or more dependent clauses:

I like the country because I was born here.
When she came in she could see that I had not been well.

A dependent clause is another name for a 'subordinate clause' and an 'embedded sentence'.

See also CLAUSE

sentence adverbs

Adverbs normally modify adjectives:

I'm <u>very</u> warm.

other adverbs:

He drove <u>very</u> erratically.

and verbs:

He drove <u>erratically</u>.

Some adverbs, however, function as sentence modifiers – that is, they modify an entire sentence rather than a word. Such adverbs are normally separated from the rest of the sentence by one comma, if the adverb comes at the beginning or end of the sentence, and by two commas if it occurs within the sentence:

<u>However,</u> we shall try to fulfil our promise.
We shall try to fulfil our promise, <u>however</u>.

We shall, <u>however</u>, try to fulfil our promise.

The list of sentence adverbs includes:

actually, fortunately, frankly, hence, however, moreover

and the set involving the suffixes '-fully', '-wise':

hopefully, thankfully, foodwise, timewise.

Many users dislike the second set of sentence modifiers.

See also ADVERB, HOPEFULLY

sentential, sentientious

These adjectives are often confused. *Sentential* means 'related to a sentence'. The sentential meaning is often different from the meanings of the individual words in the sentence. This is particularly true of idiomatic sentences. The meaning of 'It blew up' (i.e., exploded) cannot be deduced from the meanings of 'it' + 'blew' + 'up'.

The adjective *sentientious* tends to be used negatively. It suggests 'pompous judgements':

We don't want another sentientious speaker. This year, let's invite a good-natured, good-humoured speaker who will entertain us and not judge us.

See also IDIOM

sentiment, sentimentality

These nouns are often confused. *Sentiment* is positive. It suggests 'strong feelings allied to opinion':

This is a sentiment with which I can wholeheartedly agree.

The sentiments of shock and horror were shared by everyone who had witnessed the atrocity.

The noun *sentimentality* tends to have negative implications. It suggests 'false emotions and exaggerated feelings':

Many modern readers are put off by the sentimentality of the description of Little Nell's death. We should, however, remember that what we find sentimental was judged to be sensitive by the majority of Dickens's contemporary readers.

separate

Separate is one of the most frequently misspelled words in the language. It differs from 'desperate' in that there is 'a-r-a-t' in *sepa-r-a-te*. The word can function as an adjective or a regular verb:

separate tables

separate(s), separated, separating

We separated the wheat from the chaff.

septic

See SCEPTIC/SKEPTIC/SEPTIC

sepulchre, sepulcher

People rarely use the word *sepulchre*, which means 'a tomb', but it is often found in biblical language and in fixed phrases such as:

whited sepulchre

for a hypocrite. The British spelling ends in '-re'; the American spelling in '-er'.

seraph, serif

These nouns are pronounced alike but have different meanings and plurals. A *seraph* is one of the highest orders of angels. The correct plural is 'seraphim' but many people also use 'seraphs':

I wrote a story about a seraph once. Aisling was a bit like Superman in being able to fly.

A *serif* is a small line at the end of a stroke of a letter:

I prefer to select a typeface with serifs. I find the sanserif typeface a little too stark.

serf, surf

These nouns are homophones. In the past, a *serf* was an unfree land servant. If the lord of the manor sold his land, the serfs were sold with it. The word comes from *servus*, 'a slave', but serfs had more privileges than slaves:

There were serfs in parts of eastern Europe until the middle of the twentieth century.

Surf refers to the action of waves breaking or to the foam caused:

Matthew Arnold described surf as 'wild white horses foam[ing] and fret[ting]'.

sergeant

This noun refers to a non-commissioned army officer above the rank of corporal. The first syllable rhymes with 'barge' and not 'serge'. The term 'serjeant-at-arms', with a 'j', not a 'g', is occasionally used for an officer who performs ceremonial duties.

serial

See CEREAL/SERIAL

serial verb

Some languages, like English, can have several full verbs co-occurring in a sequence:

I wanted to go to try to finish my washing.

These chains are known as *serial verbs*.

See also PIDGIN AND CREOLE

series

A *series* is a number of things of similar kind, usually occurring one after the other:

We've had a series of disastrous polls. We must do something to change our ratings.

The plural is also *series*:

The Post Office issued three series of stamps last year.

serif
See SERAPH/SERIF

serve, service
These verbs are occasionally confused. *Serve* can mean 'work for someone else':

He served the family for thirty-six years.

'spend time in the armed forces':

He served in Germany and Bosnia.

'distribute food at a meal':

I served breakfasts and lunches for six months.

'deliver formally':

I was served with a summons.

and 'put the ball into play in tennis':

He served five aces in a row.

Service can mean 'maintain and repair a vehicle':

They have serviced my car since I bought it.

and 'pay interest on a loan':

we are not earning enough to service our debts.

serviceable
This adjective means 'able to be used':

My jacket is old but it's still perfectly serviceable.

Many people misspell this adjective by omitting the 'e' before '-able'. This 'e' is not optional.

serviette
Many people dislike the word *serviette*, preferring 'napkin':

I bought some lovely green serviettes for the party.

See also U AND NON-U

sett
A *sett*, with double 't', is the name of a badger's burrow. This noun is so frequently misspelled that the 'set' spelling may become standard.

settee
See COUCH/DIVAN/SETTEE/SOFA

sew, sow
These verbs are homophones. They both rhyme with 'go'. *Sew* is an irregular verb meaning 'join pieces of fabric together by means of stitches':

sew(s), sewed, sewing, sewn.

There is a tendency to regularize the past participle to 'sewed' although many people regard such usage as sloppy:

Have you sewn the buttons on my shirt yet?

Sow is also irregular and is being regularized in a similar way. *Sow* means 'scatter seeds in such a way that they will grow':

sow(s), sowed, sowing, sown (sowed)

Behold a sower went forth to sow, and as he sowed some seeds fell by the wayside ...

sewage, sewerage
These nouns are frequently misused. *Sewage* is waste matter that is carried away in sewers. The first syllable is pronounced 'sue':

There are some excellent schemes now to use sewage rather than simply dumping it.

Sewerage comprehends the network of sewers that carry sewage:

The major sewerage systems in England are still, basically, Victorian.

sexist language
Sexist language refers to sexual prejudice made overt in language. All societies have prejudices. Western society tends to associate female beauty with slimness whereas until recently Nigerian Igbos, for example, associated it with fatness.

Societies stereotype people, roles and relationships, often along sexist lines. In England, for example, many people unthinkingly subscribe to such stereotypes as:

- Women talk more than men.

- Women and men talk about different things, women discussing cooking, families, homes, men; men concentrating on business, sport, women and work.

- Women are more particular about their speech.

- Women use more intensifiers, such as 'absolutely', 'ever so' and 'quite' (as in 'quite interesting').

- Women are naturally good listeners.

- Men are good at keeping secrets.

- Women are poor drivers and know little about cars.

- Men are mechanically minded.

- Women choose cars for their shape and colour.

- Men choose cars for their size and mechanical performance.

- Girls are good at languages and subjects that depend on memory.

- Boys are better at mathematical and scientific subjects.

- Women are intuitive.

- Men are logical.

Some stereotypes contain an element of truth. British Telecom, for example, has considerable evidence that women talk much longer on the phone than men do, but most stereotypes are based on prejudice rather than fact.

Apart from such stereotypes, there are a number of ways in which users of English were linguistically conditioned along sexist lines although many expressions and attitudes have already been changed and continue to be changed.

Except for words that by definition refer to females ('girl', 'ewe') English speakers tended to define everyone as male. This is clear from expressions such as:

John Doe
the man on the street
Uncle Sam.

Unless they were prefixed by 'lady' or 'woman', many nouns were assumed to refer to men. These included:

beggar, doctor, poet, professor.

Patriarchal assumptions are reinforced by books and commentaries that refer to our 'forefathers' or 'early man'. The noun 'foremother' still does not exist. Women previously took, and frequently still take, their husband's surname and nationality after marriage, with the result that it is harder to trace the history of women.

Terms for women often reduce women in age, status or humanity:

babe, bird, broad, cheesecake, doll.

Men, too, are reduced but there are fewer male terms:

babe, beefcake, toyboy.

Verbs of attribution in novels can be sexist. Women often 'chatter' and 'scream' whereas men 'thunder' or 'roar'.

'He/his' are often used when 'he or she', 'his or her' are implied:

A writer must aim to engage his audience.
I'm sure everybody did his best.

See also EVERYBODY/EVERYONE, HE OR SHE, PREJUDICE, RACIST LANGUAGE

Seychelles

An inhabitant of the island republic in the Indian Ocean is a 'Seychellois'; the derived adjective is the same. The capital is Victoria.

shake

Shake is an irregular verb:

shake(s), shook, shaking, shaken
I was badly shaken by the news of the accident.

Shakespearean, Shakespearian

These spellings are both acceptable as adjectives derived from 'Shakespeare':

You will never appreciate how much powerful feeling can be carried in fourteen lines until you have read a Shakespearean sonnet.
Shakespearian English differs considerably from what we now classify as Standard English.

shall, will

Shall and *will* are modals that are used to express the future:

Shall I ask the neighbours to come round?
They will be leaving next Monday.

Traditional grammarians insisted that *shall* normally accompanies first-person subjects:

I shall come on Friday.
We shall go to France this year.

and *will* normally accompanies second- and third-person subjects:

You will find the keys in the left-hand drawer.
She will not be able to attend.
Will they be coming to Leeds?

The above rules are reversed for emphasis:

I will go to France and there is nothing you can do about it.
You shall not get permission!
They shall eat it or they will go hungry.

Today *will* is much more widely used for all persons, although *shall* remains a common choice in courteous questions such as:

Shall I close the window for you?

In colloquial statements, the form *'ll* is frequently used:

I'll do it later.
You'll get your death of cold.

and *won't* is more widely used than *shan't*:

We won't be able to buy much for £5.

See also AUXILIARY, MODALITY, SHOULD/WOULD

shammy

See CHAMOIS/SHAMMY

shampoo

Shampoo can function as a noun and a regular verb:

I'd like shampoos for dry hair and for normal hair, please.
shampoo(s), shampooed, shampooing
I've noticed quite a difference since I started shampooing with this new shampoo.

shard, sherd

These are alternative forms for fragments of pottery. The *shard* form is more widely used:

We spent the summer collecting shards from the newly unearthed Saxon settlement.

shave

Shave has become a regular verb:

shave(s), shaved, shaving

although 'shaven' is still occasionally used as a past participle:

The young monks have shaven their heads to remind them that they have turned away from the pleasures of the flesh.

In most current examples, 'shaved' is used as the past participle:

He hasn't shaved this morning.

and 'shaven' is used as an adjective:

clean-shaven
a shaven head.

See also DRINK, SINK/SANK/SUNK

she

See HE OR SHE

sheaf

A *sheaf* is a bundle of corn or a bundle of objects tied together. The plural is 'sheaves':

The corn used to be reaped, tied in sheaves and taken to be threshed.

shear

Shear is a verb that is in the process of being regularized:

shear(s), sheared, shearing, sheared/shorn
We sheared fifty sheep yesterday.

When *shear* is used to mean 'remove fleece', it is still possible to use 'shorn' as the past participle:

Have all the sheep been shorn now?

although 'sheared' is also used:

Have all the sheep been sheared now?

but when *shear* means 'break off, fracture' as in:

The extra tension has caused the head to shear off.

then 'shorn' cannot be used.

'Shorn' is regularly used as an adjective, especially in the fixed phrase:

a shorn lamb.

shears

Shears is a plural noun referring to very large scissors:

The shears are in the toolshed if you'd like to trim the hedge.

As with 'scissors' and 'trousers', *shears* is often prefaced by 'a pair of':

Have you got a pair of shears that I could borrow?

sheath, sheathe

These words are related in meaning but distinguished in pronunciation and function. *Sheath* is a noun rhyming with 'heath'. It means a cover or case for a sharp instrument:

Has anyone seen the sheath for my scout knife?

Sheathe is a verb rhyming with 'seethe'. It means 'cover with a sheath':

That sharp knife should be sheathed immediately.

These words are part of a set where the noun ends

in '-th' and the verb in '-the'. The best known of these are:

Noun	Verb
breath	breathe
teeth	teethe
wreath	wreathe

sheikh

This noun was popularized with the success of the Rudolph Valentino films. In the 1920s the BBC took the decision to pronounce it as a homophone of 'shake' not of 'chic' and, although both pronunciations are still heard, the one rhyming with 'take' is still regarded as the more acceptable. The variant spelling *sheik* is acceptable but not as widely used as *sheikh*.

shelf

The plural of *shelf* is 'shelves' and the related regular verb is 'shelve':

Put the novel on the top shelf.
shelve(s), shelved, shelving
I've shelved that project for the time being.

sherd

See SHARD/SHERD

sheriff

Sheriff is often misspelled. It has one 'r' and ends in '-iff' like 'bailiff', 'mastiff' and 'pontiff'. In Britain a *sheriff* is a county representative of the Crown. In the United States of America a *sheriff* is a law enforcement officer.

Most people learn about sheriffs from films about the Wild West.

shew, show

In the past, *shew* was an acceptable alternative spelling of *show*:

shew(s), shewed, shewing, shewn
show(s), showed, showing, shown
We haven't been shown the evidence yet.

Now, the '-ew-' forms are archaic.

shibboleth

The noun *shibboleth* derives from a Hebrew word meaning 'ear of grain'. According to the Book of Judges xii:5ff., the Gileadites tested people to find out if they were Ephraimites:

Then said they unto him, Say now Shibboleth: and he said Sibboleth: for he could not frame to pronounce it right.

Then they took him, and slew him at the passages of Jordan: and there fell at that time of the Ephraimites forty and two thousand.

Today, *shibboleth* refers to a practice, often a linguistic practice, that is regarded as marking one group out from another. Thus, the pronunciation of the eighth letter of the alphabet is a *shibboleth* in Northern Ireland, where Catholics tend to say 'haitch' and Protestants 'aitch'; the rolled 'r' in the pronunciation of 'bairn' and 'burn' usually denotes speakers from Scotland; the identical pronunciation of 'chatted' and 'chattered' suggests that the speaker is Australian or South African; and the use of 'railway' or 'railroad' could be enough to distinguish a British speaker from an American.

shine

The irregular verb *shine* means 'emit a light' or 'direct the light of a torch or lamp':

shine(s), shone, shining, shone
He shone the light in my face.

In British English, *shone* rhymes with 'gone'; in American English, it rhymes with 'bone' and is a homophone of 'shown'.

Some speakers use *shine* as a regular verb when it means 'polish until shining':

He shined all the shoes on a Saturday night.
but many careful speakers object to such usage.

shingles

Shingles, like other diseases such as 'measles' and 'mumps', looks like a plural but functions as a singular noun:

Shingles is related to chickenpox but is usually much more severe than the childhood illness.

ship

See BOAT/SHIP

ship's name

The usual convention in printed texts is for ships' names to be italicized:

I travelled on the *Queen Elizabeth II*.
Darwin's ship was the *Beagle*.

See also PUNCTUATION

shoe

Shoe can function as a noun and an irregular verb:

I bought three pairs of shoes last week.
shoe(s), shod, shoeing
The horses were shod recently.

shoot

See CHUTE/SHOOT

should, would

The traditional rule was that *would* is the normal choice of conditional modal after all but first-person subjects. *Should* is the normal choice for first-person subjects:

I should go if I had the money.

We should go if we had the money.
He would go if he had the money.
They would go if they had the money.

In other words, *would* and *should* were thought of as the conditional equivalents of 'will' and 'shall':

I shall go if I have enough money.
You will go if you have enough money.
She will go if she has enough money.

Traditionally, too, when direct speech was turned into reported speech, *would* replaced 'will' and *should* replaced 'shall':

'We shall go home at noon,' he suggested.
He suggested that we should go home at noon.

Today, 'would' is used as a general marker of the conditional:

I would go if I could.

and *should* is regularly used with all subjects to mean 'ought to, must':

You should work a bit harder.
She should train more regularly.
I should write home once a week.

Should is also used with 'I' to suggest that one is being tentative:

I should think so but I'm not certain.
I shouldn't have thought so myself but you may have more of the facts.

See also MODALITY, SHALL/WILL, VERB

shovel

Shovel can function as a noun meaning 'an implement like a spade' and as a regular verb:

We need a shovel to get rid of all this snow.
UK: shovel(s), shovelled, shovelling
US: shovel(s), shoveled, shoveling.

show

See SHEW/SHOW

shrewd

Shrewd is an excellent example of SEMANTIC CHANGE. This adjective is related to 'shrew' and used to mean 'spiteful'. Nowadays, its link with 'shrew' is virtually unknown and the adjective has the positive meanings of 'astute', 'showing good judgement':

He's a shrewd politician.

shrink

Shrink is an irregular verb meaning 'get smaller':

UK: shrink(s), shrank, shrinking, shrunk
US: shrink(s), shrunk, shrinking, shrunk
My thermals shrank in the wash. Now, they would fit a doll.

The American film *Honey, I shrunk the kids* has encouraged the use of 'shrunk' as a past tense form but this is still not widespread in Standard British English.

See also SINK/SANK/SUNK

shrivel

Shrivel is a regular verb that means 'become dry and wrinkled'. It regularly collocates with 'up':

The apples were all shrivelled up.
UK: shrivel(s), shrivelled, shrivelling
US: shrivel(s), shriveled, shriveling.

shut

See CLOSE/SHUT

shy

Shy can function as an adjective meaning 'bashful':

shy, shyer/shier, shyest/shiest
She is the shyest person I have ever met.

as a noun meaning 'throw, at a fair':

I won a coconut at the coconut shy.

and as a verb meaning 'move suddenly':

shy(shies), shied, shying
The horse shied away from the snake.

sibling

The term *sibling* was revived in the nineteenth century to refer to a person's brother or sister where the specification of gender is not significant. *Sibling* comes from Old English *sib*, 'relative', + *ling*, 'relative'. The diminutive '-ling' used to be an active suffix and still occurs in words such as 'duckling' and 'darling':

I have two siblings, a sister and a brother.
My parents' siblings are all still alive.

sic

Sic is Latin and means 'so', 'thus'. It is normally inserted in brackets in a printed text to indicate that an odd, incorrect or questionable form has been quoted correctly:

Tomorrow to fresh fields [sic], and pastures new.

The above is a popular misquotation. Written as above, *sic* draws attention to the fact that the writer is quoting an incorrect form. John Milton actually wrote 'fresh woods', not 'fresh fields'.

sick

See ILL/SICK

siege

This word is frequently misspelled although it follows the rule 'i' before 'e' except after 'c':

The city was under siege for three months.

See also SPELLING

Sierra Leone

An inhabitant of the West African republic is a 'Sierra Leonean'; the derived adjective is the same. The capital is Freetown.

sight

See CITE/SIGHT/SITE

signal

Signal can function as a noun and a regular verb and, as with many verbs ending in 'l', there is a difference in spelling between British and American norms:

Lowering the blinds was a signal meaning that the house was in mourning.
UK: signal(s), signalled, signalling
US: signal(s), signaled, signaling.

significant

Significant is an adjective whose meaning has been weakened by overuse. It is related to 'sign' and used to suggest 'full of meaning':

His comment was infinitely more significant than any of us realized.

It has recently become a synonym of 'big', 'important':

The football match was won by a significant margin.

signor

See SENHOR/SEÑOR/SIGNOR

silhouette

This noun is frequently misspelled. It refers to a picture in solid black or, by extension, a shadow, and derives from the surname of Etienne de Silhouette (1709–67). The 'h' is not pronounced.

silicon, silicone

These nouns are often confused. *Silicon* is a chemical element that combines freely with oxygen and is found in quartz. It is used to make microchips or *silicon* chips.

Silicone is the general term for certain chemical compounds of *silicon* that are used in plastics and paints:

His research is into the amount of information that can be stored on a silicon chip.
She thought about having silicone implants but then worried about the possible side-effects.

simile

The noun *simile* comes from Latin *similis*, 'like'. In English, a *simile* is a figure of speech that overtly expresses a likeness between two beings, objects or ideas:

She's like a tornado.
He's as tall as a tree.

The comparison usually involves the words 'as' or 'like' and often combines unequal partners, such as 'human' + 'inanimate':

She's as deaf as a post.

or 'human' + 'animate':

He's as sick as a parrot.

There are regional preferences in similes. In the north of England, for example, a foolish person might be described as being:

as daft as a brush

whereas an Australian might use:

as awkward as a pig with a prayerbook.

Similes are common in colloquial speech where they are often fixed:

as good as gold
run like the wind

and in poetry, where originality is prized:

My love is like a melody …
    Robert Burns

Like flies to wanton boys are we to the gods …
    William Shakespeare

If the comparison is implicit rather than overt, it is called a METAPHOR. Thus:

She sang like a bird.

is a simile, whereas:

She warbled.

is a metaphor.

See also FIGURE OF SPEECH

simplistic

The adjective *simplistic* means 'oversimplified', 'naïve' and it tends to be used negatively:

Your solution is too simplistic. It does not take all the necessary factors into account.

Care should be taken with *simplistic* because it has been overused in the media as an emphatic form of 'simple':

What we provide is a simplistic description of how the currency markets work.

simply

The adverb *simply* can occasionally lead to ambiguity. Its main meaning now is 'merely':

I simply said that I didn't want to go.

but it can still be used to mean 'plainly, in a straightforward manner':

He described the event simply and clearly.

Simply is used frequently in colloquial speech as an intensifier meaning 'absolutely':

She was simply stunning.

simultaneous

Simultaneous is an adjective meaning 'happening at the same time':

They put on simultaneous performances in London and New York.

British speakers tend to rhyme the first syllable with 'Tim' whereas many Americans rhyme it with 'time'.

since

Since can be used as an adverb:

I came to Leeds in 1988 and I've lived here ever since.

as a subordinating conjunction, implying time, cause or reason:

I have trained as a musician since I was six.
I knew that, since you were exhausted, you needed to rest.

and as a preposition:

I have been on vacation since the beginning of May.

In all uses of *since* except for those where it means 'because', *since* involves looking at a specific point of time in the past.

Since sometimes causes problems when it is used as a subordinating conjunction because speakers are unsure about the verbs that co-occur with it. The rules are as follows.

- *Since* is followed by the simple past when the verb in the main clause is in the present perfect:

I have loved Scotland since I read Robbie Burns.
*I have loved Scotland since I have read Robbie Burns.

- *Since* is followed by the simple past when the verb in the main clause is in the past perfect:

We had worked in the mill since it opened.
*We had worked in the mill since it had opened.

- *Since* can co-occur with the present tense and the past tense in the pattern 'It is/was + length of time + since':

It's ten years since we bought the house.
It's a long time since we heard from Robert.
It was six months since I had seen him.
It had been a long time since we had seen him.

- *Since* does not normally co-occur with a negative:

*It's ten years since we hadn't seen them.

See also AGO/SINCE, AS/BECAUSE/FOR/SINCE

sine qua non

The Latin phrase *sine qua non*, 'without which not', tends to be used in formal contexts to denote an essential condition or feature:

A willingness to take risks for peace is the *sine qua non* of all successful negotiations.

There is a range of possible pronunciations. *Sine* may rhyme with 'see May' or 'cine-(camera)'; the *qua* may rhyme with 'bah' or 'bay' and the 'non' may rhyme with 'shone' or 'shown'.

sing

Sing is an irregular verb:

sing(s), sang, singing, sung.

Although the form 'sung' is occasionally used as a past tense form in such sentences as:

*He sung his heart out.

it is only acceptable as a past participle in structures such as:

He has already sung in Paris and Milan.

He had sung in all the main opera houses by the time he was thirty.

Singapore

An inhabitant of the island republic is a 'Singaporean'; the derived adjective is the same. The capital is Singapore (occasionally known as Singapore City to distinguish it from the republic).

singe

Singe is a regular verb meaning 'scorch':

singe(s), singed, singeing

I've singed my blouse. The iron was too hot.

It is important to remember that the present participle 'singeing' has an 'e'.

singular and plural

In theory, the concept of *singular and plural* is easy to understand. It can be applied to anything that is countable. An individual entity is singular; two or more together are plural.

The majority of English nouns form their plurals by adding 's':

bat, bats

dog, dogs

horse, horses

and we can offer rules to explain why 'fly' becomes 'flies' and 'monkey' becomes 'monkeys'. In addition to these regular nouns, we have a number of irregular nouns in English. These fall into three categories.

■ Nouns that form their plurals by a change of vowel:

foot, feet

man, men

mouse, mice

■ Relics of older plurals, some only used in regional dialects:

child, children (double plural 'child' + er + en)

cow, kine

shoe, shoon

■ Plurals borrowed from other languages:

cherub, cherubim

ellipsis, ellipses

formula, formulae

index, indices

phenomenon, phenomena

plateau, plateaux.

In English, pronouns can also be singular or plural:

I, we

you, you

he/she/it, they

that, those

this, these.

In theory, this pattern is very clear, but there are complications.

Many nouns can be singular in form but plural in meaning:

a brace, a couple, a dozen

a class, a group, a team.

Some 'noun + noun' phrases are treated like singulars:

Fish and chips is my favourite food.

Law and order is high on the contemporary political agenda.

In spoken English, people often use singular nouns in measurements or amounts of money:

He's six foot tall.

That's five pound twenty.

Many nouns ending in '-s' are treated as singular. This is especially true of the names of games, illnesses and certain academic subjects:

Draughts is good fun.

Measles is not so bad, if you catch it as a child.

Linguistics is the scientific study of language.

See also PLURAL

sink, sank, sunk

Sink is an irregular verb meaning 'go below the surface of the water'. It has *sank* as a past tense form and *sunk* as a past participle:

sink(s), sank, sinking, sunk

The model boat sank, leaving only a row of bubbles behind it.

The *Titanic* sank in under an hour.

We have sunk our differences.

Many people now use *sunk* as a past tense form and many dictionaries claim that:

The ship sunk.

is acceptable. Careful writers and speakers continue to maintain the distinction, but the likelihood is that *sunk* will soon be more widely used than *sank* as a past tense form.

This verb has been unstable for some time. The earlier forms were:

sink, sank, sinking, sunken

but 'sunken' is now used as an adjective:

We used to dream of finding sunken treasure.

See also SHRINK

siphon, syphon

These are both acceptable spellings for the noun and verb associated with drawing off liquid:

We bought a new soda siphon.

They siphoned the petrol out of our car while it was parked outside the restaurant.

-sis, -ses

Nouns ending in *-sis* usually form their plurals by changing *-sis* to *-ses*:

diagnosis, diagnoses

emphasis, emphases

thesis, theses.

sit, sat, sitting

Sit is an irregular verb:

sit(s), sat, sitting

We were sitting in the garden when they rang.

Many people are uncertain about when to use *sat* and *sitting* and yet the rules are very simple. *Sat* is the past participle of 'sit' and can be used only after the auxiliary 'have':

I have sat here long enough.

She has sat outside my office for weeks.

and, rarely, in a passive construction:

He was taken into the room and sat (i.e., made to sit) in a corner.

Sitting is the present participle and follows the auxiliary 'be' when this indicates continuous action:

I've been sitting here for two hours.

The regional variant:

*I've been sat here for two hours.

is not acceptable in Standard English.

See also AUXILIARY

site

See CITE/SIGHT/SITE

sitting room

In British English social class can sometimes be revealed by the terms used for meals or for rooms. Some people use *sitting room* for the room in which they relax or entertain guests; others use LOUNGE; and a few still use the term PARLOUR.

See also LIVING ROOM, U AND NON-U

situate

Situate is sometimes used in descriptions of houses where 'situated' would be more correct:

*The house, situate in extensive gardens, is close to schools, churches and shops.

This is a form of affectation, possibly derived from legalese, and used to make the advertised house sound more imposing.

situation

Situation has become disliked as a buzz word because of its overuse:

a no-win situation

a war situation.

There is nothing intrinsically wrong with words such as 'charisma', 'important', 'nice' and 'situation', but overuse means they are drained of meaning and so an alternative should be sought.

sixth

The number *sixth* and its plural 'sixths' involve complex consonant clusters, which are often simplified in speech. Careful users invariably pronounce the cluster in its entirety.

See also CONSONANT CLUSTER

sizeable, sizable

These are alternative spellings for this adjective meaning 'quite extensive':

She has sizeable estates in several countries.

See also -ABLE/-IBLE

skeptic

See SCEPTIC/SKEPTIC/SEPTIC

ski

The 'sk' in *ski* is now regularly pronounced like the beginning of 'skin'. The once acceptable pronunciation where 'sk' was pronounced like 'sh' in 'shin' is now regarded as old-fashioned or affected.

When *ski* is used as a verb, it has the following forms:

ski(s), skied/ski'd, skiing

where the past tense and the past participle may be either 'skied' or 'ski'd'. The 'ski'd' form has the merit of avoiding confusion in that 'skied' is a form of 'sky' as in 'grey-skied'.

skilful, skillful

This adjective means 'possessing an ability':

She's wonderfully skilful at avoiding awkward topics.

In Britain, the normal spelling ends in '-ful' but most Americans prefer '-full'.

skull

See SCULL/SKILL

slander

See LIBEL/SLANDER

slang

We are not certain of the etymology of the word *slang*, although we know that the term was first used in the eighteenth century. *Slang* refers to words and phrases peculiar to a particular group and is often regarded as nonstandard and inferior. There are two main types of slang: *slang* that is relatively ephemeral:

fab (fabulous)

pillshooter (doctor)

and *slang* that has existed for centuries:

booze (alcohol)

moll (from Molly).

Slang can be witty and expressive but it is usually regarded as inappropriate in writing and in formal speech.

The main subvarieties of slang are abbreviations:

pop (popular)

back slang:

yob (boy)

borrowings:

kushti (Romani = fine, okay)

coinages:

thingamajig

compounds:

bigshot

euphemisms:

drat!

phrases or sentences:

on the razzle; hit the trail

rhymes:

to hobnob; nitty gritty

and Cockney/RHYMING SLANG:

boracic (lint) = skint; dicky (bird) = word.

See also COLLOQUIAL ENGLISH, JARGON

slay
Slay is an irregular verb that is now regarded as somewhat archaic:

slay(s), slew, slaying, slain

He slew them with the jawbone of an ass.

sled, sledge, sleigh
These words are regional variants for a snow vehicle on runners rather than on wheels. *Sled* is more widely used in America whereas *sledge* is preferred by many in England, and *sleigh* is increasingly reserved for Santa Claus:

Rudolph, with your nose so bright
Won't you guide my sleigh tonight?

sleep
Sleep can function as a noun and as an irregular verb:

I had a lovely sleep last night.

sleep(s), slept, sleeping

Have you ever slept in the open?

sleight, slight
These words are often homophones. *Sleight* is rarely used except in the fixed phrase:

sleight of hand

referring to the manual dexterity necessary to perform conjuring tricks. It can be rhymed with 'light' or, less frequently, 'late'.

A *slight* suggests an act indicating neglect or indifference:

It's not easy to overlook calculated slights. They are both hurtful and offensive.

slide
Slide can function as a noun and as an irregular verb:

We built a slide for the children.

slide(s), slid, sliding

We slid quietly into our places, hoping that she wouldn't notice we were late.

sling
Sling has two main meanings, 'throw' and 'put into a sling'. *Sling* meaning 'throw' is irregular:

sling(s), slung, slinging

He slung the bag quickly and carelessly through the window.

When *sling* is used to mean 'put into a sling', it is sometimes regularized:

We slinged the load to the lorry.

but, since many speakers would regard this as incorrect, it is probably wiser to write something like:

We used a sling to load the lorry.

slink
Slink is an irregular verb:

slink(s), slunk, slinking

He slunk out of the house when we weren't watching.

slough
This word is not now widely used except in two well-defined circumstances. It occurs in the phrase:

the slough of despond

meaning 'in a state of dejection and depression'. In this context, it rhymes with 'now'.

When *slough* is used to mean 'shed a skin':

Snakes slough their skins once a year.

it rhymes with 'rough'.

Slovak Republic
An inhabitant of the European republic is a 'Slovak'; the derived adjective is 'Slovakian'. The capital is Bratislava.

Slovenia

An inhabitant of the country in south central Europe is a 'Slovene'; the derived adjective is 'Slovenian'. The capital is Ljubljana.

slow, slowly

In colloquial speech, many speakers use *slow* as both adjective and adverb:

I'm a slow starter.
Drive slow when you get to the school.

In formal contexts, however, the adverb is *slowly*:

Drive slowly when you get to the school.

See also ADJECTIVE, ADVERB

sly

Sly keeps the 'y' when suffices are added:

slyer, slyest, slyly.

smear

Smear is now widely used with two distinct meanings. In the phrases:

cervical smear, smear test

it refers to a secretion placed on one side of a glass for analysis under a microscope.

It is also widely used in popular headlines as a shorthand equivalent of 'defamatory remarks':

NO SMEARS NO COVER UPS.

smell

Smell can function as a regular verb:

smells(s), smelled/smelt, smelling, smelt.

In Britain, 'smelt' is perfectly acceptable as a past tense form and is more widespread than 'smelled'. The 'smelled' form is the acceptable one in America.

When *smell* functions in a neutral sense of 'emit an odour', it is followed by the adjective form:

This perfume smells sweet.
The food smells wonderful.

When it means 'emit an obnoxious odour', the adverbial form is sometimes used:

The H_2S experiment smells foully.

although, in speech, the adjective is more likely:

The H_2S experiment smells foul.

See also ADJECTIVE, ADVERB, -ED/-T

smite

Smite is a little-used, irregular verb:

smite(s), smote, smiting, smitten
He smote the enemies of the Lord.

It is currently found most frequently in the sense of 'infatuated':

He's badly smitten – a case of love at first sight.

smoky, smokey

Smoky is an adjective meaning 'emitting excessive smoke':

She should not have to work in a smoky atmosphere.

The comparative and superlative forms are 'smokier' and 'smokiest':

I have never worked in a smokier environment.

Although *smoky* is the standard spelling, 'smokey' is also found, partly because the spelling rules for turning a noun or verb ending in 'e' into a '-y' adjective are not absolutely fixed:

cage: cagey or cagy
edge: edgy
poke: poky or pokey.

See also SPELLING

smooth

Smooth can function as an adjective:

The wood had been planed and was so smooth it felt like silk.

and as a verb:

His parents won't always be there to smooth his path for him.

The verb is frequently misspelled and given an 'e' by analogy with:

breath, breathe

but, with *smooth*, the analogy does not work.

smoulder, smolder

Smoulder is a regular verb meaning 'burn slowly without flame':

The fire smouldered for a further week but it was now a spent force and was no longer a cause of worry.

The verb is often used metaphorically to mean 'have strong feelings that have been hidden':

His anger smouldered for years as he served in the house that was rightfully his.

The American spelling is *smolder*:

UK: smoulder(s), smouldered, smouldering
US: smolder(s), smoldered, smoldering.

so

So has a variety of uses. It can occur as an intensifying adverb:

I was so tired I couldn't keep my eyes open.

and as a conjunction that can be prefaced by 'and':

It was raining (and) so we decided to stay at home.

So co-occurs with 'that' to introduce clauses of purpose:

She worked at night so that she could spend the days with her children.

So can be used as a colloquial sentence modifier:

So off he went!

So here we are!

It can occur in spoken questions to belittle a statement:

He's the cleverest person in the group.
So? (So what?)

So can function as a verb phrase substitute when combined with 'do':

She wanted to travel in India although to do so meant putting off university for a year.

and with verbs such as 'hope' and 'think' as a clause substitute:

Will they be pleased to see you?
I hope so.

So combines with '-and-so' to form a noun phrase substitute for an expletive:

If I catch the so-and-so who did this, I won't be responsible for my actions!

and *so* is reduplicated to mean 'not very well':

How are you feeling today?
Oh, just so-so.

See also SUCH

so-called

The adjective *so-called* tends to call into question the noun that follows:

We have learned to distinguish between real friends and so-called friends.

He was my so-called supporter but he did my campaign more harm than good.

sociable, social

These adjectives are occasionally misused. *Sociable* means 'affable, friendly':

She's a very sociable young woman, well adjusted and good natured.

Social means 'pertaining to society' or 'consisting of friendly groups':

She's a social worker.
He goes to his social club every Wednesday.

sociolinguistics

Sociolinguistics is a subdivision of linguistics and a discipline that concentrates on the study of language in society. Sociolinguists examine how and why people use particular forms of language in their interactions with others.

sofa

See COUCH/DIVAN/SETTEE/SOFA

soirée

A *soirée* (with or without the acute accent) is an evening party or social gathering, often to listen to music:

They held a soirée every Thursday. Georgina played the piano, Dora the cello and Agnes the violin.

solecism

A *solecism* is the term used to describe incorrect usage in grammar or idiom, whether in speech or in writing:

*They invited Peter and I to lunch. (Peter and me)
*I was just stood there waiting. (standing)

The term has been extended to refer to breaches of social etiquette:

It is something of a solecism to light a cigarette in someone's home without first asking for permission to smoke.

solidus

A solidus is a short oblique stroke used to separate items:

I should be grateful if copies could be sent to Dr Smith and/or Dr Jones.
16/x/1998

The plural of *solidus* is 'solidi' and it is also called a 'diagonal', a 'slash', a 'stroke' and a 'virgule'.

See also PUNCTUATION

Solomon Islands

An inhabitant of the nation in the southwestern Pacific is a 'Solomon Islander'; the derived adjective is 'Solomon Island'. The capital is Honiara.

Somalia

An inhabitant of the republic in northeast Africa is a 'Somali'; the derived adjective is either 'Somali' or 'Somalian'. The capital is Mogadishu.

sombre, somber

These are variant spellings of the adjective meaning 'gloomy', 'dark'. *Sombre* is the English variant and *somber* the American:

He's so pessimistic! Even at his brightest, he takes a sombre view of people and their behaviour.

some, -some

Some can function as a determiner:

I'd like some cheese, please.

as a pronoun:

Some like to sing while others do aerobics.

and, in certain idiolects, as an adverb:

I like her some, but not a lot.

The SUFFIX *-some* can be used to form adjectives:

awe + some = awesome
tire + some = tiresome

and it can be added to simple numbers to indicate a group of that size:

two + some = twosome
four + some = foursome.

When *some* is used as a determiner, it tends to suggest an unspecified amount. There is a growing tendency, however, for journalists to use *some* to mean 'almost exactly':

She lives some four miles from the nearest town.

See also DETERMINER, PRONOUN

some time, sometime

Although these were once identical in meaning, they have become differentiated and the use or non-use of a space allows us to make a useful distinction. *Sometime* is used occasionally as an adjective meaning 'former':

He's dancing with his sometime fiancée.

and frequently used as an adverb meaning 'at an unspecified time':

I'll call in to see you sometime.

The plural 'sometimes' means 'now and then, occasionally':

Sometimes I go to the cinema or the theatre.

Some time means 'a period of time':

He'll need some time to adjust to the tragedy.

In the spoken medium the two are differentiated by stress. *Sometime* has one main stress on the 'some'; *some time* has two equal stresses.

somebody, someone

The compounds *somebody* and *someone* mean 'a particular individual' and are interchangeable in all contexts:

Somebody has stolen my car!

They both trigger off the use of a singular verb:

Somebody/someone is watching over me!

and, in the past, they were followed by the singular possessive 'his' in such sentences as:

Somebody has left his notes in my desk.

There is a tendency now to replace the 'his' with 'their' or with 'his/her':

Somebody has left their notes in my desk.
Somebody has left his/her notes in my desk.

or the sentence is restructured so that a possessive adjective is unnecessary:

I've found somebody's notes in my desk.

See also GENDER, SEXIST LANGUAGE

somersault

This word is frequently misspelled. It is a homophone of 'summer salt'. The spelling 'summersalt' is so widely used that some dictionaries offer it as an acceptable alternative:

He turned two somersaults when he heard how good his results were.

sonar

Sonar is an abbreviation of:

so(und) na(vigation) r(anging)

The submarine's sonar was not working.

sooner

Sooner can function as an adverb in such expressions as:

No sooner had I closed the paint tin and washed the brush than I noticed a spot that I had missed.

In this context, we have 'no *sooner* ... than' and not 'no *sooner* ... when'.

See also BARELY/HARDLY/SCARCELY

sophisticated

When the adjective *sophisticated* is applied to people, it usually means 'having refined, cultured tastes':

She's a highly sophisticated young woman.

although it sometimes carries overtones of snobbery:

He likes to think he's sophisticated but he's merely pretentious.

When applied to machines or computer technology, *sophisticated* can mean 'advanced, complex':

It was a sophisticated new engine.

sort

See KIND/SORT/TYPE

sort of

See KIND OF/SORT OF

soufflé(e)

A *soufflé(e)* is an egg dish. It is stressed on the first syllable in British English and on the second in American English:

Isabelle said that a soufflée is a bachelor's standby because it is so easy to make.

sound symbolism

Every language seems to have a set of words where there seems to be a direct link between the sound and the meaning. Such a link is known as *onomatopoeia* or *sound symbolism*. In English, for example, words such as:

bang, crash, thump, wallop

can suggest the noise of one item colliding with another and:

cuckoo

imitates the sound the bird makes.

The term *sound symbolism* also includes the less well-known fact that certain sounds are regularly associated with certain meanings. Many words beginning with 'fl-' and 'gl-' suggest light and movement:

flash, flicker, flow, gleam, glitter, glow

and words beginning with 'sl-' are often unpleasant:

slam, slime, slump.

See also ONOMATOPOEIA, SYNAESTHESIA

soupçon

This word is used in English to mean 'a trace'. It tends to be pronounced in the French way with a nasalized 'o' in the second syllable:

I think I'd like just a soupçon of salt.

Many people regard the use of such borrowings as precious or pedantic.

source

The word *source* meaning 'informant' has been popularized by journalists as a means of quoting claims without having to mention names:

A source close to the Prime Minister has indicated that he is furious with the squabblers.

south, South, southern, Southern

People are often uncertain about when to use capital letters on these words. When *south* represents a simple direction or compass point, it is not capitalized:

We went south for the winter.
The cardinal points are north, south, east and west.

When *south* is part of a name, it is capitalized:

South Africa
South America
the South Pole.

The word *southern* is less specific than *south*:

They are travelling in southern Africa.

It is capitalized when it is part of a name:

the Southern Cross.

See also COMPASS DIRECTIONS

South Africa

An inhabitant of the country is a 'South African'; the derived adjective is the same. The seat of legislature is Cape Town; the seat of government is Pretoria.

sow

See SEW/SOW

spacious, specious

These adjectives are occasionally confused. *Spacious* derives from 'space' and means 'roomy':

What I'd really love is a beautifully fitted, spacious kitchen.

Specious is an adjective meaning 'apparently right but actually false':

His argument was specious but it convinced many of his listeners.

Spain

An inhabitant of the European country is a 'Spaniard'; the derived adjective is 'Spanish'. The capital is Madrid.

speak

Speak is an irregular verb:

speak(s), spoke, speaking, spoken
I have spoken to him twice this week.

-speak

Recently, *-speak* has been used as a suffix to indicate a variety of English. Among the compounds recorded are:

computerspeak, DOUBLESPEAK, mediaspeak, NEWSPEAK, SEASPEAK, technospeak.

spearhead

Spearhead has been popularized by the popular press with the meaning of 'lead':

The thinktank will be spearheaded by John Jones.

Like all overused words, *spearhead* should be avoided in formal contexts.

See also CLICHÉ

special

See ESPECIAL/SPECIAL

speciality, specialty

These nouns are regionally marked, *speciality* being the preferred form in Britain. A *speciality* can refer to a special interest or skill:

I'm a linguist but usage is my speciality.

a product or service specialized in:

Short-run printing is their speciality.

and a renowned dish at a restaurant:

Irish Stew is today's speciality.

Americans prefer the form *specialty* and this form is gaining in use in Britain.

specie, species

The noun *specie*, pronounced to rhyme with 'wee she', means 'coin money' and comes from the Latin phrase *in specie*, 'in kind':

The kidnappers wanted the money in specie to prevent its being traced.

Specie is rarely used now.

Species has the same form for singular and plural. *Species* rhymes with 'leash ease':

Each one of the groups into which a genus is divided is called a species.
It is rare for members of different species to breed successfully.

specious

See SPACIOUS/SPECIOUS

spectre, specter

A *spectre* is an apparition, ghost or phantom:

I don't know what it was. It was a thin, spectre-like thing!

Americans prefer to use the *specter* spelling.

spectrum

The noun *spectrum* has been popularized by the press in its meaning of 'range':

This programme represents the entire spectrum of human relationships.

speculate

Speculate can function both transitively and intransitively. The transitive verb means 'conjecture':

We speculated that David was about to be promoted.

The intransitive verb usually means 'buy or sell in the hope of large profits':

He speculated on property when prices were low and made a fortune when they went up.

speech and writing

Many people equate 'language' with *speech* but this equation is invalid. Language is an abstract system that can be realized in a variety of mediums, including signs, *speech* and *writing*. The varieties we use for speech are not always appropriate for writing and vice versa. *Speech and writing* differ in a number of ways and these differences can be summarized as follows:

Speech	Writing
acquired effortlessly	acquired with effort
addressee usually present	addressee usually absent
involves sound	involves marks on a surface
marked by hesitations,slips	marked by punctuation, syntactically smoother
message aided by gesture	message made explicit
organized in time	organized in space
perceived by ear	perceived by eye
produced by vocal organs	produced by hand + tool
usually spontaneous	usually prepared
usually transitory	usually more permanent

Speech is the primary medium in the sense that it is acquired first and apparently without effort. It is also the most frequently used medium. *Writing* develops when speech is no longer adequate to fulfil all the linguistic needs of a society. *Writing* allows easier and wider dissemination of knowledge and ideas.

See also FILLER

speed

Speed can function as a noun:

Kill speed. Save children.

and as a verb:

speed(s), sped/speeded, speeding, sped/speeded.

The verb was originally irregular but is being regularized. In theory, it is correct to say:

He sped round the corner.

but most users now probably say:

He speeded round the corner.

See also VERB

spell

Spell has two acceptable past tense and past participle forms:

spell(s), spelled/spelt, spelling, spelled/spelt.

The '-ed' forms are more acceptable than the '-t' forms in America.

See also -ED/-T

spelling

Spelling involves the forming of words with letters according to convention and accepted usage. Many people have commented on the fact that English spelling is often irregular. 'Pair', 'pare' and 'pear', for example, are spelled differently but pronounced the same; 'beat' and 'great' have the same ending but sound different; and a word such as 'read' can, depending on context, rhyme with 'head' and 'heed':

I read her a story last night.

I read her a story every night before she goes to sleep.

George Bernard Shaw once pointed out that 'ghoti' could spell 'fish' if we took the sound 'gh' in 'enough', the sound 'o' has in 'women' and the sound 'ti' in 'motion'.

Many attempts have been made to reform English spelling. During the fifteenth and sixteenth centuries, scholars changed spellings to make spelling conform to etymology. Thus 'dette' became 'debt' to show that it derived from Latin *debitum*. Three centuries later, Noah Webster tried to reform American spelling. He ironed out many inconsistencies but many more remained.

Spelling and pronunciation diverge in three main ways. First, many words have silent letters:

damn, gnaw, hour, knob, lamb, mnemonic, night, psalm, rhesus, walk.

Second, there are many ways of spelling the same sound. The vowel sound of the pronoun 'I' can appear as:

aye, dye, guy, high, my, Thai, thigh, tie

and the 'k' sound of 'kin' can be represented by:

can, cholera, khaki.

Finally, different sounds are often represented by the same sequence of letters. The best known example is '-ough', which can rhyme with the second word in the following pairs:

bough: cow

bought: taut
cough: off
dough: show
enough: snuff
though: go
through: do.

Because of Webster's work and the prestige of his dictionaries, a number of differences exist between British and American spellings. The most commonly occurring differences are summarized below.

Common abstract nouns usually end in '-our' in the United Kingdom and '-or' in the United States.

behaviour, behavior
colour, color
rumour, rumor.

Both countries use '-or' for people and for medical/scientific nouns:

censor, governor, pallor, tremor.

Many nouns that end in '-re' in the United Kingdom have '-er' in the United States.

centre, center
meagre, meager
theatre, theater.

Both countries use '-er' for people, for medical/scientific terms and for many verbs:

adviser/or, cater, peter out.

Many verbs that end in '-ize' may be spelled with '-ise' in Britain:

apologize/apologise
hospitalize/hospitalise
traumatize/traumatise.

Many users of British English use '-ize' for such recent coinages as 'transistorize'. In addition, both British and American users have '-ise' in a number of verbs including:

advertise, advise, apprise, arise, chastise, circumcise, comprise, compromise, despise, devise, disguise, excise, exercise, improvise, incise, revise, supervise, surmise, surprise, televise.

We often find consonants doubled before the morphological endings '-ed', '-ing', '-or/-er' in British English but left single in American writing:

councillor, councilor
kidnapped, kidnaped
levelling, leveling.

Often, the doubling is optional in American English, although many Americans follow the rule that a consonant is doubled when it occurs in a stressed syllable containing a short vowel:

rebelling, rebutting.

American English prefers '-ense' in nouns where British English has '-ence' although both forms occur in America:

UK: defence, licence, pretense

US: defense/defence, license/licence, pretense/pretense.

Both countries have the noun 'incense' and the adjectives 'immense' and 'intense'.

Often, words or morphemes that end in 'l' in British English have 'll' in the United States:

UK: fulfil, fulfilment, instal, instalment, skilful
US: fulfill, fulfillment, install, installment, skillful.

The British causative morpheme 'en-' is often replaced by 'in-' in America:

UK: enclose, endorse, ensure
US: inclose/enclose, indorse/endorse, insure/ensure.

The spellings '-ae-/-oe-' are regularly replaced by '-e-' in US English:

UK: anaesthesia, haemorrhage, manoeuvre
US: anesthesia, hemorrhage, maneuver.

A number of words ending in '-ogue' in the United Kingdom are regularly '-og' in the United States, although the 'ogue' spelling is also found:

UK: analogue, catalogue, diaologue
US: analog, catalog, dialog.

The following miscellaneous list includes the words that normally have different spellings in the UK and the United States:

UK	US
ageing	aging
aluminium	aluminum
analyse	analyze
buses	busses/buses
cheque	check
disc	disk
draught	draft
instalment	installment
mould	mold
moult	molt
moustache	mustache
plough	plow
programme	program
sulphur	sulfur
tyre	tire
waggon	wagon
woollen	woolen

Note that in Britain, 'disk' and 'program' are correct in all instances referring to computers and computing.

Some informal US spellings are popular, especially in advertising, but are not acceptable in formal contexts in either country:

donut: doughnut
sox: socks
tonite: tonight
thru: through.

The following words frequently cause spelling problems in both countries:

aberration, accommodation, align, Caribbean, commitment, committee, desiccate, desperate, diphthong, ecstasy, embarrass, exaggerate, forehead, grievous, honorary, khaki, idiosyncrasy, Massachusetts, Mediterranean, Mississippi, mortgage, parallel, pejorative, pronunciation, pus, queuing/queueing, reconnaissance, seize, separate, siege, silhouette, soliloquy, stationary (not moving), stationery (paper), supersede, vaccination, weird, wintry.

See: -ABLE/-IBLE, -IZE/-ISE, PRONUNCIATION, SPELLING PRONUNCIATION, UK AND US ENGLISH

spelling pronunciation

The spelling system of English is arbitrary and the link between spelling and the way a word is pronounced is often tenuous. There is, for example, no logical reason why the English place-name 'Mousehole' should not be pronounced the same way as 'mouse hole' instead of 'mow-zel'.

Often, when people meet a word in the written medium, they are influenced by the orthography and pronounce it the way it looks. Thus, we often find *spelling pronunciations* side by side with more acceptable pronunciations, and often the spelling pronunciation becomes standard:

Word	Spelling pronunciation	Usual pronunciation
gnu	gnu	nu
often	of-ten	off-en
tortoise	tor-toize	tor-tuss

spend

Spend is an irregular verb:

spend(s), spent, spending
We've spent all our money!

spill

Spill is like 'spell' in that it has two acceptable past tense and past participle forms:

spill(s), spilt/spilled, spilling, spilt/spilled.

The 'spilt' form is unusual in American English, where the '-ed' form is preferred.

See also -ED/-T

spin

Spin is an irregular verb:

spin(s), spun, spinning
And he spun a web of the purest gold ...

The earlier past tense form 'span' is no longer acceptable.

spiral

When *spiral* is used as a verb, it doubles the 'l' in British English:

UK: spiral(s), spiralled, spiralling (The rocket spiralled out of control.)
US: spiral(s), spiraled, spiraling.

spiritual, spirituous

These adjectives derive from 'spirit' in its two meanings of 'non-corporeal' and 'alcohol'. *Spiritual* means 'relating to the spirit or the soul' and it is sometimes equated with 'religious':

She has always been interested in spiritual matters so we were not surprised when she decided to become a nun.

Spiritual is used as a noun especially in the context 'negro spiritual':

Spirituals are now popular with choirs all over the world.

Spirituous means 'containing alcohol':

Don't drink it. It looks like lemonade but it seems to have a spirituous content.

spirt

See SPURT/SPIRT

spit

Spit is an irregular verb that is currently under going change. At the moment, the acceptable verb forms are:

spit(s), spat, spitting, spit
He spat the tablet out.

Increasingly, the form 'spit' is also used as a past tense form:

He spit it out.

but this is still not acceptable. It is likely, however, that *spit* will be influenced by such verbs as 'hit' and 'set'.

See also FIT, PUT

splendour, splendor

These are alternative spellings of the same noun. *Splendour* is the preferred British form and *splendor* is the American form:

The title of the American film *Splendor in the Grass* (1961) was spelled *Splendour in the Grass* in Britain.

split infinitive

A *split infinitive* is the use of a modifier between 'to' and the verbal part of the INFINITIVE:

To boldly go where no one has gone before
Students are asked to kindly refrain from smoking in seminar rooms.

In many languages, the infinitive is a single form of the verb and it is usually translated by the infinitive including 'to':

Latin	French	English
ire	aller	to go
venire	venir	to come

The infinitive cannot be split in Latin or French and so normative grammarians claimed that the English infinitive should not be split. This claim ignored two facts. First, English infinitives are different from Latin or French infinitives in both form and usage:

French	English
Je veux aller chez moi.	I want to go home.
Puis-je aller chez moi?	May I go home?

Second, English speakers and writers have been inserting modifiers between 'to' and the infinitive since the fourteenth century and the custom has been condemned only since the nineteenth century.

There is still prejudice against split infinitives in English, and although such prejudice is illogical and grammatically unfounded, it is important to exercise care in the use of split infinitives in formal contexts.

---

spoil

Spoil is one of the verbs that has two acceptable forms for its past tense and past participle:

spoil(s), spoilt/spoiled, spoiling, spoilt/spoiled.

The 'spoilt' form is widely used in Britain but the 'spoiled' form is preferred in America.

See also -ED/-T

---

spontaneity

The noun *spontaneity*, meaning 'behaving in a natural, unpremeditated way', has two main pronunciations. The third and fourth syllables are sometimes rhymed with 'knee + it' and, increasingly, with 'nay + it'.

---

spoonerism

A *spoonerism* is most likely to occur when a speaker is tired or talking rapidly. *Spoonerisms* involve the unintentional transposition of the initial sounds of two (or occasionally more) words:

Mig Bacs (Big Macs)

trall tees (tall trees)

brite wead (white bread).

Unintentional spoonerisms are usually meaningless but the term is often applied to humorous transpositions such as:

hushing his brat (brushing his hat).

riding on a well-boiled icicle (well-oiled bicycle).

thud and blunder (blood and thunder).

The name comes from the Reverend W.A. Spooner (1844–1930), who was well known for his eccentric behaviour.

---

spoonful

The noun *spoonful* is normally pluralized as 'spoonfuls' although some purists insist that 'spoonsful' is more accurate:

Take two teaspoonfuls every four hours.

See also -FUL

---

spouse

The noun *spouse* can refer to either a husband or a wife:

Her spouse is in Saudi Arabia.

His spouse is at the office.

It has, however, old-fashioned overtones and is much less widely used than 'partner'. *Spouse* has two main pronunciations. It may rhyme with 'mouse' or with 'vows'.

---

spring

Spring is an irregular verb:

spring(s), sprang, springing, sprung

He sprang to her defence.

There is a tendency among certain speakers to use 'sprung' as the past tense:

The weeds sprung up overnight.

but many traditionalists dislike it except when *spring* means 'put springs into':

He resprung the chair last night.

---

spurt, spirt

These are variant spellings of the noun and verb. The noun means 'sudden burst of energy':

He put on a spurt and went over the line first.

The verb is regular and means 'gush forth, make an effort':

The water spurted all over me.

Both forms rhyme with 'hurt' and the *spurt* form is more widespread.

---

squalor

The noun *squalor* means 'disgustingly dirty'. It is often misspelled because it ends in '-or' in both Britain and America and never in '-our'.

Sri Lanka

An inhabitant of the south Asian republic, which was formerly known as Ceylon, is a 'Sri Lankan' or a 'Sinhalese'; the derived adjectives are the same. The capital is Colombo (not Columbo).

---

staid

This adjective is normally used to mean 'humourless' although it derives from 'stay' and originally meant 'settled', 'permanent', 'steady':

She's staid and solemn but utterly reliable.

---

stalactite, stalagmite

These nouns, which refer to calcium carbonate outcroppings, are often confused. A stalactite, with a 'c' in it, hangs from the ceiling of a cave. A stalagmite, with a 'g', grows up from the ground.

Sometimes stalactites meet stalagmites and form pillars of calcium carbonate.

stanch, staunch

These are variant forms of a regular verb meaning 'stem the flow of a liquid'. *Stanch* rhymes with 'ranch' and *staunch* with 'haunch':

I tried desperately but I could not stanch the blood.

standard

The term *standard* has several meanings. It can refer to an accepted or approved example of something:

They have set the standard for open-air concerts.

a principle or level of excellence:

We must fight to preserve our standards no matter what anyone says or does.

a flag:

The standard flies when the sovereign is in residence.

or the value of a metal:

the gold standard.

Standard English

Standard varieties of language exist in most communities. Usually, they have greater prestige than other varieties and may even be regarded as more expressive or more easily comprehended. *Standard English* is the term given to the spectrum of Englishes taught in schools, described in grammars and dictionaries, used by the media and written with relatively little variation throughout the English-speaking world. (Occasionally the term 'General American English' is used as a synonym for standard US English.)

Standard English developed from a regional dialect spoken in and around London in the fifteenth century. Prestige varieties had existed before this time but, from the fifteenth century onwards, people outside London began to write in a variety that approximated not to their own speech but to the norms of educated speakers in the London region.

This southeastern dialect was further enhanced by the establishment of printing houses in London towards the end of the fifteenth century and by the publishing of literature and the Bible in this variety. By the middle of the sixteenth century, the beginnings of a written standard had emerged, and the vocabulary and syntax of this standard began to be spread throughout England and, eventually, around the world by education, travel and, more recently, by the media.

The existence of a standard written language did not entail a spoken standard. All educated speakers could write 'aunt' but some might pronounce it to rhyme with 'haunt' while others rhymed it with 'rant'. Standardized pronunciations became widespread only with the introduction of universal education and because of the influence of radio, films and television.

Standard English is not absolutely clearcut and discrete. One might even argue that we now have several forms of *Standard English*, African standards, an American standard, an Australian standard, a British standard and indeed a local standard in each country where English is a significant language. Yet, even within one regional standard, there is variation. In the written form it comprehends varieties that allow a speaker to indicate friendship or formality, casualness, intimacy or aloofness. Formal spoken styles are often close to written norms, with fewer reductions and weak forms than are found in colloquial speech, but regional origins are often indicated in speech.

Standard English has changed steadily over the last three hundred years, but the syntax has changed less than the vocabulary and both syntax and vocabulary have changed less in the last three centuries than in any similar period for which we have written records.

See also ACCENT, DIALECT, PRONUNCIATION, RECEIVED PRONUNCIATION

star, stare

These verbs are both regular and they are distinguished by spelling:

star(s), starred, starring
stare(s), stared, staring
She starred in the New York production of *Cats*.
She stared longingly at the wonderful food.

start

See BEGIN/START

stationary, stationery

These words are often confused. *Stationary* is an adjective meaning 'not moving':

There was gridlock in the centre of town. My bus was stationary for over twenty minutes.

Stationery is a noun and refers to the items sold by a stationer and needed for the written medium, such as paper, pens and envelopes.

stative and dynamic

Verbs in English are sometimes described as being either *stative* or *dynamic*. *Stative* verbs normally express states (e.g., 'be', 'seem'), senses (e.g., 'hear', 'see') and mental processes (e.g., 'know', 'remember'), whereas dynamic verbs tend to express actions. The majority of verbs in English are DYNAMIC.

See also VERB

status quo

The Latin phrase *status quo*, 'the state in which', is used to mean 'the existing state of affairs':

It won't be easy to re-establish the status quo.

The Latin phrase, like many borrowings, can be useful, but it is better avoided if one is not sure how or when it should be used.

staunch

See STANCH/STAUNCH

stave

Stave is a back formation of 'staves', the original plural of 'staff'. It is most frequently used today as a noun in musical contexts:

In Britain, the term stave is used for a group of five lines and four spaces on which notes are written.

As a verb *stave* co-occurs with 'off' and means 'avert', 'hold at bay':

He staved off his thirst by eating snow.

stay, stop

In some regional varieties of English *stop* rather than *stay* is used with the meaning of 'reside':

We stayed in Port Moresby for a year.
We stopped in Port Moresby for a month.

steal

See BURGLE/BURGLARIZE/ROB/STEAL

step-

Step- occurs as a prefix and indicates a relationship caused by a previous marriage. A *stepson* is the son of one's spouse and is not a blood relation. The prefix is used in:

stepbrother, stepchild, stepdaughter, stepfather, stepmother.

Occasionally, this prefix is misused when 'half-' is the correct term. Half-brothers have one parent in common; stepbrothers are not related by blood.

See also AFFIX, FAMILY RELATIONSHIP, PREFIX

stereo-

Stereo- comes from Greek *stereos*, 'solid', and can be used as a noun meaning 'stereophonic equipment' or sound:

Has anyone moved my stereo?
Will the concert be broadcast in stereo?

More frequently, it occurs as a prefix indicating three-dimensional quality:

stereochemistry (study of the arrangement of atoms)
stereophonic (sound system using two or more microphones and/or loudspeakers).

Some speakers rhyme *stereo* with 'berry + oh'; others rhyme it with 'cheerio'. Both are acceptable but the first is more widespread.

See also AFFIX

stick

Stick is an irregular verb:

stick(s), stuck, sticking
I was stuck in a traffic jam for three hours!

stigma

Stigma comes from Greek *stizein*, 'to tattoo', and meant 'a distinguishing mark'. It now has two plurals and two meanings. A *stigma* can mean 'a mark of social disgrace':

How will I ever live with the stigma of having been in jail?

The plural of this meaning is 'stigmas':

Debt and bad behaviour are not seen as the stigmas they once were.

The alternative plural 'stigmata' is usually reserved for marks resembling the wounds of the crucified Christ:

He had the stigmata and always wore bandages on his hands and feet.

although it is very occasionally used for injuries that result in scarring for life:

He carried the stigmata of his injuries for the rest of his life.

stile, style

These words are occasionally confused or misspelled. A *stile* is a set of steps in a wall or hedge that lets people, but not animals, through:

Isn't there a stile or gate somewhere here?

Style means 'manner', 'design' or method of writing:

I don't like this style of singing.
We are interested in a new style of house that is energy-efficient.

A person's *style* is often defined as a distinctive method of writing or speaking. Our individual styles involve selection from options available in the language, and the selection may involve:

■ Vocabulary: we might choose 'television', 'telly', 'TV' or 'the box'

■ Phrases: we might choose 'very hard', 'not easy', or 'frightfully difficult', or we might never select 'frightfully'

■ Sentence structure: we might prefer simple, compound or complex sentences in different circumstances:

I read it in the paper. It must be true!
I read it in the paper and so it must be true.
If I read it in the paper it must be true.

Ultimately, every linguistic choice is a stylistic choice since it affects the style of an utterance or a text. Each person has an individual *style* or IDIOLECT, but there are also 'genre' *styles* such as those associated with journalism or advertising.

See also JOURNALESE, SCIENTIFIC ENGLISH

still
See ALREADY/STILL/YET

stimulant, stimulus
These nouns are occasionally misused. They both derive from Latin *stimulare*, 'to urge on'. A *stimulant* is a drug or substance that increases certain activities:

All stimulants have potential side-effects but his need of a heart stimulant outweighs any problem that the drug may induce.

A *stimulus* is an incentive. The plural is 'stimuli':

Such children need to be exposed to all kinds of stimuli; use music, bright colours, lovely shapes, anything that will trigger off a response.

sting
Sting is an irregular verb:

sting(s), stung, stinging, stung

The wasp stung me.

There is potential confusion between the use of 'stingy' meaning 'capable of stinging' and 'stingy' meaning 'ungenerous':

The garden is full of stingy nettles.

He was extremely stingy, unwilling to share his good fortune with anyone.

The first adjective, however, is very rare. The second is colloquial and, therefore, unlikely to occur in writing. In the spoken medium, the first rhymes with 'ring + ee', the second with 'hinge + ee'.

stink
Stink is an irregular verb:

stink(s), stank, stinking, stunk

The pond was so polluted that it stank.

There is a growing tendency for 'stunk' to be used as both the past tense and the past participle form, on analogy with verbs such as STING and SHRINK. Although such usage may well become standard in time, it is better to err on the side of tradition.

Stone Age
The *Stone Age*, with capital letters, refers to a period in human development characterized by the use of stone implements. The *Stone Age* is normally divided into three stages:

Paleolithic, Mesolithic, Neolithic.

The term is sometimes used adjectivally, often without capital letters, to mean 'primitive, uncivilized':

I don't know why you put up with such stone-age behaviour.

stop
See STAY/STOP

storey, story
In British English, these homophones are distinguished in usage and meaning. A *storey* is a floor or level of a building:

We've just moved from the fourth to the second storey.

The building has six storeys.

A *story* is a narrative:

Tell me a story.

and its plural is 'stories'. In American English, *story/stories* is used for both meanings.

See also FLOOR

straight, strait
These homophones are occasionally confused. *Straight* comes from Old English *streccan*, 'to stretch', and *strait* from Old French *estreit*, 'narrow', 'constricted'. *Straight* can function as an adjective and, occasionally, as a noun:

The road was straight as far as the eye could see.

When I was a child, I wanted straight hair because my curly hair was hard to comb.

It is important for children to be brought up to follow the straight and narrow.

A *strait* is a narrow channel of water. It tends to be used in the plural:

We sailed through the Straits of Gibraltar.

straight away, straightaway
This compound means 'at once' and may be written as either one word or two:

I'll do it straightaway.

I'll do it straight away.

straitlaced, straightlaced
These are now acceptable variants and mean 'prudish'. In the past, only the *strait-* form was acceptable:

She seems straitlaced until you get to know her but she is a great believer in courtesy and decorum.

Another word that now has acceptable variants in 'straight' and 'strait' is 'straightjacket' or 'straitjacket'. Many careful users prefer to use the 'strait-' forms for both of these words since they involve the meaning of 'narrow', 'constricted'.

See also STRAIGHT, STRAIT

strata
Strata is a plural noun meaning 'layers'. The standard singular is 'stratum':

We could see the distinct strata in the sedimentary rocks.

Because it is a plural noun, care should be taken with verb agreement:

The strata are clearly visible.

*The strata is clearly visible.

The word is frequently used to mean 'levels of society':

Some sociologists distinguish nine class strata, from 'upper upper' to 'lower lower'.

stratagem, strategy

These nouns both derive ultimately from Greek *strategos*, 'one who leads an army', but they have developed different meanings in English. They both involve planning, but *stratagem* is less attractive. A *stratagem* is a 'plan' or 'trick', especially one designed to fool an enemy:

We'll have to devise a stratagem or ruse to beat her at Scrabble. We'll never beat her otherwise.

A *strategy* is 'a plan', usually an intricate plan designed to succeed in war or business:

Our new strategy has taken months to develop but it will allow us, ultimately, to take over our business rivals.

street

See ROAD/STREET

stress

The word *stress* is used in language studies in relation to the degree of prominence given to a syllable. In English certain syllables are produced with more force than others, and these are called 'stressed syllables'. Syllables that receive less stress are called 'unstressed syllables'. In a word such as 'impressive', for example, '-press-' is the stressed syllable whereas 'im-' and '-ive' receive less stress. Thus, English is called a 'stress-timed' language, while French is described as 'syllable-timed' because all syllables are pronounced with similar degrees of force.

strew

Strew is an irregular verb meaning 'spread, scatter':

strew(s), strewed, strewing, strewn
The children strewed flowers in the temple.
The floor of the temple was strewn with flowers.

The past participle 'strewn' is often replaced by 'strewed', thus making the verb fully regular. Although this is not fully acceptable now it is likely that it will become acceptable in the future.

stride

Stride is an irregular verb meaning 'walk with long, regular steps'. It patterns like 'ride':

stride(s), strode, striding, stridden
He strode angrily out of the house and across the moors.

Although dictionaries give 'stridden' as the past participle of *stride*, most speakers avoid it and replace the theoretically correct:

He had stridden all over the moors.

with:

He has walked/trudged all over the moors.

The dislike of speakers for 'stridden' is related to the tendency to regularize irregular verbs.

strike

Strike is an irregular verb meaning 'hit' and may be used literally or metaphorically:

strike(s), struck, striking
I was struck by a falling branch.
The full significance of her remarks has just struck me.

The related adjective 'stricken' means 'afflicted', 'laid low':

a stricken child.

string

The verb *string* is irregular:

string(s), strung, stringing, strung
We spent the morning stringing beads.

The adjective 'stringed' can be applied to any instrument with strings:

Stringed instruments are found in a wide range of cultures.

strip, stripe

These words can function as both nouns and verbs. A *strip* is a long narrow piece of something or the clothes worn by members of a team:

He tore a strip of cloth and used it as a bandage.
United's new strip is green.

A *stripe* is a band that differs in colour or texture from the surrounding background:

Have zebras black stripes on a white background or white stripes on a black background?

The verbs are both regular and are differentiated by spelling:

strip(s), stripped, stripping
He stripped the bark from the trees.
stripe(s), striped, striping
The council refused to provide a new zebra crossing so the residents striped the road themselves.

strive

Strive is an irregular verb meaning 'make considerable efforts':

strive(s), strove, striving, striven
He strove for years to improve their standard of living.

strong and weak form

Many words in English have two pronunciations, depending on whether or not they are stressed. Thus, the 'a' in 'a prize' would be pronounced 'ay' if one wished to emphasis that it was one prize and not more, but reduced to a short 'a' in most contexts. The emphasized or fully pronounced form is called *strong* and the reduced form is called *weak*.

The words in English that tend to have both strong and weak forms are:

articles: 'a, an, the' and 'some'

auxiliary verbs

conjunctions, especially 'and' and 'but'

'not'

some prepositions

some pronouns.

The following list includes the most frequently used examples in the language:

a, am, and, are, as, at, be, been, but, can, could, do, does, for, from, had, has, have, he, her, him, his, is, must, not, of, shall, she, some, than, the, to, us, was, we, were, will, would, you.

See also STRESS

strong and weak verb

The terms *strong* and *weak* are also applied to verbs. Irregular verbs, such as 'go', 'see' and 'write', which form their past tense and past participles by means of vowel (and consonant) changes, are called *strong*:

Verb	Past tense	Past participle
go	went	gone
see	saw	seen
write	wrote	written

Regular verbs that form their past tense and past participle by the addition of '-ed/-d' are called 'weak'. The majority of English verbs are regular:

Verb	Past tense	Past participle
cook	cooked	cooked
like	liked	liked
type	typed	typed

structuralism

The term *structuralism* is usually applied to linguistic analyses that describe languages in terms of their form and their function. In structural analyses, various different levels are distinguished. We normally have such levels as:

■ Phonology: the level that deals with sounds

■ Morphology: the level that deals with combinations of sounds

■ Lexicology: the level that deals with words

■ Syntax: the level that deals with combinations of words

■ Semantics: the level that deals with meaning.

The methods of *structuralism* is also occasionally applied to other aspects of human behaviour (including friendship, religion and storytelling)

that can be analysed in terms of a network of recurring and interconnected relationships.

See also GRAMMAR, TRANSFORMATIONAL GRAMMAR

student
See PUPIL/STUDENT

sty, stye

These homophones rarely occur in contexts where they can be confused and so, increasingly, we find that the same spelling is used for both. A *sty* has the plural 'sties' and refers to a pen where pigs are kept:

The noun sty comes from Old English *stig* meaning 'pen' or 'fold'.

Stye, meaning 'swelling on the eyelid', has the plural 'styes' but it is often spelled *sty* and 'sties':

Stye comes from Old English *styanye* meaning 'rising, swelling'. It was re-interpreted as 'stye-on-eye'.

See also FOLK ETYMOLOGY, SEMANTIC CHANGE

style
See STILE/STYLE

stylistics

Stylistics studies the use of language in specific contexts and it also attempts to account for the regularities found in the language used by both individuals and groups.

See also RHETORIC, STILE/STYLE

sub-

Sub- is a very frequently used prefix deriving from Latin *sub*, 'under'. It occurs in adjectives:

subcutaneous

adverbs:

subliminally

nouns:

submarine

and verbs:

subdivide.

See also AFFIX, PREFIX

subconscious, unconscious

These words can both be used as adjectives and nouns. *Subconscious* can be used as an adjective meaning 'without one's awareness or conscious knowledge':

I don't know why I said it. Perhaps it was the result of a subconscious desire to be taken seriously.

It is also used as a noun, mainly in psychology, to refer to the part of the mind that is outside our awareness or only partially within our conscious awareness:

We may not be able to control our subconscious fully but we can learn to understand it.

As an adjective, *unconscious* means 'totally unaware', 'in a faint':

He's unconscious. You'd better ring for an ambulance.

As a noun, it means 'the part of the mind that does not ordinarily enter an individual's awareness':

The preoccupations of the unconscious frequently reveal themselves in dreams.

subject
In English, the *subject* of a sentence is one of its major constituents:

Subject	Predicate	Object
John	loves	his parents.
He	loves	them.

The subject of a sentence (underlined in the following examples) is the noun, pronoun, phrase or clause that precedes the predicate in declarative sentences:

Trains are very comfortable.
They are very comfortable.
The Eurotrains are very comfortable.
Travelling by train is very comfortable.

that normally occurs within the predicate in questions:

Are trains becoming more comfortable?
Are they becoming more comfortable?

and that agrees with verbs in the present tense and with 'be' in both past and present:

The train travels at 150 miles an hour.
The trains travel at 150 miles an hour.
The train is on time.
The trains are on time.
The train was on time.
The trains were on time.

The most frequently occurring subjects are noun phrases:

The android is almost human.

pronouns:

He is almost human.

proper names and phrases:

Data, the android in *Star Trek: The Next Generation*, is almost human.

-ing forms:

Smoking can seriously damage your health.

'to' forms:

To err is human. To forgive is divine.

nominalizations (nouns derived from other parts of speech):

The highs will be replaced by feelings of depression.

finite clauses:

What you said was very hurtful.

Subjects occur in active sentences:

John trained Bill.

in passive sentences:

Bill was trained by John.

and in sentences with a COPULA:

John is a trainer.

Subject pronouns are often distinguishable from object pronouns:

Subject	Both	Object
I		me
	you	
he		him
she		her
	it	
we		us
they		them
	that	
	this	
who		whom
	which	

Subject pronouns occur in tag questions:

She likes her job, doesn't she?
He didn't do it, did he?
It's very hot, isn't it?

and subject relative pronouns cannot be omitted:

The man who sat over there was my father.
The book (that) we read was excellent.

See also NOUN, OBJECT

subjective
See OBJECTIVE/SUBJECTIVE

subjunctive
Descriptions of English that were based on Latin models often classified the verb phrase according to three categories: declarative/ indicative:

I like coffee.
I don't like coffee.

imperative/command:

Go home.
Don't go home.

and *subjunctive*, the verb form used in subordinate clauses:

If this be the case, then justice has not been served.

In English there is usually no difference between the form of the verb used in main and subordinate clauses:

I like coffee.
If you like coffee, you'll enjoy this brand.

However, there are three types of construction where the verb used may be classified as subjunctive:

■ Hypothetical statements:

If I were a blackbird, I'd whistle and sing.
I'd follow this up if I were you.

Colloquially, speakers often use 'if I was ...' and some speakers actually distinguish between 'if I was' and 'if I were', using the second construction to indicate the impossibility of the hypothesis:

If I were on Mars, I'd be much younger because the years are longer.
If I was at home now, I'd be watching the news on television.

■ Formulaic expressions:

Be that as it may, I still think I'm right.
Long live the King!

■ Formal, often legal, statements involving subordinate clauses:

We formally request that she be allowed to serve her sentence in Britain.
We recommend that he be remanded in custody.

In English, meanings involving doubt, suggestion and wishes, that are expressed in some languages by the subjunctive, are often carried by modal verbs.

See also MODALITY

submit

Submit is a regular verb that doubles the 't' before '-ed' and '-ing':

submit(s), submitted, submitting
I could never submit to such a tyrannical regime.

subnormal

See ABNORMAL/SUBNORMAL

subordinate clause

A *subordinate clause* is one that cannot usually occur on its own but depends on a main clause. It is another term for 'dependent clause':

Main clause	Subordinate clause
I heard	that you were leaving.
You arrived	as I was going to bed.

There are several types of *subordinate clause* (which are underlined in the following examples), including:

■ Adverbial clauses. These provide information on when, where, why or how the main clause occurred:

He resigned because he found a better job.

■ Noun clauses. These can be replaced by pronouns or noun phrases:

I believe that she is very intelligent.
I believe this/that/the following.

■ Relative clauses. These are really adjectival clauses and they modify nouns:

The book that I ordered has still not arrived.

See also CLAUSE, DEPENDENT CLAUSE

subordinating conjunction

Subordinating conjunctions are joining words that introduce a subordinate clause:

I asked [*if* she would go].
The chair [*that* I bought] is very comfortable.
[*When* you come in], please put out the light.

See also CONJUNCTION

subordination

Subordination is the term used to describe the function of subordinate clauses in a sentence. There are two examples of *subordination* in the following sentence:

[When he arrived] I asked him [where he had been].

See also SUBORDINATE CLAUSE

subpoena

Subpoena rhymes with 'cub Tina'. It derives from Latin *sub poena*, 'under penalty' and can be used as a noun and a verb. The noun means 'a writ issued by a court requiring a person to appear before it':

The court regularly issues subpoenas to people who would otherwise refuse to appear before it.

The verb is regular:

subpoena(s), subpoenaed, subpoenaing
I have never been subpoenaed.

subsequent

See CONSEQUENT/SUBSEQUENT

subsidence

The noun *subsidence* refers to the sinking of land, often as a result of earth movement or mining:

There were thousands of insurance claims for subsidence after the long, dry summer of 1995.

Subsidence has two acceptable pronunciations. In the first, the main stress is on 'sub' and 'sid' rhymes with 'did'; in the second, the main stress is on the second syllable, which rhymes with 'died'.

subsistence

The word *subsistence* is often misspelled. It is most frequently used to refer to 'the means by which we maintain life'. It can be used adjectivally in such phrases as:

subsistence farming, subsistence level

and as a noun in:

It's hardly living: it's mere subsistence.

substantial, substantive

These words both derive from 'substance', ultimately from Latin *substantia*, 'something tangible'. *Substantial* is an adjective meaning 'true', 'actually in existence', 'considerable in quantity or size or importance', 'most but not all':

There is now substantial evidence to support his plea.

a substantial inheritance

substantial buildings

A substantial part of the work has now been done.

Substantive can be used as an adjective and a noun. As an adjective it means 'having an independent existence', 'real not apparent', 'enduring', 'relating to the essence of a thing':

The new professor has published a few anthologies but nothing very substantive.

Substantive has recently taken on the meaning of 'relating to matters of national or international concern':

The two presidents met for substantive talks.

Substantive is used in grammar to refer to a noun or a pronoun that stands for a noun:

Pick out the three substantives from the sentence: 'Men and women love children.'

substitute

See REPLACE/SUBSTITUTE

subtly

The adverb *subtly* is often misspelled. It derives from the adjective 'subtle', which rhymes with 'cuttle', but it does not have an 'e':

He subtly introduced his topic.

succour, succor

This formal noun means 'help'. It is spelled *succour* in Britain and *succor* in America. It occasionally occurs in prayers:

Our Lady of perpetual succour, pray for me.

The noun is a homophone of 'sucker', one reason why the prayer was changed to:

Our Lady of everlasting help, pray for me.

such

Such has a variety of functions in English. It can occur as a determiner:

Such carvings are now highly prized.

as a pronoun:

Such is life!

and as an intensifier. *Such* occurs before uncountable and plural nouns and *such a* before singular countable nouns:

We had such fun!

They don't associate with such people!

She was such an intelligent person!

Such does not co-occur with the definite article or with demonstrative or possessive adjectives:

such a lovely girl

*such the lovely girl

*such that lovely girl

*such his lovely girl.

The pattern for a countable noun in a negative construction is often 'no + such + noun':

We recommended such an appointment.

We recommended no such appointment.

Such and such can occur, usually in informal speech, when a speaker wishes to avoid being absolutely specific:

They said they would arrive at such and such a time.

Such as is used to introduce examples:

They planted traditional trees such as beech, larch and oak.

It is regarded as being more formal, and in the written medium more correct, than 'like':

Certain adjectives such as 'unique' do not have comparative or superlative forms.

The phrase *such that* can be the syntactic equivalent of 'so that' in its ability to introduce clauses of purpose or result:

They held absolute power such that no citizen dared challenge their divine right to rule.

The adjective *suchlike* is usually regarded as informal and imprecise. It should be avoided in careful speech and writing:

Digs, entertainment and suchlike expenses make a big hole in my student grant.

See also SO

Sudan

An inhabitant of Africa's largest country is a 'Sudanese'; the derived adjective is the same. The capital is Khartoum.

sue

Sue is a regular verb meaning 'make a legal claim against':

sue(s), sued, suing

They threatened to sue us for breach of contract.

The use of *sue* meaning 'plead for' is still found in the expression 'sue for peace':

Eventually, they had to sue for peace.

suffer

In Standard English, *suffer* takes the preposition 'from' when we talk about an illness:

He is suffering from a debilitating condition.

'*Suffer* with' is not standard but is widely used:

*He is suffering with his feet.

In biblical contexts, *suffer* is occasionally used to mean 'allow' as in:

Suffer the little children to come unto me.

but this usage is archaic.

suffix

A *suffix* is a MORPHEME that can be added to the end of a word. The main suffixes are:

-en, -er, -ful, -ing, -ize, -ly, -less, -ling, -ness

Word + suffix	New word
good + ness	goodness
hand + y	handy
man + ly	manly
taste + less	tasteless

Suffixes can be used derivationally – that is, in the formation of new words that may belong to different classes:

girl (noun) + ish = girlish (adjective)
length (noun) + en = lengthen (verb)
lovely (adjective) + ness = loveliness (noun)
dread (noun) + ful = dreadful (adjective)
wide (adjective) + en = widen (verb)
plaster (verb) + er = plasterer (noun)

Inflectional suffixes, such as '-ed', '-er', '-est', '-ing' and '-s', do not create new words. Instead, they provide grammatical information with regard to adjectives:

a small girl, a smaller boy, the smallest child

adverbs:

He drives fast when he is on the motorway.
He drives faster when he is late.

nouns:

I met their daughter.
I met their daughters.

and verbs:

I usually walk to work.
He usually walks to work.
She is now walking to work.
Last week I walked to work.

All the inflectional and many of the derivational suffixes are still productive in the language, but some, such as '-ard', '-ior' are no longer used creatively:

laggard, warrior.

Occasionally, however, a dead suffix can be reactivated. This happened to '-ster' in the production of:

hipster, oldster.

The suffixes in English are a mixture of Old English forms, such as '-less' and '-ness', and borrowed forms, such as '-able' and '-ment'.

See also AFFIX, PREFIX, WORD FORMATION

suit, suite

These nouns are occasionally confused. *Suit* rhymes with 'flute' and can mean a set of matching clothes:

Have you seen her lovely new green suit?

a set of matching cards:

There are four suits: clubs, diamonds, hearts and spades.

and a law case:

He takes on a number of *pro bono* law suits.

Suite rhymes with 'treat' and refers to a number of items intended to be used together:

They bought a leather suite: two chairs and a settee.

and to an instrumental composition:

A suite can be a piece of music based on extracts from an opera or ballet.

sulphur, sulfur

In Britain, *sulphur* and its derivatives, such as 'sulphuric acid', are spelled with '-ph-'; in America, the '-f-' form is preferred:

UK: sulphur, sulphate
US: sulfur, sulfate.

summon, summons

These words are often confused. *Summon* functions only as a regular verb meaning 'order someone to come':

summon(s), summoned, summoning
I was never summoned by my bank manager when I was a student.

Summons can function as a noun or regular verb. As a noun, it means 'an official order requiring someone to attend court' and its plural form is 'summonses':

I've received a summons for speeding.

If a *summons* is taken out against a person, then such a person is said to have been 'summonsed':

summons(es), summonsed, summonsing
He was summonsed for breaking the speed limit.

sunk

See SINK/SANK/SUNK

super-

Super- is a widely-used prefix. It derives from Latin *super*, 'above', and occurs in both everyday and learned words:

superintendent, supermarket, supervise, supererogation (performance of good works), superficies (surface)

Super is used on its own as a vogue equivalent of 'excellent'.

See also SUPRA-

supercilious

This word is frequently misspelled. It derives from Latin *supercilium*, 'above + eyelid = eyebrow' and means 'disdainfully arrogant':

I don't think she intends to look so smug and supercilious.

superior

Superior is an adjective meaning 'greater or better than':

The 1966 football team was vastly superior to the 1996 team.

Superior, like its opposite INFERIOR, co-occurs with 'to', not 'than':

He thinks he's superior to all of us.

*He thinks he's superior than all of us.

superlative
See COMPARATIVE/SUPERLATIVE

supersede
This regular verb is frequently misspelled. It comes from Latin *super + sedere*, 'sit above', and means 'take the place of, supplant':

supersede(s), superseded, superseding

The typewriter has been superseded by the computer.

supine
See PRONE/PROSTRATE/SUPINE

supper
The noun *supper* is, like many words for meals, often marked for region or class. In some communities, it is the last meal of the day and may be eaten as late as nine or ten o'clock.

See also DINNER, TEA

supplement
See COMPLEMENT/COMPLIMENT/SUPPLEMENT

suppose, supposing
Both these words can be used as subordinating conjunctions to introduce hypothetical clauses:

Suppose we travel by bus, can we then afford to visit Florence?

Supposing we travel by bus, can we then afford to visit Florence?

Many people accept this usage in speech but would prefer:

If we travel by bus, can we then afford to visit Florence?

in more formal contexts.

supposedly
Supposedly is an adverb implying 'believed to be correct':

He is supposedly the fastest man in the world.

Its use in a sentence calls the claim into doubt.

supra-
Supra- is a prefix deriving from Latin *super*, 'above'. It tends to mean 'over, above' and 'greater than':

supranational (relating to more than one nation)
suprasegmental (above the level of the sound segment).

See also SUPER-

surf
See SERF/SURF

Suriname
An inhabitant of the country in South America is a 'Surinamese'; the derived adjective is the same. The capital is Paramaribo.

surmise
Surmise is a regular verb that ends in '-ise'. It means 'deduce from incomplete evidence, guess':

You are only surmising; you can't possibly know the outcome!

surplus
The plural of *surplus* is formed by adding '-es':

There were regular trade surpluses in the 1970s.

surprise
The meaning of this word has been weakened by overuse. It is now less strong than 'amaze' or 'astonish':

It surprised me when it started to rain.

When followed by 'at', 'surprised' means 'amazed':

I was surprised at his behaviour.

When followed by 'by', it means 'disturbed', 'taken unawares':

The burglars were surprised by the unexpected arrival of forty guests.

surveillance
This noun is frequently misspelled. It means 'close observation of a person or property':

The police will continue their surveillance of schools until the arsonist is caught.

Surveillance is pronounced to rhyme with 'sir may lance'.

susceptible
The adjective *susceptible* is often misspelled and misused. It can have different meanings depending on the following preposition. *Susceptible of* is formal and means 'capable of':

The utterance is susceptible of at least one other interpretation.

Susceptible to is more widely used and means 'liable to be affected or afflicted by':

I readily admit to being susceptible to flattery.
I know she is susceptible to hayfever.

swap, swop
These are alternative spellings of the informal noun and verb meaning 'exchange':

We worked out a swap: my books for his tapes.
swap(s), swapped, swapping

Would you like to swap computer games?

In America, *swap* is the more likely spelling, but *swop* is popular in Britain.

swat, swot

Swat can function as a noun or regular verb meaning 'hit, strike':

Would you like to know what a swat feels like?

swat(s), swatted, swatting

He spent hours swatting flies.

Swot is sometimes used as an alternative of *swat*, and in Britain it has the additional meaning of studying hard for an examination:

If I hadn't swotted, I would have failed Finals.

Swaziland

An inhabitant of the southern African country is a 'Swazi'; the derived adjective is the same. The capital is Mbabane.

swear

See CURSE/SWEAR

Sweden

An inhabitant of the north European country is a 'Swede'; the derived adjective is 'Swedish'. The capital is Stockholm.

sweep

Sweep is an irregular verb meaning 'clean, clear':

sweep(s), swept, sweeping

Have you swept the path?

swell

Swell is an irregular verb that is rapidly being regularized:

swell(s), swelled, swelling, swollen/swelled.

It means 'grow in size':

I could see my ankle swelling.

We continue to use 'swollen' especially when the growth is associated with pain:

My ankle has swollen.

The crowd has swelled.

swim

Swim can function as a noun and as an irregular verb:

I'm going for a swim.

swim(s), swam, swimming, swum

I swam across the bay.

He has swum the Channel twice.

People sometimes use 'swum' as the past tense form but this is not acceptable:

*I swum across the bay.

swing

Swing is an irregular verb meaning 'sway, move rhythmically':

swing(s), swung, swinging

I used to love swinging from that branch when I was a child.

swingeing

Swingeing, with an 'e' is an adjective meaning 'harsh, severe':

There are swingeing penalties for drug offences in many countries.

The first syllable of *swingeing* rhymes with 'hinge' and the 'e' is necessary to distinguish *swingeing* from 'swinging' as in:

Stop swinging that bag.

Switzerland

An inhabitant of the European country is a 'Swiss'; the derived adjective is the same. The capital is Berne.

swivel

Swivel is a regular verb meaning 'turn or swing on a pivot':

He swivelled round in his chair.

In British English, the 'l' is doubled before '-ed' and '-ing' but it is left single in American English:

UK: swivel(s), swivelled, swivelling

US: swivel(s), swiveled, swiveling.

swop

See SWAP/SWOP

swot

See SWAT/SWOT

syllable

Most of us think we know what a *syllable* is but, like 'word' or 'sentence', it is not easy to define. A useful starting point is to think of a *syllable* as a unit of language that can occur in isolation:

bee (one syllable)

behave (be + have, two syllables)

beloved (be + love + ed, three syllables).

A *syllable* in English may consist of:

a vowel alone (V): 'a' on its own or in 'afoot'

a consonant + a vowel (CV): 'be' on its own or in 'behave'

two consonants + a vowel (CCV): 'fly'/flai/

three consonants + a vowel (CCCV): 'screw' /skru/

a syllabic consonant, that is, nasals and laterals in words such as: bottom, bottle

consonant + vowel + consonant (CVC): 'ban'.

Other patterns occur such as:

CCVCC as in 'spilt'

CCCVC as in 'split'

CCCVCC as in 'splint'
CCCVCCC as in 'splints'.

In the written medium, *syllables* are marked off either by dividing the word before a consonant when only one consonant occurs:

lotus, lo-tus

between consonants when two occur:

litmus, lit-mus

after the second consonant when three or more occur:

streng-then

or according to meaning and structure:

liking, lik-ing.

See also HYPHEN, METER/METRE, MORPHEME, STRESS

syllabus

Syllabus has two acceptable plurals, 'syllabuses' and 'syllabi', but the former is much more frequently used:

Students should check that the syllabuses provided by different departments are compatible.

syllepsis

Syllepsis derives from Greek *sullepsis*, 'taking together', and it has two overlapping meanings in English. It can refer to a syntactic relationship where a number of words are, theoretically, in agreement with another word but the word cannot agree with all of them in case or gender or number:

It's either mine or her own.
Each person should collect their own form.
Does John or the children know?

It is a FIGURE OF SPEECH that involves the linking of the literal and the metaphorical use of a word or phrase:

She opened her heart and her handbag.
The bomb and I went off.

See also ZEUGMA

symbol
See CYMBAL/SYMBOL

sympathy
See EMPATHY/SYMPATHY

synaesthesia

The noun *synaesthesia* has two main applications. It can refer to the correlation between sounds and meaning. Words ending in '-ump', for example, suggest irregularity of shape and heaviness:

bump, clump, dump, thump.

It can also refer to the metaphorical extension from one sense to another. Colour, for example, is perceived by the eyes, but when we refer to 'a cold colour' we are using an adjective associated with touch to describe something we see. Similar transfers can be found in such widely-used expressions as:

a loud colour
a sharp mind
a tall tale.

See also METAPHOR, ONOMATOPOEIA, SOUND SYMBOLISM

syncope

Syncope derives from Greek *sunkope*, 'cutting off', and is the technical term for the loss of one or more sounds or letters from the middle of a word. It rhymes with 'link lippy'. Many nautical terms illustrate syncope:

boatswain is pronounced 'bosun'
coxswain is pronounced 'coxun'.

Similar syncope may be found in the British pronunciations of names:

Featherstonehaugh is pronounced 'Fanshaw'.
Leicester is pronounced 'Lester'.

See also APHESIS, APOCOPE, CLIPPING, ELISION, EPENTHESIS

syndrome

The noun *syndrome* comes from Greek *sundrome*, 'running together', and it was originally used in medical contexts to refer to a combination of symptoms that indicated a particular illness. *Syndrome*, which rhymes with 'in chrome', has been popularized by the media to mean 'any set of characteristics indicating the existence of a problem':

The indications are that we may be witnessing a new cold war syndrome.

Many people object to this metaphorical use and, because it is rapidly becoming a cliché, it is better avoided in serious or formal interaction.

synecdoche

Synecdoche comes from Greek *sunekdoche*, 'interpretation'. It is a figure of speech in which a significant part is used to represent the whole or the whole is used to represent a part:

Many hands make light work.
The university (i.e., some people in the university) objects strongly to the current underfunding by government.

Synechdoche is also used to describe the technique where the name of a material is used for the object it was used for:

She has chosen to tread the boards (i.e., the stage).

See also FIGURE OF SPEECH, METONYMY

synergy

Synergy is a medical term for the working together of two or more drugs. It derives from Greek *sunergos*, 'work together':

The hope for AIDS patients lies in synergy where a drug cocktail may produce beneficial effects greater than any of the drugs would succeed in achieving in isolation.

This noun is also used metaphorically for business mergers.

synonym

The noun *synonym* derives from Greek *syn + onyma*, 'together + name'. It describes a sense relationship in which different words seem to have the same meaning and are interchangeable in all or most contexts:

Autumn/Fall
beg/implore
big/large
clever/intelligent
conceal/hide.

When we look closely as such *synonyms*, however, we find that synonymy is always partial, rarely if ever absolute, as we see when we put 'beg' and 'implore' into a sentence:

He has been reduced to begging on the streets.
He has been reduced to imploring on the streets.

The nearest any language comes to having perfect *synonyms* is when words belong to different dialects, as with 'autumn' and 'fall' or 'elevator' and 'lift'. Yet, even here, the choice of 'fall' and 'elevator' would imply the region of origin of the speaker.

See also ANTONYM, CONNOTATION

synopsis

A *synopsis* is a condensation or summary. Its plural is 'synopses':

Your synopses must not include any of the phraseology of the original text.

See also PRÉCIS

syntax

Syntax comes from Greek *suntassein*, 'to put in order'. It describes the study of the ways in which words are combined to form sentences. In many accounts of language four levels are postulated. These are:

- Phonology, which deals with sounds and their combination

- Morphology, which deals with word formation

- Syntax, which deals with the rules for combining words into acceptable sentences

- Semantics, which deals with meaning.

Some linguists use the term 'grammar' to comprehend both morphology and syntax; others, following Chomsky, describe language in terms of three major categories: phonology, syntax and semantics, where syntax is the link between sound and meaning.

In all descriptions, however, syntax implies the rules governing acceptable arrangements of smaller units into larger ones.

See also GRAMMAR

syphon

See SIPHON/SYPHON

Syria

An inhabitant of the Arab republic is a 'Syrian'; the derived adjective is the same. The capital is Damascus.

systematic, systemic

These adjectives are derived from 'system' but they have developed different meanings. *Systematic* means 'methodical':

You won't solve any problem unless your approach is logical and systematic.

Systemic is used mainly in medical contexts to refer to a disorder that affects the entire body:

The trouble with such illnesses is that they are systemic. They affect the entire nervous system and all organs of the body are attacked.

report, reported, reporting.

See also SPELLING

table
Table can function as a noun and verb:

Put it on the table.

Will you table the motion?

It also occurs frequently in compound words some of which are hyphenated, some joined together and some written as separate words:

table-land, table-ware

tablespoon, tabletop

table salt, table tennis.

See also HYPHEN

taboo
The word *taboo* was borrowed into English from the Polynesian languages. It can function as an adjective:

That's a taboo subject with John.

as a noun:

The word 'taboo' or 'tabu' is applied to items or relationships that are simultaneously sacred and forbidden.

and as a verb:

taboo, tabooed, tabooing.

taboo vocabulary
All languages have words and expressions that are regarded as unsuitable for general use, either because they deserve particular reverence or because they are felt to be 'unclean' or vulgar. In English there are six main areas associated with linguistic taboos.

Age and size
The fear of growing old or of being obese has engendered such euphemisms as:

evergreen clubs (clubs for people who are 60+)

getting on (growing old)

senior citizens (people over 60)

fuller figure (fat)

Junoesque (tall and fat (women))

High and Mighty (tall and fat (men)).

Bodily excretions
All bodily excretions with the exception of tears and perhaps sweat have taboo associations and, like other taboo subjects, are used as expletives.

Disease and death
Many people avoid discussing serious illnesses such as cancer, often preferring to use a euphemism such as 'terminally ill'. The subject of death is not so much avoided as dealt with in euphemistic or idiomatic terms:

If anything should happen to me … (= When I die …)

the casket (= the coffin)

earthly remains (= dead body)

T

t
T is a consonant that is usually pronounced like the 't' in 'two' although, when it is followed by a 'u' sound, it is sometimes pronounced like 'ty' as in 'tune'.

-t
See -ED/-T

-t-, -tt-
The spelling rules for using *-t-* or *-tt-* are summarized below.

Monosyllables
When a monosyllabic word contains a single vowel and a single consonant, in this case 't', the 't' is doubled before a suffix beginning with a vowel and before '-y':

grit, gritted, gritting, gritty

hot, hotter, hottest.

When a monosyllabic word contains a single vowel but ends in two consonants, the 't' is not doubled before a suffix beginning with a vowel and before '-y':

belt, belted, belting

salt, salted, saltier, salting, salty.

When a monosyllabic word contains two vowels, the 't' is not doubled before a suffix beginning with a vowel and before '-y':

beat, beaten, beater

boot, booted, booting, booty.

Polysyllables
Polysyllabic words ending with a stressed syllable containing a single vowel plus 't' double the 't' before a suffix beginning with a vowel and before '-y':

allot, allotted, allotting

input, inputting.

Polysyllabic words ending with an unstressed syllable containing a single vowel plus 't' do not double the 't' before a suffix beginning with a vowel and before '-y':

billet, billeted, billeting

maggot, maggoty.

Polysyllabic words ending with a syllable containing two vowels or a consonant plus 't' do not double the 't' before a suffix beginning with a vowel and before '-y':

repeat, repeated, repeating

cash in your chips (= die)

pass on/away (= die)

put on a wooden overcoat (= die).

Mental illness and mental handicap are also taboo subjects and are often dealt with in terms of euphemisms:

He's not all there.

She's a little eccentric.

a little confused

living in cloud-cuckoo land

or 'humorous' idioms:

a screw loose/missing

a loony tune

off his rocker.

Abbreviations are frequently used so that speakers may avoid overt reference to illness:

AIDS (Acquired Immune Deficiency Syndrome)

Big C (cancer)

DTs (delirium tremens).

Religion

Words associated with God and religion are fully acceptable only in religious contexts. Even then, many orthodox Jews avoid the use of the word 'God'. In colloquial speech, terms like 'God', 'Jesus', 'damn' and 'hell' often occur but can still give offence and should be avoided. Euphemisms for these words, such as 'gosh', 'gee whiz', 'drat' and 'heck', are usually considered inoffensive but tend to be limited to colloquial speech. Latin borrowings, often abbreviated to initials, are acceptable but such forms as DG (*Deo gratias* = Thanks be to God) and DV (*Deo volente* = God willing) are rarely used now.

Sex

Words relating to sex or the sex organs are fully acceptable only in intimate relationships or in medical contexts. The most frequently used of the so-called 'four-letter words' has been reduced to an emphasizer in such contexts as:

He's ——ing stupid!

She ——ing well did!

Social stratification

Some people are embarrassed by talk about wealth or poverty, preferring understatement or idiom:

She's got a bob or two.

He's well off/rolling in it.

I'm a bit short this month.

They're down on their luck.

With regard to class, different divisions are made:

Social groups A, B, C1, C2, D and E

lower, middle, upper

working, middle, upper

but euphemisms are preferred:

I'm a domestic engineer. (= I look after a home)

the Third World (not 'poor' world)

the underprivileged.

Some occupations are judged less prestigious than others and renamed:

garbage/refuse collector = sanitation officer

electrician or other machine worker = engineer.

In the British parliament, certain 'unparliamentary expressions' are taboo. Among the terms that may not be used are:

cad, cheeky young pup, dog, jackass, liar, prevaricating rat.

This list is extended from time to time. In June 1984, for example, 'fascist' was judged 'unparliamentary' and added to the list.

Taboo words emphasize the sacredness, fear or unacceptability of certain subjects. Careless use of taboo words in the wrong contexts can result from insensitivity to language and the feelings of others.

See also EUPHEMISM, POLITICAL CORRECTNESS

tabulate

The noun from *tabulate* is 'tabulator' with '-or'.

tachograph

A *tachograph* is an instrument fitted in coaches and lorries to record the times when the vehicle was driven and the speeds at which it was driven. The word is frequently spelled incorrectly. It comes from Greek *tachos*, 'speed', and *graphein*, 'to write'.

tactics

Tactics is a plural noun:

His tactics are easy to describe.

The use of 'tactic' is incorrect.

tags

There are three main types of *tags* in English:

■ Question tags, which involve the use of an auxiliary verb + (negative) + pronoun and they are attached to statements:

She's beautiful, isn't she? (expected answer 'Yes')

He won't come, will he? (expected answer 'No')

They could make more of an effort, couldn't they?

■ Reinforcement tags, which tend to be a feature of colloquial English and are more widespread in Britain than in America:

That's a good offer, is that.

You're a prat, you are.

Funny thing, that.

■ Speech fillers, which are tags such as 'like', 'right', 'you know', 'you see'. Many speakers use them without realizing they are doing so. The tag used is often regionally marked.

Go up the road, right. Turn left at the lights, right ...

Kate was trying, like.

She was a great singer, you know.

See also AUXILIARY, FILLERS, QUESTION, SPEECH AND WRITING

Tahiti

An inhabitant of the largest of the Society Islands is a 'Tahitian'; the derived adjective is the same. The capital is Papeete.

tail-

The word 'tail' can function as a noun and a verb:

He had a tail and she had a tail
Both long and curly and fine ...
Ask the fishmonger to head and tail the trout.

The use of 'tail' meaning 'follow' or 'watcher':

We tailed them for 5 miles.
Put a tail on him.

is most likely to be found in American fiction.

Tail- occurs in a number of widely-used compounds including:

tailback (traffic queue)
tail-light (rear light)
tail off (decrease).

Taiwan

An inhabitant of the republic off the coast of China is a 'Taiwanese'; the derived adjective is the same. The capital is Taipei.

take

See BRING/TAKE

talisman

A *talisman* is a lucky charm or an object thought to be endowed with magical powers. The '-man' ending is not a suffix, like the '-man' in 'postman'. Rather, the word was borrowed whole and parallels Italian *talismano* and Spanish *talisman*. The word forms its plural by adding '-s':

One talisman is not enough for him! He has talismans by the score.

tall

See HIGH/TALL

tamarin, tamarind

A *tamarin* is a small monkey:

Like many monkeys, tamarins are becoming an endangered species.

A *tamarind*, with a 'd', is a tropical tree and its fruit, meaning 'date of India':

The fruit of the tamarind tree is a brown pod containing one to twelve seeds embedded in a soft pulp. The tamarind fruit is highly valued for its medicinal qualities.

tame

The adjective formed from *tame* + '-able' retains the 'e':

It's not so much that some animals are not tameable as that they should not have been tamed in the first place.

tango

A *tango* is a dance:

The film was called *Last Tango in Paris*.

The plural is *tangos*. The word is also used as a verb in the catch phrase:

It takes two to tango.

See also CATCH PHRASE

tantalize

Tantalize is a verb that derives from the name of a mythical king of Phrygia. The verb means 'torment by the sight or promise of something that is kept out of reach':

Don't tantalize that child by holding the ball over his head. Give it to him.

Tanzania

An inhabitant of the East African country is a 'Tanzanian'; the derived adjective is the same. The capital is Dar es Salaam.

tarantella, tarantula

A *tarantella* is a fast-moving dance:

Didn't Hilaire Belloc write a poem about a tarantella?

A *tarantula* is a large, venomous spider:

Tarantulas are not as dangerous as people think.

These words are sometimes confused, possibly because they both derive from the Italian town 'Taranto'.

target

The verb *target* as in:

He deliberately targeted the striker.

does not double the 't' before suffixes:

target, targeteer, targeting.

See also SPELLING

tariff

A number of words in English end in '-iff'. Among the commonest of these are:

pontiff, sheriff, tariff.

tart

The noun *tart* meaning 'pastry case with a fruit filling' is sometimes regarded as being marked by the age, class or region of origin of the speaker. Like many terms related to food, an Irish person's 'apple tart' may be an American's 'apple pie'. A.S.C. Ross regarded 'tart' as being more socially acceptable than any of its counterparts.

In certain regions a 'tart' can refer to a woman, usually an immoral one:

Some of the women described themselves as 'Tarts' … and said that they got their living in the best way they could.

Daily News, 5 February, 1894

tattoo

The word *tattoo* has two distinct meanings. It can refer to a military signal, usually a series of drum beats and it can also refer to body decorations, usually caused by puncturing the skin and inserting pigments. The words come from totally different origins, the military tattoo from Dutch and the body designs from Polynesian languages. The word is frequently misspelled. It has a double 't' and a double 'o'. *Tattoo* in its first meaning is used as a noun:

I particularly enjoyed watching the military tattoo.

In its second meaning, it can function as a noun or verb:

He has three tattoos on his left arm.
He was tattooed when he was in the navy.

tautology

The word *tautology*, comes from Greek *tauto-logus*, 'saying the same thing', and involves the repetition of the same idea:

2 = 2.

Often, different words are used:

It is dead, defunct, expired.

Many common catch phrases are tautological and are best avoided in formal styles. Among the commonest are:

abolish completely, actual fact ('actual' is redundant), added bonus ('added' is redundant), all alone, build up, circle round, continue on, each and every, enter into, final demise, free gift, fully comprehensive, general consensus, in close proximity, indirect allusion, join together, later on, mix together, new creation, plan ahead, raze to the ground, reduce down, repeat again, rise above, self-confessed, true facts.

Many orators and writers use tautology for effect:

He was a riddle, a mystery, an enigma.

and such repetition, even with slight semantic modification, is acceptable. It is less acceptable when used to avoid answering questions:

Our defence policy on nuclear arms is to have nuclear arms for our defence.

Even the most careful of speakers and writers is capable of using tautologies. The following occurs in a 1995 manual of usage:

You can use *team* as a verb, meaning 'to join together as a team.' [Is it possible to join apart?]

See also CIRCUMLOCUTION, CLICHÉ, PLEONASM, REDUNDANCY

taxi

Taxi can be used as a noun and a verb. It forms its plural by adding '-s':

How many taxis have you ordered?

The verb endings are '-es', '-ed' and '-ing':

taxi, taxies, taxied, taxiing
The plane taxied slowly to the end of the runway.

See also SPELLING

tea

The word *tea* comes from the Chinese (Amoy) word *t'e* and is used to describe a beverage made from the leaves of a plant such as *Thea chinensis*. The Mandarin equivalent *ch'a* provided the dialectal variant 'char'. Recently, the word has been used with prefixes for a number of beverages or infusions such as:

camomile tea, herbal tea, rosehip tea.

The word *tea* is also used in various parts of the world to refer to a meal or snack and it is, thus, potentially ambiguous. In Britain and Australia *tea* can refer to a snack in the middle of the afternoon, sometimes called *afternoon tea*; in southern Africa, *tea* or *morning tea* may refer to a mid-morning snack; in the north of England, *tea* or *high tea* may be the main meal of the day; and in Guyana, *tea* is often the first meal of the day.

Tea- occurs in a wide range of compounds, some hyphenated, some one word and some two words, including:

tea-chest, tea-leaf
teacup, teapot
tea cosy, tea party.

See also DINNER, HYPHEN, LUNCH/LUNCHEON, MEALS

teach
See LEARN/TEACH

team, teem

These words are homophones, that is, they sound the same but have different meanings. *Team* can function as a noun and a verb:

Which team do you support? Manchester United?
We teamed up to play baseball.

The noun *team* is plural in meaning but singular in form and so it should be treated as a singular noun in terms of agreement and substitution:

This team is doing well. It could win the League.

Many British people treat *team* and words like it (e.g., 'government', 'jury', 'parliament') as plural.

The following sentences were all recorded on BBC television in October 1995:

The government are doing a first-class job.

The jury brought in a not guilty verdict. How could they do that?

Parliament are not in session yet.

This team could win the double, couldn't they?

Such usage should be avoided in writing and in formal contexts.

---

tear

The word *tear* can be pronounced in two different ways. When it rhymes with 'beer', it is a noun referring to the water that comes from the eyes, usually as a result of crying or strong emotion:

I had tears in my eyes when I put down the book.

When *tear* rhymes with 'bare', it can function as a noun or verb meaning 'split, rupture':

There's a tear in my new jacket. I must have caught it on a nail.

Don't tear those papers. I haven't finished with them.

Tear is an irregular verb:

tear(s), tore, tearing, torn.

---

technical, technological

These adjectives are occasionally misused and confused. *Technical* has two meanings. It can imply 'having or relating to special knowledge of a scientific, practical or mechanical kind':

Can you tell me in plain English what is wrong with it? Don't get too technical.

I don't want any of the technical information. I just want to know how to start my car.

It can also be used to mean 'according to a strict interpretation of the rules':

a technical offence

a technical knockout.

Technological tends to be used of methods and theories associated with the sciences:

The *Tomorrow's World* programme would like to hear about any technological breakthrough.

---

technical expressions

Many of the technical and scientific discoveries of the past have resulted in the creation of specialist technical vocabulary, some of which has entered everyday speech:

catalyst, ecology, hypothermia.

Technical expressions are most apparent, perhaps, in the language associated with computers. In this we find that the expressions come from six different sources:

■ Abbreviations:

bps (bits per second)

CGA (colour graphics adapter)

PC (personal computer)

■ Acronyms:

ASCII (American Standard Code for Information Interchange)

DOS (disk operating system)

RAM (random access memory)

WIMP (window icon mouse or pointer)

■ Blends:

bit (binary digit)

modem (modulator demodulator)

pixel (picture cell)

■ Coined from already existing forms:

debug (remove the program errors or viruses)

default (initial settings of a program)

gigabyte (memory storage, 1Gb = 1024 megabytes)

■ Compounds:

daisywheel (type of printer where characters are arranged round a plastic wheel)

joystick (mechanism for playing computer games)

mailmerge (facility to produce sets of letters)

■ Words given new meanings:

abort (terminate program)

bug (error in program)

window (sectioned off area of the computer display).

Many of the words were first used in America and so are generally given American spellings, as with *disk* and *program*.

See also WORD FORMATION

---

teem

See TEAM/TEEM

---

teeth, teethe

The noun is *teeth*:

She still has her baby teeth.

The verb is *teethe* and is most frequently used to refer to the process of getting teeth:

Babies normally begin to teethe in their fourth month.

The baby is crying because he is teething.

---

teetotal

The etymology of this word is uncertain. It seems to have arisen in the United States as an emphatic form of 'total':

T-total.

It was used in England in 1833 in a speech advocating total abstinence from intoxicating drink. The noun is *teetotaller*:

I'm a teetotaller, completely teetotal.

---

telegraphese

The term *telegraphese* is given to the elliptical style often found in telegrams, *aides-mémoires*, child language, diaries, headlines, slogans and in stream-of-consciousness fiction. It is characterized by a brevity resulting from the omission of words that are not essential to the meaning. A four-word headline from the *Evening Post* helps to illustrate the technique:

BUS CRASH DRAMA REPORT.

This headline might be rewritten as:

Here is the report on the recent bus crash in Leeds.

A telegram such as:

Arriving Monday noon flight BA133

would have cost less than the longer equivalent:

I shall be arriving on Monday at noon by the British Airways flight 133.

The words that are often omitted are pronouns and auxiliary verbs:

Arriving

rather than:

I shall be arriving.

conjunctions, prepositions and articles:

(I shall be) Arriving (on) Monday (and) (I shall be) bringing (the) children.

Jane Austen uses a type of telegraphese in *Emma* to characterize the speech (and pretensions) of Mrs Elton on a strawberry-picking expedition:

The best fruit in England – everybody's favourite – always wholesome. –These the finest beds and finest sorts. – Delightful to gather for one's self – the only way of really enjoying them. – Morning decidedly the best time – never tired – every sort good – hautboy infinitely superior – no comparison – the others hardly eatable – hautboys very scarce – Chili preferred – white wood finest flavour of all – price of strawberries in London – abundance about Bristol – Maple Grove – cultivation – beds when to be renewed – gardeners thinking exactly different ...
        Volume 3, Chapter 6

See also HEADLINES, JOURNALESE, PARAPHRASE

telephone

Telephone can be used as both a noun and a verb but the abbreviated form *phone* is now the accepted form in all but the most formal of contexts:

He's on the phone at the moment.
Please write or phone if further information is required.

Often, in colloquial contexts, 'ring/call' are preferred to *phone*:

I'll ring/call you about 7:30.

Phone occurs also in a wide range of compounds, including:

phone box, phone book, phone call, phone-in.

See also ABBREVIATION

televise, television

Television is a blend of Greek *tele-*, meaning 'far

off', and Latin *videre*, 'to see'. *Televise* is a regular verb and a back formation from *television*:

It will be televised on the 13th.

There are several synonyms for *television*, reflecting its importance in the lives of many people:

the box, the telly, the TV.

See also BACK FORMATION, BLEND, SYNONYM

tell

Tell is an irregular verb. Its forms are:

tell(s), told, telling, told.

temerity, timidity

These nouns are occasionally misused or misunderstood. *Temerity* means 'cheek', 'audacity', 'boldness', 'rashness':

She had the temerity to say that the course was boring!

Timidity means 'easily frightened', 'shyness':

It is not easy to assess how much allowance should be made for his extreme timidity.

temperance

Temperance means 'restraint or moderation':

Her motto was 'temperance in all things'.

It is increasingly used to refer to abstinence from alcohol:

He belongs to a temperance society because he finds it is the surest way of controlling his problems with alcohol.

See also TEETOTAL

template, templet

These words are variant spellings and mean 'pattern'. The older form is *templet* but *template* is more widely used today particularly in the context of computer screen layouts:

Have you seen my templates for the woodwork class?

The word *template* is almost certainly a folk etymology, an attempt to make a word seem more comprehensible. For this reason, many people dislike it.

See also FOLK ETYMOLOGY

tempo

Tempo designates the speed at which a piece of music is played:

The tempo is indicated by a musical direction or metronome marking.

It has two plurals, *tempi* and *tempos* but the former is now rarely used. The word can be used metaphorically to mean 'rate, pace':

The tempo of life has quickened dramatically over the last 50 years.

The plural of this extended meaning is invariably *tempos*:

Your biological clock may be reacting against the varied tempos imposed on it by urban living.

temporal, temporary

Both these words derive ultimately from Latin *tempus* meaning 'time'. *Temporal* is an adjective with two different meanings. It can relate to time:

'Daily', 'nightly' and 'often' are temporal adverbs.

and it can be used to suggest secular as opposed to spiritual:

The House of Lords is composed of the lords spiritual and temporal.

Temporary is also an adjective meaning 'of short duration':

Prefabricated houses were intended as a temporary measure but people are still living in them fifty years after they were built!

tendency

This word is frequently misspelled. It is '-ency', not *'-ancy'. Perhaps one way of remembering the spelling is to think that there is a hidden 'den' in *ten**den**cy*. Another way is to choose a verbal structure using 'tend'. Thus, instead of:

Jane Austen has a tendency to use ...

we can use the more direct:

Jane Austen tends to ...

Tendency means 'inclination' and is used with 'to' not 'for':

She has a tendency to smugness.
*She has a tendency for smugness.

tense

The word *tense* is used in grammar to refer to distinctions of time such as past, present or future that are made overt in the verb. Thus the reference is to the present time in:

I am writing this on my computer.

It is to the past time, however, in:

I wrote this on my computer.

Often, tense and ASPECT co-occur:

I am typing this. (time = now + continuity of action)
I was typing this. (time = before now + continuity of action)

but whereas the marking of tense is obligatory in English:

I was singing in the bath.

tense may occur without aspect. A sentence such as:

I sang in the bath.

does not mark continuity overtly.

In many languages, including some English-related pidgins and creoles, aspect alone may be marked:

A singin. (I'm singing/I was singing.)

and a relic of this is found in some idiolects of Black English, where:

I singin'.

can, depending on context, mean:

I'm singing.

or:

I was singing.

In traditional grammar, three main tenses were marked:

present, past and future

and there were additional subdivisions, such as perfect and pluperfect. The usual pattern was presented as follows:

Present:	I/you/we/they see
	he/she/it sees
Past:	I/you/he/she/it/we/you/they saw
Future:	I/we shall see
	you/he/she/it/they will see
Perfect:	I/you/we/they have seen
	he/she/it has seen
Pluperfect:	I/you/he/she/it/we/they had seen.

In English, there is no absolute correlation between time and tense. The so-called 'present tense' is frequently used for expressing times other than the present. It can occur in the expression of timeless 'truths':

Water freezes at 0° centigrade.
A bird in the hand is worth two in the bush.

in oral narratives of past events (in a tense sometimes called the 'past historic'):

There was this man. He walks up to me and says ...

and with adverbials, in the marking of future time:

I leave tomorrow.
He is taking the midnight flight on Wednesday.

The so-called 'past tense' is also used for purposes other than the marking of past time. It can be used to mark hypothetical or unreal meaning:

I wish I knew (at this moment).
If I had (now or in the near future) lots of money, I'd buy a castle.
It's time they did their own dirty work (now and in the future).

and in reported speech:

'I'm tired,' John said.
John said that he was tired.

There is no 'tense' that unequivocally marks future time in English. The future can be indicated by the use of the present simple + an adverbial:

I start my new job next week.

the use of the present continuous + an adverbial:

I'm starting my new job next week.

the use of 'be' + going + infinitive + adverbial:

I'm going to start my new job next week.

the use of will/shall/'ll:

I shall start my new job next week.
I'll be starting my new job next week.

Often, it is thought that 'will/shall/'ll' always
indicate the future but this is not necessarily the
case. In spoken English, 'will/'ll' are often used
to emphasize the regularity of an action:

He'll sit there for hours just looking at her
photograph.

and 'shall' can still, occasionally, have the
meaning of 'must' as in:

You shall not break the law.

Other European languages can unequivocally
mark future time by means of verb forms. We can
contrast English and French usage in this respect:

French	English
Je porte ...	I carry/am carrying ...
Je vais ...	I go/am going ...
Je porterai ...	I shall carry ...
J'irai ...	I shall go ...

Tense usage throughout the English-speaking
world is virtually identical. The one marked
difference is that some speakers of US English
tend to use the conditional modals in consecutive
clauses (sometimes referred to as 'sequence of
tenses'):

She would have gone if she would have seen him.

whereas other speakers of English prefer:

She would have gone if she had seen him.

See also ASPECT, TIME

ter-, tri-

These prefixes both relate to 'three'. *Ter-* comes
from Latin *ter* meaning 'three times':

tercentenary (300th anniversary – i.e., three times
centenary)

tercet (a group of three lines of verse).

Tri- comes from Greek *treis*:

triangle (three-sided figure)

triaxial (having three axles).

See also NUMBERS

terminal, terminus

These words both derive ultimately from Latin
terminus, 'end'. They can both be used as nouns
to refer to the end of a transport route. In Britain,
terminal tends to be reserved for sections of
airports:

Passengers should proceed immediately to Terminal
3.

and for bus depots:

We shall reach the Leeds Terminal at 16:25.

Terminal is also used as an adjective meaning
'terminating in death':

She has terminal cancer.

Terminus can be used for railways:

When you get to the terminus, go to Platform 5,
where the London train is due to depart at 11:05.

terrible

This adjective has two 'r's and comes from Latin
terrere 'to frighten, terrify'. Originally, the word
meant 'capable of inspiring terror, or awe'. Like
many adjectives with similar meanings, such as
'awful', 'awesome', 'dreadful', *terrible* has been
weakened by frequent use and has come to mean
little more than 'unpleasant' or 'of poor quality':

a terrible bus journey
a terrible meal.

Because of its overuse, this adjective should be
avoided in formal contexts.

See also BLEACHING, SEMANTIC CHANGE

terrific

This adjective is often misspelled. It has only one
'f' and, like *terrible*, has two 'r's. It, too, derives
ultimately from Latin *terrere* 'to frighten' and its
meaning has also been altered. It is now used as
a synonym for 'good', 'pleasant':

They make terrific pizzas.
She's got a terrific head for figures.

Because of its overuse, this adjective should be
avoided in formal contexts.

See also BLEACHING, SEMANTIC CHANGE

tête-à-tête

This French phrase meaning 'head-to-head' is
used in English to refer to a private conversation:

I couldn't hear what they said. They were having a
tête-à-tête in the corner.

See also BORROWING

textual, textural

These adjectives are occasionally confused.
Textual is an adjective derived from 'text' and so
its meaning relates to 'text':

His textual analysis is impressionistic and
self-indulgent. He should refer to the original
text.

Textural is the adjective from 'texture':

The textural analysis revealed that the material was
only 65 per cent cotton and not 100 per cent, as the
label suggested.

Thailand

An inhabitant of the southeast Asian kingdom is
a 'Thai'; the derived adjective is the same. The
capital is Bangkok.

than

Than is a conjunction used in making
comparisons:

Mike is older than Peter.

He is younger than Jane was when she went to school.

It almost always follows a comparative adjective, as above, or a comparative adverb as in:

He drove faster than he should.

Less frequently, it occurs in structures with 'else' and 'other':

Where else would I go than here?
Other than this I have nothing.

Many speakers use *than* as a preposition and say:

He is taller than her.

Careful users insist that *than* is a conjunction and that it introduces a clause that is often reduced. Thus:

He is taller than she is.

becomes:

He is taller than she.

and:

He loves her more than he loves me.

becomes:

He loves her more than me.

In other words, the case of the pronoun in an elliptical sentence should be identical to the form in the full sentence. Such purism can, however, lead to ambiguity as in the last example:

He loves her more than me.
= He loves her more than he loves me.
= He loves her more than I love her.

or to stilted English as in:

He loves her more than he loves me.

In casual speech, however, many speakers treat *than* as they do words such as 'before', as conjunctions when they introduce clauses:

He is taller than she is.
He arrived before she did.

and as prepositions when they are followed by a pronoun:

He is taller than her.
He arrived before her.

See also CONJUNCTION, PREPOSITION

than I, than me

Many speakers are uncertain when to use *than I* and when to use *than me*. The rule is simple. Use *than I* when *I* would occur in the expanded sentence. Thus:

She is smarter than I am. = She is smarter than I.
He sang better than I did. = He sang better than I.

and use *than me* when *me* would occur in the expanded sentence:

He taught her a year longer than he taught me. = He taught her a year longer than me.
She loves the cats more than she loves me. = She loves the cats more than me.

Contemporary usage permits the use of 'than + object pronoun' in speech and informal writing:

She had a better education than him.

but prefers 'than + subject pronoun' in formal contexts:

She had a better education than he (had).

and demands 'than + subject pronoun' in all contexts where the pronoun is followed by a verb:

She's got more talent than we have.
They were faster than we were.

See also AS, CASE, DIFFERENT FROM/THAN/TO

thank you

Thank you is a conventional formula, expressing gratitude:

Thank you for the lovely birthday present.

Since the phrase derives from 'I thank you', it should be written as two words and not as one:

*Thankyou for all your help.

When the phrase is used as a noun or adjective, it is hyphenated:

I should like to say a warm 'thank-you' to all who contributed.
I have to write my thank-you notes yet.

The structure *I'll thank you to* is sometimes used informally as an intensifier:

I'll thank you to keep your opinions to yourself.

See also PARALINGUISTICS, PHATIC COMMUNION

thankfully

Thankfully has traditionally been used as an adverb meaning 'in a grateful way':

She accepted the gift thankfully.

Recently, *thankfully* has been used as a sentence initiator meaning 'It is a matter for thanks that':

Thankfully, we were rescued before dusk.

Many people dislike the use of *thank- fully* as a sentence initiator just as they object to:

Hopefully, we'll be able to make up for all the time we lost.

See also HOPEFULLY

thanks

Thanks can be used as a plural noun meaning 'appreciation', 'gratitude':

We should like to express our sincere thanks for all your kindness.

It also occurs as an informal interjection expressing gratitude or courtesy:

Have you eaten? Yes, thanks.
Would you like a coffee? Thanks, I would.

Thanks to can be used to mean 'because of':

Thanks to your efforts we have now have reached our target.
Thanks to you we've lost the contract!

See also THANK YOU

that

The word *that* is multi-functional in English. It can be a demonstrative adjective:

That book is mine.

a demonstrative pronoun:

That is mine.

a relative pronoun:

The hat that I wore was red.

a conjunction:

I heard that he had left.

and, in colloquial British usage, an intensifier:

I was that tired I couldn't stand up.
Surely I wasn't that fat at the time?

Often the conjunction is omitted in speech and in informal writing:

I heard he had left.

This is perfectly acceptable. It is usual, even in formal styles, to omit the conjunction *that* if it would precede a demonstrative adjective or pronoun:

I heard that that man was French.
I heard that man was French.
I heard that that was the way to do it.
I heard that was the way to do it.

See also CONJUNCTION, DETERMINER, THAT/WHICH

that, which

That and *which* can occur as relative pronouns in what appear to be identical sentences:

The cars which have air bags are very safe.
The cars, which have air bags, are very safe.
The cars that have air bags are very safe.

When these pronouns are used carefully, however, there is quite a big difference. The first sentence is potentially ambiguous. It could mean both:

Only the cars with air bags are safe.

and:

The cars are very safe and they have air bags.

Clearly, such a distinction could be of vital importance. We have two ways of disambiguating the first sentence. We can use commas to show that the clause can be omitted without fundamentally affecting the basic meaning, which is that the cars are safe. Alternatively, we can use 'that' instead of 'which'. Such a clause beginning with 'that' is a defining or restrictive clause. It cannot be omitted without fundamentally affecting the meaning.

See also DEFINING RELATIVE CLAUSE, PRONOUN, WHAT/WHICH, WHICH

the

The is one of the most frequently used words in the English language. It is a definite article and indicates that the noun so modified is either unique:

the moon, the sun

or known to the listener:

The book you ordered has arrived.

The has two pronunciations. Before a consonant, it is normally pronounced with a short 'e':

the bike

and it is pronounced with a long 'e' ('thee') before a vowel:

the awning.

The 'thee' pronunciation is also used for emphasis:

Are you really the Delia Smith?

See also A/AN, ARTICLE

theater, theatre

The normal British spelling is *theatre*:

The new Globe Theatre was first used in 1995.

Americans tend to use the '-er' spelling:

Theater tickets available in the lobby.

but some also use the '-re' spelling.

See also SPELLING, UK AND US ENGLISH

their, them

Many people are uncertain whether to use *their* or *them* before '-ing' forms as in the sentences:

He won't agree to their driving his car.
He won't agree to them driving his car.

The former is more acceptable in formal contexts; the latter is more widely used in speech. Supporters of the former point out that 'driving' is being used as a noun and so we should have:

He won't agree to their driving his car.

just as we have:

He won't agree to their plan.

See also GERUND, -ING FORM

their, there

These words are homophones, rhyming with 'hair', and they are often confused. *Their* is a possessive adjective and means 'associated with them' or 'belonging to them':

They do their best.
They have to support their parents.

The related possessive pronoun is *theirs*. Notice it does not need an apostrophe:

It is theirs. I've seen it parked outside their house.

In informal contexts, and as a method of avoiding sexism in language, *their* is used as the equivalent of 'his or her' in:

Everyone should get their essays in by Friday.

There can function as an adverb of place, as a

pronoun and as an exclamation. As an adverb, it means 'in that place':

Put the box over there.

As a pronoun, it occurs in the subject position in the sentence:

Once upon a time, there was a wicked witch.
There's a 1 in 13 million chance of winning.

As an exclamation, it often suggests sympathy or satisfaction:

There! There! Your mother will be here soon.
There! Perfect!

There's is a homophone of *theirs* but is a reduced form of 'there is' and so requires an apostrophe:

'There's a bright golden haze on the meadow.'

See also APOSTROPHE

thence

Thence is an adverb meaning 'from there', 'from that place' and 'therefore'. It is archaic but has continued to be used in very formal contexts or in fixed phrases:

… and taken thence to a place of execution …
I have shown that x = 2y and thence that *x* is an even number.

See also ARCHAISM, COLLOCATION

there are, there is

There should not be a problem with these structures. *There is* should be followed by a singular noun and *there are* by a plural:

There is an answer to every problem.
There are fairies at the bottom of my garden.

Often, however, *there's* is used where *there are* is logically required. This happens when we have a series of nouns, the first of which is singular:

There's a squirrel and two hedgehogs in the garden.

when the phrase is plural but represents a single entity:

There's bangers and mash for dinner.

when numbers or quantities are used:

There's two pounds in a kilo.
There's tons of the stuff here.

and before 'many a':

There's many a slip 'twixt cup and lip.

thesis

A *thesis* can be a theory or a dissertation:

His thesis was that nothing could travel faster than the speed of light.
His thesis was on Yeats and Irish mysticism.

The plural is *theses*:

The theses are stored in the reference section of the college library.

they're

They're is a reduced form of 'they + are':

They're just lovely!
They're reduced.

Because the 'a' is omitted, the apostrophe is essential.

See also APOSTROPHE

thief

Thief is one of a number of English words ending in 'f' or 'fe' that form their plurals in 'ves':

thief, thieves
wife, wives
wolf, wolves.

The verb from *thief* is *thieve*:

Many of those transported were thieves. They had to thieve to survive.

thingamajig

There is a group of colloquial compounds and coinages denoting a person or thing whose name we have forgotten or regard as unimportant. Their spelling is uncertain, because they tend to be restricted to speech. The commonest of these are:

thingamajig, thingamabob, thingummy, whatsit, wotsit, whatsisname, what-d'you-call-it, whatyoumacallit.

Some are regionally limited and intentionally humorous:

dingbat, oojiboo, oojimaflip.

See also COINAGE, SLANG

think

Think is an irregular verb. Its forms are:

think(s), thought, thinking, thought.

See also VERB

this, these

This can function as both a demonstrative adjective and a pronoun:

This house (i.e., the one close to us) is my sister's and that one (i.e., the one not so close) is mine.
This is the point.

The plural of both uses of *this* is *these*:

These children attend the local school.
These are my children.

See also ADJECTIVE, DEMONSTRATIVE, PRONOUN

thither

Thither is an archaic equivalent of 'to there'. It continues to be used in the fixed phrase 'hither and thither':

She ran about hither and thither.

Several Old English direction words have become obsolete and are found only in dialects, literature or fixed phrases. Among such words are HITHER, *thither*, 'yon' and YONDER.

See also ARCHAISM

though
See ALTHOUGH/THOUGH

thousand
See BILLION/MILLION/THOUSAND

thrash, thresh
These verbs are sometimes confused because of their similarity in meaning and because they derive from the same Old English verb *threscan* meaning 'to beat'. In contemporary usage *thrash* is used to mean 'beat, flog':

No matter what he did, he did not deserve to be thrashed so severely.

'defeat', 'overwhelm':

Manchester United thrashed Liverpool 7–0.

and 'move the arms and legs about wildly':

Does she always thrash about like this in her sleep?

Thresh tends to be limited to 'separate the grain from the husks and straw':

A man needed to be strong to thresh corn with a flail. Now the machine does it for you.

Occasionally, since the late 1980s, there has also been a tendency to confuse *thrash* and 'trash' in the sense of 'ruin somebody's reputation', 'diminish someone or something':

He was warned against trashing his own department in public.

This usage is still regarded by many as slang although it has been recorded in public debates in the House of Commons and used in the *Sunday Times* (29 October 1995).

See also RUBBISH, TRASH

threshold
This word comes from the Old English word *therscold* meaning 'door sill, threshold'. The word is frequently misspelled as *thresh + hold because users analogize with such compounds as 'with + hold = withhold'. The modern form *threshold* may be explained by *metathesis* (*bridd*, for example, became 'bird') or it may have been influenced by the Old Norse form *threskoldr*.

See also METATHESIS

thrive
Until recently, *thrive* was an intransitive strong verb that patterned like 'drive':

thrive(s), throve, thriving, thriven.

Increasingly, however, it is being treated as a weak verb, especially in the United States, with the forms:

thrive(s), thrived, thriving, thrived

being acceptable, even in the written medium.

See also STRONG AND WEAK FORM

throes, throws
Throe meaning 'a pang or pain' rarely occurs in contemporary English but the plural *throes* is still used often in the phrase *in the throes of*:

Little was known of internal Russian policy in 1919 because the country was still in the throes of its revolution.

This usage is often, incorrectly, replaced by *throws*.

Throw can be used as a verb and a noun meaning 'cast or project something', 'act of throwing':

John throws the ball in the air ...
How many throws of the dice did you expect?

The verb *throw* is irregular:

throw(s), threw, throwing, thrown.

through
Through is a homophone of 'threw'. It functions mainly as a preposition meaning 'starting in one place and finishing in another, via':

They walked through the woods.

In American English, and increasingly in British usage too, it means 'up to and including':

First-class passengers are in rows 1 through 8.

Occasionally, *through* is used as an adjective meaning 'continuous, unbroken':

There is no through train to Cambridge.

This usage is again more widely used in America than in Britain as is the expression 'You're through' as in:

You're through [i.e., connected] to Orlando now.

and:

He's through [i.e., finished] as a journalist.

See also UK AND US ENGLISH

thus
Thus is almost entirely confined to the written medium, where it tends to be used as a sentence modifier meaning 'consequently, in this manner':

And thus it came to pass that a child was born.

The expression 'thus far and/but no further' is found also in speech:

He was informed that he could go thus far and no further.

The use of *thusly* is found occasionally in American English, probably as a result of HYPERCORRECTION:

His grandfather left him a great deal of money and thusly, at an age when most boys have a paper-round, he had an annual income in excess of $50,000.

Tibet
An inhabitant of the autonomous region of China is a 'Tibetan'; the derived adjective is the same. The capital is Lhasa.

tie

Tie sometimes causes spelling problems. Its parts are:

tie(s), tied, tying, tied.

tilde

A *tilde* is a mark placed over 'n' especially in Spanish words such as:

mañana, señor

to indicate that the 'n' is pronounced more like the 'n' in 'news' than the 'n' in 'nose'.

It also occurs in Portuguese to indicate that the vowel is nasalized, as in São Paulo.

till, until

These two words probably came into the language because of the contact between speakers of English and the Viking languages. They both mean 'up to', 'up to the time that' and can be used as prepositions:

I waited till/until two o'clock.
He's staying till/until Friday.

and conjunctions:

Will you wait until/till he calls, please?

They are both equally acceptable in both the spoken and the written medium but many people prefer *until*, especially in formal contexts, because *till* is thought to be an abbreviation of *until* and because *till* occurs in some British dialects as the equivalent of 'to':

It's a quarter till one.
You don't have till eat it.

It is, therefore, a stigmatized feature for some users.

The cliché *until such time as* is often criticized. It means nothing more than *until*. Clichés are often used in the spoken medium but should be avoided in formal contexts.

See also CONJUNCTION, PREPOSITION,

time

The word *time* can function as a noun:

What time is it, Mr Wolf?

and as a regular verb:

time(s), timed, timings, timed.

It combines with many other words to forms compounds, some of which are hyphenated:

time-consuming, time-scale
time bomb, time zone.

Compounds that have been in existence for a long time or that have been widely used are often written as one word. The best-known examples here are:

timekeeper, timepiece, timetable.

Many nouns include a covert time reference:

past, present, youth

and kinship terms give information on generation as well as (occasionally) sex:

ancestors, grandparents, great-aunts/uncles, parents, aunts/uncles, children, cousins, descendants.

Telling the time often varies according to country or the type of watch one wears:

	UK	US
10:05	five past ten	five after ten
10:10	ten past ten	ten after ten
10:15	a quarter past ten	a quarter after ten
10:30	half past ten	half after ten
10:45	a quarter to eleven	a quarter of eleven
10:55	five to eleven	five of eleven

Some British people prefer to use a full stop instead of a colon:

10.05.

Often, people wearing digital watches say:

ten ten (10:10)
ten fifteen (10:15).

Different styles are used to refer to specific dates. The following summary illustrates acceptable usage:

■ Day + month + year = 5 October 1998. The abbreviation 5/10/98 or 5–10–98 should be avoided. In Britain, this means 5 October, but in certain other countries it means 10 May.

■ Days may be abbreviated as: Mon, Tues, Wed(s), Thur, Fri, Sat, Sun

■ Months may be abbreviated as: Jan, Feb, March, Apr, May, June, July, Aug, Sept, Oct, Nov, Dec

■ Years before Christ should be written 44BC (i.e., date, small capital letters and no fullstops). Time after Christ should be written AD56.

See also ABBREVIATION, AD/BC, A.M./P.M., UK AND US ENGLISH

timidity

See TEMERITY/TIMIDITY

tinge

The verb *tinge* means lightly coloured:

It was tinged with purple.

The '-ing' form may be either *tingeing* or *tinging*. The variation causes little trouble because this form of the word is rarely used:

The sun was tingeing/tinging the clouds pink.

tire, tyre

The rubber covering on a wheel is normally spelled *tire* in America and *tyre* in Britain:

UK: My tyre is flat.
US: My tire is flat.

titillate, titivate

These verbs are occasionally confused. *Titillate* means 'arouse', 'stimulate pleasurably but superficially':

These magazines are designed to titillate, not to entertain or educate.

Titivate is occasionally spelled *tittivate* or *tidivate* and means 'smarten up oneself or someone or something else':

You've spent the last hour titivating yourself. Are you not ready yet?

They've been titivating the house in the hope of selling at a profit.

title

The titles of books, works of art, musical compositions and films are normally italicized:

Pride and Prejudice was filmed recently.

Coronation Street has been the most successful soap opera in the history of British television.

Dali's *Crucifixion* is a masterpiece of perspective.

Newspaper titles are also italicized, but the definite article is rarely italicized except for *The Economist*, *The Independent* and *The Times*:

I want copies of the *Guardian*, the *Mirror* and the *Sun*.

The titles of long poems are italicized but those of short poems and short stories are given in quotation marks:

Have you read *Paradise Lost* and 'On his blindness'?

He's working on Joyce's 'The Dead', one of the stories in *Dubliners*.

The normal convention for titles associated with rank is that we use capital letters for titles that are followed by a proper name but not when they simply refer to a rank:

Captain Marvel but a captain in the army

King Canute but that king of Denmark

President Truman but the 13th president

Professor Bland but a professor.

See also CAPITALIZATION

titled

See ENTITLED/TITLED

to and fro

This phrase is obsolescent, but it still occurs as an adverb meaning 'back and forth' or 'here and there':

They walked to and fro.

The phrase 'toing and froing' is also used to mean 'a shifting of position':

Why don't they decide one way or the other without all this toing and froing?

See also ARCHAISM

to death

The phrase *to death* is common in three collocations:

burned to death

choked to death

starved to death.

It is not regarded as redundant because burning, choking and starving need not lead to death. A phrase such as:

*drowned to death

is unacceptable because 'drowning' implies dying.

to forms

The infinitive in English can occur with or without the *to*:

I asked her to leave.

I saw her leave.

To distinguish between these uses, linguists often refer to forms such as 'to be' as the *to form* or the 'to infinitive'.

The *to form* has the following characteristics. It can be simple, that is without an auxiliary:

to train.

It can be complex, that is, with one or more auxiliaries:

to be trained

to be training

to have trained

to have been training.

It can be clipped, that is, part can be omitted if it can be understood from the context:

I didn't train because I didn't want to [train].

I went because I had to [go] and not because I wanted to [go].

It can be used as a subject, object or complement:

To err is human.

I plan to arrive at noon.

We are to meet them soon.

The *to form* often occurs in the construction where we have a verb such as 'ask, expect, like, want' + an object pronoun + a *to form*:

They asked us to stay.

He expected me to pay for myself.

I'd like you to do it.

You wanted to go.

In these and similar examples, the pronoun looks as if it is the object of the verb it follows but it functions as the subject of the *to form*:

They asked us to stay. = We stayed.

He expected me to pay for myself. = I paid for myself.

See also INFINITIVE

tobacco

Tobacco is often spelled incorrectly. It has one 'b':

King James I wrote a treatise on tobacco.

The plural is formed by adding 's':

Some of the finest tobaccos in the world are grown in Zimbabwe.

See also SPELLING

tocsin, toxin

These words are homophones. A *tocsin* is an alarm, often sounded on a bell:

The word *tocsin* derives from Old Provençal *tocasenh*, from *tocar*, 'to touch' and *senh*, 'bell'.

A *toxin* is a poisonous substance:

Virtually all toxins are of animal or plant origin.

today, tomorrow, tonight

These words all derive from combinations of Old English words. *Today*, for example, comes from *to* + *dæge*, 'on this day'. It was common for all three to be hyphenated in the past but each is now written as one word.

See also HYPHEN

toilet

See LAVATORY/TOILET/WASHROOM

tolerance, toleration

These two nouns are related to the verb 'tolerate' but they are not synonyms. *Tolerance* means 'the state or quality of being tolerant' and 'the ability to withstand pain or hardship or poison':

She shows too much tolerance of his untidiness.

We can show some tolerance of toxins if they are absorbed gradually.

Toleration means 'the art or practice of forbearance':

The Inquisition showed no toleration.

See also INTOLERABLE/INTOLERANT

tomato

Tomato is pronounced differently in Britain and in America. In Britain, it is pronounced to rhyme with 'vibrato'. In America, it is pronounced to rhyme with 'a great O' and with the British pronunciation of 'potato'. The plural is formed by adding -es:

These dried tomatoes are very useful.

See also UK AND US ENGLISH

tomorrow

See TODAY/TOMORROW/TONIGHT

ton, tonne

In the British Imperial System of weights and measures, a *ton* weighed 2240 pounds. An American *ton* weighs 2000 pounds. A *tonne*, sometimes referred to as a 'metric ton', weighs 1000 kilograms. (A kilogram = 2.2lb.)

Tonga

An inhabitant of the island kingdom in the south Pacific is a 'Tongan'; the derived adjective is the same. The capital is Nuku'alofa.

tongs

Tongs are like 'scissors', plural in form and taking a plural form of the verb:

The tongs are in the coal scuttle.

When 'a pair of' is used with *tongs*, then the verb agrees with the singular word 'pair':

A pair of tongs is essential if you have a live fire.

tonight

See also TODAY/TOMORROW/TONIGHT

top

Top can function as a noun:

He marched them up to the top of the hill.

as a verb:

She has topped the bill at the London Palladium.

tornado

Tornado forms its plural by adding '-es':

Tornadoes occur regularly in August and September.

torpedo

Torpedo forms its plural by adding '-es':

The submarine set out with a full complement of torpedoes.

torpor

Torpor suggests inactivity, often caused by heat:

He tried to overcome his torpor but it was hard to be active in such a climate.

The word is frequently misspelled with an '-our' ending.

See also SPELLING

tortoise

This word, like 'porpoise', is frequently mispronounced. In British English, it does not rhyme with 'boys'. The second syllable is unstressed. Lewis Carroll punned on the British pronunciation, which is similar to 'taught us'.

tortuous, torturous

These words are often misused. *Tortuous* literally means 'twisted or winding':

We walked for miles along a tortuous coastal road.

It is used frequently today to mean 'devious':

Only a tortuous mind would conceive of such a plot.

Torturous is the adjective derived from 'torture' and means 'painful, inflicting torture':

There was no escape from the throbbing, torturous pain.

total
Total can function as an adjective:
a total waste of time
a noun:
My total is 87. What's yours?
and as a verb:
total(s), totalled, totalling.
The 'l' is doubled before '-ed' and '-ing' in British English but not in American English:
The bill totaled $24.
The adverb is *totally* in both countries.

toupee
The word *toupee* meaning 'man's wig' is normally not italicized or written with an acute accent:
Many television reporters wear toupees.

tourniquet
A *tourniquet* is a device to control bleeding. The final syllable rhymes with 'hay':
This tourniquet will temporarily constrict the artery and so control the bleeding.

toward, towards
The preposition *towards* is more common than *toward* in Britain:
They walked towards the river.
The reverse is true in America:
They walked toward the river.
Both forms are, however, correct.

See also UK AND US ENGLISH, -WARD/-WARDS

town
See CITY/TOWN

toxin
See TOCSIN/TOXIN

trace
The adjective formed from *trace* is 'traceable':
He's simply not traceable. It's almost as if he has vanished.

track record
This phrase has been so overused that it has become little more than a synonym for 'experience' or 'success':
We intend to appoint an academic with a proven track record in research and administration.

trade names
The rules for dealing with trade names are simple:

■ Use capital letters for proprietary names that are still in copyright:
an Everite watch, a quartz watch
an Electrolux, an electric cleaner
a Toshiba, a television
Let's have a game of Scrabble.

■ Use lower-case letters for names that are widely used in the language as generics:
Have you got an aspro, please?
Can you hoover the curtains too?

See also ABBREVIATION, ACRONYM, NEOLOGISM

trade union
A *trade union* or, less commonly, *trades union* is an association of employees. The normal plural of this phrase is *trade unions*. The TUC is, however, an abbreviation of 'Trades Union Congress'.

See also ABBREVIATION

traffic
Traffic is most frequently used as a noun:
The traffic was terrible this morning. There's virtual gridlock between eight o'clock and nine.
Traffic is increasingly used as a verb meaning 'buy and sell, trade illegally':
He traffics in drugs and arms.
When the suffixes '-ed', '-er' and '-ing' are added, the verb takes a 'k':
He trafficked in drugs.
He was a drug trafficker.
He was accused of trafficking in drugs.

See also SPELLING

trait
This word may be pronounced to rhyme with 'fray' or 'freight'. The former pronunciation is more widespread in Britain; the latter in America. The American pronunciation is, however, increasingly heard in Britain.

tranquillity
The best known use of *tranquillity* is in Wordsworth's definition of poetry as 'emotion recollected in tranquillity'. The word has '-ll-' in British English but one 'l' is more usual in America:
The aim of meditation is inner tranquility.
Both communities spell the adjective with 'l':
I felt tranquil, at peace with myself and everyone else.
See also SPELLING

trans-
Trans-, or sometimes *tran-* before 's', is a prefix meaning 'across, crossing, on the other side':
The submarines were designed for transoceanic journeys.
I've travelled on the trans-Siberian railway.

The adjective 'transatlantic' (no hyphen and no capital letter for 'Atlantic') is often used of accents that have been influenced by American speech habits:

It was common in the 1960s for British radio disc-jockeys to acquire transatlantic accents.

transcend

The noun and adjective formed from *transcend* add '-ence' and '-ent' or '-ental' respectively. They are frequently misspelled with '-ance' and '-ant(al)'.

See also SPELLING

transfer

Transfer can function as a noun and a verb:

John wants a transfer to Nottingham.
He wants to be transferred to Nottingham.

The verb doubles the 'r' before '-ed' and '-ing':

They will be transferring three of their key players.

The 'r' is also doubled in the infrequently used noun 'transferrer':

The transferrer in this case is the person who transfers property from her name to that of the transferee, her daughter.

This noun is also written 'transferor', that is, with one 'r' and with an '-or' ending. The use of the single 'r' harmonizes it with the other nouns formed from *transfer*, 'transferable', 'transferee' and 'transference'.

transformational grammar

A *transformational grammar* (often referred to as TG) is a grammar that recognizes different levels of a language and that attempts to relate these levels systematically. It aims to parallel the native speaker's linguistic abilities and to emphasize the underlying similarities in all human languages.

See also ACTIVE VOICE/PASSIVE VOICE,
COMPETENCE AND PERFORMANCE, GRAMMAR

transient, transitory

These two adjectives share the meaning of 'of brief duration'. They differ in their emotive overtones. *Transient* tends to mean 'ephemeral':

It was a passing phase, a transient passion.

Transitory has overtones of regret, suggesting that the noun described disappears rapidly:

Her poem describes the transitory nature of love and life.

See also SYNONYM

transitive

A *transitive* verb is one that can take a direct object:

I like you.
I planted the trees.

Some verbs take two objects, an indirect object and a direct object:

I bought him a car.
I bought a car for him.
I sold Mona a car.
I sold a car to Mona.

These are sometimes called 'ditransitive verbs'.

Many verbs in English can occur in both transitive and non-transitive structures:

She writes novels.
What does she do for a living? She writes.

See also ACTIVE VOICE/PASSIVE VOICE,
ERGATIVE, INTRANSITIVE, VERB

translate

The derived noun is 'translator' with '-or':

He works as a translator for UNESCO.

The derived adjective is 'translatable', without an 'e':

Prose is translatable in a way that poetry is not.

See also -ABLE

translucent, transparent

The most important difference between these two adjectives is that *translucent* objects only allow light to pass through them whereas we can see through *transparent* objects. (The 'l' in *translucent* occurs in 'light' and may thus help us to remember the difference.)

We got frosted glass in the bathroom because it is translucent without being transparent.

transmit

The verb *transmit* means 'send or pass on':

The BBC charter does not allow the Corporation to transmit advertisements.

The verb is regular and doubles the 't' before endings:

transmit(s), transmitted, transmitting.

The noun for the object that transmits is a 'transmitter'; the message sent is a 'transmission'; and the normal adjective is 'transmissable' although 'transmittable' is growing in popularity.

transpire

When *transpire* is used to mean 'become known, leak out', it occurs in an impersonal construction:

We believed that he had lived abroad for many years but it transpired that he had never been further than Calais.

The growing use of *transpire* to mean 'happen' as in:

Let's see what transpires, shall we?

is often condemned as poor usage, but semantic

changes of this nature have occurred throughout the history of the language.

Transpire can be used in biology and physiology to describe the loss of moisture:

Plants transpire through the stomata of the leaves.

See also SEMANTIC CHANGE

transport, transportation

Transport can function as both a noun and a verb meaning 'move people or things from one place to another':

The cost of the transport of the students between the campuses was not fully considered at the time of the merger.

We'll need to transport the samples by air.

The noun can also be used to mean 'the vehicle(s) employed':

Due to engineering works on the line, bus transport will be provided between Leeds and Hull each Sunday in November. (Railway announcement)

In American English, *transportation* is generally used as the noun:

Transportation costs are escalating.

Transportation from the airport will not be provided and delegates will be expected to make their own way to the Conference Center.

The use of *transportation* is growing in Britain but is still frowned on by many who think it is an unnecessary variant of *transport*.

See also BARBARISM, UK AND US ENGLISH

trapezium, trapezoid

These words are not widely used outside mathematics. In Britain, a *trapezium* is a quadrilateral with two parallel sides of unequal length. This type of figure is normally called a *trapezoid* in America, where a *trapezium* has no parallel sides.

The plural in both communities is *trapeziums*.

See also UK AND US ENGLISH

trash

Trash used to be regarded as the American equivalent of British 'rubbish':

UK: Put it in with the rubbish.

US: Put it in the trash can.

Trash is now quite widely used in Britain to mean 'foolish talk, nonsense' and 'poor writing':

Don't talk trash.

How anyone could recommend such trash for a literary award is beyond me.

As a verb, especially in journalism, it is used as a synonym for 'rubbish':

Using their conference to trash the opposition parties is not the way to maintain power.

See also RUBBISH

trauma

The word *trauma* and its derived adjective *traumatic* are widely used today as loose synonyms for 'shock' and 'upsetting':

Their trauma began when the taxi failed to arrive on time.

I've just had a traumatic interview with the bank!

This has been caused, in part, by their frequent use in tabloid journalism.

Trauma has different meanings depending on whether it is used in a medical or psychological context. In the first, it can mean 'a bodily wound or injury':

The patient arrived in A & E [Accident and Emergency] suffering from a severe trauma to the chest.

In the second, it means 'severe shock, likely to cause lasting emotional or psychological damage':

The general public has been made aware of the trauma suffered by parents whose children die in road accidents.

The usual pronunciation is for the first syllable to rhymes with 'draw', but the pronunciation that rhymes with 'trow' is also acceptable, although less common. Most dictionaries offer 'traumata' and 'traumas' as the plural of *trauma* but the first form occurs very seldom, even in medical textbooks.

See also SEMANTIC CHANGE

travel

Travel can function as a noun and a verb:

Travel broadens the mind.

I want to travel for a year before starting college.

In Britain, the verb doubles the 'l' before suffixes:

travelled, traveller, travelling

but a single 'l' is used in America:

traveled, traveler, traveling.

There are many differences in the terminology for travel in Britain and the United States, although the increase in international travel and exchanged television programmes has made many speakers of British English familiar with both varieties.

See also AMERICANISM, ANGLICISM, UK AND US ENGLISH

tread

Tread can function as a noun:

With a martial tread

Through a storm of lead ...

and as a verb:

Don't tread on the flowers.

The verb is no longer widely used. It is irregular:

tread(s), trod, trodden

and the form 'trod' is occasionally heard as the past participle.

treble, triple

These words both derive from Latin *triplus* 'threefold'. They are often used interchangeably but there are differences. *Treble* is best used to mean 'three times':

He wanted treble the amount.

The monster trebled in size between the first sighting and the third!

Triple is best used to mean 'consisting of three parts':

What were the countries involved in the Triple Alliance between 1882 and 1914?

The triple jump is very hard on the ankles.

The words are also used differently in music. A *treble* is a soprano voice or high-pitched instrument; *triple* time involves three beats to the bar.

trek

The noun and verb *trek* both came into English from Afrikaans in the nineteenth century. As a noun, it means a 'long and difficult journey':

In the Great Trek of 1833, the Boers migrated on foot and in ox wagons from the Cape to the Orange Free State.

The related verb doubles the 'k' before '-ed', '-er' and '-ing':

trekked, trekker, trekking.

tremendous

This overworked adjective is often mispronounced. It ends in '-ous' and not '-ious'. Speakers who use an '-ious' pronunciation are perhaps analogizing from adjectives such as 'tedious'.

See also GRIEF/GRIEVE/GRIEVOUS

tremor

This word, which means 'shiver', 'shake', 'vibrate', is frequently misspelled. It ends in '-or', not '-our':

Earth tremors have been reported from New Zealand to Okinawa.

See also SPELLING

Trinidad

Trinidad is the larger portion of the West Indian republic properly known as Trinidad and Tobago. An inhabitant of the island is a 'Trinidadian'. The capital is Port-of-Spain.

triple

See also TREBLE/TRIPLE

triumphal, triumphant

These adjectives are occasionally confused. *Triumphal* means 'celebrating a triumph, often a military triumph':

The triumphal processions after the Falklands War were criticized by many.

Triumphant means 'victorious, delighting in success':

Manchester United's triumphant team was greeted by thousands of cheering Mancunians.

trivia

Trivia means 'petty details, trifles':

He feels that he should not be bothered with such trivia as how to pay the rent.

The word derives from Latin *trivium*, 'junction of three roads', and is, like 'data', a plural form. We should, therefore, write:

Such trivia were not worthy of his attention.

and not:

*Such trivia was not worthy of his attention.

Some users are now treating *trivia* as a singular noun:

I can't be bothered with all this trivia.

Such usage is not, however, totally acceptable. The best advice is either to treat trivia as a plural noun or, if the structure seems pedantic, to substitute a phrase for trivia. A sentence such as:

Such trivia are time consuming.

proved unacceptable to students of English, but so did:

Such trivia is time consuming.

Acceptable alternatives were:

Such trivia can be time consuming.

I find such trivia time consuming.

Trivial matters are time consuming.

troop, troupe

These words are homophones, rhyming with 'hoop'. They both derive from French *troupe* but their meanings are distinct. A *troop* is a group of people or animals:

a troop of children

a troop of monkeys

a troop of foot soldiers.

A *troupe* is a company of actors or performers:

She used to lead a troupe of acrobats.

The derived nouns *trooper* and *trouper* are also distinguished. A *trooper* is a cavalry soldier in Britain, a mounted policeman in Australia and Canada, and a state policeman in the United States.

A *trouper* is a member of a troupe:

He has been a trouper with the company for ten years.

The expression 'trooping the colour' is almost exclusively British and means 'ceremonial parade of a flag or regimental colour':

Visitors enjoy the annual Trooping of the Colour in London, partly because it is attended by the monarch, the prime minister and other dignitaries.

trousers

The word *trousers* is plural:

These trousers are torn.

The phrase 'a pair of trousers' is singular:

A pair of trousers was produced.

The expression 'to wear the trousers' meaning to be the dominant partner tends to be British, the American equivalent being 'wear the pants':

UK: She wears the trousers in that family.
US: She wears the pants in that family.

See also TONGS, UK AND US ENGLISH

truism

A *truism* is an 'obvious truth, a tautology':

It may be a truism to say that dogs are animals but many owners treat them like children.

See also TAUTOLOGY

try and, try to

Many speakers of English use these forms interchangeably in such structures as:

I'll try and do better.
I'll try to do better.

These are both acceptable in all but the most formal of contexts, but *try to* is widely regarded as the more correct. It is certainly less restricted in its use:

He didn't try to do better.
*He didn't try and do better.
She tried to do better.
*She tried and do better.

tsar, tzar

See CZAR/TSAR/TZAR

tsetse

The word *tsetse* comes from Tswana and is sometimes spelled 'tzetze':

The tsetse fly killed thousands of cows in Africa.

tsunami

The word *tsunami* refers to a large destructive wave, especially one that is caused by an earthquake:

The tsunami often cause more devastation that the earthquakes.

The word comes from Japanese *tsu*, 'port', + *nami*, 'wave'.

tuba, tuber

These words are homophones. A *tuba* is a brass musical instrument:

The usual plural of 'tuba' is 'tubas', although 'tubae' is occasionally found.

A *tuber* is the fleshy, underground stem of a plant:

Potatoes and yams are tubers.

tumour, tumor

A *tumour* is an abnormal swelling:

She was relieved when she heard that her tumour was benign.

The word ends in '-our' in British English and '-or' in American.

See also SPELLING

Tunisia

An inhabitant of the African republic is a 'Tunisian'; the derived adjective is the same. The capital is Tunis.

tunnel

The 'l' is doubled before suffixes in British English:

tunnelled, tunneller, tunnelling

but left single in American English:

tunneled, tunneler, tunneling.

See also SPELLING

turbid, turgid

Many adjectives ending in '-id' cause problems for users. This is particularly true of *turbid* and *turgid*, because they can both be applied to liquids and to writing. *Turbid* comes from Latin *turbidus* and means 'muddy or opaque' when applied to liquids:

The children must not swim here. The water is still but turbid.

It can mean 'dense, unclear' when applied to writing:

He gained a reputation for intelligence in spite of his turbid prose.

Turgid comes from Latin *turgidus* and means 'swollen', 'congested' when applied to liquids or, more recently, traffic:

After weeks of rain, the rivers were turgid and fast flowing.

It can mean 'pompous' when applied to writing:

Osric's style might well be described as turgid.

Turkey

An inhabitant of the Europe country is a 'Turk'; the derived adjective is 'Turkish'. The capital is Ankara.

turquoise

This word, originally from Turkish, came into the language from fourteenth-century French. It is used as an adjective to refer to a colour between blue and green:

She wore a turquoise dress.

Turquoise is also used as the name for a gemstone:

The brooch was made of a single diamond surrounded by turquoises.

There are three main pronunciations of this word: where the second syllable rhymes with 'boys'; where the 'w' is omitted and where the second syllable rhymes with 'boys'; and where the second syllable rhymes with 'jars'.

Tuvalu

An inhabitant of the island group in the south Pacific is a 'Tuvaluan'; the derived adjective is the same. The capital is Funafuti.

twelfth

The CONSONANT CLUSTER at the end of this word causes many speakers to drop the 'f', causing the word to rhyme with 'health'. The 'f' should not be dropped in careful speech.

type

See KIND/SORT/TYPE

typo

A *typo* is an acceptable abbreviation of 'typographical error':

There were so many typos in the text that it was easier to retype it than to correct it.

tyre

See TIRE/TYRE

U

u

U is a vowel. It has two main pronunciations and can represent the vowels in 'put' and 'bun'. Often the letter 'o' occurs in the spelling of words that rhyme with others that have 'u'. We can compare, for example:

come with gum
done with gun
some with sum.

The capital letter *U* is used as a symbol for Uranium and occurs in the compounds:

U-boat (abbreviation of the German *Unterseeboot* = submarine)
U-bolt (bolt shaped like the letter 'u')
U-turn (change of direction).

See also SPELLING

U and non-U

The terms *U and non-U* were coined by the British academic, Alan S.C. Ross, in the 1950s. 'U' was shorthand for 'upper-class speech' and 'non-U' for all the rest. Ross wrote a number of books and articles distinguishing prestigious U forms from stigmatized non-U equivalents. He claimed, for example, that U speakers invariably put the stress on the first syllable of 'amicable', said 'rich' and not 'wealthy' and avoided clichés such as 'leave no stone unturned' and jargon such as 'pilot project'. However, he insisted that it was possible to be too affected in speech. For example, he would rule out the use of such a phrase as 'beyond a peradventure'.

Ross was correct in believing that speakers often reveal their class origins in their speech. His comments are, however, markedly classist and now very dated, although they still carry weight in parts of British society. His comment on the use of 'chalet' illustrates the snobbery of such an attitude:

CHALET – at a holiday camp – is non-U because holiday camps are non-U.

If speakers of English are to communicate freely, then certain standards of pronunciation, vocabulary and syntax are clearly desirable. Today, however, these standards are more likely to be set by radio and television than by a privileged minority.

See also RECEIVED PRONUNCIATION, SHIBBOLETH

Uganda

An inhabitant of the African republic is a 'Ugandan'; the derived adjective is the same. The capital is Kampala.

ugli fruit

An *ugli fruit* is a citrus fruit with a wrinkled skin. It is usually quite large, like a grapefruit, and is the result of cross-breeding tangerines, oranges and grapefruit. The name is a variation of 'ugly', orthographically influenced by such prefixes as:

maxi- (e.g., maxi-skirt)
mini- (e.g., mini-car)
uni- (e.g., uni-vax).

The plural of *ugli* can be either *uglies* or *uglis*.

UHF

The abbreviation *UHF* stands for 'ultra-high frequency', a frequency used for radio transmission.

See also ABBREVIATION

UK and US English

It would not be possible to describe all the differences between the varieties of English used in these two communities, but we can offer a number of comments on the differences most apparent at the levels of grammar and morphology, pronunciation, spelling and vocabulary.

Grammar and morphology

There is a range of grammatical usage in both communities that reflects a speaker's age, education, region of origin and social aspirations. As far as the standard language goes, the overlap between the varieties is large and increasing. We can, however, classify a number of potential differences under such headings as adverbial usage, article usage, nouns, prepositional usage, pronouns and verbs.

■ Adverbial usage. In colloquial American English, intensifying adjectives such as 'real' are often used instead of the adverb 'really':

He's a real smooth talker. (really)

Many Americans dislike this usage.

Adverbs ending in '-wise' are found more widely in American English:

Brainswise, she's in a class of her own.

Many Americans are as vociferous in their criticism of this usage as their British counterparts.

US speakers can use 'already' and 'yet' with the simple past:

US: Did you do it already?
UK: Have you done it already?
US: Did she see it yet?

UK: Has she seen it yet?

Adverbials such as 'momentarily' and 'presently' are used in American English to mean 'in a moment' and 'now, at present':

US: I'll do it momentarily.

UK: I'll do it in a moment/minute.

US: Presently, he's in Oregon.

UK: He's in Oregon at present.

■ Article usage is virtually identical, but there are a number of idioms that differ between UK and US speakers. Among them are the following:

UK	US
be in hospital	be in the hospital
go to university	go to a university
in future	in the future

Americans tend to use 'a half dozen', 'a half hour', 'a half pound' rather than 'half an hour/dozen/pound':

I've brought about a half dozen discs.

We'll be in Buffalo in about a half hour.

About a half pound will do.

■ Nouns. Most nouns pattern identically in British and American English, but there are a few differences. Some nouns that are plural in British English are singular in American English:

UK: innings, maths

US: inning, math.

Most speakers of American English regard collective nouns as invariably singular. The British use of:

The Labour Party are now more electable than for 20 years.

would not be acceptable even in the American tabloid press.

■ Prepositional usage. The same range of single and compound prepositions exists in American and British English, with both countries using the following list for as much as 90 per cent of their needs:

at, by, for, from, in, of, on, to, with.

There are, however, a number of differences between the two varieties, differences that are marked tendencies rather than absolutes. American English tends to differ from British English in the use of:

UK	US
behind	in back of
different from	different than
rows A to F	rows A through F

Americans often insert a preposition where one is not required in the UK:

Did you meet *with* the President?

He prevented it *from* happening.

I plan to visit *with* you guys early next month.

Americans sometimes uses a different preposition:

UK	US
to fill in	to fill out (a form)
to talk to	to talk with

Sometimes Americans omit a preposition where one would be required in Britain:

UK	US
They were not at home.	They were not home.
She works by night.	She works nights.
He fell out of the window.	He fell out the window.
It started on Monday.	It started Monday.

■ Pronouns, like nouns, are used in a very similar way in both communities. The two chief differences are related to the use of the indefinite pronoun 'one'. Americans tend to avoid the use of 'one' in all but the most formal of contexts:

UK: One should try one's best.

US: You should try your best.

Americans prefer the use of 'each other' to 'one another' in all but the most formal of styles:

UK: We love one another.

US: We love each other.

■ Verbs. Most rules of morphology are shared, but a few differences can be found. Many verbs that have '-t' as a marker of the past tense in British English have the more regular '-ed' in America:

UK: burnt, dreamt, learnt, spoilt

US: burned, dreamed, learned, spoiled.

Many people in Britain also use '-ed' endings, partly because of influence from American publications but also because of analogy with regular verbs:

burn: compare turn, turned

dream: compare team, teamed

learn: compare yearn, yearned

spoil: compare foil, foiled.

The most widely-recognized morphological difference is that most Americans use 'gotten' as the past participle of 'get', causing the verb to parallel 'forget':

I've gotten straight As.

They do, however, tend to say:

I've got it. (I understand.)

Many American speakers use 'fit', 'dove' and 'shrunk' as the normal past tense forms of the verbs 'fit', 'dive' and 'shrink':

I fit new brakes last week.

He dove head first into the ravine.

Honey, I shrunk the kids.

Many Americans use derivational suffixes more widely than is the case in Britain, resulting in greater acceptance of such verbs as:

Word	+ suffix	Derived verb
burglar	+ -ize	burglarize
city	+ -ify	citify

In American English, more nouns can be used as verbs without any derivational endings.

Noun	Verb
room	room (I'm rooming in Bodington now.)
window	window (We expect to window a house a day.)

American speakers tend to use the subjunctive more frequently in formal styles, especially in 'that' clauses:

I suggested that she be promoted.

He asked that we be informed.

It is essential that she be treated as normally as possible.

Auxiliary usage is similar in both communities, but the following generalized differences are apparent. 'Will/'ll' is preferred to 'shall' in American English:

I will be visiting with Aiko next week.

I won't try that again.

'Would' is used in American English for three purposes for which it is rarely used in Britain. These are:

to express habitual actions in the past:

When we were young, we would holiday in the mountains.

to express hypothetical expressions:

I wish I would have said the right thing.

and to parallel the use of 'would' in the main clause:

I would have gone if I would have known about it.

'Dare', 'need' and 'used' can occur as quasi-modals in Britain but not, usually, in America:

UK	US
I daren't go	I don't dare (to) go
I needn't go	I don't need to go
I usedn't to go	I didn't use to go

Pronunciation

There is a range of pronunciations in both countries but the prestigious varieties tend to be those used by newscasters on the major television channels. These tend to be known as Received Pronunciation (RP) or BBC English in Britain and General American English (GAE) in the United States of America. It should be added that several British accents, including some in Scotland and Northern Ireland, have more in common with GAE than with RP. The main differences are summarized below.

■ RP is non-rhotic; GAE is rhotic. This means that 'r' is not pronounced in words such as 'far' and 'farm' in RP but is pronounced in GAE.

■ There is a regular difference in pronunciation in words such as 'not', 'stock', 'top' and in the first syllable of 'possible'.

■ There are fewer syllable reductions in GAE.

■ The stressed syllable often differs in such words as 'ballet', 'cigarette' and 'debris'.

■ In polysyllabic words, such as 'dictionary', 'laboratory' and 'secretary', there is often a greater range of secondary stress.

■ There are a number of words that are regularly pronounced differently. These include:

Word	RP Rhymes with	GAE
ate	get	gate
lever	weaver	ever
processes	less is	less ease
shone	gone	bone

An important point to stress, however, is that we find a range of pronunciations in both communities. Some speakers from Georgia and Carolina, for example, resemble RP speakers in not pronouncing 'r' in words such as 'far' and 'farm'; and some speakers from Belfast, Glasgow and Yeovil resemble GAE speakers in pronouncing post-vocalic 'r'. The range of variation is considerable in both communities and, increasingly, because of the influence of television and films, GAE is influencing pronunciation worldwide.

Spelling

The majority of English words, especially the most irregular, are spelled the same way in both countries:

bough, bought, cough, caught, dough, eight, knock, mnemonic, pneumonia, rhythmic, should, shoulder.

There are, however, a number of systematic spelling differences, although it should be added that there is considerable inconsistency in both countries. Some of the main differences are listed below.

■ ae/oe/e

UK: anaesthetic, encyclopaedia, diarrhoea, foetus

US: anesthetic, encyclopedia, diarrhea, fetus

■ dge/dg

UK: acknowledgement, judgement

US: acknowledgment, judgment

■ ection/exion

UK: inflexion

US: inflection

■ en/in

UK: enclose, ensure

US: inclose, insure

■ ence/ense

UK: defence, licence (noun)

US: defense, license (noun)

■ gg/g

UK: waggon

US: wagon

■ **l/ll**

UK: fulfilment, instal, levelled, skilful
US: fulfillment, install, leveled, skillful

■ **mme/m**

UK: programme
US: program

■ **ou/o**

UK: mould, smoulder
US: mold, smolder

■ **our/or**

UK: colour, labour
US: color, labor

■ **pp/p**

UK: kidnapper, worshipping
US: kidnaper/kidnapper, worshiping/worshipping

■ **ss/s**

UK: buses
US: busses/buses

■ **re/er**

UK: centre, theatre
US: center, theater.

The use of '-ise' and '-ize' endings to such words as 'organize' is sometimes included as a difference between UK and US usage. It should be noted, however, that '-ize' is widely accepted in Britain and is as acceptable in all forms as '-ise'.

There are, in addition, a number of individual words that are spelled differently but that do not form a particular pattern. The best known of these are:

UK	US
cheque	check
disc	disk
jewellery	jewelry
plough	plow
sulphur	sulfur
tyre	tire

Vocabulary

The many vocabulary differences between UK and US English can be categorized under three main headings:

■ Words that are known only in one country:

Oxbridge (pertaining to Oxford and Cambridge Universities) (UK)

spanner (monkey wrench) (UK)

molasses (treacle) (US)

sophomore (second-year student) (US)

■ Words that have different meanings in the two countries:

chaps (UK men, US leggings)

homely (UK warm, friendly, US ugly)

public school (UK private, US open to all)

tights (UK pantihose, US skin-tight garment covering the body)

■ Words that are widely recognized as being equivalent:

autumn/fall; boot/trunk; entitled/titled; firework/firecracker; pavement/sidewalk; railway/railroad.

The major semantic fields in which differences occur are in clothing, education, food and drink, household and accommodation, and travel. The main differences are listed below, but many of the American terms are also heard in Britain.

■ Clothing:

UK	US
anorak	parka
bowler hat	derby
braces	suspenders
dress suit	tuxedo
dressing gown	bathrobe
duffel coat	pea jacket
handbag	purse, pocket book
jewellery	jewelry
jumper	sweater
pinafore	jumper
purse	change purse
pyjamas	pajamas
suspenders	garters
tie	necktie
trainers	sneakers
trousers	pants, slacks
(under)pants	(under)shorts
vest	undershirt
waistcoat	vest
wallet	billfold

■ Education:

UK	US
class, form	grade
curriculum vitae, CV	résumé, CV
dissertation, thesis	thesis, dissertation
essay, paper	paper, report, essay
first-year student	freshman
fourth-year, finalist	senior
homework, assignment	assignment
lecturer	assistant professor
long essay, paper	thesis
mathematics, maths	mathematics, math
(post)graduate	graduate
primary school	grade school
professor	full, senior professor
public school	private school
reader	associate professor, professor
second-year student	sophomore
secondary school	high school
senior lecturer	associate professor
staff	faculty
state school	public school

supervisor	adviser, mentor	estate agent	realtor
technical college	junior college	first floor	ground floor
term, semester	semester	flat (rented)	apartment
third-year student	junior	flat (owned)	condo(minium)
university	college, university	garden	yard
		larder	pantry

■ Food and drink:

UK	US
angel cake	plain cake, angel food cake
aubergine	eggplant
bap	hamburger bun
biscuit	cookie
chips	French fries
courgettes	zucchini
crisps	chips
grill	broil
jam	jelly
jelly	jello
kipper	smoked herring
marrow	squash
milk	cream
minced meat	chopped/ground hamburger meat
neat (without water)	straight
porridge	oatmeal
scone	biscuit
single cream	table cream
soft drink	soda, pop
spirits	liquor
sultanas	raisins
sweets	candy
Swiss roll	jelly roll
takeaway	fast food
whiskey cocktail	highball
with ice	on the rocks

Some foods are characteristically British:

bubble and squeak (mashed potato and cabbage), Cornish pasty, crumpets, Lancashire hotpot, toad-in-the-hole (mashed potato and sausage), Welsh rarebit, Yorkshire pudding.

There are also some characteristically American foods and dishes:

apple butter, blueberry pie, corn bread/dog/pone, hominy grits, lox (smoked salmon), pumpkin pie, succotash (sweet corn and lima beans), root beer.

Many of yesterday's Americanisms are now current in Britain.

■ Household and accommodation:

UK	US
aluminium	aluminum
blinds	shades
block of flats	apartment building
chest of drawers	bureau or dresser
clothes peg	clothes pin
cooker	stove
cot	crib
cupboard	closet
curtains	drapes
dustbin	ash-, trash- or garbage can
eiderdown	comforter

estate agent	realtor
first floor	ground floor
flat (rented)	apartment
flat (owned)	condo(minium)
garden	yard
larder	pantry
let	lease or rent
lift	elevator
lodger	roomer
maisonette	flat
paraffin	kerosene
power point or socket	outlet or socket
semi-detached	duplex
sideboard	buffet
tap	faucet or tap
washbasin or sink	sink
wash	wash up
wash up	do the dishes.

■ Travel:

UK	US
articulated lorry	trailer truck
bonnet (of car)	hood
book (holiday)	reserve, make a reservation
boot (of car)	trunk
caravan	trailer
car park	parking lot
carriageway	highway
central reservation	median strip or median divider
cloakroom (restaurant)	washroom or checkroom
coach	(long-distance) bus
cul-de-sac	dead-end
diversion	detour
dual carriageway	divided highway
dynamo	generator
estate car	station wagon
gear lever	gear shift
guard (railway)	conductor (railroad)
junction	intersection
lay-by	pull-off
left-luggage room	baggage room
level crossing	grade crossing
licence	license
milometer	odometer
motorway	freeway, superhighway or express way
mudguard or wing	fender
number plate	license plate
pavement	sidewalk
petrol	gasoline, gas
railway	railroad
receptionist	desk clerk
return (ticket)	round-trip (ticket)
reversing lights	back-up lights
route (pronounced 'root')	route (pronounced 'rowt')
silencer	muffler
single (ticket)	one-way (ticket)
subway	underpass
sump	oil pan

timetable	schedule
toilet	restroom or washroom
tube, underground	subway

UK English

UK is the abbreviation for United Kingdom, a term that includes England, Scotland, Wales and Northern Ireland. It is often used as a synonym for Britain or Great Britain, but the latter term does not include Northern Ireland. Because of the confusion that these terms can cause, it is advisable, when precision is required, to specify the countries being referred to.

The population of the United Kingdom is approximately 57 million and many different forms of English are spoken, the main variants being:

Standard English with a variety of accents, including RP

Scottish Englishes (e.g., Glaswegian)

Welsh Englishes (e.g., Valleys English)

Northern Ireland Englishes (e.g., Hiberno-English, Ulster Scots)

Dialect Englishes with regional accents (e.g., West Yorkshire dialect)

Creole Englishes (e.g., London Jamaican)

Asian Englishes (e.g., Bradford Bengali English)

European Englishes (e.g., Italian English).

Each variety has its own system, but all varieties are influenced by media English.

See also ACCENT, DIALECT

Ukraine

An inhabitant of the republic, formerly part of the USSR, is a 'Ukrainian'; the derived adjective is the same. The capital is Kiev.

Ulster

Ulster is one of the many regional terms that can imply different things to different people. Before 1922 the term referred to one of the four provinces of Ireland, consisting of the nine counties of Antrim, Armagh, Cavan, Derry, Donegal, Down, Fermanagh and Tyrone. After the treaty that partitioned Ireland, some people used 'Ulster' to refer to the six counties of Northern Ireland – that is, traditional Ulster without Cavan, Donegal and Monaghan.

The term *Scotch Irish* is often used in America for people from Ulster. It is rarely heard in Britain or Ireland.

ultimate

Ultimate can function as an adjective meaning 'eventual', 'final':

My ultimate goal is to make enough money to retire at fifty.

and as a noun meaning 'extreme':

That demonstration was the ultimate in bad taste.

The noun has become a vogue word in advertising, meaning 'best', 'most desirable':

The ultimate sauna – at a price you can afford.

ultimatum

The plural of this word is *ultimatums*:

He sends so many ultimatums that we disregard them now.

ultra

Ultra is a prefix meaning 'beyond or surpassing a specified limit':

ultra-conservative, ultra-modern, ultra-nationalistic.

Often, the hyphen is dropped:

UHF (ultrahigh frequency), ultraviolet.

It also occurs in a political context as an adjective meaning 'extreme', often 'immoderate':

He was proud to call himself an ultra right winger.

un-

Un- is an extremely flexible PREFIX in English. It has several meanings but tends to be associated with the negative of the unmodified form:

happy, unhappy (= not happy)

willing, unwilling (= not willing).

This prefix most frequently combines with adjectives, adverbs and verbs:

clean, unclean

likely, unlikely

do, undo

but it also combines with some participles, both past and present:

seen, unseen

loving, unloving.

See also AFFIX, NEGATIVE, PREFIX

unable

See INCAPABLE/UNABLE

unadvisable

See INADVISABLE/UNADVISABLE

unanimous

Unanimous is an adjective implying that every member of a group or committee is of the same opinion:

The decision was unanimous. We all felt strongly about the need for accommodation for the homeless. (All members of the group reached the same decision.)

This differs from a majority decision, where one or more members may disagree. A single individual cannot make a unanimous decision.

unarmed

See DISARMED/UNARMED

unauthorized

This adjective is acceptable with the endings '-ised' and '-ized', although the latter is more widespread, even in Britain.

unaware, unawares

The simple rule is that *unaware*, the form without 's', is used as an adjective, most frequently a predicative adjective:

I was unaware that you were interested in the post.

although it can, occasionally, be used attributively:

If you were unaware of my interest, you must be the most unaware employer in history.

The form *unawares* means 'without prior warning' and is used adverbially:

His angry outburst took me unawares. I would never have anticipated such behaviour.

Occasionally, the form without the 's' is used adverbially:

I don't like being taken unaware.

This usage is growing in popularity and is related to the loss of distinction between words with '-ward' and '-wards'.

See also ADJECTIVE, ADVERB, -WARD/-WARDS

unbalanced

Unbalanced can mean both 'out of equilibrium':

The argument was unbalanced; only 20 per cent of the letter discussed the less popular view.

and 'mentally unstable':

As many as one in eight of us will be unbalanced mentally at some stage in our lives.

unbelief

See DISBELIEF/UNBELIEF

unbiased

This adjective means 'fair, impartial':

I need a totally unbiased opinion on this essay.

It is usual to spell it with one 's' but *unbiassed* is also acceptable.

See also SPELLING

unchangeable

This adjective adds '-able' to 'change':

She seemed unchanging and unchangeable in a world that was otherwise falling apart.

See also SPELLING

uncle

The world *uncle* was borrowed from French and is used with the following meanings: the brother of one's mother or father (there is no distinction in English between a maternal and a paternal uncle); the husband of one's aunt; and an affectionate term for a male friend of one's parents. The word is also employed as slang for a pawnbroker.

See also FAMILY RELATIONSHIP

Uncle Tom

Uncle Tom was the eponymous hero of Harriet Beecher Stowe's novel *Uncle Tom's Cabin* (1852). Uncle Tom was a gentle, faithful, religious slave and his character did much to change the white stereotype of black people in the United States in the nineteenth century. The name began to be used as a derogatory term for any black who seems obsequious or too uncritical of white values; any member of a low-status group who is regarded as overly subservient; and anyone, including a woman, who cooperates too willingly and too uncritically with oppressive bosses or regimes.

unconscious

See SUBCONSCIOUS/UNCONSCIOUS

uncooperative

Uncooperative is normally written as one word without a hyphen.

See also HYPHEN

uncoordinated

Uncoordinated is normally written as one word without a hyphen.

See also HYPHEN

uncorrected

See INCORRECT/UNCORRECTED

unction, unguent

Unction means 'oil or ointment, usually for anointing a dying person':

Why is the Sacrament of anointing known as 'Extreme Unction'?

The related adjective, *unctuous*, meaning 'slippery, oily charm' has '-uous' not '-ious':

Chadband's unctuous manner is unattractive to the modern reader.

Unguent derives from the same Latin root as *unction* but is used for 'ointment', 'grease':

What sort of sticky unguent was he wearing on his hair?

This word is pronounced to rhyme approximately with 'young Gwent'.

under, underneath

See BELOW/BENEATH/UNDER/UNDERNEATH, UNDER WAY

under-

Under- can function as a prefix. It combines with a large range of forms:

underage, undercut, underdone, underlining.

Usually, the compounds are written without hyphens although newly-coined compounds may, at first, be hyphenated:

under-developed, under-stated.

under the circumstances

See IN THE CIRCUMSTANCES/UNDER THE CIRCUMSTANCES

under way

The phrase *under way* means 'in progress', 'on the move':

The meeting is already under way.

There is a tendency for people to write it as a single word and, although some people object to it, the tendency is likely to grow. If we modify the above example slightly to:

The meeting is already well under way.

we can see that we are treating *under way* as a compound and modifying it as we might 'undervalued' in:

The secretary is grossly undervalued.

'Under weigh' is incorrect and is either a blend or a folk etymology.

See also BLEND, ETYMOLOGY, WORD FORMATION

underdeveloped countries

Political correctness has caused a number of changes in the language. The adjectives applied to countries that were formerly colonies can provide an interesting sociological commentary on the attitudes of Europeans, in particular. Countries have been referred to as 'undeveloped', 'third-world', 'developing' and *underdeveloped*. The use of the third adjective suggests that even if the organizations necessary for Western-style capitalism are missing, they are capable of being developed.

See also POLITICAL CORRECTNESS

underhand, underhanded

These two adjectives are becoming confused. *Underhand* means 'secretive, sly, dishonest' or 'underarm':

John would never stoop to such underhand methods.

Is underhand bowling a requirement?

Underhanded means 'understaffed':

We're severely underhanded because of the flu virus.

This is a useful distinction but it is rapidly disappearing. A newspaper report in September 1995, for example, claimed:

Underhanded agreements, where money is used to oil wheels, are no longer condemned.

undernourished

See MALNOURISHED/UNDERNOURISHED

underpass

See FLYOVER/UNDERPASS

underprivileged

Underprivileged can be used as an adjective and a noun for people who do not have as many social and economic advantages as other members of society. It suggests that, although some may have more privileges than others, everyone in a particular society has some privileges. An alternative term is 'disadvantaged':

She works with children from underprivileged backgrounds.

The underprivileged, like the poor, are always with us.

See also POLITICAL CORRECTNESS

understand

Understand is an irregular verb that parallels the verb 'stand':

understand(s), understood, understanding, understood.

See also VERB

understatement

Understatement is a figure of speech, also known as LITOTES:

I'm not uninterested in him. (I'm very interested.)

It frequently occurs in speech and emphasizes a point by stressing its opposite:

He's by no means poor. (He's very well off.)

She's no chicken. (She's quite mature.)

undertake

Undertake is an irregular verb that patterns like the verb 'take':

undertake(s), undertook, undertaking, undertaken.

See also VERB

undigested

See INDIGESTIBLE/UNDIGESTED

undiscriminating

See INDISCRIMINATE/UNDISCRIMINATING

undoubtedly

Undoubtedly is a sentence adverbial, which means that it modifies a sentence, emphasizing that a statement being made is not likely to be disputed:

He was, undoubtedly, the most intelligent student I have ever taught.

This adverb does not have an unprefixed form. In other words:

*doubtedly

cannot be used. Quite a number of words exist in a negative form only:

defunct, *funct

disgruntled, *gruntled

dishevelled, *hevelled

inert, *ert.

See also AFFIRMATIVE/NEGATIVE, AFFIX, NEGATIVE PREFIX

uneatable
See INEDIBLE/UNEATABLE

unequal
When *unequal* is used to mean 'inadequate', 'insufficient', 'not up to', it is followed by the preposition 'to':

The student was unequal to the task.

There is a tendency to use the incorrect preposition 'for':

*The student was unequal for the task.

partly because of the influence from the acceptable structure 'unfit for':

The student was unfit for the task.

unequivocal
Unequivocal means 'not ambiguous', 'plain':

I was given an unequivocal promise that my vehicle would be ready for collection at noon.

unexceptionable, unexceptional
These adjectives are sometimes confused. *Unexceptionable* means 'beyond criticism':

Her behaviour has always been unexceptionable.

Unexceptional is a much less complimentary adjective meaning 'ordinary', 'usual':

She was a pleasant, unexceptional student.

unfertilized, infertile
These adjectives are often used, incorrectly, as synonyms. *Unfertilized* means 'not fertilized':

They plan to leave the field fallow and unfertilized for a year.

The phrase 'unfertilized egg' is found in texts dealing with human fertility.

Infertile means 'incapable of being fertilized or of being productive':

The land has been overused and will become infertile if immediate steps are not taken.

unforgettable
Unforgettable is an adjective:

'Unforgettable, that's what you are …'

It is frequently misspelled with only one 't' but *unforgetable is not acceptable anywhere in the English-speaking world.

See also SPELLING

unfrequented
See INFREQUENT/UNFREQUENTED

unilateral
Unilateral means 'affecting or occurring on only one side':

Rhodesia's unilateral declaration of independence in 1965 was immediately condemned by the United Nations.

The term is frequently used in diplomatic language and contrasts with 'bilateral' (on two sides) and 'multilateral' (on many sides):

The Bosnian Serbs have declared a unilateral cease-fire.

The Croats and the Serbs have declared a bilateral cease-fire.

The four groups engaged in hostilities have declared a multilateral cease-fire.

uninhabitable
See HABITABLE/INHABITABLE/UNINHABITABLE

uninterested
See DISINTERESTED/UNINTERESTED

unique
The adjective *unique* comes from Latin *unicus* (*unus* = one) and means 'being the only one of a single type', 'without equal':

The earth seems to be unique in the solar system in that it, alone, seems capable of supporting life.

Every fingerprint is unique.

Because of its meaning, *unique* cannot be graded. By definition, an object or event cannot be more or less unequalled, and therefore expressions such as:

*more unique

*most unique

*rather unique

*very unique

are logically unacceptable. However, logic is not always adhered to in usage, and the increased occurrence of sentences such as:

It was the most unique experience of my life.

suggests that its meaning is changing from 'unequalled' to 'remarkable' or 'notable'. Such a semantic shift could rob us of a useful distinction. We have many words for 'notable', few for 'unequalled', and consequently there is resistance to the change.

See also ADJECTIVE, GRADABLE

unlawful
See ILLEGAL/UNLAWFUL

unmistakable
The adjective *unmistakable* is normally spelled without an 'e' after the 'k' but the spelling *unmistakeable* is also acceptable.

See also SPELLING

unprecedented
This adjective means 'unparalleled', 'new', 'unexpected', 'without precedent':

The unprecedented success of the Apollo missions fuelled the desire for space travel.

Since *unprecedented* has been popularized by the media, its meaning has been weakened to 'great', 'very big':

Take advantage of our unprecedented offers in the MFI September Sale.

unravel
The verb *unravel* normally has 'll' before endings in British English and a single 'l' in America:

UK: unravel(s), unravelled, unravelling
US: unravel(s), unraveled, unraveling.

The verb means 'untangle', 'undo something knitted', 'solve a mystery':

I've been trying for hours to unravel this tangled wool.
We need Hercule Poirot to unravel this mystery!

See also NEGATION

unreadable
See ELIGIBLE/ILLEGIBLE/UNREADABLE

unresponsible
See IRRESPONSIBLE/UNRESPONSIBLE

unresponsive
Unresponsive is an adjective meaning 'failing to react to a stimulus':

The patient has remained unresponsive since the time of the accident.

unsociable, unsocial
See ANTISOCIAL/UNSOCIABLE/UNSOCIAL

until
See TILL/UNTIL

unused
See DISUSED/MISUSED/UNUSED

up-
Up- occurs frequently in compound words. It is found in hyphenated combinations of three words:

up-and-coming
up-and-under
up-to-date

as well as in hyphenated and unhyphenated compounds:

up-end, up-market
upbringing, upstairs.

The more widely-used the compound, the less likely it is to be hyphenated.

See also HYPHEN

up on, upon
See ON/UP ON/UPON

uphold
Uphold means 'affirm', 'defend', 'support':

I shall unflinchingly uphold the law.

It is an irregular verb; its past tense and past participle are 'upheld':

He invariably upheld the law.
He has upheld the law his entire life.

upward, upwards
In British English, *upward* is used almost exclusively as an adjective:

He seemed to be making upward movements with his head and hands.

whereas *upwards* is reserved for adverbial usage:

She moved onwards and upwards.

In American English, *upward* can function as both adjective and adverb and this usage is influencing many young speakers throughout the world.

The phrase *upwards of* meaning 'as many as' or occasionally 'more than' is now found in British as well as American English:

I counted upwards of one hundred people in the house.

See also UK AND US ENGLISH, -WARD/-WARDS

upwardly mobile
The terms *upwardly mobile* and *socially mobile upwards* were first used in sociological studies to describe people who were ambitious to move upwards in terms of class and earnings. Classes were subdivided into such categories as:

lower lower = E
middle lower = D
upper lower
lower middle = C2
middle middle = C1
upper middle
lower upper = B
middle upper
upper upper = A

on the evidence of such factors as birth, earnings and/or income, education and profession. The members of the groups B and C were regarded as being the most upwardly mobile. The modern acronyms 'dinky' (double income no kids yet) and 'yuppie' (young urban professional) are similar in connotation.

urban, urbane

The adjective *urban* contrasts with 'rural' and means 'relating to a city or a town':

I'm not cut out to be an urban dweller. I don't like the noise or the crowds or the bustle of city life.

The adjective *urbane* also derives from the Latin word *urbs*, 'city', and means 'courteous, elegant, sophisticated':

He was a cultivated, urbane person, thoughtful, courteous and unpretentious.

Uruguay

An inhabitant of the South American republic is a 'Uruguayan'; the derived adjective is the same. The capital is Montevideo.

us

See WE/US

US, USA

The *US* and *USA* are used as abbreviations for the United States of America and the unabbreviated form should be used in all formal contexts. The abbreviation 'the States' as in:

I've just arrived from the States.

should also be confined to informal contexts.

There is no derived adjective from United States of America or noun for an inhabitant so the word 'American' is frequently used:

I love American food.
She is studying the American writer Henry James.

It is important to remember that the words 'America' and 'American' do not refer only to the 50 states and their citizens. The term *America* can include Canada, Mexico and Central and South America. The term *American* can thus, in certain circumstances, be applied to Canadians, Mexicans and the people of Central and South America.

See also AMERICA/AMERICAN

US English

The United States, with a population of over 253 million, is the largest English-speaking nation in the world. It is not, however, either monolingual or monocultural. Many Americans are, to varying degrees, bilingual in English and Amerindian languages, English and Asian languages, and English and such European languages as French, German, Italian, Spanish and Yiddish. Among most Americans, however, a variety of English is

the dominant language and, because of the power and prestige of the United States, US English has influenced and increasingly influences all forms of English throughout the world. The influence is perhaps most apparent at the lexical level, with 'hotdogs' and 'coke', for example, being almost as common in New Zealand as in New York. As the power of television, in particular, grows, it is likely that US English will extend its linguistic empire.

The growth of English as a world language is welcomed by many because of its power to de-Babelize a multilingual world. It is, however, causing many others to worry because English is spreading at the expense of the languages of less powerful communities.

See also PRONUNCIATION, SPELLING, UK AND US ENGLISH

US states

Fifty states form the United States of America. In general, the name of the state should be spelled in full:

I hope to visit Wisconsin in October.

Abbreviations can be used in informal writing and in tables but the abbreviations should not be equated with the 'Zip [= Zoning Improvement Plan] Code' that is preferred for addresses. Most Americans prefer to use full stops after abbreviations but not after Zip Codes. The following list is of the names, abbreviations and Zip Codes of the fifty states:

State	Abbreviation	Zip Code
Alabama	Ala.	AL
Alaska	Alaska	AK
Arizona	Ariz.	AZ
Arkansas	Ark.	AR
California	Calif.	CA
Colorado	Colo.	CO
Connecticut	Conn.	CT
Delaware	Del.	DE
Florida	Fla.	FL
Georgia	Ga.	GA
Hawaii	Hawaii	HI
Idaho	Ida.	ID
Illinois	Ill.	IL
Indiana	Ind.	IN
Iowa	Ia.	IA
Kansas	Kans.	KA
Kentucky	Ky.	KY
Louisiana	La.	LA
Maine	Me.	ME
Maryland	Md.	MD
Massachusetts	Mass.	MA
Michigan	Mich.	MI
Minnesota	Minn.	MN
Mississippi	Miss.	MS
Missouri	Mo.	MO
Montana	Mont.	MT

Nebraska	Neb(r).	NE
Nevada	Nev.	NV
New Hampshire	N.H.	NH
New Jersey	N.J.	NJ
New Mexico	N.M(ex).	NM
New York	N.Y.	NY
North Carolina	N.C.	NC
North Dakota	N.D(ak).	ND
Ohio	O.	OH
Oklahoma	Okla.	OK
Oregon	Ore(g).	OR
Pennsylvania	Pa./Penn(a).	PA
Rhode Island	R.I.	RI
South Carolina	S.C.	SC
South Dakota	S.D(ak).	SD
Tennessee	Tenn.	TN
Texas	Tex.	TX
Utah	Ut.	UT
Vermont	Vt.	VT
Virginia	Va.	VA
Washington	Wash.	WA
West Virginia	W.Va.	WV
Wisconsin	Wis.	WI
Wyoming	Wyo.	WY

usable, useable

Both these spellings are acceptable although the former is more widely used:

The data are too corrupted to be usable.

See also SPELLING

usage

The word *usage* means 'manner of using':

I strongly object to the modern usage of 'well' instead of 'very' in such sentences as 'I'm well happy'.

The term is also used to mean the ways people do and should use the language.

As long as people continue to speak English, users will continue to worry about which usages are correct and which are not. Often there is a simple answer:

*He visited John and I.

is incorrect. It ought to be:

He visited John and me.

because the object pronoun is 'me' not 'I'.

Occasionally, there is nothing linguistically wrong with an expression, but it may be unacceptable because it is stylistically inappropriate. The expression:

Chill out.

is as grammatically correct as:

Come in.

but would not be acceptable in a formal style.

Words and phrases can come into the language because there is a need for them. A 'sibling' is a useful term for a brother or sister, when the gender is not significant, and most adults have been involved in 'a catch-22 situation'. Such words and phrases are sometimes criticized because they are either elitist or so overused that they are reduced to the status of cliché.

See also CLICHÉ, PURIST, SLANG

used

Used can be used as the past tense form of the verb 'use' meaning 'employ, utilize':

I used red ink to draw attention to the numerous errors.

Used also occurs as an adjective meaning 'second hand':

used clothing

a used car.

In both these contexts, the word *used* rhymes with 'bruised'. *Used to* also occurs as a marker of habitual action in the past:

I used to paint every summer.

In this context, *used* sounds the same as the first syllable in 'Euston'.

See also USED TO

used to

The phrase *used to* functions like an auxiliary verb in that it modifies the meaning of the main verb in the sentence:

I used to sing in the choir.

He used to be so thin.

Used to allows us to refer to habitual actions or to protracted events that occurred in the past.

Used to is restricted in its uses. Since it refers specifically to the past, it cannot be used with present or future reference. Nor can it be used in giving an order. There are also difficulties associated with using it in negative or interrogative constructions. Many people are uncertain whether to treat it like a modal verb such as 'could' or like a full verb such as 'want':

You used to play cricket.

You could play cricket.

You want to play cricket.

In other words, people are not certain whether to say:

You usedn't to play cricket. (compare: You couldn't play cricket.)

or:

You didn't use to play cricket. (compare: You didn't want to play cricket.)

or even:

You didn't used to play cricket. (compare: You didn't need to play cricket.)

All three forms are heard, yet many speakers feel uncomfortable with all of them.

A similar problem occurs in asking questions. The form:

Used you (to) play cricket?

sounds old-fashioned and pedantic but the alternative:

Did you use to play cricket?

is often decried as a 'barbarism'. Again, both forms are acceptable in the spoken medium but, since so many native speakers are uncomfortable with them, many seek alternative structures and ask:

Didn't you play cricket in the past?
Did you play cricket in the past?

See also AUXILIARY, MODALITY, QUASI-MODAL

user-friendly

The phrase *user-friendly* originated in computer texts to describe material that was easy to use because it was specifically designed to anticipate and solve a user's problems:

You've tried user-friendly programs before. Now try our software and discover a program that really lives up to its name.

Increasingly, this phrase is used to commend any product that is simple to use:

user-friendly instructions (self-assembly furniture)
user-friendly manual

and it has given rise to other adjectives such as:

environmentally friendly
student-friendly

as well as:

user-hostile
user-offputting.

See also -FRIENDLY

USSR

USSR, without punctuation marks, was the usual abbreviation for the Union of Soviet Socialist Republics. Often, the shorter phrase *Soviet Union* was used as an equivalent.

utilize

The word means 'use fully', 'make full and practical use of'. It should not, therefore, be selected as a synonym for 'use'. We can 'use' a train ticket to get from A to B but we can *utilize* the train network to avoid making unnecessary journeys by car. The spelling 'utilise' is also acceptable.

utmost, uttermost

Uttermost is a variant of *utmost* that can function as an adjective and a noun:

She paid the utmost attention to fine detail.
He did his utmost to gain promotion.

The form *utmost* is itself a superlative meaning 'of the greatest possible degree, extent, amount'. It is, therefore, unnecessary to use *uttermost*. Some users may think that the word is a blend of 'utter'(complete) plus 'most':

The Prince went to the uttermost regions of the world to find the missing key.

In other words, they have created *uttermost* by analogy with such superlatives as 'uppermost':

The desire for justice was the thing that was uppermost in their minds.

See also COMPARATIVE, SUPERLATIVE

V

v

V is a consonant that is used to represent only one sound, that is, the initial sound in 'very'.

The letter *v* is used as an abbreviation for 'versus' as in:

the Bruno v Foreman fight.

The capital letter *V* is used in such compounds as:

V-neck, V-sign.

The V-sign is made by raising the index and middle finger. In Britain, if the palm of the hand faces away from the signer, the V-sign means 'Victory'; if the palm faces the signer, the gesture is intended to be one of contempt, defiance or rudeness.

See also COMPOUND

vacant
See EMPTY/VACANT

vacation

In Britain, the term *vacation* tended to be used for the periods when parliament or the law courts were not sitting or when teaching had stopped at colleges or universities:

The Christmas vacation will begin on 22 December.

Increasingly, British speakers are using it to mean 'holiday', the normal usage in America:

We're planning a winter vacation in January.

See also UK AND US ENGLISH

vaccine

Vaccine derives ultimately from Latin vacca, 'a cow'. It rhymes with 'Maxine' and all the derived forms, such as *vaccinate*, have a double 'c'.

See also INOCULATE, SPELLING

vacuum

Vacuum comes from Latin *vacuum*, 'an empty space'. The normal Latin plural *vacua* is occasionally used but the usual and acceptable plural today is *vacuums*:

Do you think there are vacuums, regions containing absolutely no matter?

I've only had to buy two vacuums (i.e., vacuum cleaners) in twenty years.

vagary

The word *vagary* meaning 'whim' is often incorrectly spelled. It does not have an 'i' after 'g'. The incorrect spelling of *vagary* and its plural *vagaries* is possibly on analogy with such words as 'aviary' or 'intermediary'. The incorrect use of an 'i' before a suffix is also found in words such as 'grievous' being spelled *'grievious'.

See also SPELLING

vain, vane, vein

Vain is an adjective meaning 'uncritically proud of one's appearance or possessions'. The normal noun is *vanity*:

He is not only vain but he encourages vanity in others.

Vain can occur in the hackneyed phrase 'in vain' meaning 'futile':

What was that proverb of King Alfred's? It is in vain to argue with a fool, or vie in yawning with an oven.

A *vane* normally occurs in the collocation 'weather vane', a mechanism used to indicate the wind direction:

Weather vanes were normally put on church spires because they were the highest points in a village and so people could easily see when the wind was changing direction.

A *vein* is a tubular vessel that carries blood in a body or sap in a plant. This noun is also used metaphorically to refer to vein-like markings in marble or on wings.

valance, valence

These homophones are occasionally confused or misspelled. A *valance* is like a very short curtain. It is often hung across the top of a window or around a bed. Occasionally the term *valance* is applied to a short wooden fixture or pelmet fixed to the top of a window and covering the top 25 centimetres of the curtains.

Valence is less widely used than *valency* in the UK. Both nouns describe the phenomenon of chemical compounding.

valet

The noun *valet* meaning 'male servant who attends to the personal clothing and needs of his male employer' is no longer widely used, but the regular verb *valet*, *valeted* is quite widely used in garages:

We can have your car valeted as part of a major service.

The 't' in the noun is rarely pronounced; the 't' in the verb is almost always pronounced.

valid, validated

These words are related but should be clearly differentiated. *Valid* is an adjective meaning 'based on truth, legal':

Her argument was, essentially, valid.
He thought he was travelling on a valid passport.

Validated is the past participle of *validate*, 'confirm', 'corroborate', 'declare legally valid':

His papers have been validated so he is free to go.

See also ADJECTIVE, PARTICIPLE

valour, valorous

In British English, many nouns ending in '-our' lose the 'u' when the word takes the suffix '-our'. *Valour*, meaning 'courage', is one such noun:

valour, valorous
vigour, vigorous.

In American English, neither the noun nor the adjective has a 'u':

valor, valorous
vigor, vigorous.

See also SPELLING, UK AND US ENGLISH

valuable, valueless

See INVALUABLE/PRICELESS/VALUABLE/VALUELESS

van, von

The prefixes *van*, *van den* and *van der* tend to be Dutch or Flemish:

Vincent van Gogh
Marius van den Broek
Frans van der Merwe.

They are normally written with a lower-case 'v' unless they occur at the beginning of a sentence:

Van Gogh died in 1890.

Von tends to be German and, like *van*, tends to be written with a lower-case 'v' unless it starts a sentence:

Wernher von Braun
Von Braun worked on the Apollo Project.

The preferences of the owners should be taken into account when decisions are made about whether or not to use a lower-case 'v'.

See also DE, PREFIX

vanitory, vanity

In some estate agents' descriptions of houses the phrases *vanitory unit* and *vanity unit* are used to refer to a built-in hand basin with cupboard space below:

The upper bedroom also benefits from a vanitory unit with a pink-tiled splashback.

Vanuatu

An inhabitant of the island republic in the southwest Pacific, formerly the New Hebrides, is a 'Vanuatuan'; the derived adjective is the same. The capital is Vila.

vapour, vapor

Vapour is the British spelling and *vapor* the preferred American form. In both Britain and America, suffixes are added to *vapor*:

vaporize, vaporous.

See also SPELLING, UK AND US ENGLISH

variable

The adjective *variable* means 'liable to, or capable of, change':

The weather patterns have been variable over the last ten years.

Word classes in English are occasionally subdivided into words that are *variable*, that is, capable of expressing distinctions by a change of form:

big, bigger, biggest
boy, boys
bury, buries, buried, burying
she, her
take, takes, took, taking, taken

and those that are *invariable*, that is, they do not change their form in any circumstances:

and, but, so, at, from, in, how, what, where, the, my, both.

Words are occasionally described as being *free variables* when they can substitute for each other in all or almost al contexts. The words 'till' and 'until' are free variables:

Wait till/until I arrive.
I can't wait till/until tomorrow.

and so are 'hardly' and 'scarcely':

I had hardly/scarcely eaten all day.
Hardly/scarcely had I opened the window than the rain came.

The variation found at all levels of language and often corresponding to social differences can help explain how and why languages change.

See also LANGUAGE CHANGE, SHIBBOLETH, SOCIOLINGUISTICS

(at) variance

The phrase *at variance* triggers off the use of the preposition 'with':

My calculations are at variance with the bank statement.

Because *at variance* means 'different from', many people incorrectly use the preposition 'from':

*My calculations are at variance from the bank statement.

See also PREPOSITION

variegated

Variegated means 'with different colours':

The variegated leaves look attractive but the pale patches indicate infection or mutation.

The word is often spelled incorrectly with an 'a' replacing the first 'e':

*variagated.

The best way to remember the spelling is that it parallels 'variety'.

See also SPELLING

variety

The term *variety* is often used in descriptions of language because it avoids some of the overtones associated with words such as 'dialect'. A *variety* is a subdivision of a language. It may be associated with:

■ Age: the speech of teenagers often differs markedly from their parents

■ Gender: women may have a wider range of descriptive adjectives in their speech than men

■ Occupation: dockers, doctors and linguists use a jargon that is specific to their trade

■ Region: a speaker from Adelaide does not sound like a speaker from Aberdeen

■ Style: the language of religion differs from the language of national news reports.

Because *variety* can comprehend such different subdivisions of language as the speech of a region or occupation-influenced vocabulary, many scholars avoid it, preferring to use such terms as 'dialect' for regional forms, 'jargon' for occupational vocabulary and 'register' for socially influenced styles.

See also DIALECT, JARGON, REGISTER, SEXIST LANGUAGE, STILE/STYLE

VDU

The abbreviation *VDU*, 'visual display unit', has been popularized by the growth in computer technology. *VDU* is often used as a synonym for 'monitor'.

See also ABBREVIATION, COMPUTERESE

vegan

The word *vegan* is derived from '*vegetarian*' and means someone who neither eats nor uses any animal products. *Vegan* is usually pronounced to rhyme with the surname 'Keegan'.

The word 'vegetarian' is widely used: it is sometimes used to mean people who eat fruit and vegetables and no animal products; people who eat fruit, vegetables, milk and cheese; people who eat fruit, vegetables, milk, cheese and eggs; people who eat fruit, vegetables, milk, cheese, eggs and fish; and people who do not eat red meat.

vein

See VAIN/VANE/VEIN

veld

The word *veld* derives ultimately from Dutch *veldt*, a word that is cognate with 'field'. It entered the English language in South Africa because of the influence of Afrikaans. In the past, it was frequently spelled *veldt*, although the spelling without the 't' is more widespread today.

See also BORROWING

venal, venial

Neither of these words is used frequently in colloquial English, a fact that in part accounts for their occasional misuse. *Venal* means 'corruptible' or 'easily bribed':

He set out to trap the venal politicians.

Venial means 'easily excused or forgiven'. It occurs most frequently in the collocation 'venial sin':

Venial sins are less serious than mortal sins. Murder is a mortal sin; disobedience is usually venial.

vend

Vend is a synonym of 'sell'. It has become more widely used in the language since the introduction of vending machines. The seller is 'vendor' with an 'o' and, if the product is saleable, it is 'vendible' with '-ible'.

Venezuela

An inhabitant of the South American country is a 'Venezuelan'; the derived adjective is the same. The capital is Caracas.

vengeance

Vengeance is a noun meaning 'the desire for or the act of taking revenge, retribution':

You can't argue with him. He wants vengeance not justice.

'Vengeance is mine,' says the Lord.

The phrase 'with a vengeance' has become an intensifying cliché:

She cleaned the house with a vengeance.

See also AVENGE/REVENGE

venom

Venom is a noun. Literally, it is used to refer to the poisonous fluid secreted by some snakes and insects:

Some venoms can be counteracted only by snake-specific antidotes.

It is also used metaphorically to mean 'verbal spite', 'malice':

I didn't expect such venom from someone I had known all my life.

The adjective is *venomous*. (Notice the 'o' before and after 'm'):

Not all snakes are venomous. The common British grass snake is non-venomous.

venture

Venture can function as a verb meaning 'hazard', 'dare', risk':

Nothing ventured, nothing gained.

Early navigators risked their lives as they ventured into the unknown.

The noun *venture* can mean 'a risky undertaking' and also 'the money placed at risk':

My accountant thinks the venture too risky.

Venture capital schemes are not all equally risky.

Venture derives from the same source as *adventure* but, although the words both involve the meaning of 'risk', the latter is more frequently associated with pleasure:

What a wonderful adventure that was!

venue

A *venue* is a meeting place:

We haven't yet fixed the venue for the picnic.

It also has a number of legally specific meanings including 'the place fixed for a trial' and 'the locality from which jurors must be chosen'.

veracious, voracious

In rapid speech, these two words are almost homophones and so there is a tendency to confuse or misspell them. *Veracious* is an adjective related to 'veracity', 'truth':

He is essentially veracious although he has a tendency to exaggerate his management skills.

Voracious is also an adjective, deriving from *vorare* 'to devour'. It can be used literally to mean 'craving food in large quantities' or metaphorically meaning 'unremitting, hard to satisfy':

She is so thin and yet she has a voracious appetite.

Michael is a voracious reader.

veracity

Veracity is not just a synonym for 'truth'. It suggests consistent and habitual honesty and truth':

His veracity was never in question.

veranda, verandah

The noun *veranda* derives ultimately from a Hindi word meaning 'railing'. It was applied in English to a porch along the outside of a building that was sometimes partially enclosed:

Verandas are found more frequently in the tropics than in the temperate zones.

In the past, the word was often spelled *verandah*,

a spelling that is still acceptable but increasing unusual.

See also FOREIGN LOAN-WORDS

verb

A *verb* has traditionally been defined as a 'doing' word, and although this definition does not comprehend all verbs, it is a useful starting point. Verbs can be either 'weak' or 'strong'. A weak or regular verb forms its past tense by adding '-d', '-ed' or '-t':

like(s), liked

mark(s), marked

spell(s), spelled/spelt

and a strong or irregular verb often forms its past tense by means of a vowel change:

sing(s), sang

take(s), took

write(s), wrote.

The most irregular verbs in the language are the verbs 'be', 'do', 'go' and 'have'.

Regular verbs have five different forms: an infinitive (1), two present tense forms (2) and (3), a present participle (4) and a past tense form (5):

1	2 and 3	4	5
to like	like/likes	liking	liked
to mark	mark/marks	marking	marked
to spell	spell/spells	spelling	spelled

Most irregular verbs have six forms: an infinitive, two present tense forms, a present participle, a past tense form and a past participle (6):

1	2 and 3	4	5	6
to sing	sing/sings	singing	sang	sung
to take	take/take	staking	took	taken
to write	write/writes	writing	wrote	written

Some irregular verbs have the same form for the past tense and past participle:

1	5	6
to bring	brought	(have) brought
to buy	bought	(have) bought
to sit	sat	(have) sat

and many irregular verbs ending in 't' and 'd' have the same form for the unmarked present tense, the past tense and the past participle:

I bet on the winner regularly.

I bet on the winner yesterday.

I have bet on the winner once.

The main verbs in this category are the following:

1	2	5	6
to bet	bet	bet	bet
to burst	burst	burst	burst
to cast	cast	cast	cast
to cost	cost	cost	cost
to cut	cut	cut	cut

to hit	hit	hit	hit
to hurt	hurt	hurt	hurt
to let	let	let	let
to put	put	put	put
to rid	rid	rid	rid
to set	set	set	set
to shed	shed	shed	shed
to shred	shred	shred	shred
to shut	shut	shut	shut
to slit	slit	slit	slit
to split	split	split	split
to thrust	thrust	thrust	thrust

Compound forms of these verbs, such as 'broadcast' and 'upset', also belong in this category and, in America, so does 'fit':

UK: I fitted it yesterday.
US: I fit it yesterday.
UK: I had fitted it.
US: I had fit it.

In the present tense, verbs have a concordial relationship with their subjects:

I/you/we/they: make
he/she/it/Kim: make + s = makes.

The auxiliary verbs 'be', 'have' and 'do' also have a concordial relationship with their subjects:

I am making
you/we/they are making
he/she/it/Kim is making
I/you/we/they have made
he/she/it/Kim has made
I/you/we/they do make
he/she/it/Kim does make.

'Be' is unique among English verbs in showing concord in the past tense, both as a full verb and as an auxiliary:

I/he/she/it/Kim was happy
we/you/they were happy
I/she/she/it Kim was making
we/you/they were making.

English verbs can be classified in various ways:

■ They can be *intransitive*, that is, they can take a SUBJECT but not an OBJECT:

Kim arrived.
The lions died.
The milk disappeared.

■ They can be TRANSITIVE and take a subject and an object:

I like bananas.
The drought killed the trees.
I saw Michael yesterday.

■ Some transitive verbs can take a subject, a direct object and an indirect object. These are verbs such as 'build', 'buy', 'give', 'make', 'sell':

Mary built him a kennel.
Mary built a kennel for him.
John made me a cake.

John made a cake for me.
Kim sold me a pup.
Kim sold a pup to me.

■ Transitive verbs can occur in both active and passive sentences:

I followed John (active)
John was followed (by me). (passive)
Kim hugged John (active)
John was hugged (by Kim). (passive)

■ Intransitive verbs cannot occur in passive sentences:

John died. (active)
*X was died by John
Kim arrived (active)
*X was arrived by Kim.

English verbs can be divided into lexical verbs such as 'buy', 'dance', 'fly', 'swim' and auxiliary verbs such as 'be', 'can', 'could', 'do', 'have', 'must'. There can be only one lexical verb (or head verb HV) in each verb phrase but there can be up to four auxiliary verbs:

Modal	Perfective	Progressive	Passive	HV
				train
should				train
should	have			trained
should	have	been		training
should	have	been	being	trained

The verbs 'be', 'have' and 'do' can function as both lexical and auxiliary verbs:

	Lexical	Auxiliary
be	I am a nurse.	I am nursing John.
have	I have a cold.	I have heard the news.
do	I did my best.	I did not see her.

English verbs may be either finite (capable of taking a subject) or non-finite. The non-finite forms are the infinitive, the present participle and the past participle:

Infinitive	Present participle	Past participle
to be	being	been
to buy	buying	bought
to do	doing	done
to go	going	gone

All other forms are finite:

(they) go
(he) goes
(she) went.

Some English verbs take complements, not objects. These verbs are known as copulas. The most widely-used COPULA verb is 'be'. We can show the difference between copula verbs and transitive verbs by contrasting similar sentences:

Copula	Transitive
I was a teacher.	I saw a teacher.
I felt a fool.	I felt the heat.

I grew angry.   I grew tomatoes.

See also AUXILIARY, GERUND, -ING FORM, MODALITY, PARTICIPLE

verbal

The word *verbal* is ambiguous. It derives from Latin *verbum*, 'word', and can mean 'of the word' or 'related to the verb':

The verbal slot is unfilled in many slogans such as 'One person, one vote'.

The National Curriculum plans to pay as much attention to the verbal skills of speaking and listening with understanding as to the written skills of reading and writing.

verbal noun

In English, the '-ing' part of a verb can be used with a variety of functions. 'Whispering' is a nonfinite verb in:

They were whispering in class.

It is an adjective in the song title 'Whispering Grass', and it functions as a noun in:

Whispering is not very polite.

When an '-ing' form functions as a noun, it is called a *verbal noun* or a *gerund*.

Verbal noun is more self-explanatory than the term 'gerund'. It is verbal in that it is a non-finite verb form and it is a noun in that it can function as a subject and be replaced by a pronoun:

Whispering is rude.
It is rude.

and can also function as an object:

I don't like whispering.
I don't like it.

It preserves some of the attributes of a verb in that it can, for example, take its own object and be modified by an adverb:

This habit is expensive.
Smoking is expensive.
Smoking cigarettes is expensive.
Smoking heavily is expensive.

See also GERUND

verbalize

Verbalize means 'articulate, express an idea in words':

I'm not a mind reader. You'll have to learn to verbalize!

This verb may be spelled with an '-ise' suffix; both spellings are acceptable.

See also UK AND US ENGLISH

verbatim

The word *verbatim* is sometimes misused. It means 'using exactly the same words':

I want you to give the message verbatim. Use my exact words without any improvisation.

verbiage

Verbiage is a noun meaning 'excessive and sometimes meaningless use of words', 'verbosity'. People often indulge in verbiage when they have little of value to say:

When you cut through the verbiage, the verse is meaningless.

Verbiage is sometimes, incorrectly, equated with 'gossip' or PHATIC COMMUNION. These latter verbal interchanges can, however, serve a useful social purpose.

vermilion

Vermilion is a bright reddish-orange colour. The word is spelled with one 'l'.

See also SPELLING

vermin

Vermin is a singular noun meaning 'troublesome or obnoxious insects or small animals'. The word is plural in meaning and so does not need an 's'. Like other nouns that are singular in form but plural in meaning (e.g. 'parliament', 'team'), *vermin* should take a singular form of the verb:

Vermin eats into a farmer's profits.

In practice, however, most people use a plural verb:

Vermin eat into a farmer's profits.

or restructure the sentence:

Vermin can eat into a company's profits.

See also COUNTABLE AND UNCOUNTABLE

vernacular

The word *vernacular* derives from Latin *vernaculus*, 'a native', via *verna* meaning 'a slave'. It has been used to refer to languages or language varieties that are less prestigious than written, standardized languages. *Vernacular* comprehends such meanings as:

■ Nonstandard native language or dialect of an area:

There are over 400 vernacular languages in Nigeria.

■ Nonstandardized language of a speech community:

There is a vitality in vernacular speech that is rarely found in the standard language.

■ Languages without a writing system or written tradition:

As well as English, French and Arabic, Cameroonians use at least 200 vernaculars.

■ Local varieties of a language:

The Liverpool vernacular is called 'Scouse'.

The phrase *vernacular name* is given to the everyday name of a plant:

'Dane-wort' is the vernacular name of the caprifoliaceous shrub, *Sambucus ebulus*.

See also POLITICAL CORRECTNESS

vertebra

Vertebra is a singular noun referring to one of the bony joints of the spinal column. Its scholarly plural is *vertebrae* but, increasingly, the anglicized plural *vertebras* is also being used.

This CD provides a full-colour introduction to the human skeleton including recent research on the health of the vertebras.

vertex, vortex

Neither of these words is widely used. A *vertex* is the highest point, the apex:

In medicine, *vertex* is sometimes used to refer to the crown of the head.

A *vortex* is a whirling mass of liquid, gas or fire:

Houses and cars were sucked into the vortex and then discarded hundreds of yards away.

Both words have scholarly plurals ending in '-ices' and metaphorical uses ending in '-exes'.

See also SPELLING

very

Very is an intensifier, derived from the Old French form *verai*, meaning 'true' and cognate with Modern French *vrai*. It is most frequently used as an intensifying adverb, modifying adjectives and adverbs:

She is a very intelligent person.
He speaks very clearly.

Occasionally, it is used as an intensifier of a noun:

The very idea!
That's the very thing I criticized.

Very, like the adjective 'nice', is so often overused that many teachers and stylists urge writers to avoid it. The advice is valid to the extent that no word should be so overused as to become almost bleached of meaning.

Very is sometimes used before a past participle when *much* would be more appropriate:

His kindness was much appreciated.
*His kindness was very appreciated.

The rule often given is that *very* should be avoided before a past participle.

I have pleased everyone now. (past participle)
*I have very pleased everyone now.
He had a pleased expression on his face. (adjective).
He had a very pleased expression on his face.

However, *very* is often acceptable before a past participle if another adverb intervenes:

*He was very injured.
He was very badly injured.

The best rule is not to overuse *very* and to use it with special care in formal speech or writing.

veterinary

Veterinary is frequently mispronounced and misspelled. Many people omit the '-er-' syllable.

See also SPELLING

veto

Veto can be a noun:

I intend to exercise my veto.

or a verb:

I shall veto the proposal.

The plural is *vetoes* and the forms of the verb are:

vetoes, vetoed, vetoing.

VHF

VHF, increasingly *vhf*, is the normal abbreviation for 'Very High Frequency', a radio frequency.

See also ABBREVIATION, UHF

via

The Latin noun *via*, 'way', is often used as a preposition meaning 'by way of':

We went to Austin via Dallas.

The pronunciation normally rhymes with 'fire' although some speakers, approximating more closely to Latin, pronounce the 'i' as 'ee'.

See also BORROWING, FOREIGN LOAN-WORDS

viable

Viable is an adjective that is in danger of being overused. It has two main meanings: 'capable of normal growth and development, or of surviving outside the mother':

The law does not permit the abortion of a viable foetus.

and 'capable of sustaining itself without additional support':

We are looking for viable projects.
It is not a viable business.

The CLICHÉ 'viable alternative' means little more than 'alternative'. Like all clichés, it should be avoided in formal speech and writing.

vice versa

The phrase *vice versa* is used adverbially to mean 'with the order reversed'. It is not hyphenated or italicized:

Shall we go shopping and then have lunch or vice versa?

There are two frequently heard pronunciations. The first pronounces *vice* as two syllables, to rhyme with 'disa' and the second pronounces it as one syllable, a perfect rhyme for 'mice'.

vicious, viscous

These two words are often misspelled and, occasionally, confused. *Vicious* is an adjective meaning 'wicked, cruel, nasty spiteful':

We do not expect to see one footballer aim a vicious blow at the head of another.

Viscous is an adjective meaning 'thick, sticky, too thick to pour':

The paint is too viscous to use again. I left the lid off.

victimize

The verb may be spelled with '-ise'; the associated noun, 'victimization' may also be spelled with an 's'.

See also UK AND US ENGLISH

victuals

This noun, meaning 'food', is virtually obsolete, although it is frequently found in Victorian novels. The word is pronounced to rhyme with 'little' and the noun *victualler* is still found in the phrase 'licensed victualler', which rhymes with 'littler'. The form 'victual' can be used as a verb meaning 'supply with food'. The 'l' is doubled before suffixes in British English:

UK: victual(s), victualled, victualling
US: victual(s), victualed, victualing.

There is a growing tendency to pronounce the word as it is spelled on the rare occasions that it is used.

See also SPELLING

vide

This word derives from Latin *videre*, 'to see', and is pronounced 'V-day'. It is sometimes used in scholarly books or articles to give directions to the reader. Thus:

vide: see
vide ante: see before
vide infra: see below
vide supra: see above.

The word or phrase is always italicized and in lower-case letters.

See also LATIN

vie

Vie is a verb meaning 'compete for'. The forms are:

vie(s), vied, vying

and it is used with the prepositions 'for' and 'with':

John is vying with Peter for the title of *victor ludorum*.

Vietnam

An inhabitant of the southeast Asian country is a 'Vietnamese'; the derived adjective is the same. The capital is Hanoi.

vigour, vigorous

In British English, the noun ends in '-our' but the 'u' is dropped in the adjective. In American English, there is no 'u' in either the noun or the adjective.

See also SPELLING, UK AND US ENGLISH

villain, villein

These words were originally variant spellings for a 'worker on an estate'. Both nouns derive ultimately from Latin *villa*. Today, *villain* means 'criminal', 'evil person', and *villein* is obsolete, although it had the meaning of 'peasant', 'serf'. The word *villain* illustrates a change in meaning, which is often called 'semantic degradation' – that is, the meaning becomes less pleasant. We find it also in *knave*, which at one time had the same meaning as *knight* with the exception that a knave was from a poor family whereas a knight was from a wealthy one. The opposite process of 'semantic elevation' can be seen in *minister*, which used to mean 'servant, one who ministered to the needs of another'.

See also SEMANTICS

vintage

The adjective *vintage*, which derives ultimately from Latin *vinum*, 'wine', was originally only applicable to wine:

This is an example of the 1976 vintage.

Later, it was extended to an exceptionally good year for wine:

There have been only five vintage years this century.

More recently, it has been extended further to mean both 'a perfect example of the best of':

That quip was vintage Wilde.

and 'something old and usually expensive':

He collects vintage cars.

violable

The adjective from violate, 'break the law', 'assault', 'rape' is *violable* and not, as many think, *violatable. The noun is 'violator', with '-or'.

See also VULGARISM

virago

Virago means 'bad-tempered woman'. It is an example of semantic degradation in that its meaning deteriorated from 'brave', 'courageous woman' to 'shrew'. The plural is most usually *viragoes* but *viragos* is also acceptable.

See also POLITICAL CORRECTNESS, SEXIST LANGUAGE

virgule

The word *virgule* is given to the symbol /, which is used as a separator in printing:

19/7/99

Bring your partner and/or children.

Various other terms for this symbol are 'diagonal', 'slash' and 'solidus'.

virtual

Virtual is an adjective meaning 'close', 'approximating to', 'near':

This horse is a virtual certainty.

The phrase *virtual reality* is derived from computer simulations and implies that the images and sensations created are very close to life.

virtuoso

The word *virtuoso* has two plurals, *virtuosi* and the more widely-used *virtuosos*. It is applied to a person who has outstanding technical and artistic skill in music or, more recently, in dance:

Liszt is perhaps undervalued in being described as a virtuoso performer.

virus

The plural form of *virus* is *viruses*. The word originally applied to the agent of an illness:

We cannot identify the specific virus that is causing the problem.

It was then extended to the illness itself:

I've got a very unpleasant virus.

It has also been carried over into computer terminology:

I've been supplied with anti-virus software.

vis-à-vis

This French borrowing, meaning 'face to face', is normally printed in italics. In English, it is a preposition meaning 'about, regarding, in relation to':

We discussed it *vis-à-vis* his tax rebate.

In general, the English equivalents should be used as the French phrase may cause confusion.

viscera

Viscera is a plural noun meaning 'large internal organs', 'entrails' or, more recently, 'guts':

The viscera were removed in the embalming process.

viscous

See VICIOUS/VISCOUS

visible

This word meaning 'capable of being seen' has '-ible' and not '-able'. It is sometimes used in the popular press to mean 'popular', 'well known', 'high profile':

He's likely to be much less visible after such a public gaffe.

See also -ABLE/-IBLE, HEADLINES, JOURNALESE, SPELLING

visit, visitation

Visit can function as both a noun and a verb:

Our visit to Malta was arranged in a few hours.
I hope you can visit us soon.

They both mean 'stay for a short time'. Americans often use *visit with* where British speakers prefer *visit*:

UK: He visited us yesterday.
US: He visited with us yesterday.

Visitation can refer to an official, public visit:

Our university department is expecting a visitation from a group of assessors.

a supernatural apparition:

She couldn't be like everyone else and have human visitors. She experienced an angelic visitation.

or a catastrophe:

Just when the famine seemed over, there was a visitation of plagues of locusts.

visualize

The verb and its associated noun *visualization* can be spelled with 's'. Both spellings are acceptable.

See also SPELLING

vitamin

The custom is to use a small 'v' for *vitamin*:

I believe that vitamin B is good for one's nerves.

In England, the first syllable is pronounced to rhyme with 'sit'; in America it rhymes with 'site'. Both pronunciations are acceptable.

See also RECEIVED PRONUNCIATION, UK AND US ENGLISH

viz

In scholarly writing, the abbreviation *viz* (from Latin *videlicet*) is used to mean 'namely':

Here we find a number of marsupials, viz kangaroos, koalas and wombats.

There is no particular merit in using the Latin abbreviation in preference to 'namely'.

See also ABBREVIATION, BORROWING, LATIN

vocabulary

The *vocabulary* of a language is a comprehensive list of the words that occur in it. Often, these words are arranged alphabetically in dictionaries, where definitions and etymologies are also supplied. The term is also applied to the stock of words used by a specific writer or group of speakers in a particular period. When applied to an individual, a distinction is usually made between an 'active vocabulary', that is, the words actually used, and a 'passive vocabulary', which contains words that are understood but rarely used. Many users of English, for example, would never say 'concubinage' or 'desuetude' and may not even be certain of their pronunciation, but they would recognize such words as being English and might know what they meant in context.

See also DICTIONARY, LEXICOGRAPHY/ LEXICOLOGY, LEXICON/LEXIS

vocalize

Vocalize and its associated noun *vocalization* can also be spelled with 's'. Both versions are acceptable.

See also SPELLING, UK AND US ENGLISH

vocative

See EVOCATIVE/PROVOCATIVE/VOCATIVE

vogue words

Vogue words are words that are popular for a short time and are often used loosely. Many are adjectives:

in-depth, meaningful, phenomenal, pivotal, simplistic, substantive, viable.

Some are nouns:

ambiance, aspect, charisma, confrontation, dialogue, dimension, ecology, environment, escalation, framework, interface, macho, parameter, scenario, shortfall, situation, syndrome.

Some are noun phrases:

ball game, bottom line, cut-off, grass roots

and a few are adverbs:

hopefully, thankfully.

Most of these words and phrases have been popularized by the media and many have become hackneyed.

See also CLICHÉ, JARGON

voice

The term *voice* is used in two different ways in descriptions of language. It occurs in descriptions of verbs and of sentences where a distinction is made between 'active voice':

She closed the window.

and 'passive voice':

The window was closed (by her).

In phonetics, a distinction is made between voiced sounds such as vowels and voiced consonants such as /b/, /n/ and /z/, which are produced while the vocal cords are vibrating, and voiceless sounds such as /f/, /p/ and /s/, which are produced without vibration of the vocal cords.

See also ACTIVE VOICE/PASSIVE VOICE, PHONEME, VERB

volcano

The plural of *volcano* is *volcanoes*:

The ring of active volcanoes in the Pacific is sometimes referred to as the 'Ring of Fire'.

See also SPELLING

volte-face

Volte-face is hyphenated and not normally italicized. It means 'about turn, reversal':

The government has done a complete volte-face about Share Option Schemes.

The '-face' rhymes with 'gas'.

See also BORROWING, FRENCH

voluntarily

Voluntarily is normally stressed on the first syllable in British English and on the third syllable in American English.

See also UK AND US ENGLISH

voluptuous

Voluptuous and its related forms such as *voluptuousness* are often misspelled. They have '-uous' not '-ious' after 'volupt-'.

See also SPELLING

voracious

See VERACIOUS/VORACIOUS

vortex

See VERTEX/VORTEX

vote

The adjective formed from *vote* may be either *voteable* or *votable*, with the latter being more widely used.

See also SPELLING

voucher, vouchor

The *voucher* with an '-er' is a document or ticket. The form with '-or' is obsolete except in some legal transactions, where it refers to a person.

voyage

There are many words for travelling, some of them being relatively specialized. A *voyage* tends to be by sea:

A sea voyage was recommended for his health.

It is also used for 'voyages of discovery', including space travel.

vulgarism

A *vulgarism*, from Latin *vulgus* ('common people'), is a word, phrase or expression that is stigmatized as coarse or substandard. Such items may vary with time: 'kid' (child), 'sheila' (female) and 'educationalist' (educationist) have all been classified as *vulgarisms*, although many speakers would now classify 'kid' as colloquial, 'sheila' as an Australianism and 'educationalist' as an alternative to the more correct 'educationist'.

The term *vulgarism*, as its etymology suggests, has frequently been associated with class distinctions and nonstandard usages such as:

I done it.

them books

You should of called.

Today, however, it is applied, if at all, to any usage that is coarse, offensive or stylistically too colloquial for its context. The italicized items in the following sentences may be regarded as *vulgarisms*:

She told him to *f— off*.

They were determined to exclude *yobbos* and vandals.

Both the definition and the etymology were *way off beam*.

See also BARBARISM, SLANG, TABOO VOCABULARY

W

w

W is used as a consonant when it occurs at the beginning of a syllable in words such as 'wind' or 'unworkable' and when it follows another consonant as in 'dwarf' or 'twin', but it is regarded as a semi-vowel when it occurs at the end of a word or syllable as, for example, in 'now' or 'sewing'.

The letter *w* is the abbreviation for 'watt' as in:

kw = kilowatt

and for west as in:

NW = northwest.

See also ABBREVIATION

w-, wh-

In England, *wh-* is normally pronounced 'w', thus creating a considerable number of homophones:

Wales, whales
way, whey
weather, whether
were, where
witch, which.

It is important to use the correct spelling.

A few words beginning with 'wh' are pronounced as if they begin with 'h'. These are:

who, whoever, whole, wholesome, wholesale, wholly, whom, whomsoever, whooping cough, whore, whose.

wadi

A *wadi* is a dried-up riverbed. The word was borrowed from Arabic and is occasionally spelled *wady*. Its plural can be either *wadis* or *wadies*, with *wadis* being the more usual.

See also BORROWING

wage

See SALARY/WAGE

waggon, wagon

Waggon used to be the spelling favoured in Britain, whereas *wagon* was preferred in America. Now, *wagon* is the more usual spelling in Britain too:

The coal wagons are now the only traffic using the railway line.

waist, wastage, waste

Waist is a noun referring to the narrow part of the trunk between the ribs and the hips:

Many Victorian women had 18-inch waists.

Waste can be a noun, referring to careless or extravagant use, or a verb, meaning 'squander', 'spend foolishly':

What a waste! Many of these items could be recycled.
We are wasting the planet's resources.

The word *waste* is also applied to things that are thrown away:

Put it in the waste-paper basket.

Wastage implies 'loss by leakage, decay or evaporation':

We could avoid water shortages if the water companies dealt with wastage due to leaking pipes.

wait

See AWAIT/WAIT

wait for, wait on

Wait for means 'stay in a place in expectation that something will happen or someone will come':

He waited months for a reply.
She always waited for me at her aunt's house.

Wait on means 'serve':

How many courtiers waited on Elizabeth I?
He waited on Lord Cavendish for forty-six years.
She waited on him, glad to serve him in any way she could.

Many people use *wait on* when they mean *wait for* and such usage is stigmatized:

*I'll wait on you in Lewis's.

waive, wave

Waive means 'set aside one's claims or rights, forgo':

The inspector agreed to waive the interest due on the unpaid tax.

Wave means 'move something (e.g., a hand or flag) backwards and forwards':

The child waved and waved although his parents were out of sight.
On the last night of the Proms, hundreds of people wave flags and sing at the tops of their voices.

wake, waken

See AWAKE/AWAKEN/WAKE/WAKEN

Wales

An inhabitant of the UK principality is a 'Welshman' or 'Welshwoman'; the derived adjective is 'Welsh'. The capital is Cardiff.

See also CELTIC, WELSH

wallaby

A *wallaby* is a marsupial that is related to the kangaroo. It forms its plural in '-ies':

Wallabies are sometimes called small kangaroos and wallaroos are big ones.

wallop

This verb is used informally to mean 'hit hard', 'thump'. It does not double the 'p' before suffixes:

He was walloped for his trouble.

See also SPELLING

wander, wonder

Wander means 'move about aimlessly':

I wandered lonely as a cloud
That floats on high o'er vales and hills
          William Wordsworth, 'The Daffodils'

Wonder can be used as a verb meaning 'think about', 'be astonished by':

I was wondering what to have for dinner.
We wondered at the magnitude of the achievement.

and as a verb meaning 'speculate':

I wonder what she'll wear.

Wonder can be used as a noun meaning 'awe', 'surprise':

Aren't the Pyramids one of the wonders of the world?

It can be used with 'small' and 'no' as a sentence modifier:

Small wonder he would not come if he knew what you had in mind!

No wonder he would not come if he knew what you had in mind!

Modified questions often follow this verb:

I wonder who he is.
I wonder when he'll come.

They take a full stop not a question mark, even when the form of the subordinate clause is identical to the question:

I wonder who sent it.
*I wonder who sent it?

The structure 'I shouldn't wonder ...' is used to mean 'It would not surprise me ...':

I shouldn't wonder if he arrived late.

Some speakers use two negatives in sentences like this:

*I shouldn't wonder if he didn't arrive late.

This is incorrect.

wane

Wane means 'grow smaller'. It is archaic but still occasionally used in poetry and with regard to the moon:

The moon waxes for two weeks and then begins to wane.

See also WAX

want

Want can function as a noun meaning 'need', 'desire' and 'poverty':

My wants are negligible.
It is no longer only the unemployed who live in want.

Want can also be a verb with two almost opposite meanings. It can be used for 'need, desire':

I just want a little peace and quiet.

and also with 'for' to mean 'lack':

I want for nothing. I have everything that I need.

There is considerable debate among stylists and grammarians whether *want* should be followed by the present or the past participle in such constructions as:

Do you want your car washed/washing?

The sentence with the -ING FORM is widely used but regional.

want of

Want of means 'lack':

A little neglect may breed mischief, ... for want of a nail the shoe was lost; for want of a shoe the horse was lost; and for want of a horse the rider was lost.
          B. Franklin, *Poor Richard's Almanack*

war

There is considerable variation on the use of 'war' in compound words in that it may occur in one-word compounds, two-word compounds and with a hyphen:

warfare, wartime
war crime, war damage
war-cloud, war-torn.

The longer the compound has been in existence, the more likely it is to be written as one word.

See also COMPOUND

-ward, -wards

The suffix *-ward* is always used for adjectives:

a forward motion
a backward glance

whereas adverbs may use both *-ward* and *-wards*:

She looked backward and forward.
She looked backwards and forwards.

The adverbial suffix without the 's' is regular in US English:

Travelling westward, we visit Yosemite, one of the world's most beautiful parks.

It is becoming widespread in British English, too.

warn

Warn means 'give notice of danger or trouble':

I warned him that he would not be given a second chance.

It should not be used where 'advise' would be more appropriate:

I advised him that his annual bonus was larger than ever.

I warned him that there would be no annual bonus this year.

warranty
See GUARANTEE/WARRANTY

was, were
The 'be' verb is the most irregular in the language. All other verbs have one past tense form but 'be' has two, *was* and *were*. In normal references to past time, *was* occurs with first- and third-person subjects:

I was a sailor at that time and so was John.

I was singing as I walked and she was humming quietly.

and *were* occurs with 'you' and with plural subjects:

We were sailors at the time.

You were unaware that they were travelling home.

When the subordinate clause is hypothetical and begins with 'if', 'as if', 'as though' or 'suppose', then *were* is used with all subjects, especially in the written medium:

If I were a blackbird ...

She spoke as if he were not in the room.

Suppose she were the Queen. Would you speak to her that way?

Often, especially in speech, when the hypothesis is not too far fetched, the ordinary rules of agreement occur:

If I was at home now, I'd be watching *Neighbours*.

When the subject and verb are reversed in a hypothetical clause, only *were* can be used:

Were I to admit that, they would lose faith in me.

In US English, *be* is sometimes used where British speakers would prefer *is*:

If this be proved against him .... .

See also UK AND US ENGLISH

wash up
In British English, *wash up* normally implies 'wash the dishes':

That was a wonderful meal! The least I can do is wash up.

In US English, *wash up* normally implies 'wash oneself':

Have I time to wash up before supper?

See also UK AND US ENGLISH

washroom
See LAVATORY/TOILET/WASHROOM

wastage, waste
See WAIST/WASTAGE/WASTE

watch
See LOOK/SEE/WATCH

water
Water can function as a noun:

They've cut off the water!

and as a verb:

I need to water the garden.

It also occurs in a wide variety of compounds. The compounds can be single words, two separate words or hyphenated:

watercress, waterfall

water diviner, water softener

water-bed, water-lily.

There is no absolute rule for compounds involving 'water' and there can be disagreement, with some dictionaries recommending 'water-colour' and others 'watercolour'.

See also COMPOUND

wave
See WAIVE/WAVE

wax
Wax meaning 'grow' is obsolescent in English. It continues to occur in references to the moon, in poetry and in traditional religious language:

And the child waxed and grew strong ...
        Luke, 2:52

It is also found in the fixed phrase '*wax* and wane':

Their fortunes have waxed and waned over the years.

See also WANE

way-out, Way Out
Way-out (with a hyphen) is used in certain varieties of colloquial English to mean 'unusual', 'excellent':

I've never met such a way-out character.

Way-out, man!

This usage is dated and, because it is ambiguous, it should be avoided in the written medium and in careful speech.

Way Out (without a hyphen, but with initial capital letters) means 'exit'.

-ways, -wise
Both these suffixes can combine with nouns to produce adverbs or adjectives of direction:

a sideways movement

He moved sideways.

a clockwise movement

He moved clockwise.

Words with *-ways* are unhyphenated and have been in the language for a considerable time.

Words with *-wise* are often (but not always) hyphenated:

length-wise

because they are more recent creations. Occasionally, we have alternatives:

lengthways, length-wise

sideways, side-wise

and personal taste rather than correctness is involved in the choice of one rather than another. The *-wise* forms are often preferred for adjectival usage even by people who use *-ways* for adverbs, and *-wise* forms are growing in popularity.

There is a tendency to use *-wise* with nouns to mean 'with regard to':

That was a bad move, careerwise.

Moneywise, they've got no problems but healthwise they're less fortunate.

Many people dislike this usage, but it is found in both speech and writing in all parts of the English-using world.

we, us

We is the first-person plural subject pronoun. It refers to the speaker and others, but it is ambiguous in that it can be both inclusive and exclusive. If John is speaking to Sue and Tony, he can use *we* inclusively:

We've passed (i.e., John, Sue and Tony have passed).

semi-inclusively:

We've passed (i.e., John and Sue but not Tony).

or exclusively:

We've passed (i.e., John and others but not Sue and Tony).

Because of this potential ambiguity, care must be exercised when *we* is used.

We is sometimes used to refer to one person in what is called 'the royal plural':

We hereby declare ...

This is no longer customary for monarchs, but some writers use *we* as a means of involving the reader:

We have already shown that English words are multi-functional but the degree of multi-functionality varies between open and closed classes.

Older people also, occasionally, use *we* to reprimand children:

We thought we'd got away with it, didn't we?

and to express solidarity, as in a hospital:

How are we feeling today?

Many speakers worry about when to use *we* and *us*. The rule is simple. *We* is used when the pronoun is the subject of a clause:

We have not listened to our children and so we have not understood.

We adults will search outside and you children can search the house.

Us is used for objects and after prepositions:

We saw them and they saw us.

They gave the books to us.

They gave the books to John and us.

There are two occasions when virtually all speakers prefer to use *us*, even when some grammarians say that *we* would be more appropriate:

They are taller than us.

That's us in the photograph.

See also I/ME, PRONOUN

weal

A *weal* is a bump on the skin caused by a sharp stroke:

Sailors used to rub salt into weals to prevent infection.

This is sometimes also referred to as a 'wheal' or 'welt'. The spelling *weal* is now the preferred form for the injury, with 'wheal' being the form used for a Cornish tin mine.

wear

Wear is an irregular verb:

wear(s), wore, wearing, worn.

She wore a garment of white brocade. I have always worn green.

weather, whether

In many varieties of English, these words are homophones and thus they are occasionally confused in the written medium. *Weather* refers to climatic conditions and is a common topic in PHATIC COMMUNION:

We've had very unusual weather recently. First, we had hard frost and now the temperatures are 3° higher than normal.

Whether is a CONJUNCTION that introduces a choice of two:

Whether you like her or not, you have to admire her courage.

I don't know whether or not I'll go.

weave

When *weave* means 'make a fabric by interlacing yarn', it is an irregular verb:

weave(s), wove, weaving, woven

She wove the best linen in the country.

It was woven from the finest silk.

When *weave* is used metaphorically to mean 'move in and out', it tends to be treated as a regular verb:

weave(s), weaved, weaving

She weaved through the traffic in a desperate attempt to reach the hospital in time.

Both regular and irregular forms are used when *weave* means 'create a story':

She wove a spell with her storytelling.
She weaved a spell.

The irregular forms are gradually being ousted in all non-literal uses of *weave*.

See also VERB

wed

Wed is an archaic verb meaning 'marry'. It is sometimes used at weddings:

Little did I think that she would wed so soon.

It doubles the 'd' before suffixes:

I am wedding the most beautiful girl in the world.

The past tense and the past participle can be either *wed* or 'wedded':

They were wed (wedded) on a Tuesday.

The adjective is 'wedded':

Fifty years of wedded bliss!

Wednesday

Wednesday takes its name from the Old Norse god, Woden, and the word is a calque of Latin *mercuri dies*, 'Mercury's day'. There is some confusion about how the word should be pronounced. The most frequently heard pronunciation is as a disyllabic word, the first syllable rhyming with 'hens'.

weep

Weep means 'shed tears'. It is an irregular verb:

weep(s), wept, weeping, wept
I wept for joy when I heard the news.
They have wept for their country and the world has watched them weep.

weigh

Weigh means 'measure' and is related to *weight*:

She weighs 50 kilos now.

The verb is also used, sometimes with 'up', to mean 'evaluate':

They took hours to weigh (up) the evidence.

Notice the spelling. This word, like many others, breaks the rule of 'i before e except after c'.

See also SPELLING

weir

A *weir* is a type of dam. It rhymes with 'clear'.

weird

This adjective, meaning 'strange', 'uncanny', 'frightening', first appears in Shakespeare's description of the three witches in *Macbeth*. Like 'weigh', it is sometimes misspelled. The noun *weirdo* (pronounced 'weird' + 'o') is sometimes used informally for a person whose behaviour is eccentric.

See also SPELLING

welch, welsh

Both these forms are used as a verb meaning 'fail to meet a debt':

He welched on the deal.

The verb is slang and possibly racist. It is therefore better avoided.

See also POLITICAL CORRECTNESS, RACIST LANGUAGE, WALES

well

The word *well* is polysemous. It can be a noun:

They have a well at the bottom of their garden.

a verb:

The tears welled up as he walked away.

a sentence adverbial, often used in speech:

Well, I didn't know what to do.

an interjection often indicating disapproval or surprise:

Well! Well! What will she think of next!
Well! I'd never have expected such a present!

an adverb intensifier, with 'better' and 'best' as comparative and superlative forms:

He is well dressed now.
He is better dressed now than when he was young.
He knows me well but I know myself best.

and an adjective, with 'better' and 'best' as comparative and superlative forms:

She's not well today but she should be better soon.

Well is widely used as a predicative adjective:

I'm very well, thank you.

but is quite rare in the attributive position:

He's not a well man.

See also ADJECTIVE, ADVERB, GOOD/WELL, POLYSEMY

well-

When *well* is prefixed to a verb form to create an attributive adjective, a hyphen is used:

He is a well-known comedian.
She visited a well-meaning friend.

Because *well* can be used as an intensifier for many adjectives formed from verbs:

The suit was very well made.
I am well respected here.

some speakers are now using it as an intensifier for non-verbal adjectives:

*I was well happy with the result.

This usage is not acceptable.

Well is also used with a hyphen when it is part of a noun compound:

He looked after her well-being.
She was suddenly approached by a well-wisher.

Welsh

The Celts known as the Welsh (Old English

'wealh' meaning 'Celt', 'Briton', 'foreigner') now occupy an area in the west of Britain, although Welsh-derived place-names are found to the south in Cornwall, and to the north in Cumbria and Scotland, suggesting that Welsh speakers were once more widespread throughout Britain.

See also CELTIC

wench

Wench is an archaic noun for 'young woman'. It is occasionally used facetiously as in:

Come here, wench.

but it is better avoided since it may cause offence.

See also POLITICAL CORRECTNESS, SEXIST LANGUAGE

werewolf, werwolf

These two forms are used for a person who, in folk mythology, assumed the shape of a wolf at certain times, such as a full moon. The first form is more widespread in Britain, the second in America. The prefix *wer(e)-* may come from an Old English word meaning 'man'.

west, western

The noun *west* is one of the four cardinal points. When it is used in full, to refer to a compass position, we use a lower-case 'w':

Leeds lies due west of Hull.

When we use letters to refer to the compass points, we use capital letters without full stops:

N, S, E, W

When the noun is used as part of proper name, a capital letter is used:

West Africa

West Bromwich.

A capital letter is also used when 'the West' is a shorthand expression for the Western (non-Communist) world, mainly America and parts of Europe:

He defected to the West in 1976.

There are two adjectives relating to the west, *west* and *western*, which are normally written with a lower-case 'w':

It's a warm wind the west wind
    John Masefield

It's a western island, off the coast of western Ireland.

Western tends to be less geographically precise than *west*. It takes a capital letter only when it is part of a place name or fixed collocation:

Western Australia.

The noun *Western* is used as the name of a particular type of cowboy film about the western states of America.

See also ABBREVIATION

Western Samoa

An inhabitant of the island nation in the Pacific is a 'Samoan'; the derived adjective is the same. The capital is Apia.

wet

There are two acceptable past tense and past participle forms for the verb *wet*:

He wet the floor yesterday and he has wet it again today.

He wetted the floor yesterday and he has wetted it again today.

Wet, like many verbs ending in '-t' and '-d', is in the process of being simplified and so is becoming like 'put'.

Some people prefer to use *wetted* to preserve a distinction between the adjectival use of *wet* and the past participle of the verb:

The floor was wet.

The floor was wetted (i.e., deliberately made wet).

This is a useful distinction but is not always observed.

See also -ED/-T

wet, whet

In many parts of the English-speaking world, words such as 'Wales' and 'whales' or 'weather and 'whether' are distinguished in pronunciation. In England, the tendency is for such words to be homophones. Because the 'wh' words are pronounced the same as the 'w' words, there is a tendency to omit the 'h' in spelling. *Wet* means 'moisten, cover with water':

Wet the floor before putting that wax on.

Whet, on the other hand, means 'sharpen, stimulate the appetite':

Have you got a whet stone? My knife is blunt.
The wonderful smell really whetted my appetite.

See also W-/WH-

wharf

A *wharf* is a place where ships can dock to load and unload. Like some other English words that end in 'f', it can form its plural in '-ves':

hoof, hooves

wolf, wolves.

Increasingly, however, *wharf* is being treated as a regular noun that forms its plural by adding 's':

roof, roofs

scarf, scarfs

wharf, wharfs.

The two plurals, *wharfs* and *wharves*, are equally acceptable, but *wharfs* is now the more frequently used.

what

What is a multi-functional word. It can function as an interrogative adjective:

What page did you say it was on?

as an interrogative pronoun:

What did you say?

and as a non-interrogative pronoun:

What you did, you did for all of us.
I heard what you've been saying.

In such cleft sentences as:

What he wants is a nice cup of tea.

speakers sometimes worry about which form of 'be' to use. The rule is theoretically simple. If the noun after 'be' is singular, we use a singular verb:

What we need is a nice cup of tea.

If the noun after 'be' is plural, we use a plural:

What we need are more students.

Occasionally, though, the decision is not so clear cut. In a sentence like:

What we need – fish and chips.

most speakers would say 'is' because although 'fish and chips' is logically plural, it is treated like a singular collective noun. If there is any uncertainty about which form of the verb to use, it is advisable to restructure the sentence:

We need fish and chips.

See also BE, COMPLEMENT

what, which

What and *which* can both occur as interrogative adjectives and there is some overlap in their meaning:

What car did you buy?
Which car did you buy?

The main difference is that the first question is more general, whereas the second is more specific and suggests that the choice of car was more limited.

In some regions, *what* is used as a relative pronoun in such sentences as:

*The car what we bought was red.

This usage is not standard.

See also PRONOUN, STANDARD ENGLISH

what ever, whatever

Normally, *whatever* is written as one word. It can function as a pronoun meaning 'everything, no matter what':

Whatever he said, he solved our problem.

as a general all-purpose noun, similar in meaning to such forms as 'thingamajig' or 'whatsitsname':

Bring me a mallet or hammer or whatever.

as a determiner:

We'll clear whatever mess we make.

and as a postmodifier in such sentences as:

There was no need whatever to buy more food.

When the *ever* expresses incredulity and could be replaced by 'on earth' *what ever* is written as two words:

What ever will he say next?

See also DETERMINER, PRONOUN

what not, whatnot

What not, sometimes written as two words and sometimes hyphenated like the variants 'what-do-you-call it' and 'whatsit', means 'and other things like that':

She bought fruit and vegetables and what not.

A *whatnot* is a portable display unit with shelves:

She kept her souvenirs on the whatnot.

whatsoever

Whatsoever is becoming archaic. It is occasionally found in liturgical and legal language:

Whatsoever ye shall do to the least of mine, ye shall do also to me.

It still occurs as a variant form of *whatever* as an emphatic postmodifier:

There was no need whatsoever to buy more food.

It often follows such indefinite pronouns and determiners as 'any', 'anybody', 'none', 'no one':

I haven't found any whatsoever.
He took none whatsoever.

when

When can function as an interrogative adverb:

When will she arrive?

as a means of introducing a subordinate clause:

Ask her when she is arriving.

It is also used in the fixed collocation:

Say when.

meaning 'Tell me when to stop pouring.'

When should refer to time and should not be used as a loose synonym for 'in which':

*Aphasia is a condition when people lose control of language.

when ever, whenever

Whenever is normally written as one word when it means 'every time':

Whenever we meet, we talk about you.

or 'no matter when':

Call in whenever you like.

When ever functions in a similar way to 'how', 'what', 'where' and 'who' + 'ever' in that 'ever' is used as an INTENSIFIER of the word it follows:

When ever do you get time to write poetry?
Who ever could have written it?

See also EVER/-EVER

whence

Whence is now virtually obsolete, although it continues to be used in some formal contexts:

This is Brixton whence John Major came.

It is the equivalent of 'from where', which is preferable in both speech and writing.

Careful users avoid *from whence*, because the 'from' is redundant:

This is the bog from whence it came.

It should be added, however, that many acceptable collocations involve redundancy. 'Enter' means 'come in' but is frequently used with 'into':

Enter thou into the bliss of the Lord.
They freely entered into the contract.

See also REDUNDANCY

where ever, wherever

Wherever can function as an adverbial conjunction meaning 'no matter where':

Wherever you go, I'll follow.

Where ever is an emphatic equivalent of 'where':

Where ever did you put it?

Where'er is sometimes used as a poetic equivalent of 'where ever':

Where'er you walk, cool gales shall fan the glade,
Trees, where you sit, shall crowd into a shade:
Where'er you tread, the blushing flow'rs shall rise,
And all things flourish where you turn your eyes.
　　　　Alexander Pope, *Pastorals*

See also EVER/-EVER, INTENSIFIER

whereas, while

Whereas usually functions as a contrastive conjunction meaning 'but on the other hand':

I love singing whereas Michael is tone deaf.

Care should be taken not to use *while* meaning 'at the same time' if a contrast is implied. The sentence:

I played the flute whereas Michael played the organ.

contrasts actions that may not have occurred at the same time. However, in:

I played the flute while Michael played the organ.

the two actions occurred simultaneously.

Whereas is also used in legal documents as a sentence initiator meaning 'since it is the case that':

Whereas the vendor agrees to … .

whereby

Whereby tends to be limited to formal speech and writing. It is used as a relative pronoun to mean 'by which', 'because of which':

These are the techniques whereby I made a fortune.

See also PRONOUN

wherefore

Wherefore is an obsolete adverb meaning 'for what reason', but it continues to be used in legal language and as a noun in the fixed phrase 'whys and wherefores':

I'll have to know the whys and wherefores before committing myself.

whet

See WET/WHET

whether

See WEATHER/WHETHER

which

Which can function in a variety of ways in English. It can be an interrogative adjective:

Which paper is cheapest?

an interrogative pronoun:

Which did you choose?
Which of the dishes did she choose?

a pronoun implying choice:

He is either at work or on his way home. I cannot be certain which.

and a relative pronoun, either subject or object, introducing a subordinate clause and modifying a non-human noun:

This is the tree which was planted when Ruth died.
That was the letter which John wrote.

In sentences like these, the use of *which* can lead to confusion and, depending on the intended sense, the clause that it introduces should either be differentiated from the main clause by commas, dashes or parentheses or be introduced by 'that', which can, itself, be omitted without altering the sense of the sentence.

This is the tree that was planted when Ruth died.
That was the letter that John wrote.
That was the letter John wrote.

Until the seventeenth century *which* could modify human nouns and it is still found with this function in older versions of the Lord's Prayer:

Our father which art in heaven.

and, occasionally, when referring to children:

These are the babies which were born with spina bifida.

See also DEFINING RELATIVE CLAUSE, PRONOUN, THAT/WHICH, WHAT/WHICH

whichever

Whichever can function as a determiner, meaning 'any out of several':

Take whichever book(s) you like.

and as a pronoun:

Take whichever suits you.

It is always written as one word.

See also DETERMINER, EVER/-EVER, PRONOUN

while, whilst

There is no clear semantic distinction in English between *while* and *whilst*, both of which can occur as subordinating conjunctions:

Mary minds the children while I cook lunch.

Mary minds the children whilst I cook lunch.

but the use of *whilst* may be regarded as archaic, literary or regional:

Lo, as a careful housewife runs to catch
One of her feathered creatures broke away,
Sets down her babe, and makes all swift despatch
In pursuit of the thing she would have stay;
Whilst her neglected child holds her in chase ...

Shakespeare, Sonnet 143

Whilst is rarely used by mother-tongue speakers outside the British Isles.

While, but not *whilst*, can function as a noun:

Wait a while.

In the north of England, *while* is often used to mean 'until'. This usage does not cause many problems when it is used as a PREPOSITION:

I'll be here while (i.e., until) nine.

but it can result in ambiguity in such sentences as:

You won't learn anything while you listen to me.

Stop while the light is green.

See also AMONG/AMONGST/BETWEEN, CONJUNCTION, WHEREAS/WHILE

while, wile, wily

Wile, a noun meaning 'cunning', 'craftiness', and *while* are homophones for most speakers of English, although some speakers in Ireland, Scotland, Canada and the United States continue to distinguish them.

Wily looks like an adverb but is an adjective meaning 'cunning', 'crafty':

John is a wily adversary.

See also ADJECTIVE, ADVERB, PRONUNCIATION

whir, whirr

Whir is onomatopoeic in that it mimics the noise of a motor working or, more poetically, of a fluttering bird:

You don't normally hear the whir of the engine with all the other noises.

a whirr of unseen wings

R. Southey

It may be spelled with either one 'r' or two.

See also ONOMATOPOEIA

whiskey, whisky

Both these words are attempts to transcribe the first part of the Gaelic phrase *uisce beatha*, 'water of life'. In Ireland, Canada and the United States of America, the '-ey' spelling is used. In Scotland

and other parts of the English-speaking world, *whisky* is the preferred form. The abbreviation 'Scotch' is always for *whisky*.

white

White can function as an adjective:

a white sheet

and as a noun:

It's hard to believe that there can be so many shades of white.

The related verb is normally *whiten*:

Don't forget to whiten my tennis shoes.

White can also be used as a synonym for 'Caucasian'. In such usage, it is often contrasted with 'black':

The population is made up equally of blacks and whites.

In English *white* has traditionally been associated with cleanliness, goodness and light, whereas BLACK has been associated with dirt, evil and darkness. Such collocations have perhaps unconsciously contributed to racial stereotyping.

See also POLITICAL CORRECTNESS, RACIAL LANGUAGE

whither

Whither is an obsolete equivalent of 'where':

And Ruth said, Intreat me not to leave thee, or to return from following after thee: for whither thou goest, I will go ... .

Ruth, 1:16

whiz, whizz

Both these spellings are acceptable for the onomatopoeic word meaning a loud humming or buzzing sound.

See also ONOMATOPOEIA

who, whoever

Who is a subject pronoun that is used with reference to people:

Who did you see there?

It can function as an interrogative pronoun:

Who are you?

as a relative pronoun:

The man who came in was wearing a green hat.

and as a means of introducing a subordinate clause:

She doesn't know who followed her.

Whoever can be used as a pronoun:

Whoever wants it can have it.

The two-word form *who ever* occurs as an emphatic form of *who*:

Who ever did such a thing?

Notice the contrast between this sentence and:

Whoever did this will pay dearly!

There is a tendency to use *whoever* for both these usages, just as there is a tendency to compound all the other words with *-ever*, such as *however*, *whatever* and *whenever*.

See also EVER/-EVER, INTERROGATIVE, PRONOUN

who, whom

These words are variant forms of each other in the same way as *me* and *I* are, or *he* and *him* are. They are pronouns whose form is determined by grammar. *Who* is a subject pronoun:

Who is there?

I don't know who is coming.

Whom is an object pronoun – that is, the form that functions as the object of a verb or that follows a preposition:

Whom did you see?

The man, whom we have arrested, is twenty-five.

To whom did you address it?

With whom are we in touch?

As we can see from the examples above, *who* and *whom* are variants that reflect case and parallel the usage of other subject and object pronouns in English.

In colloquial speech, 'who' is frequently substituted for 'whom':

Who did you give it to?

Who will they find to do it?

but this is still not fully acceptable in the written medium.

See also CASE, PREPOSITION, PRONOUN, RELATIVE CLAUSE

who's, whose

The forms *who's* and *whose* are sometimes confused, although the rules for their use are simple. *Who's* is always a reduced form, normally of 'who is':

Who's that?

Who's in charge here?

but occasionally of 'who has':

Who's been eating my porridge?

Who's been sitting in my chair?

Whose can function as both a pronoun and a possessive adjective:

He asked me whose it was. (Whose is it?)

This is the man whose daughter is getting married.

A sentence involving *whose* as a pronoun can be rewritten with *whose* being replaced by 'to whom':

Whose is it? = To whom does it belong?

A sentence involving *whose* as a possessive adjective can be rewritten as two sentences, with *whose* being replaced by 'his', 'her', 'their':

These are the people whose daughter is getting married. = These are the people. Their daughter is getting married.

See also APOSTROPHE

whodunit

Whodunit is an informal noun for a murder mystery, usually a novel or play:

I always buy a whodunit for a long train journey.

The word is a modified form of 'who + done + it', and the term tends to indicate a 'potboiler' rather than a serious literary work.

See also COMPOUND

whole

Whole can function as an adjective meaning 'entire, complete':

… the truth, the whole truth and nothing but the truth …

and as a noun meaning 'totality':

The whole is greater than the sum of the parts.

It occurs especially in the fixed phrases:

taken as a whole

on the whole.

Whole can also occur as an adverb meaning 'completely', 'in an unbroken piece':

He swallowed the egg whole.

See also ADJECTIVE, ADVERB, COLLOCATION

wholly

See HOLEY/HOLY/WHOLLY

whoop, whooping cough

Whoop is an onomatopoeic word meaning 'cry out with joy and enthusiasm':

She whooped with delight.

The 'wh' in *whoop* is pronounced like 'w' as in 'when'. The 'wh' in *whooping cough* is pronounced like 'h' as in 'hoop'.

widow, widower

Many nouns in English have the masculine form as basic:

actor, actress

poet, poetess.

Widow is an exception in that the female form is basic and the male form *widower* is derived from it.

See also GENDER, POLITICAL CORRECTNESS, SEXIST LANGUAGE

wile, wily

See WHILE/WILE/WILY

wilful, willful

Wilful is an adjective meaning 'headstrong', 'determined to have one's own way':

She is the most wilful student I have ever taught.

The spelling *willful* is American.

See also SPELLING, UK AND US ENGLISH

will

See SHALL/WILL

will-o'-the-wisp

A *will-o'-the-wisp* is a thin phosphorescent light, *ignis fatuus*, sometimes seen over marshy ground at night. It is sometimes incorrectly spelled. The *will* is an abbreviation of 'William'. Another common name for this phenomenon is 'jack-o-lantern'.

See also COMPOUND

willy-nilly

Willy-nilly means 'whether we like it or not':

Children grow up willy-nilly.

It comes from the older English phrase 'wyle he, nyle he' meaning 'will he, will he not'. The meaning of this compound is sometimes weakened to mean 'carelessly':

She made the bed willy-nilly.

win

See BEAT/WIN

wind

There are two verbs with the same spelling. One rhymes with 'kind' and the other with 'tinned'. The verb that rhymes with 'kind' means 'turn or coil' and is irregular:

wind(s), wound, winding, wound
Wind the wool for me, please. I've wound so much that my arms are tired.

The other verb is derived from the noun that means 'a current of air' and is regular:

wind(s), winded, winding.

It can mean 'cause someone to be short of breath':

The blow winded me.

or, when used of a baby, it can mean 'help to release trapped air':

Have you winded the baby yet?

window

Window derives from an Old Norse compound meaning 'wind-eye', and it is used in many well-known expressions:

a launch window
window dressing
window shopping
the window of opportunity

In computer terminology *window* refers to software that allows the screen to be divided into several sections, each one, if required, running a different program.

wintry

The adjective from 'winter' is *wintry*, without an 'e':

I enjoy wintry weather.

wiry

The adjective from 'wire' is *wiry*, without an 'e':

He was small but strong and wiry.

-wise

See -WAYS/-WISE

wit

Wit is most frequently used now as a synonym for 'humour', but it continues to have another meaning that links it to 'wisdom'. *Wit* comes from an Old English word meaning 'knowledge'. 'Humour' comes from a Latin word meaning 'moisture'. Later, it developed the meaning of 'one of the elements found in the body that was largely responsible for personality'. Today, 'humour' is associated with moods, often a cheerful mood, and usually with laughter:

She has a wonderful sense of humour.

Wit may or may not involve laughter, but it always implies intellectual qualities. Witty language always implies inventiveness or intelligent originality.

Wit is found in a number of well-known expressions, including:

keep one's wits (about one)
quick-witted, slow-witted.

See also HUMOUR/HUMOR, PARODY, SATIRE/SATYR

witch elm, witch hazel, wych elm, wych hazel

These are variant spellings of the same words. The form *wych* is no longer common but is perfectly acceptable.

with

With is a preposition with a wide range of uses in English. It can mean 'in the company of':

He arrived with his parents.

'against', 'in opposition to':

We should not fight with our friends.

'in agreement with':

They are not with us on the important issue of pollution.

and 'in the same direction as':

You will be playing with the wind in the first half.

With is used to indicate the instrument, both

literal and metaphorical, that is involved in an action:

She hit him with her handbag.

She hit him with a lawsuit.

It can indicate the cause of a reaction:

She was mad with joy.

It can show that two or more actions or events occurred simultaneously:

He drove home with his radio blaring.

and it can indicate cause:

With his parents away, he decided to have the party of a lifetime.

Occasionally, when *with* links a singular and a plural noun in a compound subject, there is uncertainty about agreement. The rules are clear. The verb agrees with the first noun in the compound:

The archbishop together with senior bishops has reached a decision.

The senior bishops together with the archbishop have reached a decision.

See also BY/WITH, CASE, PREPOSITION

withal

Withal is an obsolescent adverb meaning 'as well', 'besides'. It still occurs occasionally in jocular speech:

He had three wives withal.

It serves no valuable function in contemporary usage but survives in the compound noun 'wherewithal', 'resources', 'means':

I haven't the wherewithal to buy a new car.

withhold

Withhold is a verb meaning 'keep back', 'refuse to give':

They withheld money for taxes.

He withheld permission for the fête.

The word retains the 'h' from 'with' and the 'h' from 'hold', unlike some other compounds where one 'h' is lost:

Church + hill = Churchill

South + hampton = Southampton.

within

Within is a preposition that is most frequently used to mean 'by the end of' and 'not beyond the limits of':

We need the proofs within a week if we are not to miss our deadline.

You must learn to live within your budget.

Often, 'in' is used instead of *within* but this can cause ambiguity:

He can come in a week.

can mean both:

It will take a week for him to get here.

He can be here in less than a week.

Within, not 'in', should be used if we wish to convey the second meaning.

See also IN

wolf, wolves

The plural of the noun *wolf* is *wolves*:

Wolves have been reintroduced into the Pyrenees.

The verb *wolf* meaning 'eat voraciously' is regular:

He wolfs his food.

He was so hungry he wolfed the food.

wolverine

Few people will need to refer to this large musteline mammal, but the alternative spelling, *wolverene*, should be avoided.

woman

See FEMALE/LADY/WOMAN

wonder

See WANDER/WONDER

wonderful, wondrous

Wonderful has become a somewhat overused adjective. It originally meant 'capable of evoking wonder':

News spread of the wonderful star that appeared to go before them.

Like many overused words, it has been bleached of much of its original meaning and has little more meaning than 'nice' or 'pleasant':

Wonderful holiday! Wish you were here!

Wondrous is literary, liturgical and obsolescent:

When I survey the wondrous Cross,
On which the Prince of Glory died ...
        Isaac Watts

See also BLEACHING, CLICHÉ, SEMANTIC CHANGE

wont

Wont is an obsolescent word meaning 'habit, custom'. It is still used jocularly and in the cliché 'as is/was my wont':

I am wont to take a walk on Sunday if the weather is good.

I went to the park as is my wont on a Sunday.

won't

Won't is an abbreviation for 'will not' and it must always be written with an apostrophe. *Won't* is perfectly acceptable in speech and in friendly or casual writing. In formal styles, abbreviations should be avoided.

See also APOSTROPHE, STILE/STYLE

woo

Woo is an obsolescent word for 'court', 'want to marry'. It still occurs in songs:

And the only thing that I ever did wrong
Was to woo a fair young maid.

Anonymous

---

wood

It is not always easy to distinguish between a *wood* and a forest although many people think of a *wood* as being smaller. The word 'forest' was borrowed from French whereas *wood* is from Old English. There are large numbers of compounds involving *wood*, the better established ones tending to be written without hyphens:

woodbine, woodcock, woodpecker, woodwork
wood-alcohol, wood-carver, wood-pigeon, wood-worm.

See also COMPOUND, HYPHEN

wool, woollen, woolly

There are two adjectives from *wool*. *Woollen* means 'made from wool':

I bought a woollen coat.

Woolly means 'like wool', 'unclear':

It had a woolly texture.
We must try to avoid woolly language.

In both British and American English, the forms with double 'o' and double 'l' occur, but American English also permits *woolen* with one 'l'.

See also SPELLING, UK AND US ENGLISH

word

Although most speakers of English have an intuitive knowledge of what a *word* is, it is not an easy concept to define. We might all agree that *tree* and *house* are words, but we might be less certain about whether *treehouse* is one word or two. In addition, although *a* and *wood* may both be recognized as words, they are clearly different in that *a* cannot normally occur alone or be pluralized, whereas *wood* can. There is no single definition of 'word' that is completely satisfactory, but we can make a number of useful distinctions:

■ In writing, a word is a group of letters with a space on either side. Thus, there are nine orthographic words in this sentence. Orthographic words can occur only in writing.

■ In speech, a word is a sound or group of sounds that can be spoken in isolation. In science fiction films, aliens and androids frequently insert pauses between words:

My # name # is # Helper.

but, in normal speech, there tends to be little or no pause between words, a fact that helps to explain such incorrect subdivision as:

an apron (derived from a naperon)
an orange (derived from a norange).

See also MORPHEME, ORTHOGRAPHY

word breaks

Often in the written medium, a full word cannot be written at the end of a line. and so it may be necessary to insert a hyphen and split it. The rules that apply are these:

■ Do not split a monosyllabic word

■ Try to avoid two-letter splits, such as:

in-fer, re-ply

■ Do not split a word if the split could cause ambiguity. An *ex-porter* is very different from an *exporter*.

■ Split a word according to its etymology, thus:

geo-graphical not *geog-raphical

■ Split a word after a prefix or before a suffix:

sub-marine not *submar-ine
relax-ation not *rela-xation

■ Split a word, if possible, between two consonants:

estab-lish

except where the consonants combine to form one sound:

Steph-anie not *Step-hanie

■ Split after the first consonant where three co-occur:

illus-trate not *illust-rate
chil-dren not *child-ren.

The most general rule of all is to avoid any split that would cause a problem to the reader.

See also HYPHEN

word formation

There are many methods of word formation in English. Of the ten techniques listed here, COMPOUNDING and DERIVATION are the most productive.

■ Acronyms

laser (*l*ight *a*mplification by *s*timulated *e*mission of *r*adiation)
posh (*p*ort *o*ut *s*tarboard *h*ome)

■ Back formation

flab (from flabby)
gatecrash (from gatecrasher)

■ Blending

chuckle + snort = chortle
stagnation + inflation = stagflation

■ Calquing

blue ribbon (from *cordon bleu*)

Break a leg! (from *Hals und bein bruch!* = Good luck)

■ Clipping
omnibus = bus
pianoforte = piano

■ Coining
pandemonium (Milton)
slithy (Lewis Carroll)

■ Compounding
hat + box = hatbox
foot + ball = football

■ Derivation
un + like + ly = unlikely
worth + less = worthless

■ Onomatopoeia
cuckoo
peewit

■ Toponyms
Kashmir = cashmere
Jersey = jersey

See also COINAGE, NEOLOGISM, NONCE

word order
Word order differs from language to language. We can illustrate this by taking the simple sentence:
I saw him (Subject Predicator Object = SPO)
and giving its equivalent in other languages. In French, we have:
Je l'ai vu (SOP)
and in Irish Gaelic we have:
Chonaic mé é (PSO).

The usual order for statements in English is SPO:
I painted it.
I did not paint it.
Imperatives generally drop the subject:
Paint it!
Don't paint it!
and questions usually involve a question word + inversion:
When did you paint it?
Why did you paint it?
The normal word order can be changed for literary effect:
Now sleeps the crimson petal, now the white,
Nor waves the cypress in the palace walk;
Nor winks the gold fin in the porphyry font.
The firefly wakens; waken thou with me.

word processor
A *word processor* is a computer program that can be loaded onto a computer to allow one to type, save, store, modify and print text. The term is also applied to a machine with a screen, keyboard and computer that is dedicated to the production of text.

work
Work is a regular verb now:
I work five days a week.
I worked here for two months.
It used to be irregular and an irregular form, 'wrought', is still associated with work in two ways. In Standard English, it is used as an adjective and applied to metals:
I bought a lovely wrought-iron gate.
and in a number of dialects it is used as a past tense form meaning 'worked hard':
His father wrought hard for him.

Work is compounded into many everyday words, some of which are written as one word and some hyphenated:
workman, worksheet, workshop
work-mate, work-people, work-to-rule.
See also VERB

World War
The forms *World War I* and *World War II* are more widely used in print than such equivalents as 'the First World War', 'the Great War' or the 'Second World War', although may people prefer 'First World War' and 'Second World War'. 'The Great War' is now regarded as archaic.

worship
Worship can function as a noun:
Such forms of worship are not to my taste.
and as a regular verb:
worship(s), worshipped, worshipping.
The 'p' is doubled before '-er' in Britain:
worshipper.
In the United States, some people spell the word with one 'p' in all contexts:
I don't get to church much but I'm a TV worshiper.
See also SPELLING

worth while, worthwhile
The rule here is quite straightforward. *Worthwhile* is used before a noun:
It was a worthwhile activity.
Worth while is used elsewhere:
Was it worth while?
Increasingly, however, it is being written *worthwhile* in all contexts.

would
See SHOULD/WOULD

would-be

Would-be functions as an adjective meaning 'aspiring'. It is always hyphenated:

Dancing in the chorus is often the only work open to would-be leading ladies.

would have

Would have most frequently occurs in such structures as 'If pronoun had X-ed, pronoun would have Y-ed':

If you had studied harder, you would have passed your A-levels.

He would have won the marathon if his shoe had not been torn.

There are two difficulties associated with the use of *would have*. First, people hear it as 'would've':

She would've gone to the top if she had persevered.

The 've sounds like 'of' and many people therefore write:

*She would of ...

which is never acceptable.

Second, some people use *would* in both clauses:

*She would have gone to the top if she would have persevered.

This is not acceptable in British English, where the *would* occurs only in the main clause.

See also MODALITY, TENSE, VERB

wrack

See RACK/WRACK

wrap

See RAP/WRAP

wrapped

See RAPPED/RAPT/WRAPPED

wreak, wreck

Wreak is a regular verb meaning 'cause something bad to happen'. It is virtually obsolete except in the phrase 'wreak havoc on':

wreak(s), wreaked, wreaking

The wrong sort of snow wreaked havoc on the train services.

Most people avoid sentences using 'wreaked' because of uncertainty about the precise form of the past tense.

Wreck is also a regular verb meaning 'destroy', 'ruin':

wreck(s), wrecked, wrecking

He wrecked all our lives.

See also WROUGHT

wreath, wreathe

Wreath, without a final 'e', is always a noun. It is most frequently applied to a circular arrangement of flowers, presented as a tribute:

Did you send a wreath to the funeral?

How many wreaths were there?

Today there is a tendency to associate a *wreath* with the arrangement of flowers that are sent to a funeral, whereas an honorary circle of leaves and flowers is called a 'garland'.

The verb *wreathe* is regular and is most frequently used metaphorically, meaning 'covered', 'encircled':

He was wreathed in smiles.

The mountain was wreathed in mist.

wring

Wring is an irregular verb but it does not pattern exactly like 'sing':

sing(s), sang, singing, sung

wring(s), wrung, wringing, wrung.

Thus, whereas we should write:

She sang the song yesterday.

we must use 'wrung' as the past tense of *wring*:

She wrung out the clothes yesterday.

write

Write is an irregular verb:

write(s), wrote, writing, written

It can be used in three acceptable structures. First, with a direct object:

He writes plays.

second, with an indirect object and a direct object:

He writes me a letter once a month.

and third, without an object:

What does he do for a living? He writes.

In US English, the structure:

He writes me once a week.

is perfectly acceptable, but in British English we must have either:

He writes me a letter once a week.

or:

He writes to me once a week.

See also UK AND US ENGLISH

wrought

Wrought is still used regionally as a past tense and past participle form of 'work':

He wrought hard for years.

She has wrought hard for her family.

These uses are no longer possible in the standard language, which uses *wrought* to mean 'shaped by hammering':

a wrought-iron gate

or, by extension, 'formed, fashioned':

She was renowned for her well-wrought prose.

Some speakers erroneously use *wrought* as the past tense of 'wreak':

*The snowstorm wrought havoc on the roads.
The snowstorm wreaked havoc on the roads.

See also WREAK/WRECK

wych elm, wych hazel
See WITCH ELM/WITCH HAZEL/WYCH ELM/WYCH HAZEL

Patients are x-rayed in the Baines Wing of the hospital.

See also <small>COMPOUND</small>

X

x

X is a consonant, usually pronounced like 'ks' as in 'fix'. It occurs rarely as the initial letter in a word, but when it does so, it is pronounced like 'z':

Xavier, xerox, xylophone.

-x-

See -CT-/-X-

x-ray

The noun is normally written with a capital 'X':

Diagnostic X-rays are never undertaken lightly. They are often expensive and always expose the patient to some degree of risk.

The verb is increasingly written with a lower-case 'x':

xenophobia

This noun means 'fear of foreigners or strangers':

Xenophobia is often a polite term for racism.

See also <small>POLITICAL CORRECTNESS</small>

xerox

Xerox is a trademark for a copying process. The word derives from Greek *xeros*, 'dry'. Increasingly, the word with a lower-case 'x' is used to mean 'reproduce' or 'copy':

Can you xerox these for me, please?
Make five xeroxes of each.

Xmas

Xmas is sometimes used informally for 'Christmas'. The custom originated in the use of *XP* as a Christian monogram for 'Christ'. The monogram was made up of *khi* and *rho*, the first two letters of 'Christ' in Greek. In most written contexts, it is preferable to use the full form, 'Christmas'.

Y

y

Y is regarded as a consonant when it begins a word such as 'you' and as a semi-vowel when it appears in words such as 'dry' and 'why'. In earlier forms of English, 'y' was used as a variant of 'I'.

-y ending

The suffix *-y* has a number of functions in English. It can be added to a name or an abbreviated name to create a diminutive:

William: Billy/Billie
John: Johnny/Johnnie
Sarah: Sally/Sallie.

It can be added to a noun or an abbreviated noun to create a familiar or affectionate form:

costume: cossy/ie
dog: doggy/ie.

It can be added to a noun or adjective to denote 'a person connected with or characterized by':

fat: fatty
group: groupy/ie
thick: thicky/ie.

It can be added to some verbs and adjectives to create nouns:

enquire: enquiry
enter: entry
jealous: jealousy
laze: lazy.

It can be added to a noun to create an adjective:

frost: frosty
green: greeny
ice: icy.

See also SPELLING

Yankee

The terms *Yankee* and *Yank* are best avoided in that they are often used disparagingly of people from the United States. There is considerable debate about the origin of the term. It may have arisen from the nickname 'Jan Kees', which some of the Dutch applied to the English settlers in Connecticut. Historically, the term has been used in America to designate a New England settler and also a Northern soldier or supporter in the American Civil War.

See also NAME, NICKNAME

Yemen

An inhabitant of the republic in the southwest of the Arabian peninsula is a 'Yemeni'; the derived adjective is the same. The capital is Sana'a.

yes/no question

A question that requires the answer 'yes' or 'no' is known as a *yes/no question*:

Are you coming?
Will you do it?

See also QUESTION

yet

Yet usually functions as an adverb. When used in sentence-final position, it is approximately equivalent to 'up to the present time':

He hasn't come in yet.

In more formal circumstances *yet* occurs after 'not':

He has not yet come in.

When *yet* occurs medially in an affirmative statement it can have negative implications:

I've yet to discover the secret of his success. (i.e., So far I have not discovered the secret of his success.)

Occasionally, in formal styles, *yet* can occur as a conjunction with the meaning of 'but' or 'nevertheless':

I tried repeatedly. Yet, in spite of trying, I failed.
They cannot win, yet they will fight on.

See also ADVERB, ALREADY/STILL/YET, CONJUNCTION

Yiddish

Yiddish is an abbreviation for *Yidish daytsh*, meaning 'Jewish German', a language that was widely used in Jewish communities in Eastern Europe. Yiddish has been carried to America, Australia, Britain and South Africa by Jews who migrated from Eastern Europe and it is one of the official languages of Israel. Yiddish influences were originally limited to the English of people who had spoken Yiddish as a mother tongue but it can now be detected in the English of many New Yorkers (of both Jewish and non-Jewish origin), of US speakers generally and in other parts of the world with sizeable Jewish communities.

Yiddish influences are most apparent in vocabulary and idiom. Among the words borrowed are items relating to religious culture:

bar/bat mitzvah (ceremony marking the religious coming of age of a boy/girl)
bris (circumcision ceremony)
kaddish or kiddush (blessing over bread and wine)
magen David or mogen Dovid (star of David)

to food:

bagel (type of bread roll)
gefilte fish (chopped fish)
matzo (unleavened bread)

to people:

goy/goyim (non-Jew/non-Jews)

shiksa (non-Jewish girl)

schmuk (fool)

and to characteristics, greetings and exclamations:

chutzpah (cheek)

kosher (genuine, correct)

schmaltz (sentimentality)

Mazel tov! (Good luck!)

Shalom! (Peace!)

Oy veh! (Heavens above!)

Keep shtoom! (Say nothing!)

See also BORROWING, FOREIGN LOAN-WORDS

yodel

This verb doubles the 'l' before suffixes:

Stop yodelling! It will ruin your voice.

See also SPELLING

yoga

Yoga with an 'a' refers to a Hindu system of philosophy that aims to promote a state of physical, spiritual and mental tranquillity by means of meditation and combined physical and mental exercises. A *yogi* with an 'i' is one who has mastered yoga. The plural is *yogis*.

yoghurt

Yoghurt has two acceptable spellings, the form with the 'h' and the form without it, *yogurt*. The spelling with the 'h' is more widespread in Britain, but *yogurt* is preferred in the United States.

yoke, yolk

A *yoke* is a wooden frame attached to the necks of beasts of burden so that they can be worked as a team. The word is also used metaphorically to mean 'burden':

... Provoke
The years to bring the inevitable yoke.
Wordsworth, *Intimations of Immortality*

A *yolk* is the yellow part of an egg:

How can anyone cook an egg so that the yolk is hard and the white runny?

yonder

Yonder can function as an adverb meaning 'over there':

Look! You can just see the river yonder.

and as a determiner:

Yonder mountains are the Pennines.

This useful word has virtually died out of the language but it continues to be used in some regional dialects.

See also ADVERB, DETERMINER, HITHER, THITHER

you

You is a pronoun that can be singular:

You tried hard, Tom.

or plural:

You have all tried hard.

It is a general second-person pronoun and does not, in itself, indicate intimacy or distance, courtesy or disrespect.

You is also used in English as a colloquial equivalent of 'one':

You can't get a parking place after 9:30.

and as a means of generalizing an individual's experience:

You try your best for your children; you work hard for them and they don't always appreciate your efforts.

Some speakers feel the need of a plural form of *you* and, since 'youse' is dialectal, use such forms as 'you all' or 'you lot'.

See also ONE

you and I, you and me

Many people are uncertain about when to use *you and I* and *you and me*. The rules are very clear. If you can replace the phrase by 'we', use *you and I*:

You and I should have a holiday.

We should have a holiday.

If you can replace the phrase by 'us', use *you and me*:

He has written to you and me.

He has written to us.

Similar rules apply to other coordinated phrases involving 'I/me':

John and I are brothers = We are brothers.

He visited John and me = He visited us.

Peter, Paul and I are brothers = We are brothers.

He left everything to Peter, Paul and me = He left everything to us.

you're, your

Your and *you're* are occasionally confused, as in the following printed sign in a hospital X-ray department:

*Ladies, if there is any possibility of you're being pregnant, please tell the radiographer before treatment.

Your is a possessive adjective. It precedes a noun or noun phrase:

I think your garden is beautiful.

Your children are your best insurance policy.

Your also precedes a present participle that is used as a noun:

Your procrastinating will have to stop.

You're is a contraction of 'you are':

You're not having another holiday, are you?

You're undoubtedly the best Scrabble player I've ever met!

See also APOSTROPHE, GERUND, PARTICIPLE

yours

Yours is a possessive pronoun:

Is this bag yours?

Yours is the one on the left.

Possessive pronouns, including *yours*, never have an apostrophe.

Yours often features at the end of a letter, either on its own:

Yours

or with an adverb:

Yours faithfully

Yours sincerely.

See also APOSTROPHE, PRONOUN

Yugoslavia

When *Yugoslavia* was a united country, there was debate about the spelling. Both the form with 'Y' and the form with 'J', as in 'Jugoslavia', were acceptable. The derived noun 'Yugoslav' was preferred for the inhabitants. Now, *Yugoslavia* is applicable only to the two republics of Serbia and Montenegro and the other republics should be referred to by their individual names.

yuppie

Yuppie is a derived acronym:

Young Urban Professional + ie.

Just as the 'p' is doubled in 'puppy', it is doubled in *yuppie*. Many acronyms were used in the 1980s for people who were socially mobile. These included:

Dinky (Double Income No Kids Yet)

Nimby (Not In My Back Yard)

and:

Woopy (Well-Off Older Person).

'zeroes', 'zeroed', but 'zeroing' does not have an 'e'.

Z

z

Z is a consonant that is pronounced to rhyme with 'bed' in British English, and with 'bee' in American English. The British pronunciation derives from Old French *zede* whereas the American pronunciation is by analogy with other consonants, 'b' pronounced 'bee', 'c' pronounced 'see' and 'd' pronounced 'dee'.

Initial *z* is rare in English, although it occurs in words borrowed from other languages:

Zeitgeist (German)
zeugma (Greek)
zombie (Kikongo).

Zaïre

An inhabitant of the African republic (currently the Democratic Republic of Congo) is a 'Zaïrean' or 'Zaïrese'. The capital is Kinshasa.

Zambia

An inhabitant of the republic in south-central Africa is a 'Zambian', and the derived adjective is the same. The capital is Lusaka.

Zanzibar

This is the name of the island that joined with Tanganyika to form Tanzania. The noun and derived adjective are 'Zanzibari'.

zero

Zero can function as both a noun and a verb:

In Britain, a billion used to have nine zeros. Now it has six.

Both 'zeros' and 'zeroes' are acceptable as plurals, but the former is more widespread. The verb, however, must have an 'e' in such forms as

zeugma

The meaning of *zeugma* overlaps that of SYLLEPSIS. *Zeugma* is a figure of speech that describes two related phenomena. A single verb or adjective may be used in relation to two nouns, only one of which would normally collocate with it:

She mislaid her handbag and her child.
He served juicy steaks and gossip.

A single word is applied with different meanings to two other words. Often one sense of the word is literal and the other metaphorical:

The housewife and the athlete both tore up the dotted line.
He closed the door and his wallet to his erring son.

See also AMBIGUITY, FIGURE OF SPEECH

zigzag

This word is an example of partial REDUPLICATION (compare *flim flam*). It doubles the 'g' before suffixes:

They zigzagged down the road.

Zimbabwe

The capital of Zimbabwe is Harare; the noun and derived adjective are 'Zimbabwean'.

zoo

Zoo is an abbreviation of 'zoological garden/s'. It forms its plural by adding 's':

There are over forty private and public zoos in England.

The word derives ultimately from Greek *zoion*, 'animal', and the Greek root is found in such words as *zoology*, 'the study of animals'. Some speakers insist that the common pronunciation of *zoology* (i.e., zoo + ology) is incorrect and that it should be 'zo' (rhyming with 'go' + 'ology'. There is some logic in this argument, but logic is unlikely to discourage the much more widespread pronunciation.